On the Road around the Capital Region USA

D0175946

THOMAS COOK

On 5 July 1841 Thomas Cook, a 32-year-old printer from Market Harborough, in Leicestershire, England, led a party of some 500 temperance enthusiasts on a railway outing from Leicester to Loughborough which he had arranged down to the last detail. This proved to be the birth of the modern tourist industry. In the course of expanding his business, Thomas Cook and his son, John, invented many of the features of organised travel which we now take for granted. Over the next 150 years the name Thomas Cook became synonymous with world travel.

Today the Thomas Cook Group employs over 14,000 people across the globe and its Worldwide Network provides services to customers at more than 3000 locations in over 100 countries. Its activities include travel retailing, tour operating and financial services – Thomas Cook is a world leader in traveller's cheques and foreign money services.

Thomas Cook believed in the value of the printed word as an accompaniment to travel. His publication *The Excursionist* was the equivalent of both a holiday brochure and a travel magazine. Today Thomas Cook Publishing continues to issue one of the world's oldest travel books, the *Thomas Cook European Timetable,* which has been in existence since 1873. Updated every month, it remains the only definitive compendium of European railway schedules.

The *Thomas Cook Touring Handbook* series, to which this volume belongs, is a range of comprehensive guides for travellers touring regions of the world by train, car and ship. Other titles include:

Touring by train
On the Rails around France (Published 1995)
On the Rails around Britain and Ireland (Published 1995)
On the Rails around Europe (Second Edition Published 1996)
On the Rails around the Alps (Published 1996)
On the Rails around Eastern Europe (Published 1996)
Touring by car
On the Road around California (Second Edition Published 1996)
On the Road around Florida (Published 1995)
On the Road around Normandy, Brittany and the Loire Valley (Published 1996)
On the Road around the Pacific Northwest (1997)
On the Road around the South of France (1997)
Touring by ship
Greek Island Hopping (Published annually in March)

For more details of these and other Thomas Cook publications, write to Passport Books, at the address on the back of the title page.

ON THE ROAD AROUND THE

Capital Region USA

Fly-drive holidays in and around Washington, D.C., Maryland, Virginia, Delaware, and Pennsylvania

Written by
Eric and Ruth Bailey

PASSPORT BOOKS
a division of *NTC Publishing Group*

Thomas Cook

A THOMAS COOK TOURING HANDBOOK

Published by Passport Books,
a division of NTC Publishing Group
4255 West Touhy Avenue,
Lincolnwood (Chicago),
Illinois 60646-1975 USA.

Text: © 1997 The Thomas Cook Group Ltd
Maps and diagrams:
© 1997 The Thomas Cook Group Ltd

ISBN 0-8442-4950-5
Library of Congress Catalog Card
    Number: 96-72600
Published by Passport Books in conjunction
with The Thomas Cook Group Ltd.

Managing Editor: Stephen York
Project Editor: Deborah Parker
Map Editor: Bernard Horton
Editorial Assistants: Kate Hopgood and
    Wendy Wood

Cover illustration by Michael Bennallack-Hart
Text design by Darwell Holland
Text typeset in Bembo and Gill Sans using
    QuarkXPress for Windows
Maps and diagrams created using Macromedia
    Freehand and GSP Designworks
Printed in Great Britain by Fisherprint Ltd,
    Peterborough

*While every care has been taken in compiling this
publication, using the most up-to-date information
available at the time of going to press, all details are
liable to change and cannot be guaranteed. The publishers cannot accept any liability whatsoever arising
from errors or omissions, however caused. The views
and opinions expressed in this book are not necessarily
those of the publishers.*

Written and researched by
Eric and Ruth Bailey

Additional research:
Stephen H. Morgan

Series Editor: **Melissa Shales**

ABOUT THE AUTHORS

Eric and Ruth Bailey, a husband-and-wife travel writing team, are experienced journalists and authors who met when working on their first newspaper. They turned to full time freelance travel writing some 16 years ago.

Members of the British Guild of Travel Writers and the Society of Authors, they have travelled widely in the USA and Canada, Latin America, Africa, the Philippines and other long-haul destinations. Closer to home, they name Ireland as their favourite European country. They have a particular interest in inland waterway boating, and are fond of animals, especially dogs.

To date, they have written nine travel books, including volumes on Ireland and New York in the *AA Thomas Cook Travellers* series and another guide in the *Thomas Cook Touring Handbooks* series, *On the Road around Florida,* in association with American travel writers Maxine Cass and Fred Gebhart.

PHOTOGRAPHS

Between pp. 32 and 33: page (i) Virginia Tourism Corporation; (ii) Super Stock; Washington, DC Convention and Visitors Association; (iii) Eric Bailey; Washington, DC CVA.
Between pp. 128 and 129: (i) Spectrum Colour Library; (ii) Eric Bailey; (iii) Eric Bailey; (iv) Eric Bailey; Spectrum Colour Library.
Between pp. 224 and 225: (i) Eric Bailey; (ii) Spectrum Colour Library; (iii) Virginia Tourism Corporation; (iv) Eric Bailey; Spectrum Colour Library.
Between pp. 288 and 289:
(i) Richard Nowitz; Tom Darden; (ii) Spectrum Colour Library; Richard Nowitz; (iii) Spectrum Colour Library; (iv) Spectrum Colour Library.

ACKNOWLEDGEMENTS

The authors would like to thank all the people who helped them during their long research tour of Washington DC and the adjacent states of Virginia, Maryland, Delaware and Pennsylvania. Among them are the directors and staff of the many city and county tourism offices and Convention and Visitor Bureaux along the way, and the proprietors of a wide variety of accommodation throughout the Capital Region.

Among all these hospitable people whom it was a pleasure to meet, the authors would like to make special mention of Hugh Barton (Arlington), Barbara Barton (Alexandria), Peter Nelson (Annapolis) and Mindy Schneeburger (Maryland).

The friendship and information given to the authors by many strangers they encountered is also greatly appreciated. These casual acquaintances provided a personal insight into the folklore, character, history and industry of their respective cities and rural areas.

Thomas Cook Publishing would like to thank all those gave assistance during the preparation of this book, in particular: Marie Tibor and her colleagues at Washington, DC Convention and Visitors Association; Sandy Walsh and her colleagues at Virginia Tourism Corporation; Peter Chambliss and Liz Fitzsimmons and their colleagues at the Office of Tourism Development, Maryland Department of Business and Economic Development; Charlotte Fenn and colleagues at Representation Plus; David Montgomery, Thomas Cook Financial Services North America; Amanda Plant, Thomas Cook Studio; Alex Goldberg, Image Select International.

5

CONTENTS

ROUTES AND CITIES

In alphabetical order. For indexing purposes, routes are listed in both directions – the reverse direction to which it appears in the book is shown in italics.
See also the Route Map, p. 8, for a diagrammatic presentation of all the routes in the book.
To look up towns and other places not listed here, see the Index, p.348.

6

7

REFERENCE SECTION

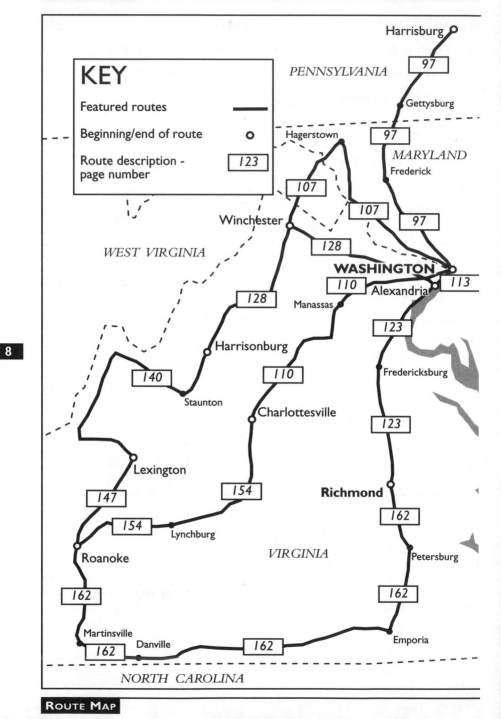

KEY

Featured routes ———

Beginning/end of route ○

Route description -
page number ⬚ 123

Harrisburg

PENNSYLVANIA

97

Gettysburg

97

Hagerstown

MARYLAND

Frederick

107

107

97

Winchester

128

WASHINGTON

110 Alexandria

113

WEST VIRGINIA

128

Manassas

123

Harrisonburg

Fredericksburg

140

110

Staunton

123

Charlottesville

Lexington

154

Richmond

147

154

162

Lynchburg

Roanoke

VIRGINIA

Petersburg

162

Martinsville

162

Danville

162

Emporia

162

NORTH CAROLINA

8

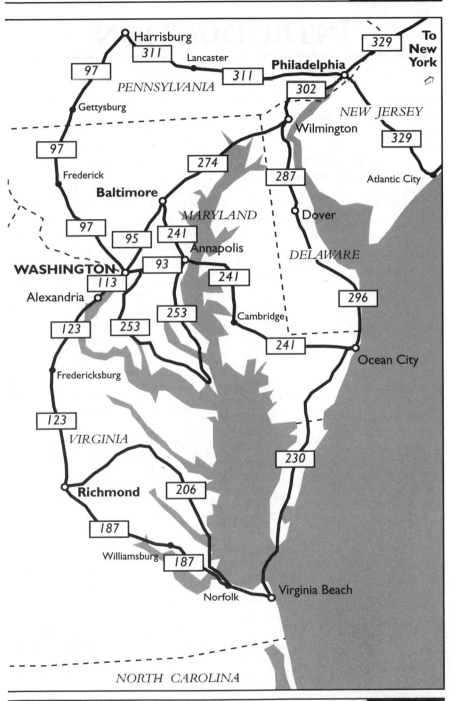

INTRODUCTION

Washington has an annual influx of 19 million visitors. They spend a few days visiting places they have seen on television or learned about at school. Some of them are unaware of the peace, beauty, history and wonders that exist on the capital's doorstep.

After the frenetic pleasures of the city, relaxed motoring can be enjoyed away from major highways. Minor roads take you through varied scenery, some pastoral, some dramatic, into the villages and small towns of Maryland, Virginia, Delaware and Pennsylvania. They lead to living colonial communities, enticing state capitals like Annapolis, MD, and Richmond, VA, the golden beaches of Chesapeake Bay and the nightlife of Ocean City and Virginia Beach.

You can meet Amish people, glimpse their unmechanised way of life and buy their apple butter and organic vegetables. You can sample foreign cuisines in lively seaports and tour caves beneath the Blue Ridge Mountains.

The range of activities is enormous. You can watch a Harley Davidson being built and assembled, then see it test-driven – all in the space of an hour. Or you may prefer to search southern Maryland cliffs for fossils up to 20 million years old. You can take a canal trip by mule-drawn barge or meet Native Americans on their reservation.

Gracious plantation homes, some with less gracious slaves' quarters still intact, can be visited. You will see places where presidents and famous generals grew up, stately mansions, country stores, wineries, historic battlefields, old taverns, barrier islands populated with wild ponies, and some of the haunts of Pocahontas.

Unless you have two or three months at your disposal, you will have to select a section of the region and leave some for another time. This book defines the Capital Region as Washington DC, Maryland, Delaware, Virginia and the south-east corner of Pennsylvania.

Wherever you go in this region, you will find yourself immersed in history.

Virginia, noted for its share of the Appalachian Trail, the Blue Ridge Mountains, the Shenandoah Valley and Civil War trail, is probably the best known part of the region among international visitors. The neighbouring states also have great charm, beauty and historic interest.

One of the joys of the region is the contrasting scenery, from Virginia's lofty but unaggressive mountains to the flat wetlands of Delaware's popular fishing country. Here tall reeds and marsh grasses stretch to the horizon beneath massive skies. All this, and bargain shopping.

Maryland's wooded hills, its beach playgrounds, its waterfronts and sailing facilities, have an appeal that few foreign visitors have yet discovered.

Pennsylvania has gently rolling green hills, small towns where you could happily spend weeks, delightful, welcoming communities and superb bed and breakfast accommodations – a trend that is growing throughout the region.

You will never be far from fascinating museums, art galleries and craft shops, excellent restaurants with much seafood on the menu, and historic sites.

Eric and Ruth Bailey

How to Use This Book

ROUTES AND CITIES

On the Road around the Capital Region provides you with an expert selection of 24 recommended routes between key cities and towns and attractions of the Capital Region (together with the gateway city of New York), each in its own chapter. Smaller cities, towns, attractions and points of interest along each route are described in the order in which you will encounter them. Additional chapters are devoted to the major places of interest which usually begin and end these routes, and some circular routes explore regions of particular interest. These route and city chapters form the core of the book, from page 65 to page 344.

Where applicable, an alternative route which is more direct is also provided at the beginning of each recommended route chapter. This will enable you to drive more quickly between the cities at the beginning and end of the route, if you do not intend to stop at any of the intermediate places. To save space, each route is described in only one direction, but of course you can follow it in the reverse direction, too.

The arrangement of the text consists of a chapter describing a large city or town of interest first, followed by chapters devoted to routes leading from that place to other major destinations; e.g. the first city to be covered is Washington, DC, (pp. 65–92), followed by routes from Washington: Washington to Annapolis (pp. 93–94), Washington to Baltimore (pp. 95–96), Washington to Harrisburg (pp. 97–106), Washington to Winchester (pp. 107–109), Washington to Charlottesville (pp. 110–112), Washington to Alexandria (pp. 113–115). Alexandria is described in the next chapter, followed in turn by routes out of Alexandria, and so on.

The order of chapters thus follows the pattern of your journey, beginning in Washington, DC, with routes radiating out. The routes then cover the state of Virginia, followed by Maryland and Delaware, before heading north into Pennsylvania, and finally making north-east towards New York City. To find the page number of any route or city chapter quickly, use either the alphabetical list on the **Contents** pages, pp. 6–7, or the master **Route Map** on pp. 8–9.

The routes are designed to be used as a kind of menu from which you can plan an itinerary, combining a number of routes which take you to the places you most want to visit.

WITHIN EACH ROUTE

Each route chapter begins with a short introduction to the route, followed by driving directions from the beginning of the route to the end, and a sketch map of the route and all the places along it which are described in the chapter. This map, intended to be used in conjunction with the driving directions, summarises the route and shows the main intermediate distances and road numbers; for a key to the symbols used, see p. 13.

DIRECT ROUTE

➡ This will be the fastest, most direct, and sometimes, predictably, least interesting drive between the beginning and end of the route, often along major highways.

SCENIC ROUTE

This is the itinerary which takes in the most places of interest, usually using ordinary highways and minor roads. Road directions are specific; always be prepared for detours due to road construction, etc.

The driving directions are followed by sub-sections describing the main attractions and places of interest along the way. You can stop at them all or miss out the ones which do not appeal to you. Always ask at the local tourist information centre (usually the Convention & Visitors Bureau or Chamber of Commerce) for more information on sights, lodgings and places to eat at.

SIDE TRACK

This heading is occasionally used to indicate departures from the main route, or out-of-town trips from a city, which detour to worthwhile sights, described in full or highlighted in a paragraph or two.

CITY DESCRIPTIONS

Whether a place is given a half-page description within a route chapter or merits an entire chapter to itself, we have concentrated on practical details: local sources of tourist information; getting around in city centres (by car, by public transport or on foot as appropriate); accommodation and dining; phone communications; entertainment and shopping opportunities; and sightseeing, history and background interest. The largest cities have all this detail; in smaller places some categories of information are less relevant and have been omitted or summarised. Where there is a story to tell which would interrupt the flow of the main description, we have placed **feature boxes** on subjects as diverse as 'The Residence of Presidents' and 'Mister Bojangles'.

Although we mention good independently owned lodgings in many places, we always also list the hotel chains which have a property in the area, by means of code letters to save space. Many travellers prefer to stick to one or two chains with which they are familiar and which give a consistent standard of accommodation. The codes are explained on p. 346, and central booking numbers for the chains are also given there.

MAPS

In addition to the sketch map which accompanies each route, we provide maps of major cities (usually the downtown area, but also the region in places like Washington, DC), smaller towns, national parks, and so on. At the end of the book is a section of **colour road maps** covering the whole area described in this book, which is detailed enough to be used for trip planning and on the road. The **key to symbols** used on all the types of map in this book is shown on p. 13.

THE REST OF THE BOOK

At the front of the book, **Driving Distances** is a tabulation of distances between main places, to help in trip planning. The use of the **Contents** and **Route Map** pages has already been mentioned above. **Travel Essentials** is an alphabetically arranged chapter of general advice for the tourist new to the Capital Region or to the United States, covering a wide range subjects such as accommodation and safety or how much to tip. **Driving** in **Capital Region** concentrates on advice for drivers on the law, rules of the road, and so on. **Background Capital Region** gives a concise briefing on the history and geography of this interesting region. **Touring Itineraries** provides ideas and suggestions for putting together an itinerary of your own using the selection of routes in this book. At the end of the book, the **Conversion Tables** decode US sizes and measures for non-US citizens. Finally the **Index** is the quick way to look up any place or general subject. And please help us by completing and returning the **Reader Survey** at the very end of the text; we are grateful for both your views on the book and new information from your travels in the Capital Region.

KEY TO MAP SYMBOLS

Route diagrams

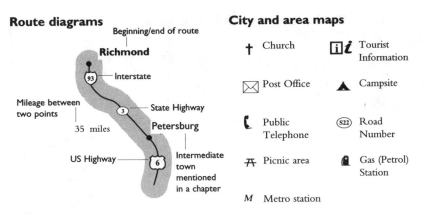

City and area maps

† Church

⊠ Post Office

☎ Public Telephone

⊼ Picnic area

M Metro station

[i]𝑖 Tourist Information

▲ Campsite

(S22) Road Number

⛽ Gas (Petrol) Station

KEY TO PRICE DESCRIPTIONS

It is impossible to keep up to date with specific tariffs for lodging and accommodation or restaurants, although we have given some general advice under 'Cost of Living' in the Travel Essentials chapter p 20). Instead, we have rated establishments in broad price categories throughout the book, as follows:

Accommodation (per room per night)		*Meal (for one person, excluding drinks, tip or tax)*	
Budget	Under $50	Cheap	Under $5
Moderate	Under $100	Budget	Under $10
Expensive	Under $150	Moderate	Under $20
Pricey	$150 and higher	Pricey	Over $20

ABBREVIATIONS USED IN THE BOOK
(For hotel chains, see p. 346)

Bldg	Building (in addresses)	min(s)	minute(s)
Blvd	Boulevard	Mon, Tues	Monday, Tuesday, etc.
Dr.	Drive (in addresses)	Rd	Road (in addresses)
hr(s)	hour(s)	Rte	Route, e.g. Rte 450
Hwy	US or State Highway, e.g. Hwy 1	St	Street (in addresses)
I–	Interstate Highway, e.g. I-95	Ste	Suite (in addresses)
Jan, Feb	January, February, etc.	SR	State Road or Highway

THOMAS COOK TOURING HANDBOOKS
The perfect companions for your holiday

These route-based guides are crammed with practical information and maps. From advice on road laws to ideas for accommodation and sightseeing, they contain all the information you need to explore the USA by car.

On the Road around New England
Price: £10.95

40 routes with side-trips and scenic drives throughout this varied region. The area covered stretches from New York up to northern Maine, with side trips into Canada to visit Montreal and Quebec.

On the Road around Florida
Price: £10.95

With clear city and regional maps and honest sightseeing advice, this book will help you to get the most out of your visit to Florida. Over 30 routes combine famous and more unusual sights.

On the Road around the Pacific Northwest
Price: £12.95   Published March 1997

Covers Washington, Oregon and the Canadian province of British Columbia as one touring region. 40 routes are accompanied by information on the cultural and historical background. Includes 16 pages of colour photographs.

On the Road around California
Price: £12.95

This practical book has just been re-researched for the second edition. 16 pages of colour photography have been added to complement a complete and fact-packed guide to the whole of California, plus the Grand Canyon and Las Vegas.

These publications are available from bookshops and Thomas Cook UK retail shops, or direct by post from Thomas Cook, Publishing, Dept (OWN), PO Box 227, Thorpe Wood, Peterborough, PE3 6PU, UK. (Extra for postage and packing.)
Tel: 01733 503571/2.
Published in the USA by Passport Books

TRAVEL ESSENTIALS

The following is an alphabetical listing of helpful tips and advice for those planning a holiday in the Capital Region.

Accommodation

The Capital Region offers accommodation of every price level imaginable, from five-star hotels and posh resorts to youth hostels and campsites. Local tourist offices can provide lodging lists and telephone numbers, but generally can't make bookings. Where available, lodging services are noted in the text.

Accommodation can be more difficult to find in major tourist destinations during high season, which is usually Memorial Day (last weekend in May), Labor Day (first weekend in Sept), plus weekends and major public holidays.

Thomas Cook or any other good travel agent can handle room bookings when purchasing air tickets and car or other local transportation. All-inclusive fly-drive arrangements, and 'do-it-yourself packages' such as Thomas Cook Holiday's *America for the Independent Traveller* programme, can provide hotel coupons, exchangeable at a range of hotel chains, which guarantee a pre-paid rate at participating chains, although they do not guarantee rooms – it's up to you to phone ahead as you go, or take a chance on availability. It's particularly important to pre-book the first and last nights' stay to avoid problems when connecting with international air flights.

Throughout the book we have indicated prices of accommodation in a comparative way by using terms such as 'moderate' and 'pricey'; see 'How to Use This Book', p.11, for an explanation of what these descriptions mean in terms of dollars.

Hotels and Motels

US hotel rates are quoted for single or double occupancy; children usually stay cheaply or for free with parents.

Once in the USA, you will find that most chain hotels and motels have toll-free reservation telephone numbers that can be reached from anywhere in North America. The list on p.346 gives a selection of these, along with the abbreviations used in the text of this book to indicate which chains are present in the town or city being described.

Advance bookings generally require a voucher or credit card number to guarantee the booking. Ask for discounts if you're a senior, a motoring club member, or travelling off-season. When checking in, always ask if there's a cheaper room rate than the one you pre-booked. It's often cost-effective to find lodging day by day, especially in off-peak seasons.

Motels are often the best bet. Literally 'motor hotels', motels are one- to three-storey buildings with a modest version of a hotel's accommodation. Most belong to nationwide chains which enforce service and safety standards.

Independent motels may not be quite as fancy, but offer even lower prices. Motels fill up fast during high season, but last-minute rooms are usually available in the off season, especially during the week.

The *AAA TourBooks* for *Mid-Atlantic* and *New Jersey/Pennsylvania* list thousands of motels and hotels; thousands more are just as comfortable and affordable. Check the motels that line major highways entering most cities and towns. Special prices are often noted on a roadside sign.

Budget hotels, especially in cities, can be dim, dirty and dangerous. Look for a motel or youth hostel instead.

Bed and Breakfast

Bed and Breakfast is not for those on a tight budget, as it can be the most expensive lodging in any area. That said, in some parts of the region, this style of accommodation can be found for between $60–80 per night. Capital Region-style Bed and Breakfast ranges from bedrooms in private homes to small inns. While most properties date from the early to mid 1800s, it is possible to enjoy stays in Colonial homes as well. Mansions are typically furnished with period antiques and reproduction linens and curtains. Breakfasts vary. A few are so healthy and calorie-conscious a songbird could go away hungry, but the standard includes fruit juice, coffee or tea, an egg dish, homemade bread, and a sweet.

Camping

Camping means a tent or a recreational vehicle (RV) in a rural campsite. KOA, Kampgrounds of America, is a private chain of RV parks that also accept tents. Many other campsites are public and operated by the National Parks and State Park systems in Virginia and Maryland. Overnight fees range from $5 to more than $20, depending on location and season. Standard facilities include a fireplace for barbecues, food storage locker, tent site, nearby showers/toilets, and, during high season, daytime guided hikes and evening educational programmes around a large campfire.

Private campsite information for Virginia is available from **Virginia Tourism Corporation**, *901 E. Byrd St, Richmond, VA 23219,* and information on private and public campsites in Maryland is available from **Maryland Office of Tourism**, *217 E. Redwood St, Baltimore, MD 21202, USA.*

Youth Hostels

American Youth Hostels (Hostelling International) was created for tight budgets, and has a handful of hostels in the Capital Region. Most hostels provide a dormitory-style room and shared bath for $8–$16 per night. Some have family rooms, all offer discounts to local attractions. When two or more people are travelling together and can share a room, cheap motels may prove even cheaper than hostels.

AIRPORTS

The three major Capital Region airports are centred within 40 miles of Washington: Baltimore/Washington International (BWI), Washington Dulles International (IAD) and Washington National Airport (WAS). However, there are numerous commuter airports located throughout the region.

Travelers Aid desks provide tourist information; **airport information** booths and touch-screen information kiosks cover airport facilities, airport-to-city transport and local accommodation, though no bookings are made.

The major airports have foreign exchange and banking services and car hire facilities. Varied and frequent public transport to Washington and Baltimore is available; specific airport arrival information is given in the chapters dealing with these cities.

BICYCLES

Cycling is popular for countryside day touring in the Capital Region – less so for overnight trips, due to geography. Bikes can be hired by the hour or the day in most wine country and beach areas. Drivers are not accustomed to sharing the street with cyclists, so try to avoid busy city streets.

For serious bikers, biking tours are available at all levels, from easy day trips to arduous pulls through the Shenandoah Valley or the Alleghany Mountains Many offer themed trips from inn to inn, incorporating wineries, historic attractions and bucolic countryside. On-your-own bike tours are also possible, but beware of unexpected distances and mountains between towns.

BOAT TRIPS

The Capital Region's maritime heritage and the importance of rivers in the area's development are reflected in the number of boat trips highlighted throughout this book. An alternative means of public transport in Annapolis and Baltimore is the water taxi, which takes visitors by boat to a number of destinations around their harbours.

Chesapeake Bay is very popular with recreational boaters, and several companies dotted around the bay offer bare-boat charters or can take visitors on water tours.

BORDERS

US Customs and Immigration has gained a reputation as one of the most unpleasant travel experiences the world has to offer. It can be, for citizens returning home as well as for first-time holidaymakers. Visitors who overstay tourist and student visas are the largest single source of illegal immigrants to the USA. C & I officials have *carte blanche* to ask any question, search anyone or anything, and do it in any manner they see fit, however unpleasant. In fact, most are polite to a fault, but the only defence against an inspector who got out of the wrong side of the bed is to have passport, visa, proof of support, and return ticket in order.

Importation of weapons, narcotics, or certain non-approved pharmaceutical products is prohibited. Carry doctors' prescriptions with documentation (such as a doctor's letter) to prove that medications are legitimate.

BUSES

Greyhound Bus Lines, *Customer Service, 901 Main St, Dallas, TX 75202; tel: (800) 231-2222*, provide information on long-distance bus services between major cities. There are discounts for seniors (over 55), disabled travellers, helpers and children (under 12) riding with a full-fare adult. The **International Ameripass** offers special discounts for adult travellers not resident in North America. Greyhound passes are obtainable through Thomas Cook travel shops in the UK.

If you're buying tickets locally ask for the Domestic Ameripass, which, depending on distance travelled, may be more economical. Local transportation companies listed in the telephone directory under individual cities and towns provide local service.

Thomas Cook publishes timetables of US buses in the *Thomas Cook Overseas Timetable* six times a year. For full details see 'Useful Reading' on p.37).

CAMPERS AND RVS

It's the freedom of the open road, housekeeping on wheels, a tinkerer's delight, a large machine hurtling down slopes and ploughing up grades. An RV, caravan, or motorhome provides a kitchen, sleeping and bathroom facilities, all integrated atop a lorry chassis.

Fly–drive holiday packages usually offer the option of hiring an RV. The additional cost of hiring an RV can be offset by the economics of assured lodging for several people, space for meal preparation and eating, and the convenience of storing comfort items and souvenirs nearby. RVs are cramped, designed to stuff you and your belongings into limited space. The economics work only if advance planning assures that the pricey spur-of-the-moment allure of a hotel shower or unplanned restaurant meal doesn't overcome RV campers! Take into account the cost of petrol – an RV guzzles 3–4 times more than a medium-sized car.

Always get operating manuals for the vehicle and all appliances before leaving the RV hire base, and have someone demonstrate how *everything* works. Systems may be interdependent, or more complex than anticipated. Be prepared to pre-plan menus and allow additional time each morning and afternoon/evening to level the RV (perfect levelling is essential for correct operation of refrigerators), hook up or disconnect electricity, water and sewer hoses, and cable television plugs. As at home, some basic housecleaning must be done; also allow time for laundry at RV parks.

Buy a pair of sturdy rubber washing gloves to handle daily sewer chores. Pack old clothes to wear while crawling under the vehicle to hook up and disconnect at each stop – many RVers carry a pair of overalls. Without hookups, water and electricity are limited to what you carry with you from the last fill-up or battery charge. If you camp in a park without hookups, locate the nearest restrooms before dark. Using showers and toilets in RV parks or public campsites will save

time cleaning up the RV shower space and emptying the toilet holding tank. Have a strong torch (flashlight) handy.

When you move out on the road, expect anything that's not secured to go flying, or to shake, rattle and roll. Quickly get into a routine of allotted tasks and assign a quick-grab spot for maps, snacks, cameras and valuables.

One final tip: know the size of your RV – some roads off-the-beaten-track don't always accommodate large vehicles.

RV travel information: **Recreation Vehicle Industry Association (RVIA)**, *Dept. RK, PO Box 2999, Reston, VA 22090-0999; tel: (703) 620-6003.* To plan RV camping, request *Go Camping America* from **Camping Vacation Planner**, *PO Box 2669, Reston, VA 22090; tel: (800) 477-8669.*

Campsite directories list private RV park locations, directions, size, number of pitches, hook-ups, laundry, on-site convenience stores and showers. Free information on private campsites is available from **Virginia Tourism Corporation**, *901 E. Byrd St, Richmond, VA 23219.*

Popular guides are: *Trailer Life Campground & RV Services Directory, TL Enterprises, 2575 Vista del Mar Dr., Ventura, CA 93001-3920; tel: (805) 667-4100* ($19.95); *Woodall's Campground Directory (Eastern Edition), 13975 W Polo Trail Dr., Lake Forest, IL 60045; tel: (800) 823-9076* ($13.70); *Wheelers RV Resort & Campground Guide, 1310 Jarvis Ave, Elk Grove Village, IL 60007; tel: (708) 981-0100,* ($15.50); *Kampgrounds of America (KOA) Directory, PO Box 30558, Billings, MT 59114-0558; tel: (406) 248-7444* ($3 or free at KOA campsites). The **AAA** have a directory and maps for Capital Region campsites. See 'Parks Information' in this chapter for campsites on state or federal land.

CHILDREN

The Capital Region, with its many theme parks and natural attractions, is both ideal for travelling with children and welcoming. From museums to transport, check for children's rates, often segmented by age, e.g. under 3 free, 6–12 years $3.00, 12–18 years $4.00. A student card must be shown to use student rates.

Travelling with children is never easy, but preparation helps. *Travel with Children*, by Maureen Wheeler (Lonely Planet) is filled with useful tips. Kids get bored and cranky on long drives. Pack favourite games and books, and pick up a book of travel games. Count dignatories' licence plates in and around Washington (official plates for Congress, the Senate etc., are marked accordingly; Diplomatic plates are red, white and blue), or foreign (out of state) plates in Virginia, Maryland and Delaware. If the children are old enough, suggest that they keep a travel diary. It will help them focus on the region and will also help them remember details later to impress friends and teachers. Collecting anything, from postcards to admission tickets, adds a new dimension to travel.

One advantage the Capital Region has as a destination, if you have children in tow, is the region's wide variety of educational and fun attractions that parents will also enjoy, all found within a relatively short distance of one another.

Any driving destination in the Capital Region is equipped for children of all ages, from nappies (diapers) to video games. Many motel chains allow children under 12, 14, sometimes 18, to stay free in their parents' room. A rollaway child's bed, often called a cot, usually comes at no or low cost.

Meals can be difficult, but picnic lunches offer flexibility. It's also a good idea to carry a small cooler filled with ice, cold drinks and snacks, especially in hot weather. Most towns have coffee shops with long hours, children's menus and familiar fast-food names. If the children like McDonalds at home, they'll like Big Macs in the USA – and vice versa.

CLIMATE

The Capital Region enjoys pleasantly hot, sunny summers, a balmy spring and autumn, and relatively mild, but crisp, winters. The region has moderate rainfall throughout the year. Average coastal temperatures in July and Aug rarely exceed the low 90s Farenheit (around 33°C), while in winter there is often a sprinkling of snow. Records show that there are 9–10 hours of daylight in summer, and 4–5 hours on winter days. On the East Coast, Sept is tropical storm season, and these storms can become hurricanes, leading to evacuation of coastal areas.

For more specific climatic information for each state in the Capital Region, see 'Background Capital Region' pp.45–53.

CLOTHING

The Capital Region has four distinct seasons, so dress appropriately for each. Summers are hot, winters are fairly mild. Coastal breezes prevail year round. In any season, take plenty of layers, from shorts for the beach to jumpers and jackets for the mountains. Cotton and wool, worn in layers, are best – one layer is cool, several layers are warm. Adding and removing layers make it easier to stay comfortable.

What to pack is a constant question. An elegant restaurant requires jackets and ties for men. Most shops and restaurants require that shirts be worn. The bottom line is: when in doubt, leave it at home. In general, US clothing prices are cheaper than those in the UK, and the region is fall of shopping malls and brand-name

Average Temperatures			
	Norfolk	Shenandoah National Park	Washington DC	Wilmington
January				
Highest	47°F/8°C	42°F/6°C	42°F/6°C	41°F/5°C
Lowest	31°F/-1°C	18°F/-8°C	27°F/-3°C	26°F/-3°C
March				
Highest	58°F/14°C	56°F/13°C	57°F/14°C	51°F/11°C
Lowest	39°F/4°C	28°F/-2°C	38°F/3°C	32°F/0°C
May				
Highest	75°F/24°C	75°F/24°C	76°F/24°C	74°F/23°C
Lowest	57°F/14°C	47°F/8°C	57°F/14°C	52°F/11°C
July				
Highest	86°F/30°C	86°F/30°C	89°F/32°C	86°F/30°C
Lowest	70°F/21°C	59°F/15°C	71°F/22°C	66°F/19°C
September				
Highest	80°F/27°C	78°F/26°C	80°F/27°C	78°F/26°C
Lowest	64°F/18°C	51°F/11°C	63°F/17°C	57°F/14°C
November				
Highest	61°F/16°C	58°F/14°C	58°F/14°C	55°F/13°C
Lowest	44°F/7°C	32°F/0°C	41°F/5°C	36°F/2°C

discount centres. Don't forget to take good, broken-in walking shoes.

COST OF LIVING

While the states that make up the Capital Region have local sales taxes and hotel/lodging taxes, the combined levy is less than the VAT charged in most of Europe. Prices are always marked or quoted *without tax*, which is added at time of purchase (see 'Sales Taxes', p.30).

Petrol prices are a special bargain, about $1.30 per US gallon (4 litres), or about $0.40 per litre. Motel rooms cost $30–$70 per night; hotels from $70 up. Restaurant meals, including soup or salad, main course, dessert, beverage, and tax are about $10–$20 per person for lunch; $20–$25 for dinner. Theme parks charge about $30 per adult for entrance; national and state parks $4–$6 per car; most museums $2–$5 per person (but a number of attractions, including the Smithsonian museums in Washington, DC, are free).

CURRENCY

US dollars are the only currency accepted in the states that make up the Capital Region. Bill denominations are $1, $2 (very rare), $5, $10, $20, $50, $100, $1000 (rare), and $10,000 (rarer). All bills are the same colour, green and white, and the same size. Take great care not to mix them up. The only differences, apart from the denominations marked on them, are the US president pictured on the front and the designs on the back. There are 100 cents to the dollar: coins include the copper 1-

cent piece, 5-cent nickel, 10-cent dime, 25-cent quarter, 50-cent half-dollar (rare), and an extremely rare Susan B. Anthony dollar.

Outside foreign exchange offices, most Americans have only a vague idea that other currencies even exist. Banks can exchange foreign currency or traveller's cheques, but expect interminable delays (and extraordinary fees) as they telephone the main office in search of exchange rates and procedures. Better to seek out one of the Thomas Cook locations noted in this book; to contact any Thomas Cook Foreign Exchange branch in North America, call *1-800-CURRENCY* (toll-free). However, traveller's cheques denominated in US dollars, from well-known issuers such as Thomas Cook, are acceptable everywhere and can be used like cash or changed easily. To report Thomas Cook Travellers Cheque losses and thefts, call *1-800-223-7373* (toll-free, 24-hour service).

A number of the Thomas Cook locations given in this book offer MoneyGram, a quick international money transfer service.

For security reasons, avoid carrying large amounts of cash. The safest forms of money are US dollar traveller's cheques and credit or debit cards. Both can be used almost everywhere. If possible, bring at least one, preferably two, major credit cards such as **MasterCard**, **American Express** or **Visa**. Thomas Cook locations will offer emergency assistance if you lose your MasterCard card.

Plastic is the only acceptable proof of fiscal responsibility. Car hire companies require either a credit card imprint or a substantial cash deposit before releasing a vehicle, even if the hire has been fully pre-paid. Hotels and motels also require either a credit card imprint or a cash deposit, even if the bill is to be settled in cash.

Some shops, cheaper motels, small local restaurants and low-cost petrol stations require cash. Automated teller machines, or **ATMs**, are a ubiquitous source of cash allowing withdrawals or cash advances authorised by debit or credit card. **CIRRUS** is the most common international system used in the US, but check terms, availability and PIN (personal identification number) with the card issuer before leaving home.

CUSTOMS ALLOWANCES

Personal duty-free allowances which can be taken into the USA by visitors are 1 US quart (approx. 0.9 litres) of spirits or wine, 300 cigarettes or 50 (non-Cuban) cigars and up to $100 worth of gifts.

On your return home you will be allowed to take in the following:
Australia: goods to the value of A$400 (half for those under 18) plus 250 cigarettes or 250 g tobacco and 1 litre alcohol.
Canada: goods to the value of C$300, provided you have been away for over a week and have not already used up part of your allowance that year. You are also allowed 50 cigars plus 200 cigarettes and 1 kg tobacco (if over 16) and 40 oz/1 litre alcohol.
New Zealand: goods to the value of NZ$700. Anyone over 17 may also take 200 cigarettes or 250 g tobacco or 50 cigars or a combination of tobacco products not exceeding 250 g in all plus 4½ litres of beer or wine and 1.125 litres spirits.
UK: The allowances for goods bought outside the EU and/or in EU duty-free shops are:
200 cigarettes or 50 cigars or 100 cigarillos or 250 g tobacco + 2 litres still table wine + 1 litre spirits or 2 litres sparkling wine + 50 g/60 ml perfume + 0.5 litre/250 ml toilet water.

DISABLED TRAVELLERS

Access is the key word. The law requires that all buildings built after 1992 should be be accessible by disabled persons, including those using wheelchairs. Many buildings built before 1992 are in the process of being converted.

Airlines are particularly hard on disabled passengers. US carriers can prevent anyone who is not strong enough to open an emergency exit (which weighs about 45lb, 20.5kg) or has vision/hearing problems from sitting in that row of seats – even if it means bumping them from the flight. Commuter airlines sometimes deny boarding to passengers with mobility problems on the grounds that they may block the narrow aisle during an emergency.

Some public telephones have special access services for deaf and disabled persons. Broadcast television may be closed-captioned for the hearing impaired, indicated by a rectangle around a double cc in a corner of the screen.

US Information: SATH (Society for the Advancement of Travel for the Handicapped), *347 5th Ave, Suite 610, New York, NY 10016; tel: (212) 447-7284.*

UK Information: RADAR, *12 City Forum, 250 City Road, London EC1V 8AF; tel: (0171) 250 3222,* publish a useful annual guide called *Holidays and Travel Abroad* (£5 including postage)which gives details of facilities for the disabled in different countries.

DISCOUNTS

Reductions on entrance fees and public transport for senior citizens, children, students, and military personnel are common. Some proof of eligibility is usually required. For age, a passport or driving licence is sufficient. Military personnel should carry an official identification card. Students will have better luck with an International Student Identity Card (ISIC), from their local student union, than with a college ID.

The most common discount is for automobile club members. TourBooks from **AAA (Automobile Association of America)** affiliates in Virginia, Maryland and Washington DC list hundreds of member discounts for the Capital Region. Always ask about 'Triple A discounts' at attractions, hotels, motels, and car hire counters. Most recognise reciprocal membership benefits. AAA and Thomas Cook have formed an alliance, see p. 34. Some cities will send high-season discount booklets on request, good for shops, restaurants or lodging.

DRINKING

You must be 21 years old to purchase or to drink any kind of alcoholic beverage in Washington, DC, Maryland or Virginia. Licensed establishments are called bars, lounges, saloons, or pubs.

Maryland and Virginia wines are growing in popularity and stature. Beer can be brewed and sold at a microbrewery, or brewpub. Convenience stores in some areas sell beer, wine, and sometimes spirits, but prices are high.

Laws against drinking and driving are very strict, and strictly enforced with fines and imprisonment. If stopped under suspicion of Driving Under the Influence (DUI), the police officer will ask you to choose between one of three tests: breath, blood, or urine. Any liquor, wine or beer container in a vehicle (RVs excepted) must be full, sealed, and unopened – or in the boot.

ELECTRICITY

The Capital Region (like the rest of the

22

USA) uses 110 volt 60 hertz current. Two- or three-pin electrical plugs are standard throughout the country. Electrical gadgets from outside North America require plug and power converters. Both are difficult to obtain in the USA because local travellers don't need them.

Beware of buying electrical appliances in the USA, for the same reason. Few gadgets on the US market can run on 220 v 50 hz power. Exceptions are battery-operated equipment such as radios, cameras, and portable computers. Tape cassettes, CDs, computer programs, and CD-ROMs sold in the USA can be used anywhere in the world.

US video equipment, which uses the NTSC format, is *not* compatible with the PAL and SECAM equipment used in most of the rest of the world. *Pre-recorded* video tapes sold in the USA will not work with other equipment unless specifically marked as compatible with PAL or SECAM. *Blank* video tapes purchased in America, however, *can* be used with video recorders elsewhere in the world. Discount store prices on blank video cassettes are very reasonable.

EMBASSIES

Australia: *1601 Massachusetts Ave NW, Washington, DC 20096; tel: (202) 797-3000.*

Belgium: *3330 Garfield St NW, Washington, DC 20008; tel: (202) 333-4000.*

Canada: *501 Pennsylvania Ave NW, Washington, DC 20003; tel: (202) 481-1740.*

France: *4101 Reservoir Rd NW, Washington, DC 20007; tel: (202) 344-6000.*

Germany: *4645 Reservoir Rd NW, Washington, DC 20007; tel: (202) 298-4000.*

Italy: *1601 Fuller St NW, Washington, DC 20009; tel: (202) 328-5300.*

Netherlands: *4200 Linnean Ave NW, Washington, DC 20008; tel: (202) 244-5300.*

New Zealand: *37 Observatory Circle NW, Washington, DC 20008; tel: (202) 328-4800.*

Republic of Ireland: *2234 Massachusetts Ave NW, Washington, DC 20008; terl: (202) 462-3939.*

South Africa: *3057 Massachusetts Ave NW, Washington, DC 20008; tel: (202) 232-4400.*

United Kingdom: *3100 Massachusetts Ave NW, Washington, DC 20008; tel: (202) 462-1340.*

EMERGENCIES

In case of emergency, ring *911,* free from any telephone. Ambulance, paramedics, police, fire brigades, or other public safety personnel will be dispatched immediately. See also under 'Health' on the next page.

If you lose your Thomas Cook Travellers Cheques, call *1-800-223-7373* (toll-free, 24-hr service). In the event of loss or theft of a MasterCard card, or for assistance with other card-related emergencies, call MasterCard Global Service at *1-800-307-7309* (toll-free, 24-hr service).

FOOD

American tradition demands huge portions and endless refills of (admittedly weak) coffee. If you're a coffee nut, try any of the coffee houses that have sprung up in mid-size to larger cities around the region. Copious consumption begins with breakfast. Thinly-sliced bacon and eggs cooked to order (fried, scrambled, boiled, poached) come with hash browns (shredded fried potatoes) or fries (chips). Toast, a flat 'English' muffin with butter and jam, or a bagel with farmer's (cream) cheese

23

and lox (smoked salmon slices) may be served alongside. Variations or additions include pancakes, French toast (bread dipped in egg batter and lightly fried), and waffles. Fresh fruit and yogurt, cereal, and porridge are other possibilities. A 'continental breakfast' is juice, coffee or tea and some sort of bread or pastry.

Hotels and some restaurants offer Sunday brunch, usually 1100–1400, with all-you-can-eat self-service buffets heaped with hot and cold dishes. The economical Sun brunch also includes coffee, tea, orange juice and cheap 'champagne' (sparkling wine).

Menus offer similar choices for lunch and dinner, the evening meal. Dinner portions are larger and more costly. Most menus offer appetisers (starters), salads, soups, pastas, entrées (main courses) and desserts. Cooking oils are not light on the palate, so avoid fried fish and ask instead for grilled seafood. Ice cream or sherbert is a lighter dessert choice.

For hearty eating, try a steak house where salad, baked potato, and beans accompany a thick steak. Italian restaurants serve pizza, pasta, seafood and steaks, with heavy doses of tomato and garlic. Mexican cooks use thin wheat or corn tortillas as the base for beans, rice, cheese, tomatoes, spicy sauce, and other ingredients. The American-Chinese cuisine offered in Chinatowns is Cantonese with bean sprout chow mein and fried rice. More authentic Chinese dishes can be found with regional variations, from spicy Hunan to rich, meaty Mandarin. Bite-size dim sum (filled dumplings) or any variety of won ton soup make a filling lunch. Japanese, Vietnamese and Thai food are other easy-to-find Asian cuisines. The Capital Region's diverse ethnic population is celebrated in the melting pot of cuisines in major cities, including German, French, Italian, Indian, Spanish, Cuban, Ethiopian, Salvadorean, and a many others.

Local seafood is a Capital Region speciality, especially blue crabs and oysters. For a regional delight, stop by one of the many crab houses that surround the Chesapeake Bay and its tributaries. This is an experience, as trays of steaming, spiced crabs are brought to your table and thrown down on to newspaper. Just grab a mallet and start cracking...

Fast food is quick and economical. Food is ordered, paid for, and picked up from a service counter, all within a few minutes. Some fast-food outlets have drive-through service, where the driver pulls up to a window, orders from a posted menu, pays, and gets the meal, all without leaving the vehicle. Hamburgers, hot dogs, tacos, fried chicken, and barbecue beef are common offerings. McDonalds' golden arches and KFC's grinning chubby colonel are easy to spot.

Other fast food chains include Arby's Roast Beef, Burger King, Carl's Jr, Del Taco, Hardee's, Jack-in-the-Box, Pizza Hut, Taco Bell and Wendy's. All are cheap.

The budget rung of the price ladder includes chain restaurants such as Denny's (common along highways and usually open 24 hours), Olive Garden (Italian), Red Lobster (seafood), and Western Sizzler. Denny's are open for all meals, the others for lunch and dinner only.

GAMBLING

Virginia and Maryland allow pari-mutuel betting at certain designated horse tracks, and both states operate highly advertised lotteries. The Pimlico Racetrack in Baltimore is home to the Preakness Stakes, the second jewel of the triple crown.

Legal gambling age is 18 years or older; when in doubt, ask at the door.

HEALTH

Hospital emergency rooms are the place to go in the event of life-threatening medical problems. If a life is truly at risk, treatment will be swift and top notch, with payment problems sorted out later. For more mundane problems, 24-hr walk-in health clinics are available in urban areas and many rural communities.

Payment, not care, is the problem. Some form of **health insurance** coverage is almost mandatory in order to ensure provision of health services. Coverage provided by non-US national health plans is *not* accepted by medical providers in the Capital Region. The only way to ensure provision of health services is to carry some proof of valid insurance cover. Most travel agents who deal with international travel will offer travel insurance policies that cover medical costs in the USA – at least $1 million of cover is essential.

Bring enough prescription medication to last the entire trip, plus a few extra days. It's also a good idea to carry a copy of the prescription in case of emergency. Because trade names of drugs vary, be sure the prescription shows the generic (chemical) name and formulation of the drug, not just a brand name.

No inoculations are required and the states covered in this book are basically healthy places to visit. Common sense is enough to avoid most health problems. Eat normally (or at least sensibly) and avoid drinking water that hasn't come from the tap or a bottle.

Sunglasses, broad brimmed sun hats, and sunscreen help prevent sunburn, sun stroke and heat prostration. Be sure to drink plenty of non-alcoholic liquids, especially in hot weather.

AIDS (Acquired Immune Deficiency Syndrome) and other sexually transmitted diseases are endemic in the US as they are in the rest of the world. The best way to avoid sexually transmitted diseases (or STDs, as they're usually called) is to avoid promiscuous sex. In anything other than long-term, strictly monogamous relationships, the key phrase is 'safe sex'. Use condoms in any kind of sexual intercourse. Condoms can be bought in drug stores, pharmacies and supermarkets, and from vending machines in some public toilets.

Rabies can be a problem in the Capital Region – do not feed any animal by hand. Always visit a doctor for a rabies shot after being bitten by any animals.

Don't wear shorts for hikes through coastal and foothill grasslands or forests. Instead, cover up with long trousers, long-sleeved shirts, and insect repellent. The risk of contracting **Lyme Disease** from ticks which thrive in moist climates is rising by the year. Lyme Disease is frequently misdiagnosed and usually mistaken for rheumatoid arthritis. Typical symptoms include temporary paralysis, arthritic pains in the hand, arm, or leg joints, swollen hands, fever, fatigue, headaches, swollen glands, heart palpitations, and a circular red rash around the bite up to 30 days later. Early treatment with tetracycline and other drugs is nearly 100% effective; late treatment often fails. Symptoms may not appear for three months or longer after the first infected tick bite, but the disease can be detected by a simple blood test.

HIKING

Walking is a favourite outdoor activity, especially in park areas. The same cautions that apply anywhere else are good in the Capital Region: know the route; carry a map and basic safety gear; carry food and water. It's also wise to stay on marked trails; wandering off the trail adds to erosion damage, especially in fragile forests and meadows.

How To Talk Capital Region

Alternate means 'alternative', not 'every other' — sometimes a source of confusion when reading timetables.

Bar-b-que sliced or chopped beef or pork served with tangy tomato-based sauce.

Bed & Breakfast (or 'B&B') Overnight lodging in a private home or small inn, usually with private facilities.

Chips Crisps, usually made from potatoes, but also from corn or other starches.

Crab A regional favourite, often steamed and picked at the table by the diner, or can be served breaded and either fried or boiled.

Downtown City or town centre

Holiday A public holiday, such as Labor Day, not a private holiday, which is a *vacation.*

Inside the Beltway People or places that are in the Washington loop, rather than outside the boundaries of Washington's political culture.

Lodging The usual term for accommodation.

Microbrewery or *brewpub* A tavern that brews its own beer.

Outlet shopping Shopping at large stores specialising in factory overruns at reduced prices. In many cases, factory outlets are simply low-priced retail stores selling direct from the factory.

Raw Bar a section found in restaurants which is filled with uncooked seafood such as oysters on the half-shell. It may include other tasty tit-bits which have been marinated but not cooked.

Resort A fancy hotel which specialises in leisure activities such as golf, tennis and swimming.

Soft-shell Crabs have shed their shell as they grow. The new shell is soft and edible and is whole crab is often served in a sandwich.

Rockfish A striped bass harvested from the Chesapeake Bay and its tributaries

Lyme Disease (see above) can be avoided by wearing long trousers and sleeves. The most common hiking problem is **Poison Oak**. This oak-like plant is usually a shrub, sometimes a vine (**Poison Ivy**), and always a trailside hazard. Variable leaf shapes make the plant difficult to identify, although the leaves always occur in clusters of three and usually look like rounded oak leaves. Leaves are bright, glossy green in spring and summer, bright red in fall, and dead in winter – but not forgotten.

All parts of the plant, leaves, stems, and flowers, exude a sticky sap that causes an intense allergic reaction in most people. The most common symptoms are red rash, itching, burning, and weeping sores. The best way to avoid the problem is to avoid the plant. Second best is to wash skin or clothing that has come into contact with the plant immediately in hot, soapy water. If you are afflicted, drying lotions such as calamine or products containing cortisone provide temporary relief, but time is the only cure.

Bears (found in western Maryland) are the only attacking animal in the Capital Region. Never feed bears, as they won't know when the meal is over. Shouting and banging pots is usually enough to persuade a curious bear to search for food elsewhere.

HITCH-HIKING

In an earlier, more trustful era, hitch-hiking was the preferred mode of transportation for budget travellers. Today, hitch-hiking or picking up hitch-hikers is asking for violent trouble, from theft to physical assault and murder. *Don't do it.*

INSURANCE

Experienced travellers carry insurance that covers their belongings and holiday investment as well as their bodies. Travel insurance should include provision for cancelled or delayed flights and weather problems, as well as immediate evacuation home in the case of medical emergency. Thomas Cook and other travel agencies offer comprehensive policies. Medical cover should be high – at least $1 million. Insurance for drivers is covered in more detail in the 'Driving in the Capital 4Region' chapter, p.43.

LANGUAGE

English is the official language, but recently arrived immigrants speak dozens of languages.

Even English can cause non-US visitors a few difficulties, and a selection of commonly encountered terms which may be unfamiliar or have a different meaning in America are set out in the box, left. The next chapter, 'Driving in the Capital Region', also provides a glossary of motoring terms for the non-US driver.

LUGGAGE

Less is more where luggage is concerned. Porters don't exist outside the most expensive hotels and luggage trolleys (baggage carts) are rare. Trolleys at airports must be hired in US currency – even though there is no *'bureau de change'* until after customs and immigration.

Luggage has to be light enough to carry. The normal trans-atlantic luggage

27

allowance is 2 pieces, each of 70 lb (32 kg) maximum, per person.

Luggage must also fit in the car or other form of transport. Americans buy the same cars as Europeans, Australians and the rest of the world, not the enormous 'boats' of the 1960s. If it won't fit in the boot at home, don't count on cramming it into a car hired in the USA.

MAPS

The best all-round maps are produced by the **American Automobile Association** and distributed through its affiliates in the Capital Region (see also p.34). State, regional, county, and city maps are available free at all AAA offices, but only to members. Fortunately, most automobile clubs around the world have reciprocal agreements with AAA to provide maps and other member services. Be prepared to show a membership card to obtain service.

Rand McNally road maps and atlases are probably the best known of the ranges available outside the USA, in the travel section of bookshops and more specialist outlets.

The most detailed road maps available are produced by **Thomas Brothers**; *tel: (800) 899-6277*, sold at most booksellers around the region.

For back-country travel, **US Geological Survey** quadrangle (topographic) maps show terrain reliably; they can be purchased at bookshops and outdoor supply shops. Before leaving civilisation behind, compare every available map for discrepancies, then check with forest or park personnel. Most are experienced backcountry enthusiasts themselves, and since they're responsible for rescuing lost hikers, they have a vested interest in dispensing the best possible information and advice.

MEETING PEOPLE

Americans are friendly, at least on the surface. As in much of the world, asking for directions, map in hand, is an 'icebreaker'. Friendliness does not extend to inviting new acquaintances to their homes, however. Yet, a bed and breakfast is an excellent place to meet 'locals' on holiday. Sports events, casual restaurants and bars can be meeting places, but most local people are wary of approaches by strangers. Professional associations, sports or interest clubs welcome visitors from abroad; contact well in advance for meeting times and venues. Check Fri or Sun newspapers for listings of events and attractions.

Street fairs, increasingly popular in the Eastern USA, and food festivals bring out crowds with a variety of interests.

Maryland World Trade Center Institute, *World Trade Center, Baltimore, MD 21202; tel: (410) 576-0022*, offers business and professional connections.

OPENING HOURS

Office hours are generally 0900–1700, Mon–Fri, although a few tourist offices also keep Sat hours. Most banks and other financial institutions are open 1000–1600 Mon–Thur, 1000–1800 on Fri, and 0900–1300 Sat. ATMs (cashpoints) are open 24 hours.

Small shops keep standard business hours. Large shops and shopping centres open at 0900 or 1000 Mon–Sat and close at 2000 or 2100. Opening hours are slightly shorter on Sun.

Many restaurants, museums, and legitimate theatres close on Mon, but most tourist attractions are open seven days a week.

PARKS INFORMATION

For specific national and state parks, monuments, and seashores, see the appropriate description among the recommended routes throughout this book.

For general information on national parks, monuments and seashores in Virginia, Maryland and Washington, DC, contact the **National Park Service**, *National Capital Region, 1100 Ohio Dr. S.W., Washington DC 20242; tel: (202) 619-7222.*

For **Virginia State Parks** information, contact *Virginia Department of Conservation and Recreation, 203 Governor St, Ste 302, Richmond, VA 23219; tel: (804) 786-1712;* for **Maryland**, **state park** details are available from the *Department of Natural Resources, State Forest and Park Service; tel: (410) 974-3771.*

PASSPORTS AND VISAS

All non-US citizens must have a valid full passport and, except for Canadians, a visa, in order to enter the United States. Citizens of most countries must obtain from a visa from the US Embassy in their country of residence in advance of arrival.

British citizens and New Zealand citizens can complete a visa waiver form, which they generally receive with their air tickets if the airline is a 'participating carrier'. Provided nothing untoward is declared, such as a previous entry refusal or a criminal conviction, which would make application for a full visa mandatory, the waiver exempts visitors from the need for a visa for stays of up to 90 days. It also allows a side-trip overland into Mexico or Canada and return.

In the UK, your local Thomas Cook branch can advise on, and obtain, US visas.

Note: Documentation regulations change frequently and are complex for some nationalities; confirm your requirements with a good travel agent or the nearest US Embassy at least 90 days before you plan to depart for the USA.

POLICE

To telephone police in an emergency, ring 911. There are many different police jurisdictions – state, city and county – each with its own force. The highways in each state of the Capital Region are patrolled by that state's police.

Washington's force is the Metropolitan Police Department and Virginia State Police patrol that state. In Maryland, the police are known as state troopers. See also under 'Security' on the next page and 'Police' in the next chapter.

POSTAL SERVICES

Every town has a least one post office. Hours vary, although all are open Mon–Fri, morning and afternoon. Postal Service branches may be open Sat or even Sun. Some big hotels sell stamps through the concierge; large department stores may have a post office; and supermarkets like Safeway sell stamps at the checkout counter. Stamp machines are installed in some stores, but a surcharge may be included in the cost. For philatelic sales, check major city telephone directories under US Postal Service.

Mail everything going overseas as Air Mail (surface mail takes weeks or even months). If posting letters near an urban area, mail should take about one week. Add a day or two if mailing from remote areas.

Poste Restante is available at any post office, without charge. Mail should be addressed in block lettering to your name, Poste Restante/General Delivery, city, state, post office's zip (postal) code, and United States of America (do not abbreviate). Mail is held for 30 days at the post office branch that handles General Delivery for each town or city, usually the main office. General Delivery zip codes include:

29

Washington, DC: 20090-9999
Baltimore: 21233-9999
Richmond: 23232-9999
Norfolk: 23503-9999
Annapolis 21401-9999

Identification is required for mail collection.

PUBLIC HOLIDAYS

America's love affair with the road extends to jumping in the automobile for holiday weekends. Local celebrations, festivals, parades, or neighbourhood parties can disrupt some or all activities in town. Independence Day and New Year's Eve bring fireworks and big celebrations, and Presidents' Day is particulary marked with large sales by retailers.

New Year (1 Jan); Martin Luther King Jr Day (third Mon in Jan); Lincoln's Birthday (12 Feb); Presidents' Day or George Washington's birthday (third Mon in Feb); Easter (Sun in Mar/Apr); Memorial Day (last Mon in May); US Independence Day (4 July); Labor Day (first Mon in Sept); Columbus Day or Indigenous Peoples Day (second Mon in Oct); Veterans Day (11 Nov); Thanksgiving Day (last Thurs in Nov); and Christmas (25 Dec).

Post offices and government offices close on public holidays. Some businesses take the day off, though department and discount stores use the opportunity to hold huge sales, well advertised in local newspapers. Petrol stations remain open. Small shops and some grocery stores close or curtail hours.

Call in advance before visiting an attraction on a public holiday as there are frequently special hours. National and state park campsites and lodging must be reserved in advance for all holidays. Easter, Thanksgiving, and Christmas are family holidays, and accommodation is available and may even be discounted (to fill hotels and motels). Other holidays are 'mobile' for Americans, so book early. The most festive holiday is 4 July, Independence Day, when most cities have public firework displays.

SALES TAXES

There is no Value Added Tax or Goods & Services Tax in the USA. Most states charge sales tax for most products and services, itemised separately on every bill, and beware, as advertised prices rarely include the tax.

In District of Columbia, sales tax is 5.75%; restaurant tax is 10%; and hotel tax is 13% plus $1.50 per night room.

In Virginia, sales tax is 3.5% and 1% local tax; food and lodging taxes are extra and vary from location to location.

In Maryland, Sales Tax is 5%; lodging tax varies. There is no state sales tax in Delaware, but accommodation taxes vary according to location.

Pennsylvania applies a 6% sales tax, plus variable lodgings tax.

SECURITY

Throwing caution to the wind is foolhardy at any time, and even more so on holiday. The US, by history and inclination, permits guns to circulate, both legally and illegally. Dial 911 on any telephone for free emergency assistance from police, fire and medical authorities.

On the other hand, millions of people travel in perfect safety each year in the USA. So can you if you take the following commonsense precautions.

Travelling Safely

Never publicly discuss travel plans or

money or valuables you are carrying. Use caution in large cities, towns, and rural areas. Drive, park, and walk only in well-lit areas. If unsure of roads or weather ahead, stop for the evening and find secure lodging. Sightsee with a known companion, or in a group. Solo travel, in urban areas or in the countryside, is not recommended.

The best way to avoid becoming a victim of theft or bodily injury is to walk with assurance and try to give the impression that you are not worth robbing (e.g. do not wear or carry expensive jewellery or flash rolls of banknotes). Use a hidden money-belt for your valuables, travel documents, and spare cash.

Carrying a wallet in a back pocket or leaving a handbag open is an invitation to every pickpocket in the vicinity. In all public places, take precautions with anything that is obviously worth stealing – use a handbag with a crossed shoulder strap and a zip, wind the strap of your camera case around your chair or place your handbag firmly between your feet under the table while you eat.

Never leave luggage unattended. At airports, security officials may confiscate unattended luggage as a possible bomb. In public toilets, handbags and small luggage has been snatched from hooks, or from under stalls. Airports and bus and train stations usually have lockers. Most work with keys; take care to guard the key and memorise the locker number. Hotel bell staff may keep luggage for one or more days on request, and for a fee – be sure to get receipts for left luggage before surrendering it.

Concealing a weapon is against the law. Some defensive products resembling tear gas are legal only for persons certified in their proper use. Mugging, by individuals or gangs, is a social problem in the USA. If

you are attacked, it is safer to let go of your bag or hand over the small amount of obvious money – as you are more likely to be attacked physically if the thief meets with resistance. *Never resist.* Report incidents immediately to local police, even if it is only to get a copy of their report for your insurance company.

Driving Safely

Have car hire counter personnel recommend a safe, direct route on a clear map before you leave with the vehicle. Lock all valuables and luggage in the boot or glove box so that nothing is visible to passers-by or other drivers. Don't leave maps, brochures, or guidebooks in evidence – why advertise that you're a stranger in town?

Always keep car doors and windows locked. Do not venture into unlit areas, neighbourhoods that look seedy, or off paved roads. *Do not stop* if told by a passing motorist or pedestrian that something is wrong with your car, or if someone signals for help with a broken-down car. If you need to stop, do so only in well-lit or populated areas, even if your car is bumped from behind by another vehicle. If your car breaks down, turn on the flashing emergency lights, and if it is safe to get out, raise the bonnet and return to the vehicle. Do not split passengers up. Expressway telephone call boxes are normally spaced half a mile apart. Lights on emergency vehicles are red or red and blue, so do not stop for flashing white lights or flashing headlights. Ask directions only from police, in a well-lit business area, or at a service station.

At night, have keys ready to unlock car doors before entering a parking lot. Check the surrounding area and inside the vehicle before entering. Never pick up hitchhikers, and never leave the car with the engine running. Take all valuables with you.

Sleeping Safely

When sleeping rough, in any sort of dormitory, train, or open campsite, the safest place for your small valuables is at the bottom of your sleeping-bag. In sleeping-cars, padlock your luggage to the seat, and ask the attendant to show you how to lock your compartment door at night. If in doubt, it's best to take luggage with you.

In hotels, motels, and all other lodging, lock all doors from the inside. Check that all windows are locked, including sliding glass doors. Ground-floor rooms, while convenient, give easier access by those intent on breaking in. Never leave the room at night without leaving a light on. Lights deter prowlers, and when you return, any disturbance will be visible.

Use a door viewer to check before admitting anyone to your room. If someone claims to be on the hotel staff or a repair person, do not let the person in before phoning the office or front desk to verify the person's name and job. Money, cheques, credit cards, passports and keys should be with you, or secured in your hotel's safe deposit box. When checking in, find the most direct route from your room to fire escapes, elevators, stairwells and the nearest telephone.

Documents

Take a few passport photos with you and photocopy the important pages and any visa stamps in your passport. Store these safely, together with a note of the numbers of your traveller's cheques, credit cards, and insurance documents (keep them away from the documents themselves). Leave another set of copies at home. If you are unfortunate enough to be robbed, you will at least have some identification, and

replacing the documents will be much easier. Apply to your nearest embassy (see 'Embassies' in this chapter for addresses and phone numbers).

SHOPPING

Virginian souvenirs include shortbread cookies, apple butter, tins of peanuts. In Washington, DC, head for the museum shops, particularly the Smithsonian, for interesting and unusual gifts. Maryland is renowned for its steamed blue crabs, so its souvenir shops are filled with stuffed crabs, toy crabs and coffee mugs and other objects bearing crab motifs. Roadside stands offer apple butter and other preserves. The state's Eastern Shore is the place to buy decoy ducks.

Clothing and shoes can be a bargain, particularly at discount or factory outlet stores, as can pewter, linens, luggage, cosmetics, sunglasses, Levi's jeans and trainers. Cameras and other photo equipment can be a fraction of UK prices, but do your homework on prices before you go, and shop around when you arrive.

Tape cassettes, blank video tapes, CDs, computer programs, and CD-ROMs sold in the USA can be used anywhere in the world. For more information on electrical goods, see 'Electricity' in this chapter.

SMOKING

Lighting up is out in public buildings and public transportation. All plane flights in the USA are non-smoking, and some hire

Colour section: (i) Re-creating a Civil War battle at Wilderness, Orange County, Virginia. Washington, DC. (see pp. 65–92):
(ii) Ford's Theatre; a view along the National Mall.
(iii) A view towards the Capitol; the Jefferson Memorial.
(iv) The Capitol Building at dusk.

cars are designated as non-smoking. Most hotels/motels set aside non-smoking rooms or floors; bed and breakfast establishments are almost all non-smoking. Restaurant dining regulations vary by locality; some forbid all smoking; others permit it in the bar or lounge only; some have a percentage of the eatery devoted to smokers. Smoking is prohibited in most stores and shops. Always ask before lighting a cigarette, cigar, or pipe. When in doubt, go outside to smoke.

TELEPHONES

The US telephone system is divided into local and long-distance carriers. Depending on the time of day and day of the week, it may be cheaper to call Los Angeles than to call 30 miles (48 km) away. After 1700, Mon–Fri, and all weekend, rates are lower. Useful phone numbers are provided throughout this book.

Public telephones are everywhere, indicated by a sign with a white telephone receiver depicted on a blue field. Enclosed booths, wall-mounted, or free-standing machines are all used. If possible, use public phones in well-lit, busy public areas.

Dialling instructions are in the front of the local white-pages telephone directory. For all long-distance calls, precede the area code with a *1*. In emergencies, call *911* for police, medical, or fire brigade response. *0* reaches an operator. For local number information, dial *411*. For long-distance phone information, dial *1*, the area code, then *555-1212*. There is a charge for information calls.

Pay phones take coins, and a local call costs $0.20–$0.25 upwards. An operator or computer voice will come on-line to ask for additional coins when needed. Many hotels and motels add a stiff surcharge to the basic cost of a call, so find a public telephone in the lobby.

Prepaid phone cards are becoming available at grocery and convenience stores. Before you travel, ask your local phone company if your phone card will work in the USA. Most do, and come with a list of contact numbers. However, remember that the USA has the cheapest overseas phone rates in the world, which makes it cheaper to fill pay phones with quarters than to reverse charges. A credit card may be convenient, but only economical if you pay the bill immediately.

For comparison, local call rates:
coin $0.20–0.25
direct dial, calling card $0.35
operator-assisted, calling card $0.95

800 and *888* numbers are toll-free. Like all long-distance numbers, the *800/888* area code must be preceded by a *1*, e.g. *1-800-123-4567*. Some US telephone numbers are given in letters, i.e. *1-800-VISIT-DC*. Telephone keys have both numbers and letters, so find the corresponding letter and depress that key. A few numbers have more than seven letters to finish a business name. Not to worry, US or Canadian phone numbers never require more than seven numerals, plus three for the area code.

Dial an international operator on *00* for enquiries or assistance.

For international dialling, dial *011-country code-city code* (omitting the first 0 if there is one)-*local number;* e.g., to call Great Britain, Inner London, from the USA, dial: *011-44-171-local number.* Some country codes:

Australia 61
New Zealand 64
Republic of Ireland 353
South Africa 27
United Kingdom 44

Generally, *(202)* is the area code for Washington, DC. In Virginia *(804)* applies for Richmond and Central Virginia, *(757)* applies to South-eastern locations such as Williamsburg, Norfolk and Virginia Beach, *(703)* to the Northern Virginia suburbs of Washington DC, and *(504)* to the mountain region.

In Maryland, *(301)* covers the western part of the state and *(410)* the east. Delaware is covered by one area code *(302)*, and the Philadelphia area of Pennsylvania is *(215)*.

TIME

District of Columbia, Virginia, Maryland, Delaware and Pennsylvania share a time zone (along with New York and New Jersey), GMT -5 hrs, called **Eastern Standard Time** (EST).

Daylight Saving Time is common to these states – from the end of April to the end of October, clocks are pushed forward one hour.

TIPPING

Acknowledgement for good service should not be extorted. That said, tipping

is a fact of life, to get or to thank someone for service.

Service charges are not customarily added to restaurant bills. Waiters and waitresses expect a tip of at least 15% of the bill before taxes are added on. In luxury restaurants, also be prepared to tip the maître d' and sommelier a few dollars, up to 10% of the bill. Bartenders expect the change from a drink, up to several dollars.

Hotel porters generally receive $1 per bag; a bellperson who shows you to the room expects several dollars; in luxury properties, tip more. Room service delivery staff should be tipped 10–15% of the tariff before taxes, unless there's a service charge indicated on the bill. Expect to hand out dollars for most services that involve room delivery.

Tip taxi drivers 15% unless the service was bad. Cloakroom attendents should receive up to $1 per coat unless a charge is posted.

Some hotels will have a chambermaid name card placed in the room: it's an unsubtle hint for a tip of a few dollars upon your departure, but never required. Ushers in legitimate theatres, arenas, and stadiums are not tipped; cinemas seldom have ushers, nor are tips expected.

Time in Capital Region (EST)	8 a.m.	12 p.m.	5 p.m.	12 a.m.
Time in				
Auckland	1 a.m.	5 a.m.	10 a.m.	5 p.m.
Cape Town	3 p.m.	7 p.m.	12 a.m.	7 a.m.
Dublin	1 p.m.	5 p.m.	10 p.m.	5 a.m.
London	1 p.m.	5 p.m.	10 p.m.	5 a.m.
Perth	9 p.m.	1 a.m.	6 p.m.	1 p.m.
Sydney	11 p.m.	3 a.m.	8 a.m.	3 p.m.
Toronto	8 a.m.	12 p.m.	5 p.m.	12 a.m.

TOILETS

There is nothing worse than not being able to find one! *Restroom* or *bathroom* are the common terms; *toilet* is acceptable; few people recognise *washroom, loo* or *WC*. Most are marked with a figure for a male or a female; *Men* and *women* are the most common terms. Occasionally, a restroom may be used by both sexes.

Facilities may be clean and well-equipped or filthy. Most businesses, including bars and restaurants, reserve restrooms for clients. Petrol stations provide keys for customers to access

Thomas Cook and AAA

The American Automobile Association (commonly referrred to as AAA, pronounced 'Triple A') is one of the largest leisure travel businesses in the United States, with 1000 travel agency locations across the country, operated by regional Automobile Clubs which in turn constitute AAA. The Thomas Cook Group has formed an alliance with AAA which, from 1 January 1997, gives visitors to the States who have booked their travel arrangements with Thomas Cook access to the benefits of the Thomas Cook Worldwide Customer Promise at AAA travel agency locations. Courtesy services available under this arrangement include changes to airline reservations and ticket revalidation, hotel and car rental reservations, travel planning and emergency local phone assistance, all free of agency service charges.

To find the nearest AAA location, check the local phone directory or Yellow Pages. AAA of Tidewater has 6 branches in Virginia; AAA Potomac has 4 agencies in Virginia and Maryland and one in Washington, DC; AAA Mid Atlantic has 19 across Delaware, Maryland and Virginia, and one in Philadelphia; and other areas of Pennsylvania covered in this book have 5 AAA locations, operated by Central Penn Automobile Club and AAA Southern Pennsylvania.

restrooms. Public toilets are sporadically placed, but well-marked. Parks, roadside rest stops and welcome centres have toilet facilities. Carry toilet paper.

TOURIST INFORMATION

Each state in the US is responsible for its own tourism promotion:

Maryland Office of Tourism, *217 E. Redwood St, Baltimore, MD 21202; tel: (410) 333 6611.* Their UK office is at *Spittal Barn, Main Street, Great Bourton, Oxon OX17 1QL.*

Virginia Division of Tourism, *901 E. Byrd St, Richmond, VA 23219; tel: (804) 7862051.* In the UK, **Virginia Division of Tourism**, *1st Floor, 182–184 Addington Rd, Selsdon, Surrey, CR2 8LB; tel: (0181) 651-4743.*

Washington DC Convention & Visitors Association; *1212 New York Ave, NW Washington, DC 20005; tel: (202) 789 7000, or 375 Upper Richmond Rd West, East Sheen, London SW14 7JG; tel: (0181) 392-9187* (in the UK).

Pennsylvania Office of Tourism,

453 Forum Building, Harrisburg, Pennsylvania 17120; tel: (717) 787-5453. Their UK office is at *11/15 Betterton St, London, WC2H 9BP; tel: (0171) 470 8801.*

In addition, Maryland, Virginia and Washington, DC are represented together in the UK as **Capital Region USA**, *375 Upper Richmond Rd West, East Sheen, London SW14 7JG; tel: (0181) 392-9187*

TRAINS

Amtrak is the official passenger train transportation company in the United States; *tel: (800) 872-7245.* Its Metroliner, Northeast Direct and Clocker services run from New York via Philadelphia to Washington, with some trains running on to Richmond. Trains do not stop at each town en route, so check if there is a stop at your destination. For reservations, *tel: (800) 523-8720.*

Train times for many Amtrak and local services are published in the *Thomas Cook Overseas Timetable* (see under 'Useful Reading' in this chapter).

Websites

The World Wide Web is another source of information on the Capital Region. Listed below are a few sites you might wish to try, and if they don't have the information or attraction that your are looking for, your favourite search engine might turn up a new website.

For details of Thomas Cook and its services around the world, visit its website on *http://www.thomascook.com*. For Thomas Cook Holiday details and the latest special offers visit: *http://www.tch.thomascook.com*

District of Columbia:
Tourism: *http://washington.org*
Washington Hotel Reservations: *http://www.bot.org/buyguide.html#CODE3378*
Washington Metro System: *http://www.nim.nih.gov/directions/dir/metro.html*

Delaware
Visitor Guide: *http://www.city.net.countries.united_states/delaware/*
Tourism: *http://www.state.de.us/tourism/intro.htm*

Maryland
Tourism: *http://www.mdisfun.orf/mdisfun*
Visitor Guide: *http://www.city.net/countries/united_states/maryland/*

Baltimore: *http://www.umbc.edu/campus-resources.html#resources*

Pennsylvania
Hotels/resorts: *att.net/800/cat/h/Oc.html*
Philadelphia accommodation: *http://www.tmgroup.com/asta.hotels.html*
Philadelphia Visitors Guide: *libertynet.org/phila-visitor*

Virginia
Tourism Guide: *http://www.virginia.org*
Virginia dining guide: *http://www.infi.net/vadner/index.html*
Staunton Visitor guide: *http://www.elpress.com/staunton*

Amtrak sells a Northeast Region Rail Pass which gives 15 or 30 days of unlimited train travel on its system in the northeast at prices in the range of $165–215. This is available from **Leisurail** in the UK, *tel: (01733) 335599.*

TRAVEL ARRANGEMENTS

Given the fact that most of the world's international airlines fly into either Washington DC and New York, and the ease of hiring cars at airports, the Capital Region is an ideal destination for independently minded travellers. However, the many types of air ticket and the range of temporary deals available on the busy routes make it advisable to talk to your travel agent before booking, to get the best bargain.

In fact, taking a fly-drive package such as one of Thomas Cook's own, or one of the many others offered by airlines and tour operators, is usually more economical than making all your own arrangements. All include the air ticket and car hire element; some also follow set itineraries which enables them to offer guaranteed and pre-paid en route accommodation at selected hotels.

Programmes such as Thomas Cook

Holiday's *America for the Independent Traveller* allow the flexibility of booking the airline ticket at an advantageous rate and then choosing from a 'menu' of other items, often at a discounted price, such as car hire, hotel coupons (which pre-pay accommodation but do not guarantee availability of rooms) and other extras.

USEFUL READING

Another useful Thomas Cook publications, if you are considering using trains or buses for any part of your trip, are the *Thomas Cook Overseas Timetable* (published every 2 months, £8.40 per issue) For more details of Thomas Cook publications see p. 15).

Few guidebook series feature a volume covering all three states that make up the Capital Region. A number of series, such as *Lonely Planet,* do produce a volume that covers only Washington, DC.

If you are arranging your own accommodation as you travel, a comprehensive guide such as the *AAA TourBooks for the Mid-Atlantic* and for *New Jersey and Pennsylvania,* or one of the *Mobil Regional Guides* can often be obtained through specialist travel bookshops outside the USA.

To find out more about the region's history, then any volumes featuring this area from *National Geographic Books* or *American Heritage Publishing* are worth seeking out. Bruce Catton is an authority on the Civil War. Recently published is his *American Heritage New History of the Civil War* (published by Viking in the UK). An earlier publication by the same author is *Civil War*, from American Heritage Publishing.

For a fuller account of the Revolutionary War from National Geographic, try *The Revolutionary War: America's Fight for Freedom* by Bart McDowell.

Other books, fact or fiction, that reflect parts of the Capital Region or have been written by one of the region's famous sons or daughters are:

Bay Tripper, A Chesapeake Bay travel Guide, Whitey Schmidt
Chesapeake, James Michener
The Fall of the House of Usher, Edgar Allan Poe
Maryland, the Seventh State, John T Marck
North and South, John Jakes
Oral History, Lee Smith
Primary Colours, Anon
Red Coat, Bernard Cornwell
The Red Badge of Courage, Stephen Crane
The Pelican Guide to Maryland, Victor Block
The Virginian, Owen Wister
Washington, Gore Vidal

WHAT TO TAKE

Absolutely everything you could ever need is available. In fact most US prices will seem low: competition and oversupply keeps them that way. Pharmacies (chemists), also called drug stores, carry a range of products, from medicine to cosmetics to beach balls. Prepare a small first aid kit before you leave home with tried and tested insect repellent, sun-screen and soothing, moisturising lotion. Carry all medicines, glasses, and contraceptives with you, and keep duplicate prescriptions or a letter from your doctor to verify your need for a particular medication. Other useful items to bring or buy immediately upon arrival are a water-bottle, sunglasses, a hat or visor with a rim, a Swiss Army pocket knife, a torch, a padlock for anchoring luggage, a money belt, a plug adapter, string for a washing line, an alarm clock and a camera. Those planning to rough it should take a sleeping-bag, a sheet liner and an inflatable travel pillow.

DRIVING IN THE CAPITAL REGION

This chapter provides hints and practical advice for visitors taking to the road in the Capital Region, whether in a hire car or RV, or in their own vehicle.

ACCIDENTS AND BREAKDOWNS

Holidays should be trouble-free, yet **breakdowns** can occur. Pull off to the side of the road where visibility is good and you are out of the way of traffic. Turn on hazard flashers or indicators, and, if it is safe, get out and raise the bonnet. Change a tyre only when safely out of the traffic flow.

For emergencies dial **911** (free) on any telephone to reach police, fire, or medical services. Emergency call boxes are placed about every half-mile on some highways and can be used to report breakdowns or a need for petrol. Give your phone number, location, problem, and need for first aid.

If involved in a **collision**, stop, and if there are no serious injuries move your vehicle out of the travel lane onto the side of the highway. Call the state police if there are injuries or excessive physical damage to either vehicle. Show the police your driver's licence, car registration, car insurance coverage, address and contact information. It is also a legal requirement to show your licence to the other party in the accident, if requested.

Fly-drive travellers should bear in mind the effects of **jet-lag** on driver safety. This can be a very real problem. The best way to minimise it is to spend the first night after arrival in a hotel at the airport or in the city and pick up your hire vehicle the next day, rather than to take the car on the road within hours of getting off the plane.

CAR HIRE

Hiring a car or RV (camper) gives you the freedom of the road with a vehicle you can leave behind after a few weeks. Whether booking a fly-drive package with an agency or making independent arrangements, plan well in advance to ensure you get the type and size of vehicle your heart desires. Free, unlimited mileage is common with cars, less so with RVs.

Sheer volume in airport rental car turnover means that in the USA it's usually cheaper to pick up the vehicle from an airport than from a downtown site, and to return it to the airport. A surcharge (called a drop fee) may be levied if you drop the car off in a different location from the place of hire. When considering an RV, ask about one-way and off-season rates.

You will need a valid credit card as security for the vehicle's value. Before you leave the hire agency, ensure that you have all documentation for the hire, that the car registration is in the glove box, and you understand how to operate the vehicle. For RVs, also get instruction books and a complete demonstration of all systems and appliances and how they interconnect. Avoid hiring a car that exhibits a hire company name on a window sticker, on the fender (bumper), or on licence plate frames. It's advertising for criminal attention.

Car size terminology varies, but general

categories range from small and basic to all-frills posh: sub-compact, compact, economy, mid-size or intermediate, full-size or standard, and luxury. Sub-compacts are rarely available. Expect to choose between two- or four-door models. The larger the car, the faster it accelerates and consumes petrol. Some vehicles are equipped with four-wheel drive (4WD), unnecessary except for off-road driving (not covered in this book).

Standard features on US hire cars usually include automatic transmission, air conditioning (a necessity for summer driving) and cruise control, which sets speeds for long-distance highway driving, allowing the driver to take his or her foot off the accelerator.

DIFFICULT DRIVING

Fog and Rain
Fog can occasionally be heavy in low-lying or coastal areas and is treacherous to drive in. Turn on the headlights, but use only the low beams to prevent blinding oncoming drivers as well as yourself with reflective glare. Lower your speed; look for reflective road markings to guide you.

Heavy downpours can begin suddenly, making driving dangerous. When travelling on the interstate, it may be advisable to pull over into a rest stop until bad weather passes. The risk of 'hydroplaning' increases on rain-slicked roads and bridges between 35–55 mph; lower your speed when roads are wet, and pump your brakes gradually when slowing or stopping.

Winter
In winter visibility can be nil due to high winds and blowing snow. Because of slower speed limits and slippery roads, plan on taking more time to get to and through areas with snow-covered streets. Local radio stations broadcast weather information. Interstates and other major highways are ploughed promptly and kept clear with sand and salt.

Useful items are an ice scraper, a small shovel for digging out, warm sleeping bags, blankets and extra clothing in case of long delays. Keep the petrol tank at least half-filled if possible, in case you're stuck for a while.

If you get stuck in a snowstorm: *Stay in the vehicle* until help arrives, put a red flag on the radio antenna or door handle and keep warm with blankets; run the engine and heater only until the car is warm, then turn it off. Open windows a little to give ventilation and prevent carbon monoxide poisoning. *Do not go to sleep.*

DISTANCES
Point-to-point distances are manageable in the Capital Region. All major tourist attractions are at most one to three hours apart. Plan on 50 mph *direct* driving time, without stops, longer in cities and in the mountains. Use the sample driving distances and times on p.345 as guidelines but allow for delays and stops.

DOCUMENTATION
In the Capital Region, your home country's driver's licence is valid. The minimum driving age is 16 in all the states of the region. Car hire companies may have higher age requirements, typically 21 or over (with additional charges for under-25 drivers).

INFORMATION
Automobile club membership in your home country can be invaluable. AAA clubs (see p. 35) provide members of corresponding foreign clubs travelling to North America the reciprocal services that

39

AAA members are eligible to receive abroad. For information on reciprocal clubs and services, contact your own club or request *Offices to Serve You Abroad, American Automobile Association, 1000 AAA Drive, Heathrow, FL 32746-5063; tel: (407) 444-7700.* Carry your own club membership card with you at all times.

For traffic reports, turn on the radio. In some areas the frequency to tune in to is indicated by roadside signs

MOTORCYCLES

If *Easy Rider* is still your idea of America, so be it. Motorcycles provide great mobility and a sense of freedom. Luggage will be limited, however; vast distances can make for long days in the saddle; and remember that potholes, gravel, poor roads, dust, smog and sun are a motorcyclist's touring companions.

Hire motorcycles locally by finding a telephone directory listing. Helmets are required by law for both driver and passenger. By custom, most motor-cyclists turn on the headlight even in the daytime to increase their visibility.

PARKING

Public parking garages (car parks) are indicated by a blue sign showing P with a directional arrow. Prices are posted at the entrance. Some city centre garages charge per 20 mins, at exorbitant rates, sometimes as much as $10.00 per hour. High daily parking changes are more likely apply in Washington, DC than in other states in the Capital Region.

In civic centres, shopping and downtown areas and financial districts, coin-operated parking meters govern kerbside parking. The charge and time limit varies with the location. Compare parking garage against meter charges for the most economic choice.

Kerbs may be colour-coded: *blue* is disabled parking; *white* is for passenger or post drop-off; *green* is limited-time parking, as indicated on the kerb; *yellow* is a loading zone, generally for lorry deliveries; and red is no stopping or parking. No parking is allowed within 15 ft of a fire hydrant, within 3 ft of a disabled person sidewalk ramp, in a bus stop area, at an intersection, crosswalk (pedestrian crossing) or sidewalk, blocking a driveway or on an expressway except in emergencies.

If you park in violation of times and areas posted on kerb signs or poles nearby, or let the parking meter expire, expect to be issued with a citation – a ticket that states the violation, amount of a fine, and how to pay it. If you do not pay it, the car hire company may charge the ticket amount (and any penalties) against your credit card. Fines range from a few dollars to several hundred dollars, depending on the violation and the locality.

Valet parking at garages, hotels, restaurants and events may be pricey, and the parking attendant will expect an additional tip of a few dollars when returning the car. Leave the car keys with the valet attendant, who will return them with the car.

PETROL

Petrol (gas) is sold in US gallons (roughly four litres per gallon). Posted prices including tax are shown in cents – as, for instance, 121.9 (= $1 and 21.9 cents) per gallon. Prices can vary from 100 to 145 cents per gallon, depending on location. In areas with many stations there can be strong price competition. Near urban areas, prices can be lower, but it's pretty much the same for rural and city areas.

Some stations offer full service, filling the petrol tank, washing the windscreen and checking motor oil, usually for about

40

$0.40 more per gallon. Most motorists use the more economical self-service.

Most US cars require unleaded petrol; due to environmental controls, leaded is very rare, and used mostly for farm equipment. The three fuel grades are regular, super and premium: use regular petrol unless the car hire company indicates otherwise. A few vehicles use diesel fuel.

When petrol stations are more than a few miles apart, normally a road sign will state the distance to the next services. Open petrol stations are well lit at night; many chains stay open 24 hours. Most stations accept cash, credit cards and US dollar traveller's cheques. Cheaper stations may only accept cash or require advance payment; check before filling the petrol tank.

POLICE

Police cars signal drivers with flashing red or red and blue lights, and sometimes a siren. Respond quickly, but safely, by moving to the right side of the road. Roll the driver's side window down but stay in the vehicle unless asked to get out. You have the right to ask an officer – politely – for identification, though it should be shown immediately. Have your driver's licence and car registration papers ready for inspection when requested. Officers normally check computer records for vehicle registration irregularities and the driver for theft, criminal record, or other driving violations. If charged, do not argue with the officer, as a bad situation can only get worse.

Remember that you can be fined for littering the highway.

ROAD SIGNS

International symbols are used for directional and warning signs, but many are different from European versions. Signs may be white, yellow, green, brown, or blue.

Stop, give way, do not enter, and wrong-way signs are *red* and *white*. *Yellow* is for warning or direction indicators. *Orange* is for roadworks or detours (temporary diversions). *Green* indicates expressway directions. *Brown* is an alert for parks, campsites, hiking, etc. *Blue* gives non-driving information, such as radio station frequency for traffic or park information, or services in a nearby town. Speed limits and distance are primarily shown in miles, not kilometres. Speed limit signs are *white* with black letters.

Traffic lights are red, yellow and green. Yellow indicates that the light will turn red; stop, if possible, before entering the intersection.

A favourite (and highly illegal) trick is to *jump* the red light, that is, enter the intersection when the signal is yellow and about to turn red. Police can cite you if you enter an intersection and you will not be clear of the intersection before the light turns red.

It is permitted to turn right at a red traffic light if there is no traffic coming from the left, i.e. as if it were a 'give way' sign, unless there is a sign specifically forbidding it ('No Turn on Red'). A flashing yellow light, or hazard warning, requires drivers to slow down; flashing red means stop, then proceed when safe.

ROAD SYSTEM

The US Interstate Highway System was built in the 1950s to streamline cargo transportation across the country. Federal funds maintain the interstates, which are usually the smoothest roads available. **Interstate** highways, designated I-(number) in the text, are the straightest and the usually least scenic route from point to point.

Expressways are fast roads with controlled access, like British motorways. **Highways** have cross traffic interrupting the flow. East–west roads have even numbers, e.g., I-10, I-8, I-80; North–south roads are odd, e.g. I-5, Hwy 1, Hwy 101.

Rest areas, commonly along highways, have restrooms with toilets and public telephones, and are usually landscaped. In Maryland and Virginia these are known as **welcome centers**, and, as well as the usual toilet and phone facilites, there are travel counsellors (usually locals) who can offer travel tips and brochures. Picnic tables are provided in scenic areas and rest stops of historic or geographical interest have explanatory signs or maps. Use caution when leaving your vehicle at night and carry a torch (flashlight).

Local roads can range from satin-smooth to pitted, depending on local spending. Dirt roads indicated on maps or described in this text may be treacherous. Ask at a petrol station about local road conditions before venturing onto them. Car hire companies may prohibit driving on unpaved roads.

Maryland Tourism can supply a **Scenic By-Way** map that shows which roads in the state head through quaint and charming towns. Roads include Rte 40 (the Old National Toll Road), which was the first federally-funded road in the country.

In some states roadsign markers give an explanation of historic points.

RULES OF THE ROAD

Lanes and Overtaking

Drive on the right. Vehicles are left-hand drive. The lane on the left, the *Number 1 Lane*, is fast; the right is slowest, and cars enter or leave traffic from the right (unless otherwise indicated by signs). Overtake other vehicles on the left side. A solid white line at least 4ft from the kerb marks a special lane for bicycles, and should be labelled 'Bike Lane'. *Cars may and will pass you on both sides in a multi-lane road.* For many drivers from the UK, this is the most unexpected and confusing feature of US roads. Use direction indicators, but don't be surprised if other drivers don't bother. Never turn against a red arrow.

Make right turns from the right-hand lane after stopping at stop signs or traffic lights. Turn left from the most left-hand of lanes going in your direction, unless the turn is prohibited by a no-turn sign. Enter bike lanes only if making a right turn. Do not drive in areas marked for public transportation or pedestrians, or HOV (High-occupancy vehicle) lanes during commuter hours – usually 0600–0900 and 1500–1800 – unless there are three or more people in the car.

Overtaking on a two-way road is permitted if the yellow line down the centre is broken. Overtake on the left. Highways, especially in mountainous areas or long, narrow stretches of road, have occasional overtaking lanes. Overtake only when oncoming traffic is completely visible, and avoid overtaking in fog or rain. Two solid yellow lines means no overtaking, and no turning unless into a private driveway or for a legal U-turn. Driving or parking on sidewalks is illegal.

Main road drivers have the right of way over cars on lesser roads, but at the junction of two minor roads cars to your right have the right of way when arriving at the same time you do.

Expressway Driving

Lanes are numbered from left to right: number one is the extreme left-hand lane, number two the next lane to the right, and so on. An 'exit' or 'off ramp' is the ramp (slip road) leading off the expressway; an 'entrance' or 'on ramp' leads onto the expressway. 'Metering lights' are traffic lights controlling ramp access.

When expressway traffic does flow, it flows smoothly and quickly. The safest speed is that which matches the general traffic flow in your lane while paying close attention to the posted speed limit.

When entering an expressway, *don't stop* on the ramp unless access is controlled by a traffic signal. Accelerate on the ramp and merge into the expressway flow. Cars that stop on the ramp are likely to be hit from the rear.

Carpool lanes

Some highways and busy commuter routes may have **carpool lanes** for vehicles carrying several passengers; signs will specify the number of passengers required to access those speedier lanes, and the effective hours. Carpool lanes, also known as diamond lanes or HOV (high occupancy vehicle) lanes, are marked on the roadbed with a white diamond symbol. Special bus lanes will be marked.

Horns

Horns should be sounded only as a safety warning, and never near a hospital.

Pedestrians

Pedestrians can legally cross at intersections, even if crosswalks (pedestrian crossings) are not indicated. Some cities or towns may cite pedestrians for jaywalking. If a vehicle is involved in an accident with a pedestrian, the presumption of error usually lies with the driver.

Speed Limits

The standard speed limit on expressways is 55 mph (65 mph in Virginia), unless otherwise indicated. Traffic may flow faster or slower than those limits, but law enforcement agencies, city, county and state police can ticket anyone going faster than the limit. You may not see the patrols. Radar guns are used from a distance to track speeds on regular roads.

Regardless of posted speed limits, police can invoke the *Basic Speed Law* that holds that no one can drive faster than is safe. The speed limit is 15–25 mph (depending on the state) around schools and 25–30 mph in most residential districts. At a railway crossing, the speed limit is 15 mph when you cannot see 400 ft down the rails. Go 15 mph in any alley. To go much faster than the posted speeds for mountain driving and when taking bends is to court disaster.

Seat Belts

Seat belts must be worn in by the driver and front-seat passenger (all passengers in DC and Maryland). Children under 5 years and weighing under 40 lb (under 4 in Maryland and Virginia, under 3 in DC) must ride in approved child safety seats. RV passengers behind the driver's area are not required to wear belts, but children should be safely seated while the vehicle is moving.

VEHICLE INSURANCE

State laws lay down varying amounts for minimum third-party liability insurance coverage. In practice, considerably more cover than the minimum is desirable, and overseas visitors hiring a car are strongly recommended to take out top-up liability cover, such as the Topguard Insurance sold by Thomas Cook in the UK, which covers liability up to $1 million. (This is not to be confused with travel insurance, which provides cover for your own medical expenses – see Travel Essentials chapter.)

Car rental agencies will also ask the driver to take out collision damage waiver,

43

or CDW (sometimes called loss damage waiver, LDW). Refusing CDW makes the renter personally liable for damage to the vehicle. CDW is strongly recommended for drivers from outside the USA, and often insisted upon as part of a fly-drive package. Sometimes it is paid for when booking the car hire abroad, sometimes it is payable locally on picking up the car. Occasionally special hire rates will include CDW. US and Canadian drivers using their own cars should ask their insurance company or auto club if their coverage extends to the states you intend to visit and meets their minimum coverage require-

ments. If not, arrange for insurance before signing the car hire contract.

VEHICLE SECURITY

Lock it when you leave, lock it when you're inside, and don't forget the windows. Never leave keys, maps, guidebooks and other tourist paraphernalia in sight. Be mindful of anyone lurking in the back seat or house part of the RV. Watch other drivers for strange behaviour, especially if you're consistently followed. Never leave an engine running when you're not in the vehicle. Keep car keys with you at all times. And always park in well-lit areas.

44

Some US Driving Terms

big rig A large lorry, usually a tractor pulling one or more trailers

boulevard stop Slowing at a stop sign, but not stopping

CNG Liquified petroleum gas used as fuel

crosswalk pedestrian crossing

connector A minor road connecting two freeways

curve bend

divided highway dual carriageway

DUI Driving Under the Influence of alcohol or drugs, aka Drunk Driving. Drink-driving laws are *very* strictly enforced

fender bumper

expressway motorway

garage or *parking garage* car park

gas(oline) petrol

grade gradient, hill

highway trunk road

hood bonnet

metering lights Traffic signals controlling access to bridges, freeways, etc.

motor home motor caravan

pavement road surface. A UK 'pavement' is a *sidewalk*

ramp slip road

rent hire

rubberneck(er) Slowing down to peer while driving past the scene of an accident or some unusual event

RV (recreational vehicle) motor caravan

shoulder verge

sidewalk pavement

sig-alert An official warning of unusually heavy traffic, usually broadcast over local radio stations

shift(stick) gear lever

switchback serpentine road

tailgate Driving too closely to the vehicle immediately in front

tow truck breakdown lorry

traffic cop traffic warden

trailer caravan

truck lorry

trunk boot

unpaved road rough gravel or dirt road – check car hire restrictions on driving

windshield windscreen

yield give way

BACKGROUND
CAPITAL REGION

The Capital Region is usually defined as Washington, DC, Virginia and Maryland. For the purposes of this book, Delaware and south-eastern Pennsylvania have been included for the historical and natural attractions that they bring to this region.

GEOGRAPHY

Some of the most varied terrain in the United States is to be found in the region surrounding the capital city. Here are majestic mountains, rolling hills, extensive forests, broad rivers, picturesque valleys and a coastal area ranging from marshland and swamps to fine, sandy beaches and the splendour of Chesapeake Bay.

The region could be a snapshot of the entire country. There are the big cities – Baltimore, Philadelphia, Washington, DC – and there are smaller, historic places – places like Alexandria, Annapolis, Gettysburg and Richmond, to name but a few. There are quaint fishing villages and remote rural communities.

The most rugged and least populated parts are those in the western part of the region, straddling the **Appalachian Mountains**, which reach northwards from Alabama to New York State. The **Blue Ridge Mountains** and the **Piedmont Plateau** both stretch across Virginia, Maryland and Pennsylvania, with the Piedmont also just touching the northern part of Delaware. The **Atlantic Coastal Plain**, which extends from Florida to Cape Cod, touches each of the

four states covered in this book. In spite of these common features, each area in the region is quite different from the others.

VIRGINIA

Covering more than 39,500 square miles, Virginia has a number of natural regions, each running from south-west to north-east and providing a richly varied landscape.

The state's western border hugs the Appalachian Mountains. In the extreme south-west, where it shares the border with Kentucky, is the **Cumberland Front** where the land lies between 2000 and 3000 ft above sea level. East of the Appalachians is the **Great Appalachian Valley**, with the **Allegheny Mountains** forming the border with West Virginia.

To the east again comes the **Shenandoah Valley**, where the famous river is divided into two sections by **Massanutten Mountain**. Next come the heavily forested **Blue Ridge Mountains**, stretching northwards from North Carolina. The range includes **Mount Rogers**, the highest peak in the state with an altitude of 5729 ft.

The **Piedmont Plateau**, a rolling upland broken by ridges and pudding-shaped hills, crosses the centre of Virginia. It encompasses some very fertile lowland belts, including the area between the **Potomac** and **Rappahannock** rivers.

The **Fall Line**, where rapids and waterfalls bring navigation to an end on rivers, follows a more or less straight line northwards from Emporia, through

45

Richmond, Fredericksburg and Arlington.

The Atlantic Coastal Plain is known to Virginians as the **Tidewater Region**. This is a lowland area, rising to about 300 ft. At sea level, much of the area is covered by marshland and swamps, the largest of which is the Great Dismal Swamp in the state's south-east corner. One of the largest wooded wetlands in the mid-Atlantic region, **Great Dismal Swamp** is now a National Wildlife Refuge with a wide range of plants, birds and animals. Cypress trees also flourish in the refuge, a reminder that Virginia is part of the South.

The waters of **Chesapeake Bay**, whose mouth separates Northampton and Accomack counties from the rest of Virginia, cover an ancient coastline to form deep tidal estuaries at the mouths of the **Potomac, Rappahannock, York** and **James** rivers.

Climate

Virginia's average temperatures are about 36°F in winter and 74°F in summer, but temperatures vary according to altitude and latitude. The state suffers heavy rainfall at times, with the average annual precipitation amounting to about 44 inches.

Wildlife

Wildlife in Virginia includes elk, black bear, wildcat and deer, with groundhog, mole, opossum, rabbit, raccoon and skunk among the smaller animals.

Birds found in the state include a wide range of wildfowl, wild turkeys, woodcock, robins, bluebirds and cardinals, the state bird. Gulls and bitterns haunt tidal waters and marshes.

Bream, catfish, perch, pickerel and pike are found in fresh waters, and flounder, herring, mackerel and shad, as well as crabs and oysters, abound off the coast.

Flora in Virginia includes broomsedge, marsh grass, wild rice, cranberries, yam and river birch. There are dozens of species of native ferns and wild flowers. The state tree and flower is the dogwood, profuse and pretty in the springtime. In autumn the forests are ablaze with colour as leaves turn red, orange and gold.

MARYLAND

Small though it is – it covers an area of only 9775 square miles – Maryland nonetheless offers great contrasts. In the west are the isolated mountain communities of the Appalachians; in southern Maryland are lowland farms, where poultry and cattle are raised and tobacco grown. Both areas have more than a whiff of Old South ambience. Around **Chesapeake Bay** are charming fishing villages. Built around an impressive natural harbour, hilly Baltimore is busy, bright and commercial, while neighbouring Annapolis moves at a leisurely pace that befits the dignity of an historic state capital.

Maryland's share of the Atlantic Coastal Plain is split in two by Chesapeake Bay. The **Eastern Shore**, fringing both Chesapeake Bay and in the south, the Atlantic Ocean, is low and flat with extensive marshes and offshore islands. The **Western Shore** rises to a rolling upland punctuated by the **Susquehanna, Gunpowder, Patapsco, Patuxent** and other rivers.

The **Piedmont** region, covering western central Maryland, has elevations ranging from less than 400 ft to around 1200 ft. The state's highest peak is **Backbone Mountain**, which rises to 3360 ft in the **Allegheny Mountains**, part of the Appalachians. Between the Appalachians and the Blue Ridge Mountains are the rich farmlands of the **Cumberland Valley** in north-west Maryland.

46

Climate

Maryland has two distinct climates. The western mountain areas have relatively cool summers (averaging 65°F in July) and very cold winters (below 28°F in January). Around Chesapeake Bay and on the Atlantic Ocean, considerably higher temperatures are enjoyed in both summer and winter. On the Eastern Shore the average January temperature is more than 35°F, with a July average of 75°F. Baltimore's average in July is 77°F, dropping to 33°F in January. Average rainfall in the state is 43 inches a year. The mountain areas see the greatest precipitation, mostly as snow.

Wildlife

Foxes, muskrats, opossums, rabbits, raccoons, skunks and squirrels are found throughout the state, and deer make their home in central and western Maryland and the lower Eastern Shore. Beavers may be found in western regions and there are some bears in the mountains.

Maryland has only two species of poisonous snakes: the copperhead (see p.48) and the timber rattlesnake. The state is home to several species of turtle; terrapins, once plentiful on the Eastern Shore, are now farmed commercially. Frogs, toads and salamanders thrive in the southern marshes.

Resident birdlife includes the blue jay, cardinal, catbird, meadowlark, mockingbird, song sparrow and wren. During the winter they are joined by the Baltimore oriole, bluebird, brown thrasher, chimney swift, peewee, warbler, woodpecker and wood thrush. In the summer red-winged blackbirds, sandpipers and upland plovers flock to the beaches, while flights of duck, geese, snipe and woodcock move to the Susquehanna River and the southern wild rice marshes in the winter.

About 40 per cent of Maryland's total area – nearly 2.5 million acres – is covered by woodland. Oak forests are found throughout the state. Hemlock, red spruce and white pine grow among the northern mountains, and fast-growing hardwoods are abundant in central Maryland. Oak, sweet gum and Virginia pine flourish in southern Maryland and the upper Eastern Shore.

DELAWARE

Less than 100 miles long, no more than 35 miles wide, and covering an area of only 1955 square miles, Delaware is the second smallest state in the Union (the smallest is Rhode Island). However, Delaware is known as the First State because it was the first to ratify the Constitution of the United States – on 7 Dec 1787.

Delaware occupies the north-eastern part of the flat, low-lying **Delmarva Peninsula** east of Chesapeake Bay. It has only three counties – New Castle, Kent and Sussex. Two-thirds of the state's population of around 669,000 live in New Castle, the northernmost county. The estuary of the Delaware River separates the state from New Jersey.

Delaware's northern tip is a region of rolling hills, valleys and wooded slopes – typical Piedmont Plateau terrain. Here, near Centerville, is the state's highest point, a dizzying elevation of 442 ft.

The **Christina River** marks the change from the Piedmont to the Atlantic Coastal Plain, which makes up most of the state. Nowhere in this region is higher than 70 ft above sea level, and there are extensive marshes and many sandy beaches.

Most of Delaware's rivers and streams rise close to the border with the Eastern Shore region of Maryland and they flow either into Chesapeake Bay or the Atlantic

47

Ocean. Navigable rivers are the **Appoquinimink, Christina, Smyrna, Mispillion, Nanticoke** and **St Jones**. There are also two canals. The **Chesapeake and Delaware Canal**, (part of the Intracoastal Waterway that follows the Gulf of Mexico and Atlantic coasts), connects Chesapeake Bay and the Delaware River, about 15 miles south of Wilmington. The **Lewes and Rehoboth Canal**, in the southern part of the state, carries smaller vessels and recreational craft.

Climate

Delaware's climate is tempered by the large bodies of water that all but surround it. In summer the mean temperature is 76°F and in winter 35°F. Rainfall averages 45 inches a year.

Wildlife

A meeting place of North and South, Delaware is blessed with an abundance of flora and fauna. Colourful wild flowers, shrubs and bushes – azalea, butterfly weed, buttonbush, honeysuckle, lady's slipper, morning glory and many-others – adorn the countryside. Orchids and swamp magnolias also grow in this state.

Deer, fox and muskrat are common, and Delaware is also home to limited populations of beaver, mink and otter. Common birds include the blue jay, cardinal, finch, grackle, oriole, robin, ruby-throated hummingbird, titmouse and woodpecker. Birdwatchers will also spot blue heron, a variety of ducks, snowy egrets, tanagers and warblers as well as hawks, owls, quail, sandpipers, turkey buzzards and woodcock.

Delaware's only poisonous snake is the copperhead. With a pattern of greyish concentric rings along a copper-coloured body, the snake – a pit viper – is poten-tially dangerous to humans. Midly venomous, its bite can cause serious illness, but is rarely fatal. Turtles flourish and oysters, clams and crabs are found in Delaware Bay. Saltwater fish include bluefish, eel, flounder, sea trout, shad and sturgeon. Blue and rainbow trout, chain pickerel, large-mouth bass and yellow perch are among the species found in fresh waters.

When the first white men arrived, Delaware was covered with virgin forests of hickory, oak, pine, walnut and yellow poplar. Today, trees cover about one third of the state, mostly second-growth forest. There are large quantities of white cedar.

Red cedar, pines, wax myrtle and beach plum grow near the beaches and elsewhere in the south there are loblolly, spruce pine, huckleberry, holly, magnolia, maple, sweet gum and other species. The northernmost stand of bald cypress is found in **Trap Pond State Park**, east of Laurel. Ash, beech, hickory, maple, oak, sycamore and walnut grow in the north.

PENNSYLVANIA

The south-east corner of Pennsylvania – the area covered by this book – covers considerably less than a quarter of the state's 44,820 square miles, yet even here there are great contrasts of terrain.

Along the **Delaware River**, from the Maryland and Delaware state lines to Philadelphia, is a narrow continuation of the Atlantic Coastal Plain. The Piedmont Plateau extends across York and Lancaster counties, separated by the broad **Susquehanna River**. This is a fertile region, with some of the state's best farms, many of them run by Amish communities. **South Mountains**, which engulf the Gettysburg National Military Park, are a continuation of the Blue Ridge Mountains.

The **Susquehanna**, which zigzags

through central and southern Pennsylvania to enter Chesapeake Bay at Havre de Grace, MD, is navigable only in parts.

Climate

South-eastern Pennsylvania enjoys a more moderate climate than the rest of the state, with an annual mean temperature of about 52°F. Rainfall in the region ranges from 38–46 inches a year, with snowfall totalling some 30 inches.

Wildlife

Wildlife in Pennsylvania includes bear, beaver, deer, fox, rabbit, skunk, wildcat and woodchuck, and bird species are similar to those found in the other three states. Copperheads and rattlesnakes are found in forest and mountain areas, but visitors are more likely to meet harmless snakes.

Bass, catfish, eels, perch, pickerel, pike and trout are among the fish found in rivers, streams and lakes.

Wild flowers include anemone, black-eyed Susan, hepatica, honeysuckle, phlox, trillium and violet. Raspberry, blackberry and elderberry are common, and dogwood, pink azalea, redbud, rhododendron and mountain laurel also grow. Trees typical of southern Pennsylvania include ash, aspen, birch, elm, hickory, maple, sycamore and wild plum.

HISTORY

The history of European involvement in what is now the United States of America begins, and is still very much reflected, in the Capital Region – a semi-circle of territory with its straight edge stretching from Virginia Beach to Philadelphia and radiating through Virginia, Maryland, Delaware and south-eastern Pennsylvania. But the Europeans, of course, were not the first people to inhabit the region.

Archaeological evidence indicates that humans were hunting and gathering food in the area as early as 8000 BC. By the time the first white men arrived, the **Eastern Woodland tribes** of Native Americans – the people a disorientated Christopher Columbus called 'Indians' – were growing vegetables, fishing, hunting and coping nicely in the climatic extremes of a densely-forested region. Their lifestyle was so well organised they even had time to play team games.

The area around Chesapeake Bay was inhabited by some 10,000 **Algonquin**-speaking Native Americans led by Chief Powhatan. The Piedmont was home to **Monacan** and **Manahoac** tribes of the Sioux nation. The Iroquoian-language **Nottoways** lived in the south-east and **Cherokees** in the south-west.

The main northern tribal groups were the **Lenni Lenape**, who lived along the Delaware River and were known as Delawares to English settlers, and the **Susquehannocks**, who had made their home along the Susquehanna Valley. By the 1670s the Susquehannocks had been decimated in attacks by white settlers and rival Native American tribes. Groups of **Shawnees** moved south into Pennsylvania in the closing decade of the 17th century, settling amicably with the Delawares.

The peaceful Delawares lived in small villages and enjoyed good relations with William Penn's colony – they were happy to sell land under treaties drawn up by the Quaker leader – but as white settlement increased and game became scarce they and the Shawnees moved away.

VIRGINIA

Named in honour of Elizabeth I, the 'Virgin Queen', Virginia received its first English colonists on 17 May 1607 when three small ships – the *Discovery*, *Godspeed*

49

and the *Sarah Constant* – sailed up the James River. The people aboard the ships had been sent out by the Virginia Company of London, chartered by James I, and once ashore they set about building **Jamestown**, the New World's first permanent English settlement.

The settlers had a hard time. The James River was infested with mosquitos and as well as malaria, they had to contend with famine and Indian attacks. Many people died, and only the firm leadership of **Captain John Smith** saved the demoralised colony.

Smith was quite the hero of his day, narrowly escaping death several times in an action-packed life. He went to sea at the age of 16 and was only 26 when he was placed in charge of the Jamestown project. In addition to leading the colony, he explored Chesapeake Bay and almost died after being stung by a stingray. On another occasion he was falsely accused of murder, but reprieved within sight of the gallows. Later, he was captured by pirates, but subsequently released. And everyone knows the story of how the Indian princess **Pocahontas** is supposed to have saved him from execution.

When he wasn't evading death, Smith made careful notes and maps during his expeditions and wrote books about his adventures and the history and geography of the regions he explored.

In 1612, **John Rolfe,** who later married Pocahontas, began to grow tobacco, improving it by selective breeding until it reached a standard commercially acceptable in England. The smoking habit caught on and the settlers found themselves in possession of a highly profitable cash crop.

The **Virginia Company**, which was in financial difficulties, granted land to all free settlers in 1618 and gave colonists the

right to hold a general assembly. A year later the New World's first elected legislative body met at Jamestown – and the first black slaves arrived in the colony.

Internal disputes among stockholders and the massacre of some 350 settlers by Native Americans prompted James I to revoke the company's charter and make Virginia a royal colony in 1624. Freed from the yoke of company restrictions, the settlers established tobacco farms along the James River and began to enjoy prosperity.

By 1700 Virginia's population had reached 75,000, making it the largest English colony in North America. It was a prosperous colony, too: its tobacco profits were boosted by the slave trade, which provided a constant stream of cheap labour for the plantations.

Virginia was in the forefront of opposition to Britain's voracious taxation demands on the American colonies. Among those who took the first steps towards independence were Virginians **Patrick Henry, Thomas Jefferson, Richard Henry Lee** and **George Mason.** Patrick Henry persuaded the colony's legislature to adopt the Virginia Resolves, declaring that it was the only authority entitled to tax its people.

Things came to a head in April 1775 when the governor appointed by the British Crown seized the colony's stocks of gunpowder. Patrick Henry raised an armed band and chased the governor to a warship in Chesapeake Bay, effectively, ending British government in Virginia. A month later the colony declared itself to be a free and independent state.

Virginians continued to play leading roles in the activities of the **Continental Congress**, which met in Philadelphia. On 7 June 1776, Richard Henry Lee introduced the motion for separation from

Britain, and the **Declaration of Independence** was drafted primarily by Thomas Jefferson. The man chosen as commander in chief of the Continental Army was **George Washington**, a Virginian

There was little fighting on Virginian soil in the **Revolutionary War**. Portsmouth and Suffolk were taken by the British in 1779, and Richmond, the capital, fell to them in January 1781. But the sweetest victory came later that year when George Washington defeated **Lord Cornwallis** at **Yorktown**.

During independent America's early days, Virginia provided four of the first five presidents: George Washington, Thomas Jefferson, **James Madison** and **James Monroe.**

It was a different story during the **Civil War**. **Bull Run**, the first great battle, was fought at Manassas on 21 July 1861, and the final surrender of the Confederates took place at **Appomattox** on 9 April 1865. Between those two events, Virginia took centre stage in the war and many other major battles were fought in the state. When the fighting ended, much of Virginia lay in ruins; recovery took most of the remainder of the 19th century.

MARYLAND

Chesapeake Bay was known to all the early European explorers. **Giovanni da Verrazano**, the Italian navigator working for France, landed there in 1524 and the intrepid Captain John Smith made a thorough survey of the bay in 1608. But no one showed further interest in the area until 1632 when **George Calvert**, first Lord Baltimore, won a grant from **Charles I** of the land on both sides of the bay and north to the 40th parallel. Calvert wanted to develop a haven for oppressed fellow Catholics.

It was left to **Cecil Calvert,** the second Lord Baltimore, to found the colony, which was named to honour Henrietta Maria, the wife of England's king, Charles I. With his brother **Leonard** as proprietary governor, he sent two ships, the *Ark* and the *Dove*, with 200 settlers. They sailed into the mouth of the Potomac River, landing near a Native American village on 25 Mar 1634. The village of bark huts and the surrounding land was bought from the Native Americans and named **St. Mary's**.

The Calvert family lost control of the colony to the Crown between 1654 and 1658, and again from 1688 to 1715, but it was restored to them when they became Anglicans. Maryland remained a proprietary colony in their hands until the American Revolution.

A number of towns were founded – and foundered – in the early 18th century. **Baltimore**, established in 1729, succeeded as a port. **Frederick**, founded in 1745, prospered in the fertile valley of the Monocacy River. **Georgetown**, now part of DC, was laid out at the head of navigation on the Potomac River in 1751.

Maryland's proprietorial family found themselves in frequent boundary disputes with their neighbours, Virginia and Pennsylvania, and in 1732 had to give up some 3 million acres, including all of present Delaware. Because of continued land quarrels between the Calverts and Penns in the 1760s, the British surveyors **Charles Mason** and **Jeremiah Dixon** drew up the present boundary between Pennsylvania, Delaware and Maryland. The **Mason-Dixon Line** was later regarded as the border between the free and slave states, and extended westward is now seen as the line between North and South.

The colony joined the resistance against

British taxes. In Oct 1774, ten months after the Boston Tea Party, the owner of the *Peggy Stewart* was forced to burn his own ship in Annapolis harbour because he had paid the tax on its cargo of tea. Representatives from each county formed an independent convention at Annapolis in 1774, and two years later a state constitution was drawn up by elected delegates.

Although Maryland troops fought throughout the eastern seaboard and the southern colonies, no important Revolutionary battles were fought in Maryland.

When the war ended, the Continental Congress met at Annapolis to receive Washington's resignation as commander-in-chief and to ratify the Treaty of Paris. Maryland approved the **US Constitution** on 28 Apr 1788 and later ceded territory and gave funds to the federal government to form the **District of Columbia**.

The state prospered in the early years of independence. Speedy clippers designed by Chesapeake Bay shipbuilders carried supplies to countries affected by the Napoleonic Wars, and during the War of 1812, clippers fitted as warships harried the British fleet.

The most northern of the Southern states, Maryland was divided in its attitudes during the **Civil War**. On 19 April 1861 Massachusetts troops were mobbed as they passed through Baltimore on their way to reinforce Washington. As a result, Union forces occupied Maryland for the rest of the war. Thousands of Marylanders fought in the Union and Confederate armies and the three major battles of the conflict – **South Mountain**, **Antietam** and **Monocacy** – were fought within the state.

DELAWARE

The English navigator **Henry Hudson** discovered Delaware in 1609 and claimed it for the Dutch, for whom he was working at the time. The Dutch tried to establish a colony near the present site of Lewes in 1631, but failed. However, they laid claim to the Delaware Valley and maintained a military presence.

The first permanent European settlement was planted by a group of Swedes, assisted by some Dutchmen, in the Delaware Valley at Wilmington in 1638. It was called New Sweden and survived only through the determined leadership of its governor, **Johan Printz,** who fended off English and Dutch claims for ten years from 1643. Printz' successor, **Johan Rising,** was less diplomatic. In 1655 he attacked a Dutch fort at New Castle. The Dutch responded by seizing New Sweden and annexing to their own colony, New Netherland.

In 1664 New Netherland was conquered by an English fleet sent by the **Duke of York**, later James II, and for 18 years Delaware was governed as part of New York. In 1682 Delaware was given to **William Penn**.

Delaware gained its name from the bay and river on its eastern side. These in turn were named to honour **Thomas West,** Lord De la Warr, governor of Virginia.

Penn's efforts to absorb Delaware's three counties into Pennsylvania were resisted by the Delawareans, who feared they would come under the control of Quakers. Penn allowed Delaware its own assembly, which made it clear in 1704 that it would have its own separate political authority.

Lord Baltimore's claim that Delaware was part of Maryland was rejected by an English court and the matter was settled once and for all when the English surveyors Mason and Dixon completed a proper boundary between the two colonies in 1768 (see p. 51).

Delaware joined the **Revolution** by declaring independence in 1776. In Sept 1777 it was invaded by British troops marching on Philadelphia. After the British seized Philadelphia and cleared the river, Delaware became the front line of the war for almost a year.

The war over, tiny Delaware enthusiastically supported efforts to establish a strong national government. After obtaining a guarantee that, despite its size, it would have an equal voice in the Senate, Delaware ratified the Constitution unanimously on 7 Dec 1787 – the **first state** to do so.

Nominally at least, Delaware remained a slave state until after the Civil War. In fact, however, most slaves had already been freed as the result of a law which made it illegal for their owners to make a profit by selling slaves out of the state. By 1860 only 1800 slaves remained in Delaware. Although many Delawareans sympathised with the Confederates and thought secession should be tolerated, the prospect of Delaware itself seceding was never considered.

SOUTH-EAST PENNSYLVANIA

When William Penn arrived in his colony in 1682, armed with a charter from Charles II which made him proprietor and governor of Pennsylvania, he set out to develop a refuge from religious intolerance. To underline his intention, he named the capital **Philadelphia** – 'city of brotherly love'.

The colony made rapid progress, its population boosted by immigrants from the British Isles, the Low Countries and Germany. By the mid-18th century a prosperous farming area had developed in south-east Pennsylvania, and by 1776 Philadelphia was the leading city in colonial America.

Pennsylvanians bitterly resented the imposition of British taxes and other infringements of their rights. They prevented the unloading of tea ships in Philadelphia in 1773. A year later the first **Continental Congress** met at Philadelphia. The Declaration of Independence was adopted in the city's **State House (Independence Hall)** in 1776.

Congress continued to meet in Philadelphia except during the British occupation of the city (Sept 1777–June 1778) when it moved first to Lancaster, then to York, where the **Articles of Confederation** were drafted.

The state contributed heavily to the **Revolution** and several battles were fought on Pennsylvania soil.

After the war there was strong support for the convention that drafted the new Constitution. Pennsylvania was the second state to ratify the Constitution on 12 Dec 1787.

As development increased in the western part of the state, the capital was moved from Philadelphia to Lancaster in 1799, and from there to Harrisburg in 1812.

Pennsylvania was a fervent opponent of slavery even before the Revolution. Its first anti-slavery society was founded in 1775 and in 1780 the state passed a gradual emancipation act which ended slavery in the state in a generation.

Some 400,000 Pennsylvanians served in the Union forces during the **Civil War** and an abundance of arms, ships and supplies was produced by the state's industries. In 1863 **Gen. Robert E. Lee** led the Confederate Army into Pennsylvania. On 3 July his troops were defeated in the decisive battle of **Gettysburg**.

TOURING ITINERARIES

Few places in the world, let alone the USA, can match the range of scenery and interests presented by the Capital Region, and you can derive much pleasure from tailoring the itinerary of a driving holiday there to match your tastes and interests. This chapter begins with some practical advice on tour planning, followed by three ready-made circular itineraries designed to show you as much as possible of the Capital Region's variety, during trips of 14 or 21 days, using the recommended routes in this book. Feel free to vary our suggestions, using the full range of information contained in the route descriptions. The remaining pages list features of the region which you can study to create a self-planned 'themed' tour.

PRACTICAL HINTS

Here are a few tips to make practicable routes easier to plan and more fun to follow:

1. Use the most detailed maps available. The colour map section at the end of this book is useful for planning itineraries and will enable you to follow the routes while driving, but a more detailed road map will be invaluable if you want to mix routes. Each of the four states covered by the region has excellent, free road maps available at tourist information centres and chambers of commerce.

2. Don't schedule too much driving each day. Allow 50 miles per hour of freeway driving, 40 miles an hour on secondary roads, to allow for breaks and unplanned stops. Each route description in this book gives information not only about mileage but also likely driving times.

3. Unless accommodation is pre-booked, plan to arrive at each destination with enough time to find a place to sleep. The Capital Region is a compact area and communities are not separated by large distances; nevertheless, it is better to be safe than worn out and sorry.

4. If you have a flight home at the end of your holiday, remember to build in time to get to your airport city without having to rush.

5. Give serendipity a chance by not planning in too much detail. Allow time to spend an extra few hours – or an extra day – in some unexpected gem of a place, or to explore an interesting byway.

THE BEST OF THE CAPITAL REGION

Compact though it is, the Capital Region offers such a diversity of attractions and historic sites that it is unlikely it could be covered sensibly in much less than three months.

Each of our three suggested circular itineraries can be shortened or lengthened – after all, you can always come back. The tours combine many recommended routes, with a few digressions and short cuts added. Suggested overnight stops are in **bold type**.

DC AND VIRGINIA HIGHLIGHTS

21 days

Day 1–3: **Washington** (pp. 65–89). Day 4: Washington to **Fredericksburg** (pp.

54

125–127). Day 5: Fredericksburg to **Richmond** (pp. 173–186). Days 6–8: **Richmond**. Day 9: Richmond to Petersburg and **Lynchburg** (route p.162–172; Lynchburg pp. 155–157). Day 10: **Lynchburg**. Day 11: Lynchburg to **Roanoke** (route p. 162–172; Roanoke p. 149–153). Days 12–13: **Roanoke**. Day 14: Roanoke to **Lexington** (pp 147–152). Day 15: **Lexington**. Day 16: Lexington to Covington, Hot Springs and **Staunton** (p. 141–144). Day 17: **Staunton**. Day 18: Staunton to Harrisonburg, Luray and **Front Royal** (p. 133–135). Day 19: **Front Royal**. Day 20: Front Royal to **Leesburg** (p. 111–112). Day 21: Leesburg to **Washington**.

MARYLAND AND VIRGINIA

14 days

Days 1–2: **Washington** (p. 65–89). Day 3: Washington to **Annapolis** (pp. 93–94). Day 4: **Annapolis**. Day 5: Annapolis to **Solomons** (p. 254). Day 6: **Solomons**. Day 7: Solomons to St. Mary's City, Waldorf and **Alexandria** (pp. 116–122). Day 8: **Alexandria**. Day 9: Alexandria to **Richmond** (route pp. 123–127); Days 10–11: **Richmond** (pp. 173–186). Day 12: Richmond to **Charlottesville** (p. 159–161). Day 13: **Charlottesville**. Day 14: Charlottesville to **Washington**.

AROUND CHESAPEAKE BAY

21 days

Days 1–2: **Baltimore** (pp. 261–273). Day 3: Baltimore to **Alexandria** (pp 116–122). Days 4–5: **Alexandria**. Day 6: Alexandria to **Richmond** (route pp. 123–127); Days 7–8: **Richmond** (pp. 173–186). Day 9: Richmond to **Williamsburg** (route pp.187–195; Day 10: **Williamsburg** (pp. 196–205). Day 11: Williamsburg to Yorktown and **Virginia Beach** (route pp. 187–195). Days 12–14: **Virginia Beach**

(pp. 217–229). Day 15: Virginia Beach to **Ocean City** (route pp. 230–240). Day 16: **Ocean City**. Day 17: Ocean City to **Dover** (route pp. 296–301); Day 18: **Dover** (pp. 292–295). Day 19: Dover to **Annapolis** (pp 246–252). Day 20: **Annapolis** (pp. 246–252). Day 21: Annapolis to **Baltimore** (pp. 261–273).

THE REGION'S NORTH

14 days

Days 1–2: **Philadelphia** (pp. 319–328). Day 3: Philadelphia to Lancaster and **Harrisburg** (route pp. 311–318). Day 4: **Harrisburg** (pp. 306–310). Day 5: Harrisburg to York and **Gettysburg** (route pp. 103–106). Day 6: **Gettysburg**. Day 7: Gettysburg to Frederick and **Annapolis** (pp. 100–102). Day 8: **Annapolis** (pp. 246–252).

Day 9: Annapolis to Easton, Cambridge, Salisbury and **Ocean City** (route pp. 241–245). Days 10–11: **Ocean City**. Day 12: Ocean City to Rehoboth Beach and **Dover** (pp. 296–301). Day 13: **Dover** (pp. 292–295). Day 14: Dover to **Philadelphia** (pp. 319–328).

MAJOR CITIES

VIRGINIA

Lynchburg

Set in the foothills of the Blue Ridge Mountains, Lynchburg takes its name from its founder, John Lynch, whose story is told in the Old Court House Museum. The city's steep streets are rich in varied 19th and early 20th century architectural styles.

Roanoke

Presenting itself as the Capital of the Blue Ridge, this metropolis of 230,000 people is marked by a star – a 100 ft man–made

55

star that has shone out from the top of Mill Mountain since 1949. Like New York's Central Park and the French Quarter in New Orleans, Roanoke's downtown is in the top 63 of America's Great Public Places..

Fredericksburg

This is where America's first president was born and where he allegedly chopped down that cherry tree. You can visit his boyhood home, Ferry Farm, his mother's final home and the George Washington Masonic Museum, where he was initiated in 1752. Fifty miles south of the capital, this old tobacco port retains a 40-block National Historic District.

Alexandria

Visitors are spoilt for choice, with dozens of traditional bars and taverns and a wide range of restaurants in fascinating old buildings. Shoppers can seek out the quaint and unusual. The waterfront is a pleasant place to stroll all year round.

Charlottesville

One name dominates the place – Thomas Jefferson. Visitors flock to his home, Monticello, and the University of Virginia which he founded. Still serving food and drink in the style of the time is the Michie Tavern.

Norfolk

A busy port with some interesting museums and a new centre, Nauticus, where the accent is on marine matters and fun. Allow at least half a day. Ships of the US Atlantic Fleet can be seen at the Naval Base.

Hampton

Settled in 1610, this is the oldest surviving English town in the USA. Jefferson Davis,

president of the Confederate States, was imprisoned here. Among other sights are the missiles, rockets and military aircraft at the outdoor Air Power Park.

Newport News

Newport News claims the only international maritime museum in the USA. It has a large collection of ships' figureheads and model ships among its hundreds of exhibits.

Portsmouth

Trolleys and horse-drawn carriages convey people around the antique shops and 18th- and 19th-century architecture of the restored Olde Towne. The Lightship Museum and Naval Shipyard Museum have much of interest. For youngsters there are the Pokey Smokey Steam Railroad and a high-tech children's museum.

Lexington

This 19th- century college town is home to Washington and Lee University and Virginia Military Institute. Robert E. Lee's office at the university, where he was head, is as he left it. Stonewall Jackson's pre-Civil War home can also be visited. The huge Virginia Horse Center with its many events adds to the tourist's pleasure.

Richmond

Thomas Jefferson designed the Old State Capitol in Virginia's capital. There's a wealth of historical attractions and museums. The Annabelle Lee paddlewheel riverboat runs plantation cruises from Apr to Dec. King's Dominion is famous for its white-knuckle rides and water park experiences.

Virginia Beach

The place for sun, sea and sand and family holidays, with 28 miles of beaches and extensive boardwalks. For fun there's plenty, including a Mirror Maze and the Haunted Mansion.

MARYLAND

Annapolis
Capital of Maryland – and of the nation for several months during the 1780s – Annapolis is also the home of the US Naval Academy. The State House, its bright dome dominating the city, is worth a visit. A guided walking tour of the historic district is worthwhile, and there's a very attractive waterfront with boat trips and many sailing craft.

Baltimore
A large and lively port city with much waterfront activity and an Inner Harbor. A World War II submarine is one of the old craft which can be explored. Visits to outstanding art galleries and museums, like the National Aquarium and the National Science Center, and shopping at the Top of the World Trade Center are enjoyable activities.

Ocean City
A long beach of white sand, a three-mile boardwalk, an amusement park, great fishing and some fine accommodations give this well-kept resort family appeal.

PENNSYLVANIA

Philadelphia
The nation was born here in 1776:. Independence National Historic Park is a must-see. Some of George Washington's personal possessions are displayed in Independence Hall. The Liberty Bell, symbol of freedom, is now housed in a pavilion. Places of interest include the historic ships moored at Penn's Landing.

Harrisburg
Extensive gardens and walks by the Susquehanna River are overlooked by the imposing Capitol Buildings.

York
For nearly a year during the War of Independence, this city of restored Colonial homes was the capital of the 13 colonies. Today there are many historic places to visit, and the world-renowned Harley-Davidson motorcycle plant.

DELAWARE

Dover
Guided tours of the historic district of Delaware's small capital city include the Old State Capitol, the Delaware State Museum and some lovely Colonial homes.

Rehoboth Beach
Delaware has 24 miles of Atlantic coastline, with lively Rehoboth at its heart. Its family attractions and nightspots make it a Mecca for summer weekenders and holidaymakers from Washington DC. Rehoboth also has a large complex of outlet stores.

Wilmington
There's a lot to enjoy in and around Wilmington, with the beautiful Brandywine Valley at its doorstep. Longwood Gardens is alive with colour all year. Industrial archaeology of the 19th century is the theme at the riverside Hagley Museum.

MUST-SEE ATTRACTIONS
The Capital Region presents the visitor with a diverse range of attractions. Some are natural, some man-made, some free – all are worth experiencing. The following

57

shortlist of must-see sights is intended to illustrate this diversity. It could be very much longer.

In Delaware, The **Winterthur Museum** houses Henry du Pont's world-renowned collection of decorative arts and furniture made or used in America from 1640–1860. Five miles south is the lovely old city of **New Castle**, with its cobbled streets, Colonial brick houses, elegant courthouse and Delaware River frontage.

Maryland also has streets steeped in history. Picturesque **Annapolis**, spread around the oldest state capitol in continuous use, carries a powerful whiff of the ocean with its yacht-filled City Dock and United States Naval Academy. In southern Maryland, **St. Mary's City** goes back to the state's very beginnings. Here, you can see how Lord Baltimore's settlers lived in the 17th century and inspect replicas of the tiny ships in which they crossed the Atlantic Ocean. On **Baltimore's** Harborplace, the stunning **National Aquarium** leads visitors around a massive pool to marine life at different levels. At the top is an artificial rain forest with exotic birds, reptiles and plants.

Outside **Philadelphia**, which has a plethora of historic sights, southern Pennsylvania is rich in contrasting attractions. On one side of the Susquehanna River, in the area around Lancaster, are the Amish communities whose members have turned their backs on modern life. You can learn about them at the **Amish Homestead**, *on Lincoln Highway E., Lancaster*. Across the river, at York, is the **Harley-Davidson Factory**, where you can join a tour to see the famous motorcycles being assembled and test-ridden. And near Harrisburg, the state capital, is **Hershey**, home of the American chocolate manufacturer. **Hersheypark** is a family theme park, while **Chocolate World**

leads visitors through the history and process of making chocolate.

Among Virginia's natural attractions are the **Luray Caverns**, on *Rte 211* just west of *Skyline Drive*. Guided tours through stupendous rock and mineral formations climax with music from the Stalacpipe Organ, which produces sound by striking tuned stalactites with hydraulic hammers. **Natural Bridge**, *on Hwy 11*, about 12 miles south of Lexington, is a 90-ft span of rock up to 150 ft wide and crossing Cedar Creek at a height of 215 ft. A 45-minute sound and light show is presented nightly. **Colonial Williamsburg** is well known, but it is still a surprise and a delight to walk its 18th century streets with more than 500 public buildings, private homes, stores and taverns. In stark contrast, nearby **Busch Gardens**, *on Hwy 60,* east of Williamsburg, is one of the country's largest theme parks.

NATURE AND WILDLIFE

Parks operated by the National Parks Service are listed first, followed by parks, preserves, shores and recreational areas administered by State authorities.

DELAWARE

Bombay Hook National Wildlife Refuge, *Rte 9,* five miles east of Smyrna; *tel: (302) 653–6872*. Thousands of resident and migrating wildfowl are attracted to 15,000 acres of marshes, ponds and fields. **Prime Hook National Wildlife Refuge**, *Rte 16,* seven miles east of Milton; *tel: (302) 684-8419*. Although it is smaller than Bombay Hook, Prime Hook is more accessible, with a boardwalk through the marshes, canoe trails and boat ramps.

State Parks
For information contact **Delaware**

58

Division of Parks and Recreation, *99 King's Highway, P.O Box 1401, Dover, DE 19903; tel: (302) 739-4413.*

Brandywine Creek State Park, five miles north of Wilmington at the intersection of Rtes 92 and 100; *tel: (302) 655-5740.* The park covers 800 acres of open ground and woodland and has 12 miles of hiking trails and a nature centre.

Cape Henlopen State Park, *Rte 9, Lewes; tel: (302) 645-8983*, has extensive camping facilities among coastal pine woods.

Delaware Seashore State Park, Rte 1, between Dewey Beach and Bethany Beach, south of Rehoboth Beach; *tel: (302) 227-2800*, is on a narrow neck of land with the Atlantic Ocean on one side and the calmer waters of Rehoboth Bay on the other.

DISTRICT OF COLUMBIA

National Mall, extends from the Capitol to the Washington Monument; *tel: (202) 426-6841* (metro: *Smithsonian*). A monument to the grand ideas of Washington's planner, Pierre-Charles L'Enfant, the Mall is a wide swathe of green bordered by shady elms and major buildings of the Smithsonian Institution.

Rock Creek Park has a visitor centre on *Military Rd NW*, about a mile east of Connecticut Ave or half a mile west of *16th St; tel: (202) 426-6832* (metro: *Friendship Heights*). This is the capital's major playground – a twisting ribbon of green that writhes northwards from Georgetown. There are picnic sites, nature walks, cycling, jogging and horse-riding trails and boating, as well as Civil War forts, a planetarium and a restored grist mill where corn and wheat are ground by water power. Admission: free.

Theodore Roosevelt Island *lies in the Potomac River between the Francis Scott Key*

and *Theodore Roosevelt Memorial bridges; tel: (703) 285-2598* (metro: *Rosslyn*). Accessible by footbridge from a car park off the George Washington Memorial Parkway on the Virginia shore, the 88-acre island commemorates the conservation policies of the 26th President. A mini-wilderness, the island has more than two miles of nature trails and provides a habitat for frogs, birds, squirrels, foxes and raccoons. It is freely accessible year-round during daylight hours.

MARYLAND

Assateague Island National Seashore, *7206 National Seashore Lane, Berlin, MD 21811.* An Atlantic barrier island, Assateague extends south for 37 miles from Ocean City to Chincoteague, VA. There are visitor centres in both state sections. Maryland *tel: (410) 641-1441*; Virginia *tel: (804) 336-6577*. To reach the Maryland entrance, take Hwy 50 from Berlin or Ocean City to Rte 611. For the Virginia entrance take Hwy 13 then Rte 175 East through Chincoteague. Admission: $4 per vehicle for seven days.

Catoctin Mountain Park, is just south of Thurmont, two and a half miles west on Rte 77 from Hwy 15; *tel: (301) 663-9388*. The park offers 10,000 acres of forested mountain country with hiking trails, scenic drives, camping, picnicking, fishing, swimming, rock-climbing and horse-riding (you'll need to take your own horse).

Chesapeake and Ohio Canal National Historic Park extends 185 miles from Georgetown to Cumberland. The park headquarters is on Rte 34, four miles west of Sharpsburg; *tel: (301) 739-4200*, and there are visitor centres at **Great Falls Canal Tavern Museum,** *11710 MacArthur Blvd, Potomac; tel: (301) 299-3613; 326 E. Main St, Hancock; tel:*

(301) 678-5463, and **Western Maryland Railroad Station Center**, *Canal St, Cumberland; tel: (301) 739-4200.* The canal has 74 locks which raise it from near sea-level to 605 ft.

Piscataway Park, *Bryan's Point Rd, Accokeek; tel: (301) 763-4600,* is a six-mile stretch of riverfront across the Potomac from Mount Vernon. The park was created in the 1950s to preserve the view that George Washington would have enjoyed. There are facilities for fishing and bird-watching, and there are tours of the National Colonial Farm, which preserves pre-Revolution agricultural techniques. The park is open daily during daylight hours.

State Parks

For information contact **Maryland Office of Tourism Development**, *217 E. Redwood St, Baltimore, MD 21202; tel: (410) 333-6611 or (800) 543-1036.*

Assateague State Park, accessible from Berlin by Rte 50 East and Rte 611; *tel: (410) 641-2120.* The state's only ocean park has 2 miles of Atlantic frontage with marshes and forest on Sinepuxent Bay.

Calvert Cliffs State Park, *on Rtes 2/4,* 14 miles south of Prince Frederick in Calvert County; *tel: (301) 888-1410.* The park covers more than 1300 acres and gets its name from the massive cliffs which contain fossils up to 15 million years old. A hiking trail leads to the Chesapeake Bay beach.

Patapsco Valley State Park. Centred on Ellicott City, the 12,700-acre park sprawls along the Patapsco River Valley from the Liberty Dam, north of I-70, to Baltimore Harbor. A western arm starts from Sykesville; *tel: (410) 461-5005.* It winds through Howard, Carroll and Anne Arundel counties and has recreation areas at Glen Artney, Hilton, Hollofield and

McKeldin.

Susquehanna State Park, accessed from Rte 155, three miles north of Havre de Grace; *tel: (410) 557-7994.* Located in the Susquehanna River Valley, the 2,640-acre park is heavily forested and has massive rock outcrops.

For informatio on State Parks, contact **Bureau of State Parks**, *P.O Box 8551, Harrisburg, PA 17105-8551; tel: (800) 63-PARKS.*

Codorus State Park, on Rte 216, four miles east of Hanover, York County; *tel: (717) 637-2816.* This 3324-acre park surrounds a 1275-acre lake with fishing and boating facilities. Ice fishing and skating is available in winter; camping mid Apr–late Oct.

French Creek State Park, from the Pennsylvania Turnpike (I-76) take Exit 22. Head west on Rte 23 for four miles, then take Rte 345 north to reach the park in less than two miles; *tel: (215) 582-9680.* French Creek covers 7335 acres of Berks and Chester counties.

Gifford Pinchot State Park, in York County, about ten miles south of Camp Hill; leave I-83 south at Exit 14 and head south on Rte 177, which reaches the park in six miles. Covering 3394 acres, the park has a visitor centre and a 340-acre lake. It offers extensive, modern campsites and cabins mid-Apr–late-Oct.

Marsh Creek State Park, on *Rte 282* off Hwy 30, just north of West Chester in Chester County; *tel: (215) 458-8515.* The 1705-acre park has boating, fishing, swimming, hiking and horse-riding trails.

George Washington Memorial Parkway may be accessed from Exit 14 of the Capital Beltway, from the Chain

Bridge on Rte 123 or from downtown Washington via the 14th Street, Memorial or Theodore Roosevelt bridges. The parkway connects the historic sites from Mount Vernon to the Great Falls of the Potomac and preserves the natural scenery along the river's course.

Prince William Forest Park, is on Rte 619 at Triangle (accessible from I-95 or Hwy 1; *tel: (703) 221-4706*. This Piedmont forest area is the home of a wide range of wildlife and offers opportunities for birdwatching, wildlife viewing, fishing and camping. There are nearly 40 miles of trails for hiking and cycling.

Shenandoah National Park lies along a section of the Blue Ridge Mountains between Waynesboro and Front Royal and is traversed by the *Blue Ridge Parkway Skyline Drive*. The park headquarters is on Hwy 211, four miles east of Luray. There are visitor centres at Dickey Ridge and Big Meadows. Heavily forested, with many streams and waterfalls.

Wolf Trap Farm Park for the Performing Arts, *1551 Trap Rd, Vienna; tel: (703) 255-1800*. The Filene Center in the first national park devoted to the performing arts can seat an audience of almost 7,000, including 3,000 on a sloping lawn among rolling hills and woodland. The stagehouse is as tall as a 13-storey building with a stage 125 ft wide and 60 ft deep.

State Parks

For information on Virginia's state parks, contact **Virginia Department of Conservation and Recreation**, *203 Governor St, Suite 302, Richmond, VA 23219; tel: (804) 786- 1712*.

Douthat State Park, seven miles north of Clifton Forge on Rte 629 (Exit 27 off I-64); *tel: (703) 862-8100*. Located among some of Virginia's most outstanding mountain scenery, Douthat has been

the focus of family outdoor activities for more than half a century. A 50-acre lake is stocked with trout and there is a sandy bathing beach.

Fairystone State Park, on Rte 57 16 miles north-west of Martinsville in south-central Virginia; *tel: (703) 930-2424*. The park gets its name from the staurolites, or 'fairystones' found in the area.

First Landing Seashore State Park, *Shore Dr (Hwy 60), two miles north of downtown Virginia Beach; tel: (804) 481-2131*. Cape Henry was where the British colonists who were to settle at Jamestown first set foot on American soil. Today, the park covers more than 2,700 acres with 27 miles of nature trails. It has more than 500 plant species, including cypress, live oak and Spanish moss.

Kiptopeke State Park, on the Eastern Shore, Rte 704 off Hwy 13, three miles north of *Chesapeake Bay Bridge-Tunnel*. The park is a major flyway for migratory birds and there are opportunities to view rare animal species and a coastal dune environment.

Lake Anna State Park, accessed from Rte 601, 20 miles south-west of Fredericksburg; *tel: (703) 854-5503*. Located on one of Virginia's most popular lakes, the park has a visitor centre in which the area's gold mining history is featured. Visitors can try their hand at panning for gold.

Smith Mountain Lake State Park, *Rte 626*, off Rte 43, about 25 miles south of Bedford; *tel: (703) 297-6066*, is on the state's second largest body of fresh water .

HISTORY

DISTRICT OF COLUMBIA

Mary McLeod Bethune Council House National Historic Site, *1318 Vermont Ave NW; tel: (202) 332-1233* (metro: *McPherson Sq*). Established in by Mary McLeod Bethune in 1935 as headquarters of the National Council of Negro Women, the site contains five galleries of artefacts, paintings, photographs and manuscripts, as well as audio-visual exhibits.

Pennsylvania Avenue National Historic Site, extends from the Capitol to the White House; *tel: (202) 426-6720* (metro: *Federal Triangle* or *Metro Center*). Including streets on either side of *Pennsylvania Ave*, the site encompasses **Ford's Theatre**, the **Old Post Office Tower**, a number of Federal buildings and several blocks of the commercial district which also include structures and architectural and historical significance. Scheduled tours of the area are conducted by **Architours**, a non-profit educational organisation; *tel: (202) 265-6454*).

Sewall-Belmont House National Historic Site, is near the Capitol at 144 Constitution Ave NE; *tel: (202) 546-3989* (metro: *Union Station*). One of the oldest houses on Capitol Hill, the site has been headquarters of the National Women's Party since 1929 and commemorates the party's founder, Alice Paul. Exhibits trace the story of suffrage and equal rights campaigns. Tours take place Tues–Fri 1000–1500, Sat, Sun and holidays 1200–1600, except Thanksgiving Day, Christmas Day and 1 Jan. Admission: free.

MARYLAND

Antietam National Battlefield, one mile north of Sharpsburg on Rte 65; *tel: (301) 432-5124)*. This is the place where the course of the Civil War was altered on 17 Sept 1862 when Gen. Robert E. Lee's first advance on the North was halted. But the clash is remembered as the bloodiest single-day battle of the Civil War, with a total of more than 23000 casualties in less than 12 hours. Some 4000 men were killed or wounded between 0930 and 1300 in the sunken country road now known as Bloody Lane. The story of the battle is told at the Visitor Center where there are film and slide shows and museum exhibits. The centre is open daily 0830–1830 (June–Aug); 0800–1700 (Sept–May); closed Thanksgiving Day, Christmas Day, 1 Jan. Admission: $4 per family or $2 per person.

Clara Barton National Historic Site, *5801 Oxford Rd, Glen Echo; tel: (301) 492-6245*. The founder of the American Red Cross spent the last 15 years of her life in this house.

Fort McHenry National Monument and Historic Shrine, *Fort Ave, Baltimore; tel: (410) 962-4290*. The flag still flying above the fort at the end of a 25-hour bombardment by the British during the War of 1812 inspired Francis Scott Key to write *The Star-Spangled Banner*. The story of the gallant defence, which foiled a British attack on Baltimore, is told in a 16-minute film. Members of the Fort McHenry Guard, in 1812 uniform, perform drills and demonstrations during the summer months and in July and Aug there are military tattoos, Sun 1830.

Monocacy National Battlefield, *4801 Urbana Pike, Frederick; tel: (301) 662-3515* - the Visitor Center is on Hwy 355, about one-tenth of a mile south of the Monocacy River. In a decisive Civil War battle fought here on 9 July 1864, Confederate Gen. Jubal T. Early defeated Union troops led by Brig. Gen. Lew Wallace. It was a hollow victory, however, because the battle delayed the Confederates long enough for a defence of Washington to be prepared. The centre is open daily 0830–1630 (Memorial Day–Labor Day); Wed, Sun 0830–1630 (rest of year). Admission free.

PENNSYLVANIA

Benjamin Franklin National Memorial, *Franklin Institute*, 20th St and Benjamin Franklin Parkway, Philadelphia; *tel: (215) 448-1329*. Located in the Rotunda of the Franklin Institute science museum, the massive seated figure of Benjamin Franklin is the focal point of the memorial to the inventor-statesman who played a number of significant roles in the early history of the US. There are exhibits of Franklin artefacts. Open daily 1000–1700 (May–Sept); Mon–Fri 0930–1630, Sat–Sun 1000–1700 (Oct–Apr). Admission: free (charge for entry to science museum).

Edgar Allan Poe National Historic Site, *532 N. 7th St; tel: (215) 597-8974*. This was the author's home from 1843–44. Now exhibits of artefacts and documents trace his life and work. Admission: free.

Eisenhower National Historic Site, *off West Confederate Ave, Gettysburg; tel: (717) 334-1124*, but all visits to the site are by shuttle bus from the **Gettysburg National Military Park Visitor Center** on *Taneytown Rd*. This is the farmhouse into which President Dwight D. Eisenhower and his wife Mamie retired. The house is built around the preserved features of a 200-year-old log cabin. Tickets covering admission and the shuttle must be obtained from the Eisenhower Tour Information Center in the lower level of the National Military Park Visitor Center.

Gettysburg National Military Park, *Taneytown Rd, Gettysburg; tel: (717) 334-1124*. One of the world's best-known battlefields, where there were 51,000 casualties in three days of fighting – more than in any other battle fought in North America before or since – has been carefully preserved, albeit embellished with many statues, monuments and memorials. The Visitor Center incorporates an informative museum and well-stocked book and gift shop.

Gloria Dei (Old Swedes') Church, is on the Delaware River at *Columbus Blvd* and *Christian St Philadelphia*, north of the *Walt Whitman Bridge* and south of the *Ben Franklin Bridge; tel: (215) 597-8974*. Founded in 1677, this is the second oldest Swedish church in the US. The present structure dates from around 1700 and is an excellent example of 17th-century Swedish church architecture.

Independence National Historical Park, *downtown Philadelphia; tel: (215) 597-8974*. Said to be 'America's most historic square mile', the park covers 24 separate sites, including **Independence Hall, Carpenter's Hall, Congress Hall,** the **Liberty Bell Pavilion** and **Christ Church** and other structures connected with the nation's Colonial, Revolutionary and Federal heritage. Visitor centre at *Third and Chestnut Sts*. Open daily 0900–1700.

Thaddeus Kosciuszko National Memorial is at *Third* and *Pine Sts,* three blocks south of the Independence NHP visitor centre; *tel: (215) 597-8974*. This small townhouse, in which the Polish-born patriot and hero of the American Revolution rented a room in the winter of 1797–98, has been restored as a memorial, with a slide presentation and exhibits.

VIRGINIA

Appomattox Court House National Historic Park, three miles north-east of the town of Appomattox on Rte 24; *tel: (804) 352-8987*. Although the Court House itself has been reconstructed – it houses the visitor centre – there is still a strong air of poignancy among the fields, lanes and buildings where Gen. Robert E.

63

Lee surrendered the Confederate army to Gen. Ulysses S. Grant.

Arlington House, accessible by shuttle bus or 10-min walk from the parking area at the Arlington National Cemetery Visitor Center. Officially known as the Robert E. Lee Memorial, this is the house in which the Confederate general lived for 30 years. Standing on a hill, the Greek Revival plantation home commands a superb view across the Potomac River to Washington.

Booker T. Washington National Monument, is on Rte 122, 20 miles south of Roanoke via Rte 116, and 21 miles south of Bedford; *tel: ((703) 721-2094.* The leading African–American educator was born here in 1856. Today, demonstrations of pre–Civil War farm life help to convey the feeling of his childhood at the now re-constructed tobacco farm.

Colonial National Historic Park. Jamestown National Historic Site and Yorktown Battlefield are accessed from Rte 17 and I-64 and connected by the 23-mile Colonial Parkway; *tel: (804) 898-3400.* A living history museum, the Jamestown Settlement depicts life in America's first permanent English colony. At Yorktown the story of the battle that won America's independence is told in the visitor centre and museum. There is an admission charge at Jamestown, but entrance to Yorktown is free.

Fredericksburg and Spotsylvania National Military Park commemorates four major actions of the Civil War – the Battle of Fredericksburg, the Chancellorsville Campaign, the Battle of the Wilderness and the Battle of Spotsylvania Court House. The park's headquarters are in Chatham Manor, *120 Chatham La, Fredericksburg; tel: (703) 371-0802.* The **Fredericksburg Battlefield Visitor Center** is at *1013 Lafayette Blvd,*

Fredericksburg, and the **Chancellorsville Battlefield Visitor Center** is *on Rte 3, eight miles west of I-95.*

George Washington Birthplace National Monument is on the Potomac River, 38 miles east of Fredericksburg and reached by way of Rtes 3 and 204; *tel: (804) 224-1732.* Located on the banks of Popes Creek, this is the 18th century tobacco farm where America's first President was born and raised.

Maggie L. Walker National Historic Site, *110½ E. Leigh St, Richmond; (804) 780-1380.* The rowhouse home of a slave's daughter who became a bank president, a leading African American and a champion of self-help initiatives.

Manassas National Battlefield Park. The park is 26 miles south-west of Washington and the visitor centre is on Rte 234, just north of exit 47B off I-66; *tel: (703) 361-1339.* This was the scene of two bloody Civil War clashes. In the first battle, staged on 21 July 1861, some 900 men died as members of Washington society looked on as if attending a race meeting. The second battle, in August 1862, lasted three days and claimed 3300 lives.

Petersburg National Battlefield, two and a half miles east of downtown Petersburg on Rte 36; *tel: (804) 732-3531.* The site commemorates the Civil War siege of Petersburg (1864–65) when Gen. Grant's army gradually encircled the important rail city to cut the Confederates' supply lines. Costumed rangers give demonstrations of mortar and cannon fire during the summer.

Richmond National Battlefield Park. The visitor centre, *3215 E. Broad St, Richmond; tel: (804) 226-1981,* is on the site of the Confederacy's largest military hospitals. Civil War battlefield sites are in the surrounding counties of Henrico, Hanover and Chesterfield.

WASHINGTON, DC

Unlike most major cities in the USA, Washington, DC has no skyscrapers. Another distinction is its wedding cake architecture in dazzling white marble with neo-classic columns. Founded in 1791, Washington is uniquely a federal district, constructed specifically to be the nation's seat of government. It is not a state, nor a part of any state, although it stands on the north bank of the Potomac River on land donated by the state of Maryland. The 'District of Columbia' (DC) refers to Christopher Columbus.

Admission to most of the city's historic buildings, museums and galleries is free.

TOURIST INFORMATION

Washington, DC Convention & Visitors Association, *1212 New York Ave, NW, Washington, DC 20005; tel: (202) 347-2873*. Open Mon–Fri 0900–1700. This office carries a wide range of free literature – including maps, brochures, events calendars and information about sightseeing, the arts, entertainment and shopping. Accommodation information is available, but there is no reservations service.

The **Washington Visitor Information Center** at *1455 Pennsylvania Ave, NW*, listed on the back of the Washington, DC Visitor Map, closed in 1989. It is now the **White House Visitor Center**.

Maps and brochures are freely available in most hotels, where you may also obtain copies of the monthly magazine, *Where Washington* and *Washington, DC Quick Guide*, published four times a year. Both publications contain maps and give shopping, dining, nightlife and events listings, as well as sightseeing details. Similar information is in *Washington Flyer*, published by Metropolitan Washington Airports Authority and available at Washington Dulles and National Airports and on Washington Flyer express buses.

Safety

Everyone is aware of Washington's lofty position on the ladder of homicide and serious crime statistics. Visitors on the general tourism trail are unlikely to stray into no-go areas. For reassurance ask your hotel concierge which areas to avoid.

Since the 1994 Crime Bill, which introduced improved crime-fighting technology and re-assigned more police to the beat, the serious crime rate has dropped considerably. Revitalisation of deteriorated neighbourhoods has also helped.

WEATHER

Washington's climate is generally temperate, with spring, early summer and autumn the most comfortable seasons. Late summer tends to be hot and humid; the average high temperature in July is 87°F. Winter can be severe, although moderate winters are not uncommon. Snowfalls, often heavy, occur mainly in Jan and Feb.

ARRIVING AND DEPARTING

By Air

The metropolitan area is served by three

65

airports: Washington Dulles International Airport, Washington National Airport and Baltimore/Washington International Airport.

Washington Dulles; *tel: (703) 661-2700*, is located in Loudon and Fairfax counties in Virginia, about 26 miles from downtown Washington. It serves more than 30,000 passengers a day with flights to US cities and foreign destinations.

The main terminal at Dulles is currently being more than doubled in size. Midfield concourses house various airlines, airline clubs, restaurants, stores and duty-free shops. The international arrivals building houses state-of-the-art Customs and Immigration services.

There are six **Thomas Cook Currency Services** locations at Dulles Airport; *tel: (800) CURRENCY*.

Transport between the airport and downtown Washington is provided exclusively by the **Washington Flyer** service contracted by Metropolitan Washington Airports Authority. The taxi fare is about $45. Washington Flyer express buses and vans operate every half-hour between the airport and **Downtown Airports Terminal**, *1517 K St, NW; tel: (703) 685-1400*. Seven downtown hotels are on the route. The fare is $16; round trip $26; children under six, free. Washington Flyer also operates a half-hourly bus service between Dulles and the West Falls Church Metrorail station on the Orange Line in suburban Virginia. Fare: $8.

Baltimore/Washington International Airport; *tel: (410) 859-3960*, (see p. 261) is 28 miles from downtown DC – a drive of about 45 min. Taxis operated by the airport authority; *tel: 1-800-I-FLY-BWI*, cost about $30. BWI Airport buses and vans; *tel: 1-800-809-7080*, operate every hour from 0700–2200 daily between the airport and Washington's

Downtown Airports Terminal. Fare: $19; round trip $29. Door-to-door services between BWI and any location in Washington cost from $21 to $26 one way. Some 40 trains a day travel between BWI and Washington's Union Station. Services are provided by **Amtrak**; *tel: 1-800-USA-RAIL*, and **MARC**; *tel: 1-800-325-7254*.

Washington National Airport; *tel: (703) 685-8000*, is less than 5 miles from downtown DC. A short-haul airport, it serves destinations in the US. Opened in 1941, the airport is being expanded with the construction of a new 35-gate terminal with direct connections to Metrorail. There are two **Thomas Cook** offices at the airport; services include foreign currency transactions.

Taxis operated by various companies charge $12–15 for the 15-min trip downtown. Washington Flyer express buses and vans operate a half-hourly service to the Downtown Airports Terminal, calling at seven downtown hotels. Fare: $8; round trip, $14; children under six, free. The airport is also served by Metrorail's Blue and Yellow lines, with fares from $1.10.

Travelling between Dulles and National takes some 45 min by taxi and costs about $40. Washington Flyer Inter-Airport express buses and vans operate an hourly non-stop service. Fare $16; round trip, $26; children under six, free. You can also make the trip by combining the Washington Flyer service between Dulles and West Falls Church Metro station and the Blue Line between Rosslyn and National Airport.

By Car

Washington is encircled by the Capital Beltway, formed by interstates I-95 and I-495. I-95 joins the circle from Virginia to the south and leaves it to head north for

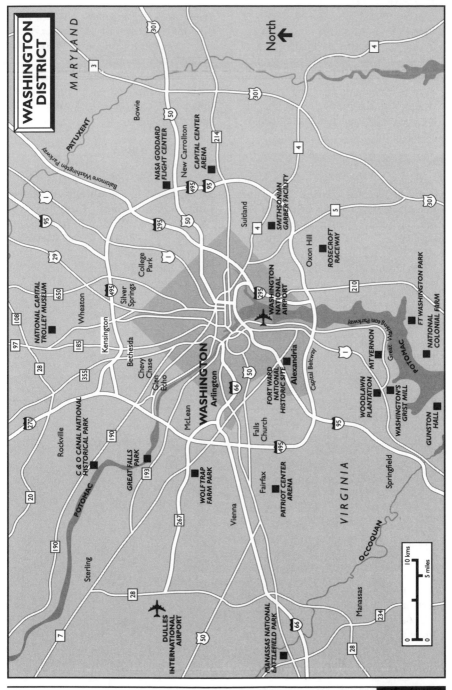

Baltimore, Philadelphia and New York. I–270 starts from the circle's north-west sector and heads north to Frederick, MD. I-50 leads west from Washington to Annapolis, MD, and I-66 goes west into Virginia. Washington's peculiar layout and a dearth of public parking ensure that driving is generally impractical and unenjoyable within the city.

A gridiron of streets is confused by an overlay of diagonal avenues. This causes some strange intersections which can lead even the most experienced travellers to lose their sense of direction, whether on foot or in a car.

The District of Columbia is a diamond shape covering ten square miles and divided into four quadrants – NE, NW, SE, SW – with the US Capitol at the centre. *North Capitol St, South Capitol St, East Capitol St* and the *National Mall* set off in cardinal directions from the Capitol. When setting out for a particular place, make sure you are heading in the right direction because the same address can turn up in more than one quadrant.

Streets running north and south are numbered – *1st St, 2nd St* and so on – while those running east and west carry letters of the alphabet – *A St, B St,* etc – but there are no J, X, Y or Z streets. After *W St,* the east-west thoroughfares continue with two-syllable names (*Adams St, Belmont St...*) then with three syllables (*Allison, Buchanan* and so on).

The diagonal avenues are named after American states – *Maryland, Pennsylvania, Rhode Island,* etc – and intersect with streets at traffic circles, a rarity in the US.

If you would like to see what kind of a pattern all this makes, take an elevator ride to the top of the **Observatory Tower** of the **Old Post Office Pavilion**, *1100 Pennsylvania Ave at 12th St NW; tel: (202) 606-8691* (metro: *Federal Triangle*). Open daily 0800–2245 (summer), 1000–1745 (winter). Admission free.

Washington's best-known sights are easily accessible. Many are within walking distance of each other and most can be reached by metro.

Public Transport

Transportation services throughout DC and in the Maryland and Virginia suburbs are operated by **Washington Metropolitan Area Transit Authority**, *600 5th St NW; tel: (202) 637-7000* (metro: *Judiciary Sq.*). **Metrorail** and **Metrobus** are both clean, safe and efficient means of getting around. In the main, they are run as separate services, although you can obtain a transfer from rail to bus. A Bus/Rail Superpass is obtainable for $65.

Metrorail

Quiet, high-speed electric trains, mainly running underground, cover much of the metropolitan area on five inter-linked lines – Red, Orange, Blue, Yellow and Green. Trains operate Mon–Fri 0530–midnight; weekends 0800–midnight. Last trains leave some stations before midnight, so check timetables displayed at stations.

Station entrances are identified by a brown pillar topped with a letter 'M' and coloured stripes indicating the lines available. Route maps are displayed in stations and aboard trains. Each train clearly displays its final destination. Flashing lights at platform edges signal an approaching train.

Fares vary according to distance travelled and time of day. Up to two children under five travel free with a fare-paying adult. Peak hours are Mon–Fri 0530–0930 and 1500–2000. A Metrorail One Day Pass costing $5 gives unlimited travel from 0930 to closing time Mon–Fri and all day

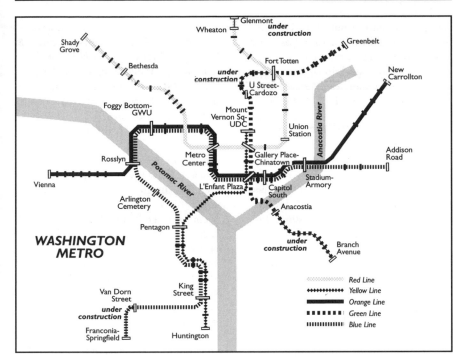

WASHINGTON METRO

Legend:
- Red Line
- Yellow Line
- Orange Line
- Green Line
- Blue Line

Sat, Sun and federal holidays. The pass is available at Metro Center and Pentagon stations, Metro headquarters and most Safeway, Giant and SuperFresh stores.

Colour-coded maps at each station concourse show fares and travel times. Farecards are purchased at machines which accept coins and bills up to $20 and give change up to $4.95. Clear instructions on buying a farecard are shown on the machines. You'll need a card to gain access to trains and to exit from your destination station. If you are continuing your journey by Metrobus, obtain a transfer slip at a dispenser near the turnstile. A transfer serves as a credit towards the bus fare.

Metrobuses

Washington and the suburbs in Maryland and Virginia are covered by a wide network of Metrobus routes. Routes and timetables are freely available in fold-up leaflets in the lobby of the Metro headquarters (see above). Most journeys cost $1.10. The dearer routes are those crossing state lines. **Flash Passes** allowing unlimited travel during a 14-day period are available at Metro headquarters and at *Metro Center* station, Mon–Fri 0800–1800, Sat 0900–1600.

Taxis

DC taxis operate on a zone system instead of meters. By law, a map showing zones and fares should be displayed in the cab. Nevertheless, it's a good idea to check the fare before getting in – and remember there is a $1.25 surcharge for each additional passenger. Taxis can usually be found near larger hotels and may be hailed from street corners. Taxis from Maryland and Virginia are equipped with meters and can take you into or out of the city. But they are not allowed to carry passengers from point to point within DC.

Washington's best-known taxi companies are **Capital Cab**; *tel: (202) 546-2400*, and **Diamond Cab**; *tel: (202) 387-6200*.

STAYING IN WASHINGTON

Accommodation

The Washington metropolitan area offers nearly 64,000 rooms in some 320 properties, including hotels, bed and breakfast establishments and inns. No district of the city is favoured with either expensive or cheap accommodation and it is possible to find somewhere to suit most pockets within easy reach of the major attractions.

July and Aug, when Congress is in recess and business and convention travel slows down, are the low-occupancy months, and this is the time when you can find the best deals. In addition, many hotels extend their low weekend rates to cover a 7-day basis and some offer free rates and complimentary meals for children. Similar low-priced packages are available during holiday periods such as Thanksgiving, Christmas, New Year's Eve and the Fourth of July. Information about special discounts and packages is available from **Washington, DC Convention & Visitors Association** (see p. 65).

Special rates and complete packages for weekend getaways are available across the accommodation spectrum throughout the year. Regular daily rack rates are substantially reduced and most hotels offer complete packages with special amenities such as breakfast, newspapers and parking.

A free brochure detailing all weekend packages offered by DC hotels is available from **Washington Weekends**, *PO Box 27489, Washington, DC 20038-7849; tel: 1-800-422-8644* or *(202) 724-4091*.

The following offer reservation services:

Capitol Reservations Tour & Travel Services, *1730 Rhode Island Ave NW, #506, Washington, DC 20036; tel: 1-800-VISIT-DC* or *(202) 452-1270*. Free service offering discounts at 70 hotels in the Washington area.

DC Hotel Reservations, *tel: 1-800-700-HOTEL*, is a multilingual lodging reservation service providing travellers with accommodation generally at discount rates. **Washington DC Accommodation**, *1534 U St NW Lower Level, Washington, DC 20009; tel: 1-800-554-2220* or *(202) 289-2220*, provides a free service offering discount rates.

Hotel chains in Washington include *BW, CI, CM, DI, ES, HI, Ma, QI, RC, Rd, Rm, Rn, Sf, Sh, ST*.

Three major hotels are so much a part of the Washington power scene that each one, though pricey, has become a tourist attraction in itself – even if the tourist does no more than stand outside and stare.

Hay–Adams Hotel, *16th and H Sts NW, Washington, DC 20006; tel: 1-800-424-5054* or *(202) 638-2260* (metro: *McPherson Sq.*), gazes across *Lafayette Sq.* at the White House. Solemnly Italian Renaissance in style, it has a lobby draped with 17th-century Medici tapestries while its 120 rooms are decorated in English manor styles.

The Jefferson Hotel, *1200 16th St NW, Washington, DC 20036; tel: (202) 347-2200* (metro: *Farragut North*), is just four blocks from the White House and is a favourite with politicians and political journalists. Each of its 100 elegantly decorated rooms and suites, many furnished with genuine antiques, has a fax machine and state of the art telephones with computer data ports.

Willard Inter-Continental Hotel, *1401 Pennsylvania Ave NW, Washington,*

The Neighbourhoods

Washington's 67 sq. miles divide into a number of neighbourhoods, each with its own distinctive character. Here are the ones most likely to appeal to visitors: **Adams-Morgan**, a few blocks north of Dupont Circle, is the capital's equivalent of New York City's Greenwich Village. Life here is played out on the streets, among corner shops, Victorian brownstone houses, colourful markets, cafés, bars and clubs. Restaurants here reflect the ethnic diversity of the neighbourhood and in the length of a street you can savour the aromas of Africa, the Mediterranean, the Caribbean or Latin America.

Capitol Hill is the Washington in everyone's mind's eye: the grand buildings of government dominated by the majesty of the US Capitol's dome; the awesome dignity of the Supreme Court; the monumental intellect of the Library of Congress and the Folger Shakespeare Library. 'The Hill' has another face. Real people live here, too, in charming streets of Victorian brick townhouses and they shop in one of the city's oldest farmers' markets. At weekends crowds flock to a sprawling flea market. Here, also are small speciality shops, intimate cafes, fine restaurants and raucous Irish pubs.

Downtown, with *Pennsylvania Ave* serving as its artery, runs from Capitol Hill to the White House and encompasses the National Archives, the National Gallery, the Navy Memorial and the White House Visitor Center and Chinatown, with its colourful Friendship Arch and bilingual street signs. Downtown has smart stores, shopping malls and restaurants.

Dupont Circle, two stops north of Metro Center on the metro's Red Line, is named after the circular park marking the intersection of Connecticut, Massachusetts and New Hampshire avenues. The lively neighbourhood has sidewalk cafés, bars, art galleries, book stores and the Philips Collection.

Foggy Bottom, stretching along the Potomac River south-west of Downtown, gained its name during the steamy summers of the 18th century when its misty marshes wrought malarial havoc. Tamed by drainage, medicine and air-conditioning, Foggy Bottom today encompasses George Washington University, the Lincoln Memorial, the Federal Reserve, World Bank, the State Department and the Vietnam Veterans' Memorial. Here, too, are the John F. Kennedy Center for the Performing Arts and the infamous Watergate complex.

Georgetown is Washington's oldest neighbourhood. Originally an Indian trading post and later a colonial port – the place where George Washington and Pierre L'Enfant met in a tavern to plan the future capital city – Georgetown today is a throbbing cosmopolitan district with brick sidewalks and a wealth of Federal townhouses. The streets are lined with boutiques, art galleries, antique shops, taverns, restaurants – and pleasure-seeking throngs.

Southwest Waterfront, along the Potomac's Washington Channel, is the city's maritime district. Smart yachts and cruisers, fishing vessels, sleek trip boats and old-time steamboats are moored alongside the piers and jetties running parallel with Maine Ave. Here you will find the Arena Stage theatre, seafood restaurants and the Maine Ave Fish Market.

DC 20004; tel: (202) 628-9100 (metro: McPherson Sq.). Two blocks east of the White House, the Willard is known as 'the Residence of Presidents' – several, including Presidents Lincoln, Grant and Coolidge, have stayed there, either waiting for their inauguration or after their term of office. In 1861, Julia Ward Howe, sat at the desk in her room at the Willard and wrote the stirring words of *The Battle Hymn of the Republic,* and in 1968 the Rev. Martin Luther King Jr wrote his 'I have a dream' speech in the hotel.

The Willard has now been restored to its Beaux-Arts elegance. It has 341 rooms, including 38 suites. The Secret Service and Protocol Office had a hand in designing the hotel's sixth floor, which is frequently occupied by visiting heads of state.

Coming down-to-earth, the budget-priced **Allen Lee Hotel**, *2224 F St NW, Washington, DC 20037; tel: 1-800-462-0186* or *(202) 331 1224* (metro: *Farragut West*), is a quaint establishment with 85 rooms close to the Lincoln Memorial, Kennedy Center and the White House.

Best Western Downtown Capitol Hill, *724 3rd St NW, Washington, DC 20001; tel: 1-800-242-4831* or *(202) 842-4466* (metro: *Judiciary Sq.*) is a moderately priced hotel handy for the US Capitol and Union Station.

The moderate–expensive **Ramada Plaza Hotel**, *10 Thomas Circle NW, Washington, DC 20005; tel: 1-800-272-6232* or *(202) 842-1300* (metro: *McPherson Sq.*), is 5 blocks from the White House. It offers room service, restaurants, covered parking and an outdoor pool.

Further out, **Adams Inn**, *1744 Lanier Pl NW, Washington, DC 20009; tel: (202) 332-3600* (metro: *Woodley Park–Zoo*), is a 25-room budget establishment in the Adams-Morgan neighbourhood. It has a laundry and limited off–street parking.

The moderate-expensive **Latham Hotel**, *3000 M St NW, Washington, DC 20007; tel: (202) 726-5000* (metro: *Foggy Bottom*) has 143 rooms, lounge, restaurant, outdoor pool, sun deck and valet parking and lies right at the busy heart of Georgetown, with shopping, dining and entertainment on the doorstep.

The budget-priced **Falls Church Motel**, *7155 Lee Hwy, Falls Church, VA 22046; tel: (703) 533-8600* (metro: *East Falls Church*) is in a quiet, secluded location only 20 min from downtown. Its 55 rooms include 18 non–smoking rooms and 33 rooms accessible to disabled people. It offers free parking and an outdoor pool.

Bed and breakfast is an increasingly popular option in DC, as it is throughout the Capital Region. The following agencies can help with reservations:

Bed and Breakfast Accommodations, *PO Box 12011, Washington, DC 20005; tel: (202) 328-3510*, has a full range of accommodation, from budget to luxury, at more than 75 locations in DC, Maryland and Virginia. Rates: $50-$250.

Bed and Breakfast League/Sweet Dreams and Toast, *PO Box 9490, Washington, DC 20016; tel: (202) 363-7767*, offers lodging in private homes and apartments in Washington. Rates: $40-$125.

Mrs Jay's Bed and Breakfast, *2951 Upton St NW, Washington, DC 20008; tel: (202) 364-0228* (metro: *Van Ness–UDC*) has two guest rooms and is located on a tree-lined residential street one block from Rocky Creek Park and two blocks from the metro. Off-street parking is available. Moderately priced.

Windsor Inn, *1842 16th St NW, Washington, DC 20009; tel: 1-800-423-9111* or *(202) 234-3309* (metro: *Dupont Circle*), is a bed and breakfast style hotel with 46 rooms, 12 blocks north of the White House. It serves complimentary breakfast and evening sherry.

Capital KOA Campground, *768 Cecil Ave, Millersville, MD 21108; tel: (410) 923-2771*, is about 20 miles north-east of Washington (free shuttle service between campsite and MARC station at Odenton). The 50-acre woodland site has 150 tent and RV pitches with full hook-up facilities, camp store, two laundrettes, recreation room, pool and playground. Open Apr–Nov.

Cherry Hill Park, *9800 Cherry Hill Rd, College Park, MD 20740-1210; tel: (301) 937-7116*, is 14 miles north of Washington, close to I-95, and has a Metrobus service from the campsite. There are 400 tent and RV pitches with full hook-up facilities, camp store, laundrette, heated pool, games room and playground.

HI: Washington International AYH Hostel, *1009 11th St NW, Washington, DC 20001; tel: (202) 737-2333* (metro: *Metro Center*). The hostel has 250 beds in dormitories for males and females, although a few rooms are available for couples. Facilities include an information desk, free tours, self-help kitchen, laundrette and limited parking. Reservations are advised for summer months when the maximum stay is six days.

Eating and Drinking

As might be expected of the world's most powerful capital city, Washington offers a culinary choice that sweeps across the international spectrum. The liveliest dining areas are Adams-Morgan, Georgetown and the area just north of *Dupont Circle*, along *Connecticut Ave, 17th St* and the side streets.

Apart from the city's diminutive Chinatown, located between *G, H, 6th* and *8th Sts,* nowhere can claim any particular ethnic inclination. There's a rash of Irish pubs building up among the intimate little cafés of Woodley Park, just northwest of Adams-Morgan, and the area surrounding *U St NW,* between *13th* and *16th Sts,* is becoming a soul food centre.

Adams-Morgan has a heavy concentration of Ethiopian restaurants, but it has a wide choice of everything else, too. Georgetown can cheerfully challenge, 'You name it...'

The place for seafood – especially crabs, oysters and other shellfish from Chesapeake Bay – is the Southwest Waterfront, fringing the Washington Channel between *4th* and *10th Sts SW* (metro: *Waterfront*).

Among the cheapest places to eat, especially for breakfast and lunch are the food courts located near major shopping malls, downtown office areas and Metro stations, such as the one next to Farragut North on *L St,* between *17th* and *18th Sts.*

The rise of the **microbrewery** in recent years has brought a revolution in economy dining. Budget–moderate meals can be had in places like the **Brickseller Inn**, *1523 22nd St NW; tel: (202) 293-1885* (metro: *Dupont Circle*). This is the most American of American restaurants, offering a cross-section of cuisine from every state in the Union and more than 600 brands of beer! Open Mon–Thur 1130–0200, Fri 1130–0300, Sat 1800–0300, Sun 1800–0200.

Swinging beer drinkers like to gather at the **Capitol City Brewing Company**, *1100 New York Ave NW; tel: (202) 628-2222* (metro: *Metro Center*). Everything served across the established big brass bar has been brewed on the premises. Cheap to budget bar food available. Open Mon–Sat 1100–0130, Sun 1100–midnight.

You can find a slot anywhere from cheap to moderate at **Garrett's**, a Georgetown restaurant and tavern with lots of shining copper and railway memorabilia at *3003 M St NW; tel: (202) 333-8282* (metro: *Foggy Bottom-GWU*). Seafood, pastas and burgers are on the menu. Open Mon–Thur 1130–0200, Fri 1130–0300, Sat 1200–0300, Sun 1200–0200.

73

Mind and body can be satisfied at **Kramerbooks and Afterwords Cafe**, *1517 Connecticut Ave NW; tel: (202) 387-1462* (metro: *Dupont Circle*). Here, customers are encouraged to read as they feed. The bookshop part is open 24 hrs while the café serves salads, sandwiches, pastas and vegetarian dishes – and brunch at weekends – daily 0730–0100. And to top it all, there's live music almost every night. Prices are budget to moderate.

Moving upmarket, **Monocle**, *103 D St NE; tel: (202) 546-4488* (metro: *Union Stn*) is a gathering place for politicos, lobbyists and journalists. Its speciality dishes – includes crab cakes and prime beef – straddle the moderate to pricey ratings. Lunch: Mon–Fri 1130–1700, dinner Mon–Fri 1730–midnight and Sat 1800–2300. A much cheaper place where you may see a famous political face feeding is the public cafeteria on the first floor, Senate-side, of the **Capitol**. It is open Mon–Fri 0730–1530, but serves Capitol staff only 1130–1300.

One of Chinatown's top restaurants is the **Golden Palace**, *710 7th St NW; tel: (202) 783-1225* (metro: *Gallery Pl.–Chinatown*). This award-winning establishment is noted for its seafood, vegetarian and traditional dishes and for its dim sum served on open carts. Prices range from budget to moderate. Open Tues–Sat 1100–midnight, Sun–Mon 1100–2200.

Among the popular Ethiopian restaurants in Adams-Morgan is **Meskerem**, *2434 18th St NW*. Budget to moderate, the menu includes meat, seafood and vegetable dishes served by costumed waiters. Live Ethiopian music is played Fri–Sun from 2330. Open Mon–Thur 1200–midnight, Fri–Sun 1200–0100.

Communications

There is a 24-hour self-service (stamp machines, scales for packages) post office at Washington-Dulles Airport. Probably the most convenient post office in the city is the one attached to the **National Post Museum**, *2 Massachusetts Ave NE, Washington, DC 20560-0001; tel: (202) 357-2700* (metro: *Union Stn*). A computer in the museum helps you to print and send personalised postcards franked with the museum postmark and you can buy special issue stamps. The entrance to the post office and museum is directly opposite Union Stn at the corner of *Massachusetts Ave* and *1st St NE*, just a few yards from the metro exit.

The telephone area code for Washington, DC is *202*. Nearby Maryland suburbs use *301*.

Money

Thomas Cook bureau de change: *1800 K St NW, Washington, DC 20006; tel: (800) CURRENCY* or *(202) 872-1427* (metro: *Farragut North*). Open Mon–Fri 0900–1700. The office at *Union Station* (opposite Gate G) *50 Massachusettes Ave N.E., Washington, DC 20002; tel: (202) 371-9219*, opens at weekends.

ENTERTAINMENT

New plays are often tried out in Washington before going on to Broadway. World class drama, music, opera and dance performances take place at the **Kennedy Center's** theatres, where entertainment ranges from Shakespeare to up-to-the-minute political satire.

Classic and contemporary plays and ethnic productions are staged in the capital, and music for all tastes is offered. As well as the major theatres, there are numerous small progressive theatres and university groups staging entertainment.

Most of Washington's nightspots open at 2100 and close their bars at 0200 – later at weekends. Exotic dancers perform on stage at some of the downtown clubs. Dinner dances are held at a number of restaurants and on river cruises, and there are at least half a dozen popular comedy clubs.

In summer free concerts by military bands and chamber orchestras take place, some of them outside.

At the other end of the scale, you can expect to pay up to $110 for one of the best seats at the **Washington Opera**.

Listings of current shows, drama and concerts are given in a number of publications, including *Where Washington*, the *Washington Post* and the *Washington Times*. Up-to-date information on performances at theatres, nightclubs, comedy clubs and other venues is available from Washington Convention and Visitors Association.

Tickets for concerts, shows and plays are obtainable through **TicketMaster** outlets at **Tower Records**, *200 Pennsylvania Ave, NW* and **Hecht's** department stores. To pay by credit card, *tel: (202) 432-7328.*

Discounted day-of-show tickets are sold by **Ticketplace**, *Lisner Auditorium, 21st and H Streets, NW; tel: (202) 842-5387* or *(202) TIC-KETS*. Open Tues–Fri 1200–1800, Sat 1100–1700.

Tickets for performances at the **Kennedy Center** can be charged by phone, *tel: (202) 467-4600* and picked up at the designated box office. Half-price tickets are sometimes available for students with ID, senior citizens, disabled people and military personnel.

The Arena Stage, founded more than 40 years ago, is Washington's leading repertory theatre, and incorporates two other theatres. Set on the waterfront at *6th St* and *Maine Ave SW, Washington, DC 20024; tel: (202) 488-3300* (metro: *Waterfront*), Arena presents drama, com-

edy, new works and classic revivals in its Oct to June season.

President Abraham Lincoln was fatally shot at **Ford's Theatre** on the night of 14 April, 1865. The theatre, which has been restored to that period, offers musicals, drama and comedy (see box, p.85). Beneath the theatre is the **Lincoln Museum**, containing the assassin's diary as well as exhibits relating to Lincoln's life. The theatre is at *511 10th St NW; tel: (202) 347-4833*; for tour information *tel: (202) 426-6924* (metro: *Metro Center*).

There are six theatres within the **John F. Kennedy Center for the Performing Arts**, with two rooftop restaurants, the Center presents drama, dance, music, comedy and film. Free guided tours take place daily 1000–1300. *Virginia and New Hampshire Aves NW; tel: (202) 467-4600* (metro: *Foggy Bottom-GWU*).

Originally built in 1921 as a movie and vaudeville house hosting the black talent of the day, the **Lincoln Theatre**, *1215 U St NW; tel: (202) 328-6000* (metro: *U St-Cardoza*), has been renovated as a performing arts centre offering film shows as well as hosting live theatre, dance and music.

The newly-renovated 1500-seat **Lisner Auditorium**, at the *George Washington University, 730 21st St NW; tel: (202) 994-1500/994-6800* (metro: *Foggy Bottom-GWU)* has a programme of more annually covering jazz, rock, classical music, opera, comedy, ballet and modern and traditional dance.

The **National Theatre**, *1321 Pennsylvania Ave NW; tel: (202) 628-6161* (metro: *Metro Center*), dating from 1835, is one of the oldest continually operating theatres in the USA. It hosts touring companies of top Broadway plays and musicals, and pre-Broadway shows.

75

Some of America's leading actors perform with the **Shakespeare Theatre's** resident company. The season is from Sept–June. The intimate, 449-seat theatre has up-to-the-minute technology. *450 7th St NW; tel: (202) 393-2700* (metro: *Archives*).

The superbly-restored **Warner Theatre**, *1299 Pennsylvania Ave NW; tel: (202) 783-4000 ext 1* (metro: *Metro Center*), a 1920s movie palace and vaudeville house provides a stage for a variety of top-line music and comedy performances and productions.

Variety

Gross National Product is a comedy group based at Arena Stage (see above), skilled in the art of pulling the rug from beneath politicians' feet. *Tel: (202) 783-7212* (metro: *Waterfront*).

Still running after more than eight years, *Shear Madness* is a comic-whodunit in which the audience helps to discover whodunit. In the **Theatre Lab** at the Kennedy Center (see above) Tues–Sun; *tel: (202) 467-4600*.

Music

The **Washington Opera** is recognised as one of the foremost opera companies in the USA, and early reservation is recommended. Performances take place in different theatres at the Kennedy Center according to the requirements of the production. *Tel: (202) 416-7800*.

The **National Symphony Orchestra** plays throughout its Nov–June season at the Kennedy Center's Concert Hall. Guest conductors and soloists are featured.

Washington Symphony Orchestra features highly-regarded musicians performing at the 3746-seat **DAR Constitution Hall**, *18th and D Sts NW; tel: (202) 857-0970*.

Ballet

Not all performances by the award-winning **Washington Ballet** take place at the Kennedy Center, so check local listings. *Tel (202) 362-3606*.

Nightlife

Dancers take the stage at **Archibald's**, a popular club for nearly 30 years, which is open daily for dinner and daily (except Sun) for lunch. Showgirls and sports TV; *1520 K St NW; tel: (202) 638-5112* (metro: *McPherson Sq.* or *Farragut North*).

Bugs are served as appetisers, the decor majors on insects and there's a highly populated ant farm at the **Insect Club**, *625 East St NW; tel: (202) 347-8885* (Metro: *Judiciary Sq.*). There's dancing to rock music, pool tables and a great atmosphere in the evenings, Wed–Sat.

The long-established **Blues Alley** jazz supper club, in Georgetown, presents the top names in jazz. Reservations essential. The cuisine is Creole. Shows are twice-nightly Sun–Thur, thrice Fri and Sat. Entrance is at the rear of *1073 Wisconsin Ave NW; tel: (202) 337-4141*.

Singing waiters and waitresses provide Broadway revue entertainment and there's dancing to live bands aboard the **Spirit of Washington** on the Potomac River. *Pier 4, 6th and Water Sts SW; tel: (202) 554-8000* (metro: *Waterfront*).

Space age decor looms large at **Planet Fred**, a place to dance, with bars at three levels; *1221 Connecticut Ave NW; tel: (202) 466-2336*, (metro: *Dupont Circle*).

EVENTS

Washington has annual events every month, and most of them appeal to visitors. Exact dates of events can be verified by contacting **Washington, DC Convention & Visitors Association,** *1212 New York Ave, NW; tel: (202)*

347-2873. Information on events can be obtained through a recording; *tel: (202) 737-8866.*

January
National Symphony Orchestra Pops (two days, early Jan), at the Kennedy Center. Admission charge. *Tel: (202) 467-4600.* **Martin Luther King, Jr.**, civil rights leader, is honoured (3rd Mon) throughout the metropolitan area. *Tel: (202) 619-7222.*

February
Black History Month. Museum exhibits and special events illustrating African Americans' contribution to US history. *Tel: (202) 619-7222.*

Abraham Lincoln's Birthday (Feb 12). Wreath-laying ceremony and the Gettysburg Address at the Lincoln Memorial. *Tel: (202) 619-7222.* **George Washington's Birthday** (3rd Mon). Wreath-laying ceremony and posting of colours by guard of honour at Washington Monument. *Tel: (703) 838-4200.*

Chinese New Year Parade (date variable). Lions, dragon dancers and fire-crackers in Chinatown's decorated streets. *Tel: (202) 393-2280.* **Washington Boat Show** (late Feb), everything that's new in pleasure craft and chandlery, at *Washington Convention Center, 900 9th St, NW; tel; (202) 789-1600* (metro: *Metro Center*).

March
St Patrick's Day Parade (Mar 17) along *Constitution Ave, NW*. Celebrate Irish heritage with bands, dancers and tableaux. *Tel (202) 637-2474.* **US Botanic Gardens Spring Flower Show** (late Mar/Apr). Free show of blossoms. *Tel: (202) 225-7099.* **Smithsonian Kite Festival** (late Mar) *National Mall.* Great free sport at Washington Monument grounds for participants of all ages and spectators. *Tel: (202) 619-7222.*

April
National Cherry Blossom Festival (sometimes starts late Mar). Two-week exultation of more than 6000 Japanese cherry trees in bloom at various historic monument locations. Grand parade on penultimate day. *Tel: (202) 547-1500.*

White House Easter Egg Roll. Eggs and entertainment are provided free for this fun event for tots at the White House South Lawn; *Tel: (202) 456-2200.* **White House Spring Gardens tours** (mid April). A free stroll through the Jacqueline Kennnedy Rose Garden and the West Lawns. *Tel: (202) 456-2200.*

Thomas Jefferson's Birthday (mid Apr). Wreath laying ceremony at Jefferson Memorial. *Tel: (202) 619-7222.*

William Shakespeare's Birthday (Sat nearest to Apr 23). Free music, theatre, children's events and exhibits at the Folger Shakespeare Library and its Tudor banqueting hall; *tel: (202) 544-7077.*

Georgetown Garden Tour. Full-day tour of private gardens. Admission charge in aid of a children's charity. *Tel: (202) 333-4953.* **Georgetown House Tour.** For two days (late Apr) 1200–1700, about a dozen homes are open for viewing to raise funds for local church work. Ticket price includes high tea at St John's Episcopal Church. *Tel: (202) 338-1796.*

Earth Day (late Apr), at *National Mall*, celebrates the planet and looks at ways of keeping it healthy. Various free events and displays. *Tel: (202) 619-7222 or (603) 924-7720.*

Washington, DC International Film Fest, in late Apr/early May, theatres all over the city screen outstanding international and local films. Tickets required. *Tel: (202) 274-6810.*

77

May

Tour of Foreign Embassies. Some of these lovely properties open to the public in aid of Davis Memorial Goodwill Industries. Reservations required. Ticket price includes tea and shuttle bus rides between embassies. *Tel: (202) 636-4225.*

Malcolm X Day (around May 19). The assassinated Civil Rights leader and orator is honoured in Anacostia Park; *tel: (202) 724-4093.* **Workfest**. This two-day event in late May showcases the ethnic diversity of the capital, with an outdoor presentation of music, food and family fun on *Pennsylvania Ave*, from *9th–14th Sts NW*, 1100–2000. Free except for modestly priced tickets for refreshments.

Memorial Day (last Mon in May). Wreath laying ceremony at the Tomb of the Unknown Soldier in Arlington Cemetery; *tel: (202) 475-0856.* Tributes also paid at Vietnam Veterans Memorial, *tel:(202) 619-7222;* and US Navy Memorial, *tel: (202) 737-2300.*

June

Dance Africa, DC. Two days of presentations of African arts, crafts and foods, with concerts in the evening. Some events free, some ticketed. *Tel: (202) 269-1600.*

Festival of American Folklife (late June/early July). Music, arts, crafts and cuisine attract more than a million people. Several selected American and international cultures are highlighted in the free event, sponsored by the Smithsonian Institution's Office of Folklife Programs. *Tel: (202) 357-2700.*

July

Fourth of July, Independence Day. Washington celebrates with a parade along *Constitution Ave*, free entertainment at the *Sylvan Theatre* on the Washington Memorial grounds, including a big-scale fireworks display and music played by the National Symphony Orchestra on the west steps of the Capitol. *Tel: (202) 619-7222.* **Bastille Day Waiters' Race** (mid July). More free fun as the city's waiters take part in the race carrying trays of champagne glasses. **Hispanic Festival** (late July). People with roots in Latin American countries showcase their cultures with free outdoor music and merry making. *Tel: (202) 835-1555.*

August

The US Army Band's 1812 Overture Concert (mid Aug) is played in the evening outside the Sylvan Theatre adjacent to the Washington Monument, with the 3rd US Infantry Salute Gun Platoon. *Tel: (703) 696-3718.* **Georgia Avenue Day**. In fact a whole weekend in late Aug, with a parade, carnival attractions, rides, live music and festive foods. *Tel: (202) 723-5166.* **Children's Festival** (late Aug) in which music, performing arts and various activities with child appeal take place in the Carter Barron Amphitheatre, *16th and Colorado Ave NW; tel: (202) 260-6836.* Admission charge

September

National Frisbee Festival (early Sept), in the *National Mall,* with frisbee champions demonstrating their skills. *Tel: (301) 645-5043.* **Labour Day Weekend Concert** in which the National Symphony Orchestra bids farewell to the summer season with a free concert at the US Capitol. *Tel: (202) 416-8100.* **Elderfest** (early Sept). Senior citizens enjoy entertainment, crafts and food at *Freedom Plaza, 1300 Pennsylvania Ave NW; tel: (202) 289-1510/ext. 120.* **DC Blues Festival** (early Sept). Top performers provide free entertainment at Carter Barron Amphitheatre; *tel: (202) 828-3028.*

Black Family Reunion (early Sept), *National Mall*. Weekend of free big-name performances and exhibits celebrating the African American family. *Tel: (202) 659-0006.* **Adams Morgan Day** (Sun following Labour Day). This culturally diverse neighbourhood presents live music, handicrafts and cuisine of its people. *Tel: (202) 332-3292 or 832-4274.* **Constitution Day Commemoration** (17 Sept), *National Archives*. The original US Constitution is displayed on the anniversary of its signing. *Tel: (202) 501-5215.*

October

Taste of DC (mid Oct). One of the most popular annual events, encouraging citizens and visitors to sample the wide range of American and international cuisines offered in *Pennsylvania Ave* between *9th* and *14th Sts, NW*. Tickets must be purchased for food tasting. *Tel: (202) 724-4093.* **Columbus Day Ceremonies** (second Mon). Wreath laying in tribute to Christopher Columbus by the Knights of Columbus, at *Columbus Memorial Plaza* outside Union Station; *tel: (301) 434-2332.* **White House Fall Garden Tours** (mid Oct). Free tours of the gardens. *Tel: (202) 456-2200.* **Washington International Horse Show** (late Oct) at *USAir Arena*. Teams from the USA, Canada and Europe compete. Tickets on sale from mid Aug. *Tel: (202) 432-SEAT.* **Marine Corps Marathon** (late Oct). Thousands of world class runners take part. *Tel: (703) 640-2225.*

November

Veterans' Day Ceremonies (Nov 11). Wreath laying, possibly by US president, at Arlington National Cemetery. Military bands honour the nation's war dead. *Tel: (202) 475-0843.* Ceremonies also held at the Vietnam Veterans Memorial; *tel: (202) 619-7222*, and the US Navy Memorial; *tel: (202) 737-2300.*

December

Pearl Harbor Day (early Dec). Wreath laying ceremony. *US Navy Memorial, 701 Pennsylvania Ave NW; tel: (202) 737-2300.* **National Christmas Tree Lighting/Pageant of Peace** (mid Dec–early Jan). The President switches on the lights on the large Christmas tree at The Ellipse. Carols are sung, and nightly choral performances follow with nativity scenes, burning yule logs and a display of illuminated Christmas trees representing every state in the USA. *Tel: (202) 619-7222.* On the evening before this ceremony, military bands perform in concert at the **People's Christmas Tree Lighting** at the west side of the US Capitol. *Tel: (202) 224-3069.*

Washington National Cathedral Christmas Celebration (Dec 24 and 25). Carols and Christmas choral works take place at special services. Free admission but tickets required. *Tel: (202) 537-6200.*

SHOPPING

Half a dozen major shopping areas – including the downtown area itself – are within easy reach of the capital's sightseeing centre. Each can be reached by metro.

Downtown shops are concentrated between *Pennsylvania Ave* and *G St NW* bordered by *7th* and *15th Sts*.

Right at the heart of the downtown area, with *Metro Center* metro station handy, are the **Shops at National Place**, three floors of boutiques, restaurants and stores like **Banana Republic** and **The Sharper Image**. National Place is between *13th and F Sts NW; tel: (202) 783-9090.* The two leading downtown department stores are also nearby. **Hecht's**

79

is at *12th and G Sts; tel: (202) 628-6661* and **Woodward and Lothrop** is at *11th and F Sts; tel: (202) 347-5300*.

The **Old Post Office Pavilion**, a former post office at *1100 Pennsylvania Ave NW; tel: (202) 289-4224* (metro: *Federal Triangle*), houses more than 80 shops and restaurants and stages daily entertainment.

Union Station, *40 Massachusetts Ave NE; tel: (202) 289-1908* (metro: *Union Stn*) looks more like a Greek temple than a working rail station, and within its elegant confines are 125 stores, restaurants, a food court, nine-screen cinema complex and a Thomas Cook currency exchange.

Between *K St* and the north of *Dupont Circle, Connecticut Ave* (metro: *Farragut North* or *Dupont Circle*) is lined with stores of all kinds, including **Burberry**, the posh London clothing store, and **Filene's Basement**, the bargain store from Boston. The area is also renowned for its concentration of private art galleries offering paintings, sculptures and other objets d'art for sale.

Washington's busiest shopping area is probably along *Wisconsin Ave* and *M St NW* in Georgetown. Crowds flock to boutiques and shops selling everything from designer clothes to second-hand books. One of the newest superstores in Georgetown is a branch of **Barnes and Noble**, the massive booksellers that never seems to close. It stands at *M St and Thomas Jefferson St*, opposite the **Old Stone House**.

Bethesda, MD, north-west of downtown Washington and reached by *Wisconsin Ave* or the metro's Red Line to *Bethesda*, has become an established shopping centre thanks to an eclectic selection of small speciality shops, art galleries and retail outlets.

Chevvy Chase, straddling the DC–Maryland line around the intersection of

Wisconsin Ave and *Western Ave* (metro: *Friendship Heights*) is the home of two major shopping centres. **Chevvy Chase Pavilion**, *5345 Wisconsin Ave; tel: (202) 686-5335*, features shops selling clothing, jewellery, home furnishings, books, gifts and toys. **Mazza Gallerie**, *5300 Wisconsin Ave; tel: (202) 686-9515*, has **Neiman Marcus, Filene's Basement** and some 50 shops, as well as restaurants and a cinema. **Saks Fifth Avenue**, the New York fashion store, is at *5555 Wisconsin Ave; tel: (301) 657-9000*, and **Gucci** is a neighbour at no *5225; tel: (301) 951-4400*.

One of the most popular shopping destinations in the DC area is the **Potomac Mills Mall**, *2700 Potomac Mills Circle, Woodbridge, VA; tel: 1-800-VA-MILLS*. It has more than 220 outlet stores, 3 restaurants and a food court under one roof. Among the stores offering goods at bargain prices are **Benetton, Bugle Boy, Laura Ashley, Levi Strauss** and **Calvin Klein**. A bus shuttle service runs from *Metro Center, Rosslyn* and *Pentagon City* metro stations on Sat.

SIGHTSEEING

Washington has diverse ways of enabling visitors to see the sights. Easy access to most of the city's most popular attractions is provided by narrated bus tours, with convenient hop-on-hop-off stops.

Tourmobile Sightseeing, *1000 Ohio Dr. SW; tel: (202) 554-5100*, offers a narrated shuttlebus service with free and unlimited re-boarding at 18 major sites. The service runs daily every 15 mins 0930–1630. Fare: $10; children 3–11 $5.

Goldline/Grayline of Washington DC *5500 Tuxedo Rd, Tuxedo, MD; tel: 1-800-862-1400* or *(301) 386-8300*, has sightseeing tours of Washington and other historic parts of the Capital Region.

Old Town Trolley Tours, *5225*

Kilmer Place, Hyattsville, MD; tel: (301) 985-3021 or (202) 872-1765. Two-hour narrated tours leave half-hourly daily 0900–1600. Free re-boarding at 17 sites. Fare: $16; children 5–12 $8.

Walking tours offer a chance to be more thorough, popping into food markets or antiquarian bookshops, or more specialist, depending on your interests.

Among new offerings are **DC Bike Tours**; tel: (202) 466-4486, who provide exercise as well as visits to historic and fascinating parts of the capital.

For something completely different, try the only amphibious tour in Washington with **DC Ducks**; tel: (202) 966-3825. The 90-minute narrated tours aboard a boat on wheels take you through city streets before transferring to the water at the Columbus Island Marina for a different perspective on the city.

Potomac Pedicabs; tel: (202) 332-1732, carry one or two passengers. The company claims to present the only driving tour that passes by the White House. These human–powered three-wheelers operate from 7th St and Pennsylvania Ave to Georgetown and Adams-Morgan districts.

Private tour companies which provide a morning or afternoon of visits to places of interest include **A Tour de Force**; PO Box 2782, Washington, DC 20013; tel: (703) 525-2948. Tours are personally conducted by Jeanne Fogle, a fourth-generation Washingtonian.

Odyssey Cruises; tel: (202) 488-6010, takes passengers under the Potomac River bridges in historic and scenic areas and offers dinner cruises aboard Odyssey III. Several other companies also offer dinner cruises on the Potomac River. A 50-min sightseeing cruise aboard Nightingale II, leaving Georgetown Harbor hourly, is operated by **Capital River Cruises**, 14101 Parkvale Rd, Rockland, MD 20853;

tel: (301) 460-7447. **Spirit Cruises**, 6th and Water Sts SW, Pier 4; tel: (202) 554-8000, has daily cruises to Mount Vernon aboard Potomac Spirit. Other cruise companies are based in neighbouring Alexandria.

The Potomac is not the capital's only waterway. The 185-mile **Chesapeake and Ohio Canal**, built by George Washington, used to carry crops between western Maryland farmland and Washington, where the produce was loaded on to clipper ships. From mid Apr–mid Oct you can take a mule-drawn barge trip with costumed guides recounting tales of long ago. Tours, departing from Georgetown, are operated by **C&O Canal Barge Rides**, PO Box 4, Sharpsburg, MD; tel: (301) 739-4200.

Other tours
All About Town, 519 6th St NW; tel: (202) 393-1618. Scheduled full-day, half-day and evening tours of Washington, Arlington and Mount Vernon by air-conditioned coaches. 24-hour reservations service; picks up at most hotels.

Capital Entertainment Services, 3629 18th St NE; tel: (202) 636-9203. Regular scheduled sightseeing tours, including speciality tours of African-American sites.

DC Foot Tour, PO Box 9001, Alexandria, VA; tel: (703) 461-7364. Personal walking tour of major historical sites. Time for picture-taking.

Scandal Tours, 1602 South Springwood Dr., Silver Spring, MD; tel: (301) 587-4291. A troupe from the Gross National Product comedy entertainment offer a 'misguided' tour exposing some of Washington's low life and scandal sites, including Watergate. Tours leave the Old Post Office Pavilion, 1100 Pennsylvania Ave NW Sat 1300 and by appointment. Tickets: $27.

Guided Walking Tours of Washington, *9009 Paddock Lane, Potomac, MD; tel: (301) 294-9514.* A selection of tours covering celebrity houses, movie location sites and the private homes of former presidents.

Washington Area Minibus Tours, *5025 13th Place NE; tel: (202)526-2049*, provides daily guided, narrated tours of historic sites and offers hotel pick-ups. **America Limousine Services Inc**; *tel: (703) 280-8123* (24 hours). Sightseeing by sedan or stretched limo.

Foggy Bottom History Tours; *tel: (202) 994-0175.* Free walking tours around George Washington University and Kennedy Center. Departs Sat 1130 from GWU Visitors Centre, *801 22nd St NW.* **Black History Tours**; *tel: (202) 554-5100.* Three-hour tour taking in abolitionist Frederick Douglass's home, the Navy Yard and other sites. Tour departs daily at 1200 from the Washington Monument. Tickets: $6; children $3.

General Attractions

Capital Children's Museum, *800 3rd St NE; tel: (202) 543-0600* (metro: *Union Station*). Children can try craftwork, cooking and computer projects and learn through hands-on exhibits relating to the arts, sciences and humanities. Through videos and interactive devices, the story of Bugs Bunny's animator is traced. Open Tues–Sun and public holiday Mon 1000–1700. Admission $6.

Corcoran Gallery of Art, *17th St* and *New York Ave NW; tel: (202) 638-3211* (metro: *Farragut West*). A fine collection of American art and some Dutch and Flemish masterpieces. A Sunday Gospel Brunch is held 1100–1400. Open Mon, Wed, Sun 1100–1700, Thur 1000–2100. Suggested donation $3 each or $5 for families.

National Building Museum, *401 F St NW; tel: (202) 272-2448* (metro: *Judiciary Sq.*). The world's largest Corinthian columns can be seen in the Great Hall of this huge former Pensions Building. The museum presents exhibitions on all aspects of the building arts and urban planning. Models of such buildings as the Capitol and the White House enable the visually impaired to discover their detail. Free lunchtime jazz concerts every Thurs. Open Mon–Sat 1000–1600. Admission free.

Library of Congress, *10 1st St SE; tel: (202) 707-2905* (metro: *Foggy Bottom*). The research library was created in 1800 to serve Congress. More than 25 million books, including the Gutenberg Bible, in what claims to be the world's largest library, housed in three impressive buildings. Items that have been copyrighted are featured. These range from Martin Luther King's 'I Have a Dream' speech to the original Barbie and Ken dolls. Open Mon–Fri 0830–2130, Sat 0830–1800. Admission free.

National Geographic Society, *1600 M St NW; tel: (202) 857-7588* (metro: *Farragut North*). Exhibits in the Explorers Hall cover early humans, the Earth, its geography and the fragile balance between its inhabitants. Open Mon–Sat 0900–1700, Sun 1000–1700. Admission free.

Textile Museum, *2320 S St NW; tel: (202) 667-0441* (metro: *Dupont Circle*). Founded in 1925, this small museum displays Third World and American Indian hand-made textiles. Open Mon–Sat 1000–1700, Sun 1300–1700. Suggested $5 donation.

US Holocaust Memorial Museum, *100 Raoul Wallenberg Pl. SW; tel: (202) 488-0400* (metro: *Smithsonian*). Through photographs, artefacts, film, videotaped histories and other exhibits, the harrowing story of the Nazi genocide is told. The

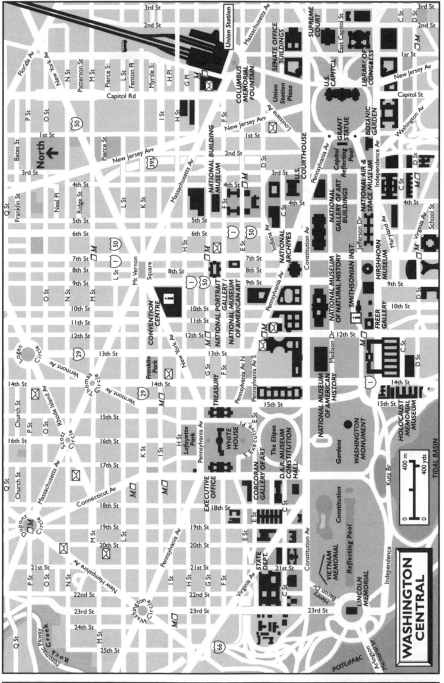

Tower of Faces, an actual barrack building from Auschwitz, is featured. Open daily 1000–1730. Admission free, but timed tickets required for crowd control.

National Aquarium, *US Dept of Commerce Building, 14th St and Constitution Ave NW; tel: (202) 482-2826* (metro: *Federal Triangle*). Rare sea turtles are among the inhabitants. Shark and piranha feedings can be watched and a touch tank contains hermit crabs and sea urchins. Open daily 0900–1700. Admission charge.

National Archives and Records Administration, *8th St and Pennsylvania Ave NW; tel: (202) 501-5000* (metro: *Archives-Navy Memorial*). The US Constitution, the Declaration of Independence and the Bill of Rights are permanently displayed. Open daily Apr–early Sept 1000–2100, rest of year 1000–1730.

Phillips Collection, *1600 21st St NW; tel: (202) 387-0961* or *387-2151* (metro: *Dupont Circle*). Museum of 19th- and 20th- century paintings, including Renoir's *Luncheon of the Boating Party* and works by Georgia O'Keeffe, Paul Klee and Jacob Lawrence. Open Tues–Sat 1000–1700, Thur –2030, Sun 1200–1900. Admission charge, weekends: $6.50, $3.25 students and seniors; weekdays: donation.

National Museum of Women in the Arts, *1250 New York Ave NW; tel: (202) 783-5000* (metro: *Metro Center*). More than 1500 works by 400 women from 28 countries. Open Mon–Sat 1000–1700, Sun 1200–1700. Donation.

DAR Museum, *1776 D St NW; tel (202) 872-3239* (metro: *Farragut West*). More than 30 rooms furnished in pre-1840s style in this museum of the Daughters of the American Revolution. A gallery with changing exhibits opens Mon–Fri 0830–1600, Sun 1300–1700. Closed Sat and two weeks in Apr. Admission free.

Washington Dolls' House and Toy Museum, *5236 44th St NW; tel: (202) 244-0024* (metro: *Friendship Heights*). Beautifully furnished dolls' houses with dolls, games and other toys. Open Tues–Sat 1000–1700, Sun 1200–1700. Admission $3, children under 14, $1.

Woodrow Wilson House Museum, *2340 S St NW; tel: (202) 387-4062* (metro: *Dupont Circle*). President and Mrs Woodrow Wilson lived here after their White House term. The original furnishings and are on view. Open Tues–Sun 1000–1600. Admission charge.

United States Botanic Gardens, *245 1st St SW; tel: (202) 225-8333* (metro: *Smithsonian*). tropical, sub-tropical and desert plants are among the exhibits. Open daily 1000–1730. Admission: free.

Folgar Shakespeare Library, *201 East Capitol St SE; tel: (202) 544-7077* (metro: *Capitol South*), is a recreation of Shakespeare's original Elizabethan theatre and one of the world's greatest collections of Shakespeare and Renaissance material. Mon–Sat 1000–1600. Admission: free.

Navy Museum, *901 M St SE; tel: (202) 433-4882* (metro: *Navy Yard*). Hands-on exhibits range from anti-aircraft guns to periscopes trained on a destroyer moored in the harbour, *USS Barry*. Changing naval art displays. Open Mon–Fri 0900–1600 (to 1700 in summer), weekends and public holidays 1000–1700.

Marine Corps Museum, *Washington Navy Yard, 9th and M Sts SE; tel: (202) 433-3534* (metro: *Navy Yard*). Displays of weapons, uniforms and documents and a diorama of battles. Letters and art, mainly relating to the Vietnam War, are also on show. Open Mon–Sat 1000–1600, Sun and public holidays 1200–1700.

Monuments and Memorials
Washington Monument, *National Mall*

'Jinxed' Theatre

A structure built by the Baptist Church in 1833 in *Tenth Street*, Washington, was leased to John Ford in 1859. He converted it into a theatre bearing his name, much to the chagrin of some members of the former congregation. In 1861 the building was destroyed by fire. Ford re-built his theatre, and all went well until a performance of a play called *Our American Cousin* on 14 Apr 1865.

President Abraham Lincoln, attending the performance with a few friends, was fatally shot by one of the actors, 27-year-old John Wilkes Booth, an avid Confederate. Instead of delivering his lines in the play, he shouted the motto of the state of Virginia: 'Thus Always to Tyrants', fired shots and the president lay mortally wounded.

People began to voice the thought that there was a curse on the building. For a period after the assassination Ford shut it down, and was about to re-open it when the government closed it officially.

Years later, having bought the building, the government converted it to office use. In June 1893 disaster struck again. The third floor collapsed, killing 22 employees and injuring 60 others. Once more it was closed. In 1932 a small museum dedicated to Lincoln opened in the building, and in 1968, after reconstruction work, Ford's Theatre re-opened. Successive presidents have attended performances without coming to any harm, and today the Lincoln Museum lives on beneath the theatre.

at 15th St NW; tel: (202) 426-6839 (metro: *Smithsonian*). See p.91.

Jefferson Memorial, *Tidal Basin, south end of 15th St SW; tel: (202) 426-6822* (metro: none close, *Smithsonian* is nearest, memorial is on tour buses' route). A 19-ft statue of Thomas Jefferson stands on the south bank of the Tidal Basin, surrounded by a white-domed marble building, the interior walls of which are inscribed with some of Jefferson's pronouncements. Open 0800–midnight. Admission free.

Lincoln Memorial, *23rd St NW between Constitution and Independence Aves; tel: (202) 426-6895* (metro: *Foggy Bottom*). The seated statue of Abraham Lincoln, 16th president, overlooks the Reflecting Pool. Many public demonstrations have taken place on the steps by the Grecian-style memorial temple. Open 24 hrs, ranger on site 0800–midnight. Admission free.

National Law Enforcement

Officers' Memorial, *605 East St NW; tel: (202) 737-3400* (metro: *Judiciary Sq.*). Lion sculptures guard each of the four entrances to this marble wall of remembrance which bears more than 13,000 names of officers who lost their lives in the line of duty. Names date from 1794 to the present. Those of recent casualties are engraved during Police Week in mid May. Among the names are those of officers killed by such notorious characters as Billy the Kid and Bonnie and Clyde. A free walking tour brochure is available at the Visitor Centre at *605 East St*, open Mon–Fri 0900–1700, Sat 1000–1700, Sun 1200–1700. Memorial open 24 hours. Admission free.

Korean War Veterans' Memorial, *West Potomac Park on the Mall,* adjacent to Lincoln Memorial at *Daniel French Dr.* and *Independence Ave SW; tel: (202) 426-6842* (metro: *Foggy Bottom*). Impact-making memorial (and Washington's newest, dedicated in 1995) with stainless steel sculptures of 19 ground troops moving towards victory in Korea. Open 24 hrs, park ranger on site 0800-midnight. Admission – free.

US Navy Memorial, *Pennsylvania Ave between 7th and 9th Sts NW; tel: (202) 737-2300* (metro: *Archives*). Those who have served in the US Navy are honoured. There is an impressive statue of the *Lone Sailor* and an amphitheatre where outdoor summer concerts are held. A film show is available. Open Mon–Sat 0930–1700, Sun 1200–1700. Admission free but charge of $3.50 to see film.

Vietnam Veterans' Memorial, near Lincoln Memorial, just north of Reflecting Pool; *tel: (202) 634-1568* (metro: *Foggy Bottom*). More than 58,000 names of those who died or remain missing in the Vietnam War are inscribed on the black granite V-shaped memorial, and there's a sculpture by Frederick Hart. Accessible 24 hrs, park ranger on site 0800–midnight. The **Vietnam Women Veterans' Memorial** is nearby.

The Potomac Powerhouse

Government of the nation has gone a long way since 1800 when President John Adams moved into a White House deliberately set far enough away from the Capitol to underline the separation of powers between the executive and legislative arms. Fundamentally, the system of government today is exactly the same as it was 200 years ago, but the pace – the size of it all – has undergone a tremendous change.

In those early days Congress assembled, as the Constitution says it shall, at 1200 on the third day of Jan, but as spring advanced and warm weather made assembly uncomfortable and concentration difficult, members frequently went into long recess. Today, air-conditioning and the pressure of national and international affairs keep Congress at work for much of the year.

Congress consists of the **Senate** and the **House of Representatives**. The Senate chamber is in the north wing of the Capitol and the House chamber is in the south wing. The Senate has 100 members, two from each state. A senator must be at least 30 years old, a resident of the state, and a US citizen for 9 years. Senators are elected for six-year terms.

The House of Representatives has 435 members. States are assigned a number of representatives based on their population. Numbers are reviewed after the national census every 10 years. A representative must be at least 25 years old, a resident of the state, and a US citizen for 7 years. Representatives serve two-year terms. Legislative procedure in begins when a member introduces a bill which is subsequently considered by a committee and after a second and third reading put to a vote. If it is passed it goes to the Senate.

If the Senate approves, the bill is signed by the Speaker of the House and the President of Senate, then sent to the President of the United States. If the President rejects it, the bill is returned to Congress and must be passed by a two-thirds vote to beat the veto. If it receives Presidential approval, the bill becomes law.

The President has a staff of about 2000 working in the White House and in the adjacent Executive Office Building. Elected for a four-year term, the President receives an annual salary of $200,000. The Vice-President, also elected for four years, gets $160,000 a year. If the President dies or becomes incapable, the Vice-President takes over. Next in line of succession is the Speaker of the House of Representatives.

Albert Einstein Memorial, *2101 Constitution Ave NW* (metro: *Foggy Bottom*). A 21-ft high statue of Einstein sculpted by Robert Berk. It depicts the genius contemplating a galaxy of 3000 stars carved on black granite. Always accessible.

Public Buildings

Two not-to-be-missed tours for first-time visitors are the **White House** and the **US Capitol**. Both are free.

The White House, *1600 Pennsylvania Ave NW; tel: (202) 456-2322* (metro: *Federal Triangle* or *McPherson Sq.*). Tours Tues–Sat 1000–1200. In summer free same-day timed tickets are distributed at the **White House Visitor Center**, *Baldrige Hall, US Dept of Commerce, 1450 Pennsylvania Ave NW; tel: (202) 208-1631 or 456-7041* (metro: as above). The Visitor Center is open 0730–1600 (extended in summer).The ticket system operates mid Mar–end Aug. Because of heavy demand it is important to arrive early, as all tickets, issued on a first come, first served basis, may have gone by 0830. Each applicant may request up to 6 tickets for the 20-min self-guided tour of the White House. No advance tickets are available.

Tours depart from *The Ellipse*, on the south side of the White House. It is suggested that tourists arrive 10 mins before the time on their ticket. Musical performances may entertain them in summer while they wait. The White House Visitor Center, operated by the National Parks Service, is worth seeing in its own right. The large, newly renovated hall has historical exhibits, displays of photographs showing life and special functions at the White House down the years, a souvenir sales area and an information kiosk.

Because of the nature of the White House, as the official residence of the US

president, all tours may be subject to change or cancellation. To check the latest schedule, call the White House Visitor Office recorded information lines: *(202) 456-2200* (special events) or *(202) 456-7041* (tours).

US Capitol, *between Capitol Hill and Independence Ave NW; tel: (202) 225-6827* (guide service) or *(202) 543-8919* for information from US Capitol Historic Society (metro: *Capitol South*). Guided tours lasting 20 min start daily from the Rotunda 0900–1545. The Capitol is open to 1630. Congress maintains it as a building with few restrictions on visitors. Tours and assistance for disabled visitors are available from the Special Services Office in the Crypt. The guided tour is a useful introduction to the building, but because of the amount of magnificent art works and historic associations, visitors may also spend time in the galleries and look around on their own. The *Washington Post* records when Senators and Representatives are sitting. To get a Congressional pass and watch proceedings, Americans can apply to their senator or representative several weeks in advance. Foreign visitors may obtain House passes at the gallery check-in desk on the third floor and Senate passes at the Senate appointment desk on the first floor. But again several weeks' notice may be required. The passes do not include a tour. A brief ride on a small subway train in the basement takes politicians, staff and visitors to the corridors of offices.

Other Public Buildings

Bureau of Engraving and Printing, *Dept of the Treasury, 14th and C Sts NW; tel: (202) 874-3019* (metro: *Capitol South*). Watching dollar bills being printed at the rate of 7000 sheets an hour, totalling well over $2 million a day, fascinates everyone. This is such a popular 25 min self guided

87

> # The Residence of Presidents
>
> It is probably the most famous address in the world – *1600 Pennsylvania Ave NW, Washington, DC*, better known as the White House. It has been the official residence of every President, except George Washington. The White House – or the President's House, as it was first known – was first occupied by America's second President, John Adams, who moved in with his family in November 1800, just a few months before the end of his term. Much of the building's interior was still unfinished and the Adams family wash was hung out to dry in the East Room.
>
> President James Madison and his wife, Dolley, introduced a more sophisticated tone when they moved into the White House in 1809. The architect Benjamin Latrobe was commissioned to decorate the Oval Room and design new furnishings. Unfortunately, his work was totally destroyed in Aug 1814 when the British raided Washington and set fire to the White House in retaliation for an American attack. After considerable reconstruction the building was ready for President James Monroe in 1817, and as the nation expanded in the 19th century so the Executive Mansion – as it was now officially known – was extended and improved.
>
> Porticos were added to the north and south ends by 1829. An indoor bathroom came in 1833, by which time running water had been added. Gas lighting was installed in 1848 and central heating in 1853. Electric lights arrived in 1891.
>
> Theodore Roosevelt changed the building's name to the White House – the name most people gave it, anyway – when he became President in 1901 and persuaded Congress to provide funds for extensive repairs and extensions. In 1948, during President Harry Truman's term, a survey revealed that the building was in an alarming condition, with many of the old wooden beams and interior walls weakened by constant structural alterations. The Trumans moved across the street to Blair House while the White House was completely reconstructed – a job that took four years.

88

tour that from May–Aug a same-day timed ticket system operates for crowd control. It means calling for a free ticket early in the day and returning at the time assigned to you. You can come away with a thick wad of (shredded) money for $1.50. Open Mon–Fri 0900–1400 except federal holidays. Admission free.

FBI Headquarters, *J. Edgar Hoover Bldg, Pennsylvania Ave NW; tel: (202) 324-3447* (metro: *Archives*). The tour reveals latest crime-fighting techniques. Open Mon–Fri 0845–1615 except public holidays. Admission free.

Supreme Court, *1st St and Maryland Ave NE; tel: (202) 479-3030* (metro: *Capitol South*). Displays and a film outline procedures in the nation's highest court. Lectures every hour on the half-hour Mon–Fri 0930–1530 when not in session, or self-guided tours. Court hearings may be watched on a first come, first served basis, but public seating is limited. For a brief look, join the 3-min line, to attend an entire case, join the regular line. The court sits 0900–1630.

Churches
Washington National Cathedral, *Massachusetts and Wisconsin Aves NW; tel: (202) 537-6200 or 6247* (metro: none; nearest is *Tenleytown*, or use *Metrobus numbered in 30s*). Twentieth century craftsmen used 14th- and 15th-century skills to build

and adorn this Gothic cathedral. The Episcopal cathedral is in fact in interdenominational use. It was completed in 1990 and is the world's sixth largest cathedral. The cathedral, which has gift shops and gardens, is set in 57 acres. Open daily 1000–1630. Guided tours Mon–Sat 1000–1515, Sun 1230–1445. Admission free, donations appreciated – $2, children $1.

St John's Church, *1525 H St NW; tel: (202) 587-0144* (metro: *McPherson Sq.* or *Farragut North*). This is the Church of the Presidents – every one of them since Madison has worshipped here. Pew 54 is reserved for the president. The Episcopal church was designed by Benjamin Latrobe – who re-built the White House after the British set fire to it – and completed in 1816. Both St John's and the adjacent Parish House, built 20 years later, are national landmarks. Tours are available after the 1100 Sunday service. St John's is open daily 0840–1600 except during regular services and federal holidays.

Ebenezer Methodist Church, *420 D St SE; tel: (202) 544-1415* (metro: *Capitol South*). Designated an historic landmark, the site was the original school for African Americans. Open Mon–Fri 0830–1500. Tours available.

Metropolitan African Methodist Episcopal Church, *1518 M St NW; tel: (206) 331-1426* (metro: *Brookland-CUA*). Dedicated in 1886, the Gothic building is noted for its stained-glass windows. Open Mon–Sat 1000–1800 and for 0800 and 1100 Sunday services.

St Augustine Catholic Church, *1419 U St NW* (metro: *U Street-Cardozo*). The church, founded in 1858, has served African American Catholics longer than any other in Washington.

Islamic Mosque and Cultural Center, *2551 Massachusetts Ave NW; tel: (202) 332-8343* (metro: no convenient station). Built among the foreign embassies in the city after World War II to meet the needs of diplomats and staff from Islamic countries, the mosque faces Mecca and has a 162-ft minaret. The Center, with its library, auditorium and gift shops, is open daily 1000–1700. The mosque is open for prayers five times a day and by appointment. To enter, women must be fully clothed, with head, legs and arms covered. Everyone must take off their shoes.

New York Avenue Presbyterian Church, *1313 New York Ave NW; tel: (202) 393-3700* (metro: *McPherson Sq.* or *Metro Center*). Two presidents, John Quincy Adams and Abraham Lincoln, worshipped here. The Lincoln pew and 19 stained-glass windows are of special interest. Open daily. Guided tours Sun after 0900 and 1100 services.

Washington Mormon Temple Visitors' Center, *9900 Stoneybrook Dr., Kensington, MD; tel: (301) 587-0144*. The Temple of the Church of Jesus Christ of Latter-Day Saints is closed to non-members, but a film about the temple can be seen in the Visitors' Center. Thirty acres of grounds are especially colourful in spring. Visitors' Center open daily 1000–2100.

National Shrine of Immaculate Conception, *4th St and Michigan Ave NE; tel: (202) 526-8300* (metro: *Brookland-CUA*). The largest Catholic church in the US, with more than 50 chapels and a wealth of stained glass. The enormous dome is nearly 240 ft high, and the 329-ft Knights' Tower has a carillon of 56 bells. Open 0700–1800 daily (to 1900 Apr–Oct). Guided tours by appointment.

Franciscan Monastery, *1400 Quincy St NE* (metro: *Brookland-CUA*). A retreat in the Byzantine style with replicas of Holy Land shrines. A statue of St Francis stands in the enclosed garden. Open daily 0900–1700.

89

WASHINGTON NATIONAL MALL

A mile of greensward lined with elm trees, museums and monuments lies grandly between the Capitol and the Washington Memorial. The National Mall was included in Pierre L'Enfant's original plan for the capital, but for 80 years it remained a marshy wasteland. It was not until the beginning of this century that L'Enfant's dream of a 'Grand Avenue' became reality.

Today, the Mall is criss-crossed with footpaths and cycle trails and adorned with information kiosks and refreshment stands. Surrounded by nine of the Smithsonian Institute's 13 museums, it makes a complete tour in itself – a tour which can be undertaken on foot or by Tourmobile trolley.

The directions given below are aimed at those travelling on foot, but a word of warning: circuiting the Mall can be tiring, especially in the heat of summer, so it would be best to spread your sightseeing over a couple of days – longer if you intend to do full justice to the Smithsonian's museums.

TOURIST INFORMATION

Five Metro stations are handy for access to the Mall at different points, but the most convenient is *Smithsonian*, close to the high-tech **Visitor Information Center** at the **Smithsonian Castle**, *Jefferson Dr.,* on the south side of the Mall; tel: (202) 357-2700; open daily 0930–1730. You can sort out your priorities at the Castle and find out where free timed tickets are required.

All the Smithsonian museums and galleries are free and open daily except for Christmas Day. Regular opening hours are 1000–1730 unless otherwise stated. Museum shops and dining facilities close half an hour before the museum closing time.

WALKING TOUR

Behind the Castle, actually beneath the four-acre **Enid Haupt Memorial Garden** is the **Arthur M. Sackler Gallery**, *1050 Independence Ave SW; tel: (202) 357-2700* (metro: *Smithsonian*), featuring 6000 years of beautiful craftsmanship from Asia and the Near East – jade, bronzes, lacquerware, sculpture, paintings, furniture...

Immediately to the east, on the corner of *Independence Ave and 12th St*, is the **Freer Gallery of Art**, (metro: *Smithsonian*) tel: (202) 357-4880. Here the emphasis is on Japanese, Chinese and Korean art and works by American artists, including Whistler. The only surviving example of his interior design work – the opulent Peacock Room – is on permanent display.

Between *12th and 14th Sts on Independence Ave*, are the two buildings of the **Department of Agriculture**. The older building (closest to *14th St*) was built in 1905 and has cornices appropriately

90

The Smithsonian Institution

The Smithsonian Institution, originating from a bequest made in 1829 by a London chemist and mineralogist, is the largest museum complex in the world.

James Smithson had amassed a fortune equal to $500,000. He had never crossed the Atlantic, but left his estate to the United States of America specifically to create 'an institution for the increase and diffusion of knowledge among men'.

The bequest inspired people from throughout the US to donate more funds, and today the Smithsonian Institution has custody of more than 78 million artefacts. Only about one per cent of these can be displayed at any one time.

James Smithson's one stipulation accompanying his generous gesture was that the institution should bear his name. Today, the name 'Smithsonian' is one of the most frequently used words in the Washington tourist vocabulary.

The oldest Smithsonian Institution building, known as **The Castle**, a red-brick edifice in the National Mall, was designed by James Renwick and completed in 1855. Its Great Hall now houses the Institution's Visitor Information and Associates' Reception Center.

James Smithson's tomb – his remains were taken to Washington in 1904 – and a small collection of memorabilia may be viewed in the Crypt Room at The Castle. Also within the building is the Woodrow Wilson International Center for Scholars.

decorated with carvings of woodlands, grains, flowers and fruit.

Cross the western end of the Mall, with the Washington Memorial to your left. The **Washington Monument**, *National Mall at 15th St NW; tel: (202) 426-6839* (metro: *Smithsonian*). is a 555-ft marble obelisk dedicated to the first president, and the world's highest free-standing masonry structure. Take the lift to the top for a spectacular view of the city. Open daily 0900–1700. Admission free, but a free timed ticket scheme may be operating, especially in summer, on a first come, first served basis. For information *tel: (202) 619-7222.*

Behind the Washington Monument, in West Potomac Park, is the **Lincoln Memorial** (see p 85) and the **Vietnam Veterans memorial**, (p 86).

Returning to the National Mall, the next attraction you come to the **Museum of American History**, *14th St and Madison Dr.; tel: (202) 357-2700* (metro: *Smithsonian* or *Federal Triangle*). This is the place for true Americana, like Henry Ford's original Model-T car, Dorothy's ruby slippers from *The Wizard of Oz*, a selection of First Ladies' inaugural gowns, the original Star-Spangled Banner – and George Washington's false teeth. A History Room for children is open Tues–Sun, 1200–1500. Free tickets may be required for this at busy times.

Between *12th St and 9th St* lies the massive **Museum of Natural History**, *tel: (202) 357-2700* (metro: *Federal Triangle*). The Hope Diamond – all 45.5 carats of it – can be seen here. Dominating the foyer is the world's largest African elephant, which died in the 1950s. Dinosaurs' skeletons, a live coral reef, anthropological displays and an insect zoo with live occupants from all over the world offer as many fascinating hours as you can spare. The Dinosaur Room, with activities for children, is open Mon–Thur 1200–1430 and Fri–Sun 1030–1530.

91

The space between *9th and 7th Sts* is taken up by the **National Sculpture Garden Ice Rink**, where skates maybe rented in winter. In summer you may be glad to cool off with an ice cream bought at the refreshment kiosk.

Next come the West and East Buildings of the **National Gallery of Art**, separated by *4th St* (but cunningly connected by an underground people-mover) *tel: (202) 737-4215* (metro: *Archives*). The gallery is recognised as one of the world's finest art museums, and both sections warrant many hours of browsing. The older West Buildings features an outstanding collection of American and European Old Masters from the 13th to 19th centuries. Modern art is in the East Building, designed by I.M. Pei and opened in 1978. For many of the 'blockbuster' special exhibitions frequently held, a free timed-ticket admission system is often imposed for crowd control. These tickets are usually available from the East and West Buildings or, for a service charge, from TicketMaster locations, or *tel: (202) 432-SEAT*. Open Mon–Sat 1000–1700, Sun 1100–1800. Admission: free.

At the eastern end of *Madison Ave*, turn right on 3rd St from where you will get an excellent view of the **Capitol** (see p.87) with the **Reflecting Pool** and **Ulysses S. Grant Memorial** in the foreground. Face the opposite direction and your gaze covers the full length of the Mall to the Washington Memorial.

Back on *Jefferson Dr.*, head west and cross *4th St* to reach the **National Air & Space Museum**; *tel: (202) 357-2700* (metro: *L'Enfant Plaza* or *Federal Center*). From the Wright Brothers' 1903 Flyer to a moon rock you can touch, the history of flight is demonstrated in 23 galleries. Films on flight, including space travel, are shown continuously in a five-storey IMAX theatre (admission charge $4, children/senior citizens $2.75). Free planetarium programmes. For information on film and planetarium details *tel: (202) 357-1686*. To avoid congestion, admission is by free tickets, available each day on a first come, first served basis, near the museum's *Independence Ave* entrance. For information *tel: (202) 786-2122*.

Across *7th St*, lie the **Hirshhorn Museum and Sculpture Garden**; *tel: (202) 357-2700* (metro: *L'Enfant Plaza*). The focus is on 18th- and 19th-century paintings in a spectacular cylindrical structure known to Washingtonians as 'the Doughnut on the Mall'. The latest art trends are explored in changing exhibitions. On the opposite side of *Jefferson Dr.*, the Sculpture Garden displays Rodin's *Burghers of Calais* as well as works by Max Ernst, Alberto Giacometti, Pablo Picasso, Henry Moore and Man Ray.

Next on the south side of Jefferson Dr. is the **Arts and Industries Building**, *tel: (202) 357-4880* (metro: *Smithsonian*). The Victorian era in America is represented here, with emphasis on a re-creation of the Philadelphia Centennial Exhibition of 1876. Steam engines and a printing press are on show.

Back at last to the Enid Haupt Memorial Garden, where this time the subterranean attraction is the **National Museum of African Art**; *tel: (202) 357-2700* (metro: *Smithsonian*. This is the only museum in the country devoted entirely to the collection, study and exhibition of African art. Ceremonial clothing and altars are among exhibits in the permanent collection.

WASHINGTON–ANNAPOLIS

Maryland's state capital, Annapolis, can be reached in little more than 40 minutes from Washington – a distance of only 35 miles. The route itself is not one of the world's most exciting journeys, but the reward for undertaking it is Annapolis itself: charming, historic, relaxed.

> DIRECT ROUTE: 35 MILES

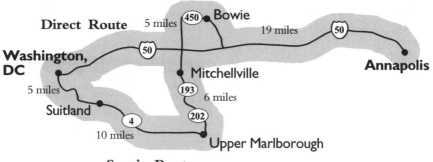

Direct Route — Washington, DC — 5 miles — **Bowie** (450) — 19 miles — (50) — **Annapolis**
(50) — **Mitchellville** (193) — 6 miles
5 miles — **Suitland** — (4) — (202) — 10 miles — **Upper Marlborough**

Scenic Route

93

ROUTES

DIRECT ROUTE

➡ From downtown Washington, take *Pennsylvania Ave* east, then continue east on *New York Ave*. This becomes Hwy 50 – at first, seemingly under constant reconstruction – soon after crossing *Florida Ave*, then continues past the **National Arboretum** and **Kenilworth Aquatic Gardens** to **Cheverly**, just across the Maryland state line. From here the highway continues almost exactly due east to

Annapolis, bypassing **Bowie** on the way. Don't miss Exit 24, where *Rowe Blvd* leads straight into downtown Annapolis, or you may soon be heading across the Severn River towards Chesapeake Bay.

SCENIC ROUTE

➡ This extends the journey to a distance of 51 miles, but takes you away from Hwy 50, which can be busy with trucks at times, and leads you on an admittedly circuitous route to take in some of the few sightseeing attractions between the two cities.

For the scenic journey, continue east

on *Pennsylvania Ave,* which continues for about 5 miles, passing through **Suitland**, under the Capital Beltway and around the northern edge of **Andrews Air Force Base** to become Rte 4. Continue east to **Upper Marlborough**, then head north on Hwy 202 *(Largo Rd)* to **Oak Grove.** From here turn on to Hwy 193 and continue north for three miles, crossing Rte 214 at **Mitchellville** before passing under Hwy 50. In half a mile turn on to Rte 450 east to Bowie, where a turn south on to *Collington Rd* leads to Hwy 50. Follow this east to Annapolis, remembering not to miss Exit 24.

SUITLAND

Tourist Information: Prince George's County Convention & Visitors Bureau, *9475 Lottsford Rd, Suite 130, Landover, MD 20785; tel: (301) 925-8300.* Landover is located north-east of Cheverley, between Hwy 50 and the Baltimore-Washington Parkway. The bureau provides general tourist information on each of the places along this route.

SIGHTSEEING

Each of Suitland's attractions is connected with aviation. The **Airmen Memorial Museum,** *5211 Auth Rd; tel: (301) 899-8386,* is a privately run museum that tells the story of the men and women involved in the development of aviation. Open Mon–Fri 0800–1700. Admission free.

Andrews Air Force Base, *Camp Springs; tel: (301) 981-4511,* home of *Air Force One,* the Presidential aircraft, may be visited by appointment.

Paul E. Garber Facility, *3904 Old Silver Hill; tel: (202) 357-1400,* is the workshop of the Smithsonian Institute's **Air and Space Museum,** and where restoration and preservation take place.

About 140 aircraft are displayed in five cavernous hangars. Open Mon–Fri 1000–1700; Sat–Sun 1000–1300. Admission free.

UPPER MARLBOROUGH

Prince George's Equestrian Center, *14955 Pennsylvania Ave; tel: (301) 952-7900.* Site of more than 40 equestrian and entertainment events a year. Open daily 0830–1600. Admission price varies.

MITCHELLVILLE

Adventure World, *13710 Central Ave (Hwy 214); tel: (301) 249-1500.* Slide shows, games and more than 50 white-knuckle rides. Open daily 1030–1800 (closes later mid June–early Sept), Oct daily 1600–2200. Admission charge gives access to everything.

BOWIE

Huntington Railroad Museum, *8614 Chestnut Ave; tel: (301) 805-4616.* A collection of restored historic Pennsylvania Railroad buildings tells Bowie's history in photographs and artefacts. Open fourth Sun in month 1200–1600 Oct–Mar. The museum also holds special event days. Admission free.

Love's Labours

Suitland's love affair with the airplane is demonstrated at the Paul E. Garber Facility.

Working sometimes from no more than a faded old photograph and what seems to be a heap of rubbish, the facility's craftsmen re-build shining classics of the air so well that many a veteran flier has been heard to say that they look better than the originals.

WASHINGTON–BALTIMORE

Three routes lead from Washington to Baltimore, Maryland's biggest and busiest city – I-95, Hwy 1 and I-295. But each follows the same north-easterly course within a couple of miles of the others and each leads into the interstate tangle that surrounds Baltimore. The easiest route is I-295, also known as the Baltimore-Washington Parkway, which picks its way across the rolling Maryland countryside once the drab streets of north-east Washington have been left behind. The places listed below are spaced neatly along the route's 40 miles.

DIRECT ROUTE: 40 MILES

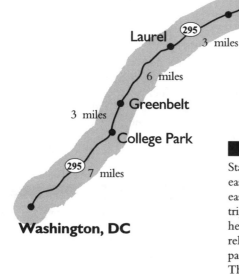

Baltimore

21 miles

Fort George G. Meade

Laurel (295) 3 miles

6 miles

Greenbelt

3 miles

College Park

(295) 7 miles

Washington, DC

95

ROUTE

Starting in downtown Washington, head east on *Pennsylvania Ave*, then continue east on *New York Ave*. This part of the trip can be a dreary experience, with heavy traffic heading for the Beltway, but relief soon comes at Cheverley and the parkway begins to live up to its name. The attractions described in this route lie either side of the Baltimore-Washington Parkway.

The chances of getting lost increase greatly as the parkway becomes involved with Baltimore's engulfing skein of interstates – 95, 195, 295, 395 and 695 – with I-83 and I-97 adding to the confusion. Be resolute: stick with I-295 through thick and thin until it runs into *Russell St*. Continue north to *Pratt St*, where a right turn will lead you within eight blocks to Inner Harbor and the heart of downtown Baltimore.

COLLEGE PARK

College Park Airport and Museum, *6709 Cpl Frank Scott Dr.; tel: (301) 864-1530.* The world's oldest continuously operated airport has been in use since Oct 1909, when Wilbur Wright, who pioneered heavier-than-air flight with his brother Orville, began teaching Army officers to fly. This cradle of military aviation saw the first experiments with bomb-dropping devices, the first mile-high flight and the first aerial use of machine guns. Photographs of these and other 'firsts', as well as aviation equipment and memorabilia, are on show at the museum, and there is a special exhibition devoted to the development of the air-mail service. The museum is open Wed–Fri 1100–1500, Sat–Sun 1100–1700. Admission free.

Nearby is the **94th Aero Squadron Restaurant**, rigged out like a French farm used by US forces in World War I. Tables overlook the runway and some are equipped with headsets so you can eavesdrop on flyers.

GREENBELT

NASA/Goddard Visitor Center and Museum, *Greenbelt Rd; tel: (301) 286-8981.* The title of NASA's Visitor Center honours Dr Robert Hutchings Goddard, accredited with launching the world's first rocket at Auburn, Massachusetts, on 16 Mar 1926. There are film shows and displays of the equipment used in space exploration. Open daily 1000–1600, admission is free. Model rockets are launched on the first and third Sun of each month at 1300. Bus tours of the NASA complex are available on the second and fourth Sun of each month at 1100 and 1400.

LAUREL

Montpelier Cultural Arts Center, *12826 Laurel-Bowie Rd; tel: (301) 953-1993.* Some 50 resident artists – including painters, potters, photographers and sculptors – produce and display their work at the centre. Open daily 1000–1700. Admission free.

The adjacent **Montpelier Mansion**, dating from the 1770s, is open Sun 1200–1515 Mar–Dec. Grandly set in picturesque gardens, the mansion was built by Thomas and Ann Snowdon. Their combined wealth, when they married in 1774, was such an embarrassment that fellow Quakers banned them from religious services until they could assume a more modest lifestyle. The Snowdons went downmarket by selling 100 slaves. Their faith is reflected in a number of design features in and around the mansion. The main door has panels depicting biblical scenes, and in the grounds a boxwood hedge grows in the shape of a cross.

SEVERN

East of I-295, and just south-west of the town of Severn is **Fort George G. Meade**, *Griffin Ave; tel: (301) 677-6966.* Exhibits feature the history of the fort and the US Army from World War I to the present. Open Wed–Sat 1100–1600, Sun 1300–1600. Admission free.

96

WASHINGTON–HARRISBURG

This route leaves the Washington political powerhouse, heads north into Maryland, then crosses the Mason-Dixon line into Pennsylvania. The journey passes through the sprawling suburbs of the metropolis, but soon reaches the rolling, wooded countryside of the Potomac Valley before moving on beside the grand Catoctin Mountains. It takes in

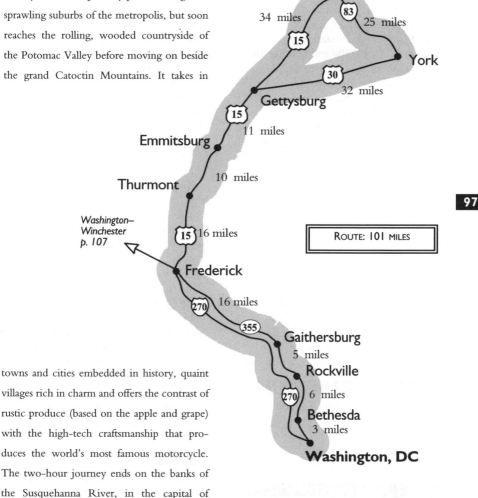

97

ROUTE: 101 MILES

Washington–
Winchester
p. 107

towns and cities embedded in history, quaint villages rich in charm and offers the contrast of rustic produce (based on the apple and grape) with the high-tech craftsmanship that produces the world's most famous motorcycle. The two-hour journey ends on the banks of the Susquehanna River, in the capital of Pennsylvania.

ROUTE

If you enjoy interstate driving, you can leave downtown Washington on *Connecticut Ave NW*, pick up the Capital Beltway at Exit 33 in North Chevy Chase, head west to Exit 34, then take I-270 north for 30 miles to Frederick, MD. Alternatively, take *M St NW* to Georgetown, then turn right on to *Wisconsin Ave*.

As Rte 355, *Wisconsin Ave* crosses the Capital Beltway then runs parallel with I-270, reaching Frederick by way of **Bethesda**, **Rockville** and **Gaithersburg**. The northern end of Bennett Regional Park, which Rte 355 skirts, lies on the line between Montgomery and Frederick counties. From **Frederick**, Hwy 15 leads north, passing Frederick Municipal Forest and Catoctin Mountain Park on the left and extensive farmlands on the right to reach **Thurmont** in 16 miles, then **Emmitsburg**, almost on the Mason–Dixon Line, after another 10 miles.

Gettysburg, and its oddly pacific battlefield, is 11 miles further along Hwy 15. To reach downtown, you need to follow Hwy 15 Business. From Gettysburg, Hwy 15 continues north beyond Camp Hill, where you may cross the Susquehanna River to Harrisburg, but a more interesting route is to take Hwy 30 east from Gettysburg to historic **York**, 32 miles away. From here, you can pick up I-83 north and reach Harrisburg after 25 miles.

MONTGOMERY COUNTY

Tourist Information: Convention & Visitor Bureau of Montgomery County, Inc, *12900 Middlebrook Rd, Suite 1400, Germantown, MD 20874-2616; tel: (301) 428-9702.*

BETHESDA

Tourist Information: as for Montgomery County, above.

ACCOMMODATION AND FOOD

The first community across the line between DC and Maryland, Bethesda offers a good range of accommodation, eating places and shopping. Hotel chains include *Hd, Hy, Ma* and *Rm*.

One of the best places for cheap to budget eating is the food court at **Bethesda Metro Center**; *tel: (301) 652-4988*. A dozen restaurants with a total seating capacity of 1000 serve breakfast, lunch and dinner Mon–Sat. The food court at **Montgomery Mall**, *7701 Democracy Blvd; tel: (301) 469-6000*, can seat more than 700 diners.

Cafe Bethesda, *5027 Wilson Lane; tel: (301) 657-3383*, has been listed in the *Washington Post* Top 50 Restaurants. Prices are moderate–budget. Lunch served Mon–Fri 1130–1400, dinner daily from 1700.

Meal prices are in the budget–moderate band at the **Cottonwood Cafe**, *4844 Cordell Ave; tel: (301) 656-4844*, with décor and cuisine in the style of the Old South-West. **La Panetteria**, *4921 Cordell Ave; tel: (301) 951-6433*, specialises in budget–moderately priced dishes from northern and southern Italy. **Positano**, *4840-48 Fairmont Ave; tel: (301) 654-1717*, is a family–run restaurant serving moderately priced authentic Italian cuisine. Adjoining it, under the same management, is the **Aldo Cafe**; *tel: (301) 986-0042*, a budget-priced trattoria. **St Elmo's Cafe**, *7820 Norfolk Ave; tel: (301) 675-1707*, is an elegant, art deco restaurant serving moderate–pricey French and New American cuisine.

SHOPPING

For shoppers, **Montgomery Mall** (see above) offers everything from banking services to women's fashions. Its 165 stores include **Hecht's, Nordstrom, Sears** and

Woodward and Lothrop. Open Mon–Sat 1000–2130, Sun 1100–1800.

ENTERTAINMENT

Concerts are staged all year round at **Strathmore Hall Arts Center**, *10701 Rockville Pike Rd, North Bethesda; tel: (301) 530-0540*. This turn-of-the-century mansion is also a venue for other performing, visual and literary arts.

SIGHTSEEING

Exhibitions of contemporary drawings, prints and water-colours are mounted in the gallery at **McCrillis Gardens**, *6910 Greentree Rd, Bethesda; tel: (301) 365-5728*. The gardens are noted for the thousands of azaleas, rhododendrons and exotic plants that bloom Apr–June.

A working laboratory, slide show and exhibits can be seen in the Visitor Information Center at the **National Institutes of Health**, a world-renowned Federal health research complex in *Cedar Lane; tel: (301) 496-1776*. Open Mon–Fri 0900–1600. Admission free. Visitors may also tour the adjacent **National Library of Medicine**; *tel: (301) 496-6308*, and visit the reading room which contains many rare and historic books. Open Mon–Thur 0830–2100, Fri–Sat 0830–1300. Free tours Mon–Fri 1300.

ROCKVILLE

Tourist Information: see also Montgomery County, left. The city has been the Montgomery County seat since 1776. A booklet featuring self-guided walking tours, with descriptions of its historic buildings, is available from the **Beall-Dawson House** (see Sightseeing, right).

ACCOMMODATION

Hotel chains in Rockville include *Cr, Ma* and *QS*.

EATING AND DRINKING

Rockville's restaurants are in the budget–moderate price range, with the emphasis on North American dishes. **Chi-Chi's**, *895 Rockville Pike; tel: (301) 251-0544*, serves Mexican cuisine and is noted for its margaritas. Hickory-smoked beef, pork and chicken are cooked in an authentic Texas-style closed-pit barbecue at **O'Brien's Pit Barbecue**, *387 East Gude Dr.; tel: (301) 762-9455*. Old-style diner meals are served at the **Silver Diner**, *1806 Rockville Pike; tel: (301) 770-2828*. **Paolo's Ristorante**, *1801, Rockville Pike; tel: (301) 984-2211*, offers pasta and pizzas.

ENTERTAINMENT

Studebaker's, *1750 Rockville Pike; tel: (301) 881-7340*, is a nightclub where you can dance to favourite tunes from the 1950s to the 1990s. A complimentary dinner buffet is served Wed–Fri 1630–2000.

Tennis, hiking, picnic and playground areas may be enjoyed at **Cabin John Regional Park**, *7400 Tuckerman Lane; tel: (301) 299-4160*. There is also a nature centre with classes and exhibits, and a year-round ice-skating rink. Open Tues–Sun 0700–sunset.

SIGHTSEEING

Beall-Dawson House, *103 W. Montgomery Ave; tel: (301) 762-1492*. Maintained by Montgomery County Historical Society, this Federal-style brick house dates from around 1815 and is furnished in early 19th-century style. Fearsome medical instruments are displayed in the **Doctor's Museum**, which stands in the grounds of the Beall-Dawson House. The museum was the office of Dr. Edward E. Stonestreet, who practised in Rockville 1852–1903 and acted as examining surgeon to Maryland draftees during the Civil War. Both properties open Tues–Sat 1200–1600; first Sun in month 1400–1700. The admission fee covers both sites.

F. Scott Fitzgerald Burial Place; the author and his wife, Zelda, are buried in *St. Mary's Church Cemetery, corner of Veirs Mill Rd* and *Church St.* Freely accessible. Archaeological artefacts from the Middle East, fine arts and antique and contemporary Judaica are on show at the **Weiner Judaic Museum**, *6125 Montrose Rd; tel: (301) 881-0100*. Open Sun–Thur 0900–2230, Fri 0900–1700. Closed Jewish holidays. Admission: donation.

GAITHERSBURG

Tourist Information: see Montgomery County, p. 98

ACCOMMODATION

Hotel chains in Gaithersburg include *EL, Hd, Hn, Ma, RR*.

100

EATING AND DRINKING

Fegan's Seafood Grille, at Rio Entertainment Center, *9811 Washingtonian Blvd; tel: (301) 948-0900*, has a budget–moderately priced menu featuring seafood, steaks, chicken and pasta. The moderately priced **Le Paradis Restaurant**, at the Festival Shopping Center, *347 Muddy Branch Rd; tel: (301) 208-9493*, serves French cuisine in casual surroundings.

For Italian fare, try the moderate–pricey **Ramino's**; *407 S. Frederick St; tel: (301) 926-7500*, or the budget-priced **Shakey's Pizza and Buffet Restaurant**, *74 Bureau Dr.; tel: (301) 977-1600*. **Olde Towne Tavern and Brewing Co**, *227 E. Diamond Ave; tel: (301) 948-4200*, is Montgomery County's first and only microbrewery pub and restaurant. Located in the county's oldest commercial property – a former general store, post office and meeting hall in the heart of the Olde

Towne district – the three-storey tavern specialises in on-site brewed ales, fresh Maryland seafood, grilled beef and pasta dishes. Budget–moderate.

FREDERICK COUNTY

Tourist Information: Tourism Council of Frederick County, Inc, *19 East Church St, Frederick, MD 21701; tel: (301) 663-8687* or *(800) 999-3613*. The council is based in a charming Federal rowhouse in downtown Frederick, with a parking garage handily placed next door. The offices also serve as a tourism information centre and the ground floor is well stocked with brochures and leaflets containing information about attractions, accommodation and dining facilities throughout the county. The centre is well signposted from all approaches.

FREDERICK

Tourist Information: see Frederick County, above.

ACCOMMODATION

The city is served by a dozen or so reputable hotels and motels and about half a dozen bed and breakfast establishments and country inns, mostly in the moderate–expensive category. Hotel chains in Frederick include *CI, DI, Hd*. The nearest campsites are in Catoctin Mountain National Park, Cunningham Falls State Park and at Thurmont (see p. 102).

EATING AND DRINKING

There's no shortage of eating places in Frederick. Cafés and restaurants cover the price spectrum, with a good choice in the budget–moderate band. Here are a few suggestions:

Barbara Fritchie Candystick Restaurant, *1513 W. Patrick St; tel: (301) 662-2500*. Run by the same family since

1920, this budget-priced restaurant serves a complete American menu for breakfast, lunch and dinner. Open daily 0700–2300.

For seafood buffs the moderately-priced **Bentz Street Raw Bar**, *6 S. Bentz St; tel: (301) 694-9134,* serves fresh Maryland crabs and oysters, as well as steaks, ribs and home-made soups. Open Mon–Sat 1100–0200, Sun 1200–0200.

Bob's Big Boy Family Restaurant, *1300 W. Patrick St; tel: (301) 695-9111,* offers budget-priced all-you-can-eat buffets and has special deals for youngsters and senior citizens. Take away meals available. Open Sun–Thur 0700–2200, Fri–Sat 0700–0300.

You can eat in or take away at **Crabapples Delicatessen**, *101 W. Patrick St; tel: (301) 694-0208.* Budget-priced, it is open Mon–Fri 0730–1630, Sat 0830–1530.

Jennifer's Restaurant, *207 W. Patrick St; tel: (301) 662-0373,* serves sandwiches, salads and full-scale meals in a comfortable pub atmosphere. Cheap–moderate.

ENTERTAINMENT

Frederick has three performing arts theatres. **Brodbeck Music Hall**, *Hood College, 401 Rosemont Ave; tel: (301) 663-3131,* is the home of the Maryland Lyric Opera. Seasonal performances. The **Jack B. Kussmaul Theater**, *7932 Opossumtown Pike; tel: (301) 846-2400,* presents regular performances, exhibitions and educational programmes.

The Weinberg Center for the Arts, *20 W. Patrick St; tel: (301) 694-8585,* is a restored 1926 cinema now featuring performing and visual arts programmes all year round.

SHOPPING

Shoppers should find most things in Frederick's three major shopping centres.

Everedy Square & Shab Row, *8 East St; tel: (301) 662-4140,* is a 19th-century factory reincarnated as a modern centre with 35 shops offering antiques, clothing, general goods, home furnishings, gifts and fine dining. **Francis Scott Key Mall**, *5500 Buckeystown Pike; tel: (301) 662-5152,* has more than 75 stores, including Leggett, Sears, Value City and Hecht's. **Frederick Towne Mall**, *Rte 40 West; tel: (301) 662-9300,* contains more than 60 shops, including Bon-Ton, J.C.Penney and Montgomery Wards.

SIGHTSEEING

Founded in 1745, the city of Frederick features a 33-block historic district with fine examples of architecture from the 18th and 19th centuries. It stands at the heart of an area which was fiercely contested during the Civil War and witnessed numerous skirmishes and extensive troop movements connected with the nearby battles of Antietam, Monocacy and Gettysburg.

Guided **walking tours** of Frederick's historic district start at 1330 from the Visitor Information Center on Sat, Sun and most Mon holidays, Apr–Dec. Tickets: $4.50.

Barbara Fritchie House, *154 W. Patrick St; tel: (301) 698-0630.* This is the reconstructed home of the 96-year-old woman who defied Gen. Stonewall Jackson and his Confederate troops by waving a Union flag as they marched by. She earned immortality in the eponymous poem by John Greenleaf Whittier. Open Mon, Thur–Sat 1000–1600, Sun 1300–1600. Admission charge.

Hessian Barracks, *101 Clarke Pl.; tel: (301) 662-4159.* Built in 1777, this stone building was used first as an arsenal and barracks, then as a prison for Hessian mercenaries who had been fighting for the

British. In the Civil War it served as a prison and hospital for captured Confederates. Open by appointment only: free.

Historical Society of Frederick County, *24 E. Church St; tel: (301) 663-1188*, is a restored Federal mansion housing a museum of period furniture, artefacts and historical documents. Art exhibitions are staged periodically. Open Tues–Sat 1000–1600, Sun 1300–1600. Admission charge.

Monocacy Battlefield, *Rte 355 South; tel: (301) 662-3515* or *663-8687*. Two miles south of Frederick, this is the site of a battle believed to have saved Washington, DC. In July 1864, Union Gen. Lew Wallace pitted 5800 men against 18,000 Confederates led by Gen. Jubal Early. Although Early triumphed, the action delayed his progress long enough for Union troops to strengthen the capital's defences. The **visitor centre** has an electronic map of the battle and displays of artefacts. Open daily 0800–1630 (late May–early Sept), Wed–Sun 0800–1630 (rest of year). Admission free.

Roger Brook Taney and Francis Scott Key Museum, *121 S. Benz St; tel: (301) 663-8687*. Built in 1779, this was the home of Chief Justice Taney who administered the oath to Abraham Lincoln. His brother-in-law, Francis Scott Key, author of *The Star-Spangled Banner*, was a frequent visitor. There are period furnishings, memorabilia and original slave quarters. Open Sat 1000–1600, Sun 1300–1600 (Apr–Oct). Admission charge.

Rose Hill Manor, *1611 N. Market St; tel: (301) 694-1648*. Dating from around 1792 and built in Georgian Colonial style as the residence for Maryland's first elected Governor, Rose Hill houses a 'touch and see' children's museum. Also featured are a carriage museum, farm museum and a log cabin. Open Mon–Sat 1000–1600, Sun 1300–1600 (Apr–Oct); Sat 1000–1600 (Mar, Nov–Dec). Admission charge.

Schifferstadt Architectural Museum, *1110 Rosemont Ave; tel: (301) 663-3885*. Frederick's oldest dwelling (built 1756) provides an insight into the lifestyle of 18th-century immigrant farmers from Germany. Open Tues–Sat 1000–1600, Sun 1200–1600 (Apr–mid Dec). Admission charge.

Utica Mills Covered Bridge, *Utica Rd*, off Hwy 15, 4 miles north of Fredericksburg. Built around 1850, the 101 ft long bridge originally spanned the nearby Monocacy River, but was washed away in a severe storm in 1889. Local people rebuilt it at its present location across Fishing Creek.

Tourist Information: see Frederick County, p. 100.

ACCOMMODATION AND FOOD

This pleasant community on the edge of Catoctin Mountain National Park has two motels and an inn, each in the moderate category. **Cozy Country Inn**, *103 Frederick Rd, Thurmont, MD 21788; tel: (301) 271-4301*, has 21 rooms and a restaurant and offers room service, cable television and complimentary continental breakfast Mon–Fri. The restaurant at the Cozy Country Inn serves lunch and dinner daily and breakfast Sat–Sun. **Rambler Motel**, *426 N. Church St, Thurmont, MD 21788; tel: (301) 271-2424*, has 30 rooms. **Super 8 Motel**, *300 Tippin Dr., Thurmont, MD 21788; tel: (301) 271-7888*, has 46 rooms. **Mountain Gate Family Restaurant**, *133 Frederick Rd; tel: (301) 271-4373*, serves all three meals daily and has a take-away service. There's a **Roy Roger's** restaurant at *203 Frederick Rd; tel: (301) 271-3252*.

Crow's Nest Campground, *PO Box 145, 335 W. Main St, Thurmont, MD 21788; tel: (301) 271-7632*, has sites for RVs and tents, a fishing lake, hiking, flush toilets and hot showers. **Ole Mink Farm Recreation Resort**, *12806 Mink Farm Rd, Thurmont, MD 21788; tel: (301) 271-7012*, offers one- and two-bedroomed luxury log cabins and campsites. Fishing, outdoor pool, playground and game room.

SIGHTSEEING

Thurmont's major attractions are the **Catoctin Mountain National Park** – home of the Presidential Camp David – and the adjoining **Cunningham Falls State Park**, both easily accessed and signposted from Hwy 15 and Rte 77. The **National Park Visitor Centre**, on Rte 77, 2.5 miles west of Hwy 15; *tel: (301) 663-9388*, provides information on both parks, which cover about 10,000 acres and offer hiking trails, scenic drives, camping and water sports. **Blue Blazes Whiskey Still**, a 15-min walk from the visitor centre, was used by moonshine men during Prohibition. It was closed after a shoot-out with Treasury agents in 1929. Rangers tell the tale and demonstrate moonshine-making (no samples!) at weekends. **Cunningham Falls**, 1.2 miles further along Rte 77 from the visitor centre, is a 78-ft cascade easily accessible in sylvan surroundings.

Catoctin Furnace, *Rte 806,* off Hwy 15 S.; *tel: (301) 271-7574*. Built in 1774, the old ironworks produced iron for armaments in the Revolutionary and Civil Wars. Admission charge.

Catoctin Mountain Zoological Park, *13019 Catoctin Furnace Rd; tel: (301) 271-7488* or *662-2579*. More than 300 specimens of native rare and endangered mammals, birds and reptiles are housed in the park. Open daily 0900–1700 (Apr and Oct), 0900–1800 (May–Sept), 1000–1600 (Nov–Mar). Admission charge.

EMMITSBURG

Tourist Information: Maryland Visitor Center, *Hwy 15,* 1 mile south of Pennsylvania state line; *tel: (301) 447-2553*. Surrounded by farmland and with a spacious car park, the centre is a semi-circular, two-storey building with toilets on the ground floor. The upper floor, reached by stairs and a ramp for disabled visitors, contains the information room with brochures on accommodation and attractions throughout the state. Friendly staff take a careful note of where visitors are from. A separate building contains vending machines dispensing snacks and soft drinks.

SIGHTSEEING

Emmitsburg has two important Roman Catholic shrines. The **Grotto of Lourdes**, a replica of the site in France, was constructed after the discovery of a cave by a priest in 1805. The grotto is on *Hwy 15,* easily recognisable from the 120 ft high campanile crowned by a gilded statue of the Virgin Mary. In the town itself, 2 miles north, is the **National Shrine of St. Elizabeth Ann Seton**, *333 S. Seton Ave; tel: (301) 447-6606*. This honours the first American-born saint, canonised in 1975. She first arrived at Emmitsburg in 1809 and died in 1821.

GETTYSBURG

Tourist Information: Gettysburg Travel Council, *35 Carlisle St, Gettysburg, PA 17325; tel: (717) 334-6274*. Located in the city's historic rail station, the information centre is well stocked with brochures, leaflets and maps, and staff are on hand to deal with specific

103

inquiries. Accommodation information is available, but there is no reservation service. The place for information connected with the Battle of Gettysburg is the Visitor Centre at the **Gettysburg National Military Park**, *Taneytown Rd* (1 mile south of downtown, near the intersection with Hwy 15 Business)*; tel: (717) 334-1124.*

ACCOMMODATION AND FOOD

About two dozen hotels and bed and breakfast establishments are to be found within easy reach of Gettysburg's compact downtown – about half of them within walking distance of *Lincoln Sq.,* the town centre. The most distant of five campsites is only 6 miles out of town.

Hotel chains in Gettysburg include *BW, CI, DI, EL, Hd, HJ, QI.* The most central establishment is the **Best Western Gettysburg Hotel**, *1 Lincoln Sq., Gettysburg, PA 17325; tel: (717) 337-2000.* Moderate–expensive, the hotel dates from 1797 and has hosted many distinguished guests, including President and Mrs Dwight D. Eisenhower, Henry Ford and Gen. Ulysses S. Grant.

Gettysburg KOA, *20 Knox Rd; tel: (717) 642-5713.* The campsite is 3 miles west of Gettysburg, off Hwy 30. Set in woodland, it has sites for tents and RVs. Services include laundry, games room, store and heated pool.

Artillery Ridge Camping Resort, *610 Taneytown Rd; tel: (717) 334-1288,* invites campers to bring their own horses – there are stalls and corrals on site. There are also pitches for tents and RVs.

Drummer Boy Camping Resort, *1300 Hanover Rd; tel: 800-336-3269,* has 300 sites and cabins on 100 acres of woodland. It is 1 mile east of town at the intersection of Hwy 15 and Rte 116.

Gettysburg Campground, 2030

Fairfield Rd; *tel: (717) 334-3304,* is 3 miles west on Rte 116. There are tent and RV sites and facilities include a store, snack bar, games room and playground.

Granite Hill Campground and Waterpark, *3340 Fairfield Rd; tel: 800-642-TENT or (717) 642-8749.* Six miles west on Rte 116, the resort is in 147 acres and has 300 sites for tents and RVs. Cabins to rent are available.

Round Top Camping Resort, *180 Knight Rd; tel: (717) 334-9565.* Full camping facilities are supplemented by a recreation room, snack-bar, store and pool. The resort is near the intersection of Hwy 15 and Rte 134, 4 miles south of Gettysburg.

ENTERTAINMENT AND SIGHTSEEING

There are plenty of cafés and restaurants in the streets leading off *Lincoln Sq.*

The city's major event is **The Real Fury of Gettysburg**, the annual re-enactment of the famous battle staged 1–2 July; *tel: (717) 337-0717.*

You can hire the services of a **licensed guide** at the National Military Park Visitor Centre (see 'Gettysburg', above). Driving your car, the guide will lead you on a tour of the battlefield. The cost is $20 for two hours (more for RVs). With a cassette from CCInc Autotape Tours, you can take self-drive tours around the battle sites. Cassettes can be purchased ($12.95) or rented ($12.00, with player) from the National Civil War Wax Museum (see p. 105).

Battlefield Bicycle Tours; *tel: 800-830-5775 or (717) 691-0236,* takes groups of up to ten cyclists on a 12-mile tour. Mountain bikes and helmets are provided. Costs are $20 single, $35 for a couple and $45 for a family. Tours start at the Baladerry Inn at the junction of *Blacksmith Shop Rd* and *Hospital Rd* off Rte 134 south.

Gettysburg Tour Center, *778 Baltimore St; tel: 800-447-8788 or (771) 334-6296,* offers open-top bus and trolley tours of the battlefield and other attractions.

Ghosts of Gettysburg; *tel: (717) 337-0445.* Guides lead groups on candlelit tours of Gettysburg's streets, pointing out reputedly haunted sites. Hundreds of ghosts of those who fell in the great battle are said to have been seen in the town. Cost: $6.

Eisenhower National Historic Site; *tel: (717) 334-1124.* The farmhouse to which President and Mrs Eisenhower retired in 1961 may be visited by shuttle bus from the National Military Park Visitor Center. Admission (includes shuttle): $3.60.

Gettysburg Battle Theatre, *571 Steinwehr Ave; tel: (717) 334-6100.* An animated colour film of those fateful first three days of July 1863. Admission charge.

Gettysburg National Military Park, *Taneytown Rd; tel: (717) 334-1124.* The **Visitor Center** incorporates a museum of the Civil War and an Electric Map presentation showing troop movements during the **Battle of Gettysburg**, in which 569 tons of ammunition were discharged and 51,000 men killed or injured in three days. Adjacent to the Visitor Center is the **Cyclorama Center**, which includes a spectacular sound and light programme in a circular auditorium. Open daily 0800–1800 (mid June–mid Aug), 0800–1700 (rest of year). Admission to visitor centre free; Electric Map $2, Cyclorama $2.

Gettysburg Steam Railroad, *106 N. Washington St; tel: (717) 334-6932.* Old-fashioned whistles and bells on 16- and 50-mile rail trips. Fares: from $7.50. Dinner trips also take place.

Jenny Wade House, *Baltimore St* (near Holiday Inn); *tel: (717) 334-4100.*

The only civilian casualty in the battle was killed by a stray bullet while baking bread. Open daily 0900–2100 (May–Sept), 0900–1700 (Oct–Apr). Admission charge.

Lincoln Room Museum, *12 Lincoln Sq; tel: (717) 334-8188.* The room in which President Lincoln wrote the final draft of his famous Gettysburg Address. Open Sun–Thur 0900–1900, Fri–Sat 0900–2000.

Lincoln Train Museum, *Steinwehr Ave* (opposite National Military Park Visitor Center); *tel: (717) 334-6296.* Simulated ride aboard the train that brought the president to Gettysburg; dioramas illustrate the role of railways during the Civil War. Open daily 0900–2100 (May–Sept), 0900–1700 (Oct–Apr). Admission charge.

National Civil War Wax Museum, *297 Steinwehr Ave; tel: (717) 334-6245.* More than 200 life-size figures in 30 scenes tell the story of the war, including the Gettysburg battle and Lincoln's speech.

National Tower, *999 Baltimore Pike; tel: (717) 334-6754.* High-speed elevators whisk visitors to a height of 307 ft to get the best view of the battlefield. Maps, telescopes and displays. Admission charge.

Soldiers National Museum, *777 Baltimore St; tel: (717) 334-4890.* Dioramas trace the progress of the Civil War from the first shot fired at Fort Sumter to the surrender at Appomattox. Open daily 0900–2100 (May–Sept), 0900–1700 (Oct–Apr). Admission charge.

YORK

Tourist Information: York County Convention & Visitors Bureau, *1 Market Way East, York, PA 17401; tel: 800-673-2429 or (717) 848-4000.*

The first capital of the USA – the Continental Congress was based here in

1777 – York has plenty to offer the visitor in the way of attractions, accommodation, restaurants and shopping.

ACCOMMODATION

Hotel chains in the city include *BW, CI, DI, Hd, Ra, RR, TL.*

The White Rose Bed and Breakfast Association, located at the Convention & Visitors Bureau (see above), can help with reservations for the 30 or so inns in the county.

One of the most recently converted inns, the **Kolter House,** *403 N. Main St, Shrewsbury, PA 17361; tel: (717) 235-5528,* is a former farmhouse built in 1876 and now offering rooms in the budget–moderate band.

The Altland House, *Center Sq, Rte 30, Abbottstown, PA 17301; tel: (717) 259-95395,* offers lodging and dining and was established as a tavern in 1790.

EATING AND DRINKING

More than 60 cafés and restaurants in the city alone are listed in York County's *Visitor Guide,* and there are many others in the immediate surroundings. Some are in delightfully quaint locations, like the **Glen Rock Mill Inn,** *50 Water St, Glen Rock; tel: (717) 235-5918,* which presents moderate–expensive dining – both casual and formal – in a stone building which once served as a woollen mill.

SIGHTSEEING

Agricultural Museum of York County, *480 E. Market St; tel: (717) 852-7007,* has displays of farm machinery and artefacts. Open Tues, Thur 1000–1600. Admission $2.

Golden Plough Tavern, Gen. Horatio Gates House, Bobb Log House, *157 W. Market St; tel: (717) 755-9290.* Three historic buildings in one compact location. The **tavern** is the city's oldest surviving structure, built in 1741. The **Gates House** was occupied by the hero of the battle of Saratoga while attending the Continental Congress, and it was here, also, that the French Gen. Lafayette thwarted a plot to replace Washington with Gen. Gates as commander of the Continental Army. The **log house,** built around 1812, is a typical Pennsylvania frontier dwelling. Open Mon–Sat 1000–1600, Sun 1300–1600. Admission: $4 (includes admission to York County Colonial Courthouse – see below).

Harley-Davidson Motorcycle Museum, *1425 Eden Rd; tel: (717) 848-1177,* provides tours of the antique motorcycle museum and of the only plant in the world where the famous machines are assembled. Visitors can watch the whole process, from bare frame to test ride and packing. Tours: Mon–Fri 1230, Sat 1000, 1100, 1300 and 1400. Admission free.

Historical Society of York County Museum, *250 E. Market St; tel: (717) 848-1587.* Permanent exhibits trace the area's history from the days of the Indians and early settlers, including a life-size village square. Open Mon–Sat 0900–1700, Sun 1300–1600. Admission: $2.50.

Industrial Museum, *217 W. Princess St; tel: (717) 852-7007.* Exhibits featuring the county's major industries. Open Tues, Thur, Sat 1000–1600. Admission: $2.

York County Colonial Courthouse, *205 W. Market St; tel: (717) 845-2951.* The Articles of Confederation were adopted here in 1777 by the Continental Congress. Open Mon–Sat 1000–1600 (last tour 1500). For admission see under Golden Plough Tavern, left.

HARRISBURG

See Harrisburg chapter, pp. 306–310.

WASHINGTON–WINCHESTER

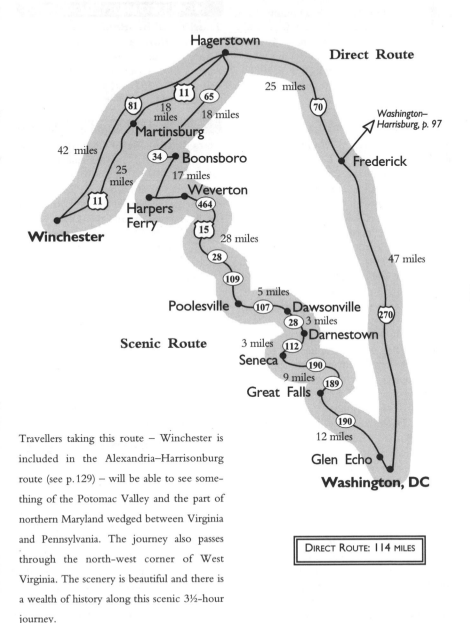

Hagerstown

Direct Route

25 miles

(11) (65)

(81) 18 miles 18 miles

Martinsburg

42 miles

(70)

Washington–Harrisburg, p. 97

(34) Boonsboro

Frederick

25 miles

17 miles

Weverton

(11) (464)

Harpers Ferry

Winchester

(15)

28 miles

(28)

47 miles

(109)

5 miles

Poolesville (107) Dawsonville

(28) 3 miles

(270)

Scenic Route Darnestown

3 miles (112)

Seneca (190)

9 miles (189)

Great Falls

(190)

12 miles

Glen Echo

Washington, DC

Travellers taking this route – Winchester is included in the Alexandria–Harrisonburg route (see p. 129) – will be able to see something of the Potomac Valley and the part of northern Maryland wedged between Virginia and Pennsylvania. The journey also passes through the north-west corner of West Virginia. The scenery is beautiful and there is a wealth of history along this scenic 3½-hour journey.

DIRECT ROUTE: 114 MILES

ROUTES

DIRECT ROUTE

➡️ Leave downtown Washington by *Connecticut Ave NW* and join the Capital Beltway at North Chevy Chase (Exit 33). Head west to Exit 34 and take I-270 north to **Frederick** (see p. 100). Join I-70 west to Hagerstown, then I-81 south to reach Winchester in 2½ hours

SCENIC ROUTE

➡️ From downtown Washington follow *M St NW* to Georgetown and continue beyond the Frances Scott Key Bridge and head along *McArthur Blvd,* which passes though the village of **Glen Echo** and on to **Great Falls State Park**. From the park head north on Rte 189 and after 2 miles turn on to Rte 190 west (*River Rd*). This reaches Seneca in 7 miles. From Seneca take Rte 112 for 3 miles to Darnestown, then follow Rte 28 west. After 3 miles, at **Dawsonville**, divert on to Rte 107 to see the 1793 **John Poole House** at **Poolesville** and the only ferry still operating across the Potomac River: **White's Ferry** (6 miles east of Poolesville) transports vehicles and passengers back and forth daily 0600–2300 (to 2000 in winter).

From Poolesville Rte 109 takes you back to Rte 28 which continues west for 12 miles where it meets Hwy 15. Turn north on to Hwy 15, then follow Rte 464 for 15 miles, then head west into **Weverton** on Rte 180. From Weverton you can cross the Potomac to **Harpers Ferry** in West Virginia, then return to continue north on Rte 67. After 15 miles, at Boonsboro, Rte 34 west heads into Sharpsburg and the **Antietam Battlefield**. From Sharpsburg you can continue north on Rte 65 for 12 miles to Hagerstown. From there Hwy 11 runs through **Martinsburg**, West Virginia, to reach Winchester in 52 miles.

MONTGOMERY COUNTY

Tourist Information: Convention & Visitor Bureau of Montgomery County, Inc, *12900 Middlebrook Rd, Suite 1400, Germantown, MD 20874-2616; tel: (301) 428-9702*, provides information for the first half of this route.

GLEN ECHO

Clara Barton National Historic Site, *5801 Oxford Rd at McArthur Blvd; tel: (301) 492-6245*. The 35-room home of the founder of the American Red Cross – known as the 'Angel of the Battlefields' for her work during the Civil War – overlooks the Chesapeake and Ohio Canal and the Potomac River. Open daily 1030–1630. Admission free.

Glen Echo Park, *McArthur Blvd and Goldsboro Rd; tel: (301) 492-6282,* was originally the centre of the Chautauqua Movement, a late-19th-century group of artists and liberal educationists. For the first half of this century it served as an amusement park and is now a centre for arts and entertainment. The old hand-carved carousel, one of the finest in the USA, is still in use. Open daily, with frequent special events and festivals.

GREAT FALLS PARK

The park is part of the Chesapeake and Ohio Canal National Historical Park and straddles both the Maryland and Virginia sides of the **Great Falls of the Potomac**. The best view of the falls is from the Virginia side, unfortunately inaccessible from this part of the park, but you can get a superb view by crossing the Olmsted Bridges to an island in the river.

The falls can be seen from a viewing platform at the **Great Falls Tavern**

108

Visitor Center; *tel: (301) 299-3613.* Built in 1830, the tavern – no longer used for refreshment – now features displays on the history of the canal. There are mule-drawn barge trips Apr–Oct. Open daily 0900–1700. Admission: $4 per vehicle; $2 per person without vehicle.

HARPERS FERRY

The **National Historic Park**; *tel: (304) 535-6223,* encompasses ruined industrial sites, Civil War forts and camps and restored buildings of the once thriving town that stood at the confluence of the Shenandoah and Potomac rivers. Easy access by canal, road and rail, as well as water power, helped establish Harpers Ferry as an industrial community. By the mid-19th century its population was 3000 and armaments the main industry. The abolitionist John Brown – whose mouldering body featured in the original words of *The Battle Hymn of the Republic* – was hanged after launching an attack on the arsenal in 1859. The town changed hands eight times during the Civil War.

The park's **Visitor Center** issues an informative leaflet on Harpers Ferry and rangers can help with information on hiking trails and self-guided walking tours – the Appalachian Trail passes through the park. Costumed re-enactments are frequently staged. Open daily 0800–1800 (to 1700 in winter). Admission: $5 per vehicle or $3 per person (includes shuttle bus between visitor centre and town site).

HAGERSTOWN

Tourist Information: Washington County Convention & Visitors Bureau, *1826-C Dual Highway, Hagerstown, MD 21740; tel: (800) 228-7829* or *(301) 791-3130.*

Hager House and Museum, *City Park, 9 Key St; tel: (301) 739-8393.* Residence of Capt. Jonathan Hager, the city founder, built in 1739. Open Tues, Sat 1000–1600, Sun 1400–1700 (Apr–Oct). Admission by donation.

Hagerstown Roundhouse Museum, *300 S. Burhans Blvd; tel: (301) 739-1998,* has rail memorabilia, a library and model layouts. Open Fri–Sun 1300–1700. Admission: $2. **Washington Museum of Fine Arts**, *City Park, 91 Key St; tel: (301) 739-5727.* The museum's permanent collection includes works by 19th-century American artists. Open Tues–Sat 1000–1700, Sun 1300–1800. Admission free.

MARTINSBURG

Tourist Information: West Virginia Division of Tourism, *2101 Washington St E., Charleston, West Virginia 25305; tel: (800) 225-5982* or *(304) 348-2286.*

Belle Boyd House and Museum, *126 E. Race St; tel: (304) 267-4713.* Home of Belle Boyd, the Confederate spy in the Civil War, built by her father in 1853. The building houses a County History and a Civil War musuem. Open Fri 1000–1800, Sat 1000–1600, Sun 1300–1600 (mid May–early Sept). Free admission.

Gen. Adam Stephen House, *309 E. John St; tel: (304) 267-4434.* Built 1774–1789 as the home of Martinsburg's founder, who served in the French and Indian Wars and in the American Revolution. The house has period furnishings 1750–1830. Open Sat–Sun 1400–1700 (May–Oct). Admission free.

Morgan Cabin, *Rte 26,* off Hwy 11, eight miles south of Martinsburg; *tel: (304) 229-8946.* The home of West Virginia's first permanent settler, the log cabin was built in 1731 by Col. Morgan Morgan. Open Sat–Sun 1400–1700 May–Aug. Admission free.

109

WASHINGTON–
CHARLOTTESVILLE

This route crosses the Potomac River, swings west and passes through the delightful countryside of northern Virginia, where the sound of the hunting horn may be heard across the hills and woodlands. From Leesburg the route heads south through the wooded contours of the Piedmont.

> DIRECT ROUTE: 120 MILES

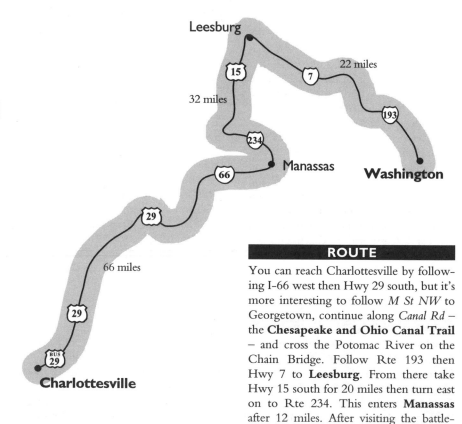

ROUTE

You can reach Charlottesville by following I-66 west then Hwy 29 south, but it's more interesting to follow *M St NW* to Georgetown, continue along *Canal Rd* – the **Chesapeake and Ohio Canal Trail** – and cross the Potomac River on the Chain Bridge. Follow Rte 193 then Hwy 7 to **Leesburg**. From there take Hwy 15 south for 20 miles then turn east on to Rte 234. This enters **Manassas** after 12 miles. After visiting the battlefields, return on Hwy 234 for five miles, pick up I-66 west, then follow Hwy 29 south. Be sure to follow Business 29 to reach downtown Charlottesville.

LEESBURG

Tourist Information: Loudoun Tourism Council, *108-D, South St SE, Leesburg, VA 22075; tel: (703) 777-0518.* Open daily 0900–1700.

ACCOMMODATION

Leesburg accommodation is in *BW, Rm* and *DI* – all in *Market Street* – or in smaller establishments like the **Norris House Inn**, *tel: (703) 777-1806,* a bed and breakfast home in the historic district, where the **Stone House Tea Room** is a popular meeting place.

EATING AND DRINKING

There are more than five dozen restaurants and eateries, from chains like McDonald's and Burger King to a restored 19th-century grain mill, the **Tuscarora Mill** at Market Station, which has an extensive wine list.

SIGHTSEEING

Chartered in 1758 as the county seat of Loudoun, set in the rich pastoral beauty of Virginia's Hunt Country, Leesburg has a **historic district**, an imposing **Courthouse Square** and a wide choice of restaurants, antique shops and stores selling crafts and collectables.

Situated between the Potomac River and the Blue Ridge Mountains, it makes an ideal base for the leisurely exploration of stately mansions, vineyards, Civil War history and the attractive little towns of the region.

Steeplechase meetings are held in several locations in the horseracing season, polo is played at Middleburg and a number of festivals take place.

In 1995 the region around Leesburg was designated the John Singleton Mosby Heritage Area, after the Civil War hero. Route 50 is now the **John S Mosby Highway.**

During the Civil War Leesburg was bounced back and forth under the control of one army or the other, emerging with little damage, although the **Battle of Ball's Bluff** early in the war resulted in more than 1000 casualties, most of them Northern troops.

Loudoun Museum, *16 Loudoun St SW, Leesburg; tel: (703) 777-7427,* tells the story of the Battle of Ball's Bluff and smaller Civil War conflicts in the county, illustrating the 'brother fights brother' aspect of the war. More distant history is outlined in a display of Indian arrowheads and axe heads. Furniture and artefacts from colonial times to the present are exhibited. See the video programme first. There are walking tours and a gift shop. Open Mon–Sat 1000–1700, Sun 1300–1700. Donations welcome.

George C Marshall International Center, *Dodona Manor, Edwards Ferry Rd, Leesburg; tel: (703) 777-1880.* George Marshall, Chief of Staff of the US Army, who gave his name to Marshall Aid in World War II and later to the Marshall Plan, lived at Dodona Manor from 1941 until his death in 1959. In 1995 the house was bought from Marshall's daughter by a preservation fund organisation set up for the purpose. The house would otherwise have been demolished and replaced with a shopping mall. After a period of limited opening, Dodona Manor, restored to its 1950 state, re-opened in spring, 1996, and was scheduled to have fully-established public hours by 1997. The house reflects the simple lifestyle of Marshall, a keen gardener, and his wife. Phone for opening times. Admission charge.

III

Oatlands, *Rte 15, Leesburg; tel: (703) 777-3174.* Tours of this 1803 mansion and its English gardens, six miles south of the city, are available. It was formerly the centre of a 3400-acre plantation. Open Mon–Sat 1000–1630, Sun 1300–1630 (Apr–Christmas). Admission $6.

Morven Park, *Rte 3,* west of Leesburg *(Old Waterford Rd); tel: (703) 777-2414.* Former governors of Maryland and Virginia have lived in this Greek Revival mansion. Both the house and its formal boxwood gardens are open for tours. As well as a foxhunting museum, there's a collection of more than 100 phaetons, sulkies, landaus and other carriages. Open Tues–Sat 1200–1700 Apr–Oct. Admission charge.

MANASSAS

Manassas National Battlefield Park, *12521 Lee Hwy, Manassas; tel: (703) 361-1339.* More than 4000 troops were killed here in two Civil War battles. 900 lost their lives in July 1861 and 3300 more during a three-day battle in August the following year. The 4500-acre park commemorates these two major battles.

The **Visitor Center** on Rte 234, just north of I-66 at Exit 47B, shows a 13-min slide programme on the hour and half-hour. A battlefield map programme is shown continuously. Artefacts from the battles are displayed.

The first major battle of the Civil War took place in July 1861 at **Bull Run**, the Manassas site south of Washington. Some of the men and women in the city's leading social set thought it would be fun to see a real-life battle, and arrived at Manassas to stand on the sidelines. But it was all far bloodier than they expected, with deafening gunfire, mud flying from horses' hooves and the troops dropping

like flies. The spectators soon headed for home in shock.

From the Visitor Center you can take a one-mile self-guided walking tour of **First Manassas** and a 12-mile self-guided driving tour of **Second Manassas**. Conducted tours are available in high season. Grounds open dawn–dusk except Christmas Day. Visitor Center open daily 0830–1700 (except Christmas Day). Admission $2 or $4 maximum per family.

Manassas Museum, *9101 Prince William St; tel: (703) 368-1873.* This well-presented museum reflects the development and history of a small Northern Virginia town which grew in importance with the arrival of the railway. The collection includes prehistoric tools, Civil War weapons and uniforms, railway memorabilia, quilts, Victoriana and a wealth of old photographs. Pamphlets detailing self-guided walking and driving tours of Old Town Manassas are also available. Open Tues–Sun 1000–1700.

Rorh's Store & Museum, *corner of Center and West Manassas; tel: (703) 368-3000.* Nostalgia rules at this third-generation family business founded in 1934. It stocks flypapers, washboards, lamp wicks and chimneys, has an old-time candy counter and also stocks modern requirements. There are two floors of museum exhibits – motor vehicles dating from 1905, household utensils, toys, music boxes, victrolas and a variety of gadgets. A doll collection has exhibits from 150 years ago, including rag, celluloid, wooden, china and bisque dolls in their original clothing. Store open Mon–Sat 0900–1800, museum open Sat and Sun 1100–1600, variable hours on weekdays. Admission $2, children $1.

WASHINGTON–ALEXANDRIA

The shoreline facing Washington, on the opposite bank of the Potomac River, is in Virginia. Alexandria is no longer part of the District of Columbia, and although it is only five miles from the capital by the shortest route, it is quite different in character.

DIRECT ROUTE: 5 MILES

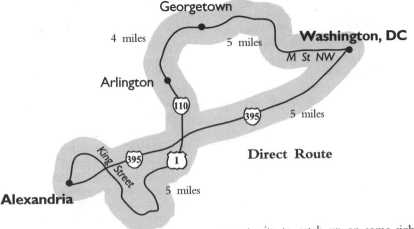

ROUTES

DIRECT ROUTE

The quickest and shortest route between Washington and Alexandria is by way of *14th St SW* to join I-395 across the river. Exit 5 leads to King St, which in turn leads straight into Old Town Alexandria.

SCENIC ROUTE

The route we recommend covers about 14 miles, but provides an opportunity to catch up on some sight-seeing on the way. From downtown Washington take *M St NW* all the way to Georgetown. At *35th St* turn left and cross the **Francis Scott Key Bridge**. Follow Rte 110 South to pass the entrances to the Marine Corps Memorial, Arlington Cemetery and the Pentagon. From there follow Rte 1 to *King St,* where a left turn will take you into Old Town Alexandria.

ARLINGTON

Tourist Information: Arlington Visitor Center, *735 South 18th St, Arlington;* tel: *(703) 358-5720 or (800) 677-6267.* Open Mon–Sun 0900–1700.

GETTING AROUND

The Metro Blue Line (see p.69) has stations at *Arlington Cemetery*, the *Pentagon*, *Pentagon City* and *Crystal City*. Arlington is also served by the Yellow Line.

ACCOMMODATION

Arlington County has nearly three dozen hotels and inns. Chains include *BW, CI, CM, DI, EL, ES, Hd, HJ, Hy, Ma, QI, Rm, Sh, SR, TL*.

EATING AND DRINKING

Arlington has more than 400 restaurants and eateries from fast food to fine dining. Most are in the budget to moderate range and they cover a variety of cuisines.

SHOPPING

Some of the best shopping within a brief metro ride of downtown Washington, DC, is at Arlington.

Fashion Center at Pentagon City, *11 Hayes St, Arlington; tel: (703) 415-2400* (metro: *Pentagon City*). The four-storey complex, with its sunlit food court and six movie theatres, is connected to Pentagon City Station. Its 130 stores include Macy's and Nordstrom. Open Mon–Sat 1000–2130, Sun 1100–1800.

Crystal City Shops, *1608 Crystal Sq. Arcade, Arlington; tel: (703) 892-4680* (metro: *Crystal City*). Connected to the metro station, this centre, with a climate-controlled walkway, has a plaza and a section below street level. It has more than 125 speciality stores and restaurants and a food court. Open Mon–Sat 1000–1800, some stores open Sun. Underground shops open Mon–Fri 1000–1900.

The Village at Shirlington, *2700 South Quincey St, Arlington; tel: (703) 379-0007*, has shopping along the main street. There are 7 movie theatres and a number of restaurants in the area.

Ballston Common, *North Glebe Rd and Wilson Blvd, Arlington; tel: (703) 243-8088* (metro: *Ballston*). Four floors of speciality stores – about 100 in all, including Hecht's and J.C. Penney, and a ground floor food court. Open Mon–Sat 1000–2130, Sun 1200–1800.

SIGHTSEEING

Arlington County is known worldwide as the home of the National Cemetery and the Pentagon, said to be the world's largest office building.

Arlington National Cemetery; *tel: (703) 692-0931* or *0937*. More than 200,000 war dead, government officials and their dependents are buried in this 612-acre hilly graveyard dotted with shady trees. Rows of neat white crosses stretch into the distance. Crowds arrive daily to see the graves of **President John F. Kennedy** (where an eternal flame burns), and those of his wife, Jacqueline, and his brother, Robert. Every half-hour there's a Changing of the Guard ceremony at the Tomb of the Unknown Soldier. There is also a memorial to those who died in the Challenger Space Shuttle, and a wall bears the names of thousands of people who died defending the US.

Tourmobile buses call at the cemetery. Open daily Apr–Sept 0800–1900, Oct–Mar 0900–1700. Admission free. Charge for parking and for tours.

Robert E. Lee Home, *Arlington House, Arlington National Cemetery; tel: (703) 557-0613* (metro: *Arlington Cemetery*). This was the home of Confederate General Robert E. Lee and his wife. Part of the land which went with the estate was taken over as a matter of urgency to be used for the burial of Civil War casualties. Soon after the war started, the house was requisitioned for use as federal headquarters for the defence of Washington. It is

---

News as History

One of the most exciting museum projects in the US was (at the time of going to press) scheduled to open in Arlington in the early summer of 1997. Called **The Newseum**, the $32 million educational facility is the only major museum in the world dedicated exclusively to news. It tells the story of the past, present and future of news-gathering and presentation through state-of-the-art multimedia techniques and interactive archives.

A **News Wall** as long as a city block presents news and front pages from every state – and all parts of the world – as it happens, through satellite and fibre optics.

The Newseum is operated by the Freedom Forum, a media-operated private foundation and a non-partisan international organisation dedicated to a free press and free speech.

Visitors can produce their own news items or weather forecasts, cruise the information highway, discuss news issues in broadcast programmes at the News Forum/TV Studio and see films on the large high-definition video screen in the 220-seat domed theatre.

The Newseum complex, occupying the first four levels of the **Freedom Forum World Center** at *Wilson Blvd*, overlooking the Potomac River, includes the Freedom Park. As well as providing a peaceful place for relaxation, the high-level park has a Berlin Wall exhibit, with sections of the wall and a guard tower that stood near Checkpoint Charlie. *Tel: (703) 284-3530.* Admission free.

---

now a memorial to Lee. Open daily Apr–Sept 0930–1800, Oct–Mar 0900–1700. Admission free.

National Inventors Hall of Fame, *2021 Jefferson Davis Hwy, Arlington; tel: (703) 557-3341* (metro: *Crystal City*). Displays featuring many of America's inventors shown in part of the US Patent & Trademark Office's headquarters. Open Mon–Fri 0830–1700. Admission free.

Marine Corps Memorial, *Iwo Jima, Marshall Dr., Arlington*, between Rte 50 and Arlington National Cemetery (metro: *Rosslyn*). Dedicated to all US Marines who died in the service of their country since 1775, this is said to be the largest cast bronze statue in the world. Every year in late Oct, the Marine Corps Marathon, attracting some 17,000 world class runners, starts from the Memorial. Registration fee; *tel: (703) 784-2225.*

The Pentagon, *Arlington; tel: (703) 695-1776* (metro: *Pentagon*). The 6.5 million sq. ft five-sided building covering 583 acres, claimed to be the world's largest office building, is the home of the **US Dept of Defence**. IDs with photographs are required for visitors taking one of the tours which take place every half-hour. Open Mon–Fri 0930–1530 except federal holidays. Admission free.

Old Guard Museum Building, *249 Sheridan Ave, Fort Myer, Arlington; tel: (703) 696-6670.* The only Army museum in the Washington, DC area, this relates the story of the oldest US Army Infantry Regiment from 1784 to the present. Open Mon–Sat 0900–1600, Sun 1300–1600. Admission free.

Netherlands Carillon, *Marshall Dr.*, between Rte 50 and Arlington National Cemetery; *tel: (703) 285-2598 or 2225* (metro: *Rosslyn*). In gratitude for the help and support of the US during World War II, the Dutch people presented this 49-bell tower to the American nation. Carillon concerts take place in summer. Open dawn–dusk.

ALEXANDRIA

Alexandria is only a few miles from Washington, but where the capital's grandeur is suitably staid and solemn, Alexandria lets its hair down and the ambience is more relaxed. There is plenty of history to explore – nearly 250 years of it – and it comes nicely diluted with places for pure enjoyment. Cheerful little shops, undaunting art studios, an interesting waterfront and a plethora of bright and busy restaurants make Alexandria a memorable city.

TOURIST INFORMATION

Alexandria Convention and Visitors Bureau, Ramsay House Visitor Center, *221 King St, Alexandria, VA 22314; tel: (703) 838-4200.* Open daily 0900–1700. Maps, brochures, leaflets, walking guides, restaurant and accommodation lists and calendar of events available. Accommodation, dining and entertainment reservations can be made through the bureau. Itineraries for shopping tours and historic interest tours are suggested and parking passes are available. A video show highlights the city's places of special interest and special events.

ARRIVING AND DEPARTING

Easily accessible by car from any direction, Alexandria, 5 miles south of Washington, is bounded by I-395 on the north and west sides and I-95 on the south side. It is bisected by US Hwy 1 and State Rte 7.

GETTING AROUND

Alexandria has four subway stations on the

Metro (see p. 69) – *King St, Braddock Rd, Eisenhower Ave* and *Van Dorn St.* There is also an Amtrak station.

Two bus systems serve the city – **Metrobus**; *tel: (202) 637-7000* and the Alexandria Transit Company's **DASH** buses; *tel (703) 370-DASH.* DASH buses provide a comprehensive, low-cost service in and around the city, with routes to all the city's Metro stations and to the Pentagon Metro station. Free transfers, valid for 4 hrs, are available. Just ask the driver for one when you board.

STAYING IN ALEXANDRIA

Accommodation

Hotel chains in Alexandria include: *CM, BW, CI, DI, EL, ES, Hd, HJ, Rd, Rm, Sh.*

Reservation services: **Alexandria Hotel Association**; *tel: (800) 296-1000.* **Princely Bed & Breakfast**, *819 Prince St; tel: (703) 683-2159.* There are more than 30 guest houses in and around Old Town; moderate. **Bed 'n' Breakfast Ltd**; *tel: (202) 328-3510* offers accommodation in private homes and inns convenient to Old Town; continental breakfast included. Minimum two-day stay preferred. Private homes in the moderate range may be rented. Inns are also moderately priced but slightly dearer than private homes. **Alexandria Lodgings**, *10 Sunset Dr,, Alexandria, VA 22314; tel: (703) 836-5575,* has furnished apartments, plus some rooms in the budget bracket.

YMCA, *420 E Monroe Ave; tel: (703) 549-0850.* Rooms, each with private shower, for men, women and families. Pool, free parking. Budget.

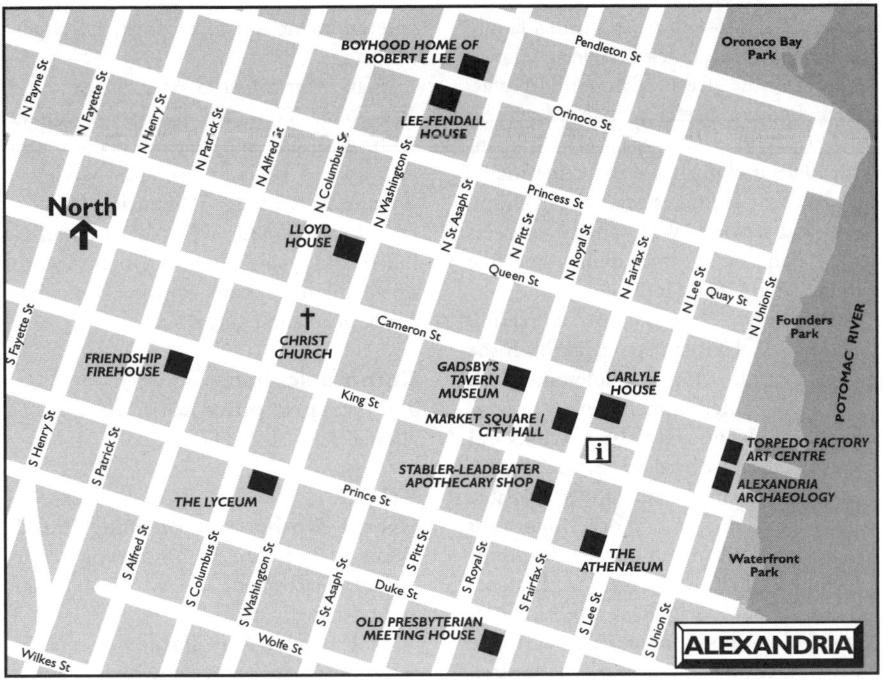
BOYHOOD HOME OF
ROBERT E LEE
LEE-FENDALL
HOUSE
LLOYD
HOUSE
CHRIST
CHURCH
FRIENDSHIP
FIREHOUSE
GADSBY'S
TAVERN
MUSEUM
CARLYLE
HOUSE
MARKET SQUARE /
CITY HALL
STABLER-LEADBEATER
APOTHECARY SHOP
THE LYCEUM
TORPEDO FACTORY
ART CENTRE
ALEXANDRIA
ARCHAEOLOGY
THE
ATHENAEUM
OLD PRESBYTERIAN
MEETING HOUSE
Oronoco Bay
Park
Founders
Park
Waterfront
Park
POTOMAC RIVER
North
Pendleton St
Orinoco St
Princess St
Queen St
Quay St
Cameron St
King St
Prince St
Duke St
Wolfe St
Wilkes St
N Payne St
N Fayette St
N Henry St
N Patrick St
N Alfred St
N Columbus St
N Washington St
N St Asaph St
N Pitt St
N Royal St
N Fairfax St
N Lee St
N Union St
S Fayette St
S Henry St
S Patrick St
S Alfred St
S Columbus St
S Washington St
S St Asaph St
S Pitt St
S Royal St
S Fairfax St
S Lee St
S Union St
ALEXANDRIA

Morrison House, *116 S Alfred St; tel: (703) 838-8000,* is a small luxurious hotel with four-posters beds and elegant dining. Pricey. **Radisson Plaza Hotel at Mark Center**, *5000 Seminary Rd; tel: (703) 845-1010*, has pools, tennis, fitness centre, two restaurants, airport and metro shuttles. Pricey.

Ramada Plaza Hotel Old Town, *901 N Fairfax St; tel: (703) 683-6000.* Pool, health club, airport and metro shuttles, non-smoking rooms, restaurant. Pricey. **Towne Motel**, *808 N Washington St; tel: (703) 329-1800.* Weekend and seasonal special rates. Budget.

Towers Hotel Suites, *420 N. Van Dorn St; tel: (703) 370-1000*; free parking, a health club, pool and shuttle to metro. Moderate. **Howard Johnson Hotel**, *5821 Richmond Hwy; tel: (703) 329-1400.* Pool, health club, free parking. Moderate.

Executive Club Suites, *610 Bashford Lane; tel: (703) 739-2582*; 76 suites with kitchen, bathroom, bedroom and living room with sofa bed. No extra per person cost. Moderate–expensive.

Eating and Drinking

There are nearly 300 restaurants, cafés and eating places, with the biggest cluster in Old Town. Many offer a take-away service. Among cuisines available are Japanese, Italian, Irish, Greek, Afghan, Creole, French, Moroccan, Thai and Vietnamese. You can even try colonial-style game pie and hot apple cider or planter's punch, brought to you by a costumed 'serving wench' at **Gadsby's Tavern**, *138 N. Royal St; tel: (703) 548-1288*, and enjoy appropriate live entertainment with dinner.

King Street Blues, *112 N St Asaph*

St; tel: (703) 836-8800, has a casual family atmosphere and quick service. Choice includes ribs, fresh fish and pastas. Cheap–budget. **Stella's**, 1725 Duke St; tel: (703) 519-1946, a spacious restaurant with 1940s movie photos and other memorabilia of the period, specialising in chops, steaks and seafood. Wide choice of beers served. Patio for summer dining, and free parking after 1700. Moderate.

Murphy's, 713 King St; tel: (703) 548-1717. Relaxed ambience in this Irish-American pub serving wholesome Irish stew. Live entertainment every night. Budget–moderate. **Kristos Charcoal House**, 608 Montgomery St; tel: (703) 548-9864. Set prime rib dinner available nightly for $7.95. Among other options is the lobster salad in summer in this long-established Old Town restaurant. Budget.

The Wharf, 119 King St; tel: (703) 836-2834. Seafood restaurant with live entertainment nightly in the Quarterdeck Lounge. Brunch sessions 1100-1600 Sat and Sun. Moderate. **Two Nineteen Restaurant**, 219 King St; tel: (703) 549-1141. Reservations advised for this Creole-cuisine restaurant in a Victorian setting. Award winning wine list. Live jazz nightly. Moderate.

Bullfeathers, 112 King St; tel: (703) 836-8088, has been voted Best Alexandria American restaurant and named as one of the ten best bars in the nation. Also revered for its burgers. Budget–moderate.

Pasta Peasant, 1024 Cameron St; tel: (703) 519-8755. If the locals swarm in, you know it's good – and they do. Flavour and healthy eating are the keynotes, with soups, salads, seafood, vegetarian and pastas. Open from breakfast (0800) to dinner (1730–2130), closed for dinner Mon. Budget. **Casablanca Restaurant**, 1504 King St; tel: (703) 549-6464. Traditional Moroccan cooking plus belly dancing

entertainment and folk dancing. Budget–moderate.

Fish Market, 105 King St; tel: (703) 836-5676. The city's largest restaurant, with 500 covers. Marine décor, fresh seafood and landlubber menu. Moderate. **Armand's Chicago Pizzaria**, 111 King St; tel: (703) 683-0313. All-you-can-eat lunch and 'midnight munch' buffets for $4.99 in the upstairs Penalty Box sports bar. Cheap and Budget.

Communications
The main **post office** is at 1100 Whyte St, Alexandria, VA 22314.

George Washington Birthday Parade (Mon nearest Feb 22) has Revolutionary War re-enactments, an Old Town parade and other activities.

St Patrick's Day Parade (second Sat in Mar) is a major event with restaurants holding parties with live entertainment after the parade.

Tour of private hand gardens, fourth Sat in Apr. Fee charged.

Alexandria Red Cross waterfront festival (second weekend in June) celebrates the importance of the city's seaport and its life ashore. Historical ships, boat trips, art displays, entertainment, food booths and general merry-making. Admission charge.

Scottish Christmas Walk, first Sat in Dec (see box, p 121).

Alexandria's extensive **Old Town** has many antique shops, gift shops, art and craft shops, fashion stores, shops selling music, books and ceramics. There are speciality shops, one-of-a-kind shops, boutiques and places where you can find all sorts of unusual and delightful purchases.

More than 150 shops are grouped in the revitalised **Landmark Mall** and there are major stores among the speciality shops near *King St* Metro Station.

It is worth getting up early for the **Farmers' Market,** *Market Square, 301 King St; tel: (703) 838-4770,* which is held every Sat all year round and lasts 4 hrs – starting at 0500. George Washington sent wagon loads of produce to the market from Mount Vernon. Stalls sell fresh vegetables, fruit and flowers, plants, homemade breads and cakes, preserves, crafts and other goods.

SIGHTSEEING

Alexandria, across the Potomac River from Washington DC, covers 15.75 sq miles and has a population of 115,000. Much of the city is an attraction in itself, notably the **Waterfront** and the extensive **Old Town**, with street upon street of 18th-and 19th-century buildings and cobblestoned alleyways off roads like *Prince* and *Princess Sts*.

Named after a Scotsman, John Alexander, and founded by Scotsmen in 1749, Alexandria still has strong Scottish connections.

Tours
Walking tours of the Old Town, with costumed guide, reveal the history and happenings of the seaport city and its famous sons. Tours start from **Ramsay House Visitors Center,** *221 King St; tel: (703) 838-4200* (see also box, p. 122). Fee charged. Inquire about a Ghost and Graveyard tour and a lantern-light walking tour on Saturday evenings in summer.

Old Town Experience; *tel: (703) 836-0694.* Walking tour of the Historic District, including visits to three museums, for individuals or groups. Fee charged.

Potomac Riverboat Company, *205*

The Strand; tel: (703) 684-0580, offers sightseeing tours afloat in Alexandria waters or taking in some Washington landmarks, aboard the 80-seat *Admiral Tilp* or the *Matthew Hayes* (capacity 149). The paddle-wheeler *Cherry Blossom* (capacity 400) can be chartered. Cruises operate Apr–Sept.

Potomac Party Cruises Inc, *Zero Prince St; tel: (703) 683-6076* (reservations) and *683-6000* (24-hour information line). Year-round lunch and dinner sightseeing cruises aboard the *Dandy,* operating a round trip between Alexandria and Washington. Dinner dances afloat.

Historical attractions
Visitors interested in historical attractions can save money by buying a $12 combination ticket for five Alexandria museums – Carlyle House, Gadsby Tavern Museum, Lee-Fendall House, Boyhood home of Robert E Lee and the Stabley-Leadbeater Apothecary Shop. Details from Ramsay House Visitors Center.

Alexandria Archaeology, *105 N Union St* (Torpedo Factory, 3rd floor); *tel: (703) 838-4399.* This research laboratory museum, operated by the city, is dedicated to the preservation of urban sites. Visitors can watch archaeologists piecing together parts of Alexandria's past. Open Tues–Fri 1000–1500, Sat 1000–1700, Sun 1300–1700. Admission free.

Lloyd House, *220 N Washington St; tel: (703) 838-4577.* Built in 1796, this Federal home was bought by John Lloyd, a merchant who married a cousin of Gen. Robert E Lee. It remained in the family for more than 85 years, until 1918. It now houses an important collection of Virginia's genealogical and historical material. Open Mon–Fri 0900–1800, Sat 0900–1700. Admission free.

Lee-Fendall House, *614 Oronoco St;*

119

tel: (703) 548-1789. In this 1785 mansion 'Light Horse Harry' Lee, Robert E. Lee's father, wrote the farewell address from Alexandria to George Washington when he left Mount Vernon to become first president of the nation. There is a permanent exhibition of dolls' houses and miniature architecture and a large and lovely garden. Guided tours. Open Tues–Sat 1000–1545, Sun 1200–1545. Closed occasionally for private parties. Admission: $3, students aged 11–17 $1, children under 11 free.

Boyhood Home of Robert E Lee, *607 Oronoco St; tel: (703) 548-8454.* Yet another Lee property, this 1795 town house was home to the boy who was to become a Confederate general. He lived there from the age of 5 to 18. It has authentic period furniture and much Lee family memorabilia. Open Mon–Sat 1000–1600, Sun 1300–1600. Last guided tour 1530. Admission charge.

Torpedo Factory Art Center, *105 N Union St; tel: (703) 838-4565.* Nearly 160 professional artists can be seen at work in 83 studios at this former government munitions factory which once provided shell cases and torpedoes used in World War II. The Art Center, by the Waterfront, attracts more than 850,000 visitors a year. Artists work, display and sell their creations, which include paintings and drawings, sculpture, print making, enamel work, stained glass, jewellery, ceramics and animation work. Open daily (except some public holidays). Admission free.

Fort Ward Museum and Historic Site, *4301, W. Braddock Rd; tel: (703) 838-4848.* One of the major defences of Washington during the Civil War, Fort Ward was restored and its earthwork walls preserved as a Civil War centennial project. Its north-west bastion was restored

---

Streets of Honour

Many of Alexandria's streets in the extensive historic district are named after illustrious figures from the past. *Pitt Street* honoured a British prime minister, *Wolfe Street* was named after the British Gen. James Wolfe, *Gibbon Street* after the historian, and so on.

The odd one out is *Oronoco Street*, which took its name from a variety of tobacco stored in the city's first warehouses.

Alexandria was established by the Virginia Assembly in 1749. Building lots were auctioned off in July of that year. A substantial tract of land that included the area on which the city was later built had been bought in 1669 by a Scotsman, John Alexander, for 'six thousand pounds of tobacco and cask.'

By the time of the Civil War, Alexandria had become a thriving seaport, but in 1861 was one of the first sites to be captured and occupied by Federal troops. It became a major base for the care of the war wounded. Many public buildings and homes were converted into military hospitals, and fortifications were built in strategic positions for the defence of Washington.

Campgrounds were set up for thousands of Union soldiers awaiting field duty.

Today Alexandria's role in the Civil War can be traced at dozens of sites around the Old Town, and bullets, still being excavated in the area, can be bought in souvenir shops.

---

and its ceremonial gate was reconstructed on the original site. Self-guided tours start from the gate. The Fort Ward Museum has Civil War exhibits and memorabilia. The museum, fort and amphitheatre are in a 45-acre park with picnic tables. Historic site open daily 0900–sunset, museum open Tues–Sat 0900–1700, Sun 1200–1700. Admission free.

Alexandria Black History Resource Center, *638 N. Alfred St; tel: (703) 838-3456*. The history of the city's African American community is documented here. Open Tues–Sat 1000–1600. Admission free but donations welcome.

Carlyle House, *121 N. Fairfax St; tel: (703) 549-2997*. Built of stone in symmetrical Scottish manor-house style, Carlyle House, owned and occupied by Scottish merchant John Carlyle, was completed in 1753. Two years later the British Gen. Edward Braddock used it as a base to plan his campaign against the French. Open Tues–Sat 1000–1630, Sun 1200–1630. Admission charge.

Gadsby's Tavern Museum, *134 N Royal St; tel: (703) 838-4242*. The tavern, built about 1770, was a centre of social, cultural and political life for nearly a century and was patronised by nearly all the founders of American Independence. George Washington was a frequent visitor to the tavern and the adjoining City Hotel (built in 1792), where lavish balls were held. The tavern now houses the museum, containing colonial furnishings, and the restaurant and ballroom are in the City Hotel. Colonial-style dishes – Martha's Omelette, Gadsby's Colonial Pye, Buttermilk Pye, Scottish Apple Gingerbread with Cinnamon Icing – are served by maids in period costume. An Englishman, John Gadsby, ran the two buildings from 1796 to 1808. The properties were saved from demolition in 1928 by veteran service organisations, acquired by the City of Alexandria in 1972 and restored for the bi-centennial of American Independence. Museum open Tues–Sat 1000–1700, Sun 1300–1700, tours available, last one at 1615. Admission charge.

121

Tartan City

Alexandria's strong Scottish ties go back to its founding in the mid-18th century, and continue to this day. The city is twinned with Dundee, on the Firth of Tay in eastern Scotland. Its tartan is the red, green and yellow weave of the Camerons – named after Lord Fairfax, Baron Cameron.

The City of Alexandria Pipes and Drums performs at public functions. One of the biggest of these, the **Virginia Scottish Games**, is held annually in the fourth weekend of July. This Celtic country fair, with Highland athletics, Scottish dancing, harp competitions, dog events and the serving of Scottish fare, takes place at the Episcopal High School, *390 W Braddock Rd*.

In defiance of the Church of England, the Presbyterian founders of the city built their church – the **Old Presbyterian Meeting House**, *321 S Fairfax St; tel: (703) 549-6670* – shortly before the Revolution. George Washington's funeral oration was held there, and it is the site of the Tomb of the Unknown Soldier of the American Revolution. **Carlyle House**, the first of Alexandria's mansions (see above) was completed in 1753 in the style of Craigiehall in West Lothian, Scotland.

On the first Sat in Dec, a **Scottish Christmas Walk** parades through the Old Town, featuring pipe bands and clan members wearing the tartan.

The **Scotland Yard** restaurant in *King St* serves such fare as fynnon haddock, bridies and leek soup, and there are at least two shops specialising in Scottish goods – **Scottish Merchant** in *King St* and **Smith's of Bermuda** in *Washington St*.

Christ Church, *118 N Washington St; tel: (703) 549-1450*. George Washington and, later, Gen. Robert E. Lee, were regular worshippers in this lovely building. Lee was confirmed and married here. Construction of the church began in 1767 and it was completed six years later. The churchyard was Alexandria's burial ground until 1809. By tradition, most presidents attend a service at Christ Church at some time during their administration. President Franklin D. Roosevelt and British Prime Minister Winston Churchill were there together on New Year's Day, 1942, for the World Day of Prayer for Peace in World War II. Guided tours available.

House of History

Ramsay House Visitor Center in King St is recognised as the oldest house in Alexandria.

It is believed to date from around 1724 – nearly a quarter of a century before Alexandria was founded – and may have possibly stood some miles down the Potomac River in an early Scottish settlement called Dumfries. It would have been transported by barge to the new port of Alexandria.

William Ramsay, a Scots-born merchant and friend of George Washington, was a founder of Alexandria. At that time the river was broader, and one theory offered is that Ramsay placed his house on its present site so that he could see his trading vessels entering and leaving the harbour.

Since those days Ramsay House has been a tavern, a grocery store, a rooming house and a cigar factory. In 1942 it was purchased by the city and, with contributions from organisations and individuals, restored. It was dedicated as a historic site in 1956.

Open Mon–Sat 0900–1600, Sun 1400–1630. Admission free.

Stabler-Leadbeater Apothecary Shop, *105-107 S. Fairfax St; tel: (703) 836-3713*. The shop was founded in 1792 and continued as a family business for 141 years, until the 1930s Depression forced its closure. More than 8000 items include a fascinating collection of hand-blown glass phials and bottles, documents, drug mills, mortars and pestles, breast pumps, carboys, herbs and potions and medical aids. Open Mon–Sat 1000–1600. Admission charge.

The Atheneum, *201 Prince St; tel: (703) 548-0035*. This prime example of Greek Revival architecture, built as a bank around 1850, houses the gallery of the Northern Virginia Fine Arts Association. Open Wed–Sat 1000–1600, Sun 1300–1600. Admission free.

Alexandria Seaport Foundation, *Jones Point Park, S. Lee St; tel: (703)549-7078*. The historic three-masted schooner *Alexandria*, 125 ft long, can be visited when in port. Open Sat–Sun 1200–1700, winter 1100–1600.

George Washington Masonic National Memorial, *101 Callahan Dr.; tel: (703) 683-2007*. This large 333 ft high building on Shooters Hill is visible from many corners of Alexandria, and the tower's enclosed observation deck gives a view of the city, river and surrounding area. The memorial was dedicated to George Washington in 1932. It contains a 17 ft bronze statue of him as Charter Worshipful Master of the Alexandria Lodge. The Memorial Museum contains some of Washington's personal possessions, including the field trunk he used in the Revolutionary War. Guided tours of the Tower Rooms are available on the half-hour in the mornings and on the hour in the afternoons. Open daily 0900–1700. Admission free.

ALEXANDRIA–RICHMOND

Most of the first half of this route follows the course of the Potomac River, which is seen in all its splendour from Mount Vernon. At historic Fredericksburg – a significant place in Colonial, Revolutionary and Civil War times – the route reaches another river, the Rappahannock. Beyond the Rappahannock, we move south through rustic scenery to reach our third river, the James, which passes through Virginia's elegant capital, Richmond.

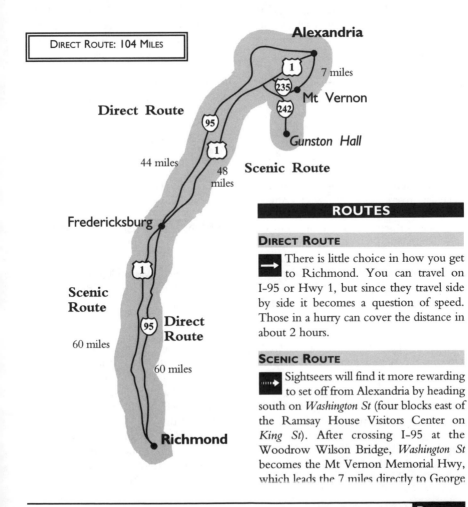

DIRECT ROUTE: 104 MILES

Alexandria

1

7 miles

235

Mt Vernon

242

Direct Route

95

1

Gunston Hall

44 miles

48 miles

Scenic Route

Fredericksburg

1

Scenic Route

60 miles

95   Direct Route

60 miles

Richmond

ROUTES

DIRECT ROUTE

There is little choice in how you get to Richmond. You can travel on I-95 or Hwy 1, but since they travel side by side it becomes a question of speed. Those in a hurry can cover the distance in about 2 hours.

SCENIC ROUTE

Sightseers will find it more rewarding to set off from Alexandria by heading south on *Washington St* (four blocks east of the Ramsay House Visitors Center on *King St*). After crossing I-95 at the Woodrow Wilson Bridge, *Washington St* becomes the Mt Vernon Memorial Hwy, which leads the 7 miles directly to George

Washington's home. From **Mount Vernon**, Rte 235 continues for 3 miles to join Hwy 1. Woodlawn Plantation is very close to the intersection. Continue south on Hwy 1 for 5 miles, where Rte 242 (*Gunston Rd*) leads to **Gunston Hall**. Returning to Hwy 1, **Fredericksburg** is 40 miles to the south, with Richmond a further 60 miles.

MOUNT VERNON

Mount Vernon, *George Washington Memorial Parkway, Mount Vernon, VA; tel: (703) 780-2000.* Whether you approach Mount Vernon from the George Washington Memorial Parkway, or along the Potomac River on a trip from Washington, you will be faced with a beautiful aspect of George and Martha Washington's hilltop home, set in 500 acres.

Mount Vernon is 16 miles south of the capital, in Fairfax County. Visitors can tour the restored home, garden – where humming birds may be seen – slaves' quarters and family tombs, and sit on the verandah overlooking the river. Attendants are on hand to answer questions.

Much of the furniture was in the mansion in Washington's day. A number of 18th-century dignitaries were entertained in the Banqueting Hall. One of them, Gen. Lafayette, presented Washington with the key to the Paris Bastille, which is displayed in the central hall. Two parlours, the family dining room, the library and a downstairs bedroom can be viewed. Upstairs, the Washingtons' bedroom contains the bed on which the president died in 1799.

A recent addition in the grounds is a meticulous reconstruction of George Washington's innovative 16-sided threshing barn, built using hand-made bricks and hand-forged nails. The almost circular design served as an indoor arena for a

horse to trample the straw, causing the grain to sift through to the floor below. Seasonal wheat-threshing demonstrations are held at the barn.

Mount Vernon is open daily 0900–1700 (Mar, Sept/Oct), 0800–1700 (Apr–Aug), 0900–1600 (Nov–Feb). Admission $7, children 6–11 $3. **Spirit Cruises**, *6th and Water Sts, Pier 4, Washington DC; tel: (202) 554-8000,* operate cruises to Mount Vernon all year round, except Feb.

Woodlawn Plantation, *PO Box 37, Mount Vernon; tel: (703) 780-4000.* Guided tours of the home of George and Martha Washington's granddaughter, Nelly Custis Lewis, are held hourly. The plantation was formerly part of the Mount Vernon property. Open Mon–Fri 0930–1630 all year, also weekends Jan and Feb only. Admission charge.

⮣ SIDE TRACK TO GUNSTON HALL

Five miles south of Woodlawn Plantation, Rte 242 leads south-east 7 miles to Gunston Hall.

GUNSTON HALL

Gunston Hall Plantation, *Gunston Rd, Mason Neck; tel: (703) 550-9220.* Gunston Hall was built from 1755 by George Mason, author of the Virginia Declaration of Rights and one who helped frame the US constitution. One of the renowned houses of pre-Revolutionary Virginia, Gunston Hall was constructed to a design by Mason, assisted by a British carpenter on his staff, William Buckland, who was responsible for much of the woodwork, including that in the Palladian drawing room. Mason designed the formal gardens. Some of Mason's original furniture can be seen in the house. Open daily 0930-1700. Admission charge. ⬛

124

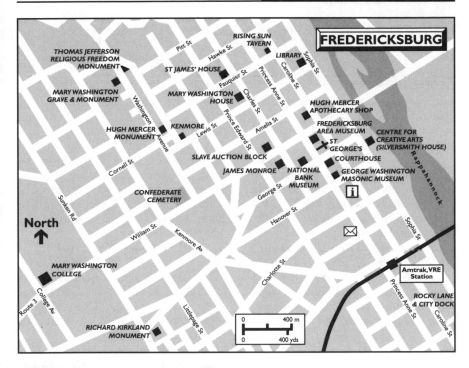

THOMAS JEFFERSON
RELIGIOUS FREEDOM
MONUMENT

MARY WASHINGTON
GRAVE & MONUMENT

HUGH MERCER
MONUMENT

CONFEDERATE
CEMETERY

MARY WASHINGTON
COLLEGE

RICHARD KIRKLAND
MONUMENT

RISING SUN
TAVERN

Pitt St
Hawke St

ST JAMES' HOUSE

Fauquier St
Charles St

MARY WASHINGTON
HOUSE

KENMORE

Lewis St

Prince Edward St

SLAVE AUCTION BLOCK

JAMES MONROE

George St

Hanover St

Charlotte St

LIBRARY

Princess Anne St

Caroline St

Sophia St

Amelia St

HUGH MERCER
APOTHECARY SHOP

FREDERICKSBURG
AREA MUSEUM

ST
GEORGE'S

COURTHOUSE

NATIONAL
BANK
MUSEUM

GEORGE WASHINGTON
MASONIC MUSEUM

CENTRE FOR
CREATIVE ARTS
(SILVERSMITH HOUSE)

FREDERICKSBURG

Rappahannock

Washington Avenue

Cornell St

Sunken Rd

William St

Kenmore Av

College Av

Route 3

Littlepage St

North

Sophia St

Princess Anne St

Caroline St

Amtrak, VRE
Station

ROCKY LANE
& CITY DOCK

0   400 m
0   400 yds

125

FREDERICKSBURG

Tourist Information: Fredericksburg Visitor Center, *706 Caroline St; tel: (703) 373-1776*, open daily 0900–1700, extended summer hours. As well as maps, leaflets, and brochures listing dining and lodging options, the centre issues free parking passes for visitors and shows a short video on the city and its history. It also provides a **Hospitality Pass**, giving admission to seven attractions at 30% discount, and a **Pick Four** pass, giving a similar discount at four attractions. The Hospitality Pass costs $16 ($6 for children 6–18) and the Pick Four Pass $11.50 ($4 for children). Sites covered are Kenmore, Mary Washington's House, Rising Sun Tavern, Hugh Mercer Apothecary Shop, James Monroe Museum, Fredericksburg Area Museum and Belmont.

Spotsylvania County Visitor Center, *4704 Southpoint Parkway, Spotsylvania; tel: (703) 891-8687*. A 10-min video introduces the region, including Lake Anna and the battlefields. Tickets for historic tours and events, regional and state maps, brochures, and information on dining and lodging are available. Open daily 0900–1700; extended hours in summer.

Stafford County Dept of Economic Development, *PO Box 339, Stafford; tel: (703) 659-8681*, has general tourist information relating to county-wide accommodation and attractions.

ACCOMMODATION

Hotel chains in the area include *BW, CI, DI, EL, Hd, HJ, Rm, Sh* and *TL*. There are also a variety of independent hotels and motels, six bed and breakfast inns in the Old Town and six more in the area.

Among campsites is **Fredericksburg/**

Washington DC South KOA, *7400 Brookside Lane, Fredericksburg; tel: (703) 898-7252.*

EATING AND DRINKING

The Old Town alone has nearly three dozen eateries and there are countless more around the highway exits serving the area.

But in town the choice nosedives in the evening, with few places open after 2200. Many are shut by 2000. **Irish Brigade**, *1005 Princess Anne St; tel: (703) 371-9413,* opens until 2100 on weekdays and 2200 Fri and Sat, but its pub, with live entertainment, opens 1700–0200. **Sammy T's**, *801 Caroline St; tel: (703) 371-2008,* is open Mon–Sat to 2300 (2100 Sun), serving a range of food, including vegan and vegetarian, and offering a separate room for non-smokers. The southwestern cuisine at the **Santa Fe**, *216 William St; tel: (703) 371-0500,* is available till late – Mon–Thur to 0200 – the time when **Mother's Public House** closes its doors at *406 Lafayette Blvd; tel: (703) 371-7070.* It serves hamburgers, snacks and salads.

SIGHTSEEING

Fredericksburg, founded as a tobacco-trading port on the Rappahannock River in 1728, was the site of four major Civil War battles. It is also the place which nurtured George Washington during most of his childhood.

In spite of heavy artillery fire from both Union and Confederate troops in the Civil War, Fredericksburg has retained a 40-block National Historic District, with more than 350 original 18th- and early 19th-century buildings.

The **Battle of Fredericksburg** and three more Civil War battles in the area claimed many lives – Fredericksburg National Cemetery is the last resting place of more than 15,000 Union soldiers.

The city can be seen by guided walks, 75-min trolley tours or 45-min horse and carriage tours.

George Washington's Boyhood Home, *Ferry Farm, Rte 3 E., Ferry Road, Falmouth; tel: (703) 372-4485.* George Washington was six when he and his family moved into Ferry Farm, just across the Rappahannock River from Fredericksburg. He inherited it at the age of 11 and lived there until he was 20, attending school and church in Fredericksburg. The house is open Mon–Sat 1000–1600, Sun 1200–1600. Free.

Masonic Lodge No 4, *803 Princess Anne St; tel: (703) 373-5885.* George Washington became a Mason here in 1752. Relics and memorabilia can be seen in the lodge museum. Open Mon–Sat 0900–1600, Sun 1300–1600. Admission: $2, children up to 19: $1.

Mary Washington House, *1200 Charles St; tel: (703) 373-1569.* George Washington bought the property for his mother in 1772, when she moved out of Ferry Farm. She lived here until her death 17 years later. Some of her personal possessions are on display. Open daily 0900–1700 (Mar–Nov), 1000–1600 (Dec–Feb). Admission $3, children $1.

Kenmore, *1201 Washington Ave; tel: (703) 373-3381.* Betty Washington (George's only sister), married Fielding Lewis, who built her this elegant mansion containing elaborately decorated rooms. Kenmore is especially noted for its ornate plasterwork ceilings. Open Mon–Sat 1000–1700, Sun 1200–1700 (Mar–Dec), Mon–Fri reservation only, Sat 1000–1600, Sun 1200–1600 (Jan, Feb). Admission $5, children $2.50, family rate $12.

Rising Sun Tavern, *1304 Caroline St; tel: (703) 371-1494.* George's younger brother, Charles, built this property as his home in 1760. It later became a tavern in the thriving port city. Today 'wenches' welcome visitors to an interpretation of 18th-century tavern life. Open daily 0900–1700 Mar–Nov, 1000–1600 Dec–Feb. Admission: $3, children: $1.

Hugh Mercer Apothecary Shop, *1020 Caroline St; tel: (703) 373-336;* 18th-century medical practices and popular remedies of a past age fascinate the visitor. Open daily 0900–1700 (Mar–Nov), 1000–1600 (Dec–Feb). Admission: $3, children: $1.

James Monroe Museum, *908 Charles St; tel: (703) 899-4559.* Long before becoming the nation's fifth president, James Monroe practised law in Fredericksburg. In the Museum and Memorial Library are Louis XVI furniture which he bought while Minister to France, and which he used in the White House. Also exhibited are documents and personal items owned by Monroe and his wife, Elizabeth, including some of her gowns and jewellery. Open daily 0900–1700 (Mar–Nov), 1000–1600 (Dec–Feb). Admission: $3, children: $1.

Belmont, the Gari Melchers Estate and Memorial Gallery, *224 Washington St; tel: (703) 654-1015,* is a lovely 18th-century home with studio and 27 acres, where Gari Melchers painted for the last 16 years of his life. The stone studio, which he built in 1924, contains many of his works, and others are shown in two adjoining galleries. A video on Melchers is shown in the Visitor Centre in the former carriage house. Information on Stafford County is also available. Open Mon–Sat 1000–1700, Sun 1300–1700 (Mar–Nov), Mon–Sat 1000–1600, Sun 1300–1600 (Dec–Feb). Admission: $4, children: $1.

Fredericksburg Area Museum & Cultural Center, *Old Town Hall and Market House, 905 Princess Anne St; tel:*

(703) 371-3037. The city's past, from prehistoric times through Indian and Colonial settlement to the Civil War and modern days, unfolds in six galleries. Exhibits range from silver snuff boxes and Civil War uniforms to slave chains and weapons. Open Mon–Sat 0900–1700, Sun 1300–1700 (Mar–Nov), Mon–Sat 0900–1600, Sun 1300–1600 (Dec–Feb). Admission: $3, children: $1.

Fredericksburg/Spotsylvania National Military Park, *Fredericksburg Battlefield Visitor Center, 1013 Lafayette Blvd; tel: (703) 373-6122,* and **Chancellorsville Battlefield Visitor Center**, *Rte 3 W; tel: (703) 786-2880.* Both open daily 0900–1700, plus extended hours in summer. Maps, brochures, audio-visual presentations and museum exhibits relating to the four battlefields, and assistance from park historians, is available. As well as **Fredericksburg Battlefield** (11–15 Dec 1862) – 'Lee's most one-sided victory' – and **Chancellorsville Battlefield** (27 Apr–6 May 1863), **Wilderness Battlefield** (5–6 May 1864) and **Spotsylvania Court House Battlefield** (8–21 May 1864) are open to visitors. On a self-guided tour of the battlefields, the visitor will find wayside exhibits, interpretive trails and historic buildings – all part of the Civil War story, involving such names as Robert E. Lee, Ulysses S. Grant and Stonewall Jackson. From early June to early Sept special interpretive programmes are held. Open daily dawn to dusk. Free.

Lake Anna State Park, *6800 Lawyers Road, Spotsylvania* (adjacent to Rte 601 off State Rte 208, Spotsylvania); *tel: (703) 854-5503.* The Visitor Center provides a history of gold-mining in the area, and visitors can try their luck at gold-panning. Also on offer are beach and picnic facilities, fishing, pontoon boat rides and eight miles of hiking trails. Freely accessible.

127

ALEXANDRIA–HARRISONBURG

Leading through places rich in Colonial and Civil War history, this route crosses the top of northern Virginia, giving the traveller a chance to sample the state's varied terrain – from the rolling hunt country of Loudon County, across the Piedmont, along part of the Blue Ridge Mountains, towards the rustic splendour of the Shenandoah Valley.

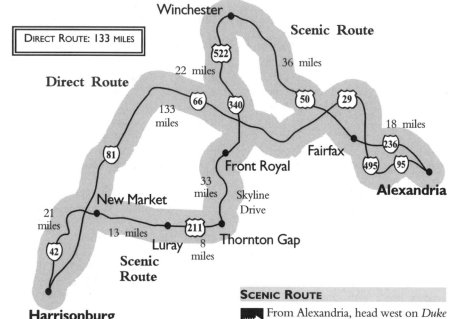

DIRECT ROUTE: 133 MILES

Winchester

Scenic Route

522

22 miles

36 miles

Direct Route

66 340

133 miles

81

New Market

33 miles

Front Royal

50 29

18 miles

236

Fairfax

495 95

Alexandria

Skyline Drive

21 miles

42

13 miles

Luray

211

8 miles

Thornton Gap

Scenic Route

Harrisonburg

128

ROUTES

DIRECT ROUTE

➡️ By following the interstates – 95, 495, 66 and 81 – you can complete the journey in a little over two hours, but you will miss much of interest along the way. The scenic route avoids the interstates, adding some 20 miles and as much time as you want.

SCENIC ROUTE

➡️ From Alexandria, head west on *Duke St*, which joins Rte 236 after 3 miles, just after I-95. Rte 236 continues through

Colour section: (i) Gettysburg Battlefield (see p.104).
(ii) York (p.106): Harley Davidson Museum and Gen. Gates House
(iii) Arlington National Cemetery; Guards at the Tomb of the Unknown Soldier (p.114); Confederate burial ground, Lynchburg (p.155).
(iv) View from Skyline Drive (p.136); the Blue Ridge Mountains, Virginia (p.147).

Fairfax where it becomes Hwy 50, which passes Washington Dulles Airport and reaches **Winchester** after 51 miles.

At Winchester, follow Rte 522 south for 22 miles to **Front Royal**, where Rte 340 leads south for 2 miles to the **Blue Ridge Parkway Skyline Drive** at the northern end of the **Shenandoah National Park**. After 31 miles, exit at **Thornton Gap** on to Hwy 211 west, which reaches **Luray** in 8 miles, and **New Market** in another 13. Six miles beyond New Market, Hwy 211 joins Rte 42, which reaches **Harrisonburg** in 15 miles.

FAIRFAX

Tourist Information: Fairfax County Convention & Visitors Bureau, *8300 Boone Blvd, Ste 450, Tyson's Corner; tel: (540) 550-2450.*

ACCOMMODATION

Holiday Inn Fairfax City, *3535 Chain Bridge Rd; tel: (540) 591-5500.* **Wellesley Inn**, *10327 Lee Hwy; tel: (540) 359-2888.*

The Bailiwick Inn, *4023 Chain Bridge Rd; tel: (540) 691-2266.* Dinner is served at this historic bed and breakfast inn.

Campsite: **Lake Fairfax Park**, *1400 Lake Fairfax Dr., Reston; tel: (540) 471-5414.*

SIGHTSEEING

City of Fairfax, Fairfax Museum & Visitors Center, *10209 Main St, Fairfax; tel: (1-800) 545-7950.* Housed in a school building dating from 1873, the museum contains local history exhibits. General information on accommodation, shopping and attractions is available at the centre.

Fairfax, 20 mins west of Washington, DC, claims to have in its area the biggest concentration of premier shopping outside New York – such shopping centres as **Fairfax Square** and the malls of nearby

Tyson's Corner, attract people from the capital and beyond.

WINCHESTER

Tourist Information: Winchester-Frederick County Chamber of Commerce and Visitor Center, *1360 S Pleasant Valley Rd* (near I-81); *tel: (540) 662-4135.* An 18-min video outlines the city's history, attractions and festivals. The centre is decorated with large colour photographs of the area and events, and has much information on local events, sightseeing, entertainment, restaurants and accommodation. Open daily 0900–1700.

Old Town Welcome Center, *The Kurtz Building, 2 N. Cameron St; tel: (540) 722-6367.* As well as tourist and business information, the centre has gifts for sale. Open daily.

At the northern end of the Shenandoah Valley, at the 'top of Virginia' and less than 80 miles from Washington, DC, Winchester is a lively city of about 30,000 people, with some famous names in its history.

George Washington had his surveyor's office here in the 1740s. In the 1860s Gen. Thomas 'Stonewall' Jackson was headquartered here – Winchester was heavily involved in the Civil War, changing hands 72 times.

Winchester was the home town of Patsy Cline, Country and Western singer, who achieved fame while still in her teens; see box feature, p. 131.

Admiral Richard Byrd, the polar explorer who, in 1929, was the first person to fly over the South Pole, was a Winchester man.

With thousands of acres of apple orchards around it, the city stages a mammoth four-day Apple Blossom Festival in early May every year. It attracts a quarter of a million people.

Winchester is proud of its shopping

129

facilities. Especially attractive is **Millwood Crossing**, a complex of about a dozen antiques and speciality shops at *381 Millwood Ave; tel: (540) 662-5157*. Handmade jewellery, engraved and stained glass, flags, candles, artworks and hand-made quilts are among items offered. **Apple Blossom Mall**, *1850 Apple Blossom Dr.; tel: (540) 665-0201*, has stores like Sears and J.C. Penney as well as a pushcart market – decorated carts stocked with T-shirts, sunglasses and fancy goods.

ACCOMMODATION

Hotel chains include *BW, DI, Hd, HJ, QI, TL*. Budget Inn and Shoney's Inn have properties in the city.

There are bed and breakfast homes in the area, notably the **Inn at Vaucluse Spring**, *140 Vaucluse Spring Lane, Stephen City; tel: (540) 869-0200*. The 100-acre property has six air-conditioned rooms, each with private bath and fireplace, in three different buildings which were the home of the American artist John Chumley. The Mill House Studio, where Chumley painted, is designed for physically handicapped guests.

Another local Bed & Breakfast is **Brownstone Cottage**, *761 McCarty Lane, Winchester; tel: (540) 662-1962*.

EATING AND DRINKING

You can eat well at remarkably modest prices at some of the area's pleasant but unassuming restaurants. There are fast-food outlets like **McDonald's**, *1801 Pleasant Valley Rd*, where you can satisfy your hunger for $5, and more atmospheric locations where you can dine in comfort with full service for a maximum of only $10, like **Cracker Barrel**, an old country store at *200 Front Royal Pike, Winchester; tel: (540) 722-3770*.

Breakfast from $2, lunches from $2.25

to $4.95 and dinners from $3.50–6.95 are served at **Bob Evans Restaurant**, *816 Millwood Ave; tel: (540) 722-5290*.

Fritter's Restaurant & Gathering Place, *1801 Dominion Ave; tel: (540) 665-4400*, has Mexican, American and Italian dishes, and on Sat and Sun a breakfast buffet is held from 0700–1200.

About 8 miles east of Winchester on Rte 7, the **Battletown Inn**, *102 W. Main St, Berryville; tel: (540) 955-4100*, provides fine dining in an historic setting. It is open for lunch and dinner but closes at 2000 Tues–Thur and 2100 Fri and Sat. Closed Mon and throughout Jan.

The Wayside Inn, *7783 Main St, Middletown; tel: (540) 869-1797*, has been providing meals and lodging since 1797, originally as Wilkinson's Tavern and later as Larrick's Hotel. It has 24 guest rooms and suites and a choice of seven dining rooms. If you've never tried peanut soup, this is the place to do so.

SIGHTSEEING

Kurtz Cultural Center, *2 N. Cameron St, Winchester; tel: (540) 722-6367*. This 1836 downtown building was originally a commodities warehouse which became a funeral parlour and then a furniture store. Local people campaigned to save it from demolition, and in 1991 it opened to the public. It is owned and operated by Preservation of Historic Winchester, Inc, serving as the Old Town Welcome Center and Gift Shop and the Civil War Information Center. There is also a 'Celebrating Patsy Cline' exhibit.

There are a number of battlefields in the Shenandoah Valley, and the **Civil War Information Center** provides an introduction to the area's role between 1861 and 1865, and a good starting point for those planning to tour Civil War sites.

Part of the town's huge cemetery holds

The Patsy Cline Pilgrimage

Every year Winchester is host to a stream of visitors from many parts of the world who go there to pay homage to Patsy Cline. Patsy died in 1963, but the Country and Western singer, who first set pulses racing as vocalist with a local Winchester group, still commands respect and adoration.

Patsy's real name was Virginia Patterson Hensley. She was born in Gore, VA, but grew up in Winchester, attending the Handley High School in *Valley Ave.* Her home, *608 S. Kent St,* is sought out by Patsy Cline pilgrims. Other places the fans visit are **Gaunt's Drug Store**, at the corner of *S. Loudoun* and *Valley Ave,* where she worked as a teenage waitress, **G & M Music** at *38 W. Boscawen St,* where she made recordings, **Winc Radio**, *520 N. Pleasant Valley Rd,* where she frequently performed, and *720 S. Kent St,* where she married Charlie Dick in 1957.

That was the year in which her success in a talent contest led to the big time. In 1958 she appeared at the Grand Ole Opry and became a regular there, moving to Nashville and being named No. 1 Female Artist 1961 and 1962. She had the No. 1 song of 1962 with *I Fall to Pieces.* The following year, on 5 March, she was killed in a Tennessee plane crash.

Ten years later she was posthumously elected to the Country Music Hall of Fame and is recognised as one of the major female vocalists of all time. Now Winchester has a **Patsy Cline Boulevard**, and Rte 522 south, which leads to the Shenandoah Memorial Park, where she is buried, is called the **Patsy Cline Memorial Highway.**

the remains of 2000 Confederate victims of the war. A statue of a soldier stands near the Old Court House, with the inscription: 'In lasting honor of every Confederate soldier from Winchester and Frederick County who faithfully served the South.'

The following three museums are operated by Winchester-Frederick County Historical Society (inquire about discounted admission if visiting all three):

George Washington's Office Museum, corner of *Braddock* and *Cork Sts, Old Town; tel: (540) 662-4412.* It was in 1748 that the youthful George Washington arrived in Winchester as part of a surveying team directed by Lord Fairfax. During the autumn and winter of 1755–56, Washington, now a colonel in the Virginia Militia, occupied the log cabin that now houses the museum while he supervised the construction of Fort Loudoun. He also had to protect the fron-

tier from hostile Indians and the advancing French. Surveying tools, documents, uniforms and Militia memorabilia are exhibited. Open Mon–Sat 1000–1600, Sun 1200–1600 Apr–Oct. Admission $3.

Stonewall Jackson's Headquarters Museum, *415 N. Braddock St; tel: (540) 667-3242.* Built in 1854 and restored and furnished to its state when Gen. Jackson led Confederate operations in the Civil War, this house contains Jackson's prayer book and wartime artefacts. It was Lt. Col. Lewis T. Moore who provided the home for Gen. and Mrs Jackson during their time in Winchester. In 1993 Moore's great-granddaughter, the actress Mary Tyler Moore, donated the reproduced gilded wallpaper used in the décor. Open Mon–Sat 1000–1600, Sun 1200–1600 (Apr–Oct). Admission $3.

Abram's Delight Museum, *1340 S. Pleasant Valley Rd; tel: (540) 662-6519.* This is the oldest house in Winchester, built of local limestone in 1754 by the son of Abram Hollingsworth, an early settler. The museum depicts life in the early settlement days in the region. Originally it was the town's first Quaker meeting house. Open Mon–Sat 1000–1600, Sun 1200–1600 Apr–Oct. Admission $3.

Handley Library and Archives, *Braddock and Piccadilly Sts; tel: (540) 662-9041.* Winchester's public library, completed in 1913, has a stained-glass dome, glass floors and wrought iron staircases. Open Mon–Sat. Free admission.

Old Stone Presbyterian Church, *306 E. Piccadilly St; tel: (540) 662-3824.* This 18th-century church has also served as a school and an armoury – and during the Civil War it was used by troops to stable horses. Open daily. Free admission.

Winchester Little Theatre, *315 W. Boscawen St; tel: (540) 662-3331.* Local and visiting enthusiasts have been sustaining amateur theatricals here since 1929. Phone for performance times. Admission charge.

Shenandoah University Theatre, *1460 University Dr.; tel: (540) 665-4569.* Four shows a year are staged in Oct, Nov, Feb and Apr. Phone for performance times. Tickets $10, students $7.

Rinker Orchards, *1156 Marlboro Rd, Stephen City; tel: (540) 869-1499.* A chance to pick-your-own fruit. Apple picking starts in mid-Sept. Your visit may coincide with the local Lions Club boiling and selling apple butter or the United Methodist Women selling apple dumplings. Ready-picked fruit is for sale.

Old Town Winchester, *Downtown Development Board, Rouss City Hall, 15 N. Cameron St; tel: (540) 667-1815.* On summer Friday evenings live music is played on the steps in front of the **Old County Court House**. The Old Town, with its speciality shops, galleries, restaurants and, from May–Oct, sidewalk cafés on the pedestrian mall, has 45 square blocks of buildings on the National Historic Register.

Nine miles south-east of Winchester, at Boyce on US 50, is the **State Arboretum of Virginia**, *Blandy Experimental Farm, Boyce; tel: (540) 837-1758.* With a backdrop of the Blue Ridge Mountains, the 170-acre arboretum, a research centre of the University of Virginia, has one of the most extensive boxwood collections in North America. Visitors can drive a circular route through native and foreign trees or stroll through a lane of dogwoods. Magnolias, maples, beeches and half the world's pine species may be seen. A lake with wetland plants, meadowlands, native Virginia plants and a herb garden can be enjoyed. Arboretum tours are held in spring and autumn. Picnic tables and ample parking are provided and there's a shop with gifts and horticultural books. Office open Mon–Fri 0900–1700, arboretum open daily dawn to dusk. Free.

On the way south from Winchester to Front Royal, it's worth stopping at the little towns of **Middletown** and **Strasburg**. Each has a battlefield site.

Cedar Creek Battlefield Site, *PO Box 229, Middletown; tel: (540) 869-2064.* A wealth of information about one of the most dramatic Civil War battles, which took place in Oct 1864, can be found in the Visitor Centre and bookshop here and at the neighbouring Hupp's Hill Battlefield Park (see below). Every Oct a re-enactment of the battle on the site is a major event attracting tens of thousands of people. Open Mon–Sat 1000–1600, Sun 1300–1700 Apr–Oct. Free admission; donations welcome.

Belle Grove Plantation, *PO Box 137, Middletown; tel: (540) 869-2028.* This imposing mansion was built in 1794 by Major Isaac Hite, with architectural advice from Thomas Jefferson. Gen. Philip Sheridan used Belle Grove as his head-quarters in the autumn of 1864. Union soldiers camping here were a sitting target when Confederate Gen. Jubal Early led a surprise attack. Sheridan had gone to Washington but returned in time to organise his troops in battle – the Battle of Cedar Creek. Hundreds of men were slain in that last major battle for control of the Shenandoah Valley. There is a museum and quilt shop with products of the region. Open Mon–Sat 1000–1600 (tours 1015–1515), Sun 1300–1700 (tours 1315–1615) mid Mar–Oct. Admission charge.

Wayside Theatre, *Rte 11 S., Middletown; tel: (540) 869-1776.* For more than 30 years this professional company has presented contemporary and classic drama, comedies and musicals. Open May–Oct and Dec. Admission charge.

Hupp's Hill Battlefield Park and Study Center, *Rte 11 north, Strasburg; tel: (540) 465-5884.* A unique Civil War museum with a hands-on approach. A map table in the Study Center enables vis-itors to follow the movements of Union and Confederate troops and to see how these were helped and hindered by the terrain and natural obstacles. Children can dress up in Civil War uniforms, sit astride wooden war horses and go inside military tents. Earthworks dug by Union troops can still be seen at Hupp's Hill. A 100 ft hand-painted mural in the Visitor Center depicts scenes from the Civil War. Exhibits include weapons, medical equip-ment, documents and relics dug up from battlefields. Open daily Mon–Sat 1000–1600, Sat, Sun 1100–1700. Admission to museum $3.50, seniors $3, children $2.

FRONT ROYAL

Tourism Information: Front Royal-Warren County Chamber of Commerce, *414 E. Main St; tel: (540) 635-3185.* A visitor centre is housed in the old Southern Railroad station, *Main St.*

ACCOMMODATION AND FOOD

As well as a **Budget Motel** and **Quality Inn**, both budget to moderately priced, Front Royal has 9 or 10 other motels in a similar price bracket. There are a number of Bed and Breakfast homes and guest houses out of town. In Front Royal itself is the **Chester House Inn** (moderate–expensive), *43 Chester St; tel: (540) 635-3937*, situated in the historic district.

Several campsites serve the area, includ-ing the **Front Royal-Washington DC KOA** with 150 sites, on *Rte 340 S.; tel: (540) 635-2741*. Cabin rentals are also available, though mostly nearer to Luray than to Front Royal.

Plenty of budget fast-food facilities can be found in Front Royal. **Dominos Pizza** (budget) at the *Royal Plaza Shopping Center; tel: (540) 635-4171*, stays open to 2300 (0200 Fri and Sat). Lunches and din-ners are served daily at the **Feedmill Restaurant** (moderate), *500 E. Main St; tel: (540) 635-3123*, local entertainment is a bonus. The **Fox Diner** (budget to mod-erate), *20 South St; tel: (540) 635-3325*, serves good, unpretentious food. **McDonald's, Pizza Hut** and **Kentucky Fried Chicken** are in town.

SIGHTSEEING

Once a small village, Front Royal grew quickly from the mid-1930s, when the entrance to the Shenandoah National Park and the start of the Skyline Drive opened at its doorstep. In the 1980s its historic dis-trict was restored to give a Victorian vil-lage atmosphere.

Skyline Caverns, 1mile from Front Royal on Rte 340 S.; tel: (540) 635-3185. This is one of the few places in the world

133

where the rare calcite formations known as anthodites can be seen – flower-like shapes which some call 'orchids of the mineral kingdom'. Underground streams and the **Rainbow Falls** – a 37 ft waterfall – are among the special features of the caverns. From Mar–mid Nov, weather permitting, a miniature train carries passengers along woodland tracks. Open daily 0900–1700 (mid Mar–mid June); Mon–Fri, Sat, Sun 0900–1800 (mid June–Labour Day), 0900–1700 (Labour Day–mid-Nov); Sat, Sun 0900–1800, daily 0900–1600 (mid Nov–mid Mar). Admission charge.

Belle Boyd Cottage, *101 Chester St; tel: (540) 636-1446.* During the Civil War Belle Boyd stayed here for two years while spying on Union forces and reporting back to the Confederates. Open daily May–Oct, rest of year Mon–Fri. Admission charge. **Warren Rifle Confederate Museum**, *Chester St; tel: (540) 639-6982.* A collection of weapons, battle flags, cavalry equipment, uniforms, pictures and personal items belonging to major Civil War figures. Admission charge.

NEW MARKET

Tourist Information: Shenandoah Valley Travel Association, *PO Box 1040; tel: (540) 740-3132.*

ACCOMMODATION

Hotel chains in the town include *QI.*

SIGHTSEEING

Hall of Valor Civil War Museum & New Market Battlefield State Historic Park, *PO Box 1864, Rte 305, Collins Parkway; tel: (540) 740-3101.* This is the battlefield where some 350 cadets from the Virginia Military Institute at Lexington were ordered into combat by the desperate Confederate Gen. John Breckenridge, whose troops were confronted by a pow-

erful Union force. The cadets helped win the day. For them it was a muddy and bloody initiation. Rain poured for almost all four days of their march to the battle-front, and 10 were killed and nearly 50 wounded in the fighting. **Hall of Valor** tells the poignant story of the day – 15 May 1864. Also on the site is a 19th-century-style farm. Open daily 0900–1700. Admission charge.

Meem's Bottom Covered Bridge, Rte 11, 4 miles north of New Market and about 2 miles south of Mount Jackson, on Rte 720. The 204-ft bridge spanning the north fork of the Shenandoah River carried traffic for more than 80 years before arsonists vandalised it in 1976. It has been rebuilt using some of the original timbers.

Endless Caverns, *PO Box 859, New Market* (5-mile drive from I-81); *tel: (540) 896-CAVE.* Guided tours of the caverns last 75 min, through a variety of colourful rock formations. Open daily. Admission charge.

LURAY

Tourist Information: Luray-Page County Chamber of Commerce, *46 E. Main St, Luray, Suite 1001; tel: (540) 743-3915.*

An attractive town within 10 miles of Shenandoah National Park. The population is greatly enlarged by the daily influx of visitors to the Luray Caverns.

ACCOMMODATION

A handful of local motels and inns, a 101-room **Ramada Inn**, the **Luray Caverns Motel** (one east and one west of the caverns' entrance) and one or two very hospitable Bed and Breakfast homes provide more than 1000 guest rooms, mostly in budget to moderate range. There are also self-catering cottage options in the area, including the riverside **Deerlane**

Cottages and Cabins, *PO Box 188; tel: (540) 567-3036*, where dogs are welcome. The romantic **Woodruff House B & B**, *330 Mechanic St, Luray; tel: (540) 743-1494*, described as 'fairytale Victorian', is popular with honeymoon and wedding anniversary couples – and with others, as the gourmet chef cooks breakfast and high tea.

EATING AND DRINKING

The town has fast-food outlets and privately-owned eateries. The **American Presidents Gallery Restaurant** is at the *Ramada Inn, Luray; tel: (540) 743-4521*.

SIGHTSEEING

Luray Caverns, 15 mins from I-81, Exit 264 on Rte 11, *PO Box 748, Luray; tel: (540) 743-6551*. Amid the huge and weird formations, the world's only 'stalacpipe' organ plays. After the caverns tour and a visit to the extensive gift shop, call at the **Car and Carriage Museum** next door (no extra charge) which has horse-drawn and early motorised vehicles and 19th-century baby perambulators. Open daily. Admission charge.

Luray Singing Tower, *PO Box 748, Luray* (adjoining Caverns)*; tel: (540) 743-6551*. Recitals from the 47-bell carillon on some afternoons and evenings in summer. Free admission.

Luray Reptile Center and Dinosaur Park, *Rte 1, Box 481, Luray; tel: (540) 743-4113*. A petting zoo, dinosaur park and various animals, birds and reptiles. Open daily mid Apr–Oct. Admission charge.

HARRISONBURG

Tourist Information: Harrisonburg-Rockingham Convention & Visitors Bureau, *800 Country Club Rd; tel: (540) 434-2319*.

This workaday city's main attraction is its proximity to a number of the state's lovely recreational areas within a half-hour drive. Harrisonburg also offers good shopping.

ACCOMMODATION AND FOOD

Motel chains include *CI, DI, EL*. Among other budget-priced motels are **Shoney's Inn, Hampton Inn, HoJo Inn** and the **Village Inn**. In the moderate range is the **Sheraton Harrisonburg Inn**. Ten miles east of the city is the up-market **Massanutten Resort**; *tel: (540) 289-4954*, with winter skiing and a range of leisure activities in the other seasons. There are also nearby out-of-town Bed and Breakfasts.

For dining try **Purgo's**, *1691 E. Market St, Harrisonburg; tel: (540) 433-5000*.

SIGHTSEEING

Eastern Mennonite University, two miles north-west on Rte 42; *tel: (540) 432-4000*. A number of Mennonites live in the Harrisonburg region. The University library has Mennonite books dating from the 16th century. Visitors may see the Art Gallery and shows in the Planetarium by appointment. Open daily in term time except Sun. Free admission.

James Madison University, *S. Main St, Harrisonburg; tel: (540) 568-3621*, has the Sawmill Art Gallery and the Miller Hall Planetarium on campus and accessible to the public. Phone for opening times. Free.

George Washington National Forest, *PO Box 233, Harrisonburg; tel: (560) 564-8300*. More than a million acres offering scenic drives, camping, picnicking, fishing, boating, cycling, hiking and lake swimming. Part of the Appalachian Trail passes through the forest. Free admission in most areas.

SHENANDOAH NATIONAL PARK

The names of two geographical features are inescapably and romantically linked to Virginia by song in the public mind: the Shenandoah River and the Blue Ridge Mountains. The link is strengthened by the fact that the Blue Ridge Parkway Skyline Drive, which covers the length of the Shenandoah National Park, is Virginia's second most popular tourist attraction, drawing some two million visitors a year.

Straddling the crest of the Blue Ridge Mountains, Shenandoah national park covers 195,000 acres and extends for about 80 miles, from Front Royal south to Waynesboro, varying in width from one mile to about 13 miles. With a maximum speed limit of 35 mph, it can be crossed from end to end in less than three hours – but only those with a soul of stone could fail to stop and take in the many stunning views. For those with time on their hands, there are places to stay and eat.

The Blue Ridge Parkway – better known in Virginia as the Skyline Drive – extends much further: from Waynesboro it continues south for about 350 miles to link up with the Great Smokey Mountain National Park in North Carolina.

In many places, the Parkway runs close to the great Appalachian Trail, which extends some 2000 miles from Maine to Georgia. About 95 miles of the trail wind through the Shenandoah National Park.

Concrete posts located every tenth of a mile help travellers to know exactly where they are. Distances are measured from Front Royal and the posts are on the right-hand side of the highway as you drive south. The park is open 24 hours a day, all year round, although Skyline Drive may be closed at times because of snow or other bad weather conditions. Admission: $5 per vehicle or $3 per person.

TOURIST INFORMATION

Shenandoah National Park, *Rte 4, PO Box 348, Luray, VA 22835; tel: (540) 999-2266.* The park headquarters is 4 miles east of Luray (see p.134) on Hwy 211. There are **visitor centres** at **Dickey Ridge** (Mile 4.6) and **Big Meadows** (Mile 51).

The free news-sheet, *Shenandoah Overlook*, obtained at park entrances, visitor centres and concession lodges, gives information about the park and current activities and events.

ARRIVING AND DEPARTING

There are four entrances to the park. From **Front Royal** (Alexandria–Harrisonburg route, p.133) access is via Hwy 340. **Thornton Gap** (see also p.128) entrance (Mile 31.5) interchanges with Hwy 211.

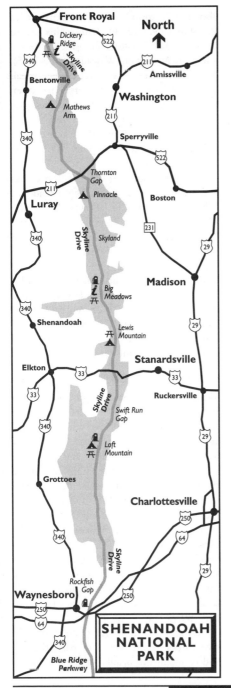

Swift Run Gap entrance interchanges with Hwy 33 at Mile 65.5. The park's southern entrance is at **Rockfish Gap**, accessed at Mile 105.4 from Hwy 150 and I-64.

GETTING AROUND

There are really only three ways of travelling through the park: by car, horseback or on foot. Cycling is frowned on and allowed only in specially designated parts of fire roads, campground roads and on Skyline Drive.

There are **petrol stations** just outside the north and south entrances to the park. From mid May–early Nov you can fill up at **Elkwallow Wayside**, **Big Meadows** and **Loft Mountain Wayside**, 0900–1800.

Horse riders should be in their element with more than 150 miles of trails and fire roads where riding is permitted. The trails are marked with a yellow blaze. Visitors may bring their own horses (May–Oct) or rental is available from **ARAMark Skyline**, *PO Box 727, 21 N. Broad St, Luray, VA 22835; tel: (540) 999-2210.* The stables are at **Skyland** (Mile 42.5) and a guide accompanies all trips. Another company offering guided trail rides in the park is **Skyline Ranch**, *Rte 4, PO Box 205, Front Royal, VA 22630; tel: (540) 636-6061.*

The park has some 300 miles of varied hiking trails, including a section of the **Appalachian Trail**, which is marked with a white blaze. All other trails, except for a few short, easy walks, are marked with a blue blaze.

A number of private companies offer hiking holidays in the park and surrounding countryside. **Hiking Holidays**, *PO Box 750, Bristol, VT 05443; tel: (802) 453-4816*, organises five-day hiking trips within the park. **Mountain Memory**

137

Walks, *PO Box 164B, North Conway, NH 03860; tel: (800) 869-0949*, has five-day trips in the park and elsewhere in the Blue Ridge Mountains, as does **North Wind Touring**, *PO Box 46, Waitsfield, VT 05673; tel: (800) 496-557*. **Wayfaring Travelers**, *27 Sunnyview Dr., Phoenix, MD 21131-2036; tel: (410) 666-7456*, offers two-week trips through the Shenandoah Valley.

STAYING IN SHENANDOAH NATIONAL PARK

Accommodation

Two **lodges** – at Skyland (Mile 41.7) and Big Meadows (Mile 51.2) - offer motel-type accommodation and rustic cabins for rent. A few **cabins** are also available at Lewis Mountain (Mile 57.5). The lodges are usually open early April-Nov and Lewis Mountain cabins May-late Oct. For summer it is advisable to book as early as possible with **ARA Virginia Skyline Co, Inc.**, *PO Box 727, Luray, VA 22835; tel: (800) 999-4714*.

The park has four campsites, each with pitches for tents and RVs. **Big Meadows campground** is the largest, with a total of 227 sites, but reservations are recommended May-Oct (the campsite is open Mar-Dec); *tel: (540) 999-2221*. The other campgrounds – **Mathews Arm** (Mile 22.2), **Lewis Mountain and Loft Mountain** (Mile 79.5) – are on a first-come first-served basis and are open May-Oct. Mathews Arm is the only campsite without showers and laundry facilities, and Lewis Mountain is the only one without an RV sewage disposal site.

Eating and Drinking

Meals and groceries may be purchased within the park. There are **dining halls** at Skyland and Big Meadows (where there is also a grill room) and a **restaurant** at Panorama (Mile 31.6). **Cafeterias** are to be found at Elkwallow Wayside (Mile 24) and Loft Mountain Wayside (Mile 79.5). The dining halls are closed between meals and after 2100. The cafeterias are open 0900–1800, and the Big Meadows grill room serves breakfast, lunch and snacks, but closes at 1730 during the summer. The Panorama Restaurant opens 1000–1800 and sometimes later.

Groceries, camping supplies, soft drinks and beer are available at Big Meadows, Elkwallow Wayside, Lewis Mountain Campstore and Loft Mountain Campstore.

The park has seven **picnic areas**, each with picnic tables, fireplaces, drinking fountains and toilets. They are at **Dickey Ridge** (Mile 4.7), **Elkwallow**, **Pinnacles** (Mile 36.7), **Big Meadows**, **Lewis Mountain**, **South River** (Mile 62.8) and **Loft Mountain**. Picnic tables can also be found at **Skyland** and at a number of places beside Skyline Drive.

SIGHTSEEING

Whether you travel through Shenandoah National Park by car, on horseback or on foot, sightseeing will be your principal activity. The park is in an area of heavily forested ridges and valleys and there are many stunning views. There are more than 60 peaks reaching more than 2000 ft – the highest, **Hawksbill**, is 4049 ft and is located about halfway along the park.

There are many **waterfalls**, some plunging more than 80 ft, but only one is visible from Skyline Drive. Unnamed, it is at Mile 1.4 and is dry at certain times of the year. The 70-ft **Dark Hollow** cascade is a 0.7 mile walk from the Drive at Mile 50.7.

Along the Drive there are about 70 **overlooks** where you can park the car and drink in the beauty of the Piedmont spread out below or gaze across the Shenandoah River at the forested ridges marching westwards towards the Allegheny Mountains.

Wildlife

The park is home to a wide range of wildlife, including an estimated 500 **black bears**. Some experts believe that the **mountain lion**, officially believed to be extinct in Virginia, still roams the park. There are two species of poisonous snake: the **copperhead** and **rattlesnake**.

Less fearsome species found in the park are Virginia white-tail deer, red and grey foxes, skunk, bobcat, raccoon, groundhog and chipmunk.

The birds most commonly seen, especially from Skyline Drive, are the **turkey vulture** and **black vulture**. The turkey vulture, also known as a buzzard, has a wingspan up to six ft, a red head and soars in a rocking motion with its wings forming a shallow 'V'. The smaller black vulture has a pale patch on the underside of each wing and flaps its wings more frequently than the buzzard.

Wild turkeys, the largest of the park's bird species, are frequently seen, especially in the northern section. Other prominent species are the **ruffed grouse**, sometimes mistaken for a chicken as it scurries across the Drive, and the **woodcock**, well camouflaged with its mottled plumage but unmistakable once you see its disproportionately long beak.

More than 1000 species of plantlife are found in the park, including 18 types of orchid. Picking flowers is forbidden. Most of the park's trees are deciduous, with oaks and hickories predominating.

WAYNESBORO

Tourist Information: Augusta-Staunton-Waynesboro Visitors Bureau, *PO Box 446, Rte 1, Afton, VA; tel: (540) 943-5187.*

Waynesboro–East Augusta Chamber of Commerce, *301 W. Main St, Waynesboro, VA 22980; tel: (540) 949-8203.*

ACCOMMODATION AND FOOD

The closest community to the park's southern entrance, Waynesboro has limited facilities, but standards are reasonable.

Comfort Inn Waynesboro, *640 W. Broad St; tel: (540) 942-1171,* has a pool and 75 rooms in the budget-moderate range. **Days Inn,** *2060 Rosser Ave; tel: (540) 943-1101,* is also in the budget-moderate category, with a pool, restaurant and 98 rooms. The moderately priced **Holiday Inn,** 4 miles east on Hwy 250 at the junction with Skyline Drive and I-64; *tel: (540) 942-6201,* has 118 rooms, heated pool, restaurant and bar.

The Iris Inn, *191 Chinquapin Dr.; tel: (540) 943-1991,* is a moderately priced Bed and Breakfast inn, non-smoking, with seven rooms and balconies overlooking the Shenandoah Valley.

The **Fox and Hounds Pub,** *533 W. Main St; tel: (540) 946-9200,* offers budget–moderate dining in a house which both sides used as a hospital during the Civil War.

SIGHTSEEING

Waynesboro has two art galleries. The **Moss Museum,** *2150 Rosser Ave; tel: (540) 949-6473,* is dedicated to the work of the artist P. Buckley Moss. Open daily 1000–1600. Admission free.

Shenandoah Valley Art Center, *600 W. Main St; tel: (540) 949-7662,* displays local and visiting exhibits and has studios with working artists. Open Tues-Sat 1000–1600, Sun 1400–1600. Admission: free.

HARRISONBURG–LEXINGTON

This route reveals the diversity of Virginia's picturesque scenery as it moves from the upper reaches of the Shenandoah Valley (see also pp. 136–139) to the rail city of Staunton, renowned as the birthplace of Woodrow Wilson and for its splendid Museum of American Frontier Culture. From Staunton the route heads west through the George Washington National Forest, then climbs into the highlands of the Shenandoah and Allegheny Mountains before descending again to Lexington, home of the Virginia Military Institute and final resting place for Generals Robert E. Lee and Stonewall Jackson.

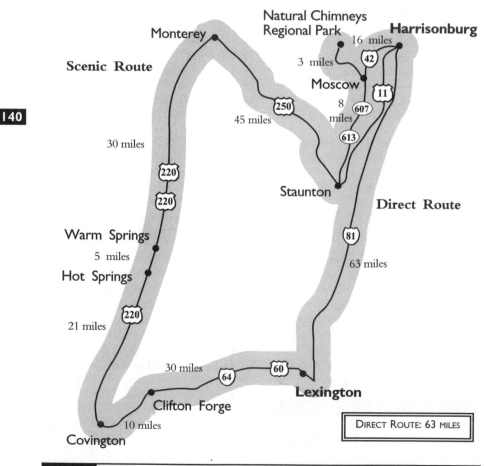

Natural Chimneys Regional Park

Monterey

Harrisonburg

16 miles

Scenic Route

3 miles

42

Moscow

11

250

8 miles

607

45 miles

613

30 miles

Staunton

Direct Route

220

220

81

Warm Springs

63 miles

5 miles

Hot Springs

220

21 miles

30 miles

64

60

Clifton Forge

Lexington

10 miles

DIRECT ROUTE: 63 MILES

Covington

ROUTES

DIRECT ROUTE

From downtown Harrisonburg, take Hwy 33 east for 2 miles, then I-81 south for a further 59 miles. A final 2-mile stretch west on Hwy 60, and you will be in Lexington in around an hour.

SCENIC ROUTE

This adds about 100 miles to the trip, which will take about three hours if you keep going. But the scenery is almost certain to slow you down, and you may want to make an overnight stop.

Between Harrisonburg and **Staunton** (pronounced 'Stanton') you can choose Hwy 11, which runs more or less alongside I-81 – though it is a quieter, more scenic route – or the rustic Rte 42, which you can take for 16 miles to the village of **Moscow**.

From Moscow you can make a 3-mile detour by turning right on to Rte 731 to **Natural Chimneys Regional Park**; *Rte 1, Mount Solon; tel: (540) 350-2510*. The park is named after the strange limestone formations which look like factory chimneys. A campsite in the park has 120 pitches with water and electricity hookups. To continue from Moscow, head south on Rte 607 for 5 miles. After crossing Rte 612, continue south on Rte 613, which leads into *Spring Hill Rd,* Staunton, after 3 miles. A left turn onto *Churchville Ave* leads into downtown Staunton, where the visitor bureau is well signposted. Heading west, *Churchville Ave* becomes Hwy 250, which winds its way up and down for 45 miles through the **George Washington National Forest**, past the 3760-ft **Shenandoah Mountain** and on through alpine scenery to the neat little town of **Monterey**, seat of Highland County. From here Hwy 220 heads south

across open country, with the West Virginia state line never far away, to reach **Covington** in 56 miles. On the way Hwy 220 passes through the spa towns of **Warm Springs** and **Hot Springs**, and the spectacular Homestead resort.

From Covington, Hwy 60 and I-64 combine, heading east to Lexington passing **Clifton Forge** on the way. Some 23 miles after Clifton Forge, take Exit 50, where Hwy 60 south leads into downtown **Lexington** after 6 miles. Again, the way to the visitor center is well marked.

STAUNTON

Tourist Information: Augusta–Staunton–Waynesboro Travel Information Center, *1303 Richmond Ave at I-81* (Exit 222); *tel: (540) 332-3972* or *(800) 332-5219*; open daily 0900–1700; **Augusta–Staunton–Waynesboro Visitors Bureau**, *116 W. Beverley St; tel: (540) 332-5219*; Mon–Sat 0900—1700, Sun 1200–1700 (summer), Mon–Sat 1000–1600, Sun 1200–1600 (winter). Although it is small, the bureau is well stocked with brochures on attractions, dining and accommodation in the city and surrounding area. The staff are friendly and extremely helpful.

141

ACCOMMODATION

An important rail city – Amtrak trains still stop there – Staunton has a good selection of accommodation. Hotel chains include *BW, CI, DI, EL* and *Hd.* **Shoney's Inn**, *Rte 4 at I-81 (Exit 222); tel: (540) 885-3117* or *(800) 222-2222*, has budget-priced accommodation as well as a restaurant open Sun–Thur 0600–2300, Fri–Sat 0600–0100. Among the city's inns, **Belle Grae**, *515 W. Frederick St; tel: (540) 886-5151*, is moderately priced with 15 rooms, some with private patios and balconies, in a restored Victorian mansion.

Thornrose House, *531 Thornrose Ave; tel: (540) 885-7026*, is a relaxed, family-style bed and breakfast establishment in a Georgian-revival house with wrap-around verandah and four-poster or brass beds in its five guest rooms. Non-smoking, it straddles the budget–moderate categories.

Ten independently owned country inns in the area are represented by **Virginia's Inns of the Shenandoah Valley**, *PO Box 1387, Staunton; tel: (800) 334-5575*.

Shenandoah Valley KOA, *PO Box 98, Verona, VA 24482; tel: (540) 248-2746* or *(800) 562-9949*. The campsite is 5 miles north of Staunton. From I-81, Exit 227, head west on Rte 612 for 1½ miles to Hwy 11, then head north for half a mile and follow Rte 781 west for 1 mile to the entrance. The site has pitches for RVs and tents and cabins for rent and offers swimming and fishing.

EATING AND DRINKING

Staunton has been an important rail centre since 1854, so it is not surprising that two of its most popular restaurants – in the budget–moderate category – are actually part of the station.

The Depot Grille, *42 Middlebrook Ave; tel: (540) 885-7332*, is located in the station's old freight depot and features a 50-ft antique oak bar. The menu features fresh fish, Black Angus sirloin and seafood platters. There is a wide selection of beers and wines from around the world. Open Sun–Thur 1100–2230, Fri–Sat 1100–2330. **The Pullman Restaurant**, *36 Middlebrook Ave; tel: (540) 885-6612*, at the passenger end of the station, has a Victorian ice-cream parlour and a magnificent polished brass and shiny wood buffet area, seen at its best for Sunday brunch. Its menu includes dishes based on old time dining-car meals and includes steaks,

seafood, chicken, sandwiches and lighter fare. The Pullman is open daily for lunch and dinner.

About 12 miles west of Staunton, at **Churchville** on Rte 250 (the road to Monterey), the **Buckhurst Inn**; *tel: (540) 337-6900*, is a moderately priced establishment serving traditional Shenandoah Valley dishes. Open Tues–Thur 1100–2000, Fri 1100–2100, Sat 1600–2100, Sun 1200–2000. The Buckhurst also has Bed and Breakfast accommodation.

Staunton's visitor bureau has a dining and lodging leaflet which lists about 30 eating places in the area, in addition to a similar number of hotels and inns.

SIGHTSEEING

An informative leaflet, with map and details of self-guided walking tours through the city's five historic districts – each listed in the National Register – is available from the visitor bureau.

Jumbo Antique Fire Engine, *500 N. Augusta St; tel: (540)332-3884*. This beautifully restored 1911 Robinson pumper – the only one surviving – will appeal to those who admire antique vehicles. Admission free.

Museum of American Frontier Culture, clearly signposted on *Hwy 250 west* (Exit 222 from I-81); *tel: (540) 332-7850*. One of the best 'living museums' in the Capital Region tells the story of American pioneer settlement in four reconstructed authentic farms. The extensive and attractive site includes a large and informative visitor centre. The lifestyle of an English yeoman and his family is brought to life in a 17th-century farmhouse and rural buildings shipped from Worcestershire and Sussex, England. Life in the early 18th century is depicted in an 18th- century town farm from Hördt in Germany, and a 19th-century Ulster farm shows what life was like for many people in Northern Ireland before they moved to the Shenandoah Valley. The museum's fourth farm shows the influence of European cultures on a Virginian farm just before the Civil War. Demonstrations of traditional crafts and special festivals and events take place year-round. Open daily 0900–1700 (mid Mar–end Nov), 1000–1600 (Dec–mid Mar). Admission: $7.

Trinity Episcopal Church, *214 W. Beverley St; tel: (540) 886-9132*, was built in 1855 on the site of the 18th-century Augusta Parish Church. It contains several stained-glass windows by Louis Comfort Tiffany. Open Mon–Fri. Admission free.

Woodrow Wilson Birthplace and Museum, *18 N. Coalter St; tel: (540) 885-0897*. The 28th president of the US was born in the Greek Revival manse in 1856 when his father was a Presbyterian minister. It includes 7 galleries featuring the life and times of the president who introduced prohibition and women's suffrage. Open daily 0900–1700 (Mar–Nov), 1000–1600 (Dec–Feb). Admission charge.

MONTEREY

Tourist Information: Highland County Chamber of Commerce, *PO Box 223, Main St, Monterey, VA 244465; tel: (540) 468-2550*. The chamber maintains a visitor centre, offering advice and literature on attractions, dining and lodging throughout the Western Highlands area. Open Mon–Fri 0900–1600.

Monterey is a small town, so amenities are thin on the ground. The best place for accommodation and dining is the budget–moderate Victorian **Highland Inn**, *Main St; tel: (540) 468-2143*, a Virginia Historic Landmark listed on the National Register of Historic Places. The town has one motel, the **Montvallee Motel**, *Main St; tel: (540) 468-2500;* budget.

A major industry in the area is maple syrup production, and the chamber of commerce runs the **Little Highland Maple Museum**, *Rte 220 south; tel: (540) 468-2550*. It is located on the outskirts of town in a replica old-time sugar house, where exhibits feature traditional and modern processes in making maple syrup and sugar. Admission by donation. During the second and third weekends in Mar each year, Monterey is the centre of the **Highland County Maple Festival** when tastings, demonstrations and exhibitions are staged throughout the area.

The area's chief attractions are its magnificent alpine scenery (Monterey has an elevation of 2881 ft), and outdoors activities. The visitor centre has details.

WARM SPRINGS

Tourist Information: see Hot Springs, p. 144.

Thirty miles south of Monterey, Hwy 220 becomes 'Thermal Springs Alley'. Warm Springs is closely followed by Hot Springs, Healing Spring and Falling Spring. Warm Springs has a number of historic buildings and lies at the foot of Little Mountain. During spring and autumn it is a particularly attractive centre for hiking and sightseeing.

The moderately priced **Inn at Gristmill Square**, *PO Box 359, Rte 619, Warm Springs, VA 24484; tel: (540) 839-2231*, has 17 apartments in five restored 19th-century buildings. It has a pool, sauna and bar (open 1700–2200) and the moderate–pricey **Waterwheel Restaurant**. Complimentary continental breakfast. **Three Hills Inn and Cottages**, *PO Box 9, Hwy 220, Warm Springs, VA 24484; tel: (540) 839-5381*, offers a wide range of accommodation in the budget–expensive brackets. **Warm Springs Inn**, *PO Box 99, Hwy 220,*

143

Warm Springs; VA 24484; tel: (540) 839-5351, has budget-priced rooms and moderately priced suites; restaurant. Ten other bed and breakfast inns are listed in a leaflet published by Bath County Chamber of Commerce.

Bath County Historical Society Museum, located in a cottage in *Courthouse Sq; tel: (540) 839-2543,* has a genealogical library as well as exhibits of local historical artefacts. Open Mon–Fri 1000–1600 (May–Oct). Admission free.

HOT SPRINGS

Tourist Information: Bath County Chamber of Commerce, *PO Box 718, Main St, Hot Springs, VA 24445; tel: (540) 839-5409,* offers tourist information and leaflets on accommodation and lodging throughout the county.

An attractive village with an alpine ambience (elevation 2238 ft), Hot Springs is dominated by the massive presence of **The Homestead**, *tel: (540) 839-1766 or (800) 838-1776.* What began as a spa pool and bathhouse in 1776 has developed into a monolithic resort hotel with 521 rooms and suites, a dozen cafés and restaurants, meeting facilities and shops. Recreation facilities spread over 15,000 acres include three golf courses – The Cascades is regarded as the finest mountain course in the US – shooting, tennis, horse-riding, trout fishing, biking, hiking, skiing and skating. The hot springs are still in use. Other amenities include a library, cinema and a mile-long airstrip. Expensive–pricey.

Roseloe, *Rte 2,* off Hwy 220, 3 miles north of Hot Springs; *tel: (540) 839-5373,* is a 14-room motel with budget-priced accommodation and a restaurant nearby. **Vine Cottage Inn**, *Hwy 220,* near The Homestead entrance; *tel: (540) 839-2422,* is a budget–moderate Bed and Breakfast establishment.

Sam Snead's Tavern, *Main St; tel: (540) 839-7666,* is a prominent pub-cum-restaurant offering such specialities as fresh mountain trout and Black Angus steaks on a budget–pricey menu.

COVINGTON

Tourist Information: Alleghany Highlands Chamber of Commerce, *241 W. Main St, Covington, VA 24426; tel: (540) 962-2178 or (800) 628-8092.*

The largest community in the Highlands area, Covington (population 7000) is a commercial and industrial centre, with companies involved in robotics, fibre optics, paper board, plastics, computer technology and communications.

Hotel chains in Covington are *CI, Hd.* **Milton Hall**, *207 Thorny Lane, Callaghan, Covington, VA 24426; tel: (540) 695-0196,* is an English-style manor offering moderate–expensive Bed and Breakfast. Callaghan is 5 miles west of Covington and the manor, built by Viscountess Milton in 1874, is off Rte 600.

A downtown focal point is **The Craft Shops of Covington**, a regional craft market for handmade pottery, textiles, glass and other collectables, at *120 W. Main St; tel: (540) 962-0557.* Open Mon–Sat 1000–1800, Sun 1300–1800.

Fort Young, *W. Riverview Dr., I-64 Exit 14,* is a reconstruction of the fort designed by George Washington for the French and Indian war in 1756. **Humpback Bridge**, *Midland Trail, I-64 Exit 10,* is the only surviving curved-span covered bridge in the US. The mid 19th-century structure is 100 ft long and its centre is 8 ft than each end.

Lake Moomaw, 13 miles north of Covington on Rte 600 (follow signs to Gathright Dam); *tel: (540) 962-2214,* is 12 miles long and is surrounded by recreation areas with facilities for boating, fishing, camping, picnicking and hiking. Open daily. Admission charge.

CLIFTON FORGE

Tourist Information: Alleghany Highlands Chamber of Commerce, *403 E. Ridgeway, Clifton Forge, VA 24422; tel: (540) 862-4969.*

The town's name reflects the time when for more than a century this was the centre of a flourishing iron industry.

Alleghany Highlands Arts and Crafts Center, *439 E. Ridgeway; tel: (540) 862-4447.* Galleries feature work produced by Highlands artists and crafts-people whose work in pottery, wood, glass, needlework, water-colour, oils and other media, may be purchased in the shop. Open Mon–Sat 1030–1630 (May–Dec); Tues–Sat 1030–1630 (Jan–Apr).

C & O Historical Society Archives, *312 E. Ridgeway; tel: (540) 862-2210.* With its collection of Chesapeake and Ohio Railroad artefacts, uniforms, photographs and memorabilia, this is the place for railway buffs. Open Mon–Sat 0800–1700. Admission free.

Stonewall Theatre, *510 Main St; tel: (540) 862-7407.* Built circa 1905, this is now a performing arts centre specialising in Appalachian music and drama.

LEXINGTON

Tourist Information: Lexington Visitors Center, *106 E. Washington St, Lexington, VA 24450; tel: (540) 463-3777.* Exhibits and a slide show introduce visitors to the city and its heritage. Travel advisers are on hand to help with information, directions, maps and a calendar of events. An accommodations gallery has information on local hotels and inns, a direct-dial phone to some establishments and a pay phone. The centre has toilets, a water fountain and soda machine and there are picnic tables in the grounds. Open daily 0900–1700; 0830–1800 (June–Aug).

ACCOMMODATION

Lexington and the surrounding area has a total of more than 40 hotels, motels, inns, Bed and Breakfast establishments and tourist homes. Hotel chains include *BW, CI, DI, EL, Hd, HJ, Rm*. There is a good concentration of inns and Bed and Breakfast homes in the downtown area.

Blue and Grey B&B, *401 S. Main St; tel: (540) 463-6260.* Four blocks south-west of the visitor centre, this graceful Victorian house is furnished with Civil War period antiques, has a wrap-around porch and an outdoor pool. Moderate. **Brierley Hill Country Inn**, *Borden Rd; tel: (540) 464-8421.* Located on eight acres off Rte 6, 1½ miles west of the visitor centre, the tastefully decorated inn has a verandah and magnificent country views. Country breakfast, dinner by reservation. Moderate–expensive. **The Keep**, *116 Lee Ave; tel: (540) 463-3560.* This 1891 house in the downtown historic district has one double room and one suite and offers off-street parking. Moderate.

Seven Hills Inn, *408 S. Main St; tel: (540) 463-4715*, is a restored Southern Colonial manse with seven deluxe rooms individually furnished with antiques or reproductions. Moderate–expensive.

Natural Bridge/Lexington KOA Campground, *PO Box 148, Natural Bridge, VA 24578* (Hwy 11, 9 miles south of Lexington); *tel: (540) 291-2770 or (800) KOA-8541.* Full hook-up RV sites, tent pitches and cabins; store, laundry, recreation room, pool. **Long's Campground**, *PO Box 127A, Lexington, VA 24450* (Rte 39, 5 miles west of Lexington), has RV sites with full hook-ups, cabins and trailer rentals. Store, laundry, playground, 18-hole mini-golf.

145

EATING AND DRINKING

The area has more than 50 eating places, ranging from fast-food establishments to fine dining restaurants, with a choice of regional and ethnic cuisines.

Blue Heron Cafe, *110 W. Washington St; tel: (540) 463-2800*, has home-made vegetarian dishes and daily specials. Open Mon–Fri 1130–1430. Budget–moderate.

Country Cookin', *439 E. Nelson St; tel: (540) 463-3044*, offers unlimited salad, vegetables and dessert with every meal at no extra cost. Open Sun–Thur 1100–2100, Fri–Sat 1100–2200. Cheap–budget.

Harb's Bistro, *19 W. Washington St; tel: (540) 464-1900*. A lively café with patio service featuring filling sandwiches in freshly-baked bread; candlelit dinners. Open Sun 0900–1500, Mon 0800–1500, Tues–Thur 0800–2100, Fri–Sat 0800–2200. Budget–moderate.**Hunan Garden Restaurant**, *401 E. Nelson St; tel: (540) 463-3330*. Authentic Chinese cuisine; take-away and delivery service. Open daily 1100–2200. Budget–moderate.

Il Palazzo, *24 N. Main St; tel: (540) 464-5800*. Traditional Italian cuisine, featuring pasta dishes, fresh seafood and pizza. Open daily 1100–2300. Moderate. **Willson–Walker House**, *30 N. Main St; tel: (540) 463-3020*, offers creative American cuisine in an 1820 Classic Revival house. Open Tues–Sat 1130–1430, 1730–2100. Moderate–pricey.

SIGHTSEEING

Lexington's chief attraction is the city itself, with its pleasant streets of quaint shops and houses, its gracious southern-style homes, and the Greek Revivalist splendour of the Virginia Military Institute. Half a dozen routes are detailed in a **walking tours** leaflet available at the visitor centre.

An excellent introduction is given by

Lexington Carriage Company; *tel: (540) 463-5647*, whose horse-drawn carriage tours begin at the visitor centre. Daily 0900–1730 (June–Aug), 0930–1630 (Apr–May, Sept–Oct). Tours last about 50 mins and cost up to $9 depending on age.

George C. Marshall Museum and Library, *Virginia Military Institute; tel: (540) 463-7103*. Exhibits trace the career of the World War II General who won the Nobel Peace Prize. Open daily 0900–1700 (Mar–Oct), 0900–1600 (Nov–Feb). Admission: $3.

Lee Chapel and Museum, *Washington and Lee University; tel: (540) 463-8768*. The chapel was built in 1867 under the supervision of Gen. Robert E. Lee, later president of the university. Open Mon–Sat 0900–1700 (Apr–Oct), 0900–1600 (Nov–Mar), Sun 1400–1700 (all year round). Admission free.

Stonewall Jackson House, *8 E. Washington St; tel: (540) 463-2552*. The only home the Civil War hero ever owned interprets his life as a citizen of Lexington, professor at the Virginia Military Institute, church leader and family man. Open Mon–Sat 0900–1700, Sun 1300–1700; Mon–Sat 0900–1800 (June–Aug). Admission: $4. **Stonewall Jackson Memorial Cemetery**, *S. Main St.* The cemetery contains the grave and a statue of Gen. Jackson and is the burial place of more than 100 Confederate soldiers. Open daily dawn–dusk. Admission free.

Virginia Military Institute and Museum; *tel: (540) 464-7232*. Founded in 1839, the VMI is the nation's oldest state-supported military college. Full dress parades are staged most Fri afternoons. Exhibits in the museum, in the Jackson Memorial Hall, illustrate the history and traditions of the institute. Open Mon–Sat 0900–1700, Sun 1400–1700. Admission free.

LEXINGTON–ROANOKE

This is a short, but very attractive route through beautiful countryside flanked by the George Washington and Jefferson National Forests. It links the small academic city of Lexington with lively Roanoke and provides an opportunity to view one of the great natural wonders of the world – the massive Natural Bridge.

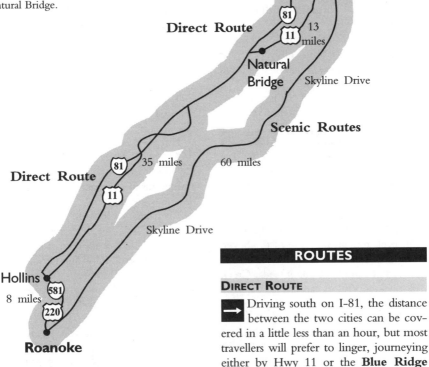

DIRECT ROUTE: 54 MILES

ROUTES

DIRECT ROUTE

Driving south on I-81, the distance between the two cities can be covered in a little less than an hour, but most travellers will prefer to linger, journeying either by Hwy 11 or the **Blue Ridge Parkway Skyline Drive**. All three are reached from downtown Lexington by way of Hwy 60 east. With a 35 mph speed limit, Skyline Drive is the slowest route. Hwy 11 is a good compromise – it runs alongside the interstate, switching sides now and then, and of course it takes you to **Natural Bridge**. The mileage for each route is more or less the same.

SCENIC ROUTE

From Lexington's visitor centre, travel north along *E. Washington St* for three blocks, turning left on to *Jefferson St* for one block, then left again on to *Nelson St* (Hwy 60 east). This reaches Hwy 11 in ½ mile, or you could continue 6 miles to **Skyline Drive** at **Buena Vista** and follow this route through the **Blue Ridge Mountains** to Roanoke. From Hwy 60 (east), **Natural Bridge** is 12 miles south on Hwy 11.

Hwy 11 continues to the outskirts of Roanoke, where it joins Hwy 220 near the suburb of **Hollins** for about a mile and a half before peeling off to the left as *Williamson Road*, which leads into downtown **Roanoke** in less than 4 miles.

NATURAL BRIDGE

Tourist Information: Natural Bridge Village, *PO Box 57, Natural Bridge, VA 24578; tel: (540) 291-2121 or (800) 533-1410.*

The 90-ft span of Natural Bridge is part of Rte 11, but you may scarcely be aware of it, even though it is one of the Seven Natural Wonders of the World, until you marvel at it from the bank of Cedar Creek 215 ft below. Visitors can also see the Wax Museum and, in summer, explore the deep caverns beneath the bridge area. In spite of its tourist attractions, Natural Bridge remains remarkably rural. The resident population is only about 200.

ACCOMMODATION

On the privately-owned Natural Bridge complex is the **Natural Bridge Inn and Conference Center**, Hwy 11 and Rte 130 (exits 175 and 180 off I-81), *PO Box 57, Natural Bridge; tel: (540) 291-2121 or (800) 533-1410.* There is a mix of corporate guests and family vacationers, who can visit the Natural Bridge, Caverns and Wax Museum at discounted rates. There are hiking trails and an indoor pool at the inn. Rates, mainly moderate, vary from budget to expensive.

Budget Inn, Rte 2, Rte 11 south, *PO Box 603, Natural Bridge; tel: (540) 291-2896*, is a small inn with rooms at budget rates.

Fancy Hill Motel, *Rte 2, PO Box 590, Natural Bridge; tel: (540) 291-2143.* Budget to moderate. Newly renovated property in a rural setting at intersection of Rte 11 and I-81.

Red Mill Inn Bed and Breakfast, *Rte 1, Box 447, Natural Bridge; tel: (540) 291-1704.* Formerly a working tavern and mill, this attractive property is newly restored and furnished with antiques. Children are welcome. Expensive.

Burger's Country Inn, *Rte 2, Box 564, Natural Bridge; tel: (540) 291-2464*, has four rooms (each with fireplace and antique furniture) priced at $55, based on double occupancy.

Breford Cottage Bed and Breakfast, *PO Box 1, Natural Bridge; tel: (540) 291-2217*, a modern non-smoking home, charges $95 for one person or two sharing, with $10 for each extra person in a room which sleeps up to five – a very modest price for a family.

There are at least two handy campsites. **Campground at Natural Bridge**, (exit 180 off I-81, then follow signs) *PO Box 266, Natural Bridge Station; tel: (540) 291-2727.* Set by the James River adjoining Jefferson Natural Forest, it has 175 sites and full hook-up facilities. Canoeing, fishing, hiking and mini-golf are among the activities, and there's a games room.

Cave Mountain Lake Recreation

Area, *Rte I-81, PO Box 10, Natural Bridge Station; tel: (540) 291-2188.* A 22-pitch campsite in Jefferson National Forest with showers, toilets, picnic tables. Open May–Oct.

EATING AND DRINKING

On site at Natural Bridge, the **Colonial Dining Room** at the **Natural Bridge Inn and Conference Center**, *tel: (540) 291-2121,* offers fine dining with seafood specials on Fri, rib specials on Sat and Sun buffets. Moderate.

Fancy Hill Restaurant (see Fancy Hill Motel, above), *tel: (540) 291-2860,* is a full service family restaurant with plenty of choice on the menu and beer and wine available. Budget to Moderate.

Corner Grill and Restaurant, *Rte 130, Natural Bridge Station; tel: (540) 291-2521.* Sandwiches, burgers and sundaes daily, Mon–Wed 0700–2000, Thur–Sat 0700–2100 and Sun 0800–2000. Budget.

SIGHTSEEING

Natural Bridge itself cannot fail to impress. Indians many centuries ago worshipped it as 'the Bridge of God'. It is 90 ft long and its width varies from 50 ft to 150 ft.

George Washington was a young assistant surveyor in a team employed by Lord Fairfax, to survey his vast holdings in Virginia in which the Natural Bridge was situated. Washington carved his initials 23 ft up on the bridge wall. They can still be seen nearly 250 years later. Thomas Jefferson was so enraptured by the bridge's natural limestone arch that in 1774 he bought it, and more than 160 acres around it, for 20 shillings. It remains in private ownership to this day.

When you've bought your ticket at the admission desk in the gift shop, you can either board the **shuttle bus** which will transport you to the bridge or, preferably, take the short downhill walk beside the creek which tumbles over its rocky bed. On the way, if you walk, you will see *abor vitae* trees said to be more than 1600 years old. (You can use the shuttle bus for the uphill trip back.)

A nightly performance of a music and light show, **Drama of Creation**, provides a different perspective of the Natural Bridge.

Natural Bridge is open daily, summer 0800–2200, winter 0800–1800. Drama of Creation is show presented nightly after dark. Admission $8, children $4.

Further natural attractions at the site are the **Caverns of Natural Bridge**; *tel: (540) 291-2121,* the deepest on the east coast, equal to 34 storeys beneath the earth's surface. Guided tours are held between Mar and Nov. Open daily mid Mar–Nov 1000–1700, closed Dec–mid Mar. Admission $7, children $3.50.

Another part of the complex is the **Wax Museum**; *tel: (540) 291-2426,* with more than 125 figures from history – much of it local history – set in appropriate scenery and animated with some clever sound, lighting and electronic techniques. A tour of the Wax Museum factory is included in the admission charge.

Natural Bridge Zoo; *tel: (540) 291-2420,* has more than 400 reptiles, birds and animal. There's a petting area, a breeding centre for endangered species, a gift shop and picnic area. Open daily in summer from 0900, closed in winter. Admission $6, seniors $5, children aged 3-12 years $4, under 3 free.

ROANOKE

Tourist Information: Roanoke Valley Convention and Visitors Bureau, *Marketplace Center, 114 Market Place; tel: (540) 342-6025 or (800) 635-5535*

149

Information and brochures are available on all aspects of tourism, and the bureau is open daily 0900–1700.

Roanoke Valley Visitor Information Center, off I-81 and exit 143 and mile post 120 off *Blue Ridge Parkway* (signposted); *tel: (540) 345-8622.* Visitor services include reservations. Open daily 0900–1700.

A go-ahead city set between the Blue Ridge Parkway and the Appalachian Trail, Roanoke offers the best of both worlds – the culture, shopping, entertainment and services of a city and the recreational pursuits and beauty of the nearby mountains. The city has a population of nearly 100,000, and more than twice that number live in the communities of the Roanoke Valley.

ACCOMMODATION

With nearly a dozen hotels, motels and inns handy for the downtown area, another 10 near Roanoke Municipal Airport, others in Salem and other parts of the metropolis, and a number of bed and breakfast houses, the district offers a wide choice of accommodation. In the valley area and along the I-81 and Blue Ridge Parkway corridor are more than a dozen campsites, some of which are open year-round.

Hotel chains in Roanoke include *BW, CI, DI, EL, Hd, HJ, Ma, QI, Rd, Rm* and *TL.*

Top of the range in the downtown area is the **Hotel Roanoke and Conference Center**, *110 Shenandoah Ave, Roanoke; tel: (540) 985-5900.* The hotel, in the expensive category, has been welcoming guests since 1882. The present structure, dating from the 1930s, has been completely restored, with nearly 350 rooms and suites. The Conference Center is new, providing high technology meeting space. A $6.5

million glass–enclosed bridge, completed in 1995, gives easy access over the Norfolk-Southern railway tracks to Roanoke's award-winning market area.

Radisson Patrick Henry Hotel, *617 S. Jefferson St, Roanoke; tel: (540) 345-8811,* is a fully restored historic landmark, with kitchenettes. Moderate–expensive.

Holiday Inn has properties in Roanoke and Salem, including one at the airport. **Holiday Inn at Civic Center**, *Williamson Rd at Orange Ave; tel: (540) 342-8961,* has an outdoor pool and meeting room. Moderate.

Jefferson Lodge, *616 S. Jefferson St; tel: (540) 342-2951,* has a restaurant, guest laundry and outdoor pool. Budget.

Hampton Inn Tanglewood, *3816 Franklin Rd SW, Roanoke; tel: (540) 989-4000,* offers free continental breakfast. Budget.

Hampton Inn Airport, *6621 Thirlane Rd N.W., Roanoke; tel: (540) 265-2600.* Microwave and fridge in rooms. Free continental breakfast. Budget.

Colony House Motor Lodge, *3560 Franklin Rd, Roanoke; tel: (540) 345-0411.* Convenient for local shopping and restaurants. Suites available. Budget–moderate.

Best Western Inn at Valley View, *5050 Valley View Blvd, Roanoke; tel: (540) 362-2400.* Indoor pool, in-room coffeemakers, complimentary continental breakfast. Moderate.

The Inn at Burwell Place, *601 W.,Main St, Salem; tel: (540) 387-0250.* Four bedrooms with private baths, luxury suites, breakfast included. Moderate to expensive.

The Mary Bladon House, *381 Washington Ave S.W., Roanoke; tel: (540) 344-5361,* has three guest rooms and provides full breakfast. Close to Blue Ridge Parkway and downtown. Moderate.

The Old Manse, *530 E. Main St,*

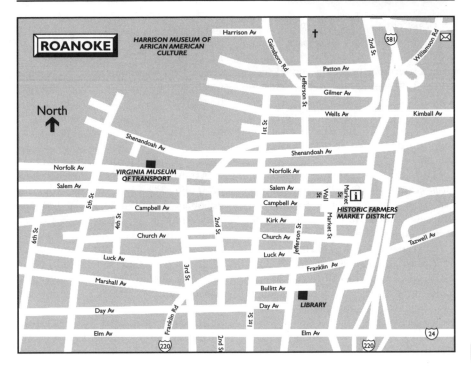

Salem; tel: (540) 389-3921. Furnished with antiques, this two-guest room inn dating from 1847 is on the National Historic Register. Full Southern breakfast included. Budget.

Walnuthill Bed and Breakfast, *436 Walnut Ave S.E., Roanoke; tel: (540) 427-3312.* Gourmet breakfast, coffee all day. Phone and fax. Moderate.

Dixie Caverns and Pottery Campground, *Salem; tel: (540) 380-2085.* Open all year with 75 tent sites and 53 trailer sites, with showers, hook-ups and sanitary station. $14–$16 per night.

Peaks of Otter Campground, *Blue Ridge Parkway, Mile Post 86; tel: (540) 586-4357.* Tent and trailer sites. Open May–Oct, $9 per night.

EATING AND DRINKING

Awful Arthur's, *108 Campbell Ave,*

Roanoke; tel: (540) 344-2997, is spacious, with speedy service, extensive raw bar and fresh seafood. Live entertainment Wed and Thur evenings. Open 1100–0200. Budget to moderate.

Billy's Ritz, *102 Salem Ave, Roanoke; tel: (540) 342-3937.* Steaks and good American cuisine served in early 20th century-style surroundings. Moderate.

Townspeople have voted **Szechuan**, *5207 Bernard Dr.; tel: (540) 989-7947,* Roanoke's best oriental restaurant and best take-away for at least five years in a row. Open daily for lunch and dinner. Budget–moderate.

Star City Diner, *118 Campbell Ave, Roanoke; tel: (540) 344-8850.* A fun place, popular with families. Open 20 hours a day Fri and Sat (0700–0300) and from 0700–0030 Sun–Thur. Cheap to budget.

Carlos Brazilian International

Cuisine, *312 Market St S.E., Roanoke; tel: (540) 345-7661*. Not a lot of space but this restaurant is very popular, so it's wise to make a reservation, especially at weekends. Closes 2130 Mon–Thur, 2200 Fri and Sat. Closed Sun. Moderate to expensive.

Sunnybrook Inn, *Plantation Rd, Roanoke; tel: (540) 366-4555*. Casual eating, American food, buffets. Cheap to budget.

The Library, *3117 Franklin Rd, Roanoke; tel: (540) 985-0811*. Formal special occasion dining. Wine list and service officially voted the best in town. Reservations required. Expensive.

Charcoal Steak House, *5225 Williamson Rd, Roanoke; tel: (540) 366-3710*, offers more than 50 entrée choices, including charcoal-cooked steaks, prime ribs, veal, seafood and authentic Greek dishes. Moderate.

Eden's Vegetarian Cafe Deli, *104 Church Ave S.E., Roanoke; tel: (540) 344-3336*. All-vegetarian cuisine, eat in or take away. Budget.

La Maison, *5732 Airport Rd, Roanoke; tel: (540) 366-2444*. The locals go to this Georgian house for celebratory meals. Continental cuisine. Outdoor dining available. Moderate–expensive.

Old Country Buffet, *4335 Starkey Rd, Roanoke; tel: (540) 776-0718*. Home cooking served in all-you-can-eat buffet style. Budget–moderate.

Regency Room, *Roanoke Hotel, 110 Shenandoah Ave, Roanoke; tel: (540) 985-5900*. Probably the city's most elegant restaurant. There are usually some traditional Virginian dishes on the menu. Moderate–expensive.

SIGHTSEEING

Roanoke has made it easy for visitors to wallow in culture for hours at a time without flagging. Three independent museums

and a theatre are housed under one roof at the **Center in the Square**, *1 Market St; tel: (540) 342-5700*, a restored and converted 1914 warehouse. Lifts, or a white spiral staircase that rises like an open tower, lead to the different floors. The concept of the Center was formulated in the late 1970s – and it opened in the City Market district in the heart of the downtown area shortly before Christmas 1983.

Art Museum of Western Virginia; *tel: (540) 342-5760*, displays nationally important American art of the 19th and 20th centuries, as well as folk art of the Southern mountain region are displayed. International works of art are introduced in changing exhibitions. The Art Museum store specialises in Virginian arts and crafts. Open Tues–Sat 1000–1700. Admission free.

Science Museum of Western Virginia and Hopkins Planetarium; *tel: (540) 342-5710*. More than 40 interactive exhibits in five galleries on two keep visitors busy. Even the exhibit demonstrating the human blood circulatory system has a hands-on aspect. Visitors can try forecasting at the Weather Station and broadcast their prediction on closed circuit TV. A touch tank enables people to meet a spider crab and some of the other occupants of Chesapeake Bay face to face. Open Mon–Sat 1000–1700, Sun 1300–1700. Admission $5, senior citizens $4, children $3. Extra charge for some planetarium shows.

Roanoke Valley History Museum; *tel: (540) 342-5770*. Two or three hours spent here give a fascinating insight into the development of the area from the days before Colonial settlement, through wars (including World War II), and the arrival of the railway which brought prosperity and expansion. Artefacts from prehistoric times, the re-creation of an 1890 store and a fashion parade through history enlighten the visitor. Open Tues–Fri 1000–1600, Sat 1000–1700 and Sun 1300–1700. Admission $2, seniors and children $1.

Lavish musicals, strong dramas and Shakespearean classics have led the **Mill Mountain Theatre**; *tel: (540) 342-5740* to be regarded as one of the best regional theatres in the country. The year-round professional theatre also performs free script-in-hand productions of new plays each month. Admission charge.

Historic Farmers' Market, *First St, tel: (540) 342-2028*. The open-air farmers' market has been operating since 1882, selling local produce and flowers. Set in the downtown area, it is surrounded by speciality shops, art studios, coffee houses and restaurants. Open Mon–Sat 0730–1700.

Virginia Museum of Transportation, *303 Norfolk Ave S.W., Roanoke; tel: (540) 342-5670*, is housed in the old Norfolk and Western freight station. The museum displays giant steam, vintage electric and classic diesel locomotives. Early cars, fire engines, carriages and aircraft are also exhibited. Expansion work that began in 1996 includes railway dining cars used as restaurants. Open Mon–Sat 1000–1700, Sun 1200–1700. Closed Mondays in Jan and Feb. Admission $5, seniors $4, children $3.

Salem Museum, *801 E. Main St, Salem; tel: (540) 389-6760*. Exhibits on Salem, in the Roanoke Valley west of Roanoke, outline its past, including the Civil War. Open Tues–Fri 1000–1600, Sat 1200–1700. Free admission.

Harrison Museum of African American Culture, *523 Harrison Ave, Roanoke; tel: (540) 345-4818*. Art by local African Americans is on show as well as

changing displays which include exhibits from Africa. Open Tues–Fri 1000–1700, Sat, Sun 1300–1700. Free admission.

Mill Mountain Zoo, Star and Overlook, access from I-581, or Blue Ridge Parkway; *tel: (540) 343-3241*. Mountain-top site with nearly 50 species of native and exotic creatures. Open daily 1000–1700. Admission $4, senior citizens $3.60, children $2.75. A 100-ft star, erected high up the mountain in 1949 and lit up nightly, is visible from 60 miles away. An overlook provides a panoramic view of the Roanoke Valley.

Dixie Caverns and Pottery, *5753 W. Main St, Salem; tel: (540) 380-2085*. As well as the wonders of the caverns, there is a rock and mineral shop and a Christmas shop. Open daily 0900–1800, tours 0930–1700. Extended hours in summer. Admission $6, children $3.50.

Virginia's Explore Park, *Blue Ridge Parkway, mile post 115; tel: (540) 427-1800*. Living history museum in 1300 acres, featuring a settlement from the 1800s, with costumed interpreters. Frontier days and a Native American village are featured. Bluegrass musicians entertain. Open Apr–Oct, Sat–Mon only, 0900–1700. Admission $4, students 6-18 $2.50, children under 6 free.

To The Rescue Museum, *Tanglewood Mall, (second level), Roanoke; tel: (540) 776-0364*. A tribute to the nation's first medical and rescue services, whose story is told in inter-active exhibits. Through a video programme visitors can 'experience' racing to the scene of an accident in a rescue truck, see rescues and learn training techniques. Open Mon–Sat 1000–2100, Sun 1300–1800. Admission $2, children $1.

153

ROANOKE–CHARLOTTESVILLE

This route takes us through the western part of central Virginia, through the foothills of the Blue Ridge Mountains and across the undulating countryside of the Piedmont, to places bearing the firm stamp of history. Lynchburg, named after its Quaker founder, bears witness to the horror of war with 2701 Confederate soldiers buried in its Old City Cemetery. The serene village of Appomattox Court House, where the Civil War ended, reflects the hopes of peace. In stately Charlottesville they remember more tranquil times when Thomas Jefferson was the 'Sage of Monticello'.

154

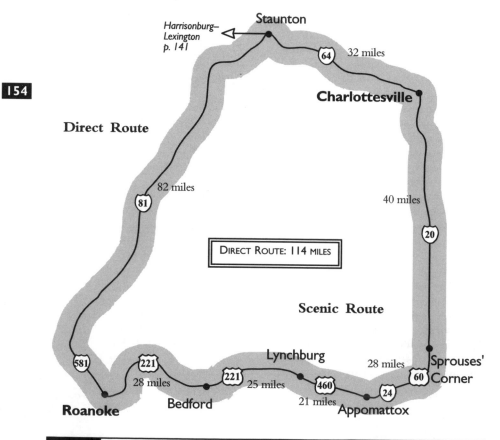

Harrisonburg–
Lexington
p. 141

Staunton

64 32 miles

Charlottesville

Direct Route

82 miles

81

40 miles

20

DIRECT ROUTE: 114 MILES

Scenic Route

Lynchburg 28 miles Sprouses'
60 Corner

581 221 221 25 miles 460 24
28 miles 21 miles

Roanoke **Bedford** **Appomattox**

ROUTES

DIRECT ROUTE

➡ Travellers in a hurry can cover the distance in about 2 hrs by joining I-581 at *Orange Ave*, near Roanoke Civic Center, heading west for 5½ miles to I-81 north, which intersects with I-64 after 76 miles near **Staunton** (see Harrisonburg–Lexington chapter p.141).

I-64 east reaches Charlottesville in 32 miles. Take exit 121 for the Monticello Visitor Center and the Charlottesville/Albermarle Visitor Bureau.

SCENIC ROUTE

▪▪▶ From Roanoke Civic Center head east on *Orange Ave* which becomes Hwy 221/460. The city of **Bedford**, founded as Liberty in 1782, is reached after 28 miles. From Bedford continue east on Hwy 221 for a further 25 miles to **Lynchburg**. Hwy 221 becomes *Lakeside Dr.* and leads downtown. From downtown, *Campbell Ave* leads south to intersect with Hwy 460 east, which reaches Appomattox after 21 miles. **Appomattox Court House National Historic Park** is on Rte 24 north, which you should follow for 20 miles, then turn right on to Hwy 60 east. After 8 miles, at **Sprouses' Corner**, turn left on to Rte 20 north. This leads to **Charlottesville** and the Monticello Visitor Center after 40 miles.

BEDFORD

Tourist Information: Bedford Area Chamber of Commerce, *305 E. Main St, Bedford, VA 24523; tel: (540) 586-9401 or (800) 933-9535*. Open Mon–Fri 0900–1700, Sun (Apr–Nov) 1000–1500.

SIGHTSEEING

Established as the town of Liberty in 1782, Bedford is listed on the National Register

of Historic Places. In Centertown's largely intact 19th-century streets the architecture is predominantly Italianate, but the city's residential areas contain some 15 architectural styles ranging from Greek Revival to Victorian.

Bedford City/County Museum, *201 E. Main St; tel: (540) 586-4520*. Exhibits and memorabilia housed in this 1895 masonic building tell Bedford's story from the early Native American era to modern times. Open Mon–Sat 0900–1700. Admission charge.

Bedford Historic Meeting House, *153 W. Main St; tel: (540) 586-8188*. Listed in the National Register of Historic Places, this church building was built in 1838 as Liberty's first Meeting House for Methodists. From 1886 it served a black congregation for 82 years as St Philip's Episcopal Church. Admission: donation.

Historic Avenel, *413 Avenel Ave; tel: (540) 586-8180*. Another structure on the National Register of Historic Places, this stately mansion was built around 1838 as the dominant feature of a 40-acre plantation, and served as the focal point of social, cultural and political life in the area. Distinguished visitors included Gen. Robert E. Lee and Edgar Allen Poe. The building is said to be haunted. Restoration is being carried out and tours are by appointment.

155

LYNCHBURG

Tourist Information: Lynchburg Visitors Center, *216 Twelfth St, Lynchburg, VA 24504; tel: (804) 847-1811*. Operated by the Greater Lynchburg Chamber of Commerce, the office is well stocked with information on historic tours, lodging and restaurants.

ACCOMMODATION

Lynchburg has more than 1700 guest

rooms in hotels and bed and breakfast inns. Hotel chains include *BW, CI, DI, EL, Hd, Hn, Rm, S8*.

Federal Crest Inn, *1101 Federal St; tel: (804) 845-6155*, located in the Federal Hill historic district, is a spacious Georgian revival mansion, built in 1909. It features exceptionally comfortable rooms with gas fireplaces and private baths. Gourmet breakfast is served in an elegant dining room. Moderate.

Lynchburg Mansion Inn, *405 Madison St; tel: (804) 528-5400 or (800) 352-1199*, is in Garland Hill historic district, on a street with brick sidewalks. A full silver service breakfast is served. Moderate.

The Madison Bed and Breakfast, *413 Madison Ave; tel: (804) 528-1503 or (800) 828-6422*, also in Garland Hill, is an elegant Victorian mansion with lavish decor. Afternoon tea and gourmet breakfast served. Moderate.

EATING AND DRINKING

The city has about 60 eating places with cuisines ranging from traditional Old South to exotic Oriental.

Cafe France, *3225 Old Forest Rd; tel: (804) 385-8989*, is a combined delicatessen, wine shop and restaurant with an enormous selection of wines and beers. The restaurant specialises in slow-cooked prime rib, lamb and a wide choice of seafood. Lunch is served Mon–Sat 1130–1500, dinner Tues–Sat 1730–2200. Moderate–pricey

Cattle Annie's, *4009 Murray Place; tel: (804) 846-BOOT*. The style is Southern Americana with smoked meats, fresh salads and barbecue sandwiches. Live country music and dancing. Open Tues–Fri 1130–2200, Sat 1600–2200. Moderate.

Morrison's Family Dining, *3405 Candler's Mountain Rd; tel: (804) 237-*

6549. Home-made Southern cooking with cafeteria service. Take-out available. Open Mon–Fri 1100–1430 and 1600–2030; Sat 1100–2030; Sun 1100–2000. Budget–moderate.

Philippine Delight, *Community Market, Main and 12th Sts; tel: (804) 384-5654*. Oriental fast food, including authentic Philippine pork or chicken kebab. Open Tues–Fri 1100–1400, Sat 0900–1400. Budget.

SIGHTSEEING

Settled in 1727, Lynchburg sprawls across seven hills overlooking the James River. The city began as a ferry crossing and developed as a tobacco town; for more than a century tobacco was processed, auctioned and made into cigarettes and plugs for chewing.

During the Civil War, the city was a major Confederate storage depot and a burial place for the war dead. Six Confederate generals lie here, including Jubal Early who commanded the Confederate forces during the brief Battle of Lynchburg. Streets on five of the city's seven hills – **Diamond, Court House, Federal, Garland** and **Daniel's** – are designated historic districts.

Anne Spencer House and Garden, *1313 Pierce St; tel: (804) 846-0517*. Restored home of the noted poet who was part of the Harlem Renaissance and is the only black woman and Virginian included in the *Norton Anthology of Modern American and British Poetry*. Visitors to the house during the 72 years she lived there included Paul Robeson, H.L Mencken and Martin Luther King Jr.

The garden, which contains her writing cottage, 'Edankraal', is open without charge Mon–Sat 1000–1600. The house is open by appointment. Admission charge.

City Cemetery, *Fourth and Taylor Sts*.

The cemetery dates from 1806 and the earliest section contains the graves of men who fought in the Revolutionary War, but the most poignant part is the Confederate section with the graves of 2701 soldiers from 14 states who died in the Civil War.

Within the cemetery is the **Pest House Medical Museum**, which grimly portrays the work of the Civil War surgeon, Dr John J. Terrell and his efforts to treat smallpox. The cemetery is freely accessible daily dawn–dusk. Information on cemetery tours and interior tours of the Pest House from the Lynchburg Visitors Center.

Community Market, *Bateau Landing, Main and 12th Sts; tel: (804) 847-1499.* The market was founded in 1783 and was a favourite with Thomas Jefferson on his frequent visits to Poplar Forest (see below). Trading year-round, stallholders sell fruit and vegetables, baked goods and handmade craftware, and there are plenty of eating places. Open Mon–Fri 0700–1400, Sat 0600–1400.

Miller-Claytor House, *Riverside Park, Rivermont Ave; tel: (804) 847-1459.* Dating from 1791, this is believed to be the fourth house built in the city. It is now a 'living history' museum, with demonstrations of early crafts. Open Thur–Mon 1300–1600 (May–Sept). Admission free.

Old Court House, *901 Court St; tel: (804) 847-1459.* The 1855 building, which contains the restored courtroom, houses three museum galleries in which exhibits outline the city's history. Open daily 1300–1600. Admission charge.

Point of Honor, *112 Cabell St; tel: (804) 847-1459.* This stately brick mansion, set on Daniel's Hill high above the James River, was built on an old duelling ground by Dr George Cabell, physician to the Revolutionary hero, Patrick Henry.

Open daily 1300–1600. Admission charge.

Poplar Forest, *Rte 661,* five miles south-west of Lynchburg; *tel: (804) 525-1806.* Thomas Jefferson's obsession with the octagon is demonstrated in the country retreat he designed and built in 1806. Considerable restoration work is now in progress. Open Wed–Sun. Major holidays 1000–1545. Admission: $5.

APPOMATTOX

Tourist Information: Appomattox Visitor Information Center, *in* former rail station, *Main St; PO Box 704, Appomattox, VA 24522; tel: (804) 352-2621.* The center provides information on local attractions and on destinations throughout the state, and features displays highlighting the heritage of Appomattox County. Open daily 0900–1700.

ACCOMMODATION

Tent and RV pitches are located in **Holliday Lake State Park**, *Buckingham-Appomattox State Forest, Rte 692* (9 miles north of Appomattox on Rte 24, then 6 miles east on Rte 626); *tel: (804) 248-6308.* The 250-acre park has a swimming beach, hiking trails, picnic sites and visitor centre.

SIGHTSEEING

Appomattox County Historical Museum, *Court House Sq; tel: (804) 352-7510.* Formerly used as the county jail, the building now houses a collection of artefacts and memorabilia. Open Tues, Thur, Sat 1300–1600 (May–Oct). Admission free.

Appomattox Court House National Historical Park, 3 miles from Appomattox on Rte 24 north; *tel: (804) 352-8987.* This quiet little community of 19th-century homes, a law office, store, court house and jail was the scene of one

The War Ends

The Civil War ended miserably for the 28,000 Confederate soldiers in Gen. Robert E. Lee's Army of Northern Virginia. On 3 April 1865 Grant led his men into retreat from Petersburg (see p.171) which had suffered a ten-month siege. The Confederates' progress westward across south-central Virginia was slow and painful. The troops were exhausted and hungry, their uniforms in rags. Heavy rain added to their misery. Three days later, at **Sailor's Creek**, near the town of Farmville, they fought what proved to be the last major battle of the war.

There was still enough fight left in them, however, to launch an attack on the Union army at Appomattox at dawn on 9 Apr, but their resolution was short-lived. By 1000 it was clear to the Confederate command that further fighting was useless. Lee and Ulysses S. Grant met in the parlour of the McLean House in Appomattox Court House village and by 1500 the surrender terms had been agreed and signed.

One Northern and 18 Southern soldiers who died on the day of surrender are buried in the Confederate Cemetery on the edge of the village.

After so much bloodshed and horror, the surrender was a dignified, gentlemanly agreement. Grant asked only that the Confederates should pledge not to take up arms against the United States. Three days later, at the spot now known as **Surrender Triangle**, the Southern troops laid down their weapons. Printing presses were set up to produce passes that would allow them to return home.

Although Lee's capitulation brought an effective end to the war, it did not bring the Confederacy down at once. It was 26 April before an army, commanded by Joseph E. Johnston, surrendered in North Carolina to Gen. William Sherman. The Confederate States of America continued until 2 June when the flag was hauled down at Galveston, Texas.

The village that came to symbolise the reunification of the states was originally known as Clover Hill, a tiny settlement with a few houses nestling around the tavern, which served as a stage-coach stop-over on the road between Richmond and Lynchburg. It was chosen as the county seat and renamed in 1845 when the new county of Appomattox was formed. There had been little competition for the honour: with a population of 150, it was the only village – let alone town – in the new county. The remaining 8750 inhabitants, 54% of whom were black, lived on plantations and farms.

And what of the people who owned the house in which Gen. Lee surrendered? Wilmer McLean and his family originally lived at Manassas in northern Virginia (see p. 112), where the first battle of the Civil War was fought almost on their doorstep. They moved south hoping to find peace.

of the most significant events in the history of the US – the ending of the Civil War. Here, on 9 Apr 1865, Gen. Robert E. Lee surrendered the Army of Northern Virginia to Gen. Ulysses S. Grant, commander of the Union forces. (See box feature, above).

Restored to its appearance in 1865, the village is now the focal point of a 1700-acre national park. Uniformed park rangers and costumed guides are available to discuss the surrender and those people involved with visitors. The reconstructed court house houses the visitor centre which contains a museum. An audiovisual slide programme is shown every 30 mins. Other buildings which may be visited on a self-guided tour are the **McLean House**, where the surrender document was signed, **Clover Hill Tavern**, the **Confederate Cemetery, County Jail, Meeks' Store** and the **Woodson Law Office**. Open daily 0900–1730. Admission: $2.

CHARLOTTESVILLE

Tourist Information: Charlottesville/ Albermarle Convention & Visitors Bureau, *PO Box 161, Charlottesville, VA 22902; tel: (804) 977-1783*. The bureau shares a large modern building on Rte 20 south, off I-64 Exit 121, with the **Monticello Visitor Center**; *tel: (804) 984-9822*. The bureau's office is roomy and well stocked with literature covering attractions and events, lodging and dining in the area, and staff are on hand to deal with enquiries. *Charlottesville Monthly*, a free arts and entertainment publication, and the complimentary *Charlottesville Guide* are both available.

The Monticello center has a permanent exhibition of memorabilia, architectural models and drawings connected with the life and times of Thomas Jefferson and his family who lived at nearby Monticello (see p.160). A 35-min film, *Thomas Jefferson: the Pursuit of Liberty*, is shown at the centre which also has a tasteful gift shop and a study section.

GETTING AROUND

Charlottesville Transit System; *tel: (804) 296-RIDE*, operates Mon–Sat with routes throughout the city and parts of Albemarle County. Reduced fares are available for the elderly and disabled; children under five travel free.

The downtown district is a compact six blocks square and its tree-lined streets are full of interest, with many shops and restaurants and more than 200 historic buildings and landmarks.

There are six downtown car parks as well as on-street parking.

ACCOMMODATION

The city has a good range of lodgings, including hotels belonging to international groups and a number of bed and breakfast inns, many of which are in or near downtown. Hotel chains in Charlottesville include *BW, CI, CM, Hd, HJ, Om, Ra, Sh*.

English Inn, *2000 Morton Dr.; tel: (804) 971-9900* or *(800) 977-8008*, is a moderately-priced motor hotel which offers a complimentary breakfast buffet.

200 South Street, *200 South St; tel: (804) 979-0200*, is a gracious Southern home, built in 1853. The spacious inn has 20 well-furnished rooms. Complimentary wine and tea is served in the afternoon. Moderate-expensive.

Silver Thatch Inn, *3001 Hollymead Dr.; tel: (804) 978-4686*, is said to be Charlottesville's oldest country inn – a rambling white clapboard building dating from around 1780. It has seven rooms, some with fireplaces and canopy beds, all with private baths. Locally grown foods and Virginia wines are served in the candlelit restaurant. Completely non-smoking. Moderate–expensive.

Charlottesville KOA, *Rte 1, PO Box 144, Charlottesville, VA 22903; tel: (804) 296-9881* or *(800) 336-9881*, is close to Monticello, Ash Lawn and Historic Michie Tavern and has pitches for RVs and tents in a quiet wooded setting. Open begining Mar–end Oct.

EATING AND DRINKING

There should be no need to go hungry in Charlottesville. The downtown area has

159

nearly 30 restaurants and cafés offering a range of cuisines and prices.

Awful Arthur's, *333 W. Main St; tel: (804) 296-0969*, serves a wide choice of seafood dishes, including oysters, shrimps, clams and crab. Pasta dishes, chicken, steaks and sandwiches are also available. Open daily until 0200. Budget.

Blue Ridge Brewing Company, *709 W. Main St; tel: (804) 977-0017*. Beer made on the premises is served in this pub-cum-restaurant where Caribbean dishes are among the specialities. Lunch is served Wed–Sun 1130–1400, dinner daily 1700–2200. Bar open daily to 0200. Cheap–moderate.

C&O Restaurant, *515 E. Water St; tel: (804) 971-7044*. A choice of dining styles is offered in this French-American restaurant: formal upstairs or casual in the downstairs bar and bistro. Open Mon–Fri 1130-0200, Sat–Sun 1700–0200. Lunch: budget; dinner budget–pricey.

Guadalajara, *805 E. Market St; tel: (804) 977-2676*, is the area's only authentic Mexican restaurant, offering beef, poultry and vegetarian dishes and 26 combination platters. Budget.

Hardware Store Restaurant, *316 E. Main St; tel: (804) 977-1518*. A century ago this really was a hardware store and some of the old ironmongery and advertising signs are on display. Specialities include seafood, chicken and huge deli sandwiches. Budget–moderate.

SIGHTSEEING

An elegant yet lively city dating from Colonial times – it was founded in 1762 – Charlottesville is dominated by the University of Virginia, which was founded by Thomas Jefferson. The city is is also an important centre for agricultural produce, wine, apples, peaches and light industry.

Details of a self-guided walking tour of Charlottesville's historic downtown can be obtained from the visitors bureau.

The President's Pass, a combination discount ticket giving admission to Ash-Lawn Highland, Historic Michie Tavern and Monticello, for $17 (senior citizens $15.50) is also available from the bureau.

Jefferson in Charlottesville

Monticello, *Thomas Jefferson Parkway, Rte 53; tel: (804) 984-9822* or *984-9800*. Charlottesville's *pièce de résistance* is the stately, though eccentric home designed by Thomas Jefferson, third president of the United States. Maintained and preserved as a national monument to Jefferson, the house is located on a mountaintop and commands a fine view of the Virginia countryside. Inside you will find many of the original furnishings and the grounds – which include an orchard, vineyard and 1000-ft long kitchen garden – are well worth a visit, allowing an insight into the mind of the squire who has become a revered American icon. Open daily 0800–1700 (Mar–Oct), 0900–1630 (Nov–Feb). Admission: $8.

University of Virginia, *W. Main St; tel: (804) 924-7969*. Another Jefferson brainchild, the 'academical village' is a complex of dignified red brick, smooth green lawns and carefully placed trees. Room 13, in the West Range, was occupied by the young Edgar Allan Poe, and is open to the public. Guided tours daily 1000–1600. Admission free.

Ash Lawn-Highland, Rte 795, 4 miles south-east of downtown; *tel: (804) 293-9539*. This 535-acre estate was the plantation home of James Monroe, fifth president of the US, who allowed Thomas Jefferson not only to choose the site, but also to design the house and gardens – a project that cost him more than he could afford. There are tours of the house and grounds, where visitors are treated to demonstrations of spinning and weaving. Open daily 0900–1800 (Mar–Oct), 1000–1700 (Nov–Feb). Admission: $7.

Jefferson is also connected to two of the regions vineyards – Barboursville and Jefferson Vineyards – detailed below.

Other Attractions

Albemarle County Court House, *Court Sq.* In the 1820s the north wing of the court house was shared as a place of worship by Baptists, Episcopalians, Methodists and Presbyterians, and worshippers included Jefferson, Monroe and Madison. Next to the building is a statue by Charles Keck of Gen. Stonewall Jackson on his horse Little Sorrel.

Historic Michie Tavern, *683 Thomas Jefferson Parkway, Rte 53; tel: (804) 977-1234.* Scotsman William Michie opened his home as an 'Ordinary' – a tavern – in 1784. Today, the reconstructed building serves as a museum of life in an 18th-century inn and visitors can enjoy Colonial hospitality and dishes in an optional lunch. Open daily 0900–1700. Admission: $6. Buffet lunch served 1130–1500. Cost: $9.75

McGuffey Art Center, *201 Second St; tel: (804) 295-7973,* is a co-operative of artists with three galleries and a shop. Visitors may view work in progress in the artists' studios. Open Tues–Sat 1000–1700, Sun 1300–1700. Admission free.

Virginia Discovery Museum, east end of Downtown Mall (opposite Post Office); *tel: (804) 977-1025.* Children and adults can find out how things work or happen through weird and wonderful contraptions. Open Tues–Sat 1000–1700, Sun 1300–1700. Admission: $4.

Vineyards

Charlottesville lies at the heart of Virginia's wine-producing country. The following vineyards welcome visitors for tours and tastings.

Barboursville Vineyards, *Rte 777, Barboursville,* 17 miles north-east of Charlottesville off Rte 20; *tel: (540) 832-3824.* Barboursville mansion was designed by Thomas Jefferson but was gutted by fire on Christmas Day, 1884. Today, the Barboursville estate is known for the production of quality wines. Open Mon–Sat 1000–1700, Sun 1100–1700.

Horton Cellars, *6399 Spotswood Trail, Gordonsville,* off Hwy 33 west; *tel: (540) 832-7440.* Tastings are held daily in a magnificent stone winery. Open daily 1100–1700 (weekends only during Mar).

Jefferson Vineyards, *between Ash Lawn and Monticello on Rte 53; tel: (804) 977-0800.* The vineyard stands on the site where Jefferson planted the colony's first vines. Open daily 1100–1700 (Mar–Nov).

Oakencroft Winery, *Barracks Rd, west of Emmet St (Rte 29 north); tel: (804) 296-4188.* Charlottesville's nearest vineyard is said to be one of Virginia's most picturesque. Tours and tastings offered Jan–Feb by appointment only; Mar: weekends only 1100–1700; daily 1100–1700 (Apr–Dec).

Prince Michel de Virginia Vineyards and Restaurant, *Rte 29, Leon,* 37 miles north of Charlottesville; *tel: (800) 869-8242.* The winery houses an extensive museum, and visitors may take a self-guided tour through the state-of-the-art 200,000-gallon winery. Open daily 1000–1700. Admission free. Restaurant serves lunch and dinner Thur–Sat, lunch Sun.

161

ROANOKE–RICHMOND

This route leaves the foothills of the Blue Ridge Mountains, heads south-west into the Piedmont, the speedway city of Martinsville and onto Danville, known as 'the Last Capital of the Confederacy'. It continues east to the extensive lake district that straddles the border between Virginia and North Carolina, then continues to Emporia, a crossroads community on the edge of the Tidewater district, where it heads north to historic Petersburg and the state capital, Richmond.

ROUTE: 258 MILES

162

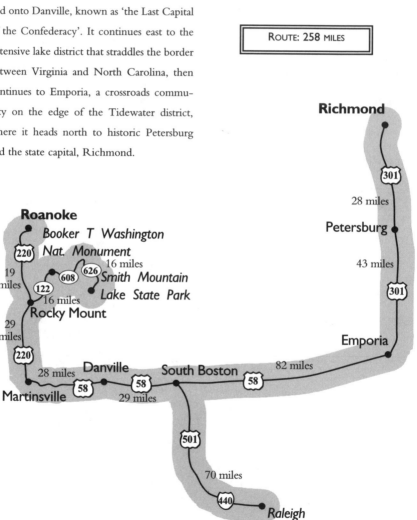

Richmond

301

28 miles

Petersburg

43 miles

301

Emporia

Roanoke

Booker T Washington
Nat. Monument

220

16 miles

19 miles

608 626 Smith Mountain
Lake State Park

122

16 miles

Rocky Mount

29 miles

220

28 miles Danville South Boston 82 miles

Martinsville 58 58 58

29 miles

501

70 miles

440 Raleigh

ROUTE

From downtown Roanoke head south on I-581 for 3 miles then take Hwy 220 south to **Martinsville**, 48 miles on. From here Hwy 58 heads east all the way to **Emporia**, passing through **Danville** (at 28 miles) and **South Boston** (29 miles). From South Boston to Emporia the distance is 82 miles. From Emporia I-95 and Hwy 301 head side by side north to **Petersburg**, 43 miles away, then continue for another 28 miles to **Richmond**. The journey takes around 5 hrs.

Two Side Tracks are offered as options on this route. The first – from **Rocky Mount**, halfway between Roanoke and Martinsville on Hwy 220 – provides an opportunity to visit the **Booker T. Washington National Monument** and the attractive **Smith Mountain Lake State Park**. The second, from South Boston, provides a big city break in **Raleigh**, capital of the neighbouring state of North Carolina.

ROCKY MOUNT

Tourist Information: Franklin County Chamber of Commerce, *PO Box 158, Rocky Mount, VA 24151; tel: (540) 483-9542.* The chamber dispenses information about the 'Land Between the Lakes and the Blue Ridge'.

The Hales Ford Academy, *102 Bernard Rd; tel: (540) 483-5138,* is a one-room school restored as a museum displaying an 1880s curriculum and furnishings and presenting hands-on experiences.

SIDE TRACK FROM ROCKY MOUNT

Rte 122 heading north from Rocky Mount gives travellers the chance to visit two off-the-beaten-track attractions – the **Booker T. Washington National Monument** and **Smith Mountain Lake State Park**.

The monument, birthplace of the African American educator, is on Rte 122, 16 miles north of Rocky Mount; *tel: (540) 721-2094.* Rural life in pre-Civil War Virginia is depicted on the 207-acre restored tobacco farm, and living history demonstrations take place mid June–early Sept. Books and craftware are for sale in the **visitor centre**, and there are areas for picnics and environmental study. Open daily 0830–1700. Admission: $2.

The state park is on the north shore of **Smith Mountain Lake**. From the national monument continue north for 10 miles on Rte 122 to **Moneta**, then turn right on to Rte 608. After 6 miles turn right again on to Rte 626, which leads to the park entrance.

Smith Mountain Lake, a man-made reservoir completed in 1966, is 40 miles long and has 500 miles of shoreline with 5000 acres of woodland. It was created by the Appalachian Power Company to generate electricity, but also has great recreational opportunities. There are three yacht clubs, more than two dozen marinas along the shoreline, and several boat ramps where people can launch their own craft. Boat rentals are also available.

Fishing is a major pursuit, with a number of tournaments taking place. The lake is noted for its trophy-size striped bass and other game fish. Nature lovers and hikers have miles of trails to follow.

The Appalachian Power Company has provided picnic areas with tables, large shelters, charcoal grills and toilets. Campsites are dotted around the lake and there are cabins which can be rented. For information *tel: (804) 786-*

163

1712 and for reservations *tel: (800) 933-PARK*. Luxurious condominiums have been built around the shore, some with tennis courts, and several PGA championship golf courses are in the area. Most golf courses are available to visitors on a daily green fee basis.

Inquiries about condos, cottage and townhouse accommodation should be addressed to **Lakeshore Rentals and Sales**, *Rte 5, PO Box 114, Moneta, VA 24121; tel: (540) 721-5253*.

Smith Mountain Lake Visitors Center is at *2 Bridgewater Plaza, Moneta; tel: (800) 676-8203*. Information packs are available there.

Appalachian Power Company's visitor centre – **Smith Mountain Dam Visitors Center**, *Rte 1, PO Box 311, Sandy Level, VA 24161; tel: (540) 985-2587* – has exhibits showing how electricity is produced, a three-dimensional terrain map of the lake area, its roads and communities, and a slide show about the dam's construction. The lake was created by the damming of a gap in Smith Mountain. Open daily 1000–1800, except on some public holidays. From the visitors' centre, people can walk to an esplanade and overlook for a stunning view of the dam and gorge.

Smith Mountain Lake State Park, *Huddleston; tel: (540) 297-6066*, is a 1500-acre wilderness reserve on the lake's north shore in Bedford County. It offers swimming, primitive camping, boat launching, miles of hiking trails, picnicking, interpretive programmes and paddleboat rentals. Its visitor centre opens at weekends late May–Sept 1000–1900, but such amenities as hiking trails, fishing and boat launching are accessible outside these times.

There are also bed and breakfast and country club options.

The Manor at Taylor's Store Bed and Breakfast Inn, *Rte 122, Smith Mountain Lake; tel: (800) 248-6267*. Moderate–expensive. It offers luxurious amenities, gourmet food and a range of recreational activities.

The Water's Edge, *PO Box 540, Smith Mountain Lake; tel: (800) 858-4653*, is a private country club community of luxurious homes with views of the Blue Ridge Mountains and a challenging golf course. Expensive.

MARTINSVILLE

Tourist Information: Martinsville-Henry County Chamber of Commerce, *Broad and Market Sts, Martinsville; tel: (540) 632-6401*. Open Mon–Fri 0900–1700.

Martinsville is a business-like, well organised and good-looking industrial city. Its challenging speedway, built as a dirt track half a century ago and now a modern facility with seating for 66,000, placed it on the international map. Martinsville is also the home of the excellent **Virginia Museum of Natural History** and the **Piedmont Arts Association**, whose frequent workshops, shows and special events have enhanced community pride and involvement and produced a very high standard of work.

ACCOMMODATION

Al Groden's Dutch Inn, *626 Virginia Ave, Collinsville; tel: (540) 647-3721*. Catering for business and leisure guests, this inn situated at the edge of town has a sauna, exercise equipment, pool and whirlpool, and meeting rooms. It has a restaurant open daily from 0600–2230. Budget to moderate – rates increase during Martinsville Speedway meetings, held four times a year.

Best Western, *Rte 220 N., Villa*

Heights, Martinsville; tel: (540) 632-5611, features a fitness centre and coin-operated launderette. Budget to moderate.

Innkeeper of Martinsville, Rte 220 N; tel: (540) 666-6835, has non-smoking rooms, two telephones in each room and offers complimentary continental breakfast. Budget to moderate.

Accommodation in the budget–moderate category is also available at: **Travel Inn of Martinsville**, Rte 220 S.; tel: (540) 956-3141; **Red Carpet Inn**, Rte 220 S.; tel: (540) 638-3914 ; and **Econo Lodge**, Rte 220, 800 S. Virginia Ave, Collinsville; tel: (540) 647-3941.

Motels include **King's Court Motel**, Rte 220 S., Ridgeway; tel: (540) 956-3101; **Fairystone Motel**, Rte 220 N., Collinsville; tel: (540) 647-3716, and **Super 8 Motel**, 960 N., Memorial Blvd; tel: (540) 666-8888.

EATING AND DRINKING

The city is liberally sprinkled with low-cost quick-service chains – **Taco Bell, Subway, Shoney's, Pizza Hut, Burger King, Hardee's, Kentucky Fried Chicken** and **McDonald's**. There are nearly 40 other places to eat, all at

---

Fairystones

Fairystone State Park in Henry County, within 20 miles of Martinsville, is named after the staurolites, or fairystones, that are found in the area.

These fascinating little stones, no bigger than an inch long and some much smaller, are in the form of a Maltese, Roman or St Andrew's Cross.

According to local legend, the stones are the crystallised tears of fairies, who wept on hearing of Christ's crucifixion.

---

prices in the budget to moderate range. In the **Liberty Fair Mall**, W. Commonwealth Blvd, Martinsville – a shopping centre opened in 1990 with Sears, J.C. Penney and Wal-Mart among its 50 stores – are half a dozen popular eateries, including **Country Cookin'**; tel: (540) 666-0678, **China Sea**; tel: (540) 632-6161; and **Fuzzy's Bar-B-Q**; tel: (540) 647-4479.

SIGHTSEEING

Virginia Museum of Natural History, 1001 Douglas Ave, Martinsville; tel: (540) 666-8600. The state museum has more than a million exhibits, including genuine dinosaur tracks, demonstrating that Virginia sustained animal life 210 million years ago. The museum also offers an educational outreach programme featuring lectures, tours of research sites and excavations, visits to special events and field trips in which people of all ages can clamber around disused quarries finding fossils, for example. There is more participation in annual events such as Earth Day in Apr and the Virginia Indian Heritage Festival in Sept.

The prehistoric dinosaur tracks were discovered in recent years at Culpeper, tracks of a giant ground sloth – see them in the museum's mammal section, – were found at Saltville, andancient whale skeletons have been dug up near Richmond .

A zoom video camera can be operated by visitors to the museum to see greatly magnified images of creatures on a 32-in television monitor.

As well as the Martinsville 'museum without walls' there are branches at Virginia Tech in Blacksburg and at the University of Virginia in Charlottesville.

The Virginia Museum of Natural History at Martinsville is open Mon–Sat 1000–1700. Free admission.

Piedmont Arts Association,

165

Speeding to Success

Located about halfway down the eastern side of the US, Martinsville (pop. 16,162) is as close to the middle as Middle America can get. It is a pleasant little city which significant history has largely by-passed since its establishment in 1793. Like many another community in this part of the world, commerce in its early days depended solely on tobacco. The city's major industries today are textiles, furniture manufacture and man-made fibres, although tobacco remains an important cash crop.

A quiet place, then, quietly going about the business of doing business. But several times a year Martinsville plays host to thousands of people from every state in the Union – and beyond – and the peace is shattered by the sound of screaming tyres and the clash of metal on metal.

Martinsville Speedway is one of most important and demanding tracks on the NASCAR (National Association of Stock Car Racing) Winston Cup Circuit. Covering just over half a mile, the paper clip-shaped track is one of the shortest, but its tight turns with 12-degree banking produce wild push-and-shove racing. Here, driver-ability rather than horsepower wins races.

The track began as a dusty, rough-hewn dirt course built by H. Clay Earles in Sept 1947. Since then it has developed into one of the most sophisticated modern racing facilities in existence – for the spectators, that is. The track was paved in 1955, but it is as challenging as ever and competitors still have to drive 263 miles to complete 500 laps. For those watching, there are modern grandstands with seating for 66,000, six corporate suites and a hospitality village.

Robert 'Red' Byron, winner of the inaugural race in 1947, took home $500. Today's leading drivers can take away more than $170,000. The city gains a sizeable purse, too. It has been estimated that with each visiting racegoer spending an average of $90 a day – excluding the cost of tickets – Martinsville gains some $60 million a year.

166

Schottland House, 215 Starling Ave, Martinsville; tel: (540) 638-3963. This non-profit-making association, formed in 1961, is housed in a bright, airy mansion in which works in various media of local, regional and national artists are displayed to great effect. The association aims to encourage and develop community awareness and appreciation of the arts and to provide opportunities for participation. Also in the building is a craft centre where people can attend courses in such subjects as calligraphy and pottery. The PAA centre is open Mon–Fri 0900–1700, Sun 1330–1660. Free exhibitions.

Martinsville Speedway, PO Box 311, Speedway Rd (on Rte 220 S. 2 miles south of Martinsville, near the North Carolina border); tel: (540) 956-3151. Major stock car events are held several times a year (see box feature, below). Admission charge.

DANVILLE

Tourist Information: Danville Area Chamber of Commerce Visitor Center, 635 Main St, PO Box 1538, VA 24543; tel: (804) 793-5422. Clearly signposted from the city approaches, the chamber has brochures and leaflets on attractions, lodgings and dining throughout the area, including parts of North Carolina whose state line touches the city's southern outskirts.

ACCOMMODATION

The city has about a dozen hotels and motels and a few bed and breakfast inns. Hotel chains include *BW, DI, HJ, S8*.

Innkeeper Motor Lodge West, *3020 Riverside Dr., tel: (804) 799-1202 or (800) 822-9899.* Continental breakfast is complimentary in this budget-priced motor hotel. An adjoining restaurant is open daily 0600–midnight.

Similar facilities are available at **Innkeeper North**, *1030 Piney Forest Rd; tel: (804) 836-1700*, which also offers buget-priced accommodation.

Stratford Inn, *2500 Riverside Dr.; tel: (804) 793-2500 or (800) 326-8455.* Budget. Complimentary full breakfast is served and the restaurant is open daily 0630–2200. The bar closes at midnight. Other facilities include a coin-operated laundry and exercise equipment.

Bed and Breakfast inns include **Broad Street Manor**, *124 Broad St; tel: (804) 792-0324*; **Red Maple Bed and Breakfast**, *2203 Franklin Turnpike; tel: (804) 836-6361*; **The Wedding Cake House**, *1020 Main St; tel: (804) 799-4644*; **Woodside Inn**, *Rte 57 North, Milton, NC; tel: (910) 234-8646.*

EATING AND DRINKING

Danville has almost 100 eating places, ranging from cafeterias and fast-food establishments to ethnic and themed restaurants, family dining and seafood specialists. A complete list is available at the visitor centre.

One of the most popular of the themed restaurants is the **Rock-Ola Cafe Grille and Bar**, *140 Crown Dr.; tel: (804) 793-1848*. The rock 'n' roll memorabilia does not measure up to that found in a Hard Rock Cafe, but the music is as good and the food better. Budget.

Other budget–moderate favourites are

Texas Steakhouse and Saloon, *2925 Riverside Dr.; tel: (804) 791-4419*; **Mayflower Seafood**, *2320 Riverside Dr.; tel: (804) 792-8817*; **Casa Perez** (Mexican), *1227 Franklin Turnpike; tel: (804) 836-5129*; **Fireside Country Kitchen** (Southern), *816 Westover Dr.; tel: (804) 792-3843.*

SHOPPING

With 15 major shopping centres and plazas and a commercially active downtown, Danville is an attractive place for shoppers. One of the city's major industries is textiles and **Dan River Inc**, a company established more than a century ago, maintains a store on *W. Main St*, open Mon–Sat 0800–1700. A list of shopping centres – and individual stores located on each – can be obtained from the visitor centre. There is also a leaflet giving details of antiques dealers in the area.

SIGHTSEEING

Two brochures that visitors must make sure they collect from the visitor centre are *Victorian Walking Tour* and *A Self-Guided Tour of Civil War Sites*. Each contains a wealth of information. The walking tour, especially, provides details of some 50 historic or architecturally interesting properties in the downtown area.

Three adjoining cemeteries on *Lee St* give an interesting sidelight on to Danville's past. **Freedman's Cemetery**, established in 1872 and occupying 11 acres, was intended, as its name implies, for recently freed slaves and other black citizens. **Green Hill Cemetery**, established in 1863, is typical of the Romantic layout of municipal burial grounds of the time. 'Confederate Row' leads to the city's Confederate Soldiers Monument, a 16-ton obelisk of Virginia granite. The **United States National Cemetery** created just

167

after the Civil War in 1867, contains the graves of 1323 Union troops – 148 of them unknown – who died as prisoners of war in Danville.

Danville Museum of Fine Arts and History, *975 Main St; tel: (804) 793-5644*. The museum is housed in the 1875 **Sutherlin Mansion**, said to be one of the finest examples of Italian-villa architecture in Virginia. Rooms in the restored house feature silver ornaments, crystal chandeliers, oriental rugs, 19th-century portraits and elegant furniture. Three galleries containing the museum's collection of 18th- and 19th-century American decorative art – including furniture and textiles – historic documents and costumes; Civil War artefacts and paintings are housed in two modern wings.

During the final week of the Civil War the Confederate President Jefferson Davis and his Cabinet occupied Sutherlin Mansion. For that reason, Danville is known as the 'Last Capital of the Confederacy'. Open Tues–Fri 1000–1700, Sat-Sun 1400–1700. Admission: donation.

Danville Science Center, *677 Craghead St; tel: (804) 791-5160*. Housed in Danville's old rail station, the centre is loaded with hands-on exhibits to help visitors find out how things work. Open Mon–Sat 0930–1700, Sun 1300–1700. Admission: $4.

Langhorne Legacy, *117 Broad St.* This large but simple weatherboarded house is the birthplace of Nancy Langhorne, Viscountess Astor (the first woman to sit in the British House of Commons), and her sister Irene, who was immortalised by her artist husband, Charles Dana Gibson, as the Gibson Girl. Their father, Col. Chiswell Dabney Langhorne, was a colourful tobacco auctioneer who is said to have originated the

sing-song chant of modern auctioneers. The house was saved from destruction in 1988 and is being restored by the **Lady Astor Preservation Trust**, *PO Box 3518, Danville, VA 24543*. The trust's aim is to create a museum with a one-bedroom facsimile of an 1870s Southern home, with other rooms featuring various interpretations of the Langhorne family and its legacy. At present public access to the house is limited.

Tobacco auctions: Danville was founded as a tobacco inspection centre in 1793 and is the birthplace of the colourful loose-leaf auction system known as the Danville System, now used throughout the south-eastern US. Auctions take place Mon–Thur (mid Aug–early Nov) in seven warehouses in the city. The chamber of commerce visitor center issues a leaflet detailing a tour of the auctions. Admission free.

SOUTH BOSTON

A quiet stopover 29 miles east of Danville, South Boston has accommodation at the **Best Western Howard House Inn**, *2001 Seymour Dr.; tel: (804) 572-4311*, and **Days Inn**, *Hwy 58 west; tel: (804) 572-4941*.

South Boston Historical Museum, *801 N. Main St; tel: (804) 572-9200*, houses a collection of local memorabilia. Open Thur–Fri 1000–1600, Sun 1400–1630. Admission: donation.

Staunton River State Park, *Rte 344, Scottsburg* (take Hwy 360 north for 7 miles, then Rte 344 south for 10 miles); *tel: (804) 572-4623*. In a remote location with acres of woodland, meadows and shoreline on Buggs Island Lake, the park has a visitor centre, hiking trails, swimming and wading pools, boating and tennis. There are cabins and campsites. Groceries and snacks are available in summer.

Beautiful though it is, this part of southern Virginia has no sizeable communities and very little in the way of tourist amenities, so travellers might consider heading south across the state line into North Carolina, where Raleigh, the state capital, beckons from a distance of 85 miles with a good selection of accommodation and restaurants and some interesting attractions.

From South Boston head south on Hwy 501 to reach the North Carolina line in 12 miles. Continue on Hwy 501 for a further 31 miles to the outskirts of Durham. Head east on I-40 for 25 miles. At the junction with I-440 take exit 4 to Hwy 401 (*Wade Ave*) and continue east for two miles into downtown Raleigh.

You can return to Virginia by continuing on Hwy 401 north for 50 miles to Macon, NC, then heading east on Hwy 158 for 28 miles to Roanoke Rapids, a lakeside resort town also good for a stopover. From Roanoke Rapids to Emporia, VA, is 18 miles north on either I-95 or Hwy 301.

RALEIGH

Tourist Information: Capital Area Visitor Center, *301 N. Blount St; tel: (919) 733-3456*. This time the term 'Capital Area' means Raleigh and environs, but this well-stocked, well-staffed bureau is the place for maps, brochures and information on accommodation and dining. Here, too, you can join tours of the State Capitol, museums and other attractions.

Greater Raleigh Convention and Visitors Bureau, *225 Hillsborough St, Suite 400, PO Box 1879, NC 27602-1879; tel: (919) 834-5900*, also provides information.

Named after Sir Walter Raleigh, the city was founded in 1792. The original Governor's Residence was destroyed by Union troops during the Civil War, but many attractive antebellum homes and estates remain. Today, Raleigh has a population of around 208,000 and is a centre for education and technological research.

ACCOMMODATION

As befits its size and importance as state capitol, Raleigh has a good selection of accommodation covering the price spectrum. Hotel chains include *CI, DI, ES, Hd, Hn, Ma, Rd, R I, RR, QS, Sh.*

Oakwood Inn, *411 N. Bloodworth St; tel: (919) 832-9712* or *(800) 267-9712*. Built in 1871 and listed on the National Register of Historic Places, this six-room inn offers bed and breakfast and Victorian furnishings. Moderate.

William Thomas House, *530 N. Blount St; tel: (919) 755-9400* or *(800) 653-3466*, dates from 1881 and is furnished with antiques. A totally non-smoking bed and breakfast inn. Moderate–expensive.

Velvet Cloak Inn, *1505 Hillsborough St; tel: (919) 828-0333* or *(800) 334-4372*. With 168 rooms and two restaurants, this elegant hotel is a Raleigh institution. The tropical garden surrounding the pool is a popular spot for wedding receptions. Live entertainment is a frequent feature of the Charter Room restaurant. Moderate.

EATING AND DRINKING

Dining is a similar picture to the accommodation scene.

42nd St Oyster Bar, *508 W. Jones*

St; tel: (919) 831-2811, draws diners from all social strata. The attraction is superb oysters and seafood meals. Open Mon–Fri 1130–2300, Sat 1700–2300, Sun 1700–2200. Live jazz Fri–Sat evenings. Budget–moderate. **Est Est Est Trattoria**, 19 W. Hargett St; tel: (919) 832-8899, serves pasta with the authentic taste of northern Italy. Open Mon–Thur 1100–2200, Fri–Sat 1100–2300. Budget–pricey.

Irregardless Cafe, 901 W. Morgan St; tel: (919) 833-8898, serves vegetarian dishes in addition to chicken and seafood. Totally non-smoking. Open Mon–Sat 1130–1430 and 1730–2200, Sun 1000–1430. Cheap–moderate.

SIGHTSEEING

Most of downtown Raleigh's attractions are within strolling distance of each other. Admission to many of the state buildings, historic sites and museums is free.

Mordecai Historic Park, Mimosa St and Wake Forest Rd; tel: (919) 834-4844, contains a number of reconstructed buildings dating from 1785 to 1826, including the house in which Andrew Johnson, 17th President of the US, was born. There is also a herb garden dating from the 1830s. Open Mon–Fri 1000–1700, Sat–Sun 1330–1530. Tours $3.

North Carolina Museum of Art, 2210 Blue Ridge Rd; tel: (919) 833-1935. Galleries house collections of European and American paintings and sculpture, Judaica and Egyptian, Greek, Roman, African and pre-Columbian objects. Open Tues–Thur and Sat 0900–1700, Fri 0900–2100, Sun 1100–1800. Admission free.

North Carolina Museum of History, 1 E. Edenton St; tel: (919) 715-0200, tells the state's history through artefacts, interactive displays and audiovisual programmes. There are special exhibits on sports, folklife and women who made history. Open Tues–Sat 0900–1700. Admission free.

North Carolina Museum of Natural Sciences, 102 N. Salisbury St; tel: (919) 733-7450. Skeletons of dinosaurs and whales are on show as well as fossils and exhibits depicting the state's natural resources. Open Mon–Sat 0900–1700, Sun 1300–1700. Admission free.

State Capitol, Capitol Sq; tel: (919) 733-4994. The legislative chambers in this stately Greek Revival building have been restored to their appearance in the 1840s. Open Mon–Fri 0800–1700, Sat 0900–1700, Sun 1300–1700. Admission free.

State Legislative Building, Salisbury and Jones Sts; tel: (919) 733-7928. Visitors may get the chance to see the law-makers at work during guided tours arranged through the visitors center. Open Mon–Fri 0800–1700, Sat 0900–1700, Sun 1300–1700. Admission free.

EMPORIA

This crossroads community (I-95 and Hwy 58 intersect here) is another useful stopover. Budget-priced accommodation with complimentary continental breakfast can be found in four chain hotels:

Best Western, 1100 W. Atlantic St; tel: (804) 634-3200, has a pool and a restaurant open 0600–2200. **Comfort Inn**, 1411 Skipper's Rd; tel: (804) 348-3282, has an adjoining restaurant open 0530–2300.

Days Inn, 921 W. Atlantic St; tel: (804) 634-9481, also has an adjoining restaurant is open 24 hours daily.

Hampton Inn, 1207 W. Atlantic St;

tel: (804) 634-9200. A restaurant is nearby.

Village View, *221 Briggs St* (off *S. Main St); tel: (804) 634-2475,* is a restored 1790s mansion with exhibits featuring family life of the rural southside and Confederacy. Tours available. Admission charge.

PETERSBURG

Tourist Information: Petersburg Visitors Center, *PO Box 2107, 425 Old Cockade Alley, Petersburg, VA 23804; tel: (804) 733-2400 or (800) 368-3595.*

Located in the McIlwaine House in Old Towne Petersburg, the centre has information on attractions throughout Virginia as well as those in the city. Travel counsellors are available to answer individual inquiries and help arrange itineraries. Open daily 0900–1700.

The city also maintains a visitors centre at the **Carson Rest Area** on I-95 north, about 12 miles south of Petersburg; *tel: (804) 246-2145.* where visitors will find maps, attraction brochures and information on attractions and hotels. Again, travel counsellors are on hand. Open daily 0900–1700.

ACCOMMODATION AND FOOD

Hotel chains in Petersburg include *DI, EL, HJ, QI*.

Alexander's, *101 W. Bank St; tel: (804) 733-7134,* specialises in Greek, Italian and American cuisine. Budget. Open Mon, Tues 0900–1530, Wed–Sat 0900–2030.

Pumpkins Restaurant, *S. Crater Rd* (near Days Inn, exit 45, I-95 south); *tel: (804) 732-4444.* Budget–moderate fare. Open daily 0530–2200. **Steven Kent Restaurant**, *S. Crater Rd* (near Quality Inn); *tel: (804) 733-0600,* is another budget–moderate establishment. Open daily 0530–2200.

SIGHTSEEING

Petersburg's roots go back to 1645 when the Colonial authorities at Jamestown ordered the building of Fort Henry at the falls of the Appomattox River. By 1675 a prosperous trading post at the fort operated by Peter Wood was known as 'Peter's Point', which later evolved into Petersburg.

The city has played a major role in each of the three wars fought on American soil. During the Revolutionary War its economy was all but destroyed when it fell to the British in the spring of 1781. In the War of 1812 volunteers from the city served with such valour in Canada that President Madison dubbed Petersburg 'Cockade City', a reference to the ribbons the men wore on their hats. And in the last year of the Civil War, the city was devastated in the crippling ten-month siege in which 28,000 Confederates and 42,000 Union troops were killed.

Blandford Church, *111 Rochelle Lane; tel: (804) 733-2400.* Dating from 1735, the church was restored in 1901 as a memorial to the Southern soldiers who died in the Civil War. It has 15 stained glass windows designed by Louis Comfort Tiffany. Some 30,000 Confederate soldiers are buried in the cemetery, where other tombstones date from the early 1700s. Open daily 1000–1700.

Centre Hill Mansion, *Centre Hill Court; tel: (804) 733-2400.* Petersburg's grandest home was built for the Bolling family in 1823. Ornate woodwork, plaster motifs and chandeliers accompany period furnishings. A service tunnel connects the basement to the city. Presidents Tyler, Lincoln and Taft visited the house as guests. Open daily 1000–1700. Admission charge.

Farmers Bank, *19 Bollingbrook St; tel: (804) 733-2400.* Built as a branch of the

Farmers' Bank of Virginia in 1817 – it is one of the oldest bank buildings in the US. The museum contains banking memorabilia, including a heavy safe and a press and plates used for printing Confederate banknotes. Accommodation areas for the cashier and his family and the bank's slaves are preserved. Open daily 1000–1600 (Apr–Sept). Tours start at the *Cockade Alley* visitors centre. Admission charge.

Lee Memorial Park, *Johnson Rd; tel: (804) 733-2394*. This 864-acre park on the south side of the city has a lake with fishing facilities, game fields and courts and a picnic area. Open daily 0830–dusk. Admission free (charge for fishing and games facilities).

Old Towne Petersburg. A collection of wooden homes and warehouses along the Appomattox River, the old town of Petersburg was razed when fire broke out on a hot summer night in 1815. The brick-built commercial district that took its place became a crossroads for bateaux on the canals, trading ships on the river and the major rail lines which extended north and south of the city.

Today, Old Towne is a place of antique galleries, boutiques, craft shops and restaurants.

Petersburg National Battlefield, *Visitor Center, Rte 36,* 2½ miles east of downtown Petersburg; *tel: (804) 732-3531*. Covering more than two square miles, the park has Union and Confederate fortifications and trenches and **The Crater**, a hole 170 ft long, 60 ft wide and 30 ft deep created when Union forces tunnelled under the Confederate lines and set off four tons of gunpowder. Tactics following the massive explosion were botched with the result that Union casualties totalled 4400 against the Confederates' 1500. During the summer living history programmes and demonstrations of mortar

and cannon firings and 19th-century military life take place. A 17-min map presentation is shown hourly at the visitor centre. The park has are cycle, hiking and self-guided car trails, as well as picnic areas and toilets. The battlefield is open daily 0800–dusk; visitor centre daily 0800–1700 (1900 in summer). Admission: $4 per vehicle or $2 per person.

Quartermaster Museum, *Fort Lee,* 3 miles from downtown on Rte 36 east; *tel: (804) 734-4203*. Fort Lee was a US Army training centre in World Wars I and II, and the museum has displays of military artefacts going back to the Revolutionary War. Uniforms, flags, equipment and weapons are on show. Open Tues–Sun 1000–1700. Admission: free.

Siege Museum, *15 W. Bank St; tel: (804) 733-2400*. Exhibits show how the citizens of Petersburg lived before, during and immediately after the Civil War and how they endured the hardship of the ten-month siege. *The Echoes Still Remain*, a film with narration by Joseph Cotten, is shown hourly. The museum building, a Greek Revival structure, opened in 1839 as a commodities market. Open daily 1000–1700. Admission charge.

Trapezium House, *244 N. Market St; tel: (804) 733-2400*. Charles O'Hara, an eccentric Irishman, built this house with no right angles and no parallel walls in 1817. O'Hara is said to have been influenced by his West Indian servant who believed that right angles attracted evil spirits. Open daily 1000–1600. Admission fee. Tours start from the Siege Museum.

U.S. Slo-Pitch Softball Hall of Fame, *3935 S. Crater Rd; tel: (804) 732-4099*. The history, personalities and accomplishments of the nation's most popular amateur team sport are honoured in exhibits, photographs and a 7-min film. Open daily 1000–1700. Admission: $2.

RICHMOND

Virginia's state capital since 1780 and capital of the Confederacy between 1861 and 1865, Richmond offers an almost inexhaustible supply of museums, shopping, live entertainment, historic homes and buildings, outdoor attractions and recreational pursuits.

In the area are Civil War sites, riverside plantation homes, places associated with Pocahontas, and Paramount's King's Dominion theme park with its white-knuckle excitement.

Richmond's magnificent Monument Ave, with its statues of Civil War generals and others, is regarded as one of the most beautiful streets in America. In another part of this city of more than 200,000 people is a monument to black entertainer Bill 'Bojangles' Robinson.

Old and new sit happily together. The Fan, the area of streets fanning out westward from Monroe Park and downtown Richmond, is arguably the largest intact Victorian neighbourhood in the US. Shockoe Slip, with its cobblestoned, gas-lit streets bounded by 15th, 21st, Dock and Broad Streets, now house nightclubs, restaurants, boutiques and entertainments.

Visitors can go white-water rafting on the James River, or take a sedate dinner cruise aboard a paddlewheel riverboat. They can also discover how a place settled in the 17th century can contain examples of architecture from the 12th and 16th centuries.

TOURIST INFORMATION

Metro Richmond Convention and Visitors Bureau, *550 E. Marshall St, Richmond; tel: (804) 782-2777 or (800) 365-7272.* Brochures and maps on attractions, entertainment, events, accommodation, dining and shopping are available at the bureau, where travel counsellors can assist with lodging reservations and give directions. Information on tours is also available.

Visitor Center, *1710 Robin Hood Rd, Richmond* (Exit 78 on I-95); *tel: (804) 358-5511.* Open daily 0900–1700 (to 1900 June–Aug). Gift items, including Virginia products and souvenirs, are on sale. There is also a visitor centre at **Richmond International Airport** (Exit 197 off I-64, east of Richmond); *tel: (804) 236-3260.* Open daily 0900–1700 (to 1900 June–Aug).

For visitor information for **Chesterfield County** contact *PO Box 40, Chesterfield; tel: (804) 748-1161*, and for **County of Henrico**, *PO Box 27032, Richmond; tel: (804) 672-4257.*

For accommodation reservations throughout the Richmond metropolitan area, *tel: (800) 444-2777.*

Lodging taxes range from 6.5 per cent to 9.5 per cent, depending on the location of the accommodation.

ARRIVING AND DEPARTING

Richmond is centrally situated at the Falls of the James River and is named after its sister city on the River Thames in Surrey,

173

England. Metropolitan Richmond is at the intersections of I-95, I-64 and I-295.

GETTING AROUND

The first successful commercial trolley car system in the US was in Richmond, and there is still an efficient public transport system in the city today.

Buses

Greater Richmond Transport Co; *tel: (804) 358-4782*, provides a bus service throughout the Metropolitan Richmond area and operates buses equipped to take disabled travellers. **Greyhound/Trailways'** terminal is near downtown at *2910 N. Boulevard; tel: (800) 232-2222*.

Ground transport between Richmond Airport and the city is provided by **Groome Transportation**, *5500 Lewis Rd, Sandston; tel: (804) 222-7222*.

Trains

The **Amtrak** station is at *7519 Staples Mill Rd*, close to I-95 and I-64. Accessibility for disabled travellers and special assistance are available. Eight trains a day link Richmond with Washington DC.

Taxis

More than 40 taxicab companies, including **Yellow Cabs**, serve the Richmond area. Most major hotels have an adjacent cab stand, and there are cab stands (taxi ranks) at the airport, rail station and bus terminal. Rates are around $1.50 a mile. For Yellow Cabs *tel: (804) 222-7300*. For **Veterans Cab Assn** *tel: (804) 329-3333*. The telephone directory lists independent operators.

STAYING IN RICHMOND

Accommodation

Hotels, motels, suites, inns, bed and breakfast homes and campsites provide a variety of lodging options at all price levels. Some of the chains have more than one hotel or motel in the metropolitan area – Holiday Inn has nine properties.

The hub of Richmond's social life for most of the past 100 years – its centenary was celebrated in 1995 – is the **Jefferson Hotel**. (See feature, right). Located midway between the business and residential districts at *Franklin and Adams Sts; tel: (804) 788-8000 or (800) 424-8014*, it has the AAA Five Diamond rating. The Jefferson features a Grand Ballroom with a proscenium stage, and a wide double staircase in marble. In Palm Court, the registration area, a statue of Thomas Jefferson presides, created for the hotel before the turn of the century by Richmond sculptor Edward Valentine. The 248 guest rooms and 26 suites include two presidential suites. A health centre, 24-hr room service and a choice of formal or casual dining are available. The property is on the list of National Historic Places and is a charter member of Historic Hotels of America. Pricey.

Linden Row Inn, *100 E. Franklin St; tel: (804) 783-7000 or (800) 348-7424*. A row of 1847 Greek Revival townhouses form this warmly hospitable and elegant inn. Large rooms and suites furnished with antiques, business services, courtyard dining, complimentary continental breakfast and a cocktail bar make this a popular overnight and dining option for leisure and business guests, including state politicians. Moderate to expensive.

Berkeley Hotel, *1200 E. Cary St; tel: (804) 780-1300*. A comfortable Four Diamond hotel in historic Shockoe Slip. Overnight guests get complimentary valet parking. Restaurant and bar. Expensive to pricey.

Commonwealth Park Suites Hotel,

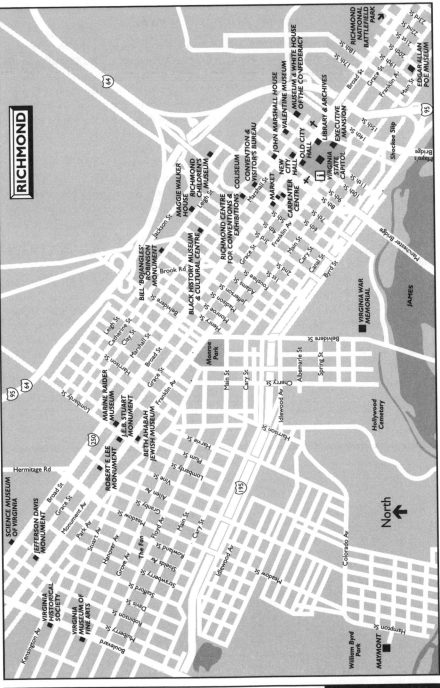

RICHMOND

Science Museum of Virginia
Jefferson Davis Monument
Virginia Historical Society
Virginia Museum of Fine Arts
Hermitage Rd
Robert E Lee Monument
Marine Raider Museum
J.E.B. Stuart Monument
Beth Ahabah Jewish Museum
Bill "Bojangles" Robinson Monument
Black History Museum & Cultural Centre
Maggie Walker House
Richmond Children's Museum
Richmond Centre for Conventions & Exhibitions
Coliseum
Convention & Visitor's Bureau
John Marshall House
Valentine Museum
Museum & White House of the Confederacy
New City Hall
Old City Hall
Market
Carpenter Centre
Library & Archives
Executive Mansion
Virginia State Capitol
Richmond National Battlefield Park
Edgar Allan Poe Museum
Shockoe Slip
Virginia War Memorial
Monroe Park
Hollywood Cemetery
William Byrd Park
Maymont
JAMES
Manchester Bridge
Mayo's Bridge

Leigh St, Catherine St, Clay St, Marshall St, Broad St, Grace St, Franklin Av, Harvie St, Plum St, Lombardy St, Vine St, Allen Av, Granby St, Floyd St, Meadow St, Main St, Cary St

Hanover Av, Grove Av, Shields Av, Strawberry St, Stafford Av, Davis St, Robinson St, Mulberry St, Boulevard

Kensington Av, Broad St, Grace St, Monument Av, Park Av, Stuart Av, The Fan, Rowland St

Lombardy St, Belvidere St, Brook Rd, Jackson St, Leigh St, Henry St, Monroe St, Madison St, Jefferson St, Adams St, Foushee St, 1st St, 2nd St, 3rd St, 4th St, 5th St, 6th St, 7th St, 8th St, 9th St, 10th St, 11th St, 12th St, 14th St, 15th St, 17th St, 18th St, 19th St, 20th St, 21st St, 22nd St, 23rd St

Marshall St, Grace St, Franklin Av, Main St, Cary St, Canal St, Byrd St

Broad St, Grace St, Franklin Av, Main St

Belvidere St, Spring St, Albemarle St, Cherry St, Cary St, Idlewood Av, Harrison St, Colorado Av, Meadow St, Idlewood Av, Hampton St

North

175

One Man's Dream

A multi-talented multi-millionaire, whose dream was to construct the finest hotel in America, built the **Jefferson Hotel** in Richmond. He spent around $8 million on the project – and that was more than 100 years ago when the sum was astronomical.

New York-born Lewis Ginter, the son of Dutch immigrants, arrived in the city in 1842 when he was 18. By the time the Civil War broke out he had made his first million as a fabric merchant. He served in the war as a major in the Confederate Army. After the war he added to his wealth with success as a banker, tobacco tycoon and land developer. As a civic leader and philanthropist he was one of Richmond's most highly esteemed citizens.

Ginter had turned 70 when his no-expense-spared hotel opened in 1895. It had electric lighting, elevators operated by electricity, hot and cold water and a system that pre-dated the telephone for room service. It had Turkish baths, Russian baths, billiard rooms, palm trees from South America and hundreds of antiques from around the world. The Gay Nineties were in full swing, and rich and famous guests from show business, politics and many other spheres were among the merrymakers who danced on the newly opened hotel's rooftop.

The Jefferson has hosted headline-makers of successive generations, among them nine presidents of the USA – and Elvis Presley.

Major Ginter died in 1897, only two years after his dream came true. In 1901 a large part of the hotel was destroyed by fire. Nobody was killed, but one of the casualties was a marble statue of Ginter's hero, Thomas Jefferson, whose head came off. Fortunately the sculptor, Edward Valentine, was able to re-attach it. The hotel re-opened after a couple of months; during the period of closure 20 rooms were added to the 100 which survived the fire, and the fountains in the Palm Court were replaced by a pool in which live alligators lurked. Nearly 50 years ago their place was taken by cast iron alligators.

A second fire in 1944 took its toll, and the hotel went into a state of gradual decline, culminating in closure in 1980. A massive three-year $34 million reconstruction programme began in 1983, and in 1986 it re-opened, restored to splendour as a Sheraton hotel. In 1991 it was bought by Historic Hotels. Today, people still marvel at the magnificence of its two lobbies.

PO Box 455, 9th and Bank Sts; tel: (804) 343-7300. Opposite the State Capitol; expensive.

Brandermill Inn, *13550 Harbour Pointe Parkway, Midlothian* (off Rte 360); *tel: (804) 739-8871 or (800) 554-0130*. A 20-min drive south-west from downtown Richmond takes you to the 1700-acre **Swift Creek Reservoir**, on the wooded banks of which stands this highly regarded inn. Accommodation is in suites overlooking the lake. The inn has a restaurant serving Italian cuisine, a piano bar, exercise room, pool, sauna, Jacuzzi and jogging trails. There are five golf courses in the area. Expensive.

Sheraton Inn Richmond Airport, *4700 S. Laburnum Ave; tel: (800) 628-7601*. The hotel offers a restaurant open daily 0600–0100, indoor pool, barber's shop, beauty salon, gift shop, exercise equipment and sauna. Rooms are moderately priced, suites moderate–expensive.

Courtyard by Marriott, *6400 W. Broad St; tel: (804) 282-1881*. This motel provides coffee-making facilities in its rooms and has a bar, exercise equipment, outdoor pool and laundry. Moderate.

Red Roof Inn, *4350 Commerce Rd; tel: (804) 271-7240* or *(800) THE ROOF.* Over the James River, south of downtown Richmond. Rooms in this motel have TV and basic facilities. Budget. A restaurant is nearby.

Holiday Inn Airport, *5203 Williamsburg Rd, Sandston; tel: (804) 222-6450* or *(800) 964-6886.* Free transport to the nearby airport and free continental breakfast are offered. The inn has a restaurant and bar, with entertainment and dancing Thur–Sat. Moderate.

Emmanuel Hutzler House, *2036 Monument Ave; tel: (804) 353-6900.* This inn with a non-smoking policy has four rooms for guests. Coffee, served in the library, and continental breakfast are complimentary. Moderate–expensive.

West-Bocock House, *1197 Grove Ave; tel: (804) 358-6174.* Built in 1871, this bed and breakfast home is conveniently located close to museums, restaurants and shopping areas. Rooms are moderately priced, and each has a private bath. Full breakfast is served.

Americamps, *396 Air Park Rd, Ashland* (on Hwy 1); *tel: (804) 798-5298,* is roughly halfway between Richmond and Paramount's King's Dominion theme park, about 20 miles north of the city.

Two other campsites in the area are the **Bowling Green/Richmond N. KOA**, *Box 1250, Exit 104 Bowling Green; tel: (804) 633-7592* or *(800) 562-2482,* open all year, and **Paramount's King's Dominion Campground**, *10061 King's Dominion Blvd, Doswell; tel: (804) 876-5355,* off I-95 half a mile east on Rte 30. A free shuttle service operates to the theme park.

Eating and Drinking

Visitors should have little difficulty finding somewhere to have a meal whether they want fine dining, fast food or something in between. Several establishments offer live entertainment and many have great character. A 9.5% meal tax is imposed by restaurants in the City of Richmond. Outside the city limits the meal tax falls to 4.5%.

For one of the largest concentrations of restaurants in Richmond, head for the Fan District or Shockoe Slip, where many former warehouses now contain restaurants and bistros.

Strawberry Street Cafe is in the Fan, at *421 N. Strawberry St; tel: (804) 353-6860,* and is famous for its bathtub salad bar and diverse menu. Moderate.

Mystery Dinner Theatre, *Governor's Inn, Midlothian Turnpike; tel: (804) 649-CLUE.* Comic who-dunnits are staged Fri–Sat at 1930. Four-course dinners are served – by the suspects – one course between each of five acts. Moderate–pricey.

The Tobacco Company Restaurant, *1201 E. Cary St; tel: (804) 782-9431,* has continental cuisine in an award-winning restaurant housed in a former 1800s tobacco warehouse. Live music and dancing. Moderate.

Hugo's Bistro, in the *Hyatt Richmond, 6624 W. Broad St; tel: (804) 285-1234.* The continental cuisine is given an Italian accent. Moderate.

Delaney's Cafe and Grill, *10622 Patterson Ave, tel: (804) 740-1921.* Seafood is one of the specialities at this lunch and dinner venue. It closes at 2130 weekdays, 2230 Sat, 2100 Sun. Budget–moderate.

Farouk's House of India, *3033 W. Cary St; tel: (804) 355-0378.* Curries and other Indian dishes are on the menu in budget category, though you might just creep into the moderate bracket choosing from the dinner menu.

Lemaire, *Jefferson Hotel, Franklin and*

177

Adams Sts; tel: (804) 788-8000. Named after Thomas Jefferson's White House *maître d'hôtel*, who introduced Americans to the art of cooking with wine, the Lemaire – actually seven small dining rooms seating from 12 to more than 50 – is today presided over by Swiss-trained chef Mark Langenfeld. Lemaire is open to the public Mon–Sat for breakfast, lunch and dinner. Prices are surprisingly down to earth, with some items on the menu under $10, though you can pay considerably more for regional game dishes.

The Frog and the Redneck, *1423 E. Cary St; tel: (804) 648-3764.* Trendy and popular, with bright decor and continental menu, this restaurant, open Mon–Sat, encompasses budget to pricey gradings.

O'Toole's, *4800 Forest Hill Ave; tel: (804) 233-1781.* A family-owned eatery with Irish decor. Barbecued dishes are a speciality. Prices mainly cheap to budget or just over. Open to 0200 weekdays, midnight Sun.

Matt's British Pub, *109 12th St; tel: (804) 644-0848.* In a late 19th-century grain warehouse in Shockoe Slip, this place offers lunch for under $10 and dinner in the budget–moderate bracket, with comedy entertainment Fri and Sat.

Peking Pavilion, *1302 E. Cary St; tel (804) 649-8888.* As well as serving great value Peking duck and other Chinese dishes, the restaurant sells Oriental goods. You can eat at lunchtime for under $5. Dinner ranges from budget to pricey.

Sorrento, *5604 Patterson Ave; tel: (804) 282-9340.* Italian restaurant specialising in veal recipes and serving its own pasta. Budget to moderate.

Communications

The main **post office** is at *1801 Brook Rd; tel: (804) 775-6143.*

ENTERTAINMENT

Theatre, opera, ballet, music, comedy and historical presentations contribute to the performing arts scene in Richmond. There is also a range of spectator sports.

Carpenter Center for the Performing Arts, *600 E. Grace St; tel: (804) 782-3930.* This restored 1920s theatre, seating more than 2000, stages orchestral concerts, opera, dance and major Broadway shows.

Barksdale Theatre at Hanover Tavern, *PO Box 7, Hanover* (north of Richmond on Rte 301); *tel: (804) 731-4860.* This 1723 stage-coach inn presents professional dramas, comedies and Broadway musicals all year round. It claims to be the nation's oldest dinner theatre. Its five Colonial dining rooms are separate from the theatre.

The State Ballet of Virginia, *614 N. Lombardy St; tel: (804) 359-0906.* Five professional productions are staged in the Sept–May season.

Virginia Opera, *300 W. Franklin St; tel: (804) 643-6004.* Performances, by one of the nation's largest opera companies, take place at the Carpenter Center Oct–Mar.

Swift Creek Mill Playhouse, *17401 Jefferson Davis Hwy, PO Box 41, Colonial Heights, Chesterfield County; tel: (804) 748-4411.* South of Richmond, the 17th-century grist mill offers year-round Southern dining and/or Broadway entertainment and theatre in a setting of art works and historic artefacts.

Theatre Virginia, *2800 Grove Ave, Richmond; tel: (804) 353-6161.* Located in the Virginia Museum of Fine Arts, this professional theatre presents five shows each season – musicals, comedies, dramas and classics.

Top-name entertainers perform at the outdoor **Classix Amphitheatre**, *State*

Fairgrounds, Strawberry Hill; tel: (804) 228-3213.

The Mosque, *Laurel and Main Sts; tel: (804) 780-4213*, is a near-Eastern theatre more than 70 years old, presenting Broadway productions, concerts and lectures. **Theatre IV**, *114 W. Broad St, Richmond; tel: (804) 344-8040*. A highly esteemed resident professional company performing all year in a lovely old theatre, which incorporates a children's theatre.

Performances also take place throughout the year at the area's universities; *tel: (800) 365-7272* for details.

Spectator Sports
Richmond Braves Baseball Club, *The Diamond, 3001 N. Blvd, Richmond* (off I-95); *tel: (804) 359-4444*. The stadium seats nearly 13,000. The Richmond Braves are affiliates of the National League team, the Atlanta Braves. Open Apr–Sept.

Stock-car racing takes place at the three-quarter mile **Richmond International Raceway**, *Strawberry Hill, Laburnum Ave; tel: (804) 329-6796* The one-third mile oval track at *Genito Rd, Midlothian; tel: (804) 358-9875*, has a regular Fri evening meeting Apr–Sept.

Ice hockey matches take place in winter when the **Richmond Renegades** play at the *Richmond Coliseum* in the downtown area; *tel: (804) 780-4956 or (804) 643-PUCK*.

Three university teams share the basketball scene. They are **Virginia Commonwealth University**; *tel: (804) 828-7267*, **University of Richmond;** *tel: (804) 289-8388* and **Virginia Union University**; *tel: (804) 257-5790*.

Richmond Kickers are the area's professional soccer team. Home games are played in summer at the University of Richmond Soccer Complex, *tel: (804) 282-6776*.

Drag racing meetings are held at **Virginia Motorsports Park**, *Hwy 1 at Dinwiddie* (four miles south of I-85); *tel: (804) 732-RACE*.

SHOPPING
There are a number of malls in the city, but the place for boutique shopping is Shockoe Slip (see feature on 'Special Places', p.181). For antiques collectables, head north of Richmond to Mechanicsville, detailed in the box feature on p.180.

The **Farmers' Market**, *17th and Main St; tel: (804) 780-8597*, has operated since the 1740s on the site of an Indian trading post, and is open daily.

SIGHTSEEING
A good place to get your bearings in downtown Richmond is from the **Skydeck** at the multi-storey City Hall at *9th and Broad Sts; tel: (804) 780-7000*. It's open Mon–Thur 0800–2000, Fri–Sun 0800–1700. Free admission.

Tours
A number of organised tours are available by bus or mini-van, limousine or on foot. There are seasonal themed walking tours, tours with costumed guides and tours by aircraft over Civil War sites and battlefields. Operators of these tours include:

Historic Ashland, a walking tour featuring some of Richmond's most gracious Victorian homes; *tel: (804) 798-1722*.

Historic Richmond Tours, *707A E. Franklin Rd; tel (804) 780-0107*, has daily guided tours by mini-van. People can board at the visitor centre in *Robin Hood Rd* or at major downtown hotels. Seasonal themed tours are also held by mini-van or on foot.

Living History Associates; *tel: (804) 353-8166*. History is conveyed in an entertaining way by costumed guides.

179

Annabel Lee Riverboat, *4400 E. Main St; tel: (804) 644-5700*. The replica paddlewheeler runs lunch and dinner cruises on the James River, plus trips with live music, entertainment and dancing and, on Tues, a cruise past Plantation Row, with guided tours of plantation homes. Admission charge.

Richmond Discoveries; *tel: (804) 795-5781*. Group tours with historical entertainment, step-on guide service available.

Civil War Air Tours; *tel: (804) 649-1861*. 'Flightseeing' by plane over battlefields and other sites.

Historic Districts

Valentine Riverside, *500 Tredegar St; tel: (804) 649-0711*. On the site of the old Tredegar Iron Works, which supplied Civil War armaments for the Confederate Army, this urban history museum has state-of-the-art living history displays, rafting trips at the falls of the James River, a sound and light show, cycle tours and archaeological digs. Open Mon–Sat 1000–1700 (summer months only). Admission charge.

Court End, *c/o 1201 E. Clay St; tel: (804) 649-1861*. Dedicated history buffs

can take in four National Historic Landmarks, four museums and 11 other historic buildings, including St John's Church (see below) in a self-guided walking tour. Block tickets for the museums, valid for 30 days, and a map, are obtainable from the museums. Admission charge.

Virginia State Capitol, at the heart of Court End, *9th and E. Grace Sts; tel: (804) 786-4344*, was designed by Thomas Jefferson in 1785 as the first neo-classical building in the New World. Open Mon–Sun 0900–1700. Free.

Museum and White House of the Confederacy, *1201 E. Clay St* (Court End); *tel: (804) 649-1861*. Confederate President Jefferson Davis lived in the mansion during the Civil War. The adjacent museum claims to have the world's largest collection of Confederate artefacts, including Gen. Robert E. Lee's military tent. Open daily, Mon–Sat 1000–1700, Sun 1200–1700. Admission charge.

Valentine Museum and 1812 Wickham House, *1015 E. Clay St* (Court End); *tel: (804) 649-0711*. The life and history of Richmond are recorded and illustrated here. Urban and social history, decorative arts, costumes and architecture are among the subjects covered. The

---

Yesterday for Sale

Anyone who collects tobacco tins, old Valentine cards, antique farm implements or who wants a flag designed should take a 25-min drive to **Mechanicsville**, north of Richmond on US 301.

Sixteen shops here form **Antique Village**; *tel: (757) 746-8914 or 746-1008,* where all sorts of off-beat collectables can be found. One shop specialises in papers and documents – old labels, theatre programmes, postcards, sheet music, magazines from long ago, political manifestos full of forgotten promises, and pin-ups which once adorned the walls of wartime US servicemen stationed in the east of England.

Another shop offers arts and crafts, African carvings, and fine ceramics from the Orient, Toys, model trains and kitchen items of a past age are the speciality of another.

One shop features a huge collection of flags; you can have a banner hand-made to your own or someone else's design.

Special Places

Downtown Richmond has a selection of historic districts which everyone seeks out for an evening meal, some entertainment, a nightclub. some special shopping or to absorb the culture.

The **Fan District** is regarded as the largest intact Victorian neighbourhood in the US, with some 2000 townhouses of diverse architectural styles.

Shockoe Slip is the city's oldest mercantile district. Carefully restored, it is now a fashionable area for shopping, galleries and entertainment.

The 19th-century buildings of **Shockoe Bottom** now house restaurants, nightclubs and one-of-a-kind shops and boutiques. The restoration of this district is more recent than that of Shockoe Slip – for a long time floodwater from the James River made redevelopment difficult. Work went ahead as soon as a multi-million dollar flood barrier was completed, and now the district is alive with activity day and night.

Even taller than the converted warehouses is **Main Street Station**, and there are plans to revive rail travel to and from the spectacular building.

The ever-popular **Farmers' Market** – one of the country's oldest, having been operating for nearly three centuries – is on 17th Street.

There are fewer than 2000 National Historic Landmarks in the whole of the USA, and Richmond's **Court End** has seven of them, 11 other buildings on the National Register of Historic Places. Antebellum houses fill **Church Hill.**

Virginians are justifiably proud of their **Capitol Square** and its hilltop position, set among great trees and wide lawns. In the Rotunda of the Virginia State Capitol is the only statue of George Washington sculpted from life. The sculptor was Jean Antoine Houdon.

181

museum incorporates the architecturally important 1812 Wickham House, which has one of the finest neo-classical wall paintings in the nation. Open all year round Mon–Sat 1000–1700, Sun 1200–1700. Admission charge.

Monument Avenue is a thoroughfare of impact-making statues. Travelling from east to west, you will first see **Gen. J.E.B. Stuart**, the Confederate general who was fatally wounded at the Battle of Yellow Tavern. Then the magnificent statue of **Gen. Robert E. Lee**, astride his steed, Traveller, comes into view. Dedicated in 1890, this was the first monument in the Avenue. Next is a monument of Confederate **President Jefferson Davis** by Richmond sculptor Edward Valentine. In the work he included 13 Doric columns representing the 11 states that seceded and the two that sent delegates to the Confederate Congress. **Gen. Thomas 'Stonewall' Jackson** comes next. He was accidentally fatally injured by a shot from one of his own men at the battle of Chancellorsville. Finally, you encounter not a Civil War figure, but the oceanographer and scientist **Matthew Fontaine Maury**, inventor of the electric torpedo. This statue, the last of the quintet to be sculpted, was unveiled in 1929. *Monument Ave* is lined with turn-of-the-century mansions.

Church Hill is an historic neighbourhood of some 70 antebellum homes, many with cast iron ornamentation, bounded by *Broad, 29th, Main and 21st Sts.* Within it are St John's Church (see p. 182) and, at the eastern end, the headquarters of **Richmond National Battlefield Park**. The Park's **Visitor Center**, *3215 E. Broad St; tel: (804) 226-1981*, is open daily 0900–1700 (on US 60 in Richmond). See the film presentation and exhibits and use the map guide for a 97-mile self-guided motoring tour of the preserved battlefields and other sites in and around Richmond. **Civil War Tour** information also available from *(800) 365-7272*. Sites in adjacent Chesterfield and Henrico counties and in Richmond encompass nearly 100 miles of roads. McClellan's 1862 Peninsula campaign and Grant's 1864 attack at Cold Harbor are highlighted. Chickahominy Bluff, Beaver Dam Creek, Gaines Mill, Malvern Hill and Fort Harrison are among the names you encounter which may be familiar from history books. Parks open dawn to dusk. Free admission.

St John's Church, *2401 E. Broad st; tel: (804) 648-5015*. Dating from 1741, St John's is the church in which Patrick Henry delivered his famous 'Give me liberty or give me death' speech. A re-enactment of the 1775 occasion takes place every Sunday in summer (late May–early Sept). The city's oldest burial ground is at St John's. Open Mon–Sat 1000–1600, Sun 1300–1600. Admission charge.

Historic Buildings and Attractions

Virginia War Memorial, *Belvidere St* (just north of Lee Bridge) honours Virginians who gave their lives in World War II, in Korea, Vietnam and the Persian Gulf conflict. It is in the form of a glass structure with the figure of a mourning woman, and contains more than 12,000 names. Open daily. Free admission.

James River and Kanawha Canal Locks, *12th* and *Byrd Sts*. Restored locks on America's first canal system, in which George Washington was involved, with

audio-visual presentation. Picnic area. Open daily. Free admission.

John Marshall House, *818 E. Marshall St; tel: (804) 648-7998*. The house was built in 1790 for Chief Justice John Marshall, who lived there with his family for 45 years. The authentic furniture of the period includes some used by the Marshall family. There is a gift shop in the wine cellar. Open Tues–Sat 1000–1700, Sun 1300–1700 (summer), 1000–1630 Oct–Dec. Admission charge.

Hollywood Cemetery, *Albemarle and Cherry Sts; tel: (804) 648-8501*. As well as 18,000 Confederate soldiers, US Presidents James Monroe and John Tyler and Confederate President Jefferson Davis are buried here. Open daily 0800–1800. Free admission.

St Paul's Episcopal Church, *9th and E. Grace Sts*. Jefferson Davis and Robert E. Lee worshipped at this Richmond church, known as the Church of the Confederacy. It is noted for its Tiffany glass windows. Open daily. Free admission.

St Peter's Parish Church, *8400 St Peter's Lane, New Kent* (about a 20-mile drive east of Richmond); *tel: (804) 932-4846*, is the church where George and Martha Washington were married. Open daily. Tours by appointment.

Agecroft Hall, *4305 Sulgrave Rd; tel: (804) 353-4241*. This 15th-century English Tudor manor house – a superb example of its period – was dismantled, shipped across the Atlantic in the late 1920s, and carefully reconstructed by the James River in Richmond. Set in 23 acres of gardens, lawns and woodland, the richly timbered house and its furnishings reflect the lifestyle of a wealthy English family in the reign of King Charles I. The new museum shop is stocked with British goods. Open Tues–Sat 1000–1600, Sun 1230–1500. Admission charge.

Mister Bojangles

Bill 'Bojangles' Robinson, whose statue stands at the corner of Adams and Leigh streets in Richmond, was Jackson Ward neighbourhood's most famous son. Known throughout the pop music world as 'Mister Bojangles' – thanks to a popular song of the 1980s – he was a legendary tap dancer who became a popular vaudeville performer and screen star.

Born in 1878, he achieved worldwide fame when he danced with Shirley Temple in the film, *The Little Colonel*, but his career had begun at the age of six when he danced for nickels and dimes at Richmond beer gardens. At nine he ran away to Baltimore, where he fell in with a vaudeville performer named Elly Leonard. His first professional appearance was three years later as a dancer in the chorus of a Richmond show called *The South Before the War*.

Robinson is said to have been working as a waiter at Richmond's Jefferson Hotel when he was discovered by a New York agent. He was a great success in New York theatres and in 1930 he went to Hollywood. During the 1930s and 40s he starred in a number of Broadway musicals and made more films.

The famous dancer never forgot his beginnings in Jackson Ward. He was a regular contributor to charities and other causes. His statue stands at the corner of *Adams* and *Leigh Streets*, the intersection where he paid for a traffic light to improve safety for local children.

Bojangles died in 1949 at the age of 71.

Virginia House, *4301 Sulgrave Rd; tel: (804) 353-4251.* Next door to Agecroft Hall, this English priory said to date from 1125 was also transported across the ocean in the 1920s and re-assembled as a residence with terraced gardens, pools and pathways. It is owned and operated by the Virginia Historical Society. Open Tues–Sat 1000–1600, Sun 1230–1700. Admission charge.

Egyptian Building, *1223 E. Marshall St.* Demonstrating the diversity of architectural styles in Richmond, this unusual structure is considered the finest example of Egyptian Revival architecture in the country. Free admission.

Citie of Henricus Historical Park, Dutch Gap Landing on James River, Chesterfield County (reached via Rte 10 and *Old Stage Rd*); *tel: (804) 748-1623.* This was the second permanent English settlement in the New World, established in 1611 by Sir Thomas Dale. A mile-long riverside path leads to the site. Boat trips on the James River are available. Open daily dawn to dusk. Park free, there is a charge for river trips and there are living history interpreters.

Museums and Galleries
Richmond Children's Museum, *740 Navy Hill Dr; tel: (804) 643-KIDO.* Children as young as two years and up to 12 can enjoy learning by participating in exhibits and being introduced to the arts, nature and humanities. There's an 'In My Own Back Yard' feature. Activities are organised in the Art Studio. Open Tues–Sat 1000–1700, Sun 1300–1700. Admission charge.

Richmond Railroad Museum, *Hull and First Sts; tel: (804) 233-6237.* Artefacts and photographs from the area's railway history are displayed in a restored Railway Express Agency car. Open Sat and Sun.

Science Museum of Virginia, *2500 W. Broad St; tel: (804) 367-1013.* Presenting the modern mix of education

183

and fun, this popular museum has more than 250 hands-on exhibits, a planetarium and space theatre. Open Mon–Sat 0930–1700, Sun 1200–1700. Admission charge.

Virginia Museum of Fine Arts, *280 Grove Ave; tel: (804) 367-0844.* The Fabergé collection, for which this extensive art museum is renowned, includes five Easter eggs of Imperial Russia. Works displayed range from Renaissance paintings to Picasso and Andy Warhol. Open Tues–Sun 1100–1700 (Thur to 2000). Admission by donation.

Edgar Allan Poe Museum, *1914 E. Main St; tel: (804) 648-5523.* The life and literary works of Poe chronicled in the **Old Stone House**, said to be Richmond's oldest building (1737), and a model of Richmond as it was in Poe's time – the first half of the 19th century. Open Tues–Sat 1000–1600, Sun 1100–1600. Admission charge.

Money Museum, *Federal Reserve Bank, 7th and Byrd Sts; tel: (804) 697-8000.* Rare old bills, other forms of currency and gold and silver ingots can be seen. Open Mon–Fri.

American Historical Foundation Museum, *1142 W. Grace St; tel: (804) 353-1812*, contains personal possessions of Civil War figures Gen. J.E.B. Stuart and John S. Mosby and a large collection of military bayonets and knives. Open Mon–Fri 0830–1700. Free admission.

Lora Robins Gallery of Design from Nature, *University of Richmond; tel: (804) 289-8237.* A delightful collection of gems, fossils and rare seashells. Phone for opening hours. Admission charge.

Center for Virginia History, *428 N. Boulevard; tel: (804) 358-4901.* Virginia Historical Society's pride and joy, this museum contains everything the researcher into nearly four centuries of the state's history could wish to find. The museum has seven galleries displaying Virginia treasures and a library for general and genealogical research. Events from World War II up to the present decade are represented. Museum shop. Open Mon–Sat 1000–1700, Sun 1300–1700. Admission $3, children $2.

Virginia Aviation Museum, *Richmond International Airport, 5701 Huntsman Rd, Sandston; tel: (804) 236-3622 or 222-8690.* Vintage aircraft from 1914 to the 1930s, exhibits on World War II, navigational aids and other items are on show at this division of the Science museum of Virginia. Open daily 0930–1700. Admission $3.50, children $2.50.

Virginia Fire and Police Museum, *200 W. Marshall St; tel: (804) 644-1849.* Vintage equipment and memorabilia of these two emergency services are on display, and a safety education programme operates. Open Tues–Sat 1000–1600, Sun 1300–1700. Admission charge.

Chesterfield Museum Complex and Magnolia Grange, *Chesterfield Courthouse, 6805 W. Krause Rd; tel: (804) 748-1026.* A variety of interests are covered here. The museum displays ancient fossils and Indian artefacts, early coal-mining and Revolutionary and Civil War history and many other aspects of life in Chesterfield County down the centuries. The complex includes the **Old Jail** (1892). Museum open Mon–Fri 1000–1600, Sun 1300–1600. Free admission. **Magnolia Grange** is a plantation house built in 1822, and has furnishings of the period. Open Mon–Fri 1000–1600, Sun 1300–1700. Admission $2, senior citizens $1.50, children $1.

Wilton House Museum, *215 S. Wilton Rd; tel: (804) 282-5936.* A Georgian mansion dating from 1753 typi-

---

Birthplace of Black Capitalism

The first African American to win Wimbledon, Arthur Ashe, lived in Richmond. The first black woman to become a bank president, Maggie Walker, lived there. So did Lawrence Douglas Wilder, who was the nation's first elected black governor. Another famous son was the entertainer Bill 'Bojangles' Robinson (see box, p.183), whose statue stands at the corner of *Adams* and *Leigh Streets*.

All made their contribution to the rich African American heritage. One of the city's finest athletic and trade show facilities, the Arthur Ashe Center, honours the champion tennis player.

A leading force in the city's black community and a champion of self-help initiatives, Maggie Lena Walker became a bank president in 1903, founding the oldest surviving black-operated bank in the US at *110½ Leigh Street*. She lived there for 30 years, and it is now a National Historic Site; *tel: (804) 780-1380*, and is managed by the National Park Service. Open Wed–Sun 0900–1700. Free admission.

Richmond's African American heritage is centred on **Jackson Ward**. A free black man, Abraham Skipwith, a plasterer by trade, built a small cottage in *Duval St* nearly 200 years ago, and was the first resident. Jackson Ward flourished after the Civil War, and was soon recognised as one of the most important black residential and commercial districts in the nation. It became known as Little Africa and is often called the Birthplace of Black Capitalism.

Jackson Ward Historic District claims to have more cast iron porches and ornamental work on its homes and buildings than anywhere outside New Orleans. Much restoration work is taking place. The district's *Second Street* and famous **Hippodrome Theatre** are undergoing a major restoration programme. Such performers as Ella Fitzgerald and Duke Ellington have received standing ovations here.

Second Street Festival, held in October, is one of Jackson Ward's major annual events celebrating African American culture.

The **Black History Museum and Cultural Center of Virginia**, *Clay Street, Jackson Ward; tel: (804) 780-9093*, depicts the major developments in the history of black people in Virginia from James Town in 1619 onwards. One section illustrates Jackson Ward as the Birthplace of Black Capitalism. The museum is open Tues and from Thur–Sat 1100–1600. There is an admission charge.

The **Virginia E. Randolph Museum**, *2200 Mountain Rd; tel: (804) 262-3363*, commemorates the career of a pioneer in the field of vocational education. Virginia Randolph was supervisor of a fund set up by a wealthy Quaker to further the cause of education for black people in the US. The museum, with free admission, is open Mon, Wed, Fri and Sat 1300–1600 and Sun 1500–1700.

A marker on the site of a Civil War fortification, on US 1 north of *Broad St* at Brook Run shopping centre, commemorates an ill-fated slaves' revolt. The site is known as **Gabriel's Insurrection**.

---

fies the opulent family homes built by wealthy planters. Standing on a bluff overlooking the James River, this one has some noted interior panelling and contains many antiques. Open Tues–Sat 1000–1630, Sun 1330–1630. Admission charge.

Meadow Farm Museum, *Mountain and Courtney Rds, Glen Allen (12 miles* north of the city off Woodman Rd); *tel: (804) 672-5106* or *672-9496.* The living historical museum reflects the life of a middle class rural family in the 1860s, during the Civil War years. First watch the video in the new orientation centre, then see costumed interpreters at work in the farmhouse, barn, doctor's surgery, blacksmith's forge, schoolhouse and stables. Grounds with picnic shelters open daily, dawn to dusk. Free admission. Museum open Tues–Sun 1200–1600 mid Mar–mid Dec. Admission charge.

Shockoe Bottom Arts Center, *2001 E. Grace St; tel: (804) 643-7959.* Artists work in various media here, and the public can survey the results. Open Tues–Sat 1000–1700, Sun 1200–1700. Admission free.

Three Lakes Nature Center and Aquarium, *400 Sausiluta Dr; tel: (804) 262-4822.* Wetland flora and fauna, creatures of the forest and aquatic wildlife and plants are on view. Open Tues–Sun 1200–1700. Free admission.

Gardens and Theme Parks

Lewis Ginter Botanical Garden, *1800 Lakeside Ave; tel: (804) 262-9887,* has an extensive display of flowers in season, starting in spring with an array of daffodils, followed by azaleas and rhododendrons. In the garden, which has a three-acre lake, are the Henry Flagler Perennial Garden, the Grace Arents Garden, Children's Garden, a mansion – Bloemendal House – and a teahouse. Open Mon–Sat 0930–1600, Sun 1300–1600. Admission charge.

Maymont, *1700 Hampton St; tel: (804) 358-7166.* A 100-acre estate in which people can wander by the James River, around herb beds and Japanese and Italian gardens, visit a nature centre with native wildlife, enjoy a children's farm, tour the restored late-Victorian home and see a large collection of antique carriages. Tram tours and carriage rides are available. Open all year round Tues–Sun 1200–1630. Closed Mon. Grounds free, admission charge for some sections.

In the 287-acre **William Byrd Park** is a 240 ft high brick carillon tower, a memorial to those who served in World War I.

Pocahontas State Park, south on US10 then west on Rte 655; *tel: (804) 796-4255 or 786-1712.* A 20-min drive south of downtown Richmond, the park provides more than 7000 acres of recreational area, with Swift Creek Lake at its heart. Seasonal camping and interpretive programmes. Boating is restricted to man-powered or electric motor craft. Canoe and paddle boat rentals are available. Freshwater fishing, hiking trails, cycle paths (and bicycle hire), swimming pool and picnic facilities are popular. The visitor centre has wildlife exhibits. Admission charge and parking fee.

Paramount's Kings Dominion, off I-95 at Doswell, 20 miles north of Richmond; *tel: (804) 876-5000.* With more than 100 exciting rides, live shows, the Hurricane Reef water park, racing car simulators and other attractions, this is one of the most popular theme parks in the US. Since the summer of 1996 the whoops and shrieks have been even more shrill with the introduction of The Outer Limits: Flight of Fear. Passengers in a 24-seat train are propelled around steep turns and plummeted down seven storeys in complete darkness. Speeds of more than 50 mph and high-tech special effects make it a never-to-be-forgotten experience. Open Mar–May and Sept/Oct weekends only, daily June–Aug. Admission charge.

RICHMOND–VIRGINIA BEACH

Following the James River from Virginia's capital to its outlet at the mouth of Chesapeake Bay, and on to the popular Atlantic Ocean resort, this route visits those parts of the state which saw the arrival of the first English settlers. About half the route follows one of Virginia's loveliest by-ways, Rte 5, along which lies a string of historic plantation homes – some offering bed and breakfast accommodation. Beyond Williamsburg (see pp. 196–205) we reach the busy conurbation of sea ports and resort areas around the Hampton Roads, where the James, York, Elizabeth and Nansemond rivers enter Chesapeake Bay.

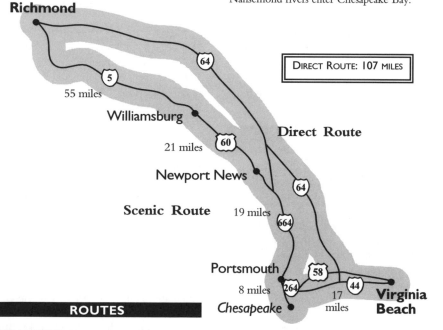

Richmond

64

5

55 miles

DIRECT ROUTE: 107 MILES

Williamsburg

Direct Route

21 miles 60

Newport News

64

Scenic Route 19 miles

664

Portsmouth

58

8 miles 264

17 miles

44

Virginia Beach

Chesapeake

ROUTES

DIRECT ROUTE

The quickest route between the state's capital and its most popular resort is by way of I-64 and Rte 44 east, which will take you into downtown Virginia Beach in about 1 hr 45 mins. But this means you will miss the beauty of Rte 5 and the chance to visit some of the James River Plantations, which would mean adding a mere 20 miles to the journey.

SCENIC ROUTE

From Richmond's *Capitol Sq.* take *E. Franklin St* through Shockoe

Bottom then turn right on to *27th St.* Turn left on *E. Main St,* which leads directly into Rte 5. The first of Charles City County's plantations is reached in 18 miles. Rte 5 winds its tree-lined way for a further 35 miles to **Williamsburg**. From Williamsburg head south along Hwy 60 – the Pocahontas Trail – for 21 miles, through **Newport News**, to cross the James River on I-664 by way of the 6-mile long Monitor-Merrimac Memorial Bridge-Tunnel. Exits 11 and 13 from I-664 both lead on to roads into downtown **Portsmouth**. Neighbouring **Chesapeake** can be reached from I-64. I-264 cuts through the centre of Portsmouth, crossing the Elizabeth River to the outskirts of Norfolk, where Hwy 58 *(Virginia Beach Blvd)* and Rte 44 *(Virginia Beach-Norfolk Expressway)* travel side by side to downtown **Virginia Beach** (p. 217), 13 miles to the east.

188

CHARLES CITY COUNTY

This is a county without a city. The tiny community that provides its name surrounds an early 18th-century courthouse at the intersection of Rtes 5 and 155.

Located between the James and Chickahominy Rivers, the county was founded in 1616 and marked the first westward expansion of English-speaking America. Agriculture – especially highly profitable tobacco farming – led to the establishment of a number of splendid plantations along the James River. Many of the gracious manor houses have survived the Revolutionary War, the War of 1812 and the Civil War. Privately owned, a number of them are open to visitors. Each property is clearly signposted from Rte 5.

ACCOMMODATION AND FOOD

Four plantation properties offer bed and breakfast lodging in the moderate–expensive range.

Belle Air Plantation, *11800 John Tyler Hwy, Charles City, VA 23030; tel: (804) 829-2431,* was built in 1670 and includes what is said to be America's finest Jacobean stairway. Its landscaped grounds overlook extensive farmland.

Edgewood Plantation, *4800 John Tyler Hwy, Charles City, VA 23030; tel: (804) 829-2962,* is an 1849 Gothic Revival home which has served as a church, post office and Confederate signal post. Features include a free-standing double spiral staircase, formal gardens and a 1725 gristmill.

North Bend Plantation, *12200 Weyanoke Rd, Charles City; tel: (804) 829-5176,* is a Greek Revival manor built in 1819 for Sarah Harrison, sister of William Henry Harrison, 9th president of the US. It served as Gen. Sheridan's headquarters in 1864. Its large rooms with private baths are furnished with original antiques.

Piney Grove at Southall's Plantation, *16920 Southall Plantation Lane, Charles City; tel: (804) 829-2480,* was built around 1800 and is a rare survival of early Tidewater log architecture. Guest rooms feature original antiques and the grounds include gardens, a pool and a nature trail.

Fine dining is available in moderate–pricey restaurants, both open daily for lunch and dinner. **Indian Fields Tavern**, *9220 John Tyler Hwy, tel: (804) 829-5004,* serves Virginia ham, Chesapeake Bay seafood and other regional specialties in a turn-of-the-century farmhouse on Rte 5. **Coach House Tavern**, *12602 Harrison Landing Rd; tel: (804) 829-6003,* is located in a restored outbuilding on Berkeley Plantation. Dinner (reservations essential) is served by candlelight, and staff in period costume serve lunch.

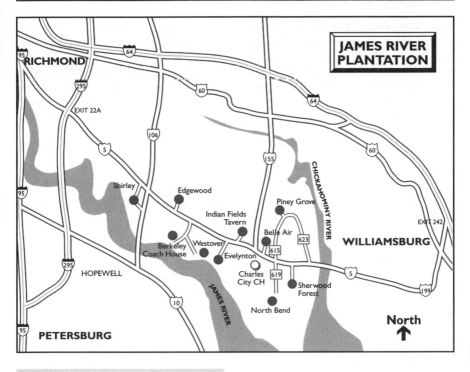

JAMES RIVER PLANTATION

North ↑

SIGHTSEEING

Berkeley Plantation, *12602 Harrison Landing Rd; tel: (804) 829-6018*. The site of the first official Thanksgiving in 1619, Berkeley was the birthplace of Benjamin Harrison, a signatory to the Declaration of Independence, and William Henry Harrison, 9th president of the US, and ancestral home of the 23rd president, Benjamin Harrison. Open daily 0800–1700. Admission: $8.50.

Evelynton Plantation, *6701 John Tyler Hwy; tel: (804) 829-5075*. Home of the Ruffin family since 1847, this Georgian Revival manor house is furnished with heirlooms and is noted for its outstanding floral arrangements. The family patriarch, Edmund Ruffin, fired the first shot on the Civil War. Open daily 0900–1700. Admission: $7.

Sherwood Forest Plantation, *14501 John Tyler Hwy; tel: (804) 829-5377*. Known to be the longest frame house in the country, Sherwood Forest was the home of John Tyler after he served as president of the US from 1841–45, and has been restored and furnished with his possessions. Open daily 0900–1700. Admission: $7.50.

Shirley Plantation, *501 Shirley Plantation Rd; tel: (804) 829-5121*. Settled in 1613 by Sir Thomas West, this is Virginia's oldest plantation. The present house was built in 1723. It has original portraits, silver and furniture and a unique flying staircase which rises three stories with no visible means of support. Open daily 0900–1630. Admission: $7.50.

NEWPORT NEWS

Tourist Information: Newport News Tourism Development Office, *50 Shoe

Lane, Newport News, VA 23606; tel: (800) 333-7787, has information on local attractions, historic sites, dining and lodging and a copy of the free *Newport News Visitors Guide* and discount coupons. **Newport News Tourist Information Center**, *13560 Jefferson Ave; tel: (804) 886-7777*. Located within Newport News City Park, which may be accessed from *Jefferson Ave* or *Fort Eustis Blvd* at the northern end of the city, the centre dispenses maps, brochures and information on local and state attractions and accommodation. From I-64 take exit 250B to Rte 105 east (*Fort Eustis Blvd*). The park entrance is within half a mile. From Hwy 60 take Rte 105 east for 1½ miles.

Newport News is named after Captain Christopher Newport, commander of the ships that brought the first English settlers to America in 1607, and the news he took back to the Old World.

ACCOMMODATION

The city boasts 30 hotels and hotel chains include: *CI, DI, EL, TL, Om, Ra* and *S8*.

Host Inn, *985 J. Clyde Morris Blvd (Hwy 17); tel: (804) 599-3303 or (800) 747-3303*, has a pool and a 24–hour restaurant opposite. Budget.

Mulberry Inn, *16890 Warwick Blvd; tel: (804) 887-3000 or (800) 223-0404*. Some rooms have self-catering facilities; amenities include a fitness centre, laundry, pool, restaurant and lounge. Moderate.

Omni Hotel, *1000 Omni Way; tel: (804) 873-6664 or (800) 843-6664*, features an indoor pool. The restaurant is open daily 0630–2300, and the bar 1100–0200. Expensive.

Ramada Inn and Conference Center, *950 J. Clyde Morris Blvd (Hwy 17); tel: (804) 599-4460 or (800) 2-RAMADA*, has a restaurant, fitness centre and a heated indoor pool. Moderate.

A campsite with more than 180 RV and tent sites is located in **Newport News Park**, *13564 Jefferson Ave, Newport News, VA 23603; tel: (804) 888-3333*. Each site is equipped with picnic table and charcoal grill, and many have electrical and water hook-ups. Facilities include hot showers, laundry room, camp store and pay phones. Camping is available all year round, with a 21-day limit Apr–Oct.

EATING AND DRINKING

Some 50 establishments, mostly in the budget price range, are listed in a restaurant guide published by Newport News Tourism Development Office and obtainable from the tourist information centre.

Chris' Steak House, *3506 Washington Ave; tel: (804) 380-1380*, serves Greek and American dishes at lunch and dinner. Budget.

Cracker Barrel, *12357 Hornsby Lane; tel: (804) 249-3020*, specialises in country cooking and serves breakfast, lunch and dinner. Budget.

Kappo Nara Sushi, *550A Oyster Point Rd; tel: (804) 249-5395*, serves Japanese cuisine. Moderate.

A good choice of budget fast food is available in the **Patrick Henry Mall Food Court**, *12300 Jefferson Ave*.

SIGHTSEEING

Harbor Cruises at Waterman's Wharf, *917 Jefferson Ave; tel: (804) 245-1533*. Two-hour narrated cruises of the Hampton Roads Harbor start from the Small Boat Harbor at *12 St* and *Jefferson Ave*. Passengers are able to view the massive **Newport News Shipyard** where aircraft carriers and submarines are built, the site of the famous Civil War battle between the ironclads *Monitor* and *Merrimac*, and the Norfolk Naval Base. There are daily departures at noon and

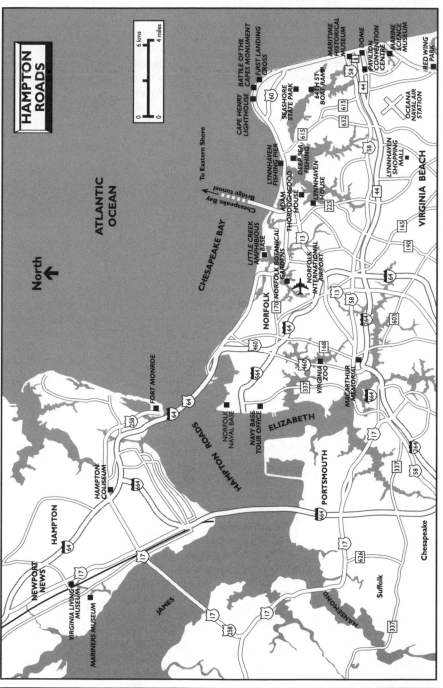

HAMPTON ROADS

North ↑

ATLANTIC OCEAN

CHESAPEAKE BAY

To Eastern Shore

Chesapeake Bay Bridge tunnel

MARITIME HISTORICAL MUSEUM
DOME
PAVILION CONVENTION CENTRE
MARINE SCIENCE MUSEUM
RED WING PARK

BATTLE OF THE CAPES MONUMENT
FIRST LANDING CROSS
CAPE HENRY LIGHTHOUSE
SEASHORE STATE PARK
64TH ST. BOAT RAMP

60
615
632
58
44

LYNNHAVEN FISHING PIER
DEEP SEA FISHING
LYNNHAVEN HOUSE
615
58

OCEANA NAVAL AIR STATION

LYNNHAVEN SHOPPING MALL
44

ADAM THOROUGHGOOD HOUSE
225

VIRGINIA BEACH
165

LITTLE CREEK AMPHIBIOUS BASE
NORFOLK BOTANICAL GARDENS
13

NORFOLK INTERNATIONAL AIRPORT
13
58

190

64

170
64

264
603

FORT MONROE

460
564

168
460

VIRGINIA ZOO
337

MACARTHUR MEMORIAL
664

NORFOLK

258
64

HAMPTON ROADS

NORFOLK NAVAL BASE
NAVY BASE TOUR OFFICE

ELIZABETH

PORTSMOUTH

17
17
264

337
58

HAMPTON COLISEUM
664

HAMPTON
64

664

17

626
Chesapeake

NEWPORT NEWS
17

VIRGINIA LIVING MUSEUM
MARINERS MUSEUM

JAMES

17
17
58

NANSEMOND
Suffolk
337

0   6 kms
0   4 miles

191

1400 mid May–mid Aug, with one daily departure at 1200 during the rest of the year. A 3-hr evening buffet cruise with dancing departs daily at 1900 June–Aug, and an 8-hr cruise of the Intracoastal Waterway departs at 0900 daily, May–Oct. Fares: from $12.50.

Mariners' Museum, *100 Museum Dr.* (intersection of *Warwick* and *J. Clyde Morris Blvds*); *tel: (804) 595-0368* or *(800) 581-SAIL.* Nautical history covering 3000 years is represented in 13 stunning galleries displaying model ships, figureheads, marine paintings and decorative arts, scrimshaw, navigational instruments and small craft. One gallery is devoted to the life of Admiral Lord Nelson. Hundreds of photographs and artefacts, work boats and a working steam engine are on show in the Chesapeake Bay Gallery, while the Age of Exploration Gallery traces the development of shipbuilding, navigation and cartography over the centuries. The evolution of the sailing ship is illustrated in the Crabtree Collection of Miniature Ships, 16 painstakingly detailed models constructed over 28 years by Dr. August F. Crabtree, grandson of a Clydeside shipbuilder. The museum is located within a 550-acre park with picnic areas, rental boats and canoes and a 5-mile walking trail. Open daily 1000–1700. Admission: $6.50.

Museum of the Harbor, *Waterman's Wharf, 917 Jefferson Ave; tel: (804) 245-1533* or *(800) 362-3046.* The museum traces the evolution of ship construction with special emphasis on the contributions made by the Newport News builders. A special section, including a giant diorama, is devoted to Civil War naval battles, including the exchange between the ironclad vessels, *Monitor* and *Merrimac.* Open daily 1000–1700. Admission: donation.

Newport News Park, *13564 Jefferson Ave; tel: (804) 888-3333.* With some 8000 acres of woodlands and two freshwater lakes, this is one of the largest municipal parks in the US. It offers year-round hiking, camping, fishing, boating, golfing and seasonal events. More than 30 species of mammals – including deer, fox, raccoon, otter and beaver – and 200 species of birds share the park's varied habitats, and there are the remnants of Civil War earthworks and fortifications. The park's Interpretive Center houses a display of Civil War artefacts recovered from sites within the grounds, and there is a wildlife rehabilitation centre where injured or orphaned animals are tended until they are fit to be released back into the wild. Admission: free.

Newsome House Museum and Cultural Center, *2803 Oak Ave; tel: (804) 247-2360.* This elegant Queen Anne-style residence, built in 1899, was the home of Joseph Thomas Newsome (1869–1942), a prominent black lawyer who edited a local newspaper, formed the Colored Voters League of Warwick County and became a respected civic leader. Open Mon–Sat 1000–1600. Admission free.

Peninsula Fine Arts Center, *Mariner's Museum Park, 101 Museum Dr.; tel: (804) 596-8175.* The center features constantly changing national and regional exhibitions of a broad range of artistic styles and media. Occupying 15,000 sq ft it can accommodate up to seven concurrent exhibitions and houses classrooms and workshops. Open Tues–Sat 1000–1700, Sun 1300–1700. Admission free.

U.S. Army Transportation Museum, *Besson Hall, Fort Eustis, Mulberry Island,* off Hwy 60 (exit 250 off I-64); *tel: (804) 878-1182.* Indoor and outdoor displays tell the story of two centuries of military transportation, from horse-drawn vehicles to mighty steam locomotives, helicopters, jet aircraft and cybernetic walking machines. Open daily 0900–1630. Admission free.

War Memorial Museum of Virginia, *9285 Warwick Blvd; tel: (804) 247-8523*. More than 50,000 artefacts document American conflicts from the Revolutionary War to Desert Storm. There are displays of uniforms, insignia, vehicles and weapons and one of the largest collections of propaganda posters in the U.S. Open Mon-Sat 0900–1700, Sun 1300–1700. Admission: $2.

PORTSMOUTH

Tourist Information: Visitors' Information Center, *6 Crawford Parkway, Portside; tel: (804) 393-5111.*

Operated by Portsmouth Convention and Visitors Bureau, the centre is on the waterfront and is identified by the British red telephone booth standing outside. The booth was a gift from the city's twin and namesake in England. The centre is a treasure house of information about the area and can assist with restaurant reservations as well as accommodation advice. There are even menus for visitors to examine.

ACCOMMODATION

Portsmouth's leading hotel is the **Holiday Inn Old Towne**, *8 Crawford Parkway; tel: (804) 393-2573*. Located on the Elizabeth River waterfront in the heart of the historic Old Towne district, it has a restaurant overlooking the river, open daily 0630–2200 and the bar 1200–0200. Facilities include a coin-operated laundromat and exercise equipment. Moderate.

Days Inn, *1031 London Blvd; tel: (804) 399-4414* has fully furnished studio suites and offers free continental breakfast Mon-Fri. Budget-moderate.

Olde Towne Inn, *420 Middle St, Olde*

Towne; tel: (804) 397-5462 is a two-storey Victorian home restored as a bed and breakfast inn. Each of its four guest rooms has a theme and a chamberpot - for decoration only. Private baths and verandas are additional features. The inn is within walking distance of the waterfront, attractions, shops and restaurants. Moderate.

The **Vagabond Inn**, *333 Effingham St; tel: (804) 397-5462*, is another moderately priced Olde Towne bed and breakfast inn.

EATING AND DRINKING

The first port of call for restaurant information has to be the Visitors' Information Centre (see left), where staff can produce menus and can also make reservations. **Portside Marketplace**, on the waterfront, is a favourite place for eating out with 11 open-air restaurants offering cuisine ranging from barbecue to seafood with musical entertainment Wed–Sun.

At the **Commodore Theatre**, *421 High St; tel: (804) 393-6962*, you can enjoy dinner and a first-run movie. **Cafe Europa**, *319 High St; tel: (804) 399-6652*, specialises in Continental cuisine. Open Tues–Thur 1130–1400, 1700–2130, Fri–Sat 1130–1400, 1700–2230 (closed mid Aug–mid Sept). Moderate.

The Max, *425 Water St; tel: (804) 397-1866*, is noted for its seafood dishes, which may be served on an outdoor patio overlooking the Elizabeth River. Open daily 1130–2200. Budget-moderate.

Scale O' De Whale, *3515 Shipwright St; tel: (804) 483-2772*, is located at the end of a pier where you can enjoy seafood or steaks surrounded by maritime antiques, model ships, scrimshaw and navigation lights.

SIGHTSEEING

The city was named after the English naval port by Colonel William Crawford, a wealthy colonist, in 1752 and it displays a rich variety of architectural styles spanning the centuries. The **Olde Towne** historic district has the largest collection of original old homes between northern Virginia and South Carolina.

The **Olde Towne Walking Tour** brochure, obtainable from the visitors' centre, contains a map and descriptive text of the square-mile area in which there are no fewer than 45 points of interest. The self-guided walk is designed to last about an hour. **Olde Towne Lantern Tours** are conducted by a guide in period costume on Tues 2030–2130, starting and ending at the Holiday Inn on the waterfront. Tickets ($3) may be purchased at the Visitors' Information Centre.

More of the city can be seen on an **Olde Towne Trolley Tour** operated by Tidewater Regional Transit; *tel: (804) 640-6300*. The tours start at Portside, opposite the visitors' information centre. **African American Heritage Trolley Tours**; *tel: (804) 393-5327*, also start from Portside. Included on these tours is the **Art Atrium**, a gallery in which the works of Hampton Roads African American artists and original arts and crafts from Africa are exhibited.

Harbor Cruises: *tel: (804) 393-4735*, operates sightseeing trips aboard the *Carrie B*, a replica 19th-century Mississippi sternwheeler river boat. Cruises depart from Portside daily at 1210 and 1410. Sunset cruises depart daily at 1810 June–Sept. Fares from $12. The company also operates cruises to the Great Dismal Swamp National Wildlife Refuge (see Chesapeake, p.195). The day-long trip includes continental breakfast, Southern-style buffet lunch and return by motor coach.

Children's Museum of Virginia, *221 High St; tel: (804) 393-8393*. The museum houses more than 60 interactive exhibits intended to challenge and inform. Among them are *The City*, where things are scaled down to child size, *Hocus Pocus*, a collection of optical illusions, and a state-of-the-art planetarium. Opening hours are Tues–Fri 1000–1700, Sat 1000–2100, Sun 1300–1700 (Sept–May); Mon–Sat 1000–1900, Sun 1300–1700 (June–Aug).

The Hill House, *221 North St; tel: (804) 393-0241*. Headquarters of the Portsmouth Historical Association, this four-storey English basement dwelling was built in the early 1800s and contains original furnishings collected by generations of the Hill family over a period of 150 years. Open Wed, Sat, Sun 1300–1700. Admission: $2.

Arts Center, *420 High St; tel: (804) 393-8983*, is located in the gallery of an 1846 court house, and features a complete spectrum of visual arts by international and regional artists in changing exhibitions. Open Tues–Sat 1000–1700, Sun 1300–1700. Admission charge.

Lightship Museum, *London Slip, Water St and London Blvd; tel: (804) 393-8741*. Commissioned in 1915, the lightship *Portsmouth* has been restored to its original condition. Visitors can board the vessel and see what life was like for the men of the Lighthouse Service. Open Tues–Sat 1000–1700, Sun 1300–1700. Admission charge.

Naval Shipyard Museum, *2 High St (on the Elizabeth River); tel: (804) 393-8591*. Exhibits capture the lifestyle of Portsmouth in the 18th and 19th centuries and there are thousands of naval artefacts, including signal flags, uniforms, maps and model ships. Open Tues–Sat 1000–1700, Sun 1300–1700. Admission charge.

Trinity Church, *500 Court St; tel: (804) 393-0431*. Built in 1762, this is the oldest church in Portsmouth. The church bell, now re-cast, is said to have cracked while ringing after the British surrender at Yorktown in 1781. Open Mon–Fri on request (enquire at office in parish hall behind the church).

Virginia Sports Hall of Fame, *420 High St; tel: (804) 393-8031*. The achievements of more than 150 of Virginia's leading sportsmen and women – including golfer Sam Snead, Olympic basketball player Nancy Liberman-Cline and tennis ace Arthur Ashe – are enshrined in the hall, which contains immortalising mementos, photographs and film clips.

SIDE TRACK
FROM PORTSMOUTH

CHESAPEAKE

Tourist Information: Public Information Dept, *PO Box 15225, Chesapeake, VA 23328; tel: (804) 547-6241*.

ACCOMMODATION

Hotel chains in Chesapeake include *CI, DI, Hd*.

Comfort Inn, *4433 S. Military Hwy; tel: (804) 488-7900*, has 93 rooms, seven with kitchen units. Continental breakfast is complimentary. Moderate. **Hampton Inn-Chesapeake**, *701A Woodlake Dr.; tel: (804) 420-1550*, has 119 rooms and a pool. Complimentary continental breakfast. An adjoining restaurant is open daily 0630–2200. Moderate.

EATING AND DRINKING

Cara's, *123 N. Battlefield Blvd; tel: (804) 548-0006*, is a restaurant specialising in Chesapeake Bay and Southern dishes. A patio dining area overlooks the Tidewater wetlands. Live music Fri, Sat. It opens Mon–Thur 1130–1430,

1600–2200, Fri–Sat 1130–1430, 1600–2300, Sun 1130–2100. Moderate.

Locke's Point, *136 N. Battlefield Blvd; tel: (804) 547-9618*, specialises in fresh seafood and presents entertainment at weekends. Open Mon–Fri 1130–1500 and 1700–2200, Sat 1700–2200, Sun 1100–2100. Lunch is budget, dinner moderate.

SIGHTSEEING

Great Dismal Swamp National Wildlife Refuge, *PO Box 439, Suffolk, VA 23439* (accessible from Hwy 17 south); *tel: (804) 986-3705*. This eerie area, 25 miles long and up to 11 miles wide, abounds with animal and bird life, including white-tailed deer, black bear, bobcats, foxes and many snakes, including copperheads and rattlesnakes.

Lake Drummond, lying in the centre of the refuge, covers 18 square miles and consists of 'juniper water', a combination of water and the juices of gum, cypress, maple and juniper that remains fresh indefinitely – a boon for sailors in the days when voyages lasted many weeks.

Timber, especially cypress and cedar, was exploited even before the Revolutionary War. George Washington and a group of businessmen formed a company which bought part of the swamp and used slave labour to dig a canal to get the timber out. The canal is in use today.

Northwest River Park, *Indian Creek Rd, off Battlefield Blvd; tel: (804) 421-3145*. This 760-acre city park has eight miles of hiking and nature trails, fishing, boating, canoeing, picnic sites and a playground. There is a campground with tent and RV pitches. Open daily. Admission free.

195

WILLIAMSBURG

There are really two Williamsburgs. One is an attractive but nonetheless everyday community of 11,500 people whose activities, concerns, interests and aspirations are much the same as those of any other Americans. The other is the 173-acre Colonial Williamsburg – a town-sized living history museum. Here, many of the houses, shops, taverns and other buildings are authentic 18th-century structures, and the broad, unpaved streets, peopled with costumed shopkeepers, craftsmen, soldiers, slaves, housewives and public officials, vividly recall the ambience of Virginia's pre-Revolutionary capital.

TOURIST INFORMATION

Williamsburg Area Convention and Visitors Bureau, *PO Box 3585, 201 Penniman Rd, Williamsburg, VA 23187; tel: (757) 229-2047.* The bureau provides information on attractions, events, accommodation and dining throughout the Williamsburg area.

The Colonial Williamsburg Foundation, *PO Box 1776, Williamsburg, VA 23187-1776; tel: (757) 220-7645 or (800) HISTORY (447-8679).* A non-profit-making educational organisation, the foundation arranges accommodation and dining reservations in the Historic Area's hotels, taverns and restaurants and arranges themed holiday packages. It maintains an extensive **Visitor Center** *on Colonial Parkway at Hwy 60; tel: (757) 220-*
7645, where visitors may purchase tickets, make reservations, obtain information and see an introductory film.

The newspaper-style *Visitor's Companion* contains information on sites, lodging, shopping and dining and a map. Published weekly, it also has details of special events. Distinctive green and white signs lead to the centre, which has plentiful, free parking. Open Mon–Fri 0900–1700, Sat–Sun 0830–1800.

ARRIVING AND DEPARTING

The principal highway leading to Williamsburg is I-64. Take Exit 238 and follow the green and white signs to the Visitor Center. Other convenient roads are Hwy 60 and Rtes 5 and 31.

Amtrak **rail** services link the Williamsburg Transportation Center with New York, Philadelphia and Washington, DC.

GETTING AROUND

Williamsburg and the Historic Area are both reasonably compact, but to get to the Historic Area you must use one of the official shuttle buses which regularly cruise a circuit from the Visitor Centre and around the old town's perimeter (the streets themselves are closed to modern traffic). Shuttle bus travel is included in the admission fee, and passengers may get on and off as they please at designated stops.

James City County Transit; *tel: (757) 220-1621,* serves most residential neighbourhoods, shopping areas and tourist attractions Mon–Sat. Flat fare (exact money only) is $1 each way. Schedules obtainable from hotel reception desks.

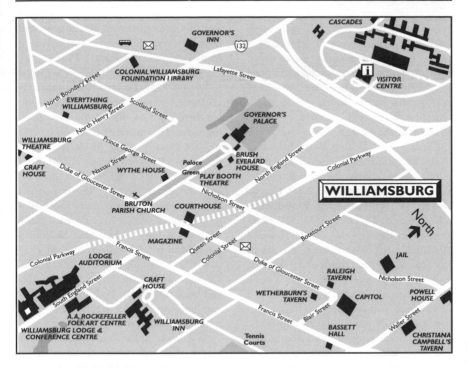

Map labels: CASCADES · GOVERNOR'S INN · (132) · COLONIAL WILLIAMSBURG FOUNDATION LIBRARY · Lafayette Street · VISITOR CENTRE · North Boundary Street · EVERYTHING WILLIAMSBURG · Scotland Street · GOVERNOR'S PALACE · North Henry Street · WILLIAMSBURG THEATRE · Prince George Street · BRUSH EVERARD HOUSE · North England Street · Colonial Parkway · CRAFT HOUSE · Duke of Gloucester Street · Nassau Street · WYTHE HOUSE · Palace Green · PLAY BOOTH THEATRE · WILLIAMSBURG · BRUTON PARISH CHURCH · COURTHOUSE · Nicholson Street · North · MAGAZINE · Queen Street · Botetourt Street · JAIL · Colonial Parkway · LODGE AUDITORIUM · Francis Street · Colonial Street · Duke of Gloucester Street · RALEIGH TAVERN · Nicholson Street · South England Street · CRAFT HOUSE · WETHERBURN'S TAVERN · CAPITOL · POWELL HOUSE · A.A. ROCKEFELLER FOLK ART CENTRE · WILLIAMSBURG INN · Blair Street · Waller Street · WILLIAMSBURG LODGE & CONFERENCE CENTRE · Francis Street · BASSETT HALL · CHRISTIANA CAMPBELL'S TAVERN · Tennis Courts

STAYING IN WILLIAMSBURG

Accommodation

One of the most popular tourist attractions in the US, Williamsburg has plenty of accommodation, ranging from upscale hotels to motels, bed and breakfast inns, private guest homes and campgrounds. A number of hotels, motels, guest houses and taverns are Colonial Williamsburg properties and are either in or near the Historic Area. The busiest periods of the year, when accommodation is hardest to find and at its most expensive, are Apr, May and Oct. The cheapest period is Jan–Feb. **Williamsburg Hotel and Motel Association;** *tel: (800) 899-9462* runs a complimentary reservations service.

Hotel chains in Williamsburg include *BW, CI, CM, DI, EL, ES, Hd, Ma, QI, QS, Ra.*

Certain benefits are available to guests staying in official Colonial Williamsburg hotels, including discounted admission tickets, complimentary guided tours, free or discounted use of fitness centre facilities and preferred seating for advanced dining reservations in hotels or colonial taverns. The following are official Colonial Williamsburg hotels (all sharing the toll-free *tel: (800) HISTORY)*: **Governor's Inn**, *506 N. Henry St; tel: (757) 229-1000.* This is a modern motel located three blocks from the Historic Area. It is a stop on the free shuttle bus route. Amenities include a pool, gift shop and games room. Moderate. **Williamsburg Inn**, *Frances St, Historic Area; tel: (757) 229-1000.* Presidents, royalty and heads of state have stayed in this five-star hotel, which combines a colonial ambience with modern amenities. Its spacious public areas are decorated in Regency style and each of its guest rooms has antique or reproduction furnishings. Complimentary tea is served each afternoon and the restaurant is open daily 0700–2200. There are swimming pool, tennis courts, fitness centre and a championship golf course. Pricey. **Williamsburg Lodge**, *S. England St; tel: (757) 229-1000.* Within strolling distance of the Historic Area, the hotel has three pools, tennis courts and a golf course. Restaurant open daily 0700–2200. Expensive–pricey. **Williamsburg Woodlands**, *Visitor Center Dr; tel: (757) 229-1000.* Located in the grounds of the Colonial Williamsburg Visitor Center, the motel has 314 rooms, each overlooking wooded grounds and gardens. There are two pools and a restaurant. Moderate–expensive.

Colonial Williamsburg also has accommodation in 26 houses and taverns in the Historic Area, ranging from rooms and converted kitchens and laundries, to cottages and larger homes. Some houses are more than 200 years old and are furnished in period style. Accommodation is on a bed and breakfast basis, with dining facilities at the Williamsburg Inn. Expensive–pricey.

Elsewhere in Williamsburg, **Kingsmill**, *1010 Kingsmill Rd; tel: (757) 253-1703*, is a resort hotel with indoor and outdoor pools, three 18-hole golf courses, a driving range and putting green and other sports facilities. Dining room open 0600–2130; room service to midnight. Expensive. **Colonial Gardens Bed and Breakfast**, *1109 Jamestown Rd; tel: (757) 220-8087 or (800) 886-9715*, is a charming 'country brick' home in a woodland setting 5 mins by car from Colonial Williamsburg and Jamestown. Heirloom antiques and original art decorate the interior and a garden theme is extended into the guest rooms. Full breakfast is served

and the innkeepers will gladly assist with dinner reservations. Non-smoking. Moderate. **Governor's Trace**, *303 Capitol Landing Rd; tel: (757) 229-7552 or (800) 303-7552.* Located right next to the Historic Area, this bed and breakfast inn has three rooms – one with a woodburning stove. Full breakfast is served by candlelight. Non-smoking. Moderate. **Indian Springs**, *330 Indian Springs Rd; tel: (757) 220-0726 or (800) 262-9165.* A quiet bed and breakfast retreat in downtown Williamsburg. Its four country suites overlook a scenic wooded ravine with plenty of birdwatching. Moderate. **Williamsburg Manor**, *600 Richmond Rd; tel: (757) 220-8011 or (800) 220-0245*, is a 1927 Georgian-style brick home with five bed and breakfast rooms. Full breakfast served and lunch and dinner are available. Non-smoking. Moderate–expensive.

Williamsburg has about a dozen private **guest homes** with accommodation priced $25–$50 a night for two people, all within easy reach of Colonial Williamsburg, some within walking distance. The homes are listed in the *Visitors Guide* published by the Convention and Visitors Bureau.

Campsites include: **Williamsburg KOA**, *5210 Newman Rd* (exit 234 off I-64); *tel: (757) 565-2907 or (800) KOA-1733.* The resort campground has pitches for tents and RVs in a landscaped location in a forest of southern hardwoods. Cabins are also available. Fishing, pool, 24-hr laundry. A free shuttle bus provides transport to Colonial Williamsburg, Busch Gardens and Water Country USA. **Anvil Campground**, *5243 Mooretown Rd; tel: (757) 562-2300 or (800) 633-4442*, offers four nights for the price of three, except during holidays. Cabins available. Facilities include pool, store, showers, games room, playgrounds laundry. **Fair Oaks**

Campground, *901 Lightfoot Rd; tel: (757) 565 2101 or (800) 892-0320*, has 450 sites on 50 acres of woodland. Full hook-ups, bathhouses, laundry and large pool. **Jamestown Beach Campsites**, *Rte 31 south*, 3½ miles from Colonial Williamsburg; *tel: (757) 229-7609 or (800) 229-3300*. Located on the James River, next to the Jamestown Settlement, the campsite has full facilities. It also has a sandy beach, a pool, take-away restaurant, grocery store and live music. **Kin Kaid Kampground**, *559 E. Rochambeau Dr.; tel: (757) 565-2010*. Five miles west of Williamsburg. Full hook-ups available.

Eating and Drinking

More than many other places, Williamsburg can boast that when it comes to dining it can provide something for everyone – even for those with a penchant for 18th-century dishes. Four colonial taverns in the Historic Area serve the kind of food that would have been familiar to Redcoats and Patriots and do their best to drum up the right atmosphere with minstrels and serving wenches. Prices in each tavern range from budget to pricey.

Vegetarian dishes and light fare are available in each tavern. Hot dogs and hamburgers may be available to suit precocious 20th century juvenile tastes. Smoking is strictly forbidden in each of the taverns – fire regulations, rather than tradition.

Chowning's Tavern, *Market Sq; tel: (757) 229-2141*, recalls an English alehouse, serving Brunswick stew and roast beef as well as prime rib with Virginia ham and roast Chesapeake Bay duck. Lots of nightly rollicking fun in the Tap Room, with colonial board games and costumed musicians. Open Wed–Sun 1100–midnight; Tap Room 'Gambols' from 2200.

Christiana Campbell's Tavern, *Waller St; tel: (757) 229-2141*, is said to have been George Washington's favourite eating place. Spoon bread and sweet potato muffins accompany crab cakes, shrimp and scallops and Chesapeake Bay jamabalaya. Open Wed–Sat 1700–2130.

Colonial balladeers entertain diners at **The King's Arms Tavern**, *Duke of Gloucester St; tel: (757) 229-2141* – 'where the best people resorted' in colonial times. Specialties include Virginia peanut soup, game pie, veal in wine sauce and filet mignon stuffed with Chesapeake Bay oysters. Open daily 1130–2130.

Shields Tavern, *Duke of Gloucester St; tel: (757) 229-2141*, has eight dining rooms, plus an alfresco dining area. Its Shields Sampler offers a taste of several 18th century dishes. Minstrels roam from room to room. Open Fri–Tues, 0830–1000, 1130–1500, 1700–2130.

There is a good choice of eating places outside the Historic Area. Here are a few suggestions.

Berret's Seafood Restaurant and Raw Bar, *199 S. Boundary St; tel: (757) 253-1847*, offers a full service menu of crab, shrimp, fresh fish, scallops, chicken and steaks, with fresh seafood, sandwiches and salads available at the raw bar. Open daily 1130–2200. Budget–moderate.

Chez Trinh, *157 Monticello Ave; tel: (757) 253-1888*. Vietnamese seafood, chicken, beef, pork and vegetarian dishes served in a casual atmosphere. Eat-in or take-away. Open daily 1130–2300. Budget–moderate.

Cracker Barrel Old Country Store, *200 Bypass Rd; tel: (757) 220-3384*. Old-fashioned country cooking in the setting of a country store. Open Sun–Thur 0600–2200, Fri–Sat 0600–2300.

Old Chickahominy House, *1211 Jamestown Rd; tel: (757) 229-4689*. Plantation cooking served in a non-

199

touristy 18th-century dining room. This is where the local people go for a breakfast of Old Virginia Ham, Country Bacon, Sausage with two Eggs and Grits, or a lunch of Chicken and Dumplings or Brunswick Stew & Hot Biscuits. Open daily 0830–1015, 1130–1415. Totally non-smoking. Budget.

Yorkshire Steak and Seafood Restaurant, *700 York St; tel: (757) 229-9790*. Fresh local seafood and steaks served in a relaxed early-American setting. Extensive wine and cocktail list. Open daily 1600–2230.

Communications

Williamsburg Post Office, *425 N. Boundary St; tel: (757) 229-4668*. Open Mon–Fri 0800–1700, Sat 1000–1400. The post office lobby provides access to vending machines for stamps 24 hours a day.

Colonial Post Office, *Duke of Gloucester, Historic Area*. Postcards mailed here are hand-cancelled with the original 18th century Williamsburg postmark. The shop sells an extensive collection of reproduction 18th-century prints and maps. Open daily 1000–1630.

ENTERTAINMENT

Much of Williamsburg's entertainment is centred on the colonial taverns. To find out what's going on outside the area get a copy of the *Great Entertainer Magazine* from the Convention and Visitors Bureau or your hotel.

The Lyric Theater; *tel: (757) 988-3133*, stages professional productions at various locations in the Williamsburg area. It specialises in the musical comedies of George and Ira Gershwin. **Old Dominion Opry**, *3012 Richmond Rd; tel: (757) 564-0200 or (800) 2VA-OPRY*, is the premier place for evening family entertainment, with year-round productions of live country music and comedy. Shows staged Mon–Sat at 2000. **Williamsburg Theatre**, *Merchants Sq; tel: (757) 229-1475*, presents a nightly programme of arts cinema, foreign films and independent productions.

America's Railroads on Parade, *1915 Pocahontas Trail (Village Shops at Kingsmill); tel: (757) 220-8725*. A must for train buffs of all ages, with 45 model trains – classic and modern – operating on more than 4000 sq ft of layouts with dynamic sound and computerised lighting. Open daily 1000–1700. Admission charge.

Family Funland, *801 Merrimac Trail - James York Plaza; tel: (757) 220-1400*, is Williamsburg's only indoor family entertainment facility. It has a two-storey playland with balls and tunnels, bumper cars, miniature golf, arcade games, a laser storm and a full menu restaurant. Open year-round. Admission free.

Events

Most annual and seasonal events are connected with and staged at Colonial Williamsburg. A season of **Colonial Weekends** with an 18th-century theme and including guided tours, a lecture and a banquet is held Jan–Mar. George Washington's birthday is celebrated in Feb, when there is also an annual antiques forum. Members of the Williamsburg Independent Company parade on Market Square Green for weekly costumed drill, mid Mar–Oct, while the Fife and Drum Corps performs in the Historic Area Apr–Oct. **Publick Times**, staged over Labor Day weekend (early Sept), is a re-creation of a colonial market, with competitions, a craft show, auctions and military displays. Early Dec–early Jan, Colonial Williamsburg and much of the rest of the city is illuminated and there are fireworks displays and parades.

SHOPPING

Nine shops within the Historic Area are working businesses offering souvenirs ranging from three-cornered hats and fifes for youngsters to colonial-style jewellery, hand-crafted leather products, ironware, pottery, basketware, soaps, candles and foodstuffs. Three gift shops are to be found near the visitor centre, where the bookshop has an extensive selection of publications on 18th-century America and Colonial Williamsburg. Sheafs of discount coupons are inserted into the *Great Entertainer Magazine*.

Bargain hunters will doubtless want to head for the town's factory outlets. **Berkeley Commons Outlet Center**, *Rte 60 west; tel: (757) 565-0702*, has more than 80 name-brand stores with savings averaging 40 per cent off normal retail prices. **Williamsburg Outlet Mall**, *also on Rte 60 west; tel: (757) 565-3378*, is a fully enclosed complex of 60 stores offering savings of 20–70 per cent.

Merchants Square, *Duke of Gloucester St, adjacent to the Historic Area; tel: (757) 220-7751*, is a colonial-revival village of 41 shops and restaurants. **Banister Shoe Store**, *Williamsburg Pottery, Hwy 60; tel: (757) 564-9802*, features top brand names in men's, women's and athletic shoes at factory-direct prices. **Boyer's Diamond and Golf**, *6564 Richmond Rd; tel: (757) 565-0747*, specialises in diamonds, Italian made gold with 40–50 per cent discounts, rings, pendants, earrings and Seiko and Citizen watches.

The Campus Shop, *425 Prince George St; tel: (757) 229-4301*, sells licensed College of William and Mary merchandise, including sweatshirts, T-shirts, baseball caps, mugs and other gifts. Similar mementos are also available at **The College Shop**, *Merchants Sq; tel: (757) 229-2082*. **The Craft House**, *Merchants*

Sq and the Williamsburg Inn; tel: (757) 229-1000, offers reproductions of antiques in the Colonial Williamsburg Foundation's collection, as well as prints, china, crystal, linens and candlesticks inspired by original colonial work. **J. Fenton Gallery**, *110 S. Henry St; tel: (757) 221-8200*, specialises in unusual handcrafts by premier artisans, including jewellery, wooden boxes and games, clothing, pottery and stained glass.

Fort Cherokee Trading Post, *8758 Pocahontas Trail; tel: (757) 220-0386*, is the largest Native American arts and crafts store in Virginia. It offers handcrafted jewellery from the Navajo, Zuni and Hopi Indians, handmade pottery, moccasins and a large selection of Dream Catchers, Mandellas toys, T-shirts and blankets.

The Porcelain Collector, *Merchants Sq; tel: (757) 229-3961*, stocks fine crystal porcelain and china collectibles bearing such world-famous names as Armani, Chase, Portmeirion, Royal Copenhagen and Waterford. **Quilts Unlimited**, *440A Duke of Gloucester St; tel: (757) 253-8700*, is filled with antique and new quilts, as well as wall hangings, fine Virginia handcrafts and cotton clothing. **Shirley Pewter Shop**, *417 Duke of Gloucester St; tel: (757) 229-5356 or (800) 550-5356*, has a variety of gifts, including many handmade by the Shirley Craftsmen of Williamsburg. Engraving is carried out on the premises. **Souvenirs and Stuff**, *1505 Richmond Rd; tel: (757) 253-8007*. T-shirts, sweatshirts, posters, prints, jewellery, books, mugs, toys, games and, of course, three-cornered hats.

SIGHTSEEING

Full details of guided tours in the area can be obtained from the Convention and Visitors Bureau and from the visitors centre at Colonial Williamsburg.

Interpre-Tours; *tel: (757) 785-2010,*

organises attractions tickets, lodgings, meals and offers guide services. Its three evening tours comprise the History Mystery Evening, Myths and Legends of Williamsburg and the Hauntings of the Old Town.

The Ghosts of Williamsburg is a fun tour – by night, of course – organised by **Maximum Guided Tours Inc**, *tel: (757) 253-2094*. Colonial Williamsburg offers an evening **Lanthorn Tour** of the streets of the Historic Area, including four candlelit shops. Tours leave Fri, Sat, Sun 2030. Admission: $10 ($5 for Patriot's Pass holders – see below).

For an overview – literally – of the area, **Historic Air Tours**; *tel: (757) 253-8185 or (800) VA-BY-AIR*, offers a 35-min light aircraft flight over Williamsburg, Jamestown and Yorktown, with narration, for $30 per person. Other tours fly over the James River Plantations and the Hampton Roads, last 55 minutes and cost $45 per person. Flights depart from Williamsburg-Jamestown Airport.

Tidewater Touring Inc; *tel: (757) 872-0897*, organises guided coach and minibus tours of the area.

Attractions

Anheuser-Busch Hospitality Center, *Hwy 60, three miles south of Williamsburg; tel: (757) 253-3036* (see Busch Gardens, below). Recently renovated, the centre highlights the history and products of the Anheuser-Busch brewing companies. In addition to viewing displays and films, visitors can take a tour of the brewing process, from ingredient selection to high-speed canning and bottling. The Hospitality Center has a gift shop, and guests over the age of 21 can enjoy a complimentary sampling of the brewery's beverages. Open daily 1100–1600 (Nov–mid Apr); during the remainder of the year, the

centre opens and closes an hour ahead of Busch Gardens Williamsburg, with 2200 the latest closing time. Admission free.

Busch Gardens Williamsburg, *Busch Gardens Blvd (three miles south of Williamsburg on Hwy 60); tel: (757) 253-3000*. A theme park operated by the Anheuser-Busch brewery conglomerate, this is a fantasy version of 17th-century Europe in a journey through nine 'hamlets' filled with more than 30 white-knuckle rides, attractions, live shows, eating places and shops.

Transportation around the park is by steam train or computerised monorail. Open Fri and Sun 1000–1900, Sat 1000–2200 (mid Apr–mid May); Sun–Fri 1000–1900, Sat 1000–2200 (mid May–early June); daily 1000–2200 (early–end June); Sun–Fri 1000–2200, Sat 1000–midnight (July–Aug); Fri–Tues 1000–1900 (Sept–Oct); closed winter. Admission: from $29.95 (late afternoon admission cheaper, special rates for two and three-day passes). Parking: $4 per vehicle.

Carter's Grove, *Hwy 60, eight miles east of Williamsburg; tel: (757) 229-1000 (ext 2973)*. Maintained by the Colonial Williamsburg Foundation, Carter's Grove is an 18th-century plantation on the James River. It includes a colonial mansion, reconstructed slave quarters, a 17th-century English settlement and the Winthrop Rockefeller Archaeology Museum. Built on an 80 ft bluff overlooking the river, **Carter's Grove Mansion** is an elegant 18th-century brick home furnished with antiques evoking the spirit of the Colonial Revival and restored to its appearance during the 1930s. Visitors are free to wander through the mansion, which was once described as America's most beautiful house. The reconstructed **Slave Quarters** at Carter's Grove consist of three dwellings which would have housed 24

Ferry to the Past

Virginia's only 24-hour state-run car ferry operation crosses the James River from Glass House Point at Jamestown to Scotland in Surry County – a 15-minute crossing – and gives passengers the chance to imagine what the first colonial settlers saw when they travelled on the river nearly four centuries ago. The first car ferry, the vessel *Captain John Smith*, made the crossing in Feb 1925. Today, there are four ferry boats – *Williamsburg, Surry, Virginia* and *Pocahontas* – and more than 90 employees keep them on schedule.

On the south side of the James River crops of cotton, peanuts and tobacco are grown as they have been since before the Revolution. And here, on Rte 10, three miles east of the town of Surry, is **Chippokes Plantation and State Park;** *tel: (757) 294-3625* (open daily 0800–dusk; admission charge). The plantation was started by Captain William Powell, one of the Jamestown settlers, and has been farmed continuously since 1619. Crops of corn, peanuts, rye, soya beans and barley are still harvested. Visitors may tour an antebellum mansion, stroll through the gardens, look in on a working sawmill and view a collection of antique farm and forestry equipment. There is a visitor centre and a recreation area which offers biking, hiking, swimming and picnicking.

A further three miles east on *Rte 10* is **Bacon's Castle;** *tel: (757) 357-5976,* said to be the oldest documented brick house in English North America. It was built in 1655 by Arthur Allen, an English immigrant. Its name stems from a rebellion in 1676, when the house was seized and fortified by troops loyal to Nathaniel Bacon. Its garden was laid out in 1680 and is the best-preserved 17th-century garden site in the US. **Smith's Fort**, Rte 31, *Surry; tel: (757) 294-3872,* is the site of the fort built by Captain John Smith in 1609 to serve as a second line of defence against attacks on Jamestown by the Indians and Spanish. The area south of the river was given by Chief Powhatan to John Rolfe on his marriage to Pocahontas.

The Jamestown Ferry is on Rte 31 south, which continues from Scotland. For schedule information and fares *tel: (800) VA-FERRY.*

203

slaves. Costumed interpreters provide introductions to the site as they carry out everyday 18th-century chores. **Wolstenholme Towne** is the partly reconstructed site of an English settlement where 49 people were killed during an attack by Indians in 1622. The site was discovered in 1979 when archaeologists unearthed the remains of a 40-year-old woman who died in the raid. The **Winthrop Rockefeller Archaeology Museum**, built underground, has a permanent exhibition of artefacts uncovered at Wolstenholme Towne, as well as electronic maps and audiovisual programmes. A one-way scenic country road winds back to the Historic Area through woodlands, meadows and marshes. Carter's Grove is open Tues–Sun 0900–1800 (mid Mar–Nov); 1000–1600 (Nov–Dec). Admission charge (included with Colonial Williamsburg passes – see below).

College of William and Mary, *Duke of Gloucester St (at junction of Jamestown and Richmond rds); tel: (757) 221-4000.* The second oldest university in the US. (Harvard is the oldest), the college was granted a royal charter in 1693. Three early presidents – Jefferson, Monroe and Tyler – were educated within its gracious walls, and it is still in use today with an enrolment of close on 8000 students. The

Sir Christopher Wren Building, designed by the great English architect and completed in 1699, is the nation's oldest academic structure in continuous use. **Muscarelle Museum of Art** stages visiting exhibitions and displays from an extensive collection. The college museum is housed in the **Earl Gregg Swem Library**. Open Mon–Fri 0900–1700, Sat–Sun 1300–1700. Admission free.

COLONIAL WILLIAMSBURG

To see everything the restored town has to offer will require more than a full day – probably two – so if time is limited the best thing is to acquire a copy of the *Visitor's Companion*, which lists all attractions, shows them on a map and provides details of events in the current week. Advice on making the most of your time is included in the *Colonial Williamsburg Trip Planning Guide*, which also gives details of package holiday plans, sports and recreation and special events throughout the year. **Orientation Walks** help first-time visitors to get their bearings in the Historic Area. The 30 min guided walks take place daily 1000–1500 and start at the Lumber House ticket office, *S. England St*. **Carriage and Wagon Rides** take place daily 1000–1600, weather permitting. (tickets from any ticket sales location).

Exhibition Sites

Brush-Everard House, *between N. England St and Palace Green*. An original building displaying aspects of life as a slave in 18th-century Williamsburg, where half the population was black. **Bruton Parish Church**, *Duke of Gloucester St, corner of Palace Green*. In continuous use since 1715, this Episcopal church may be toured Mon–Sat 0900–1700, Sun 1200–1700.

Capitol, *east end of Duke of Gloucester St*. A reconstruction of the H-shaped building in which the colonial government sat from 1701. Among the many significant events staged in the original capitol was the unanimous adoption of a resolution declaring independence from England in May 1776, nearly two months before the First Continental Congress adopted the Declaration of Independence in Philadelphia. **Courthouse**, *Duke of Gloucester St, east of Palace Green*. Built in 1770, the courthouse served as the seat of local government and housed municipal and county courts until 1932. Re-enactments are staged here.

Governor's Palace, *north end of Palace Green*. This imposing reconstruction of the 1722 palace, which was the residence of seven royal governors and the commonwealth's first two state governors, is furnished as it would have been during the residence of Lord Botetourt, who died in 1770.

Magazine, *Duke of Gloucester st, opposite Courthouse*. Built in 1715, this substantial building was where the town's arms and ammunition were stored. **Public Gaol**, *east end of Nicholson St*, is the original building in which colonial wrongdoers – including the pirate Blackbeard and his crew – were incarcerated. **Public Hospital**, *west end of Francis St*. A reconstruction of the first institution in America devoted solely to the treatment of the mentally ill.

Raleigh Tavern, *east end of Duke of Gloucester St*. A reconstruction of the 1717 tavern in which much plotting by Revolutionary patriots took place. **Wetherburn's Tavern**, *east end of Duke of Gloucester St*, is the original inn which Henry Wetherburn's family and slaves ran successfully in the 1750s. **Wythe House**, *Palace Green at Prince George St*. Built in 1755, this was the home of George Wythe, America's first professor of law and tutor to Thomas Jefferson. George

Washington used the house as his head-quarters before the siege of Yorktown.

Museums

Abby Aldrich Rockefeller Folk Art Center, *S. England St*. Established in 1957, the centre is the oldest institution in the US. devoted to the collection and preservation of American folk art. Its 18 galleries house a collection of primitives, whirligigs, weathervanes, carvings, toys, embroideries and other folk works representing many cultural traditions and geographic regions. Open daily 1000–1800. Admission charge.

Bassett Hall, *east end of Francis St*, is a two-storey 18th century frame house on 585 acres and was the home of John D. Rockefeller Jr and his wife Abby. It is furnished much as it was when the Rockefellers lived there during the 1930s. Tours by appointment (apply at ticket offices) 0900–1645. Admission charge.

DeWitt Wallace Decorative Arts Gallery, entered through *Public Hospital, Francis St; tel: (757) 220-7724)*. Twelve galleries house an exceptional collection of English and American decorative arts from 1600 to 1830, including the world's largest collection of Virginia furniture and the largest collection of English pottery outside the United Kingdom. Open daily 1000–1800. Admission charge.

Historic Trade Sites

Scattered throughout the Historic Area are about 20 workshops, offices and stores where visitors can watch craftsmen and women practising traditional skills. These include apothecary, blacksmith, carpenter, foundry, gunsmith, shoemaker, silver-smith, wigmaker, and others.

Jamestown, the Original Site, *Rte 31, five miles south of Williamsburg; tel: (757) 229-1733*. Part of the Colonial National Historical Park, which includes York-town, Jamestown is the site of the first permanent English settlement in North America. An extensive visitor centre has museum displays, information services, shop and a cinema where a 15-min introductory film is shown. Guided tours of the site start at the centre; visitors may make their own way (audiotapes available for a nominal rental fee). **Towne Site**, close to the visitor centre, encompasses the excavated ruins of the early homes and public buildings. Also nearby is the **Old Church Tower**, believed to be part of the first brick church, **Memorial Church**, built in 1907 over the foundations of the original church, and the ruins of a glass furnace built in 1608. Among monuments in the area are statues of Captain John Smith and Pocahontas. A five-mile **car trail** winding through 1500 acres of woodland and marsh gives visitors an idea of what the land was like when the settlers arrived in 1607. Open daily 0830–1700. Admission: $8 per car or $2 per cyclist or pedestrian.

Jamestown Settlement, *Rte 31, four miles south of Williamsburg; tel: (757) 253-4838*. Operated by the Commonwealth of Virginia, the Jamestown Settlement is a living museum depicting the struggles and achievements of the first settlers. There are gallery exhibits, full-sized replicas of the ships – *Susan Constant, Godspeed* and *Discovery* – which brought the pioneers across the Atlantic, a re-created fort and a reconstructed Powhatan Indian village. Open daily 0900–1700. Admission: $9.

Water Country USA, *Rte 199, three miles east of Williamsburg; tel: (757) 229-9300*. Another Anheuser-Busch enterprise, this is a park featuring more than 30 water rides and attractions, live entertainment, shopping and restaurants with a 1950s and '60s surfing theme. Open daily mid May–early Sept from 1000.

TIDEWATER TOUR

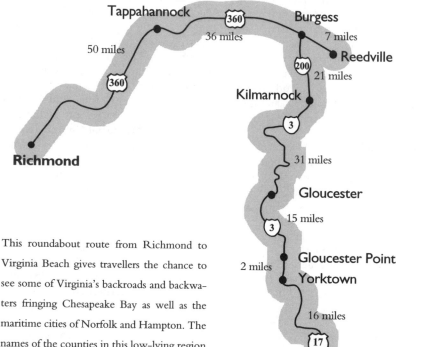

This roundabout route from Richmond to Virginia Beach gives travellers the chance to see some of Virginia's backroads and backwaters fringing Chesapeake Bay as well as the maritime cities of Norfolk and Hampton. The names of the counties in this low-lying region along the tideways of the York and Rappahannock rivers – names like King William, King and Queen, Middlesex, Gloucester, Lancaster and York – are the first clues to English colonial settlement. Two great American generals – George Washington and Robert E. Lee – were born in the region and the last major battle of the Revolutionary War was fought here.

Although this route can be done in 4 hrs, allow at least another half-day for sightseeing.

DIRECT ROUTE: 201 MILES

ROUTE

From Capitol Sq, Richmond, take *Franklin St* east and turn left on to 18th St, then turn right on to Hwy 360. Fifty miles from Richmond, Hwy 360 reaches **Tappahannock** where it crosses the Rappahannock River to the area known as the **Northern Neck**, before continuing for another 36 miles to **Burgess**. Here you can either turn right to continue our route on Rte 200 south or continue to the harbour town of **Reedville** where ferries cross to Smith and Tangier Islands in **Chesapeake Bay**.

Rte 200 continues for 14 miles to **Kilmarnock**, where you should turn left on to Rte 3. This travels south crossing the Rappahannock and Piankatank rivers to reach **Gloucester** after 31 miles.

From Gloucester head south on Hwy 17, reaching **Gloucester Point** in 15 miles.

Hwy 17 crosses the York River to **Yorktown** and continues for 11 miles to intersect with I-64. Take I-64 east. To visit **Hampton** take Exit 267 and follow the blue 'Hampton Tour' signs to the Visitor Center. Continue east on I-64, crossing the Hampton Roads to reach **Norfolk**.

To visit downtown Norfolk take exit 276 and head south on Hwy 460 (Granby St). For Virginia Beach continue on I-64 to exit 284 and take Rte 44 east. This reaches downtown Virginia Beach in 13 miles.

NORTHERN NECK

Tourist Information: Northern Neck Travel Council, *PO Box 312-A, Reedville, VA 22443; tel: (757) 453-6167.* **Westmoreland County Council for Travel and Tourism**, *Courthouse Sq, Montross, VA 22520; tel: (757) 493-8440.* A visitor information centre, museum and historic reference library share the same location.

ACCOMMODATION

There are **Days Inns** at Colonial Beach; *tel: (757) 224-0404,* and Tappahannock; *tel: (757) 443-9200.* **The Tides Lodge Resort and Marina**, *PO Box TG, Irvington, VA 22480; tel: (800) 248-4337,* offers 'informal luxury', with championship golf, sauna, exercise room, tennis and entertainment. Expensive.

Numerous waterfront inns and bed and breakfast homes are to be found in the villages. **Chesapeake Bay/Smith Island KOA**, *PO Box 1910, Reedville, VA 22539; tel: (757) 453-3430,* has wooded sites for tents and Rvs in a riverside setting half a mile from the Chesapeake Bay shore. Cabins are available. Amenities include snack bar, mini-golf, fishing and boat rentals. Daily trips are available to Smith Island, MD.

Camping and cabins are also available in **Westmoreland State Park**, *Montross; tel: (757) 493-8821.*

207

SIGHTSEEING

The Northern Neck, the jagged spit of land between the Potomac and Rappahannock rivers, has a number of quaint villages tucked away among its many bays and inlets, especially along the shores of the Potomac River and Chesapeake Bay.

George Washington's Birthplace National Monument, *Rte 1, between Colonial Beach and Montross; tel: (757) 224-1732.* Guided tours of the house and colonial farm. Open daily 0900–1700. Admission charge.

Mary Ball Washington Museum and Library, *Lancaster; tel: (757) 462-7280.* This complex of seven buildings houses a regional museum, research centre and historical and genealogical libraries. Open daily. Admission free.

Fishermen's Museum, *Historic District, Reedville; tel: (757)453-6371.* The museum is housed in a restored waterman's home. Open daily (May–Oct), weekends only (Nov–Apr). Donation.

Richmond County Museum, *Warsaw; tel: (757) 333-3607.* Artefacts are on display and visitor information is available in the historic Clerk's Office at the Courthouse. Open Thur–Sat 1100–1500. Admission free.

Stratford Hall Plantation, *Stratford; tel: (757) 493-8038.* The 1730s mansion, birthplace of Robert E. Lee, is open for tours. There is a reception centre, where visitors may view a slide presentation, museum and gift shop. Dining room. Open daily 0900–1630. Admission charge.

GLOUCESTER

Tourist Information: Chamber of Commerce: *tel: (757) 693-2425.*

Founded in 1769, this delightful village is surrounded by many old landmarks and plantation estates.

County Courthouse; *Courthouse Sq.* The 18th-century building is at the centre of the historic district, which includes a debtors' prison, the pre-Revolutionary Botetour Building. Plaques in the courthouse commemorate Nathaniel Bacon, leader of the first organised resistance to the British in 1676, and Major Walter Reed, the surgeon who brought abut the defeat of yellow fever.

Virginia Institute of Marine Science; *Gloucester Point; tel: (757) 642-7000.* A branch of Williamsburg's College of William and Mary, the institute has a small aquarium and museum with displays of sea turtles, Chesapeake Bay fish and invertebrates, and a book store. Open Mon–Fri 0900–1700. Admission free.

YORKTOWN

Tourist Information: Colonial National Historic Park Visitor Center, *Colonial Parkway, Yorktown; tel: (757) 898-3400.* The emphasis here is on the last great battle of the American Revolution, but the centre, run by the National Parks Service, has limited information on local facilities and a copy of the *Yorktown Visitor Guide* – a leaflet listing attractions, shops, lodgings and eating places – can also be obtained.

ACCOMMODATION AND FOOD

Yorktown has two motels. **Duke of York Motor Hotel**, *508 Water St; tel: (757) 898-3232*, overlooks the York River. It has a pool, restaurant and rooms with balconies. Moderate. **Yorktown Motor Lodge**, *8829 George Washington Hwy; tel: (757) 898-5451 or (800) 950-4003*, offers a mini-bar in every room, some of which are non-smoking, and a swimming pool.

Beach House Restaurant, *Water St* (foot of *Church St* steps); *tel: (757) 890-2804*, serves deli sandwiches, pizza and salads and offers outdoor waterfront dining. Open daily 1100–2100. Moderate.

Nick's Seafood Pavilion, *Water St (near bridge); tel: (757) 887-5269* has been in the same hands since 1944 and is renowned for its seafood dishes, especially lobster and seafood kebab. Open daily 1100–2200. Budget–pricey.

Sammy and Nick's Restaurant, *Alexander Hamilton Blvd; tel: (757) 898-3070.* Another long-established family concern – this time in business since 1905. It is noted for its cuts of beef, well-prepared seafood and pasta. Open 0700–2200. Moderate.

Yorktown Pub, *Water St (at Read St); tel: (757) 898-8793.* A full menu and home-made desserts served in a lively pub atmosphere. Open daily 1100–0200; live entertainment Wed, Fri, Sat 2100–0100. Moderate.

SIGHTSEEING

With a population fewer than 400, Yorktown is much smaller now than it was in colonial times when it was an important tobacco port. But it is still an active and attractive little town with many buildings from the colonial period still standing.

Grace Episcopal Church, *Church St; tel: (757) 898-9315*. Built in 1697, the church was damaged during military action in 1781 and gutted by fire in 1814. Open Tues–Sat 1100–1400 and Sunday after services.

Watermen's Museum, *309 Water St; tel: (757) 888-2623*. Boats and models, photographs and tools tell the story of the tough lives of those who earned a living sailing Chesapeake's wooden craft. The gift shop sells pottery, books, nautical clothing and the work of 43 artists. Open Tues–Sat 1000–1600, Sun 1300–1600.

Yorktown Battlefield is where the British army led by Lord Cornwallis was defeated and surrendered to Washington's allied French and American forces. The events of the siege and the story of Yorktown are featured in an audio–visual presentation and exhibits in the visitor center. Items on display include tents used by Washington and parts of a reconstructed British frigate. A panoramic view of strategic points on the battlefield can be seen from the visitor centre roof. A brochure detailing self-guided driving tours of the battlefield is available and an audio-tape commentary may be rented.

Highlights of the battlefield area are **Moore House**, where the 'Articles of Capitulation' were drafted; **Nelson House**, home of Thomas Nelson Jr, a signatory to the Declaration of Independence; **Yorktown National Civil War Cemetery**, and the **Victory Monument**, a 95-ft granite column commemorating American-French alliance which led to victory. The British surrender is celebrated at Yorktown on 19 Oct each year with re-enactments, patriotic festivities and military exercises. The battlefield is open daily 0830–1730. Admission free.

Yorktown Victory Center, *Rte 238 and Colonial Parkway; tel: (757) 253-4838;* unfolds the story of the American Revolution through a timeline walkway, exhibition galleries, a film and a re-created Continental camp and 18th-century farm where costumed interpreters demonstrate cooking, medicine, military techniques and rural skills. Open daily 0900–1700. Admission charge.

HAMPTON

Tourist Information: Hampton Visitor Center, *710 Settlers Landing Rd, Hampton, VA 23669; tel: (757) 727-1102 or (800) 800-2202.*

Overlooking the scenic Hampton River, this attractive and spacious centre has a gift shop and offers a variety of maps, attractions brochures and self-guided tour pamphlets. An accommodations directory is included in the annual *Visitor's Guide* produced by Hampton Conventions and Tourism. A restaurant guide and a calendar of events are also available. Visitors may watch an orientation video. Open daily 0900–1700.

GETTING AROUND

Some of Hampton's major attractions are downtown, within walking distance of the Visitor Center, but others – for example the Air Power Park and Buckroe Beach – are more scattered. Local bus services are provided by **Pentran**; *tel: (757) 723-3344*, which also operates a free trolley service for downtown Hampton during the summer. Taxi companies operating in the city include **Langley Cabs**, *tel: (757) 723-3377*; **Sunshine Taxi Service**, *tel: (757) 723-3316*, and **Yellow Cabs**, *tel: (757) 727-7777*.

ACCOMMODATION

The bulk of Hampton's hotel and motel accommodation is in the Coliseum area, straddling *Mercury Blvd* near exit 263-B from I-64. Hotel chains in the city include *CI, CM, DI, EL, Hd, QI, Rd, RR, S8*.

Only two establishments offer accommodation in the downtown area. The **Radisson Hotel Hampton**, *700 Settlers Landing Rd; tel: (757) 727-9700 or (800) 333-3333*, is on the waterfront, close to the Visitor Center. Rooms feature floor-to-ceiling bay windows; there are three restaurants and an outdoor pool. Expensive.

Crabtown Inn, *403 Pembroke Ave; tel: (757) 726-2673*, is a bed and breakfast establishment with two guest rooms in a charming colonial revival home built in 1915. The downtown waterfront is within walking distance. Moderate.

The city's largest hotel is **Holiday Inn Hampton**, *1815 W. Mercury Blvd; tel: (757) 838-0200*. It has 324 rooms, indoor and outdoor pools, coin laundry and a restaurant open daily 0600–2200. The bar is open 1100–midnight.

Todd's Cottages, *200 Point Comfort Ave; tel: (757) 851-7700*. Two- and three-room cottages, equipped with kitchenettes, sleep up to four or six people and are located one block from Buckroe Beach. Budget–moderate.

EATING AND DRINKING

Hampton's renovated downtown waterfront district is dotted with restaurants and pubs, and there is another concentration of eating places in the Coliseum area.

Buckroe's Island Grill, *1 Ivory Gull Cres; tel: (757) 850-5757*. Offering sandwiches, seafood and chicken dishes, the restaurant overlooks the Salt Ponds Marina. Open Mon–Sat 1100–midnight, Sun 1000–2300. Budget–moderate.

Capt. George's Seafood Restaurant, *2710 W. Mercury Blvd; tel: (757)826-1435*. Extensive seafood buffet and a complete menu. Open Mon–Fri 1630–2230, Sat 1600–2230, Sun 1200–2200. Moderate.

Fisherman's Wharf, *14 Ivy Rd; tel: (757) 723-3113*. You can watch fishing boats bringing in the latest catch as you dine beside the historic Hampton Roads Harbor. Entertainment. Open Mon–Fri 1700–2200, Sat 1600–2230, Sun 1200–2200. Moderate.

The Grey Goose, *101A W. Queen's Way; tel: (757) 723-7978*. You can sample Virginia cooking and Southern hospitality in this country store and tea room. No alcoholic beverages. Open Mon–Sat 1100–1600. Budget.

Heartbreak Cafe/Rhinestone Cowboy, *100 Newmarket Sq W; tel: (757) 245-3313*. These neighbouring clubs offer dining and dancing, with snacks served to 0200. The Heartbreak features 1950s music Thur–Sat 1600–0200; dinner served to 2200. The Rhinestone Cowboy caters for Country music lovers Thur–Sat 1700–0200 with dinner up to 2200. Moderate.

Oasis Restaurant, *3506 Kecoughtan Rd; tel: (757) 723-5736*. Leisurely dining in a casual atmosphere, with Italian and Greek dishes on a menu that includes steaks and seafood. Open Mon–Sat 0700–2100, Sun 0700–2000. Cheap–budget.

Oyster Alley, *Radisson Hotel Hampton, 700 Settlers Landing Rd; tel: (757) 727-9700*. Seafood and American cuisine served al fresco overlooking the Hampton River and downtown waterfront. Open daily 1100–2000 (Apr–Nov). Moderate.

Second Street Restaurant and Tavern, *132 E. Queen St; tel: (757) 722-6811*. One of Hampton's most popular restaurants, featuring local seafood, steaks, chicken and home-made Italian specialties, as well as burgers, sandwiches and salads. Children will enjoy the make-your-own sundae bar. Live entertainment and dining on a large outdoor deck. Open daily 1100–0200. Moderate.

Wine Street Gourmet, *22 Wine St; tel: (757) 722-VINO*. Sandwiches, take-away cuisines and boxed lunches may be purchased at this wine, cheese and gourmet food shop. Open Mon–Sat 0900–1900. Budget.

SIGHTSEEING

Exploring Hampton by car is easy. Distinctive blue 'Hampton Tour' signs mark a circular, self-guided route and point the way to the city's attractions and visitor centre. You can start the tour wherever you see a sign.

Self-guided tour pamphlets for walkers and drivers direct visitors along the city's waterfront and into the historic Queens Way district. The Hampton University driving tour details some of the National Historic Landmarks on the campus, which was founded in 1868 for newly freed African Americans. A more comprehensive overview of multi-cultural sites is provided by the Africa American heritage tour.

The dock next to the visitor centre is the starting point for cruises of the Hampton Roads Harbor and Chesapeake Bay aboard **Miss Hampton II**. The cruise passes Blackbeard's Point, Old Point Comfort and the Norfolk Naval Base and stops at Fort Wool, an island fortress built in 1819. The three-hour cruises depart daily at 1000 (mid Apr–May), 1000 and 1400 (June–Aug), 1000 (Sept–Oct). Admission: $13.50

Air Power Park, *413 W. Mercury Blvd; tel: (757) 727-1163*. Home to one of the largest civilian-owned collections of aircraft and missiles in the U.S., the park contains aircraft from the country's various service branches. Outdoor displays include a Nike surface-to-air missile and an F-100D Super Sabre, the first USAF fighter with true supersonic performance. There is an extensive collection of model aircraft and a wind tunnel is also on show. Open daily 0900–1630. Admission free.

Bluebird Gap Farm, *60 Pine Chapel Rd; tel: (757) 727-6739*. This 60-acre farm is home to goats, sheep, horses and other domesticated animals. The site includes a petting area, playground and picnic tables. Open Wed–Sun 0900–1700. Admission free.

Buckroe Beach, *end of Pembroke Ave; tel: (757) 727-6347*. Maintained by Hampton Parks and Recreation, the area borders Chesapeake Bay and offers wide beaches, gentle surf and excellent fishing. Big band concerts, outdoor films and live jazz performances take place in the park pavilion area during the summer. There are picnic shelters and seasonal lifeguards. Freely accessible.

Casemate Museum, *Fort Monroe; tel: (757) 727-3391*. Headquarters of the US Army Training and Doctrine Command, Fort Monroe is the largest stone fort ever built in the country. It was completed in 1834. Within its walls, Casemate Museum chronicles the history of the fort and the Coast Guard Artillery Corps. Visitors may see the cell in which Confederate

211

President Jefferson Davis was imprisoned after the Civil War. Open daily 1030–1630. Admission free.

Charles H. Taylor Arts Center, *4205 Victoria Blvd; tel: (757) 722-ARTS.* The centre is headquarters of the Hampton Arts Commission, which stages the highly-acclaimed annual Great Performers Series. Travelling national and regional art exhibitions are staged at the centre. Open Tues–Sat 1000–1800, Sun 1300–1700. Admission free.

Grandview Nature Preserve, *entrance at intersection of Beach Rd and State Park Dr; tel: (757) 727-6347.* Located on an estuary, this 578-acre preserve is ideal for wildlife observations, birdwatching and hiking. It includes a 2½ mile stretch of bayfront beach. Hawkins Pond, an inland body of water, is a traditional stopover for migrating waterfowl. Freely accessible.

Hampton Carousel, *610 Settlers Landing Rd; tel: (757) 727-6347.* Built by the Philadelphia Toboggan Company in 1920, the cheerful carousel has been restored to its original beauty and is housed in its own weather-protected pavilion on the downtown waterfront. It is one of only 170 antique merry-go-rounds in the US. Open Mon–Sat 1000–2000, Sun 1200–1800 (Apr–Sept), daily 1200–1800 (Oct), Sat–Sun 1200–1800 (Nov–mid Dec). Admission: $0.50.

Hampton University; *tel: (757) 727-5000.* The university is among the nation's top-ranked universities and colleges, and the waterfront campus, overlooking the scenic Hampton River, is the site of six National Historic Landmarks, including the Emancipation Oak, where Abraham Lincoln's *Emancipation Proclamation* was first read to the residents of Hampton.

The university museum houses a collection of more than 9000 artefacts and works of art from all parts of the world.

The campus is open daily until dusk. The museum is open Mon–Fri 0800–1700, Sat–Sun 1200–1600. Admission free.

Little England Chapel, *4100 Kecoughtan Rd; tel: (757) 723-6803.* A State and National Historic Landmark, the sanctuary is Virginia's only known African American missionary chapel. Built around 1879, it holds a permanent exhibition to help visitors understand the religious lives of post-Civil War blacks. Exhibits include handwritten Sunday school lessons, photographs and religious books. Open Tues, Wed, Fri–Sat 1000–1400 (other days by appointment). Admission: donation.

St John's Church, *100 W. Queens Sway; tel: (757) 722-2567.* Established in 1610, St John's is the oldest continuous English-speaking parish in the US. The present church dates from 1728. Among its prized possessions are communion silver made in London in 1618 and a stained-glass window depicting the baptism of Pocahontas. Graves in the churchyard date from 1701 and include a memorial to Virginia Laydon, the first surviving English child born in the New World. Open Mon–Fri 0900–1500, Sat 0900–1200. Admission free.

Sandy Bottom Nature Park, *1255 Big Bethel Rd; tel: (757) 825-4657.* The 456-acre park encompasses two lakes and wetland areas. Facilities include hiking and biking trails, fishing, non-motorised boating, picnic sites, a campsite and nature centre. Open Sat–Sun 0800–dusk (Jan–Mar), Tues–Sun 0800–dusk (Apr–Dec). Admission free.

Virginia Air and Space Center, *600 Settlers Landing Rd; tel: (757) 727-0900 or (800) 296-0800.* The official visitor centre for NASA Langley Research Center features more than 100 aeronautic and space exhibits, including the *Apollo 12* command module and a piece of moon rock three billion years old. Space films are shown on a massive IMAX screen.

During the summer there are coach tours of the NASA Langley Center, where visitors get a close-up look at wind tunnels and the gigantic Lunar Landing Research Center.

Open Mon–Wed 0900–1700, Thur–Sun 0900–1900 (summer); daily 1000–1700 (winter). Admission: $6 ($9 with IMAX; extra charge for coach tour).

NORFOLK

Tourist Information: Norfolk Convention and Visitors Bureau, *232 E. Main St, Norfolk, VA 23510; tel: (757) 441-5266.* Located on the ground floor of a public parking garage, behind the Marriott Hotel downtown, the bureau is well stocked with maps and brochures and staff are on hand to deal with inquiries about tours, accommodation and dining.

A more accessible – and easier to find – source of assistance is the **Visitor Center at Ocean View**, *exit 273 off I-64; tel: (757) 441-1852 or (800) 368-3097.* Staff at the centre can help with information on restaurants and attractions and assist with accommodation reservations in Norfolk and the surrounding Virginia Waterfront communities. Open daily 0900–1900 (mid June–Aug), daily 0900–1700 (Sept–mid June).

GETTING AROUND

Many of Norfolk's attractions are downtown and can be reached easily on foot. For getting around the city area generally, however, the most economical method is by **Tidewater Regional Transit** (TRT), which operates a network of bus, ferry and trolley routes. TRT's *Discover Tidewater Passport* gives unlimited access to the system. Passports are available for 1–3 days. For information, *tel: (757) 640-6300.*

Taxi companies operating in Norfolk include **Norfolk Checker Taxi**; *tel: (757) 855-3333* and **Yellow Cab**, *tel: (757) 622-3232.*

Elizabeth River Ferry, *The Waterside; tel: (757) 640-6300.* There has been a ferry crossing between Norfolk and Portsmouth since Colonial times. Although it has now been superseded by a tunnel connection, the charming little sternwheeler remains popular with pedestrians. The boats departs half-hourly on the quarter-hour. Fare: $0.75.

ACCOMMODATION

Norfolk has 46 hotels and motels and lodging options range from luxury suites on the downtown waterfront to budget rooms. For a free lodging guide *tel: (800) 368-3097.*

Hotel chains in the city include *BW, CI, DI, EL, Hn, Ma, Om, QI, Rm, S8.*

Marriott-Waterside Hotel, *235 E. Main St; tel: (757) 628-6466.* This glittering tower overlooking the waterfront is hard to miss. It has an indoor pool, coin laundry, business centre, gift shop, exercise equipment and games room. The restaurant is open daily 0600–1430 and 1730–2300 and the bar 1100–0100. Expensive.

Omni Waterside Hotel, *777 Waterside Dr; tel: (757) 622-6664.* Right on the waterfront, next to the municipal marina, the hotel features a pool, business centre, gift shop and health club. The restaurant opens daily 0630–2200 and room service is available to 0100. Bars open 1100–0200. Entertainment and dancing at weekends. Expensive.

Old Dominion Inn, *4111 Hampton Blvd; tel: (757) 440-5100 or (800) 653-9030.* This modest inn offers complimentary continental breakfast; a nearby restaurant is open 24 hours. Moderate.

213

Tides Inn, *7950 Shore Dr; tel: (757) 587-8781 or (800) 284-3035* is a 103-room motel with an outdoor pool. Kitchenettes available. Restaurants and shops nearby. Budget.

EATING AND DRINKING

There are lots of eating places downtown, especially around the waterfront. Ghent – Norfolk's answer to Washington's Georgetown – has a plethora of bistros and restaurants along its lively, turn-of-the-century streets.

The Banque, *1849 E. Little Creek Rd; tel: (757) 480-3600*, is a strange mixture: part restaurant, part dance hall, part shop. But it is all Country and Western. The restaurant is noted especially for its steamed shrimp. Free dance lessons Tues–Thur and Sun 1900–2000. Western souvenirs, clothing, belts and boots can be bought in the adjoining boutique. Restaurant open Tues–Sun 1800–0200. Moderate.

Bienville Grill, *723 W. 21st St; tel: (757) 625-5427*. A truly Southern ambience with Cajun and Creole dishes and live jazz Thur–Sat. Open Tues–Thur 1130–2200 (Fri to 0100), Sat 1730–0100, Sun 1730–2100. Moderate.

Elliott's, *1421 Colley Ave; tel: (757) 625-0259*. Down-to-earth restaurant in the Ghent neighbourhood, featuring seafood, veal, burgers and vegetarian dishes. Open daily 1100–2200 (Fri–Sat to midnight); Sun brunch served 1100–1430. Lunch budget, dinner budget–moderate.

Reggie's British Pub, *333 Waterside Dr; tel: (757) 627-3575*. Located downtown on the upper level at The Waterside Festival Marketplace, the restaurants serves such classics from old Blighty as fish and chips, mixed grill and shepherd's pie. Open daily 1130–2300. Lunch budget, dinner budget–moderate.

SIGHTSEEING

An easy introduction to the city is offered by the **Norfolk Trolley Tour**, which departs from the front of The Waterside Festival Marketplace on *Waterside Dr (opposite the Marriott Hotel); tel: (757) 640-6300*. The round trip lasts about an hour and takes in the historic downtown and the city's fashionable neighbourhoods, including Ghent, but passengers can alight and re-board a later trolley at stops along the route, taking as long as they like to explore attractions. Tours daily 1100–1600 (May–Aug), daily 1200–1600 (Sept). Fare: $3.50.

River Trips

Three vessels offer trips along the Elizabeth River.

American Rover, a three-masted topsail schooner modelled after the 19th century Chesapeake Bay craft, carries up to 149 passengers on two- and three-hour narrated cruises under sail; *tel: (757) 627-SAIL*. Spring (mid Apr–mid May) and autumn (early Sept–late Oct) departures from The Waterside marina daily at 1500 and Fri–Sun additionally at 1800 (2 hr cruises), and Sat at 1100 (3 hr cruise). Summer (mid May–early Sept) departures daily at 1100 and 1500 and Fri–Sat additionally at 2230 (2 hr cruises); daily at 1830 (3 hr cruises). Fares: $14 (2 hr), $17 (3 hr).

Carrie B; *tel: (757) 393-4735*, a Mississippi-style paddlewheeler, also departs from The Waterside marina daily at 1200 and 1400 (Apr–Oct). Fare: $12. A 2½ hour Sunset Cruise departs daily at 1800 (June–early Sept). Fare $14.

Spirit of Norfolk; *tel: (757) 627-7771*, is a modern cruise vessel offering lunch and dinner cruises with dancing and live entertainment included. Departures from Town Point Park, next to The Waterside. Lunch cruise (1200–1400)

Tues–Fri, fare: $20.50; Sat–Sun $23.75. Dinner cruise, Sun 1830–2130, fare: $33.95; Tues–Thur 1930–2230, fare: $33.95; Fri 1930–2230, fare: $34.95; Sat, 1930–2230, fare: $39.60. Moonlight Party Cruise (dancing, snacks, cocktail service) Fri–Sat midnight–0200, fare: $15.70.

Attractions

Chrysler Museum of Art, *245 Olney Rd; tel: (757) 622-Arts.* Built in the style of a Florentine-Renaissance palace, with the main entrance through an impressive covered courtyard, the museum houses more than 30,000 objects spanning some 4000 years of the history of art. Its glass collection which includes works from the fifth to second centuries BC, as well as carved and blown sculptural works by Tiffany, Gallé and Lalique, is world-renowned. Other notable collections include Art Nouveau furniture, works from African, Egyptian, pre-Columbian, Islamic and Asian cultures and European and American paintings, sculpture and decorative arts. One gallery is devoted solely to photography. Open Tues–Sat 1000–1600, Sun 1300–1700. Admission: donation.

D'Art Center, *125 College Place; tel: (757) 625-4211.* A working studio centre for the visual arts where visitors can watch sculptors, painters, jewellers and potters at work. Their work is for sale. Open Tues–Sat 1000–1800, Sun 1300–1700. Admission free.

Douglas MacArthur Memorial, *MacArthur Sq at Bank St and City Hall Ave; tel: (757) 441-2965.* Nine galleries of memorabilia surround the tomb of the controversial World War II general. Exhibits include Japanese surrender documents, the general's corncob pipe and his 1950 Chrysler Crown Imperial limousine. Open Mon–Sat 1000–1700, Sun 1100–1700. Admission free.

Fort Norfolk, *810 Front St; tel: (757) 664-6283* (Mon–Fri) *or (757) 625-1720* (weekends). Located on the banks of the Elizabeth River, near the neighbourhood of Ghent, this is one of the best-preserved sites from the War of 1812. One of the few surviving forts commissioned by George Washington in 1794, it is the scene of special events and military re-enactments throughout the year. Open Sun 1300–1600. Admission: donation.

Hermitage Foundation Museum, *7637 N. Shore Rd; tel: (757) 423-2052.* This riverside Tudor-style mansion, built in 1908, houses an outstanding collection of Eastern and Western art, including Chinese tomb figures from the T'ang Dynasty and relics from the private collection of Czar Nicholas. Open Mon–Sat 1000–1700, Sun 1300–1700. Admission: $4.

Hunter House Victorian Museum, *240 W. Freemason St; tel: (757) 623-9814.* An outstanding example of Victorian architecture, the house features Victorian furnishings, a nursery of children's toys and a collection of early 20th-century medical equipment. Open Wed–Sat 1000–1530, Sun 1200–1530 (Apr–Dec). Admission: $3.

Moses Myers House, *331 Bank St; tel: (757) 664-6283.* Built in 1792 by one of America's first millionaires and Norfolk's first permanent Jewish settler, the house holds a collection of original furnishings reflecting the French influences of the Federal period. There is also a collection of works by noted American artists. The museum is said to be the only historic house in the U.S. interpreting the traditions of early Jewish immigrants. Open Tues–Sat 1000–1700, Sun 1200–1700 (Apr–Dec); Tues–Sat 1200–1700 (Jan–Mar). Admission: $3.

Nauticus, *1 Waterside Dr; tel: (757)*

215

664-1000 or (800) 664-1080. Exhibits interpret the whole maritime scene, from marine sciences and exploration to shipbuilding, international trade and sea warfare. Computer, video and virtual reality technology enables visitors to experience navigation, take part in a submarine hunt and design a ship. Outside, a deep-water pier hosts US Navy and foreign and commercial vessels, many of which may be toured by visitors. Open Tues–Sun 1000–1700 (Oct–Apr), daily 1000–1900 (May–Sept). Admission: $7.50.

Norfolk Botanical Gardens, *Azalea Garden Rd; tel: (757) 441-5830*. Collections of azaleas, camellias, roses and rhododendrons flourish on 155 acres, thanks to Norfolk's mild climate. The gardens' 12 miles of pathways may be toured on foot or by trackless train, and there are canal boat tours between flower-covered banks. Cafe and gift shop. Open daily 0900–1900 (midApr–mid Oct), daily 0900–1700 (mid Oct–mid Apr). Train tours mid Mar–Oct, boat tours Apr–Sept weather permitting. Admission: $2.50.

Norfolk Naval Base, *Base Tour Office, 9079 Hampton Blvd; tel: (757) 444-7955*. Guided bus tours of the world's largest naval installation are led by naval personnel, and visitors get a close up view of Atlantic Fleet training centres, massive aircraft carriers and sleek submarines. At weekends there are free 'open-house' tours of selected ships from 1300–1630 – visitors should collect a map from the tour office.

Tour buses may be boarded at the tour office or downtown at The Waterside. Departures daily every half-hour 0900–1430 from the base; daily 1000, 1100, 1230 and 1330 from The Waterside (June–Aug). Telephone for departures at other times of the year. The downtown bus also picks up visitors at Nauticus (see above), 15 mins after leaving The Waterside. Fare: $2.50.

St Paul's Church, *201 St Paul's Blvd; tel: (757) 627-4353*. Built in 1739, St Paul's is Norfolk's oldest building and the only structure to survive the British destruction of the city on New Year's Day 1776. A British cannonball remains lodged in the south-eastern wall. Still in use, the church has a Tiffany stained-glass window. Open Tues–Fri 1000–1600. Admission: donation.

Virginia Zoological Park, *3500 Granby St; tel: (757) 441-2706*. The 55-acre park is home to about 300 animals, ranging from elephants and monkeys to reptiles and nocturnals. Small children especially enjoy the Virginia Farmyard exhibit. Open daily 1000–1700. Admission: $2.

The Waterside Festival Marketplace, *333 Waterside Dr*. The complex overlooks the Elizabeth river and encompasses more than 100 shops, restaurants, kiosks and nightclubs. Eight full service restaurants specialise in a variety of cuisines. Live entertainment is featured on the centre stage throughout the week, and there are spring and summer concerts in the outdoor amphitheatre.

A brick promenade along the water's edge connects The Waterside with **Towne Point Park**, venue for many free outdoor concerts and festivals. Open Mon–Sat 1000–2200, Sun 1200–2000 (June–early Sept); Mon–Sat 1000–2100, Sun 1200–1800 (Sept–May). Major restaurants and entertainment centres remain open until 0200.

Willoughby-Baylor House, *601 E. Freemason St; tel: (757) 664-6283*. Built in 1794, this classic example of Georgian and Federal architecture is furnished with authentic 18th-century pieces. Open by appointment only. Admission: $3.

VIRGINIA BEACH

With 416,000 people, Virginia Beach is the largest city in the state of Virginia. The resort attracts about 2.5 million visitors a year. It has a two-mile boardwalk on which a variety of entertainment is centred in summer, and has been featured in the record books for the extent of its sandy beaches – 28 miles of them.

There are 45 miles of bicycle trails, including one which runs alongside the boardwalk. Golf, tennis and water sports are amply provided for. Virginia Beach offers visitors a wide choice of things to do. They can go bungee jumping, get confused in a maze of mirrors, or make a serious exploration into such subjects as holistic health and reincarnation.

A cross marks the spot where America's first settlers landed in 1607.

A $60 million oceanfront improvement programme was completed in 1995.

TOURIST INFORMATION

City of Virginia Beach Information Center, *2100 Parks Ave, Virginia Beach, VA 23451; tel: (757) 437-4888, (757) 437-4700, (800) 822-3224 or (800) 446-8038.* Brochures and leaflets on attractions, accommodation and restaurants are available. The centre has an automated communication and distribution system which processes the 330,000 visitors' inquiries generated annually by the city's Department of Convention and Development marketing programme.

ARRIVING AND DEPARTING

By car: Approaching from the west, the most convenient roads are I-64, Hwy 460 or Hwy 58. From the north and south use I-85, I-95, Hwy 13 and Hwy 17.

By bus: Greyhound/Trailways **Bus Lines** serve the area; *tel: (757) 422-2998.*

By train: Virginia Beach is part of a seven-city metropolitan area (see map, p. 191) called Hampton Roads. One of these, Newport News, has an **Amtrak** station. An Amtrak bus service runs between the train station and the Radisson Hotel, *1900 Pavilion Dr.*

By water: Private navigators along the East Coast can plot a coast on the Intra-Coastal Waterway or the Atlantic Ocean. For information on local marinas and slipway fees, *tel: (800) VA-BEACH.*

217

GETTING AROUND

Major car rental companies and limousine services operate in Virginia Beach. Moped rentals are available from some locations. There are several municipal car parking lots. Of more than 5000 on-street parking spaces, some 4000 are non-metered.

Bus transport covering the area is operated by **Tidewater Regional Transit (TRT).** For information on routes, schedules and fares *tel: (757) 640-6300.*

From late spring and through the summer a local trolley service is run between *2nd* and *42nd Sts* on *Atlantic Ave,* from *19th St* and *Pacific Ave* south on *General Booth Blvd* and to *Lynnhaven Mall* via the Expressway.

A year-round service is provided by the **North Seashore Park Trolley;** *tel: (757) 428-3388,* from *19th St* and *Pacific Ave.*

Bicycles and roller blades are popular forms of transport along the boardwalk. They can be rented by the hour or half-day from several outlets and hotels in the area.

Accommodation

There are about 11,000 hotel and motel rooms and more than 2500 campsites. Several hundred cottages and other properties are available for rental. Other accommodation is in condominiums, apartments and in a small number of bed and breakfast homes.

Reservation services: **City of Virginia Beach Reservations;** *tel: (800) VA-BEACH (800 822-3224).* **Virginia Beach Central Reservations;** *tel: (800) ROOMS-VB (800 766-6782).*

Hotel and motel chains include: *BW, CI, CM, DI, EL, Hd, HJ, Hn, QI, Rd, Rm, Sh, TL.*

The price category for accommodation is based on summer rates. Generally those establishments open all year offer considerably lower rates in shoulder seasons and winter.

Comfort Inn, *Oceanfront, 20th St; tel: (757) 425-8200,* is centrally situated, has suites with kitchenettes, each with a balcony overlooking the ocean. Facilities include an indoor heated pool and exercise room. Expensive.

Beach Carousel Motel, *1300 Pacific Ave; tel: (757) 425-1700.* Heated pool. Moderate.

Belvedere Motel, *PO Box 451, 36th St and Oceanfront; tel: (757) 425-0612.* Restaurant, bike rentals. Closed in winter. Moderate.

Idlewhyle, *2705 Atlantic Ave; tel: (757) 428-9341.* Family run, this small hotel by the ocean has a courtyard with sunbeds, indoor pool, coffee shop, free bike loan and free parking. Some units are self-catering. Budget–moderate.

Founders Inn and Conference Center, *5641 Indian River Rd; tel: (757) 424-5511.* This hotel is set in 26 acres with English-style gardens and a lake, between Virginia Beach and neighbouring Norfolk. There are restaurants, a dinner theatre, deli, fitness centre, sauna, indoor and outdoor pools, tennis and racquetball. Expensive–pricey.

Dunes Family Lodge, *9th St and Oceanfront; tel: (757) 428-7757.* Children especially welcome here – there's a kiddie pool, children's host, games room, bike rentals, whirlpool, swimming pool, snack shop, and guests can use laundry and other amenities at the neighbouring (and more expensive) Dunes Motor Inn. Lodge guests pay $58-$60 for two in a double-bedded room or $76-$82 for two adults and two children.

Flagship Motel, *6th St and Atlantic Ave; tel: (757) 425-6422.* A family-owned motel across the street from the sea, it offers rooms or self-catering units, poolside and room service, sundeck, laundry and free on-premises parking. Budget–moderate.

La Quinta Inn, *192 Newtown Rd; tel: (757) 497-6620.* Accepts pets. It has a pool. Its summer rates are from $55-$62, with complimentary continental breakfast.

Lakeside Motel, *2572 Virginia Beach Blvd; tel: (757) 340-3211.* Within 5 miles of the seafront, this motel offers weekly and monthly rates. Budget.

Marjac Suites, *22nd St and Oceanfront; tel: (757) 425-0100.* All units are two-room suites with private balconies and fully-equipped kitchens. Expensive.

Murphy's Emerald Isle, *1005 Pacific Ave; tel: (757) 428-3462.* One- and two-room apartments with kitchen. Pool

and games room. Children under 12 free. Budget-moderate.

Ocean Holiday Hotel, *25th St and Oceanfront; tel: (757) 425-6920.* Pets permitted; indoor pool, exercise equipment and gift shop. Rates moderate–pricey.

Barlay Cottage Bed and Breakfast, *400 16th St; tel: (757)422-1956.* This restored historic house has six rooms for non-smokers. Children not accepted. The price includes a full breakfast. Moderate.

Church Point Manor House, *4001 Church Point Rd; tel: (757) 460-2657.* Six climate-controlled no-smoking rooms in a restored 1860s farmhouse. Outdoor pool and tennis court. Expensive–pricey.

Sheraton Oceanfront, *36th St and Oceanfront; tel: (757) 425-9000.* Facilities include restaurant, lounge, pools, exercise room and sauna. Under 18s free. Expensive–pricey.

Howard Johnson, *5173 Shore Dr.; tel: (757) 460-1151.* 52 units with fridges. Free continental breakfast. Children under 12 free. Moderate.

Dolphin Run Condominium, *3rd St and Oceanfront; tel: (757) 425-6166.* One-, two- and three-bedroom units with oceanfront balconies in luxury high-rise property. Indoor pool, gym, games room and sauna. Weekly rates $800–$1500.

Ocean II Studio Condominiums, *40th St and Oceanfront; tel: (757) 428-9021.* Café and pool. Apartments with kitchens. Free coffee and doughnuts in mornings. Budget–moderate.

First Landings/Seashore State Park and Natural Area Campground, *2500 Shore Dr.; tel: (757) 481-2131 (information only), (800) 933-7275 (reservations only).* Virginia's most visited state park has 233 sites, restrooms, showers and dumping station. There are housekeeping cabins and store on site. Pets on leashes permitted. Open Mar–Dec.

Virginia Beach KOA Kampground, *1240 General Booth Blvd; tel: (757) 428-1444.* Open all year. Live entertainment in summer. Pools. Free trolley ride to beach.

Holiday Travel Park, *1075 General Booth Blvd; tel: (757) 425-0249 (information)* or *(800) 548-0223 (reservations)* has more than 700 tree-sheltered campsites on its 140-acre grounds for tents and camper vans. There are tiled comfort stations and showers, four large pools, a kiddie pool, well-equipped playgrounds, games room with pool tables and videos, grocery stores, laundry facilities, weekend hayrides, restaurant and lounge, mini golf, volleyball, basketball, jogging trails and live entertainment.

Nearly a dozen real estate companies offer furnished cottages to rent in the main resort area and North Virginia Beach. Details of properties are given in their brochures, which can be mailed to applicants. Among these companies are:

Atkinson Realty, *5307 Atlantic Ave; tel: (757) 428-4441.* **Judy Andrassy International Realty,** *3309 Atlantic Ave; tel: (757) 428-8800.* **Hudgins Real Estate,** *3201 Pacific Ave; tel: (757) 422-6741.*

Eating and Drinking

Virginia Beach has at least 250 restaurants and eateries, and in almost all of them the dress code is casual. Finding somewhere dressy can be a problem, but such places do exist. There are steak houses, pancake houses, waffle houses, oyster bars, pasta and pizza houses. You can choose from around a dozen cuisines – Caribbean, Italian, French, Japanese, Chinese, continental, barbecue, Indian, Southern, Texan, Nouvelle American and not-so-Nouvelle American. But remember: the waters of the Atlantic Ocean and Chesapeake Bay yield supreme seafood, and this has top-of-the-menu appeal in the city.

Captain John's Seafood Restaurant, *4616 Virginia Beach Blvd at Pembroke; tel: (757) 499-7755.* Fried scallops, steamed clams, chilled mussels, Atlantic salmon, soft shell crabs in season, oysters, lobster bisque – there's a 75-item buffet and a full menu, too. Moderate.

Abbey Road Pub and Restaurant, *203 22nd St (just off Atlantic Ave); tel: (757) 425-6330.* Seafood, beef and 100 different beers. Live rock entertainment. Open 1100–0200. Budget-moderate.

Carvers Creek, *2013 Laskin Rd; tel: (757) 425-2621.* This comfortable new establishment has quickly won acclaim for its roasted Indiana duck and other meat dishes. Moderate.

The Lighthouse Restaurant, *1st St and Atlantic Ave; tel: (757) 428-7974.* Everyone gets a view of the boating and surfing activity on the water, whether they dine on the patio or in the glass-walled dining rooms. Take-outs can be ordered by phone – *tel: (757) 456-5678.*

Rudee's on the Inlet, *227 Mediterranean Ave; tel: (757) 425-1777.* Candlelit dining with a view of the inlet and raw bar serving seafood and steaks. Moderate.

Duck-In and Gazebo, *Shore Dr. at Lynnhaven Inlet; tel: (757) 481-0201.* The locals keep voting 'Best of the Beach' awards for this all-American restaurant with a view over Chesapeake Bay. On Fri and Sat there's an all-you-can-eat buffet. Moderate.

Taste Unlimited, a sandwich, box lunch and picnic specialist which has three Virginia Beach outlets – *36th St* and *Pacific*

Ave; tel: (757) 422-3399, 4097 Shore Dr.; tel: (757) 464-1566 and *Hilltop West Shopping Center; tel: (757) 425-1858.* The company has a wide selection of beers and wines. Moderate.

Shogun Japanese Steakhouse, *550 First Colonial Rd; tel: (757) 422-5150.* Japanese food prepared at the table. Sushi bar. Moderate.

The Lucky Star, *1608 Pleasure House Rd; tel: (757) 363-8410.* American regional cuisine, up-market seafood, moderate to pricey but you don't need to dress up. Reservations advised.

La Caravelle Restaurant, *1040 Laskin Rd; tel: (757) 428-2477.* French and Vietnamese cuisine. Pianist entertains at weekends. Closed Fri. Moderate-pricey.

Frankie's Place for Ribs, *408 Laskin Rd at 31st St; tel: (757) 428-7631.* Frankie wins awards for his hickory-smoked barbecue baby back pork ribs. The menu also has beef ribs, chicken, steak and burgers. Children eat for $0.99. Open every evening from 1600 with 'early bird' specials until 1830. Moderate.

Desperado's, *315 17th St; tel: (757) 425-5566.* Country and Western entertainment comes with prime rib and T-bone steak dinners. Lunch cheap–budget, dinner moderate.

Famous Uncle Al's 'At the Beach', *300 28th St; tel: (757) 425-9224.* Hot dogs – satisfying and cheap.

Maple Tree Pancake House, *2608 Atlantic Ave; tel: (757) 425-6796.* Open for breakfast, lunch and dinner, with varied menu. Cheap–budget.

Le Buffet, *2014 Atlantic Ave; tel: (757) 425-1575.* All you can eat, and the price is budget–moderate.

Chick's Oyster Bar, *2143 Vista Circle.* Casual dockside dining on fresh local seafood. Budget–moderate.

Isle of Capri, *39th and Atlantic Ave*

(6th floor at Holiday Inn); tel: (757) 428-2411. Fine Italian food with a sea view. Reservations advised. Moderate.

Henry's Raw Bar and Sea Grille, *3319 Shore Dr.; tel: (757) 481-7300.* Established in Virginia Beach in 1938, Henry's is now in a modern, two-storey building with a view of Lynnhaven Inlet. Valet parking for your car – or you can moor your boat outside. Open 1700 Mon–Sat and 1000 Sun for the popular brunch session. Moderate–expensive.

Heritage Cafe, *310 Laskin Rd; tel: (757) 428-0500.* Healthy eating with natural foods on the menu. Budget.

India Restaurant, *5760 Northampton Blvd; tel: (757) 460-2100.* Indian cuisine with classical Indian music. Budget–moderate.

Sage's, *1658 Pleasure House Rd; tel: (757) 460-1691.* Nouvelle American eclectic cuisine. The dress code is casual elegance. Reservations are recommended at weekends. Moderate–pricey.

Chix Cafe, *701 Atlantic Ave* (in Hilton Hotel); *tel: (757) 428-6836.* Raw bar, wings and burgers. Budget–moderate.

Alexander's on the Bay, *foot of Fentress St; tel: (757) 464-4999.* Formal Dress code. Seafood and sea view. Reservations required. Open daily for dinner only. Pricey.

Five O1 City Grill, *501 N. Birdneck Rd; tel: (757) 425-7195.* The dress code is smart casual, the kitchen is open, the wine list is extensive and the cuisine is Nouvelle American. Best to make a reservation. Moderate.

Areo, *981 Laskin Rd; tel: (757) 428-0111.* Italian ways with pasta, veal, seafood and chicken. Moderate.

Forbidden City, *3644 Virginia Beach Blvd; tel: (757) 486-8823.* Authentic Mandarin, Hunan and Schezuan cuisine. Smart casual or dressy. Moderate.

221

Croc's Restaurant, *19th and Cypress Ave; tel: (757) 428-5444.* A place for joyous Caribbean evenings with cuisine to match. Sunday reggae nights. Moderate.

Great Wall Restaurant, *875 Lynnhaven Parkway; tel: (757) 468-1212.* Chinese and Vietnamese cuisine. Open for lunch and dinner daily. Moderate.

Tandom's Pine Tree Inn, *2932 Virginia Beach Blvd; tel: (757) 340-3661.* Choose from a 70-item salad and raw bar. Angus beef and fresh seafood are served. Piano music nightly. Moderate–expensive.

Rosie Rumpe's Regal Dumpe, *14th St and the Boardwalk (in the Sandcastle Motel); tel: (757) 428-5858* for reservations and show times. This is where you go back a few centuries, find yourself in a London tavern and let your hair down for a themed evening of bawdy humour. A minstrel wanders, wenches serve, tables groan under generous platefuls of food and a court jester entertains as everyone awaits the arrival of King Henry VIII. Pricey.

ENTERTAINMENT

There is no shortage of movie theatres showing current releases in Virginia Beach. The Lynnhaven Mall has 11 and there are 8 new ones in Pembroke Mall.

As well as summer band concerts on the beach and the Boardwalk, where there is nightly entertainment all summer, there are more formal events at **Virginia Beach Pavilion Convention Center,** *1000 19th St.* For a recorded monthly schedule of events *tel: (757) 437-4774* and for tickets *tel: (757) 428-8000.*

Virginia Symphony; *tel: (757) 623-2310* gives performances at the Pavilion, as do. **The Community Orchestra;** *tel: (757) 426-2225.* Professional musical comedies are presented by **Commonwealth Musical Stage;** *tel: (757) 340-5446,* at the Pavilion Theatre.

A 20,000-seat **amphitheatre** hosting such international stars as Elton John and Whitney Houston was completed in 1996 on a 96-acre site at *Princess Anne Park; tel: (757) 463-1940.* Major cultural and civil events take place there.

Little Theatre at Virginia Beach, *24th St and Barberton Dr.; tel: (757) 428-9283,* is the venue for local amateur groups to stage theatrical productions from musicals to dramas.

Entertainment is also provided at **Founders Inn Dinner Theatre,** *5641 Indian River Rd; tel (757) 366-5749.* It is open all year round Tues, Fri and Sat, dinner at 1830, show 2015, Sun dinner at 1730, show 1930. Price $35.20 inclusive for dinner and show, $24.20 for show only.

Virginia Opera, *Harrison Opera House, Virginia Beach Blvd; tel: (757) 623-1223,* is an acclaimed company presenting classic and original works.

Top comedy entertainment can be enjoyed at the **Thoroughgood Inn Comedy Club,** a full-service restaurant at *Pembroke Meadows Shopping Center at Pembroke Ave and Independence Blvd; tel: (757) 499-7071.*

Listings in local newspapers provide the latest information on what's on in the club scene. There are clubs for under 21s, dance clubs and different nightclubs offering jazz, reggae, Top 40, rock, comedy or Country and Western.

Sport

Nine golf courses and 190 public tennis courts – some floodlit – enable visitors to work off their energy. **Owl's Creek Municipal Tennis Center,** just south of the resort area, is operated by the Parks and Recreation Department. It has tournament seating for 1300. For a small court fee, lessons can be taken there.

Deep-sea fishing is a major activity. Private boats can be chartered or enthusiasts can join like-minded anglers on one of the party (or head) boats that run half-day or full-day excursions. Check whether you need a saltwater fishing licence – with some companies the licence is part of the deal. Party boats leave from **Lynnhaven Seafood Marina,** *3311 Shore Dr.; tel: (757) 481-4545* and from **Virginia Beach Fishing Center,** *Rudee Inlet, 200 Winston Salem Ave; tel: (757) 422-5700.* The reservations number is *(757) 482-9777.* Scuba diving and snorkelling trips are also available.

Other private charter companies are at **Bubba's Marina,** *3323 Shore Dr.; tel: (757)481-3513;* **Fisherman's Wharf Charters,** *524 Winston Salem Ave; tel: (757) 428-2111;* and **Rudee Inlet Station Marina,** *foot of Mediterranean Ave; tel: (757)422-2999.*

For freshwater fishing in Back Bay or Lake Smith, a temporary licence can be obtained from sports supply stores or from the **Clerk of the Circuit Court Officer,** *Virginia Beach Municipal Center, Princess Anne Rd and North Landing Rd.*

Boats can be rented from several companies, among them **Lake Smith Boat and Tackle Shop,** *5381 Shell Rd; tel: (757) 464-4684* and **Sandbridge Boat Rentals,** *3713 Sandpiper Rd; tel: (757) 721-6210.* Sandbridge Boat Rentals has canoes for exploring miles of bayside waters, 14 ft sailing catamarans, 14 ft fishing boats, jet boats and motorised inflatables. Expect to pay about $16 an hour, $49 a half-day and $89 a day for a fishing boat or inflatable. Canoes are around $6 an hour or $35 a day. Lifejackets are supplied free with all craft.

Watersports in Virginia Beach include windsurfing, jet skiing, parasailing, scuba diving, snorkelling, sailing and canoeing –

there are inland waterways as well as coastal waters.

The city also has facilities for miniature golf, volley ball, bowls and roller skating.

SHOPPING

Boutiques, art galleries, antiques and collectables shops, craft shops and stores selling souvenirs and all the paraphernalia of beach and watersport activities are dotted all around the resort area, from *2nd St* through *40th St* on *Atlantic* and *Beach Aves.* These shops, and those in major malls and shopping centres, are open all week.

Lynnhaven Mall, *701 Lynnhaven Parkway,* is one of the East Coast's largest malls, with major department stores and many small shops and restaurants.

Pembroke Mall, at the intersection of *Independence Blvd* and *Virginia Beach Blvd,* was the first one built in the city. Its stores include Sears, Profitts and Upton's.

Hilltop Area, at the intersection of *Laskin Ave* and *First Colonial Rd,* embraces a number of shopping centres.

Designer labels at bargain prices can be found at the **Great American Outlet** at *3750 Virginia Beach Blvd.* Household goods and sportswear are available at outlet stores in **Loehmann's Plaza** at *Virginia Beach Blvd* and *Stepney Lane.*

For hand-made crafts and gifts, go to **Crafters Mall** at the *Baxter Run Shopping Center; tel: (757) 499-1559* (via the Virginia Beach-Norfolk Expressway). Here you will find porcelain dolls, miniatures, hand-made quilts, stained glass, ceramic, jewellery, baskets, candles, clothes and many other items.

SIGHTSEEING

Tours
A trolley tour of the historic homes and places of Virginia Beach is available Wed

223

and Thur, June–end Sept. Tickets are available at 0830 on the day of the tour from the *24th St* information kiosk. The **Passport to History** tour departs at 0900 from the *24th St* kiosk, and includes the First Landing Cross, Cape Henry lighthouse, the Life-Saving Museum of Virginia and two historic homes. Fare: $7.

Oceanfront cruises aboard the *Miss Virginia Beach* last 90 mins and cost $10 (children under 12, $8). The cruises are operated three times daily by **Virginia Beach Fishing Center**, *200 Winston Salem Ave; tel: (757) 422-5700.* Dolphins often swim alongside.

Discovery Cruises, *600 Laskin Rd; tel: (757) 422-2900 or 491-8090,* runs excursions May–end Oct and charters all year round. The company offers tours of Broad Bay and lunch and dinner cruises aboard 80 ft craft.

Attractions

First Landing Cross, *Fort Story.* A cross erected in the region where the Atlantic Ocean and Chesapeake Bay meet marks the place where the first English settlers – the Jamestown colonists – landed on 26 Apr 1607, 13 years before the Pilgrim Fathers landed at Plymouth Rock, Massachusetts. The present cross was erected in 1935.

Ocean Breeze Fun Park, *849 General Booth Blvd; tel: (757) 422-0718 or* for a recording of opening times, etc, *422-4444;* off-season *(757) 340-1616.* This is four parks in one. **Wild Water Rapids** has a wave pool and speed slides where you get a digital reading of your speed. **Shipwreck Golf** is a 36-hole mini-golf course. **Motorworld** provides thrills and skids on a realistic Formula One Grand Prix course and a gentler challenge on the twisting Family Track. **Strike Zone** puts you in a batting cage as used in the major

baseball leagues. Weekends only at shoulder seasons (most of May and last three weeks of Sept) 1200–1900 (water park open only if weather permits). Park open daily late May–early Sept; water park 1000–2000; Motorworld, golf and batting 1500–2300. Admission charges: water park $16; golf $6 (18 holes); Strike Zone $2; Motorworld charge per ride.

Christian Broadcasting Network, *I-64 at Indian River Rd; tel: (757) 579-2747.* Tours of one of the nation's most modern television stations. Be there at 0930 to join the studio audience for Pat Robertson's 700 Club or Family Channel broadcasts.

Farmers' Market, *1989 Landstown Rd; tel: (757) 427-4395.* In addition to fresh and organic produce, meat and pastries, the market also has an antique farm museum, a restaurant and some special events like carnivals and craft shows.

Maze of Mirrors, *10th St and Atlantic Ave; tel: (757) 425-5233.* Extraordinary illusions, based on the maze at the 1896 World Fair. Admission charge.

Virginia Beach Center for the Arts, *2200 Parks Ave; tel: (757) 425-0000.* Twentieth century art from America and abroad. Educational programmes, workshops and exhibitions are held. Gift shop. Open Tues–Sat 1000–1600, Sun 1200–1600. Admission free.

Adam Thoroughgood House, *1636 Parish Rd; tel: (757) 460-0007.* On the

Colour section: (i) Natural Bridge (see p. 148) (ii) Monticello (p.160); inset, George Washington Birthplace Monument, (p.208) (iii) Costumed guides in Colonial Williamsburg (pp.204–205) (iv) Solomons Island, South Maryland (p. 255); a replica of the *Susan Constant* at Jamestown (p. 205): inset, statue of Pocahontas (p.203)

A Museum Grows

N ow that Virginia Marine Science Museum has undergone a $35 million expansion project, and tripled its size, it merits at least a half-day visit. The extended area, with many additional attractions, opened in 1996, elevating the already highly regarded museum into one of the top marine science and aquaria facilities in the US.

The new area includes a large shore bird aviary, an IMAX theatre, a saltmarsh preserve with walking trails and a 300,000-gallon aquarium with sharks, large fish and other sea creatures and a re-created shipwreck.

A spacious new building at Owl's Creek, the waterway behind the museum, houses an indoor/outdoor river otter habitat and an interactive micro-marsh. Outside the museum's entrance harbour seals greet visitors. From an outdoor boardwalk visitors can see waterfowl and animal inhabitants of the saltmarsh. They can find out how Chesapeake Bay evolved, who lives in and around the area's coastal rivers, and they can watch a craftsman carve a wooden decoy duck or goose. A Chesapeake Bay touch tank enables people to handle a sea star or feed a horseshoe crab. Turtles and freshwater fish can be seen in an indoor river in the Coastal Plains River Room. Visitors can try weather forecasting, and make enough waves to start a storm in the Weather Room. And there are countless species of fish to see in the aquaria exhibits.

Boat trips are operated by the museum, taking people to see whales or dolphins, according to season – though naturally sightings cannot be guaranteed. Whale-watching trips lasting 2 hrs, with museum staff to answer questions, depart from Rudee Inlet Fri–Mon, Jan–Mar. The 2-hr dolphin-watching trips are from June–Oct, daily at first, then on selected dates in Sept and Oct. On Wed in July and Aug, collection trips in the ocean take place. Marine life is collected and brought on board for display in temporary aquaria. All trips are subject to cancellation in adverse weather conditions. Phone the museum for details of schedules and prices.

Virginia Marine Science Museum, *717 General Booth Blvd; tel: (757) 437-4949 or (757) 425-FISH (for recorded information).* Open year round. Daily Sept–late May 0900–1700, late May–early Sept Mon–Sat 0900–2100, Sun 0900–1700. Admission (subject to change) $5.25, seniors $4.75, children $4.50. IMAX theatre extra.

banks of the Lynnhaven River, this modified hall, built in English cottage style around 1680, has a collection of 17th-century decorative arts and old herb and flower gardens. Open Tues–Sat 1200–1700 (Jan–Mar); Tues Sat 1000–1700, Sun 1200–1700 (Apr–Dec). Admission by donation.

Oceana Jet-Landing Observation Points. From parks in *Oceana Blvd* and *London Bridge Rd* you can watch the US Navy's most sophisticated aircraft leaving and returning to the Oceana Naval Base.

Oceana is home to a number of aviation squadrons, including F-14 Tomcat fighter planes and A6 Intruder attack bombers.

Old Cape Henry Lighthouse, *Fort Story; tel: (757) 422-9421 (in season) or 460-1688 (recording).* The 1791 lighthouse is said to be the oldest government-built lighthouse in America. It marked the 14-mile entry to Chesapeake Bay and warned mariners entering Virginia's capes for nearly a century. Visitors who climb the winding staircase to the top are rewarded with a great view of Chesapeake

Bay. Open daily 1000–1700 (mid Mar–end Oct). Admission: $2.

Back Bay National Wildlife Refuge, *4005 Sandpiper Rd; tel: (757) 721-2412.* Migratory waterfowl make use of the 7700 acres of beach, dunes, woodland and marsh. Dec and Jan are the best months to see peregrine falcons and bald eagles. Snow geese and marsh hawks, foxes and loggerhead turtles are sometimes seen. There are 10 miles of hiking and biking trails. Open daily dawn–dusk. Visitor centre open Mon–Fri 0800–1600, Sat–Sun 0900–1600. Admission: $4 per car, $2 per bike or pedestrian.

Atlantic Wildfowl Heritage Museum, *Dewitt Cottage, 1113 Atlantic Ave at 12th St; tel: (757) 437-8432.* Opened in 1994, the centre presents artistic and educational activities relating to waterfowl. Arts and artefacts reflecting the city's rich wildfowl heritage are housed in the only existing turn-of-the-century beach cottage. Exhibits trace the art of decoy-making. Admission charge.

Life-Saving Museum of Virginia, *24th St and Oceanfront; tel: (757) 422-1587.* The history of the US Life-Saving Service (Coast Guard) is depicted, demonstrating efforts to rescue shipwreck victims and tankers blown up by German mines in the entrance to Chesapeake Bay, witnessed by strollers on the shore. Maritime instruments, paintings and scrimshaw works are exhibited. The museum is housed in a life-Saving/Coast Guard station built in 1903 and operated until 1969. Nautical brassware, art works, jewellery and books are on sale in the gift shop. Open Tues–Sat 1000–1700, Sun 1200–1700; also open Mon late May–end Sept. Admission: $2.50.

Over the Edge Bungee, *in Ocean Breeze Fun Park near Wildwater Rapids (General Booth Blvd).* Get the adrenalin

226

moving by leaping from a tower equal to 13 storeys high.

Francis Land Historic House and Gardens, *3131 Virginia Beach Blvd; tel: (757) 340-1732.* Costumed guides, the 18th-century plantation house and its period furnishing and effects show us how the rich lived. Generations of the Land family lived as planters in this late Georgian-style house. Varieties of cereals and crops which are not as prevalent now are grown, and in summer a field of flax provides a haze of blue. Special events are held occasionally, when the process of forming linen thread from the flax may be demonstrated. Gift shop. Open Tues–Sat 0900–1700, Sun 1200–1700. Admission: $2.50.

Norwegian Lady Statue, *on the Boardwalk at 25th St and Oceanfront.* This 9-ft bronze statue was a gift from the people of Moss, Norway, to commemorate the loss off the Virginia Beach shore in 1891 of the Norwegian vessel, *Dictator.* Before the statue was erected the wooden figurehead of the ship served as memorial.

Association for Research and Enlightenment, *67th St and Atlantic Ave; tel: (757) 428-3588.* This library and conference centre is the headquarters for the work of the late well-documented psychic, Edgar Cayce, regarded as the father of holistic medicine. Visitors can explore holistic health care, meditation, dreams, extra-sensory perception, reincarnation and spiritual healing. Open Mon–Sat 0900–2000, Sun 1100–2000. Admission free.

Lynnhaven House, *4405 Wishart Rd; tel: (757) 460-1688* (recorded information). Costumed interpreters escort tours of this early 18th-century home, considered one of the best-preserved houses of its period in the US. Open Sat–Sun 1200–1600 (May, Sept and Oct);

Tues–Sun 1200–1600 (June–Sept). Admission: $2.50.

Upper Wolfsnare, *2040 Potters Rd; tel: (757) 491-3490.* The brick Georgian-style house was built by Thomas Walke III in 1759, and reflects the lifestyle of a well-to-do family of the time. The Walke family, who became prominent colonial citizens, are believed to have come from Barbados. Open Wed only 1200–1600 (June–Sept). Admission: $2.50.

Battle of the Capes Monument, *Fort Story* (at northern end of the ocean-front). This statue was erected in 1976 as a gift from the French in recognition of the help they gave the colonists in the American Revolution. In 1781 a French fleet of 24 ships stood off an attack by 19 British ships, thus enabling George Washington's troops to overcome the British.

Tidewater Veterans Memorial, *1000 block, 19th St* (opposite Pavilion). This beautiful sculpture of stone and waterfall, dedicated in 1988, honours the service of the area's military forces and symbolises the vision that a world divided by war can be united in peace.

Royal London Wax Museum, *1606 Atlantic Ave; tel: (757) 491-MUSM.* Self-guided tour among scenes from history, fantasy and fiction peopled by more than 100 life-size wax figures made by the Madame Tussaud Studios in London. Open daily 1000–2200 (late May–early Sept); rest of year shorter opening times – phone for hours. Admission: $3.95.

Princess Anne Courthouse, *Princess Anne Rd (Rte 165) and North Landing Rd; tel: (757) 427-4111.* This landscaped municipal complex housing the offices of Virginia Beach's executive, legislative and judicial departments originated in 1824. There are now nearly 30 major buildings, some old, some new.

First Landing/Seashore State Park, *off 64th St; tel: (757) 481-2131.* Nearly 3000 acres of natural parkland bordering Lynnhaven Inlet, with creeks and high dunes. More than 400 species of trees and plants grow here. There are more than 27 miles of hiking and cycling trails. The park has picnic grounds, camping, beaches and a public boat ramp. Park open daily 0800–dusk; visitor centre open 0900–1800 (Apr–Nov). Parking fee $2.50 late May–early Sept; $1 rest of year.

Tom's Bike Rentals, *tel: (757) 425-8454,* is a company which delivers and picks up bicycles for riding in First Landing/Seashore State Park and on the Boardwalk. Daily rate $15 (up to 24 hours), weekly rate $45. Discount on three or more bikes.

False Cape State Park, *4001 Sandpiper Rd (5 miles south of Back Bay National Wildlife Refuge); tel: (757) 426-7128.* One of the undeveloped areas along the Atlantic coast attracts many migratory birds. The park, with forests and dunes, is accessible only on foot, by bicycle or boat. Camping is permitted, but there is no water source and open fires are are not permitted.

227

SIDE TRACK TO THE OUTER BANKS

THE OUTER BANKS

The Outer Banks are a narrow chain of sandy barrier islands stretching 175 miles from Back Bay, just south of Virginia Beach, to Cape Lookout, but by car you can only get as far as Ocracoke Island, 149 miles from Virginia Beach – about 5 hrs under normal circumstances.

The islands are full of interest. There are beaches galore and dozens of sub-merged wrecks are a joy for scuba divers. Sir Walter Raleigh founded an English colony here in 1587, but it vanished without trace. And, in an accent bearing more than an echo of Elizabethan English, local people tell tales of buried treasure – Blackbeard and his pirate gang lurked along these shores.

For generations of fishing families the islands remained isolated not only from the rest of North Carolina, but also from each other. Linked by bridges and ferries, today the quaint communities are popular with tourists.

During summer months, travel can be severely affected by heavy traffic – there is often a considerable tailback at the free ferry across Hatteras Inlet. And it should be remembered that this is an area frequently hit by hurricanes. That said, however, the Outer Banks side track is a worthwhile excursion.

From Virginia Beach take Hwy 44, then I-64 west to Rte 168 south, which passes through Chesapeake to reach the North Carolina state line in 15 miles. Continue south for a further 22 miles to just south of Maple, where Rte 168 joins Hwy 158, which carries on south to Point Harbor, where it crosses the Intracoastal Waterway to reach the Outer Banks at Southern Shores.

Tourist Information: Outer Banks of North Carolina/Dare County Tourist Bureau, *PO Box 399, Manteo, NC 27954; tel: (919) 473-2138* or *(800) 446-6262.* The bureau issues information about attractions, dining and lodgings between Duck in the north and Ocracoke, where there are ferry connections across Pamlico Sound to the mainland.

ACCOMMODATION AND FOOD

The islands have an abundance of lodging and eating places. Most accommodation is in motels, but there are also wide choices of cottage rentals and bed and breakfast inns. The greatest concentration of hotels and motels is found around Nags Head and Manteo.

Hotel chains in the Outer Banks include *BW, CI, DI, EL, Hd, QI, Rm.*

Cape Hatteras KOA, *Rodanthe; tel: (919) 987-2307* or *(800) 562-5268.* A resort park on the oceanfront, the campsite has pitches for RVs and tents and cabins may be rented. There are two pools, a poolside café, air-conditioned games room, bathhouses and a TV lounge.

There are campsites in designated areas along the **Cape Hatteras National Seashore;** *tel: (919) 473-2111,* and private campsites can be found at Hatteras, Kill Devil Hills, Manteo, Ocracoke and Rodanthe.

There is no shortage of eating places in the Outer Banks, with the emphasis very much on seafood. There is a plethora of raw bars serving oysters and clams.

SIGHTSEEING

Kill Devil Hills on *Hwy 158 south* is home of the **Wright Brothers National Memorial;** *tel: (919) 441-7430.* A granite monument marks the spot where Orville and Wilbur Wright flew their heavier–than–air machine on 17 Dec 1903. Replica of their aircraft, and of a glider they made in 1902, stand on the site and there is a visitors centre with exhibits, a bookshop, telephones and restrooms. Open daily 0900–1700 (to 1800 in summer). Admission: $4 per vehicle, or $2 per person.

The Wright Brothers would certainly approve of **Jockey's Ridge State Park;** *tel: (919) 441-7132.* Five

228

miles south of Kill Devil Hills, this is a popular place for hang-gliding. Lesser aviators are content to fly kites. Open daily 0800–dusk. Admission free.

Manteo, on *Roanoke Island,* is where the very first English colonists in North America settled, and mysteriously disappeared. **Elizabethan Gardens,** *Hwy 64; tel: (919) 473-3234,* are a lush memorial to the unfortunate settlers. Open daily 0900–1700 (Mar–Nov); Mon–Fri 0900–1600 (Dec–Jan). Admission: $2.

Elizabeth II State Historic Site, *downtown Manteo; tel: (919) 473-1144.* This is a replica of a 16th-century vessel, built to commemorate the 400th anniversary of the landing of the first colonists on Roanoke Island. Costumed guides interpret the story and there are exhibits on Elizabethan exploration. Open daily 1000–1800 (Apr–Oct); Tues–Sun 1000–1600 (Nov–Mar).

Fort Raleigh National Historic Site; *Hwy 64, 3 miles north of Manteo; tel: (919) 473-5772,* is a reconstruction of the original fort of first colony. There is an introductory film and exhibits, and rangers give conducted tours of the site in summer. There are nature and historic trails and a picnic area. Open daily 0900–1700 (to 2000 in summer). Admission free.

The Lost Colony, *Waterside Amphitheatre, Hwy 64, Manteo; tel: (919) 473-3414 or (800) 488-5012,* is an open-air drama company telling the story of the colonists who settled in 1587, then vanished totally. Performances Sun–Fri 2030 (mid June–late Aug). Admission: $12.

Pea Island National Wildlife Refuge, *northern end of Hatteras Island, between Oregon Inlet and Rodanthe; tel:*

(919) 473-1131. A must for birdwatchers, the refuge is part of Cape Hatteras National Seashore. It covers more than 5000 acres of marshland and attracts about 270 species, some endangered. Open Mon–Fri 0800–1600. Admission free.

Chicamacomico Lifesaving Station, *Rodanthe; tel: (919) 987-2203.* The restored station, now serving as a museum, features the work of the 24 stations that once covered the Outer Banks. Open Tues–Thur 1100–1700 (May–Oct); re-enactments performed June–Aug. Admission free.

About 25 miles south of Rodanthe is the 208-ft **Cape Hatteras Lighthouse;** *tel: (919) 995-4474.* The tallest on the eastern seaboard, the lighthouse was built in 1870 and for more than a century its light could be seen from a distance of 20 miles. Visitors can climb its 268 stairs for a spectacular view. Open daily 0900–1700. Admission free.

The free **ferry** that crosses the Hatteras Inlet to Ocracoke Island runs every 30 mins with a crossing time of 40 mins. Vessels can carry up to 30 cars.

The village of **Ocracoke** has shops, restaurants and motels, and the speech of local residents bears a distinctly Elizabethan accent. Edward Teach, better known as the pirate Blackbeard, had his base in Ocracoke until his capture and death in 1718. His treasure is said to be buried somewhere in the area.

Ferry services connect Ocracoke with Cedar Island and Swan Quarter on the North Carolina mainland. It takes 2 hrs 15 mins to reach **Cedar Island** and 2½ hours to reach **Swan Quarter**. A one-way crossing costs $10 per car. ◪

229

VIRGINIA BEACH– OCEAN CITY

This route takes you from one seaside resort to another, with a lot of countryside – and water – between the two. Much of the journey covers the eastern shores of Virginia and Maryland, an area so flat that the only inclines you may notice are those on the Chesapeake Bay Bridge-Tunnel, where Hwy 13 bobs and dives over and under the waves. The land on the eastern side may be flat, but it is by no means uninteresting. Woodlands restrict the horizon and narrow lanes lead to tiny but intriguing waterside communities just off Hwy 13.

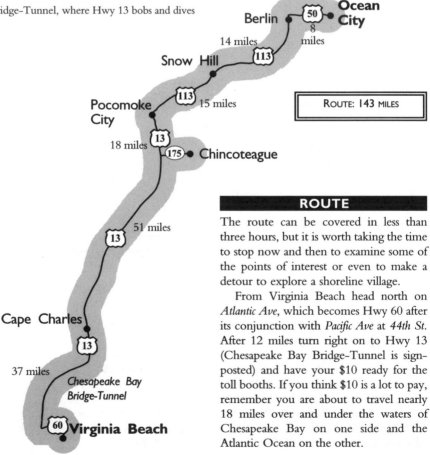

ROUTE: 143 MILES

ROUTE

The route can be covered in less than three hours, but it is worth taking the time to stop now and then to examine some of the points of interest or even to make a detour to explore a shoreline village.

From Virginia Beach head north on *Atlantic Ave*, which becomes Hwy 60 after its conjunction with *Pacific Ave* at *44th St*. After 12 miles turn right on to Hwy 13 (Chesapeake Bay Bridge-Tunnel is signposted) and have your $10 ready for the toll booths. If you think $10 is a lot to pay, remember you are about to travel nearly 18 miles over and under the waters of Chesapeake Bay on one side and the Atlantic Ocean on the other.

From the other side of the bridge-tunnel, Hwy 13 reaches the Maryland state line in 68 miles. Rte 175, the road to **Chincoteague**, is 5 miles south of the state line. Five miles into Maryland, at **Pocomoke City**, follow Hwy 113 north for 29 miles through **Snow Hill** to **Berlin**. From here, Hwy 50 heads east to the southern end of Ocean City.

EASTERN SHORE

Tourist Information: Eastern Shore Tourism Commission, *PO Box R, Melfa, VA 23410; tel: (757) 786-2460.*

Between Virginia Beach and the Eastern Shore is one of the man-made wonders of the world – the **Chesapeake Bay Bridge-Tunnel**, opened in 1964. It is 17.6 miles long and its existence brings another facet of Virginia's rural character within an easy drive.

On your way across Chesapeake bay you will see ships passing in and out of the Norfolk Naval Base, and commercial vessels going about their business.

The toll for cars, light recreational vehicles (Rvs) and light trucks using the bridge-tunnel is $10 each way – more for heavy RVs and trucks. Just beyond the southern entrance to the tunnel, on the southernmost of four man-made islands, there is a viewing point with café and gift shop and a free fishing pier, so if you want to pause before going under the waves, keep to the right of the entrance. Be sure to do a U-turn to get back to the tunnel entrance – if you follow the road round you will find yourself on the way back to Virginia Beach, and to get back on course will involve paying the toll again.

Just before reaching the 70-mile peninsula which forms the Eastern Shore, you will see **Fisherman's Island National Wildlife Refuge**, where a museum has an extensive collection of waterfowl carvings.

The barrier islands clustered along the Atlantic coast provide a sanctuary for many migratory bird species. The Eastern Shore beaches yield a variety of seashells.

Kiptopeke State Park, *Cape Charles; tel: (757) 331-2267*, is 3 miles from the southern tip of the peninsula. Turn west off Rte 13 to Rte 704. The Eastern Shore Birding Festival is held there in early Oct. The park, an area of coastal dunes, has full-service and tent campsites, a lighted fishing pier, boat ramps, picnic facilities, hiking trails and swimming. Admission charge.

CAPE CHARLES

Tourist Information: *PO Box 11; tel: (757) 331-2304.*

The sea wall of this little town (pop 1400) provides a pleasant walk with a view of Chesapeake Bay. There are antique and speciality shops and a choice of restaurants and cafés offering seafood fresh from the bay.

231

ACCOMMODATION

Day's Inn, *29106 Lankford Hwy, Cape Charles; tel: (757) 331-1000.* Budget to moderate. **Cape Charles House Bed and Breakfast**, *645 Tazewell Ave; tel: (757) 331-4920*, is handy for the beach. Bicycles available and gourmet breakfast served. Moderate. **Sunset Inn Bed and Breakfast**, *108 Bay Ave; tel: (757) 331-2424*, is on the waterfront. Full breakfast served. Moderate.

CAPE CHARLES TO CHINCOTEAGUE

US 13 has a railway line as its close companion much of the way up the Eastern Shore. **Eastville** has an old debtors' prison and claims the oldest continuous court records in America. They date from 1632 and can be seen at the Clerk's Office.

At Nassawadox you can take a wagon ride around a working farm and nursery at **Custis Farm**, *Seaside Rd; tel: (800) 428-6361* for reservations. Lunch is included in the price.

Turn east on to Rte 180 for the picturesque fishing village of **Wachapreague**; *tel: (757) 787-7117*. Flounder fishing is the big draw here. Cruises to barrier islands are available. The village has a new $1 million marina.

Returning to US 13, you will soon find yourself at **Melfa** – small but rich in restored colonial architecture. Waterfowl and other wildlife sculptures by acclaimed artists William and David Turner can be seen at a gallery in **Onley**; **Turner Sculpture**, *PO Box 128; tel: (757) 787-2818*.

Close by, westward on Rte 179, is **Onancock**, a scenic village by the bay, founded in 1680. At 2 *Market St* is the **Hopkins and Bros Store**; *tel: (757) 787-4478*, one of the oldest general stores on the east coast. **Kerr Place**, *69 Market St; tel: (757) 787-8012*, is a 1799 federal-style mansion and museum.

In summer, passenger boats go from Onancock to Tangier Island, 12 miles out in Chesapeake Bay. Trips are operated by **Tangier Island Cruises**, *1001 W. Main St, Crisfield; tel: (800) 863-2338*. **Tangier Island** dates from 1686, and was so isolated that for centuries the people retained much of the Elizabethan way of speaking. With the influence of radio and television – and air travel to the island – this is less prevalent today, but especially among the older islanders the accents of their forefathers are still evident. Few cars and trucks use the narrow streets. People get around in golf carts and other small vehicles.

On US 13 just north of Onancock is **Accomac**, whose streets have a diversity of 18th- and 19th-century architecture, including a 1784 jailer's home converted into a debtors' prison.

Parksley, 2 miles west of US 13 on Rte 176, is home to the **Eastern Shore Railway Museum**; *tel: (757) 665-RAIL*. Visitors can explore a caboose and, in late spring and fall, take a rail excursion. Open Tues–Sat 1030–1630.

Continue to a turn-off eastward on Rte 689 to **Wallops Island** and the **NASA Visitor Center**; *tel: (757) 824-1344*. Open Thur–Mon 1000–1600 (Mar–Nov) and daily in July and Aug.

North again on US 13 to **Oak Hall**. where beautifully carved and hand-painted wooden decoy geese and ducks and other waterfowl are made and displayed at **Stoney Point Decoys**; *tel: (800) 826-5883*. Decoy kits are also available.

Just north of Oak Hall, Rte 175 goes 10 miles east to **Chincoteague** and **Assateague Islands**, straddling the Virginia-Maryland border and famous for the annual wild pony swim in late July. The ponies swim from the 37-miles long Assateague Island across a channel to Chincoteague, where some are auctioned and funds are raised for volunteer fire-fighting services. The event takes on a carnival atmosphere, with crowds joining in the festivities and enjoying a variety of seafood. (See box, left). The two islands, joined by a bridge across the inlet, are worth visiting at any time of year. Biking and hiking trails and picnic facilities provide recreation at **Assateague Island National Seashore**, *PO Box 38, Tom's Cave Visitor Center, Chincoteague; tel: (757) 336-6577*. The visitor centre is open 0800–1800 mid June–early Sept, rest of season 0900–1600. It is closed in winter.

Apart from the sale of snacks in summer, the National Seashore is uncommercialised and is for day use only. Cars are restricted to designated roads.

Offshore Ponies

T he annual Assateague pony-penning and auction is important for the survival of the wild ponies. Their numbers have to be kept down or there would be too many competing for the marsh grass and scrub trees on which they live.

Two separate herds of the small but sturdy wild ponies exist on Assateague Island. According to legend, they are descended from 15th-century animals which managed to swim ashore after the Spanish galleon in which they were being transported was shipwrecked. Many people subscribe to the more mundane theory that they originate from animals put out to graze by settlers.

Short self-guided nature trails highlight the three major aspects of the island – marsh, dunes and forest. Ponies can often be seen from an observation platform near the Woodland Trail and you are also likely to encounter small groups of them on the beach, anywhere along the trails, and even in the water when they want to cool off.

Visitors are advised not to try to pet the ponies. However friendly they seem, they can kick out nervously or give a nip. And there is a strict no-feeding rule. It could encourage them on to roads, where they could be hit by a vehicle.

The rounding up of the ponies takes place on the last Wednesday of July, when they are herded across the shallow bay at low tide to Chincoteague town, where they are corralled for the night. The following day a certain number are auctioned to qualified buyers. The rest swim home to freedom.

233

As well as the wild ponies, the woods, dunes and marshes of Assateague Island sustain a unique species of squirrel, the small sika deer and a wide variety of waterfowl. Most of the island is within the **Chincoteague National Wildlife Refuge**, where more than 300 species of birds have been recorded. Birds stop there during migratory flights. You may see osprey, peregrine falcon, horned lark, snow bunting, oyster catchers, bittern, eiderduck, tern and any amount of waders, shorebirds and other waterfowl.

CHINCOTEAGUE

Tourist Information: Chincoteague Chamber of Commerce Visitor Centre, *PO Box 258, Chincoteague VA 23336; tel: (757) 336-6161.*

While Assateague is uninhabited, the smaller island of Chincoteague has well over a dozen hotels, motels and inns, and a reputation for some of the best sports fishing on the east coast. It is also renowned for its oysters.

ACCOMMODATION

Sea Shell Motel, *3720 Willow St; tel: (757) 336-6589*, offers a choice of rooms, apartments and cottages. There is a swimming pool, and guests can use a screened summer kitchen to steam crabs and clams. Open Apr–Oct $450–$500 a week, minimum two-day stay at weekends, 3 days Mon–Fri.

Island Motor Inn, *4391 Main St; tel: (757) 336-3141*. On the bay, with restaurants nearby, the inn has rooms and suites, pools and laundry facilities. Peak season rates moderate–expensive.

Refuge Motor Inn, *7058 Maddox Blvd; tel: (757) 336-5511*. Adjacent to the Wildlife Refuge, set among pines, this inn has suites, family rooms and de luxe rooms. It has a rental shop with bicycles, beach chairs and umbrellas, an exercise room, sauna and indoor and outdoor pools. Moderate–pricey.

Miss Molly's, *4141 Main St; tel: (757) 336-6686*, is where Marguerite Henry stayed while writing the children's book *Misty of Chincoteague*. The bay-side property, built in 1886, has seven guest rooms, most with private bath. Full breakfast and afternoon tea are complimentary. Open Mar–Dec. Moderate–expensive.

Duck Haven Cottages, *6582 Church St; tel: (757) 336-6290*. Secluded, minutes from the beach. Moderate.

SIGHTSEEING

Narrated 90-min boat tours aboard *The Osprey* are operated by **Island Cruises**, *c/o Refuge Motor Inn; tel: (757) 336-5511*. The company also runs motor tours of the Chincoteague National Wildlife Refuge not generally accessible to cars.

Refuge Waterfowl Museum, *PO Box 272, Chincoteague; tel: (757) 336-5800*. Carved birds, antique decoys and wildlife paintings are exhibited, and there are displays of boats and weapons. Open daily in summer, rest of year weekends, 1000–1700. Admission charge.

Oyster and Maritime Museum, *PO Box 352, 7125 Maddox Blvd, Chincoteague; tel: (757) 336-6117*. A study of the oyster and its life-cycle fascinates visitors, and there is an impressive display of live sea creatures. The seafood industry and the history of the Eastern Shore are outlined. Open daily May–early Sept, weekends only mid Sept–Nov 1100–1700. Admission charge.

Continuing north on US 13, you can prepare to bid farewell to Virginia with a visit to the **New Church Welcome Center**, a mile short of the Maryland state line.

POCOMOKE CITY

They call it the friendliest town on the Eastern Shore. They also say it is 30 miles from anywhere. The town has a lovely waterfront park on the Pocomoke River and a 1920s art deco movie theatre.

The **Cypress Park Nature and Exercise Trail**, *off Front St; tel: (410) 957-1919*, has a self-guided boardwalk trail through cypress swamp to high ground on the banks of the Pocomoke River. Open dawn–dusk.

Costen House and Hall Memorial Garden, *204 Market St; tel: (410) 957-4364*, is open to the public by appointment. Built in 1870, it is considered a fine example of the Victorian Italian style of architecture. Admission charge.

Pocomoke River State Forest and Park covers more than 30,000 acres either side of the river from Pocomoke City towards Snow Hill. Fishing, canoeing, cross-country skiing and trails for hiking, biking and horseriding can be enjoyed here.

SNOW HILL

Tourist Information: Worcester County Tourism Office, *PO Box 208, 105 Pearl St, Snow Hill; tel: (410) 632-3617*.

Snow Hill, founded in 1642 and the seat of Worcester County, has more than 100 homes over a century old. A free self-guided walking tour brochure is available.

Tillie the Tug, *Sturgis Park, Snow Hill; tel: (410) 632-0680*, provides 45-minute narrated cruises on the Pocomoke River from mid June–early Sept. Admission charge.

Furnace Town, in the Pocomoke Forest; *tel: (410) 632-2032*, is a re-creation of the 1840s village at the Nassawango Iron Furnace. It is north west of Snow Hill

234

– about 5 miles along Rte 12, then turn left on to *Old Furnace Rd* and continue for a mile. In the village are a broom maker's, a blacksmith's, a smokehouse and a print shop. A museum, gift shop and the Old Nazareth Church can also be visited. A number of events relating to history, archaeology, music, art and natural history are held during the seven-months season. There are picnic facilities and nature trails incorporate boardwalks and swampland. Open daily Apr–Oct 1100–1700. Admission $3, children $1.50.

BERLIN

Tourist Information: Worcester County Tourism, *Box 208 105 Pearl St, Snow Hill; tel: (410) 632-3617.*

A neat city, Berlin has had its red-brick, turn-of-the-century downtown restored in recent years.

Calvin B. Taylor House Museum, *208 N. Main St, Berlin; tel: (410) 641-1019*, dates from the early 19th century. The main part is a house museum, and the west wing is a gallery. Open mid May–late Sept, Mon, Wed, Fri and Sat 1300–1600. Admission charge.

Harness racing takes place in summer at **Delmarva Downs** *(Rtes 50 and 589), Racetrack Rd, Berlin; tel: (410) 641-0600.* Open nightly, Apr–Sept, 1930. Admission charge.

OCEAN CITY

Tourist Information: Ocean City Visitors and Convention Bureau, *PO Box 116, 4001 Coastal Hwy, Ocean City; tel: (410) 289-8181.* **Visitor Information**, *40th St, Ocean City; tel: (800) OC-OCEAN.*

If certain land developers had had their way, Ocean City would have been called 'The Ladies Resort to the Ocean'. That was in the early 1870s, when the place was just beginning to emerge from small fishing village status. Fortunately sanity prevailed and the less unwieldy name that it bears today was chosen.

The sports fishing fraternity and holidaymakers began to arrive in earnest when, on Independence Day, 1875, the Atlantic Hotel opened. Guests reached it by stage coach and then a ferry trip, until a railway bridge connecting the resort with the mainland opened in 1890.

In those days a portable wooden boardwalk was put in place for a few weeks in high summer. By 1915 there was not only a permanent boardwalk but a pier and an amusement park as well.

In 1918 a road bridge was built, and Ocean City and its population grew fast. A vicious hurricane hit the town in August 1933, but even that was not entirely an ill wind. It created an inlet separating Ocean City from Assateague Island, thus opening up a means for fishermen to sail through to the Atlantic Ocean.

Today the resort receives four million visitors in summer and attracts deep sea anglers, golfers and other vacationers during the rest of the year.

Ocean City has 10 miles of sandy beaches, a 3-mile boardwalk alive with shops, restaurants, attractions, music and street entertainment.

ACCOMMODATION

The hotels and motels of Ocean City provide 9500 rooms. In addition there are more than 25,000 condominium units, apartments and beach houses, and several bed and breakfast homes. There's a campground in Ocean City and eight more in the vicinity.

Hotel and motel chains include *BW, CI, DI, EL, Hd, HJ, QI, Rm, Sh*.

Castle in the Sand Hotel, *3701 Atlantic Ave; tel: (410) 289-6846.* Rooms

235

Island Life

The Hotels at Fager's Island is a luxurious five-acre complex of two hotels and a restaurant and bar beside the Isle of Wight Bay – all connected by well-li footbridges over the natural wetlands.

The 85-suite **Coconut Malorie**, 201 60th St; tel: (410) 723-6100, is furnished in Caribbean style and features displays of Haitian art.

The Lighthouse Club, 56th St; tel: (410) 524-5400, designed in the form of a typical broad-based lighthouse of the region, provides peace and comfort in 23 spacious suites, some with double Jacuzzi. A beautiful wooden staircase spirals from the lobby to the third floor. Both properties, open all year, are in the pricey bracket, but have special offers in the shoulder seasons.

Fager's Island Restaurant, 60th St; tel: (410) 524-5500, is a lively place overlooking the bay. A band plays in summer and at weekends year-round. Roast duckling is one of the specialities on the varied menu. Moderate-pricey.

---

and self-catering units are offered, including cottages. Restaurant and lounge. Open Apr–Oct. In expensive category July–late Aug, rates reduced other times. Cottages from $750–$1225 a week.

Dunes Manor Hotel, *2800 Baltimore Ave; tel: (410) 289-1100*. Opened in 1987, this year-round hotel near the Boardwalk was designed and is operated in the gracious turn-of-the-century manner. All 170 rooms and suites face the ocean and have balconies. Complimentary afternoon tea is served. In peak season a standard room for two adults costs from $175–$189; Jan–late Mar the same room would be $55.

Spanish Main Motel, *14th St; tel: (410) 289-9155*. A harbourside property, it has a pool and lawn with barbecue grills and picnic tables. Moderate.

Sea Hawk Motel, *124th St; tel: (410) 250-3191*. Half a block from the beach, the motel has fully-equipped self-catering units. Moderate.

Sun 'n' Fun Motel, *29th St and Baltimore Ave; tel: (410) 289-6060*. All 28 rooms have two double beds, refrigerator and microwave. Budget–moderate.

Eden Rock, *Oceanfront and 20th St; tel: (410) 289-6022*. Nearly 50 self-catering units of generous size, most sleeping six. Shower rooms available for use after check-out. Budget–moderate.

Harrison Hall Hotel, *15th St and Boardwalk; tel: (410) 289-6222*. Rocking chairs on the porch, restaurant, Olympic-size pool and attentive service at this hotel, established in 1951. Expensive, but money-saving package plans are offered.

Princess Royale Oceanfront Hotel and Conference Center, *9100 Coastal Hwy; tel: (410) 524-7777* is Ocean City's newest and largest oceanfront resort. The indoor Olympic-size pool is in a tropical-style atrium. Fitness facility, sauna. Expensive–pricey.

Windjammer Apartment Hotel, *Oceanfront at 46th St; tel: (410) 289-9409*. Open Apr–Oct. On a life-guarded beach, this family motel has fully-equipped kitchens. Pets permitted. Moderate.

Taylor House Bed and Breakfast, *10th St and Baltimore Ave*. Well-appointed guest rooms and a five-course breakfast. Moderate–expensive.

Annabel's Bed and Breakfast, *10th St and Boardwalk; tel: (410) 289-8894*. Breakfast on oceanfront porch. Health club and beach equipment. Expensive.

Ocean City Weekly Rentals, *7th St,*

54th St and 87th St, Oceanside; tel: (410) 524-7486. Fully equipped kitchens in apartments sleeping from 4–10, from $500 a week in season.

Sun Mark Condominiums, *No. 6, 34th St; tel: (410) 289-3451.* Spacious oceanfront condos sleep six. Fully equipped kitchens. Daily and weekly rentals. Varying prices.

Ocean City Travel Park, *105 70th St; tel: (410) 524-7601.* Year-round campsite for tents and RVs one block from the beach. Facilities include hot showers and laundry.

Bali-Hi RV Park, *St Martin's Neck Rd; tel: (410) 352-5477.* Family campsite with 178 pitches, but not for tents. Open six months from early May.

EATING AND DRINKING

More than 160 restaurants, many of them in waterside settings, serve seafood favourites – steamed crabs and clams, lobsters and oysters on the half-shell. French, Chinese, Italian, Mexican and Greek are among the cuisines offered. A number of restaurants run a take-away service.

Fish Tales, *between 21st and 22nd Sts at Bahia Marina; tel: (410) 289-0990.* Dockside restaurant boasting 'overstuffed' hot and cold sandwiches. Food is not served after 2000 but the bar stays open until 0200. Budget–moderate.

The Olive Tree, *1613 Philadelphia Ave; tel: (410) 289-4557.* Italian specialities with hot breadsticks and salad. Cocktails served. Moderate.

Dough Roller, *3rd St and Boardwalk; tel: (410) 289-2599.* Fare includes pizza, pancakes, sandwiches and subs. Open daily Apr–Nov, weekends rest of year. Budget.

Cadillac Jack's Bar and Grill, *106 S. Boardwalk; tel: (410) 289-4375.* Burgers, pizzas, subs and overstuffed sandwiches, plus dancing to golden oldies. Budget.

Paul Revere Smorgasbord, *Boardwalk and 2nd St; tel: (410) 524-1776.* All-you-can-eat buffet in colonial atmosphere. Open mid May–Sept. Moderate.

Shenanigans Irish Pub, *Boardwalk and 4th St; tel: (410) 289-7181.* Seafood and snacks. Entertainment in summer. Budget.

Bull on the Beach, *12th St and Boardwalk* (in Howard Johnson's); *tel: (410) 289-3744.* Open pit roast beef, raw bar. Moderate.

Embers Restaurant and Nite Club, *24th St and Philadelphia Ave; tel: (410) 289-3322.* All-you-can-eat seafood buffet, also a prime beef buffet, plus a la carte and full dining at this establishment. Moderate–pricey.

Brass Rail Restaurant, *4801 Coastal Hwy; tel: (410) 723-3150.* Tex-Mex buffet – as much as you like. Light fare. Summer entertainment. Open Mar–Oct. Budget–moderate.

Charlie Chiang's Restaurant, *5401 Coastal Hwy; tel: (410) 723-4600.* Hunan and Szechuan cuisine. Open all year. Moderate.

Jonah and the Whale Seafood Buffet, *Boardwalk and 26th St; tel: (410) 524-CRAB.* All-you-can-eat seafood buffet, including raw bar, salad bar, prime rib carving station. Open May–Sept. Moderate.

Reflections Restaurant, *67th St and Coastal Hwy; tel: (410) 524-5252.* Specialist French and American cuisine prepared at the table. A totally non-smoking restaurant. Moderate–pricey.

Several companies offer deli items, pastas, subs and sandwiches which you can buy for a beach picnic or have delivered. **Fat Daddy's Sub Shop**, *Dorchester and S. Baltimore Ave; tel: (410) 289-4040,* offers a choice of 20 fillings in fresh subs and will deliver within a limited area until 1600.

237

Board Wok, *on the Boardwalk between N. Division and Caroline Sts; tel: (410) 289-1514*, will deliver Chinese dishes.

A company called **Takeout Taxi**, *12817A Coastal Hwy; tel: (410) 524-MEAL*, runs a multi-restaurant delivery service, giving a choice of lunches and dinners from 35 restaurants. Orders must be for a minimum of $15. Takeout Taxi is open all year. Most hotel/motel rooms or lobbies will have a bill of fare available.

EVENTS

Jan: Two-day **Nautical Wildlife Art Festival**, *Convention Center, 40th St and Bay; tel: (410) 524-9177.*

Feb: Three-day **Seaside Boat Show**, *Convention Center; tel: (410) 352-3087.*

Mar: **St Patrick's Day Parade and Festival.**

Apr: **Ward World Championship Wildfowl Carving Competition**. *Convention Center; tel: (410) 742-4988.* Said to be the world's largest contest of its kind, with 1000 competitors and around $90,000 in prizes and awards.

May: **Springfest** four-day festival of music and art, with sky diving events and kite flying. Held at inlet parking lot and beach at south end of Boardwalk; *tel: (410) 250-0125.*

June. **Arts Atlantica.** Four-day fine arts festival on the Boardwalk; *tel: (410) 289-2800.*

July (Independence Day). **Jamboree** in the Park, *Northside Park, 125th St and Bay; tel: (410) 250-0125.* Also **Fireworks Jubilee**. Beach and boardwalk, *N. Division St (downtown); tel: (410) 289-2800.*

Aug: **White Marlin Fishing Tourney**, *Harbour Island/14th St Bayside; tel: (410) 289-9229.* The five-day event is the summer's largest ocean contest, with 200 boats expected and some $700,000 of prize money to be won.

Sept: **Gathering of Heroes**, *Ocean City Airport, Rte 611; tel: (410) 213-2471.* Two-day air show with World War II aircraft and light plane aerobatics. Also **Sunfest**, at Inlet parking lot and beach; *tel: (410) 250-0125.* Four-day event with arts and crafts booths, entertainments, beach treasure hunts, fun run and other delights.

Oct: **Ocean City Bavarian Festival**, *Convention Center; tel: (410) 524-6440.* German oom-pah bands, food and beer, puppet shows.

Nov: Tree-lighting ceremony/ **Winterfest of Lights**, throughout the city; *tel: (410) 250-0125.* More than 800,000 lights, with animated displays.

Dec: **Christmas Parade**, *Coastal Hwy, 100th–115th Sts; tel: (410) 524-9000.* Decorated floats, Santa Claus, bands and marching groups.

SHOPPING

Ocean City is well served with shopping malls. The enclosed **Gold Coast Mall**, *115th St; tel: (410) 524-9000*, has shops selling fashions, shoes, accessories, electronic goods, crafts, flowers, jewellery, gifts and other specialities.

For souvenir T-shirts, sportswear and gifts, many visitors flock to **M.R. Ducks**, *Talbot St and The Bay; tel: (410) 289-9125*, which has an attractive decoy gallery.

Ocean City Factory Outlets, *Rte 50 and Golf Course Rd; tel: (800) 625-6696 ext. 3365*, has more than 30 outlets, many of them big names, covering a wide range of goods selling at savings of 20–70% off regular retail prices.

SIGHTSEEING

Long and narrow, with the Atlantic Ocean on one side and the Assawoman, Isle of Wight and Synepuxent Bays on the other, Ocean City is most easily explored by municipal bus. It's hardly worth using the car for local journeys when you can take the bus for a dollar a day – and it's a 24-hr service. You can ride the buses as many times in a day as you wish for your dollar – all that is asked is that you offer the exact fare. The half-hourly service is increased to approximately every 10 mins in summer.

For visitors over 60, half-fare discount passes are available from the **Transportation Office**, 66th St (bayside).

Tours

Most people enjoy a **boat trip**, and there are several such options in Ocean City apart from hiring a boat from one of the marinas.

Ninety-min narrated oceanfront cruises aboard the *Judith M* are run each evening by **Bahia Marina**, located *between 21st and 22nd Sts; tel: (410) 289-7438*. The company also operates half-day fishing trips.

The *Ocean City Princess* takes passengers on offshore nature cruises with an expert to lecture on the dolphins, whales, sea turtles and marine life which may be sighted. One-hour cruises among the city's bays are available between May and September. Deep sea fishing trips aboard *OC Princess* leave at 0700 from the **Shantytown Lighthouse Pier**, *(Rte 50 and Shantytown Rd); tel: (410) 213-0926* for information or *(800) 457-6650* for reservations. The fishing trip returns at 1400.

Amusements and Attractions

Ocean City Kayak Company, *Shantytown Village; tel: (410) 213-2818*, enables you to paddle your way along the coast or to visit Assateague Island. Prices start at $30 for a 2-hr nature tour, $35 for coastal surfing by kayak and $50 for a combined four- to five-hour tour.

Parasailing and jet-skiing are provided by **Island Watersports**, *1st St and Bay;*

tel: (410) 289-2896. Another company, **OC Parasailing**, has two locations, *54th St and Talbot St Pier; tel: (410) 723-1464*, offering rides over the ocean or bay.

Laser Storm, *33rd St and Coastal Hwy; tel: (410) 524-4386*, features virtual reality in the ultimate laser tag game. Open 0900–midnight year-round. Admission charge.

Planet Maze, *3305 Coastal Hwy; tel: (410) 524-4FUN*. An indoor/outdoor maze with equipment for adults and children to climb on, slide on and jump. Open 0900–midnight year-round. Admission charge.

Trimper's Rides, on *Boardwalk between S. Division and S. 1st Sts; tel: (410) 289-8617*, was set up in 1890 and is still going strong, with more than 100 rides and amusements for family fun. Rides range from a restored 1902 Herschel Spellman carousel with hand-carved and painted animals to a Tidal Wave loop roller coaster. Open 1300–midnight Mon–Fri, weekends 1200–midnight. Admission charge.

Frontier Town, *Rte 611; tel: (410) 289-7877*. Western theme park with Indian dancing, stage-coach and steam train rides, can-can show, panning for gold and paddle boating. Open mid June–early Sept. Admission charge.

Jolly Roger Amusement Park, *30th St and Coastal Hwy; tel: (410) 289-3477*. Time Twister roller coaster, water park, mini golf and rides, shows and attractions for all age groups. Open daily late May–early Sept. Admission charge.

65th Street Slide and Ride; *tel: (410) 524-5270*. Triple flume water slide with kiddie slide, bumper boats, go-karts and other fun things to do at this family amusements and water park. Open May, June and Sept 1100–1900, July and Aug 1000–2300.

239

Ocean Gallery-World Fine Art Centers, *Boardwalk at 2nd St; tel: (410) 289-5300 and* **45th St Village***; tel: (410) 289-9300*, are antique centres offering original oil paintings and prints from many countries at keen prices. Open year-round 1000–midnight.

The Kite Loft, *Boardwalk at 5th St; tel: (410) 289-6852* and three other Ocean City locations. The shop is an attraction in itself, filled with windsocks, flags and kites of ever more imaginative aerodynamic designs. Open 0900–midnight.

Old Pro Golf operates eight miniature golf courses throughout Ocean City, including a heated indoor course at *68th St; tel: (410) 524-2645*. Open late May–early Sept 0900–0100, shorter hours rest of year. Admission charge.

Three **arcades** with coin–operated amusements, videos and electronic games – **Fun City, Marty's Playland** and **Sportland** – can be found along the Boardwalk. Marty's Playland opens all year, 0900–0100, Sportland opens all year 0900–0200, Fun City opens 0800–0100 in the season and is open at weekends only in winter.

Ocean City Life-Saving Museum, *Boardwalk at the Inlet; tel: (410) 289-4991*. Not-to-be-missed multi-faceted museum in the 1891 building which headquartered the local US Life-Saving Service and Coast Guard personnel. A 'wreck in the offing' exhibit demonstrates the work of the Service along the barrier islands of Delmarva (Delaware, Maryland and Virginia) between 1875 and 1914. Unusual items including art works recovered from wrecks are displayed with early diving suits. Pictures of ships sunk in local waters by German submarines in World War II can be seen. Raging storms which affected Ocean City's history are illustrated. Saltwater aquariums contain marine

240

Birdseye View of the Beach

P robably the most thrilling way of seeing Ocean City's beach is by joining in the action at the **Skydiving Center**, *Ocean City Airport; tel: (410) 213-1319*. No experience is necessary – you go tandem with an instructor after a half-hour training session. You get a scenic flight at 9000 ft above the beach and boardwalk before you take the plunge, free-falling for half a minute before the instructor opens the parachute.

Daily flights over the city and beaches from Ocean City Airport are available in Cloud Dancer, an open-cockpit classic Waco bi-plane from an earlier aviation age. For information and prices *tel: (410) 641-2484*.

Sky Tours, Ocean City Airport; *tel: (410) 289-TOUR*, operates daily year-round flights of varying lengths over the area from Pocomoke City to the Delaware state line, including a city-lights-at-night flight.

---

life from the region, and there is even a feature on mermaids. The all-enveloping woollen bathing costumes and bloomers of the resort's early days make an amusing exhibit, and also on show is a range of antique nautical instruments and paraphernalia. Information of shipwreck research is available by appointment. As well as marine matters, the museum traces some of Ocean City's terra firma history, with old boardwalk souvenirs and early advertisements and beautiful models of some of the hotels, homes and businesses which existed in years gone by. Open daily June–Sept 1100–2200, daily May and Oct 1100–1600, winter weekends only 1200–1600. Admission $2, children under 13, $1.

OCEAN CITY–BALTIMORE

Here is a route that truly offers a range of contrasts – from the beaches, boulevards and esplanades of Ocean City's Atlantic sea front, across the charming rustic landscape of Maryland's Eastern Shore, through the cities of Salisbury and Cambridge to heavily-indented, island-studded Chesapeake Bay. Another crossing of the bay – shorter but no less exciting than the Chesapeake Bay Bridge-Tunnel crossing to the south – leads us to quaint Annapolis (see pp. 246–252), home of the US Naval Academy, and from there it is a short hop to big, booming Baltimore (pp. 261–273).

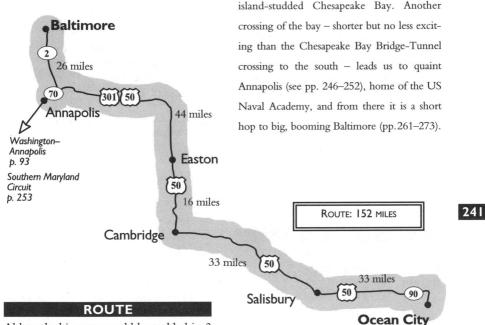

Baltimore

② 26 miles

⑦ ③①① ⑤⓪ **Annapolis** 44 miles

Washington–Annapolis p. 93

Southern Maryland Circuit p. 253

Easton

⑤⓪ 16 miles

ROUTE: 152 MILES

241

Cambridge

33 miles ⑤⓪

33 miles

⑤⓪ ⑨⓪

Salisbury

Ocean City

ROUTE

Although this route could be tackled in 3 hours, plan on three days or more to allow for sightseeing.

From Ocean City's Convention and Visitor Information Center (opposite *40th St*), head north on *Coastal Hwy* (Rte 528) for just over a mile and turn left on to Rte 90 west. This crosses the Isle of Wight in Assawoman Bay and intersects with Hwy 50 in ten miles. **Salisbury**, a busy port on the Wicomico River, is reached after a further 22 miles.

At Salisbury, Hwy 50 crosses the river on a drawbridge and traffic is held up when a vessel passes. Continuing north-

west, Hwy 50 passes through **Cambridge**, 33 miles from Salisbury, crosses the mouth of the Choptank River and continues through the community of Easton (16 miles) to intersect with Hwy 301 at **Queenstown** after a further 20 miles. The combined highways head west, crossing Chesapeake Bay by way of Kent Island and the 7-mile **William Preston Lane Jr Memorial Bridge**. A $2.50 toll is charged for eastbound vehicles crossing the bridge.

Exit 24 from Hwy 301/50 leads to Rte 70 south (*Rowe Blvd*), which reaches downtown **Annapolis** in less than two miles. If you intend to stop in the city, cross College Creek and *Rowe Blvd* veers right and leads into *Northwest St*. Turn left into *Northwest St* then right into Gotts Court parking garage at the rear of the Annapolis and Anne Arundel County Conference and Visitors Bureau.

Leave Annapolis by taking *College Ave* east to *King George St*. Turn left and continue to the end of *King George St* (about a mile), where a right turn will put you on to Rte 450. On the opposite side of the Severn River this becomes Rte 2 north which leads 25 miles to **Baltimore**. After crossing the Middle Branch of Baltimore Harbor and passing under I-95, Rte 2 becomes *Light St*. Continue north to Pratt St in downtown Baltimore. The visitors centre at Harborplace is four blocks to the right.

SALISBURY

Tourist Information: Wicomico County Convention and Visitors Bureau, *Civic Center, 500 Glen Ave, Salisbury, MD 21801; tel: (410) 548-4914* or *(800) 332-TOUR*. The bureau is located in the Wicomico Youth and Civic Center – the county's major showcase for rock concerts, circuses, exhibitions, conventions and sporting events. It provides information on local attractions, shopping, events and accommodation.

ACCOMMODATION AND FOOD

The city has a dozen motels and hotels. Hotel chains include *CI, DI, EL, Hd, Sh, S8*.

The city's largest hotel is the **Sheraton Inn**, *300 S. Salisbury Blvd; tel: (410) 546-4400* or *(800) 325-3535*, with restaurant, lounge, indoor pool and health club. The restaurant is open Mon–Fri 0630–1430 and 1730–2230; Sat–Sun breakfast from 0700. Bar opens Mon–Fri 1600–0200; Sat Sun from 1200. Moderate–expensive.

Comfort Inn, *2701 N. Salisbury Blvd* (4 miles north on Hwy 13)*; tel: (410) 543-4666* or *(800) 221-2222*, has 96 rooms and offers free continental breakfast. Restaurant nearby. Budget.

Days Inn, *2525 N. Salisbury Blvd; tel: (410) 749-6200* or *(800) 325-2525*, features a pool, and complimentary continental breakfast and coffee in rooms. Nearby restaurant opens 0600–2200. Moderate.

Holiday Inn, *2626 N. Salisbury Blvd; tel: (410)742-7194*, has a pool, coin laundry and a restaurant open daily 0630–1330 and 1700–2200. Bar open 1630–midnight. Budget–moderate.

SHOPPING

Salisbury's **Downtown Plaza**, a pedestrianised mall bordered by *Mill St, Division St, W. Church St* and *Camden St*, has a number of eating places and there is a food court with half a dozen restaurants at **The Centre** shopping mall at *2300 N. Salisbury Blvd; tel: (410) 548-1600*.

The Country House, *805 E. Main St; tel: (410) 749-1959*, is said to be the largest country store in the East. Its many departments featuring pottery, throws, tinware, paper goods and many other items – will certainly appeal to shoppers seeking gifts.

Two factories have made a name for Salisbury in the production of handcrafted pewter. **Chesapeake Pewter**, *1705 N. Salisbury Blvd; tel: (410) 860-6700* or *(800) 228-2629*, is open Mon–Fri 0700–1800, Sat 0900–1600, Sun 1100–1600. Admission free. **Salisbury Pewter**, *Hwy 13,* 3 miles north of Salisbury; *tel: (410) 456-1188*, has an observation room where visitors can watch items being made. Factory tours are available. Open

Mon–Fri 0900–1730, Sat 1000–1700, Sun 1200–1700. Admission free.

SIGHTSEEING

Situated at the head of the Wicomico River, Salisbury was laid out by a charter granted in 1732. But the city was twice ravaged by fire – in 1860 and 1886. Only a few buildings survived the second conflagration. Reconstruction began in 1887 and that neighbourhood, known to this day as Newtown, is the city's oldest area with a wealth of Victorian architecture. A self-guided walking tour leaflet is available from the visitors bureau.

Salisbury's oldest house is **Poplar Hill Mansion**, *117 Elizabeth St; tel: (410) 749-1776*. Built around 1805, it is noted for its exterior details, finely carved interior woodwork and heart of pine floors. Open Sun 1300–1600; other times by appointment. Admission charge.

Mason–Dixon Marker, *Rte 54 off Hwy 50 at Mardela Springs, 9 miles north of Salisbury*. Erected in 1768, this marks the southern end of the boundary installed to settle property disputes between the Penn and Calvert families, whose coats-of-arms it bears. Freely accessible.

Nutter's Museum, *521 N. Division St, Fruitland, five miles south of Salisbury; tel: (410) 546-1281*. The last building in the US to be used solely as a voting house is now a museum devoted to local, state and national politics. It features memorabilia from presidential campaigns dating from 1844 to the present. Open Thur 1000–1600 (May–Sept). Admission free.

Pemberton Hall and Park, *Pemberton Dr, off Rte 349, five miles west of Salisbury; tel: (410) 742-1741 or (410) 749-0124*. Built in 1741 and listed on the National Register of Historic Places, this is one of the earliest brick gambrel roofed houses in Maryland and is a typical mid

18th century Eastern Shore plantation home. Open daily 1400–1600 (May–Oct); other times by appointment. Admission: donation. The park has nature trails, picnic area and a pond. Open daily dawn–dusk. Admission free.

Salisbury Zoo, *750 S. Park Dr.; tel: (410) 548-3188*. Located on the banks of a branch of the Wicomico River. it provides naturalistic habitats for some 400 mammals, birds and reptiles. Major exhibits include spectacled bears, spider monkeys, jaguars, bison, bald eagles and waterfowl. Open daily 0800–1930 (late May–early Sept); to 1630 in other seasons.

Ward Museum of Wildfowl Art, *909 Schumaker Dr.; tel: (410) 742-4988*. Named in honour of Lem and Steve Ward, of Crisfield, MD, who elevated decoy carving to a fine art, the museum houses the world's most comprehensive collection of wildfowl carving. Interpretive galleries, leading through history and heritage, contain antique working decoys, contemporary models, acclaimed sculpture and painting. A video presentation introduces the art of decoy carving. Gifts and books are available in the museum shop. Open Mon–Sat 1000–1700, Sun 1200–1700. Admission: $4.

CAMBRIDGE

Tourist Information: Dorchester County Tourism, *203 Sunburst Hwy, Cambridge, MD 21613; tel: (410) 228-1000*. A visitor's guide to the county contains information on a range of amenities as well a list of attractions, accommodation, dining and shopping facilities. A very detailed pamphlet leads visitors on a self-guided walking tour of Cambridge Historic Area.

ACCOMMODATION AND FOOD

There are about half a dozen bed and

243

breakfast inns in Cambridge, with a similar number in outlying villages. Most are in the budget–moderate category.

Three campsites are located south-west of the city, accessible via Rte 16. The nearest is **Madison Bay Marina and Campground** on the Little Choptank River at Madison; *tel: (410) 228-4111.* **Tideland Park Campground** is on Slaughter Creek, Taylors Island; *tel: (410) 397-3473.* **Taylors Island Family Campground**, overlooking Chesapeake Bay on Taylors Island; *tel: (410) 397-3275,* has showers, laundry and restaurant.

Although accommodation might be difficult to find in Cambridge, there is no shortage of eating places and they are listed in the Visitor's Guide. The usual fast food chains are represented, but there are a few locally owned family restaurants, mostly with seafood as a prominent feature.

SIGHTSEEING

Annie Oakley House, *28 Bellevue Ave, Hambrooks Bay, Cambridge.* Annie 'Get Your Gun' Oakley and her husband Frank Butler retired here in 1912. The house has an unusual roof line, designed so that sharpshooter Annie had an uninterrupted line of fire at waterfowl flying in over the bay. The house was also built without cupboards – Annie was so used to living out of a trunk that she forgot about them when the house was built. The house is privately owned and occupied, so you can only stand outside and look.

Blackwater National Wildlife Refuge, *Rte 335,* off Rte 16, 12 miles south of Cambridge; *tel: (410) 228-2677.* Some 20,000 acres of rich tidal marsh and mixed woodland provide habitats for such endangered species as the Delmarva fox squirrel, peregrine falcon and a large nesting population of bald eagles. The refuge is a major wintering home for waterfowl

using the Atlantic flyway, and large concentrations of Canada geese and more than 20 duck species Oct–Mar. Osprey, great blue heron, hawks, muskrat inhabit it. A visitor centre contains exhibits and film presentations, and there are driving, walking and bike trails. Open daily dawn–dusk. Visitor centre open Mon–Fri 0800–1600, Sat–Sun 0900–1700. Admission charge.

Brannock Maritime Museum, *210 Talbot Ave; tel: (410) 228-6938,* showcases artefacts from Chesapeake Bay and beyond, and is dedicated to Dorchester County's maritime heritage. Open Fri–Sat 1000–1600, Sun 1300–1600; other times by appointment. Admission: donation.

Dorchester Arts Center, *120 High St; tel: (410) 228-7782 or 228-1000,* displays the work of local painters, sculptors and photographers. Open Mon–Fri 1000–1400, Sat 1100–1500. Admission free.

Dorchester Heritage Museum, *Horn Point Rd; tel: (410) 228-1899.* The museum's four main areas – Heritage Displays, the Waterman Room, Aviation Hall and Archaeology Room – highlight the county's heritage. There is also a section of children's exhibits. Open Sat–Sun 1300–1630 (mid Apr–Oct); other times by appointment. Admission free.

Meredith House and Neild Museum, *901 LaGrange Ave; tel: (410) 228-7953.* Built in 1760, the house harbours artefacts from six Maryland governors born in Dorchester County and includes a child's room with antique dolls and toys. There is an extensive collection of agricultural, maritime, industrial and Native American items. Open Thur–Sat 1000–1600. Admission charge.

Richardson Museum, *401 High St; tel: (410) 221-1871 or 228-3323,* is dedicated to the traditional wooden boats and other craft of Chesapeake Bay. Open Sat

1000–1600, Sun 1300–1600; other times by appointment. Admission free.

Underground Railroad: Harriet Tubman Museum, *424 Race St; tel: (410) 228-0401.* This is a resource centre for information on Harriet Tubman, heroine of the 'Underground Railroad', along which escaped slaves were smuggled to freedom. Harriet Tubman was born in Cambridge – the site of her birthplace is identified by a marker in *Green Briar Rd.* A museum gift shop sells items from Africa, as well as Native American and local articles. Open Tues–Fri 1300–1700, Sat 1200–1600. Admission free.

EASTON

Tourist Information: Talbot County Conference and Visitors Bureau, *PO Box 1366, Talbot Chamber Building, Tred Avon Sq, Easton, MD 21601; tel: (410) 822-4606.* Visitor guides to Talbot County and the town of Easton including information on attractions, accommodation and dining are available.

ACCOMMODATION AND FOOD

First settled in 1682, Easton is an attractive community of quaint, tree-lined streets and one of America's top 100 small towns. It has half a dozen hotels and about the same number of bed and breakfast inns.

Hotel chains in Easton include *CI, DI, EI, Hd.* Most central is the **Tidewater Inn**, *101 E. Dover St; tel: (410) 822-1300* or *(800) 237-8775.* It offers free valet parking and a pool. Restaurant open daily 0700–2200; bar 1100–0200. Moderate-expensive. Two blocks away is **The Bishop's House**, *214 Goldsborough St; tel: (410) 820-7290* or *(800) 223-7290.* This bed and breakfast inn, a restored Victorian villa furnished in period style, is in Easton's historic district. Moderate.

Comfort Inn Easton, *8253 Ocean*

Gateway (Hwy 50); tel: (410) 822-4600. Complimentary continental breakfast is offered in this 84-room motel which has a restaurant nearby. Moderate.

The town has about 30 eating places, few of which are national fastfood establishments. The best-known restaurant is **Legal Spirits**, *42 E. Dover St; tel: (410) 820-0033.* Located in a former music hall built in 1922 and decorated in Prohibition speakeasy style, it offers massive salads, seafood – including Maryland crab cakes – and prime beef. Open Mon–Thur 1130–2200, Fri–Sat 1130–2300. Lunch budget, dinner budget–moderate.

SIGHTSEEING

Academy of the Arts, *106 South Street; tel: (410) 822-5997,* is a multi-discipline arts centre presenting the work of local, regional and national artists, Open Mon–Tues and Thur–Sat 1000–1600, Wed 1000–2100. Admission free.

Avalon Theater, *40 E. Dover St; tel: (401) 822-0345.* Built in 1921 and restored in the 1980s, this art-deco theatre now functions as a year-round non-profit performing arts centre with a programme of concerts, films, seminars, plays and community events. Opening times vary. Admission free.

Talbot County Historical Society, *5 S. Washington St; tel: (410) 822-0773.* The society's museum offers three galleries of changing exhibits, and there are guided tours of 18th- and 19th-century restored houses. Open Tues–Sat 1000–1600, Sun 1300–1500. Admission free.

Third Haven Friends Meeting House, *405 S. Washington St; tel: (410) 822-0293.* Built in 1682, this is believed to be the oldest frame building in continuous use in the US William Penn preached here and Lord Baltimore attended services. Open daily 0900–1700. Admission free.

ANNAPOLIS

Founded in 1649, the entire city of Annapolis is a National Historic Landmark, with many houses and public buildings more than 200 years old. It has more surviving colonial buildings than anywhere else in the US Annapolis became the capital of Maryland in 1695, and the Maryland State House, built at the time of American Revolution, doubled as the nation's capital in 1783-84. Today, it is a charming waterside city whose nautical character is underscored by the presence of the US Naval Academy, a powerful influence since its establishment in 1845.

246

TOURIST INFORMATION

Tourist Information: Annapolis and Anne Arundel County Conference and Visitors Bureau, *26 West St, Annapolis, MD 21401; tel: (410) 280-0445*. Located at the heart of downtown Annapolis, just a few moments' stroll from *Church Circle*, the visitor centre may be accessed either from *West St* or from the car park behind, which has entrances on *Northwest St* and *Calvert St*. Visitors to the centre can receive a 50 cents discount off the first hour's charge ($1) at the car park. The centre has a pleasant, relaxed atmosphere and has photographic displays of local scenes. Information is available on local and state-wide attractions and helpful staff are on hand to answer inquiries about dining, shopping, events and sightseeing. A tourist information booth is located on the City Dock.

ARRIVING AND DEPARTING

Hwy 301/50 runs east–west across the north of the city. Head south on Rte 70 to reach the downtown.

If coming from the south, Rte 2 leads to Rte 450 W.

GETTING AROUND

Annapolis is an old city with quaint narrow streets. Cars are a problem and parking difficult. Parking meter hours are daily 1000–1930. The meter charge is $0.25 for 30 mins and most meters have a limit of two hours or less.

There are five parking garages downtown. **Gotts Court**, next to the visitor centre, costs $1 an hour with a maximum charge of $8. Reduced rates at weekends. A 'Park and Shop' scheme enables shoppers to obtain parking discounts from participating traders. You can park all day at the Navy-Marine Corps Memorial Stadium, north of College Creek, for $4 and take the Annapolis Trolley Express Shuttle downtown, with stops at the visitor centre, *Church Circle*, *Maryland Ave*, Gate 1 of the Naval Academy and *Main St*.

Most of the city's sightseeing attractions are in the downtown area, and walking is the best way to see them. Other parts of Annapolis – especially the restaurants along Spa and Back Creeks – may be visited by **Jiffy Water Taxi**, *Slip 20, City Dock; tel: (410) 263-0033*. The taxi departs hourly from City Dock and operates Mon–Thur 0930–midnight, Fri 0930–0100, Sat 0900–0100, Sun 0900–midnight (mid May–early Sept – times vary in Apr, early May, Sept and Oct). Fare: $1–$3.50 according to destination.

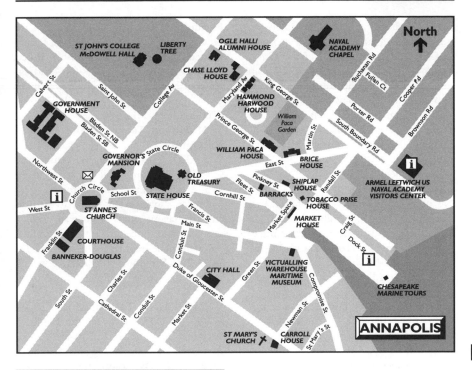

STAYING IN ANNAPOLIS

Accommodation

Annapolis has a good selection of accommodation in hotels, motels and especially bed and breakfast inns – there are 20 of these in the downtown historic district alone. Hotel chains in the city include *CM, DI, EL, Hd, Ma, RI.*

The following organisations offer reservations services for accommodation in hotels, inns, and furnished houses:

Amanda's Bed and Breakfast Regional Reservation Service, *1428 Park Ave, Baltimore, MD 21217; tel: (410) 225-0001*; **Annapolis Accommodations**, *66 Maryland Ave, Annapolis, MD 21401; tel: (410) 280-0900 or (800) 715-1000*; **B&B of Maryland**, *PO Box 2277, Annapolis, MD 21204; tel: (410) 269-6232 or (800) 736-4667.*

Historic Inns of Annapolis, *16 Church Circle, Annapolis, MD 21401; tel: (410) 263-2641.* Four inns from the 18th and early 19th centuries – the **Maryland Inn**, **Governor Calvert House**, **Robert Johnson House** and **State House Inn** – are clustered around the two circles at the heart of Annapolis and offer a total of 137 rooms.

The Maryland Inn, on *Main St* at *Church Circle*, was built in 1776. Eleven delegates to the 1786 US Congress stayed at the inn, which has a noted restaurant, as well as a tavern and pub. Expensive.

Loews Annapolis Hotel, *126 West St, Annapolis, MD 21401; tel: (410) 263-7777*, has 216 rooms and 23 suites on six floors, and is within walking distance of the Naval Academy and City Dock. The restaurant is open Mon–Fri 0630–2230, Sat–Sun to 2300; bar open daily 1100–

0200. The hotel has a pool, tennis courts, health club and business centre. Expensive.

Gibson's Lodgings, *110 Prince George St; tel: (410) 268-5555*, is half a block from the City Dock in the Annapolis historic district. It has 21 rooms and offers courtyard parking, complimentary sherry and continental breakfast and is totally non-smoking. Restaurant nearby. Moderate–expensive.

Eating and Drinking

No need to go hungry – or thirsty – in Annapolis. There is, literally, something to suit almost every taste, and eating places range from sandwich bars and cafés to chic bistros and full-blown restaurants in waterfront settings. Downtown, the greatest concentration is along *West St, Main St* and around the **City Dock**. Another area with an eclectic choice is the **Eastport/Annapolis Neck** neighbourhood on the south side of Spa Creek, which is at the end of *Compromise* and *Duke of Gloucester Streets*.

Acme Bar and Grill, *163 Main St; tel: (410) 280-6486*, serves American cuisine in a classic saloon setting. On the menu are chicken wings, home-made soups, salads, crab cakes and pastas and ice-cold draught beer. Music. Open daily 1130–0200. Budget–moderate.

Carrol's Creek, *410 Severn Ave, Eastport; tel: (410) 269-1406*. Overlooking the City Marina and facing a superb view of Annapolis, the restaurant has outside and indoor dining areas serving regional cuisine with a strong emphasis on seafood. The lunch menu offers a wide choice of sandwiches at budget prices. Wine available by the glass. Open Mon–Sat 1130–1600 and 1700–2200, Sun brunch 1000–1400. Budget–moderate.

City Dock Cafe, *18 Market Space; tel: (410) 269-0969*, is a small, casual and friendly coffee house close to the City Dock. A huge selection of coffees, freshly roasted and ground, and freshly baked confections. A great place for chatting, playing Scrabble and people-watching. Open Sun–Thur 0700–2200, Fri–Sat 0700–midnight. Budget.

Middleton Tavern Oyster Bar and Restaurant, *2 Market Space; tel: (410) 263-3323*. Traditional Maryland fare served in a restored building dating from 1750, overlooking the harbour. The ambience ranges from casual to formal, and the tavern offers a sidewalk café, a raw bar and fine, fireside dining. Live entertainment nightly. Open Mon–Fri 1130–200, Sat–Sun 1000–0200. Lunch is budget–moderate, dinner moderate–pricey.

Ram's Head Tavern, *33 West St; tel: (410) 268-4545*. Home of the Fordham Brewing Co – the first micro-brewery in Annapolis in 300 years – the traditional English-style tavern features more than 170 beers from around the world, 26 of them on draught. Full lunch and dinner menus seven days a week. Garden. Budget–moderate.

Treaty of Paris Restaurant, *16 Church Circle; tel: (410) 263-2641*. New American cuisine and continental dishes in an elegant and intimate 18th-century setting on the ground floor of the Maryland Inn. Open Mon–Thur 0700–1430 and 1730–2230, Fri–Sat to 2330, Sun to 2130. Breakfast and lunch budget, dinner moderate–pricey.

ENTERTAINMENT

Culturally, Annapolis is a busy place, with around a dozen organisations involved in the performing arts. Major performances are staged at the **Maryland Hall for the Creative Arts**, *801 Chase St; tel: (410) 263-5544*.

Entertainment and arts information is published in *The Capital*, a daily newspaper serving the Annapolis area, and *The Publick Enterprise*, published twice a month. *Inside Annapolis* is a free bi-monthly magazine available at the visitor centre, hotels, restaurants and shops. It includes a detailed map, calendar of events and details of current entertainment, dining and shopping.

Annapolis Opera; *tel: (410) 263-2710* or *267-8135*, performs opera, operettas and musicals year-round at the Maryland Hall and other Anne Arundel County locations.

The Annapolis Chorale; *tel: (410) 263-1906*, has a 150-voice full chorus, a chamber chorus, youth orchestra and the Annapolis Chamber Orchestra. 'Pops' and masterworks concerts are performed Sept–May in the Maryland Hall.

Annapolis Summer Garden Theatre, *143 Compromise St; tel: (410) 268-9212*. A programme of Broadway musicals and other shows is presented in a 200-seat outdoor community theatre. Performances are staged nightly (late May–early Sept).

Annapolis Symphony Orchestra; *tel: (410) 269-1132*. Seasoned professional players perform a classical repertoire at the Maryland Hall.

Ballet Theatre of Annapolis; *tel: (410) 263-8289*, is a professional dance company offering both classical and modern ballet productions, most of which are performed at the Maryland Hall.

Chesapeake Music Hall, *339 Busch's Frontage Rd; tel: (410) 626-7515*. A gourmet buffet and quality Broadway-style shows are presented in one of the area's largest dinner theatres. Open Thur–Sat 1800, Sun 1200.

Colonial Players, *108 East St; tel: (410) 268-7373*. Productions are presented in a 180-seat theatre-in-the-round by this established Annapolis theatre group.

SHOPPING

In spite of its popularity with visitors, Annapolis manages to maintain a small town – if not village – ambience, and strolling among the shops downtown is pleasurable. Shopkeepers welcome browsers. The major downtown shopping areas are *Main* and *West* streets, but concentrations of shops are also to be found around the City Dock and along *Maryland Ave*.

The nearest retail outlet centre is **Chesapeake Village**; *tel: (410) 827-8699*. This complex of 59 designer shops, including such names as Brooks Brothers and Nike, is on the Eastern Shore at Queenstown at the intersection of Hwys 301 and 50.

Shopping Malls

Annapolis has four shopping centres:

Annapolis Harbor Center, *2454 Solomons Island Rd; tel: (410) 266-5857*. The complex encompasses stores selling clothing, home furnishings and entertainment products and a variety of eating places and nine cinemas.

The **Pennsylvania Dutch Farmers' Market**; *tel: (410) 57300770*, is staged here every week, with stalls selling country cooking, baked goods, vegetables, cheese, meat and poultry. Open Thur 1000–1800, Fri 0900–1800, Sat 0900–1500.

Annapolis Mall, *2002 Annapolis Mall* (off Defense Hwy at the western end of *West St); tel: (410) 266-5432*. The mall features 160 specialty shops and restaurants and a food court as well as cinemas and big stores, such as Hecht's, J.C. Penny, Montgomery Ward and Nordstrom.

Fiesta at Riva, *Forest Dr.* and *Riva Rd;*

249

250

tel: (410) 381-9500, is a family shopping centre with restaurants and stores selling groceries, toys, crafts and other goods.

Harbor Square, *110 Dock St; tel: (410) 269-0884.* Located on the waterfront in downtown Annapolis, the mall has a range of shops featuring gift and souvenir items, including jewellery, painting, art prints and sculpture.

Crafts and Specialist Shops

The city has a number of specialist shops, some selling items closely related to the area.

Annapolis Antique Gallery, *2009 West St; tel: (410) 266-0635,* represents 40 merchants from Maryland, Virginia, Pennsylvania and the District of Columbia and offers antique furniture, books, china, clocks, decoys and many other collectables. Open daily 1000–1700.

Annapolis Pottery, *40 State Circle; tel: (410) 268-6153,* is located in one of the city's most historic buildings, the pottery produces and sells a wide range of items. Visitors can watch potters at work.

Annapolis Treasure Company, *161 Main St; tel: (410) 263-7074.* Certainly a treasure chest for the collector, with coins, brassware, jewellery, books and maps.

Historic Annapolis Foundation Museum Store, *77 Main St; tel: (410) 268-5576.* The heritage of Annapolis – including its architectural, social, cultural and maritime histories – is reflected in a range of distinctive products, including reproductions of 18th-century artefacts, hand-blown glassware, pottery, jewellery and books. Information about the foundation's sites and programmes is available. Open Mon–Sat 1000–1700, Sun 1200–1700.

Save the Bay Shop, *188 Main St; tel: (410) 268-8832.* Proceeds from the sale of appropriate books, clothing and gifts sup-

port the Chesapeake Bay Foundation, the largest non-profit group working to preserve the bay's unique environment. Open Mon–Fri 1000–1700; weekend and holiday hours vary.

SIGHTSEEING

Tours

Three Centuries Tours of Annapolis, *48 Maryland Ave; tel: (410) 263-5401.* Knowledgeable guides in colonial costume lead 2-hr tours of the Naval Academy and historic district. Depart daily 1030 from the visitor centre, *West St;* daily 1000 from Loews Annapolis Hotel, 1330 from City Dock information booth, 1400 from Annapolis Marriott Hotel, *80 Compromise St,* (Apr–Oct); Sat 1430 from Gibson's Lodgings, *110 Prince George St* (Nov–Mar). Admission: $7.

Annapolis Walkabout, *223 S. Cherry Grove Ave; tel: (410) 263-8253.* An architectural historian conducts walking tours, tailored to the interests and schedules of groups.

Ghost Tours of Annapolis, *214 Duke of Gloucester St; tel: (410) 974-1646.* The title tells it all: candlelit walks to the city's spookiest spots. Tours take place at weekends (Apr–Nov).

The voice of veteran broadcaster Walter Cronkite leads a self-guided tour of the city. The 45-min audio-cassette may be purchased at the **Historic Annapolis Foundation Museum Store and Welcome Center**, *77 Main St; tel: (410) 268-5576.* Open Mon–Sat 1000–1700, Sun 1200–1700.

Chesapeake Marine Tours, *Slip 20, City Dock; tel: (410) 268-7600.* The company runs a programme of cruises in Annapolis Harbor, along the Severn River and into Chesapeake Bay. A 40-min cruise, with several sailings daily

Apr–early-Oct, costs $6. A 90-min cruise costs $12 (from $21.95 with lunch).

Schooner Woodwind; *tel: (410) 263-7837*, is a 74-ft vessel reminiscent of the Chesapeake Bay schooners built as yachts at the turn of the century. There are four 2-hr cruises Tues–Sun (May–Sept). Only a sunset cruise sails Mon. Departures from Pussers Landing at the Annapolis Marriott Waterfront Hotel, next to City Dock. Fares: daytime cruise $22, sunset cruise $25. The schooner has accommodation for eight guests in four double-berth staterooms with air-conditioning. 'Boat and Breakfast', including a sunset cruise, costs $145 single, $180 double.

Museums and Historic Buildings

Banneker-Douglass Museum, *84 Franklin St; tel: (410) 974-2893*. Housed in the former Mount Moriah African Methodist Episcopal Church, the museum is named after two eminent black Marylanders, Benjamin Banneker and Frederick Douglass. It is the official state repository of African-American cultural material. Collections include artefacts and photographs relevant to black life in Maryland, as well as African and African-American art, historical documents and rare books. Open Tues–Fri 1000–1500, Sat 1200–1600. Admission free.

Barge House Museum, *Bay Shore Dr. (end of Second St), Eastport; tel: (410) 268-1802*. Exhibits feature the business and culture of the area, including boat building, and collections include historic and maritime artefacts, maps and photographs. Open Sat 1100–1600 and by appointment. Admission free.

Charles Carroll House, *107 Duke of Gloucester St; tel: (410) 269-1737*. The restored birthplace of Charles Carroll, one of the wealthiest men in colonial America and the only Catholic to sign the Declaration of Independence. The 18th-century terraced gardens overlook Spa Creek. Open Fri 1200–1600, Sat 1000–1400, Sun 1200–1600 (other times by appointment). Admission: $4.

Chase-Lloyd House, *22 Maryland Ave; tel: (410) 263-2723*. Built in 1769 by Samuel Chase, another signatory to the Declaration of Independence, the Georgian townhouse is noted for its fine interior detail. Open Tues–Sat 1400–1600 (Mar–Dec); Tues, Fri and Sat 1400–1600 (Jan–Feb). Admission charge.

Government House, *State Circle and School St; tel: (410) 974-3531*. Built during the Victorian period, the official residence of the Governor of Maryland houses a collection of art and antiques from the state. Tours by appointment Tues–Thur 1000–1400 (Apr–Dec), Tues and Thur 1000–1400 (Jan–Mar). Admission free.

Hammond-Harwood House *19 Maryland Ave; tel: (410) 269-1714*. The last work of the renowned architect, William Buckland, the house was built in 1774 for Matthias Hammond, legislator, planter and Revolutionary patriot. Considered one of the most beautiful examples of late colonial architecture, the house stands in a charming garden and features a collection of late 18th- and early 19th-century Maryland furniture and paintings. Open Mon–Sat 1000–1600, Sun 1200–1600; gift shop Tues–Sat 1100–1500. Admission: $4.

Kunta Kinte Plaque, *head of City Dock, on the sidewalk*. The marker commemorates the arrival in 1767 of the African slave immortalised in Alex Haley's book, *Roots*.

Maryland State Archives, *350 Rowe Blvd; tel: (410) 974-3914*, houses collections include original public records, church records, newspapers, photographs and maps. Exhibits, books and gifts in the

251

lobby. Open Tues–Fri 0800–1630, Sat 0830–1200 and 1300–1630. Admission free.

Maryland State House, *State Circle; tel: (410) 974-3400.* The focal point of Annapolis and the country's oldest state house in continuous use, this was the capitol of the US from 1783 to 1784. It was the setting for George Washington's resignation as Commander-in-Chief and the ratification of the Treaty of Paris, which officially ended the American Revolutionary War. Tours daily 1100 and 1500. Admission free.

St John's College, *College Ave; tel: (410) 263-2371.* Founded in 1784, the college traces its origins to the King William School founded in 1696 and today continues a long tradition of liberal arts education. It was the site of Revolutionary and Civil War encampments and George Washington's two nephews and step-grandson studied here. In the grounds are the **Liberty Tree**, the tulip poplar under which the Sons of Liberty met during the Revolution.

William Paca House and Garden, *186 Prince George St; tel: (410) 263-5553.* The restored home of William Paca, signatory to the Declaration of Independence and Governor of Maryland, was built between 1763 and 1765. It stands in a 2-acre garden featuring five terraces, a herb and vegetable area, a fish-shaped pond and a wilderness patch. Open Mon–Sat 1000–1600, Sun 1200–1600 (Fri–Sun only Jan–Feb). Admission charge.

The Naval Academy

US Naval Academy Visitor Center, *inside Gate 1, off King George St; tel: (410) 263-6933.* This is the starting point for guided tours of the academy, a 338-acre complex where more than 4,000 students prepare for a career as officers in the US Navy or Marine Corps. A small fee is charged for tours, but the grounds are freely accessible to visitors. Sights to see include:

Bancroft Hall. Home to the entire brigade of midshipmen, the hall is one of the world's largest dormitories, with 1873 rooms, five miles of corridors and 33 acres of floor space. Visitors may examine a sample midshipman's quarters.

Buchanan House, is where distinguished visitors, including royalty and heads of state, are entertained.

The Chapel. Known as the *Cathedral of the Navy*, the stately chapel contains Tiffany windows and is open to the public for interdenominational worship. Beneath the chapel is the **Crypt of John Paul Jones**, the naval hero of the Revolutionary War, whose remains were taken to the US in 1905 after more than a century of obscurity in a cemetery in Paris.

Class of 1951 Gallery of Ships, is an exhibition of model ships dating from the 17th century, constructed of bone, gold and wood by outstanding craftsmen.

Tecumseh Court, in front of Bancroft Hall, contains a bust of the Indian warrior Tecumseh, a replica of the figurehead of USS *Delaware*. The figure plays an important role in midshipmen traditions.

The Naval Academy Visitor Center is open daily 0900–1700 (to 1600 Dec–Feb). Tours: Mon–Fri 1000–1500, Sat 1000–1530, Sun 1230–1530; Mon–Sat 1100 and 1300, Sun 1230 and 1430 (Dec–Feb).

Naval Academy Museum contains a collection of some 50,000 items, including arms, artefacts, model ships and aircraft, paintings and prints. Open Mon–Sat 0900–1700, Sun 1100–1700.

SOUTHERN MARYLAND CIRCUIT

Here is a route that takes you back to where you start: Annapolis. Southern Maryland is the area south of a line between Washington DC and Annapolis bordered on the east by Chesapeake Bay and on the west by the Potomac River. It is a beautiful region with a wealth of history. At Calvert Cliffs State Park you can pick up fossils millions of years old. St Mary's City was where the first settlers from England made their home more than 350 years ago. Clinton and Waldorf witnessed dramatic consequences following the assassination of President Lincoln. There are pleasant waterfront villages and peaceful rural communities. The circuit leads through the counties of Calvert, St Mary's, Charles and Prince George's, in addition to Anne Arundel at the start/finish.

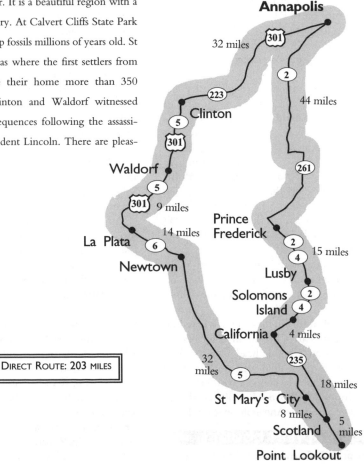

Annapolis

32 miles · 301

2

44 miles

253

223

Clinton

5

301

261

Waldorf

5

301 · 9 miles

Prince Frederick

14 miles

2

La Plata · 6

4 · 15 miles

Newtown

Lusby

2

Solomons Island · 4

California · 4 miles

DIRECT ROUTE: 203 MILES

32 miles

235

5

18 miles

St Mary's City

8 miles · 5 miles

Scotland

Point Lookout

ROUTE

From Church Circle, Annapolis, follow *West St* (Rte 450 west) for about 2miles then head south on Rte 2 and continue for 23 miles. At **Friendship** turn left on to Rte 261, which crosses into Calvert County, passes through the bayside communities of **North Beach** and **Chesapeake Beach**, then gradually turns inland again to connect with the combined Rte 2/4 a couple of miles north of the town of **Prince Frederick**.

A worthwhile diversion comes three miles south of Prince Frederick. Take a right turn on to Rte 264 and after 2 miles a left turn on to Rte 265. After another 6 miles turn right into the entrance of the fascinating Jefferson Patterson Park and Museum.

Rte 2/4 continues through **Lusby** and reaches the relaxed resort town of **Solomons Island**, at the mouth of the Patuxent River. Cross the river to **California**, in St Mary's County, turn left on to Rte 235 south. You can continue south to **Scotland** and then on to **Point Lookout**, where there is a state park, then turn back on Rte 5 north to **St Mary's City**, or you can cut through on Rte 237 and approach St Mary's City from the north.

Continue north on Rte 5 to reach **Newmarket** in 32 miles. Head west on Rte 6 for 14 miles to **La Plata**, the county seat. From La Plata, Hwy 301 north reaches **Waldorf** in nine miles, where Rte 5 continues to **Clinton** in a further 10 miles. From Clinton head west on Rte 223 for 5 miles, then west on Rte 4 for another 4 miles to connect with Hwy 301 at **Upper Marlboro**. Hwy 301 north will lead you back to Annapolis in 23 miles.

CALVERT COUNTY

Tourist Information: Calvert County

Department of Tourism, *Courthouse, 175 Main St, Prince Frederick, MD 20678; tel: (410) 535-4583.* **Solomons Information Center**, *Solomons Island's Rd South, Solomons Island (opposite Calvert Marine Museum); tel: (410) 326-6027.*

ACCOMMODATION AND FOOD

Most accommodation in Calvert County is to be found at Solomons Island, where the largest hotel is the **Holiday Inn**, *155 Holiday Dr; tel: (410) 326-6311 or (800) 356-2009.* A combined hotel, conference centre and marina, it has 326 rooms and nine acres of grounds, with an outdoor pool, tennis and volleyball. There are fine and casual dining facilities and a dockside bar. Moderate.

Comfort Inn Solomons, *Lore Rd; tel: (410) 326-6303.* A waterfront complex, some rooms with jacuzzis. Outdoor pool and restaurant; complimentary continental breakfast. Budget–moderate.

There are about a dozen bed and breakfast inns and homes in the county; again, the greatest concentration is at Solomons Island, but there are a couple in the north.

Angels in the Attic's West Lawn Inn, *Chesapeake Ave and 7th St; North Beach; tel: (410) 257-1069*, is a restored 1903 home within walking distance of a sandy beach, fishing pier, antique shops and galleries; moderate.

Tidewater Treasures, *7315 Bayside Rd, Chesapeake Beach; tel: (410) 257-0785*, is a contemporary bed and breakfast establishment offering moderately-priced accommodation.

The majority of bed and breakfast inns at Solomons Island are houses built well before the end of the 19th century. **Back Creek Inn**, *Alexander and Calvert Sts; tel: (410) 326-2022*, dates from 1880, is furnished with antiques and surrounded by gardens There are private suites with fireplaces and full breakfast is included. Open Feb–Dec. Moderate–expensive.

Hutchins Heritage, *2860 Adelina Rd, Prince Frederick; tel: (410) 535-1759.* This turn-of-the-century farmhouse is located on farmland with a view of the Patuxent River. There is a front porch and parlour and guests are served a full breakfast. Moderate.

Breezy Point Campgrounds, *Breezy Point Rd, Chesapeake Beach; tel: (410) 535-1600 ext 225.* Open mid Apr–mid Oct, this beachfront site features picnic tables, swimming, fishing and crabbing.

Patuxent Camp Sites, *4770 Williams Wharf Rd, St Leonard; tel: (410) 586-9880.* With 125 RV sites – all with water and electricity – the campground is open year round. There are full bath facilities, a boat ramp, 100-ft pier and picnic tables.

As usual in the rural US, it is much easier for the traveller to find somewhere to eat than a place to rest one's head. Prince Frederick and Solomons Island offer the widest choice, but there are fast food cafes and restaurants at North Beach, Chesapeake Beach, St Leonard and Lusby. Not surprisingly, with Chesapeake Bay never far from view, menus are heavily weighted with seafood, but Chinese and Italian cuisines are available, as well as all-American steaks, ribs and chicken.

SIGHTSEEING

Battle Creek Cypress Swamp Sanctuary, *Grays Rd, Prince Frederick; tel: (410) 535-5327.* Within this 100-acre nature centre stands America's northernmost stand of bald cypress trees. An elevated boardwalk enables visitors to tour the swamp, and the centre contains live animals and exhibits featuring the sanctuary's natural and cultural history. Films, demonstrations, field trips and special pro-

grammes are offered throughout the year. Open Tues–Sat 1000–1700, Sun 1300–1700 (Apr–Sept); Tues–Sat 1000–1630, Sun 1300–1630 (Oct–Mar). Admission free.

Calvert Cliffs Nuclear Power Plant Visitors Center, *Baltimore Gas and Electric, 1650 Calvert Cliffs Parkway, Lusby; tel: (410) 586-2200 ext 4679.* The information centre is housed in a 19th century tobacco bar and features agricultural and archaeological displays as well as a hands-on exhibit about energy and nuclear power. The Visitors' Overlook provides a view of Maryland's first nuclear power plant and on a clear day the eastern shore can be seen across Chesapeake Bay. Nearby are the ruins of an 18th-century plantation home. Open daily 1000–1600. Admission free.

Calvert Cliffs State Park, *Rte 765, Lusby; tel: (800) 784-5380.* This 1460-acre wooded park includes the majestic Calvert Cliffs on Chesapeake Bay. They were formed more than 15 million years ago and contain more than 600 species of fossils. Because of landslides, the area under the cliffs is closed, but fossil collecting is allowed along the open beach. The park is ideal for walking, hiking, picnicking, fishing and day-camping. Drinking water is unavailable, but picnic tables and grills are provided. Open daily 1000–1800 (June–Aug), Fri–Sun 1000–1800 (Sept–Oct and Apr–May). Admission: $2 donation suggested.

Calvert Marine Museum and Drum Point Lighthouse, *Solomons Island Rd South, Solomons Island; tel: (410) 326-2042.* Chesapeake Bay's rich maritime history and ecology are featured, along with boats, models, paintings, wood carvings, aquariums and fossils. Outdoor exhibits include a boat basin and a re-created salt marsh. Visitors may board the

255

Wm B. Tennison, a traditional bugeye oyster vessel built in 1899, for a cruise around the bay. Within the museum area is the Drum Point Lighthouse, one of only three remaining screwpile, cottage-style lighthouses that served the Bay at the turn of the century. Nearby, the **J.C Lore Oyster House** features boat-building and artefacts of the local seafood industry. Open daily 1000–1700. Admission: $4.50.

Chesapeake Beach Railway Museum, *Rte 261, Chesapeake Beach; tel: (410) 257-3892*. A collection of historical artefacts and photographs, displayed in an old rail station, details the history of the Chesapeake Beach Rail Company which brought holidaymakers to the resort in the early 1900s. Open daily 1300–1600 (May–Sept); Sat–Sun 1300–1600 (April and Oct). Admission free.

Flag Ponds Nature Park, *Solomons Island Rd North (Rte 2/4), Lusby; tel: (410) 586-1477*. Once a sheltered harbour, the park is now a variety of natural environments, including sandy beaches, freshwater ponds and the Calvert Cliffs. A visitors centre has wildlife exhibits and there are hiking trails, a wetlands boardwalk, a fishing pier and a beach. Picnic tables and grills are provided. Open Mon–Fri 0900–1800, Sat–Sun 0900–2000 (late May–early Sept); Sat–Sun 0900–1800 (Sept–late May). Admission: $6 (Apr–Oct), $3 (Nov–Mar).

Jefferson Patterson Park and Museum, *Rte 265, St Leonard; tel: (410) 586-0050 or 586-0055*. This 512-acre park, once a colonial plantation, is located on the scenic Patuxent River and now serves as an archaeological and environmental preserve with a visitors centre, exhibits of agricultural equipment, an archaeology trail and picnic area in a setting of rolling pastures, woodlands, fields and 2½ miles of shoreline. Open

Wed–Sun 1000–1700 (mid Apr–mid Oct). Admission free.

One-Room Schoolhouse, *Broomes Island Rd, Port Republic; tel: (410) 586-0232 or 586-0482*. Port Republic School No.7 has stood next to Christ Church for more than a century. Now authentically preserved, it is filled with memorabilia from the past. Open Sun 1400–1600 (June–Aug). Admission free.

ST MARY'S COUNTY

Tourist Information: St Mary's County Division of Tourism *PO Box 653, Leonardtown, MD 20650; tel: (301) 475-4404 or (800) 327-9023*. **Visitor Information Center**, *St Mary's County Chamber of Commerce, 6260 Waldorf-Leonardtown Rd (Rte 5), Mechanicsville, MD 20659; tel: (301) 884-5555*.

With St Mary's City, established in 1634, at one end of the historic spectrum and the US Naval Test Pilots' School at the other, it is not surprising that St Mary's County claims it is 'Still Making History'. The county has 400 miles of shoreline and acre upon acre of unspoilt parkland.

ACCOMMODATION

Accommodation options range from holiday cottages to bed and breakfast inns and motels, with the greatest concentration in the southern part of the county.

Days Inn, *Rte 235, Lexington Park; tel: (301) 863-6666*. This motel has a lounge and restaurant and offers complimentary continental breakfast. Outdoor pool. Moderate.

Scheible's Motel and Fishing Center, *Rte 5, Wynne Rd, Ridge; tel: (301) 872-5185*. Air-conditioned rooms with a waterfront view, TV and private bath. The motel has a waterside restaurant, charter fishing, a crab dock and gift shop. Budget–moderate.

Myrtle Point Bed and Breakfast, *Patuxent Blvd, California; tel: (301) 862-3090.* Located on the banks of the Patuxent River, the house has rooms with private bath and rates include full breakfast. Private beach and dock.There are special rates for a three-night stay. Open year round. Moderate.

St Michael's Manor, *Rte 5, Scotland; tel: (301) 872-4025.* Nine miles south of Historic St Mary's City and close to Point Lookout State Park, this 1805 home overlooks Long Neck Creek and has air-conditioned rooms for bed and breakfast guests. Boating, biking and swimming available. Open Feb–Dec. Moderate. Discounts Sun–Thur.

Old Kirk House, *Rte 5, Scotland; tel: (301) 872-4093.* Built around 1800, this large home overlooks Biscoe Creek and has four spacious bedrooms, two with private bath and fireplace. A second storey balcony is available for quiet reading and birdwatching. Moderate.

There are three campsites at the southern end of the county.

La Grande Estate Camping Resort, *Rte 5, Leonardtown; tel: (301) 475-8550.* Wooded sites for Rvs and tents, with electric, water and sewage hook-ups.

Point Lookout State Park, *end of Rte 5, Scotland; tel: (301) 872-5688.* RV and tent pitches on wooded and waterfront sites with full hook-up facilities. Amenities include laundromat, camp store, beach, fishing, boat ramp and rental.

Seaside View Recreation Park and Campground, *Seaside Rd, Ridge.* Rental cabins are available as well as RV sites with full hook-up facilities. The campground has a restaurant and lounge.

The county has an eclectic spread of eating places, with focal points at Mechanicsville in the north, Leonardtown – the county seat – and Lexington Park. In

the south, Ridge has around half a dozen restaurants. Again, seafood predominates, but there are a number of Chinese and Italian restaurants. Travellers planning a picnic, or eating on the hoof, could try **Crabnocker's Seafood Market**, *intersection of Rtes 5 and 234, Leonardtown; tel: (301) 475-7830.* The market specialises in all kinds of seafood, available for takeaway only.

SIGHTSEEING

Two companies run waterborne tours at the southern end of St Mary's County. **Skipjack Tours**, *Rte 249, St George Island; tel: (301) 994-0897.* Local waterways are explored aboard a locally made skipjack. The company offers a programme of environmental tours, crab feasts and oyster roasts. Open Apr–Nov. **Smith Island Cruises**, *Rte 5, southern tip of county, Scotland; tel: (301) 425-2771.* Cruises to historic Smith Island, which is then toured by bus. Departures Fri–Sun (late May–early Sept).

Historic St Mary's City, *Rte 5, St Mary's City; tel: (301) 862-0990 or (800) SMC-1534.* The place where colonists sent by the second Lord Baltimore established the fourth permanent settlement in British North America in 1634 has been restored as an exciting 800-acre 'living' museum.

Archaeologists are still at work, painstakingly excavating more than 150 sites, and authentically costumed interpreters re-live the past in reconstructed 17th century exhibits. The visitor centre, where tickets may be purchased, includes a museum shop and the Archaeology Exhibit Hall featuring artefacts recovered from the site.

The nearby **Woodland Indian Exhibit** features a longhouse, explores the relationship between native Americans

257

and their environment and illustrates how they shared their skills and knowledge with European settlers.

Farthing's Ordinary is a reconstructed 17th-century inn, typical of the kind of establishment that offered food, drink and lodging in the first capital of Maryland. **Farthing's Kitchen**, behind the ordinary, caters for the needs of modern visitors.

The reconstructed **State House of 1676** is a Jacobean-style brick structure built in 1934 as a faithful re-creation of one of Maryland's first public buildings.

The **Maryland Dove**, moored in the river below the State House, is a full-scale working re-creation of one of the two ships that brought the first English settlers to Maryland in 1634.

The **Godiah Spray Tobacco Plantation**, re-created from the 1660s, contains the main and tenant houses and tobacco barns, as well as crops, gardens, orchards, livestock and fencing of a successful plantation. Costumed staff interpret the everyday life of early Tidewater farmers. Visitor centre and Archaeology Exhibit open Wed–Sun 1000–1700 year round; museum Apr–Nov. Admission: $6.50.

Naval Air Test and Evaluation Museum, *Rte 235, Lexington Park; tel: (301) 863-7418.* The only museum in the US dedicated to the testing and evaluation of naval aviation, with photographs, vintage scale models and full-size aircraft.

Nearby is the Naval Air Warfare Center, home of the US Naval Test Pilots' School, where a number of astronauts have undergone training. Open Fri–Sat 1100–1600, Sun 1200–1700. Admission: donation.

Old Jail Museum, *Courthouse lawn, Leonardtown; tel: (301) 475-2467.* County artefacts and memorabilia are exhibited

and a 'lady's cell' may be visited. Open Tues–Sat 1000–1600. Admission free.

Point Lookout State Park, *Rte 5, Scotland; tel: (301) 872-5688.* Located at the southernmost tip of St Mary's County, at the confluence of Chesapeake Bay and the Potomac River, this 1037-acre park contains the site of Fort Lincoln, an earthen fort built by Confederate prisoners.

Two monuments honour the 3364 Confederates who died in the fort's prison camp. The park's visitor centre houses a Civil War museum. There are numerous hiking trails, a swimming beach, fishing, picnic area and a campsite. Open daily 0800–sunset; visitor centre and museum weekends only (May–Sept). Admission charge.

Potomac River Museum, *Rte 242 off Rte 5, Colton's Point; tel: (301) 769-2222.* The history of the area and life along the Potomac River is traced through archaeological exhibits and cultural events. The museum contains a 19th-century country store and the **Little Red School House**, built about 1840.

Boat tours are available to nearby **St Clement's Island**, where a cross marks the landing of the first Maryland colonists in 1634 and the celebration of the first Roman Catholic Mass in English-speaking America. Open Mon–Fri 0900–1700, Sat–Sat 1200–1700 (Apr–Sept); Wed–Sun 1200–1600 (Oct–Mar). Admission charge.

Sotterley Plantation, *Sotterley Rd, Hollywood (end of Rte 245 east); tel: (301) 373-2280.* A working colonial plantation in a magnificent setting along the Patuxent River. The mansion contains period furnishings and a Chinese Chippendale staircase. There are formal gardens, a gate house, slave cabin, farm museum and a gift shop. Open Tues–Sun 1100–1600 (June–Sept). Tours by appointment only

Apr, May, Oct and Nov. Admission charge.

CHARLES COUNTY

Tourist Information: Charles County Tourism, *PO Box 1144, 8190 Port Tobacco Rd, Port Tobacco, MD 20677; tel: (301) 934-9305 or (800) 766-3386.*

ACCOMMODATION

The city of Waldorf (pop 15,000) offers the widest choice of accommodation and eating places. It has four hotels belonging to internationally known chains.

Days Inn, *5043 Hwy 301; tel: (301) 932-9200.* This budget-priced hotel offers complimentary continental breakfast and a coin laundry. Nearby restaurant open daily 1100–2200.

EconoLodge, *4 Business Park Dr; tel: (301) 645-0022,* also offers complimentary continental breakfast and has a coin laundry. Budget.

HoJo Inn, *3125 S. Crain Hwy; tel: (301) 932-5090.* The inn includes suites with kitchenettes, and a pool. Complimentary continental breakfast. Adjoining restaurant open daily 1100–2200. Moderate.

Holiday Inn, *1 St Patrick's Dr; tel: (301) 645-8200.* The hotel has some rooms with kitchenettes. There is a pool and a coin laundry. Restaurant opens daily 0630–1400 and 1700–2200; bar open 1200–2300. Moderate.

Goose Bay Marina and Campgrounds, *PO Box 58, 9365 Goose Bay Lane, Welcome, MD 20693; tel: (301) 934-3812 or 932-0885.* Located off Rte 6, ten miles west of La Plata, the site has waterfront tent and RV pitches, with water and electricity hook-ups. The marina store stocks groceries, ice and fishing tackle.

SIGHTSEEING

Afro-American Heritage Museum, *Marshall's Corner, Gwynn Rd, Waldorf; tel: (301) 843-0371.* The museum reflects more than two centuries of black history in Maryland. Exhibits include a log cabin, ball and chain and shackles, as worn by slaves, and many other artefacts. Tours by appointment. Free.

Charles County Courthouse, *Chapel Point Rd, off Rte 6, Port Tobacco; tel: (301) 934-4313.* The reconstructed 19th-century building houses exhibits on tobacco growing and processing and features finds of the Society for the Restoration of Port Tobacco. Now a quiet village, Port Tobacco was a major river port from 1685 until the end of the Revolutionary War.

The courthouse is the focal point of **Historic Port Tobacco**, which includes **Catslide House**, a restored colonial home built around 1720, and a **one-room schoolhouse** dating from about 1890. Open Wed–Sat 1000–1600, Sun 1200–1600 (Apr–Aug); Sat–Sun 1200–1600 (Sept–Dec). Admission charge.

Dr Samuel A. Mudd House, *near intersection of Poplar Hill Rd and Dr Samuel Mudd Rd, Waldorf; tel: (301) 934-8464 or 645-6870.* The home of the physician who treated John Wilkes Booth, who had broken his leg as he leapt from the presidential box at Ford's Theatre after shooting Abraham Lincoln on 14 Apr 1865.

Although Dr Mudd knew nothing of the president's assassination and was a stranger to Booth, he was tried and convicted by a military court and sentenced to life imprisonment at Fort Jefferson in the Dry Tortugas, off the Florida Keys. He was pardoned and released by President Andrew Johnson in 1869.

The house is still owned by the Mudd family, and descendants of the doctor act as guides. Open Wed 1100–1500, Sat–Sun

259

1200–1600 (Mar–late Nov). Admission: $3.

Maryland Indian Cultural Center, *Waldorf; tel: (301) 372-1932*. The museum attempts to introduce non-Indian visitors to the cultural diversity of Native Americans through exhibits reflecting their geographic locations, tribal structures, art and lodge construction. Open Tues–Thur 0900–1500, Sun 1200–1700. Admission charge.

Mount Carmel, *5678 Mount Carmel Rd, La Plata; tel: (301) 934-1654*. The site of the first religious community for women established in the original 13 American colonies. Two of the original seven buildings are still standing. Open daily 0800–1700 (May–Oct). Admission free.

Thomas Stone National Historic Site, *6655 Rosehill Rd, Port Tobacco; tel: (301) 934-6027*. Completed in 1773, this was the plantation home of Thomas Stone, lawyer, politician and signatory to the Declaration of Independence. Open daily 0900–1700 (June–Aug); Wed–Sun 0900–1700 (Sept–May). Admission free.

PRINCE GEORGE'S COUNTY

Tourist Information: Prince George's County Conference and Visitors Bureau, *9475 Lottsford Rd, Suite 130, Landover, MD 20785-5358; tel: (301) 925-8300*.

ACCOMMODATION AND FOOD

Accommodation and dining options are thin in this part of the route, probably because we are not far from the dormitory suburbs of Washington, DC. However, Clinton has three hotels.

Colony South Hotel, *7401 Surratts Rd; tel: (301) 856-4500*, has an indoor pool, restaurant, lounge and entertainment and fitness facilities. Moderate.

Comfort Inn Clinton, *7979 Malcolm Rd; tel: (301) 856-5200*. Non-smoking. Budget.

EconoLodge/Andrews Air Force Base, *7851 Malcolm Rd; tel: (301) 856-2800*. Some units in this motel have kitchenettes. Fitness facilities available. Budget.

The **Wayfarer Restaurant** at the Colony South Hotel, Clinton, features American and Italian cuisine. Open daily 0630–2200. Lunch budget–moderate; dinner moderate–pricey.

SIGHTSEEING

Darnall's Chance, *14800 Governor Oden Bowie Dr, Upper Marlboro; tel: (301) 952-8010*. Built between 1694 and 1713, the house is the probable birthplace of Daniel Carroll, signatory to the US Constitution, and his brother John, the first bishop of the Roman Catholic Church in America. Open Sun 1200–1600 (other times by appointment). Admission charge.

Surratt House Museum, *9118 Brandywine Rd, Clinton; tel: (301) 868-1121*. Built in 1852, this was the tavern where John Wilkes Booth stopped to retrieve weapons and supplies after assassinating President Lincoln.

The tavern keeper, Mary Surratt, was tried in a military court and convicted of conspiracy. On 7 July 1865 she was hanged – the first woman to be executed by the federal government. During the Civil War the tavern had been a safehouse in the Confederate underground system which flourished in Southern Maryland. Open Thur–Fri 1100–1500, Sat–Sun 1200–1600 (Mar–mid Dec). Admission charge.

260

BALTIMORE

Developed beside a natural harbour in Chesapeake Bay, Baltimore has its roots in the needs of 18th-century Maryland grain farmers and tobacco growers who wanted to distribute their products. From the moment Baltimore was given town status in 1729, it grew fast. Shipwrights and merchants anxious to carry flour to distant reaches of the British Empire settled round the harbour fringes, and by 1768 the town had become the Baltimore County seat.

Over the next couple of centuries Baltimore's fate alternated between boom and doom, the first bad patch being the regulations on commerce which the British tried to impose on the American colonies. Today, Baltimore is the 13th largest city in the US and the fifth busiest port. It is regarded as a 'blue collar' city based on industry and commerce, but it is also a high-spirited place, with its busy Inner Harbor, restaurants, entertainment, and activities – not to mention traffic snarl-ups in the hilly streets.

TOURIST INFORMATION

Baltimore Area Visitors Center, *300 W. Pratt St, Baltimore, MD 21201* (in the Constellation Building on the Inner Harbor across from Harborplace's Pratt St Pavilion); *tel: (410) 837-INFO or (800) 282-6632*. Maps, transport schedules and information on events, accommodation,

restaurants and events are available. The bureau is perfectly located among the major waterfront attractions but it is short on space and gets crowded during busy periods. Also, parking near the waterfront is scarce and expensive.

Maryland Office of Tourism Development, *Department of Business and Economic Development, 217 E. Redwood St, Baltimore, MD 21201; tel: (410) 767-6270.*

ARRIVING AND DEPARTING

Airport
Baltimore/Washington International Airport; *tel: (410) 859-7100*, is 10 miles south of the Inner Harbor. It has five terminals, and a new pier will double its capacity for international passengers. Cash machines are located at the Main Terminal, Pier C.

Train services by **Amtrak**; *tel: (800) 872-7245*, and **Maryland Area Rail Commuter (MARC)**; *tel: (800) 325-RAIL*, connect the airport and Baltimore's Penn Station, a 20-min journey. A free shuttle bus covers the 10-min trip between the main terminal and the airport station. Bus service no.17, operated by **Mass Transit Administration (MTA)**; *tel: (410) 539-5000*, runs between downtown Baltimore and the airport; fare: $1.65. **BWI Airport Van Shuttle**; *tel: (800) 435-9294*, runs a service between the Inner Harbor hotels and the airport for $10 one way, $16 round trip. **Airport Transportation**; *tel: (410) 519-0000*, offers a limousine service, with cars costing from $23.50. Taxis charge around $17 for the airport to downtown journey.

261

By Car

Baltimore is reached by I-95, the major East Coast route, and from the north by I-83. The city is surrounded by I-695, the Baltimore Beltway, from which a number of access roads lead downtown.

GETTING AROUND .

Your hotel parking lot is the best place to leave the car in big-city Baltimore. Driving is not a pleasure in this complex of hilly one-way streets. Fortunately, most of the major attractions are within walking distance of the Inner Harbor, while sights farther out may be visited by tourist trolley (see Sightseeing, p. 267).

Public Transport

Bus, Metro, Light Rail and MARC train services are operated by **MTA**; *tel: (410) 539-5000* or *(800) 543-9809*. Baltimore's public transport system is intended to serve commuters and local residents, rather than tourists. Travelling any distance by bus may involve a number of transfers. The Metro has half a dozen stations downtown – none closer than three blocks to the Inner Harbor – but beyond Penn Station it strikes out for the north-west suburbs. The Light Rail service travels between Timonium in the north and Glen Burnie in the south; again, none of its five downtown stations is closer than three blocks to the Inner Harbor.

Probably the jauntiest – and certainly the cheapest – way to see Baltimore at its best is to travel by **Water Taxi**; *tel: (410) 563-3901* or *(800) 658-8947*. This year-round service has 15 stops giving access to major sights around the Inner and Outer Harbors. Passengers are given a useful *Waterfront Guide to Baltimore*, which contains good maps and information on attractions, bars and restaurants. Water Taxis operate Mon–Thur 1100–2100,

Fri–Sat 1100–midnight, Sun 1000–2100 (Apr and Oct); Mon–Thur 1100–2300, Fri 1100–midnight, Sat 1000–midnight, Sun 1000–2300 (May–Sept); Wed–Sun 1100–1800 (Nov–Mar). Fare: $3.50 for an all-day pass (purchased on board).

STAYING IN BALTIMORE

Accommodation

As in many major cities, budget accommodation is not easy to find, but if you are prepared to stay three or four miles from the Inner Harbor you will find lodgings much easier on your pocket. Further savings can be made through offers available to readers of advertisements in the current issue of the *Baltimore Quick Guide* and in the *Baltimore Street Map and Visitor Guide*, both available at the visitor center. There are also more than a dozen bed and breakfast homes, apartments available for short-term or longer leasing, and a hostel.

Hotel and motel chains in this city of several neighbourhoods include *BW, CI, DI, Hd, Hn, Hy, Ma, QI, Rd, Rm, S8, Sh.*

Reservation services include **Maryland Reservations Center**, *68 Maryland Ave, Annapolis, MD 21401; tel: (410) 269-5620;* and **Amanda's Bed and Breakfast Reservations Service**, *1428 Park Ave, Baltimore, MD 21217; tel: (410) 225-0001.*

The recently renovated **Holiday Inn Express**, *1401 Bloomfield Ave; tel: (410) 646-1700*, is 4 miles from the Inner Harbor. Local telephone calls are free, and the complimentary continental breakfast is a generous one. Moderate. **Days Inn Baltimore/Inner Harbor**, *100 Hopkins Pl.; tel: (410) 576-1000*, has competitively priced rooms: children under 17 stay free and the under-12s can even eat free. Moderate.

Brookshire Inner Harbor Suite

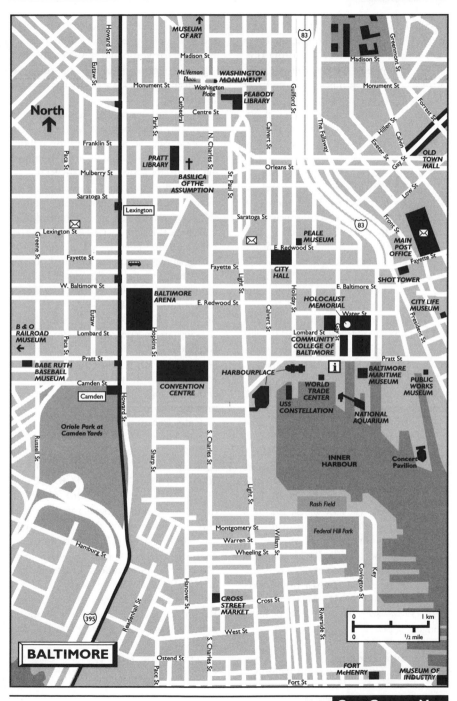

Hotel, *120 E. Lombard St; tel: (410) 625-1300.* The only all-suite hotel at the Inner Harbor. Expensive–pricey. **Comfort Inn**, *6700 Security Blvd, West Baltimore; tel: (410) 281-1800,* ten miles from the Inner Harbor, offers courtesy airport shuttle service and free deluxe continental breakfast. Check if a budget category deal is available, otherwise it is at the lower end of moderate.

Harbor Court Hotel, *550 Light St; tel: (410) 234-0550.* This hotel is Baltimore's best, and has been rated 11th in a poll of US hotels. Its rooms include 25 suites with four-poster beds and a clear view of Baltimore's harbour. The fitness centre offers a racquetball court and a rooftop tennis court, as well as fitness equipment. Pricey – double room rates start at $230, suites are from $375.

Sheraton Inner Harbor Hotel, *300 S. Charles St; tel: (410) 962-8300.* Harbour views, and one block from the many shops and restaurants at Harborplace. Expensive. **Clarion Hotel**, *Mount Vernon Sq., 612 Cathedral St; tel: (410) 727-7101.* Complimentary shuttle operates to Inner Harbor from this hotel. Expensive, but special weekend packages are available.

Admiral Fell Inn, *888 S. Broadway, Fells Point; tel: (410) 522-7377.* Historic European-style inn, with English-style pub. Expensive–pricey. **Mr Mole Bed and Breakfast**, *1601 Bolton St; tel: (410) 728-1179,* provides highly regarded non-smoking accommodation in 1870 renovated rowhouse furnished with antiques. Complimentary Dutch-style breakfast. Moderate–expensive. **Baltimore International Hostel**, *17 W. Mulberry St; tel: (410) 576-8880;* check-in is 1000–1100. Budget.

Eating and Drinking

You could spend two weeks in Baltimore,

dining in a different restaurant every night and still not sample all the ethnic cuisines available. Or you could stay a month trying out restaurants specialising in American fare and have plenty left over for another trip.

There are some 125 restaurants and eateries in **Harborplace** alone, at *Pratt* and *Light Sts*, and many more throughout the downtown area and central communities like **Fells Point** and **Little Italy**.

Seafood is abundant. Crab cakes are on many menus, and you can eat in comfortable surroundings for modest expenditure.

Kawasaki, *413 N. Charles St; tel: (410) 659-7600,* has been hailed as one of the top Japanese restaurants in the US; and serves budget lunches, dinners at budget–moderate prices. Closed Sun. **Sisson's Restaurant and Brewery**, *36 E. Cross St; tel: (410) 539-2093.* Cajun/Creole cooking and a choice of cooling brews. **Bertha's**, *734 S. Broadway, Fells Point; tel: (410) 327-5795.* The slogan 'Eat Bertha's Mussels' is worth heeding. You will have enough change from a $10 bill for a pint – they have dozens of beers.

Café Promenade, in Marriott Inner Harbor Hotel, *110 S. Eutaw St; tel: (410) 962-0202,* is a pasta bar with plenty of choice for under $10. Open daily 1700–2000. **Hampton's**, in the Harbor Court Hotel, *550 Light St; tel: (410) 234-0550;* this non-smoking restaurant has been voted top for service and second overall in the whole of the US. Reservations are essential. Men must wear jackets. Closed Mon. Pricey. **Germano's Trattoria**, *300 S. High St, Little Italy; tel: (410) 752-4515.* One of many Italian restaurants in Baltimore, but Germano's, specialising in good Tuscan fare, is always busy. Budget–moderate.

The Prime Rib, *1101 N. Calvert at Chase St; tel: (410) 539-1804.* This has been named 'Baltimore's top Steak House.' Comprehensive wine list. Men should wear jackets. A pianist plays and the décor is arresting. Pricey.

The Owl Bar, (in the Belvedere) *1 E. Chase St; tel: (410) 347-0888.* A popular and cheerful restaurant serving imaginative Continental food. Ask about the owls. Moderate–expensive.

Wayne's Bar–B–Que, *Harborplace Pavilion, 301 Light St; tel: (410) 539-3810,* is trendy place for barbecues, with a good choice of beers and wines. Country music sets the tone. Budget–moderate. **Mo's Fisherman's Wharf Inner Harbor**, *219 President St* (at *Stiles St*); *tel: (410) 837-8600,* has a wide variety of shell fish and fresh fish, plus classic pastas and prime ribs. Moderate. **Phillips**, *Harborplace Pavilion, 301 Light St; tel: (410) 685-6600* or *(800) 782-CRAB.* There is an all–you–can–eat buffet and raw bar at this waterfront seafood specialist. Piano bar. Moderate.

Bombay Grill, *2 E. Madison St at Charles St; tel: (410) 837-2973.* This classic Indian restaurant enjoys a great reputation. Budget–moderate. **Uncle Lee's Harbor Restaurant**, *44 South St at Lombard St; tel: (410) 727-6666,* has Szechuan, Hunan and Mandarin cuisine. Take-away available. Budget–moderate.

Henninger's Tavern, *1812 Bank St, Fells Point; tel: (410) 342-2172.* A variety of American dishes served at this popular bistro in a century-old tavern. Open Tues–Sat evenings. Moderate. **Lista's**, *1637 Thames St/Brown's Wharf; tel: (410) 327-0040.* Mexican food and music with colourful décor. Live jazz on Fri. Dining rooms and patios overlook the water. Moderate.

Communications and Money

There are numerous post offices and foreign exchange facilities around the city.

ENTERTAINMENT

As well as some top-class music and theatre performances, Baltimore has a diversity of entertainment on the club and pub scene, with comedy clubs, dance clubs and live vocals and bands in bars and taverns.

Baltimore Center for the Performing Arts, *1 N. Charles St; tel: (410) 625-4230.* National touring productions are presented at various locations. **Center Stage**, *700 N. Calvert St; tel: (410) 332-0033.* Theatrical productions presented by the State Theatre of Maryland.

Morris A. Mechanic Theatre, *Hopkins Plaza, Baltimore and Charles Sts; tel: (410) 625-1400,* presents a programme of popular shows, Sept–June. **Playwrights Theatre of Baltimore**, *908 Washington Blvd, Superba Arts and Commerce Center; tel: (410) 727-1847,* has professional performances of innovative new works.

The Vagabond Players, on the square at *806 S. Broadway, Fell's Point; tel: (410) 563-9135.* An attraction for more than 80 years, the Players present quality theatre at affordable prices. Performances are year-round on Fri and Sat evenings and Sun afternoon and evening. **Fell's Point Corner Theatre**, *251 S. Ann St; tel: (410) 276-7837* or *466-8341,* presents Fri and Sat evening and Sun afternoon community theatre performances in an 1859 former fire house. Premieres of off-Broadway plays are performed. **Arena Players**, *Arena Playhouse, 801 McCullen St; tel: (410) 728-6500;* a lively African-American company present classical and contemporary works.

Baltimore Opera Company, *Lyric Opera House, 140 W. Mount Royal Ave; tel: (410) 727-6000.* The city's resident company for 45 years stages grand opera with international artists and full orchestra. English translation is projected over the stage.

265

Baltimore Symphony Orchestra, *Joseph Meyerhoff Symphony Hall, 12121 Cathedral St; tel: (410) 783-8000,* presents varied high-profile programmes with guest performers.

Peabody Conservatory of Music, *1 E. Mount Vernon Pl.; tel: (410) 659-8124.* Students of the nation's oldest music school (founded 1857) and guest artists perform recitals, symphonies and operas. **Handel Choir of Baltimore,** at various locations; *tel: (410) 366-6544.* Choral works sung by a 75-strong choir, with full orchestra and guest soloists.

Orpheum Cinema, *1724 Thames St, Fell's Point; tel: (410) 732-4614.* Hollywood classics, foreign films, vintage cartoons and newsreels are screened twice nightly and on Sat and Sun afternoons.

Comedy Factory, *36 Light St; tel: (410) 752-4189.* Established stand-up comics and talented newcomers with constantly up-dated material set a high-hilarity standard. **Slapstix Comedy Club,** *The Brokerage, 34 Market Pl., Suite 260; tel: (410) 659-7527.*

Fat Lulu's, *1818 Maryland Ave; tel: (410) 685-4665.* Jazz and blues and special shows with your Cajun and Creole Meal.

Dancing

There are dance clubs and/or live music venues at a number of locations, among them:

The Oak Room, *Radisson Plaza Lord Baltimore Hotel, 20-30 W. Baltimore St; tel: (410) 539-8400.* **Da Mimmo,** *217 S. High St, Little Italy; tel: (410) 727-6876.* **Hurricane's,** *Sheraton International Hotel, 7032 Elm Rd; tel: (410) 859-3300.* **Bumpers,** *Baltimore Marriott Inner Harbor, 110 S. Eutaw St; tel: (410) 962-0202.* **Champagne and Truffles Piano Bar,** *The Belvedere (13th floor) 1 E. Chase St; tel: (410) 347-0888.* **Buddies Pub and Jazz Club,** *313 N. Charles St; tel: (410) 332-4200.*

The Harborplace Amphitheatre presents on-going daytime entertainment and many evening concerts. Open daily.

SHOPPING

More than 130 shops and eateries are in the city's **Harborplace Pavilion** and a further 60 at **The Gallery,** connected by a skywalk. Another 400 stores and street carts offer a diversity of goods at **Market Center,** Baltimore's original retail district, bounded by *Franklin, Liberty, Baltimore* and *Greene Sts.*

The **Fell's Point** neighbourhood, with its cobbled streets and historic buildings, is the place for unusual purchases – nautical instruments, original artwork, embroidered clothing, beads from far and wide, Polish dolls, Irish crystal, batik wear, incense, contemporary posters – as well as antiques. More than two centuries old, **Broadway Market** is crammed with stalls of fresh produce, baked goods, spices and flowers. **Lexington Market,** founded in 1782, houses 140 food merchants selling just about every type of snack you can think of, and a great range of comestibles.

Antique Row is where the wealthy shop for silver, porcelain, Victorian collectables and furniture in the many antique shops on *N. Howard* and *W. Reed Sts.* Or there is the **Antique Warehouse,** *1300 Jackson St; tel: (410) 659-0662,* in the Federal Hill area, where a range of antiques and collectables is offered. Closed Mon.

Baltimore Orioles fans can find all the baseball goods associated with the city team at **Stadium Sports** in the Harborplace Pavilion, *Light St.*

SIGHTSEEING

Tickets for many city museums and attractions, tours and cruises, concerts, sports and other events, can be obtained at the **City Life Tickets** kiosk, *Inner Harbor Promenade, West Shore* (between Harborplace and Maryland Science Center); *tel: (410) 396-8342.* This one-stop ticketing system offers discount admissions to many attractions. Open daily.

Tours

Baltimore Trolley Tours, *tel: (410) 752-2015 or 724-0077*, offer a narrated tour aboard replica Victorian trolleys revealing history, culture, folklore and trivia. There are 20 places to board and you can ride all day for $12 (children $4.50), boarding and reboarding as often as you like. Trolleys run daily approximately half-hourly 1000–1600 (last pick-up 1600). Limited service operates Nov–Feb.

Harbor Shuttle, *tel: (410) 675-2900.* Year-round shuttle service in weather-protected boats. **Harbor Cruises**, *tel: (410) 727-3113.* Daily lunch cruises from $21.95 and dinner cruises from $33.50. Moonlight cruises Fri–Sat cost from $17.95. DJ and dancing in the evenings.

Baltimore Defender and Guardian, *tel: (410) 685-4288.* The vessel provides a shuttle service to Fort McHenry and Fell's Point, departing from Inner Harbor Finger Piers May–Sept. **Baltimore Patriot**, *tel: (410) 685-4288*; 90-min narrated harbour cruises departing from Constellation Dock.

Clipper City, *tel: (410) 539-6277.* Two- and three-hour tours from Harborplace under sail aboard the tall ship. Sunday brunch cruise and weekend calypso and reggae parties.

Harbor Belle, *tel: (410) 764-0808.* Lunch and Sunday brunch cruises aboard a replica turn-of-the-century paddlewheel steamboat.

Minnie V. Skipjack, *tel: (410) 522-4214.* Narrated tours aboard an historic Chesapeake Bay oyster boat.

Pride of Baltimore II, *tel: (410) 539-1151.* When docked at the Inner Harbor, this replica of the famous Baltimore clipper (many of which were built between the Revolutionary War and the mid 1800s), can be visited. The 160-ft topsail schooner is Maryland's goodwill ambassador, voyaging under sail to ports around the world. **Spirit of Baltimore**, *tel: (410) 523-7447.* Two live bands and a Broadway revue are featured on dining and entertainment cruises around the harbour.

Paddle boats can be hired from Harborplace; *tel: (410) 563-3901*, and Trident **electric boat rentals** are located between the World Trade Center and the National Aquarium.

City Viewpoints

Top of the World; *401 E. Pratt St; tel: (410) 837-4515.* An observation floor on the 27th storey of the World Trade Center provides a panoramic view of the harbour and city. You can also find multimedia exhibits relating to Baltimore's history. Open Mon–Fri 1000–1600, Sat 1000–1830, Sun 1100–1730. Admission charge.

Washington Monument, *N. Charles St at Mount Vernon Pl.; tel: (410) 837-4636.* This imposing monument was the first in the nation honouring George Washington. It was designed by Robert Mills, the architect responsible for the Washington Monument in Washington, DC. A 228-step climb to the top is rewarded with a bird's eye view of the city. Freely accessible.

Museum Row

Baltimore City Life Museums: six museums and a city park form a group of sites which depict the city's history. Four of them, – **Brewer's Park**, **Carroll**

267

Museum, Center for Urban Archaeology and the **1840 House** – are at Museum Row and share a single entrance at *800 E. Lombard St.* For information and to check times of opening and admission charges, *tel: (410) 396-3523.* There is an admission charge for all sites except Brewer's Park. General opening times of the buildings are Tues–Sun 1000–1700, Sun 1200–1700 (closing 1600 Nov–Mar).

Brewer's Park, the one-acre outdoor recreation park with picnic facilities and self-guided trail is on the site of an 18th-century brewery.

Shot Tower, *801 E. Fayette St; tel: (410) 837-5424.* The 234-ft tower, built in 1828 with a million wood-fired bricks, was one of the nation's largest suppliers of lead shot and is now one of the few remaining shot towers in the US. Inter-active exhibits and a sound-and-light show illustrate how gun shot was made. Open Wed–Sun 1000–1600.

Carroll Museum. Charles Carroll, a signatory to the Declaration of Independence, wintered here from 1820 to 1832. The period furniture and decorative arts indicate the style in which the city's elite lived during the 19th-century.

The Center for Urban Archaeology has an 'Archaeologists as Detectives – Solving History's Mysteries' feature. An excavation pit, industries and shops from the past and glassware and ceramics are exhibited. Staff and volunteers can be seen identifying excavated items.

1840 House: the reconstructed rowhouse exhibits the home and its contents of a local wheelwright.

H.L. Mencken House, *1524 Hollins St.* A stately Victorian house and garden was the home for nearly 70 years of journalist and author Henry Louis Mencken,

known to the nation as the Sage of Baltimore. Open Sat, Sun 1200–1700 (to 1600 Nov–Mar).

Peale Museum, *225 Holliday St.* An important collection of historic prints, paintings and photographs of Baltimore and its people in a museum purpose-built by the painter Rembrandt Peale.

Recently opened in Museum Row as part of the City Life complex is a 30,000 sq ft **Morton K. Blaustein City Life Exhibition Center**, with temporary exhibitions and education spaces on four floors and a permanent 'I Am The City' exhibition on the second floor.

Historical Museums

Fort McHenry National Monument and Historic Shrine, end of *E. Fort Ave; tel: (410) 962-4290.* The star-shaped, brick-built fort, built in 1790, successfully thwarted the British attack on Baltimore in 1814 – an event which inspired Francis Scott Key to compose *The Star-Spangled Banner*, the national anthem. Officers' quarters, guardrooms, a restored powder magazine and other exhibits can be seen. A re-enactment of life in the garrison is presented by guardsmen in period uniform on weekend afternoons from mid June–Aug. Open daily 0800–1700 (winter), 0800–2000 (summer). Admission charge.

Flag House and 1812 Museum, *844 E. Pratt St at Albemarle St; tel: (410) 837-1793.* Built in 1793, this was the home of Mary Pickersgill, who made the flag which flew over Fort McHenry during the British bombardment. Open Mon–Sat 1000–1600. Admission charge.

Great Blacks in Wax Museum, *1601–1603 E. North Ave; tel: (410) 563-3404.* This is America's only wax museum of African-American history and culture. More than 100 life-sized figures illustrate historical scenes. Among those featured are

Clean and Safe

Strangers in a crowded and busy city centre may sometimes feel uneasy amid the crowds. Obviously, you should take the same precautions about personal possessions that you would at home, but in downtown Baltimore you can feel reassured by the presence of the Clean and Safe guides.

Downtown Partnership of Baltimore introduced these guides, who give added protection to the public by acting as extra eyes and ears for the police.

The whole of the downtown area, including elegant *Charles St*, has Public Safety Guides and Clean Sweep Ambassadors working under the Clean and Safe programme. They are identified by distinctive purple caps and black jackets with a purple and gold motif on the shoulders.

They are also a valuable source of information and can answer visitors' questions on Baltimore.

Frederick Douglass (born 1817), a Baltimore shipyard worker who escaped from slavery to become a Civil Rights orator and writer, Harriet Tubman (born 1815), another slave who escaped to become a freedom fighter on the Underground Railroad, and Dr Martin Luther King Jr. A model slave ship depicts the long history of the Atlantic Slave Trade. Open Tues–Sat 0900–1800, Sun noon–1800. Admission charge.

Mount Clare Museum House, *Carroll Park, 1500 Washington Blvd and Monroe St; tel: (410) 837-3262.* Baltimore's only pre-Revolutionary War mansion. Built in 1760, it is considered one of the finest examples of Georgian architecture in the US. The 18th- and 19th-century fur-

niture belonged to Charles Carroll and his wife. Tours start Tues–Fri every hour on the hour between 1000 – 1500, and on Sat and Sun at 1300, 1400 and 1500. Admission charge.

Maryland Historical Society Museum and Library, *201 W. Monument St; tel: (410) 685-3750.* There is much to see here. The museum includes the Radcliffe Maritime Museum, the Darnall's Children's Gallery, Enoch Pratt House and Civil War and War of 1812 galleries. The original manuscript of Francis Scott Key's *The Star-Spangled Banner* can be seen and there are important collections of American silver, decorative arts and paintings. Open Tues–Fri 1000–1700, Sat 0900–1700. Admission charge.

The Preservation Society/ Robert Long House, *812 S. Ann St; tel: (410) 675-6750.* Dating from 1765 and restored and furnished with antiques of the period, this is Baltimore's oldest surviving urban residence, and is the headquarters of the city's Preservation Society. Open Thur, tours at 1000, 1300 and 1500.

Baltimore Public Works Museum and Streetscape, *751 Eastern Ave* (Inner Harbor East); *tel: (410) 396-5565.* This revealing and unusual museum housed in an old pumping station offers presentations on public works and the urban environmental history of Baltimore. Find out 'What's Beneath the Streets' and 'The Rotten Truth about Garbage'. Open daily mid Apr to mid Oct 1000–1700, rest of year Wed–Sun 1000–1600. Admission charge.

Edgar Allan Poe House and Museum, *203 N. Amity St; tel: (410) 396-7932.* Poe lived here for three years (1832–35), at the beginning of his writing career. This was also the period of his courtship of his cousin, whom he later

269

married. The house contains Poe artefacts and furniture of the period. A video presentation can be seen. Open Wed–Sat 1200–1545. Admission charge.

Eubie Blake Gallery and National Museum at The Brokerage, *34 Market Pl.; tel: (410) 396-8128.* The work of community artists of Baltimore and its and outskirts is showcased in this museum which honours the Baltimore-born composer with displays and memorabilia of his life and work. Eubie Blake, who died in 1983 at the age of 100, was a ragtime pianist and vaudeville entertainer. He co-composed Broadway's first black musical, *Shuffle Along*, and wrote such hits as *I'm Just Wild About Harry* and *Memories of You.*

Jewish Heritage Center of the Jewish Historical Society of Maryland, *15 Lloyd St* between *Lombard* and *E. Baltimore Sts; tel: (410) 732-6400.* As well as extensive archives and collections on show, the centre includes two historic restored synagogues. One is the Lloyd St Synagogue, built in 1845. The other is the B'nai Israel Synagogue, built in 1876. Both are on the National Register of Historic Places. A research library can be visited by appointment. Open Tues–Thur and Sun, 1200–1600. Admission charge.

Holocaust Memorial and Sculpture, *Water, Gay and Lombard Sts.* This is a memorial to the millions of Jews murdered in Europe by the Nazis between 1933 and 1945.

Baltimore Museum of Industry, *1415 Key Hwy; tel: (410) 727-4808.* Housed in an 1870 oyster cannery on the harbour, the museum has a belt-driven machine shop, garment loft and print shop. Hands-on cannery activity and a 1906 steam tugboat are some of the illustrations of Baltimore's industrial history. Open daily, 1200–1700 and also

Wed evening 1800–2100 late May–early Sept. Winter Thur–Sun 1200–1700. Admission charge.

Baltimore City Fire Museum, *414 N. Gay St at Orleans st (Rte 40E); tel: (410) 727-2414 or 764-4070.* The great engine house dates from 1799, with the bell tower added in 1853. The museum displays antique fire apparatus photographs and general memorabilia. Open Fri 1900–2100, Sun 1300–1600, or by appointment.

Art Musuems and Galleries
Walters Art Gallery, *600 N. Charles St; tel: (410) 547-9000.* Works of art originated over 5000 years and from four continents are exhibited in three wings at this highly esteemed gallery, bequeathed by Baltimore-born Henry Walters. Exhibits range from medieval armour and Fabergé eggs to Ancient Egyptian and art nouveau. The Asian arts wing is at **Hackerman House**, *1 Mt Vernon Pl.* Open Tues–Sun 1100–1700. Admission charge, except for free hour Sat 1100–noon.

American Visionary Arts Museum, *800 Key Hwy; tel: (410) 244-1900.* Outstanding original works by intuitive self-taught artists, unrestricted by the teachings of established colleges of art, provide an impact-making experience. Open Wed, Thur, Sun 1000–1800, Fri and Sat 1000–2000 (winter); Sun–Thur 1000–2000, Fri and Sat 1000–2200 summer). Admission charge.

Baltimore Museum of Art and new Wing of Modern Art, *Art Museum Drive, Charles St at 31st St; tel: (410) 396-7100.* This permanent collection of 120,000 works includes the Cone collection of 20th-century paintings by Matisse, Picasso and Cezanne. Works of art from many parts of the world are displayed. Open Wed–Fri 1000–1600, Sat–Sun 1100–1800. Admission charge.

Evergreen House, *4545 N. Charles St; tel: (410) 516-0341.* This Italianate mansion built in the mid 1800s houses impressive collections of Japanese and Chinese porcelain and art works, post-impressionist paintings, 35,000 books (many rare), and period furnishings. It has a private theatre and is set in 26 acres of gardens. Open Mon–Fri 1000–1600, Sat–Sun 1300–1600. Admission charge.

Baltimore International Culinary College Cooking Demonstration Theatre, *Commerce Exchange Building, 206 Water St; tel: (410) 752-4983.* The college's chef instructors and guest chefs give 90-min, step-by-step demonstrations on a variety of dishes in a 90-seat state-of-the-art theatre. Open Mon–Thur 0915 and 1345, Wed 1700 and 1930. Admission charge.

Science and Nature Attractions

Maryland Science Center, *601 Light St; tel: (410) 685-2370.* Such diverse subjects as space exploration, television production, energy and Chesapeake Bay can be explored through hands-on exhibits on three floors. The Imax Theatre has a screen five storeys high, and the Davis Planetarium is equally impressive. Open Mon–Thur 1000–1800, Fri–Sun 1000–2000 (–1800 in winter). Admission charge.

National Aquarium in Baltimore, *Pier 3, 561 E. Pratt St; tel: (410) 576-3800.* Opened in 1981, this is a world-class aquatic museum dedicated to education, conservation and environmental improvement. More than 1½ million visitors a year flock to its collection of some 7000 creatures, representing at least 500 species of fish, birds, reptiles, amphibians and marine mammals in re-created habitats from many parts of the world. Viewing windows enable visitors to see aquatic life in huge tanks. Narrations are given as divers feed the nation's largest collection of stingrays.

Fresh water and coastal species found in Maryland – bullfrogs, diamond-back terrapins, sea robins and flounders – are seen in four exhibits.

The *Surviving Through Adaptations* gallery demonstrates how various species survive through adjusting to situations. The giant Pacific octopus, burrowing jawfish, green moray eels that lurk in caves, electric eels and seahorses occupy this gallery.

A 335,000-gallon tank contains the most authentic Atlantic coral reef ever fabricated, with colourful tropical fish swimming in shoals. An *Open Ocean* exhibit brings the visitor face to face with several shark species, sand tigers and sawfish. Puffins and black guillemots are seen on the Atlantic sea cliffs of the *North Atlantic to Pacific* gallery. An undersea kelp forest and Pacific reef formations can be seen, and a touch tank in the *Children's Cove* has starfish, crabs and many small marine animals.

Perhaps the *pièce de résistance* of the aquarium is the reproduced *South American Rain Forest*, where the sharp-eyed may spot a range of cleverly camouflaged creatures in the jungle habitat. Poison-dart frogs, sloths, monkeys, piranhas and tropical birds live among the pools, trees and lush vegetation. Through videos, graphics and innovative technology, marine mammals can be studied in the Exploration Station, and dolphins perform in the Marine Mammal Pavilion's daily 25-min shows in a 1300-seat theatre.

Near the aquarium entrance is an outdoor rock pool in which harbor and grey seals can be observed by the public without charge.

The aquarium occupies two buildings. Both buildings are accessible to disabled travellers. Open Sun–Thur 0900–1800,

Waterfront Walkway

In times to come, it will be possible to follow a continuous waterfront path linking the Inner Harbor, the south shore along Key Highway, Little Italy, Inner Harbor East, Fell's point and Canton.

The 7½-mile brick promenade is an on-going project under construction by the Baltimore Harbor Endowment, whose aims are to promote public access to the waterfront, to stimulate improvements to waterfront parks and to foster appreciation of the harbour and bay environment.

Signs gives information about the harbour and its special features. Engraved bricks in the promenade are dedicated to past and present Baltimore residents. Parts of the walkway are already complete, with dedicated bricks in place.

Fri–Sat 0900–2000 (July–Aug); Sat–Thur 1000–1700, Fri 1000–2000 (Sept–June). Admission: $11.50.

Baltimore Zoo, *Druid Hill Park; tel: (410) 396-7102.* Walk or take the zoo tram to see 1200 mammal, bird and reptile species. Rhinoceros, zebra and gazelle roam the new, free-range African habitat. There is also a children's zoo. Open daily 1000–1600. Admission charge.

National Museum of Dentistry, *31 S. Greene St; tel: Public Information Office at University of Maryland, Baltimore (410) 706-0600.* This new speciality museum educates visitors about the history of dentistry and preventative care. It is the first of a proposed group of museums related to health and science, including medicine, pharmacy and nursing.

Columbus Center – Hall of Exploration, *Piers 5 and 6, Inner Harbor; tel: (410) 576-5750.* Schedule for opening

in early spring 1997, this is a major world centre for marine biotechnology research and education. The subject is considered vital for advances in health care and the preservation of the environment, and the accent is on public education and work-force training. Open Sat–Thur 1000–1700, Fri 1000–2000 (Sept–June); from 0900 (July–Aug). Admission: $7.

Transport and Maritime Attractions

Baltimore Maritime Museum, *Pier III, Pratt St, Inner Harbor; tel: (410) 396-3453.* Three historic ships can be toured. The US Coastguard cutter *Taney* is the only ship still afloat that survived the attack on Pearl Harbour. The US submarine *Torsk* sank the last Japanese combatant ship of World War II. Lightship *Chesapeake* is a 1930s floating lighthouse which was posted in Chesapeake Bay for many years. Open Mon–Fri 0930–1700, Sat–Sun 0930–2000; Fri–Sun 0930–1700 (Dec–Feb). Admission charge.

Baltimore Streetcar Museum, *1901 Falls Rd; tel: (410) 547-0264.* Exhibits outline the history of the streetcar system in the city. Visitors can ride in streetcars built between 1859 and 1963 with clanging bell and costumed conductor. Open June–Oct, Sat and Sun 1200–1700, rest of year Sun only 1200–1700. Admission charge.

B & O Railroad Museum, *901 W. Pratt St at Poppleton St; tel: (410) 752-2490.* The birthplace of the oldest railroad in the country (the Baltimore and Ohio) dating from 1829, and the site of the first American passenger railroad station (Mount Clare Station). Many of the nation's oldest steam and diesel locomotives, as well as passenger cars and freight wagons, are displayed. Excursion trains run at weekends. The museum has a research library and shop, and there is a garden of model trains. Open daily 1000–1700. Admission charge.

U.S.S. Constellation, *Pratt St, Pier I, Constellation Dock; tel: (410) 539-1797.* (Note: At the time of writing the ship is undergoing repairs and is scheduled to be on show again in 1998. For information write to *1 E. Pratt St, Baltimore MD 21202-1038*). The *Constellation* was launched in Baltimore as a frigate in 1797 and re-built as a Sloop of War in 1854. Her missions included blocking slave ships off Africa, freeing slaves and a famine-relief voyage to Ireland. Admission charge.

Public Buildings

Basilica of the National Shrine of the Assumption of the Blessed Virgin Mary, *Cathedral and Mulberry Sts; tel: (410) 727-3564.* Dedicated in 1821, this was the first Roman Catholic Cathedral in the US. It was designed by Benjamin Latrobe, architect of the White House, and is considered one of the world's best examples of neo-classical architecture. Tours after 1045 Sunday mass or by appointment.

Baltimore Convention Center, *1 W. Pratt St; tel: (410) 659-7000.* Already recognised as one of the country's best-equipped and most flexible conference facilities, the Convention Center has been undergoing major improvements, doubling its size to 1.1 million sq ft. Scheduled to be fully complete by April 1997 – though opening before that date – it features a 38,000 sq ft ballroom, more than 40 meeting rooms and 300,000 sq ft of exhibition space on one level. Tours by appointment.

Enoch Pratt Free Library, *400 Cathedral St; tel: (410) 396-5430.* Special collections on Edgar Allan Poe, Henry Louis Mencken and the state of Maryland. This is one of the largest libraries in the US. Open Mon–Wed 1000–2000, Thur and Sat 1000–1700, also Sun 1300–1700 Oct–Apr.

Westminster Hall Burying Ground and Catacombs, *Fayette and Greene Sts; tel: (410) 706-2072.* The Presbyterian Church (1852) is now inactive and used as a cultural resource. The burial ground is one of the city's oldest. It contains the graves of Edgar Allan Poe and many prominent Maryland people. Regular scheduled tours are held for which reservations are required.

Baltimore City Hall, *100 N. Holliday St; tel: (410) 837-5424.* Noted for its 110-ft rotunda capped by a rare segmented dome, the post-Civil War hall was built between 1867 and 1875. It has a permanent exhibit on Baltimore history, plus other changing exhibits. Open Mon–Fri 1000–1630.

Sports Attractions

Oriole Park at Camden Yards, *333 W. Camden St; tel: (410) 547-6234.* A new, updated ballpark seats 48,000 spectators at baseball matches of the famous Baltimore Orioles. Between March and December daily tours of the scoreboard control room, press box and other facilities are available. Scheduled for completion in 1997 are inter-active exhibits using computer and laser technology, to enable visitors to stand in the batter's box and slam at the ball. Phone for tour times. Admission charge.

Lacrosse Foundation and Hall of Fame Museum, *113 W. University Parkway; tel: (410) 235-6882.* The sport's national museum traces 350 years of lacrosse history and big moments with artefacts, photographs, vintage equipment and uniforms. Open Mon–Fri 0900–1700 year-round, and from Mar–May also Sat 1000–1500. Admission charge.

BALTIMORE–WILMINGTON

This short route takes us around the northern shore of Chesapeake Bay. Before crossing the Susquehanna River it is worth pausing in the delightful – and delightfully named – town of Havre de Grace, before moving on to the second smallest state in the Union, Delaware. Wilmington, the state capital, gazes at New Jersey, across the Delaware River.

DIRECT ROUTE: 73 MILES

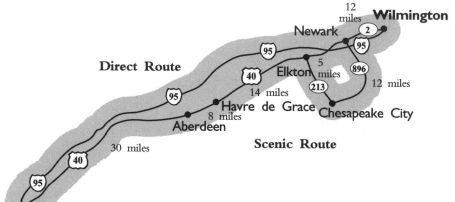

274

ROUTES

DIRECT ROUTE

You can scarcely put a foot wrong in finding your way from Baltimore to Wilmington. There are only two options – I-95 or Hwy 40 – and they run side by side, separated from each other by three miles at the most. Using I-95 stretches the distance to 77 miles, but trims the journey time to about 1 hr 20 mins.

SCENIC ROUTE

An alternative route, which follows Hwy 40 as far as Elkton then takes Rte 2 to Wilmington, can be covered in under an hour and a half. But an even better option, adding 16 miles to the journey, takes us a little way south to the charming old canal town of Chesapeake City before crossing into Delaware and moving north again to pick up Rte 2.

From downtown Baltimore take *Light St* south and, at the south end of the Inner Harbor, follow Key Hwy to connect with I-95 north. Exit 60 from I-95 leads to Hwy 40, which reaches **Aberdeen** after

30 miles. **Havre de Grace** comes after a further 8 miles and **Elkton** after another 14. A $2 toll is charged on the bridge that carries Hwy 40 across the Susquehanna River.

From Elkton head south on Rte 213 to reach **Chesapeake City** in 5 miles. From here, Rte 285 east crosses the state line in 2 miles, and intersects with Rte 896 in a further 4 miles. **Newark**, Delaware, is 6 miles north on Rte 896. From Newark, Rte 2 north reaches Wilmington after 12 miles.

ABERDEEN

Tourist Information: **Harford County Office of Economic Development**, *220 S. Main St, Bel Air, MD 21014; tel: (410) 638-3339.*

ACCOMMODATION AND FOOD

The city (pop. 13,000) has three hotels. **Days Inn**, *783 W. Bel Air Ave; tel: (410) 272-8500*, has 49 rooms and offers complimentary continental breakfast; budget.

Holiday Inn-Chesapeake House, *1007 Beards Hill Rd; tel: (410) 272-8100.* This hotel has rooms, suites and kitchenettes available. Indoor pool. The restaurant opens Mon–Fri 0600–1400 and 1700– 2200; weekends from 0700, moderate.

Howard Johnson, *793 W. Bel Air Ave; tel: (410) 272-6000*, has 124 rooms and suites, swimming pool and coin laundry. Complimentary continental breakfast. Adjoining restaurant opens daily 0600–1400 and 1700–2200. Budget–moderate.

SIGHTSEEING

Aberdeen's claim to fame is as home of the US ordnance proving grounds. Weaponry and other army material are tested under combat conditions on a 75,000-acre reservation jutting into Chesapeake Bay.

US Army Ordnance Museum, *Rte 22 E.* (off Hwy 40, 3 miles south of Aberdeen); *tel: (410) 278-3602.* This is the place for small boys and ex-Service personnel, with masses of rifles, machines guns, tanks and Jeeps. Weapons displayed range from a Civil War Gatling gun to an atomic cannon developed in the 1950s. Open daily 1000–1645. Admission: free.

HAVRE DE GRACE

Tourist Information: **Havre de Grace Chamber of Commerce**, *PO Box 339, 220 N. Washington St, Havre de Grace, MD 21078; tel: (410) 939-3303 or (800) 851-7756.*

Pick up a self-guided tour leaflet to ensure you make the most of this enchanting small town, which was severely damaged during a British attack in 1813. The British attempted to burn the place down and 60% of its buildings were damaged. Nevertheless, some 800 structures are now contained within the town's Historic District.

275

ACCOMMODATION

What Havre de Grace accommodation lacks in variety, is more than compensated for by its historic quality. There are two bed and breakfast inns, each in the Historic District and each in the moderate price bracket.

Spencer–Silver Mansion, *200 S. Union Ave; tel: (410) 939-1097 or (800) 780-1485*, provides elegant lodgings in the town's only High Victorian stone mansion. Built in 1896, it contains numerous architectural embellishments, including a tower, four gables, a dormer and a two-storey bay window.

Vandiver Inn, *301 S. Union Ave; tel: (410) 939-5200 or (800) 245-1655.* Gourmet dinners, as well as bed and breakfast, are available in this 1886 mansion in the style of a Queen Anne cottage. It is said to be the town's most extensively and expensively restored building, with original stained-glass windows located, purchased and re-installed by the present owners.

EATING AND DRINKING

Two restaurants specialise in seafood. **Bayou**, *927 Pulaski Hwy (Hwy 40); tel: (410) 939-3565*, opens daily 1130–2200. Lunch is cheap–budget, dinner budget–moderate. **Crazy Swede**, *400 N. Union Ave; tel: (410) 939-5440*, is open daily 1100–0200. Lunch is cheap–budget, dinner moderate.

SIGHTSEEING

The highlight of the town's sightseeing attractions is **Concord Point Lighthouse**, *at the foot of Lafayette St*. Located at the point where the Susquehanna River enters Chesapeake Bay, the granite lighthouse was completed in 1829 and manned by the same family – the O'Neills – until 1928, when it was automated. It is believed to be the oldest continually used lighthouse in the US. From the lighthouse you can see ocean-going shipping on its way to and from Philadelphia by way of the Chesapeake and Delaware Canal (see p. 278). Open Sat–Sun 1300–1700 (May–Oct). Admission: free.

Decoy Museum, *Giles and Market Sts; tel: (410) 939-3739*. The museum is dedicated to the art of decoy making, especially as it applies to the Chesapeake Bay heritage. There are collections of decoys made by master carvers Madison Mitchell, Charlie Joiner, Charlie Bryant and others, and displays of the various tools and equipment used in making decoys. Open daily 1300–1600. Admission charge.

Steppingstone Museum, *461 Quaker Bottom Rd* (off Rte 155, 3 miles north of

Havre de Grace); *tel: (410) 939-2299*. A 19th-century farm is the setting for this agricultural museum where traditional crafts are demonstrated. The main building is a stone farmhouse and there are farm buildings, barns and a working blacksmith's shop. Open Sat–Sun 1300–1700 (May–Sept). Admission charge.

Susquehanna Museum, *Erie and Conesteo Sts; tel: (410) 939-1800 or 939-5780*. Located in an 1840 lockhouse that once served as home and office for a lockkeeper on the Susquehanna and Tideway Canal, the museum is furnished in the style of the canal era and an audio-visual programme tells the story of the old waterway. A partly restored lock is in front of the house. Open Sat–Sun 1300–1700 (May–Oct). Admission: free.

Susquehanna State Park, *off Rte 155*, (3 miles north of Havre de Grace); *tel: (410) 557-7994*. The park covers 2639 acres fronting the Susquehanna River and has a network of hiking, cycling and horseriding trails. Within the park is a historic area containing the 1794 **Rock Run Grist Mill**, where milling demonstrations still take place, the **New Jersey Toll House**, a passing point for early settlers, and the **Archer Mansion**, built in 1804. The park's campsite has 75 pitches with facilities for tents and RVs. Open daily 0800–dusk. Admission charge.

ELKTON

Tourist Information: **Cecil County Chamber of Commerce**, *129 E. Main St, Elkton, MD 21921; tel: (410) 392-3833 or (800) CECIL-95*.

ACCOMMODATION AND FOOD

Despite its location as a crossroads town, Elkton offers little in the way of accommodation or sustenance for the traveller. **Elkton Lodge**, *200 Belle Hill Rd; tel:*

276

(410) 398-9400, is a 32-room budget motel with a restaurant nearby.

Sutton Motel, *405 E. Pulaski Hwy* (Hwy 40); *tel: (410) 398-3830*, has 11 rooms with showers and also has a restaurant nearby.

SIGHTSEEING

Elkton Historical Society Museum, *135 E. Main St; tel: (410) 398-1790*, features an early kitchen, country store, firehouse, and a long schoolhouse. Open Mon 1200–1600, Tues 1800–2030, Thur 1000–1600, fourth Sun in every month 1000–1400. Admission: $1. In the same location, with the same hours, is the **Sheriff John F. Dewitt Museum**, a collection of artefacts from all branches of the military, from the Civil War to Desert Storm. Dewitt started collecting military memorabilia at the age of 11, and went on to become the only sheriff in the history of Cecil County to be elected for four consecutive terms. Admission: free.

Elk Neck State Forest, *130 Mckinneytown Rd, North East, MD 21901* (four miles west of Elkton, off Rte 7); *tel: (410) 287-5675*. Visitors can observe forest management practices, view wildlife, hike, camp and enjoy winter sports in an area of 3465 acres. Write or phone for permit details.

Elk Neck State Park, *4395 Turkey Point Rd, North East* (Rte 272 14 miles south of Elkton); *tel: (410) 287-5333*. The park encompasses 2200 acres of varied topography – from sandy beaches and marshland to forested bluffs on the Elk Neck Peninsula, bordered by the Elk River, Chesapeake Bay and Turkey Point. There are facilities for fishing, swimming, boating and picnicking, as well as nature and hiking trails. The year-round campsite has flat pitches for tents or camper vehicles, each with lantern post, picnic table

and fire ring. A central bathroom has hot showers. Rustic cabins overlooking the Elk River are available May–Oct.

CHESAPEAKE CITY

Tourist Information: **Chesapeake City Historic District**, *PO Box 533, 103 Bohemia Ave, Chesapeake City, MD 21915-1219; tel: (410) 885-2415* or *885-2797*.

ACCOMMODATION

Blue Max Inn, *300 Bohemia Ave; tel: (410) 885-2781*. This Georgian federal-style house (built in 1854) was once the home of Jack Hunter, author of the novel *Blue Max*, on which the famous film was based. Today, it offers rooms with Laura Ashley décor, plus a full breakfast and afternoon tea. Moderate.

The Inn at the Canal, *104 Bohemia Ave; tel: (410) 885-5995*. Six bedrooms are available for bed and breakfast in this 1870 mansion overlooking the Chesapeake and Delaware Canal. Totally non-smoking. Restaurant nearby. Budget–moderate.

EATING AND DRINKING

Baker's Restaurant, *1075 Augustine Herman Hwy; tel: (410) 398-2435*. Homemade specials are served every day in this family restaurant, which was established in 1958. Open Sun, Mon, Wed 1130–2000, Tues, Thur–Sat 1130–2100. Moderate.

The Bayard House Restaurant, *11 Bohemia Ave; tel: (410) 885-5040*, serves innovative and traditional Eastern Shore cuisine in a quaint waterside setting. Specialities include Crab Imperial, Tournedos Baltimore and Lump Crab meat stuffed with green chili salsa. Open daily for lunch and dinner. Moderate–pricey.

Schaefer's Canal House, *208 Bank St; tel: (410) 885-2200*, is a seafood restaurant offering summertime outdoor dining

277

with a view of the C & D Canal. Open daily 0800–2200. Budget–pricey. Bed and breakfast accommodation also available.

SIGHTSEEING

A former centre of canal-related industry and commerce, this attractive 19th-century town has undergone extensive restoration and now encompasses restaurants and shops. Guided tours available.

Chesapeake and Delaware Canal Museum, *815 Bethel Rd; tel: (410) 885-5621.* Opened in 1829, the canal crosses the Delmarva Peninsula from Chesapeake Bay to the Delaware River, saving a 300-mile passage around Cape Charles – a short cut taken by thousands of vessels each year. An audio-visual presentation, models and displays tell the story of the canal's development and its impact on the upper Chesapeake Bay area. A working model shows how the canal's lift lock works. Open Mon–Sat 0800–1600, Sun 1000–1800. Closed Sun during winter. Admission: free.

NEWARK

Tourist Information: **Greater Wilmington Convention and Visitors Bureau**, *1300 Market St, Suite 504, Wilmington, DE 19801; tel: (302) 652-4088* or *(800) 422-1181.*

ACCOMMODATION

With a population of around 25,000, Newark offers a wider choice of accommodation and dining than elsewhere on this route. Hotel chains in the city include *BW, CI, Hd, HJ* and *Hn.*

The grandest hotel in the area is the **Hilton Inn Christiana**, *100 Continental Dr.* (exit 4B from I-95); *tel: (302) 454-1500.* The hotel has 200 rooms and suites, heated pool and a restaurant open daily 0630–2200. The bar is open 1100–0100.

Amenities include tennis, golf and fitness centre. Expensive.

McIntosh Inn, *100 McIntosh Plaza; tel: (302) 453-9100*, is a 108-room motel with a 24-hour restaurant nearby. Budget.

EATING AND DRINKING

Klondike Kate's, *158 E. Main St; tel: (302) 737-6100.* Tex-Mex dishes – and conventional American – served in a former jail and courthouse. Claustrophobic diners will be glad to learn that meals may be taken alfresco when the weather permits. Fresh seafood is a speciality. Open Mon–Sat 1100–0100, Sun 1000–0100. Cheap–moderate. **Mirage**, *100 Elkton Rd; tel: (302) 453-1711.* Fresh seafood and beef are the specialties here, and jazz is a Fri bonus. Open Mon–Fri 1130–1430 and 1730–2100, Sat 1730–2200. Lunch falls in the budget range, dinner moderate.

SIGHTSEEING

Generally considered to be part of Greater Wilmington, Newark nonetheless retains its own identity as a thriving small city. Developed around the crossroads of two major Indian trails, it is home to the University of Delaware.

University of Delaware, *Visitors' Center, 196 S. College Ave; tel: (302) 831-8123.* Tours of the elm tree-shaded campus, with its fine lawns and Georgian-style brick buildings are conducted Mon–Fri and Sat morning. Visitors are also admitted to the university's mineral collection, *Penny Hall, Academy St; tel: (302) 831-2569.* Open Mon–Fri. Admission: free.

Cooch's Bridge, *on Rte 4,* on the city's south-west outskirts, is the scene of the only Revolutionary War battle fought in Delaware. It took place on 3 Sept 1777, when the new 13-star flag, the Stars and Stripes, is believed to have been unfurled for the first time. Freely accessible.

WILMINGTON

Delaware's largest city, Wilmington (population 71,500), is midway between New York City and Washington, DC – 100 miles from each. It sits beside the great Delaware River, and two other rivers, the Brandywine and the Christina, flow within its boundaries. For tourism purposes, the area is promoted as Wilmington and the Brandywine Valley.

Wilmington was first settled in 1638 by the Swedes. Seventeen years later the Dutch took it over, and by 1665 the English were entrenched. Shipping and other industries founded on sound Quaker philosophies have flourished, and today Wilmington has a strong industrial base, with chemicals to the fore. Its port, 65 miles from the Atlantic Ocean, is visited by more than 500 ships a year and annually handles 4.5 million tons of cargo.

TOURIST INFORMATION

Greater Wilmington Convention and Visitors Bureau, *1300 Market St, Suite 504, Wilmington, DE 19801; tel: (302) 652-4088.* General information on accommodation, entertainment and attractions throughout the area; maps and brochures. The bureau has a Visitor Information Center on I-95 just south of Wilmington between Rtes 896 and 273 at milepost 6; *tel: (302) 737-4059.* Open daily 0800–2000. Travel counsellors are happy to deal with visitors' inquiries.

Delaware Tourism Office, *99 Kings Hwy, PO Box 1401, Dover, DE 19903; tel: (302) 739-4271.*

Delaware State Visitor Center, *406 Federal St, Dover; tel: (302) 739-4266.* Material on local and statewide attractions, events and activities. The centre has a museum and a gift shop selling books, jewellery, handicrafts and Delaware souvenirs. Two galleries have changing exhibitions on the state's history, fashions and arts and crafts. Admission free, donations welcome. Visitor Center open Mon–Sat 0830–1630, Sun 1330–1630.

Brandywine Valley Tourist Information Center, *Rte 1, Kennett Square, PA 19348 (at entrance to Longwood Gardens); tel: (610) 388-2900.* Open daily 1000–1800. As well as the usual range of informative literature, the centre has copies of menus from local restaurants and taverns on display.

ARRIVING AND DEPARTING

The nearest **airport** is Philadelphia International, 25 miles north of the city. By **road**, Wilmington is easily accessed from north and south via I-95. Use Exits 7 and 8 for the Brandywine Valley. Those arriving via the New Jersey turnpike will cross the river by the Delaware Memorial Bridge (I-295). For **rail** travellers, more than 50 trains a day serve Wilmington's refurbished Victorian Amtrak Station at *Martin Luther King Blvd and French St.*

GETTING AROUND

Although buses serve the city and Dart First State operates a weekday service covering all three counties in the state, Wilmington is sufficiently small and well

279

signposted for visitors to use their own cars without difficulty. Many of the main attractions are several miles out of town on good roads. Visiting motorists are helped in following their chosen routes by a system of black, white, red and blue signs.

STAYING IN WILMINGTON

Accommodation

Hotel chains in Greater Wilmington include *BW, CI, EL, Hd, HJ, Hn, Ma, QI, Ra, Rd, Sh, TL*.

Tally Ho Motor Lodge, *Rte 202 and Naamans Rd, Wilmington; tel: (302) 478-0300*. The 100–room motel, 3½ miles north of Wilmington, offers rooms with a choice of king-size or double beds, and units with kitchenettes. On-site laundry facilities. Budget. **Holiday Inn Downtown**, *700 King St, Wilmington; tel: (302) 655-0400*. Modern nine-storey hotel with 217 well-proportioned rooms, in the business district. Conference and business facilities, restaurant, indoor pool. Moderate–expensive. **Comfort Inn**, *1120 S. College Ave, Newark; tel: (302) 368-8715*. The motel's 102 double rooms cost from $62–$64. Outdoor pool. Nearby restaurant and lounge.

Best Western Brandywine Valley Inn, *1807 Concord Pike, Wilmington; tel: (302) 656-9436*. Midweek and weekend packages include admission to some major attractions; 95 rooms, some suites with kitchens. Moderate. **Sheraton Suites**, *422 Delaware Ave, Wilmington; tel: (302) 654-8300*. 230 suites in the 16-storey building. Business centre, free parking. Coupon books give free or discounted entry to some local attractions. Complimentary breakfast. Expensive–pricey.

The Boulevard Bed and Breakfast, *1909 Baynard Blvd, Wilmington; tel: (302)*

Rent-a-Camp

Delaware State Parks operate a Rent-a-Camp scheme, enabling first-timers to experience a night under canvas without investing in all the paraphernalia.

A tent and other camping equipment are supplied and park staff are available to familiarise campers with the equipment, to offer advice and answer questions.

Unlike most campsites in Delaware state parks, which operate on a first-come first-served basis, Rent-a-Camp sites can be reserved. The charge for a site is $25 a night.

656-9700. Restored city mansion in the historic district. Six rooms. Full breakfast. Business services available. Moderate. **Bed and Breakfast of Delaware** (agency), *2701 Landon Dr, Suite 200, Wilmington; tel: (302) 479-9500*. Reservation service for business or holiday travellers. Historic bed and breakfast homes in Delaware and neighbouring states, from $45–$150.

Lums Pond State Park Campsite, *1068 Howell School Rd, Bear (about five miles south of I-95 off Rte 896 near Glasgow); tel: (302) 368-6989*. The entrance to the campground, a few miles southwest of Wilmington, is on Rte 71 between Kirkwood and the Rte 896 intersection. The campground has drinking water, modern shower and sanitary facilities and sewage dumping station but no on-site utility hook-ups. Rent-a-Camp programme operates (see box p. 00). Open Apr–Oct. $11 per night.

Philadelphia/West Chester KOA, *PO Box 920D, Unionville, PA 19375; tel: (610) 486-0447*. Convenient for Philadelphia, Amish Country and brandywine Valley. Riverside tent sites, play-

280

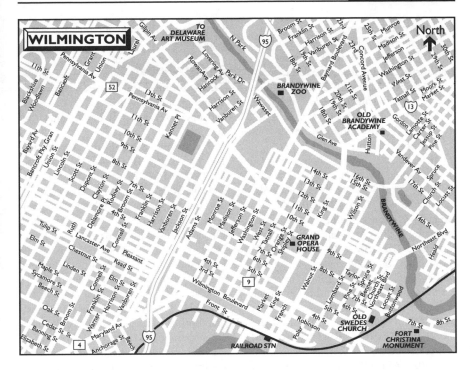

ground, planned activities and daily guided tours. Open Apr–Oct.

Eating and Drinking

Dining in Delaware comes without sales tax. As well as a wide range of cuisines from many corners of the world, there are regional delicacies like exotic mushrooms from Kennett Square and fresh crabs.

Moderate-priced options include the following:

Garden Restaurant and Tea Room at the Winterthur Museum, *Rte 52 north of Wilmington; tel: (302) 888-4855.* Traditional English-style afternoon tea, also champagne Sunday brunch 1000–1330. **Picciotti's Restaurant**, *3001 Lancaster Ave, Wilmington; tel: (302) 652-3563.* Opened more than 60 years ago, Picciotti's is famous for its filet mignon. Veal and chicken dishes are also

popular. **Harry's Savoy Grill**, *2020 Naamans Rd, Wilmington; tel: (302) 475-3000.* Fresh seafood and beef are specialities at this friendly British-style restaurant with solid mahogany mirrored bar and marble fireplaces. Open daily. **Constantinou's House of Beef**, *1616 Delaware Ave, Wilmington; tel: (302) 652-0653.* A favourite of the locals and visitors for beef and seafood dishes. Extensive wine list. **Shipley Grill Restaurant**, *913 Shipley St, Wilmington; tel: (302) 652-7797.* All-American wine list offers more than 30 wines by the glass, to accompany the beef, seafood and pasta dishes. **Griglia Toscana**, *1412 N. duPont St, Wilmington; tel: (302) 654-8001.* Authentic Tuscan cuisine in a bistro with open kitchen and award-winning wine list. Weekday lunches, dinner nightly. **Country Mouse Cafe**, *4001 Kennett*

Pike, Greenville Crossing, Greenville (about 5 miles north-west of Wilmington); tel: (302) 656-7627. Low cholesterol gourmet vegetarian specials, open for breakfast, lunch and dinner. Take-out available. **The Brass Bass**, *Radisson Hotel, Wilmington, 4727 Concord Pike, Wilmington; tel: (302) 478-6000.* Fresh seafood and health-conscious pasta dishes prepared to order.

There is also a wide choice of good budget eating, including:

Wing Wah, *3901-03 Concord Pike, Wilmington; tel: (302) 478-9500.* Award-winning Cantonese cuisine and exotic cocktails. Take-out available. Budget–moderate. **DiNarda's Restaurant**, *405 N. Lincoln St, Wilmington; tel: (302) 656-3685.* Casual tavern atmosphere with hard shell crab the speciality in a full seafood menu. Open Mon–Sat 0900–2400, Sun 1500–2200. Budget–moderate. **Govatos Restaurant and Candies**, *800 Market St Mall, Wilmington; tel: (302) 652-9082.* Frosted mugs of draught beer with platters, sandwiches or charbroiled burgers. Wines served. Candies made on premises. Open Mon–Sat 0700–1730. **Leo and Jimmy's Delicatessen**, *728 Market St Mall, Wilmington; tel: (302) 656-7151.* The place to pick up a picnic. Sandwiches packed with fresh ingredients, soft drinks, cookies and cakes. **O'Friel's Irish Pub and Restaurant**, *600 Delaware Ave, Wilmington; tel: (302) 654-0321.* Good food, good atmosphere, good entertainment with live Irish music Thur–Sat and a DJ on Tues. 'Open live mike night' is held the last Thur of the month – the microphone is handed around and those who think they can sing or tell a story (usually after a pint or two) can entertain for a few minutes. **Varsity Grill**, *837 Orange St, Wilmington; tel: (302) 656-8872.* Generous portions of low-cost tasty food. Happy

hour, evening entertainment and seven pool tables.

ENTERTAINMENT

The performing arts are well supported in Wilmington, with theatre, dance, music and opera venues and some dinner theatres, too.

Delaware Symphony Orchestra, *Box Office, 206 W. 10th St, Wilmington; tel: (302) 656-7374*, is a major orchestra and a versatile one under celebrated music directed Stephen Gunzenhauser. Its concerts range from classical at the Grand Opera House and small ensembles at Winterthur, to chamber concerts in the Hotel du Pont's Gold Ballroom and pop concerts at the Playhouse. **Grand Opera House**, *818 Market St Mall, Wilmington; tel: (302) 658-7897.* A year-round programme of classical concerts, popular entertainment and dance is presented at this restored 1871 theatre architecturally important for its unusual cast iron façade. Professional productions with full orchestra are staged here by the nationally-recognised **Opera Delaware Company**, *4, S. Poplar St, Wilmington; tel: (302) 658-8063.*

Chorus of the Brandywine, *302 Nottingham Rd, Newark; tel: (302) 737-6141*, is the Wilmington Chapter of a men's organisation dedicated to the preservation of four-part 'barber-shop' singing.

Russian Ballet Theatre of Delaware, *PO Box 263, Rockland; tel: (302) 888-2900.* Dancers trained at Russia's foremost academies give four performances a year, featuring some of classical ballet's masterpieces.

Delaware Theatre Company, *200 Water St, Wilmington; tel: (302) 594-1100.* These professional performers offer a season of five plays from Oct–Apr in a modern theatre by the Christina River.

Hotel of the Arts

The most gracious hotel in Wilmington – and one which incorporates a 1200-seat theatre – is the 12-storey, 206-room, 10-suite **Hotel du Pont**, built in the Italian Renaissance style and opened in 1913. The hotel has been given the Four Diamond Award of the American Automobile Association, and two of its four restaurants – the formal Green Room with a musicians' gallery and the more intimate Brandywine Room – hold the coveted Four Diamond Award for excellence in dining.Celebrities who have stayed there include Eleanor Roosevelt, Charles Lindbergh, John F. Kennedy, Elizabeth Taylor, Katherine Hepburn, Ingrid Bergman, Prince Rainier of Monaco and Joe diMaggio.

More than 700 original works of art, many of them renowned artists of the Brandywine Valley, are displayed in the Hotel du Pont, which features polished walnut panelling, high ceilings and Queen Anne and Chippendale furnishings. The Gold Ballroom, built in 1918 in the French Neoclassic style and accommodating up to 500 people, is richly ornate. The ceiling contains 20 medallions of famous women in history.

The hotel's Playhouse Theatre presents a yearly programme of Broadway touring shows, dance and music and also holds a children's theatre season.

The beautifully appointed guest rooms cost $139–$219. Suites are $385–$409. The Hotel du Pont is at *11th and Market Sts, Wilmington; tel: (302) 594-3100 or (800) 441-9019.*

Playhouse Theatre, *10th and Market sts, Wilmington; tel: (302) 656-4401.* Touring companies of Broadway shows and productions bound for New York give performances throughout the year at this 1200-seat theatre which has been in continuous operation within the Hotel du Pont since 1913. A children's theatre season also takes place in the Playhouse.

Wilmington Drama League Community Theatre, *10 W. Lea Blvd, Wilmington; tel: (302) 764-1172.* This company has provided community entertainment in the area for more than 60 years.

Candlelight Music Dinner Theatre, *2208 Millers Rd, Ardentown, Wilmington; tel: (302) 475-2313.* Musicals, revues and comedies presented year-round. **Three Little Bears Dinner Theatre**, *1540 Foxcroft Dr, Pike Creek Valley, Wilmington; tel: (302) 368-1658.* Live Broadway shows with your buffet dinner. **Christina Cultural Arts Center**, *800 E. 7th St,* *Wilmington; tel: (3020 652-0101.* Concerts, special events and exhibits presented in the Old Swedes Church complex.

Delaware Park Racecourse, *Rte 7, off I-95, Exit 4B, Stanton (just south of Wilmington); tel: (302) 994-2521.* Daytime thoroughbred racing Tues, Wed, Sat and Sun from 1245 (Mar–Nov); also Victorian-style Slots Casino open daily until 0200. Admission: $2.

SHOPPING

Because no state tax is imposed in Delaware, anything you buy costs six or seven per cent less than it would in neighbouring states. Greater Wilmington provides shopping malls and department stores, and many specialist shops and places where you can browse in search of unusual gifts and souvenirs of the state, such as carved wooden decoy ducks and geese and original handicrafts.

For menswear, the long-established

Wright and Simon, *911 Market St, Wilmington; tel: (302) 658-7345*, provides plenty of choice. Wilmington's West End is the fashionable area for boutiques and galleries, men's and women's fashions and gifts. **Sweeny's Irish Imports**, *1942 Gilpin Ave; tel: (302) 656-0317*, stocked with Irish crystal, woollens and tweeds, jewellery and music tapes and CDs, is in the West End. Oriental works – porcelain, objets d'art, jewellery and furniture can be chosen unhurriedly at **Jung's Oriental Antiques and Fine Arts**, *1314 W. 13th St, Wilmington; tel: (302) 658-1314*, and at *1701 N. Lincoln St* is **J.D. Kurtz Oriental Rugs**, *tel: (302) 654-0442*, one of the leading oriental rug galleries in the US.

Ninety stores are clustered at **Concord Mall**, *4737 Concord Pike, Wilmington; tel: (302) 478-9271*. They include Sears, Sawbridge and Clothier, and Boscov's. (designer label fashions at moderate and promotional prices).

SIGHTSEEING

Apart from a number of historic buildings and places of interest in the city of Wilmington, most of the sightseeing is in Greater Wilmington and the Brandywine Valley, easy to reach by car.

Tours

Several companies provide guide services:

Colonial Pathway Tours, *Marshallton Building, PO Box 879, Chadd's Ford West; tel: (610) 388-2654*. One-day or multi-day itineraries and guide service in the Brandywine Valley. **Congo Shuttle and Service**, *2902 W. 2nd St, Wilmington; tel: (302) 571-5585*. Minibus, motor coach and charter services, customised tours, group tours, step-on guide services, one-day and multi-day packages. **Red Carpet Travel**, *413 Branmar Plaza,*

Wilmington; tel: (302) 457-1220. Provides customised tours, group tour services, one-day and multi-day packages, guided walking tours. **Footloose Tours**, *2126 W. Newport Pike, Suite 203, Wilmington; tel: (302) 994-9451*. Provides custom guided walking tours of New Castle and Wilmington and van tours of Brandywine Valley. One-day and multi-day packages.

Museums and Attractions

Lincoln Collection of the University of Delaware, *Goodstay Center, 2600 Pennsylvania Ave, Wilmington; tel: (302) 573-4419*. More than 2000 exhibits relating to Abraham Lincoln's private and public life. Open Tues (Oct–May). Admission: free. **Delaware Art Museum**, *2301 Kentmere Parkway, Wilmington; tel: (302) 571-9590*. Noted Brandywine Painters are featured and one of the largest collections of English pre-Raphaelite works in the US can be seen. Open Tues–Sat 1000–1700, Sun 1200–1700. Admission: free.

Rockwood Museum, *610 Shipley Rd, Wilmington; tel: (302) 571-7776*. Designed in 1851 by English architect George Williams, the Rockwood country estate is considered an outstanding example of Rural Gothic architecture. Built for a merchant banker, Joseph Shipley, it has a manor house, conservatory, porter's lodge, gardener's cottage, carriage house and outbuildings. Furniture and decorative arts are from the 17th, 18th and 19th centuries. Open Tues–Sat 1100–1600, tours on the hour and half-hour, last tour 1500. Admission: $5.

Wilmington Maritime Center, *Christina Park at E. Front and Church Sts, Wilmington; tel: (302) 984-0472*. Cruises on the Delaware River, including sunset cruises.

Mushroom Museum at Phillips

Place, *Kennett Square, PA, Hwy 1; tel: (610) 388-6082*. This museum, half a mile south of Longwood Gardens, explains through film and slides the history, lore and mystique of mushrooms, and displays exotic varieties like Shiitake, Portabella, Crimini and Oyster mushrooms. The gift shop has china, glassware, table linen, jewellery and many other items all with a mushroom motif. Mushroom delicacies and other gourmet foods are on sale. Open daily 1000–1800. Admission: $1.25.

Delaware History Museum, *504 Market St Mall, Wilmington; tel: (302) 656-0637*. The Historical Society of Delaware operates the museum, which has changing exhibitions on the state's history and decorative arts. Open Tues–Fri 1200–1600, Sat 1000–1600. Donations accepted.

Kalmar Nyckel Foundation, *1124 E. 7th St, Wilmington; tel: (302) 429-7447*. A 17th century shipyard is a major feature of the museum, which commemorates the beginning of the permanent European settlements in the area in 1638. A model of the *Kalmar Nyckel*, one of the ships which carried Swedish settlers to the area, is on show. Tours Tues–Sat 1000–1600 (phone for details).

Longwood Gardens, *Hwy 1 (northeast of Kennett Square); tel: (610) 388-1000*. More than 1000 acres of outdoor gardens and nearly four acres under glass present one of the world's major horticultural displays. On summer evenings illuminated fountains play, and at Christmas the festive lights go on. Roses and orchids bloom all year. Longwood's woodland region includes a grove of trees planted two centuries ago. A heathland area has azaleas and other flowering shrubs. There's a water garden, rose garden and other gardens specialising in particular types of flora. An audio-visual presentation puts visitors in

Family Connections

The influence of the wealthy du Pont family, founders of the worldwide chemicals company which originated here, is evident in many of the main sightseeing options in the Wilmington area.

Hagley Museum, on the Brandywine, features the original du Pont gunpowder mills estate and first family home. Longwood Gardens, at Kennett Square, is the former country estate of Pierre S. du Pont, who developed it from a Quaker farm which he bought in 1906. The incredible nine-storey Winterthur Museum, Garden and Library was the home of Henry Francis du Pont, who accumulated an enormous collection of American fine arts and added rooms by the hundred to accommodate them. Nemours Mansion and Garden, dating from 1910, built in the Louis XVI style, was named after the du Pont ancestral home in France.

285

the year-round picture; other amenities include the Terrace Restaurant and a gift shop. Open daily, gardens 0900–1800, conservatories 1000–1800 (closed at 1700 Nov–Mar). Admission: $10 ($6 on Tues), good for all day but does not include special events.

Delaware Museum of Natural History. *Rte 52 (north-west of Wilmington, between Greenville and Centreville); tel: (302) 658-9111*. A 500 lb clam, a shell collection, an exhibition of the wildlife of Delaware and places farther afield, like an African watering hole and Australia's Great Barrier Reef, are featured. There's a Children's Discovery Room. Open Mon–Sat 0930–1630, Sun 1200–1700. Admission: $4.

Winterthur Museum, Garden and

Library, *Rte 52 (six miles north-west of Wilmington); tel: (302) 888-4600.* Period rooms and exhibition galleries house an unrivalled collection of American decorative arts from 1640–1860, amassed by Henry Francis du Pont, and include silver tankards once owned by Paul Revere and a dinner service made for George Washington. Visitors can tour the galleries or stroll in the extensive natural gardens, or pay extra for guided tours (reservations required) covering three different aspects of Winterthur – period rooms, decorative arts and garden walks. Open Mon–Sat 0900–1700, Sun 1200– 1700. Admission:

Swedish Church and Hendrickson House Museum, *606 Church St, Wilmington; tel: (302) 652-5629.* Services are still held regularly at the church – one of the oldest churches in the US, still as it was originally built by Swedish settlers in 1698. The 1690 Swedish farmhouse is now a museum. Open afternoons only Mon, Wed, Fri and Sat. Admission: free.

Hagley Museum, *off Rte 141, 3 miles north-west of Wilmington; tel: (302) 658-2400.* Water from the Brandywine River was the source of power for the mills when the du Pont gunpowder works were set up on its banks. The waterwheel still operates. Daily demonstrations with interpreters in costume depict work and home life in the 19th century, and exhibits and working models show how the Brandywine Valley developed economically and technologically. Farther upstream (transport included in admission price) visitors see the Georgian-style home, **Eleutherian Mills**, built in 1803 as the du Ponts' first family home, and its French-style gardens. Open daily 0930–1630 (Apr–Dec), weekends 0930–1630 (Jan–Mar). Admission: $26.50 per family or adults $9.75, seniors and students $7.50, children 6–14 $3.50.

Fort Christiana, *foot of E. 7th St, Wilmington.* A monument presented by the people of Sweden in 1938 marks the site of their forebears' first settlement in the area three centuries earlier. An early log cabin stands nearby.

Old Town Hall, *512 Market St Mall, Wilmington; tel: (302) 655-7161.* Built between 1798 and 1800, the Georgian-style building was the town's centre of government until 1916. It is owned and operated by the Historical Society of Delaware, whose growing museum collections are displayed there. Open Tues– Fri 1200–1600 (Mar–Dec). Admission: free.

Nemours Mansion and Gardens, *Rockland Rd, Wilmington; tel: (302) 651-6912.* The 102-room mansion, completed in 1910 for Alfred I. du Pont, contains antique furniture, rare rugs, tapestries and works of art. In the 300-acre estate are French-style landscaped gardens surrounded by woodland. Guided tours last a minimum of 2 hrs and reservations are recommended. Visitors must be over 16, and there are staircases to negotiate. Tours Tues–Sat at 0900, 1100, 1300 and 1500, Sun 1100, 1300, 1500 (May–Nov). Admission charge.

Wilmington and Western Railroad, *Greenbank Station, Rte 41 (three blocks north of junction with Rte 2); tel: (302) 998-1930.* Steam or diesel train trips through Red Clay Valley to picnic grove. Special events, such as Children's Days, Civil War troop train trips, Wild West Robberies Ride and Santa Claus trains. Diesel trains Sat (July–Aug), steam trains Sun (May–mid Nov). Phone for details. Fare: $7.

Wilderness Canoe Trips, *2111 Concord Pike, Fairfax Shopping Center, Wilmington; tel: (302) 654-2227.* Canoe or inner tube trips from two to six hours along the Brandywine River, ideal for first-timers.

WILMINGTON–DOVER

This short route is full of interest, taking us from tiny Delaware's largest city to the state capital. The quickest route between the two cities is Hwy 13, but by following Rte 9 and dodging back on to Hwy 13 from time to time travellers can enjoy the beauty of the marshlands fringeing the Delaware River without missing the places listed below.

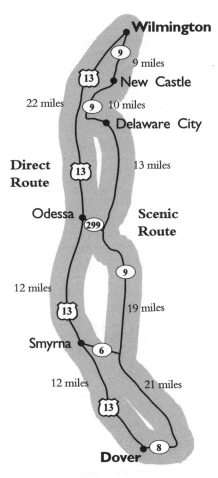

Wilmington

9 miles

New Castle

22 miles   10 miles

Delaware City

Direct Route

13 miles

Odessa   **Scenic Route**

12 miles

19 miles

Smyrna

12 miles   21 miles

Dover

DIRECT ROUTE: 46 MILES

ROUTES

DIRECT ROUTE

Following Hwy 13 all the way without stopping will take just under an hour.

SCENIC ROUTE

Following the meandering Rte 9 and slipping west to take in Odessa and Smyrna will stretch the trip to 67 miles and as many hours as you may wish to take.

From downtown Wilmington, follow *Market St* south, then head west on *Martin Luther King Blvd;* which leads to Exit 6 on

I-95. Head south on the interstate for 2 miles then take I-295 north. The last exit before the Delaware Memorial Bridge, which crosses the Delaware River to New Jersey, leads to Rte 9 south. The charming old town of **New Castle** is reached in 7 miles.

From New Castle Hwy 9 hugs the shore of the Delaware River as it continues south for 10 miles to **Delaware City**. After a further 11 miles it intersects with Hwy 299, which leads north for 2 miles to **Odessa**, then continues south for 12 miles to its intersection with Rte 6. This heads east into Bombay Hook National Wildlife Refuge and west for 5 miles to **Smyrna**.

From Smyrna you can either continue south on Hwy 13 to reach Dover in 12 miles or return to Rte 9, head south for 11 miles, then head west on Rte 8 for a final five-mile run into Dover (see p.292–295).

NEW CASTLE

Tourist Information: Mayor and Council Office, *220 Delaware St, New Castle; tel: (302) 323-4452.*

ACCOMMODATION

The town's motels and inns include EconoLodge, Travelodge, **Rodeway Inn** and **Shoney's Inn**, all with rooms in the budget category.

Quality Inn-Skyways, *147 N. du Pont Hwy, New Castle; tel: (302) 328-6666,* has 100 rooms, some non-smoking, a restaurant, lounge and outdoor pool. Pets are accepted. Moderate.

Ramada Inn, *I-295 and Rte 13 N., New Castle; tel: (302) 658-8511.* One mile from the Delaware Memorial Bridge, the inn has 131 rooms and suites, restaurant and lounge, outdoor pool and secure 24-hr parking. Moderate.

There are two bed and breakfast homes in the historic district. The **William Penn**

Guest House, *206 Delaware St; tel: (302) 328-7736,* dates from 1682, has four guest rooms, and is within walking distance of restaurants and museums. Moderate.

At **Jefferson House Bed and Breakfast**, *Strand at the Wharf; tel: (302) 325-1025,* a substantial 19th-century riverside residence, self-catering is an option and children are welcome. Moderate.

EATING AND DRINKING

Dempsey's Restaurant, *Rte 13* (opposite New Castle County Airport), *New Castle; tel: (302) 328-4879.* This establishment serves home-made food – and has a great reputation for strawberry pie. Open 24 hrs. Budget.

Air Transport Command Restaurant, *143 N. du Pont Hwy, New Castle; tel: (302) 328-3527.* An unusual and interesting restaurant with a World War II theme, a Scottish farmhouse-style setting and a view of airport runways. DJ and dancing Wed–Sun. Beef, poultry and seafood are served. Generally moderate, but it's possible to choose a budget-priced dinner.

Newcastle Inn, *1 Market St, New Castle; tel: (302) 328-1290.* In an 1809 building once used as an arsenal, the inn, in the historic district, is open for lunch and dinner. Try the chicken and oyster pie. Moderate.

Colour section: (i) Annapolis (pp.246–252); inset, *Pride of Baltimore II* sails into Annapolis harbour.
(ii) A view of Baltimore (pp.261–273); Baltimore National Aquarium (p.271) at dusk
(iii) Shopping at Hershey Chocolate World (p.310); the Delaware River at Philadelphia (pp.319–328); the Liberty Bell (p.326).
(iv) Independence Hall, Philadelphia (p.326).

Lynnhaven Inn, *154 N. du Pont Hwy* (opposite county airport); *tel: (302) 328-2041*, has crab meat, oysters, lobster, prime rib and steaks on the menu. Budget lunches, dinners moderate to pricey.

Casablanca, *4010 N. du Pont Hwy, New Castle; tel: (302) 652-5344.* Distinctive Moroccan fare – a seven-course dinner includes chicken, beef, lamb, shish kebabs and couscous – and if you're there on Fri or Sat you get belly-dancing with it. Moderate, but with a 15% service charge attached.

EVENTS

The town's main annual event, on the third Sat in May, is **A Day in Old New Castle**, when many of the historic homes are opened to the public by their owners.

Christmas candlelight tours are held in December.

SIGHTSEEING

New Castle, founded in 1651 by Dutch colonist Peter Stuyvesant, is a historic Delaware River town. It has retained many lovely old homes and buildings which have been carefully preserved while continuing as part of both the residential and business scene to this day.

Much of its development was in the 18th and 19th centuries, and visitors admire the colonial-era cobblestone streets, ironwork fences, the central green planned by Stuyvesant, and the Old Court House, now a museum.

New Castle was the first landing site, in 1682 – in North America of William Penn, the English Quaker and founder of Pennsylvania, whose statue surveys the heart of the historic district.

New Castle Court House, *211 Delaware St, New Castle; tel: (302) 323-4453.* This was Delaware's colonial capitol and meeting place of the State Assembly from 1732–77, and the first state house. It is now a museum pin-pointing the creation of Delaware's northern boundary and the way legislative and judicial practices affected the people, including slaves and free blacks. Period portraits and furnishings are displayed. Walking tours of the historic district start from the Court House. Open Tues–Sat 1000–1630, Sun 1330–1630. Admission: free.

George Read II House and Garden, *42 The Strand, New Castle; tel: (302) 322-8411.* George Read II was a lawyer and the son of a man who was a signatory of the Declaration of Independence and the US Constitution. His ambition was to construct the grandest house in Delaware, and he commissioned the finest craftsmen and imported the best materials to New Castle towards this aim. The symmetrical house, close to the river on the cobbled Strand, was built between 1797 and 1804, reflecting the height of Federal fashion with its elaborately carved woodwork, gilded fanlights, relief plasterwork and door hardware of silver. Formal boxwood gardens were designed from 1847 by the property's second owner, William Couper. Twelve rooms – three in Colonial Revival style – are open to the public. The house is run by the **Historical Society of Delaware**, who offer a walking tour of New Castle. Open Mar–Dec Tues–Sat 1000–1600, Sun 1200–1600. Admission $4, students 12–21 $3.50, children 6–12 $2.

Old Presbyterian Church, *25 E. Second St, New Castle; tel: (302) 328-3279.* The church, built in 1707, was used for services until 1854. Some 50 years ago it was restored to its original appearance and services resumed. The first congregation was Dutch – unmarked graves date from the Dutch era. Open daily. Visitors also welcome at services. Donations accepted.

289

Immanuel Episcopal Church, *The Green, New Castle; tel: (302) 322-5774.* Founded in 1689, this was the first Church of England parish in Delaware. Fire caused severe damage in 1980, and the original walls and foundations were used in the rebuilding. Open daily 1000–1700. Visitors welcome at services. Donations accepted.

Old Dutch House, *32 E. Thirs St, New Castle; tel: (302) 322-2794.* Dating from the late 17th century, this is believed to be the oldest house in Delaware in its original state. Its furnishings are colonial Dutch and authentic household equipment of early settlers is on show. Open Tues–Sun Mar–Dec. Admission charge (combination ticket available with Amstel House Museum).

Amstel House Museum, *4th and Delaware Sts, New Castle; tel: (302) 322-2794.* The 18th-century brick mansion, which includes a complete colonial kitchen, was the home of the seventh governor of Delaware. George Washington attended a wedding here. Decorative arts and colonial furnishings are displayed. Open Tues–Sun Mar–Dec. Admission charge (combination ticket available with Old Dutch House).

Old Library Museum, *40 E. Third St, New Castle; tel: (302) 322-2794.* Special exhibits depicting New Castle and Delaware history are housed in a hexagonal 1892 building. Open Sat and Sun. Admission: free.

New Castle–French Railroad Ticket Office, *Delaware St, New Castle.* This is one of the earliest railroad lines in the country. The 1832 ticket office, which is surrounded by a white wicket fence, occupied several locations before being placed here in the 1950s.

The public cannot go inside, but a section of restored track can be seen. Admission: free.

DELAWARE CITY

South of New Castle, on the Delaware River and the Chesapeake and Delaware Canal, is Delaware City, a port and commercial centre. It still has its 19th-century atmosphere.

SIGHTSEEING

In the middle of the Delaware River is Pea Patch Island, where **Fort Delaware State Park**; *tel: (302) 834-7941,* is located, reached by a 10-min ferry ride. A visit to the Civil War-era prison fort starts with an audio-visual presentation. Ramparts, soldiers' quarters, parade grounds and gun emplacements can be seen. The island is a nesting spot for egrets, herons and other wading birds, which can be watched from an observation tower. The passenger ferry *Delafort* runs chartered cruises in summer. Open weekends and public holidays from late Apr–Sept. Admission charge.

Just south of the Chesapeake and Delaware Canal is the little riverside town of **Port Penn**, where an interpretive centre at *Market and Liberty Sts; tel: (302) 834-0431,* has exhibits of wildlife, fishing, trapping and agriculture. A small country store and a schoolroom are also on site. Open May–Sept Sat and Sun afternoons. Admission: free.

ODESSA

Rte 9 follows the river and goes through the **Augustine Wildlife Park** before reaching Odessa, on Rte 13, where three historic houses and a gallery are open to the public, owned and operated by the Winterthur Museum.

Odessa is a very small village of about 300 people, but it receives many visitors attracted by demonstrations of hearth cookery, as well as the village's 18th- and 19th-century architecture and the wide, tree-lined main street.

Originally settled by the Dutch in the 1720s, Odessa, known as Appoquinimink after the creek on which it lies, became a busy grain-shipping port.

Later the name was changed to Cantwell's Bridge, and in the mid 19th-century it was changed again to Odessa, named after the Black Sea grain port in Russia. Trade, however, started to decline, and today Odessa is almost entirely residential.

SIGHTSEEING

During the first weekend in Dec a number of private homes are open to the public as a pre-Christmas house tour event.

Muskrat was a popular dish, and one of the outbuildings visitors can see is the **Muskrat Skinning Shack** (see below).

The Historic Houses of Odessa, in *Main St; tel: (302) 378-4353*, are open Mar–Dec. Admission: from $4 for one property.

The Corbit-Sharp House, is a Georgian-style country home completed in 1774. Its regional and family furnishings reflect life from 1774–1818.

The Wilson Warner House, built in 1769, is typical of Delaware Georgian architecture, and it is authentically furnished to the period.

The Federal-style **Brick Hotel Gallery**, a hotel and tavern for many years, contains an important collection of furniture manufactured in New York by John Henry Belter in the mid-1800s.

The early 18th-century **Collins-Sharp House** is where hearth cookery demonstrations and craft workshops are held on Sat (Apr, May, Sept and Oct). As well as the Muskrat Skinning Shack, outbuildings include a fieldstone stable.

SMYRNA

Tourist Information: Smyrna Visitors Centre, *5500 du Pont Hwy; tel: (302) 653-8910.*

Follow Rte 13 south to **Smyrna**, settled by English Quakers around 1700 and known for many years as Duck Creek Village. By the mid-1800s it had become a thriving shipping centre, despatching produce from the fertile land of central Delaware, and changing its name to Smyrna, after the important Turkish seaport.

Smyrna has some well-maintained historic homes and buildings, some of which are open to the public by appointment. For information call at or phone the Smyrna Visitors' Centre, details above. The attractive centre offers local information and has restrooms, a petting zoo, picnic area and playground. The town has a small **museum** with changing exhibits at *11 S. Main St; tel: (302) 653-8844*. Hours are limited. Admission: free.

Bombay Hook National Wildlife Refuge, *Rte 9*, about 8 miles south-east of Smyrna; *tel: (302) 653-6872*. The 15,000-acre expanse of grass and ponds attracts thousands of Canada geese and vast white clouds of snow geese. Various species of ducks and other waterfowl use the refuge for food and rest during spring and fall migration. Bald eagles and several species of shorebird are seen there, and mammals include muskrat, deer and fox. There are observation towers for watching wildlife, foot trails and a 12-mile car route.

A **visitor centre** offers interpretive and environmental education programmes (summer and winter Mon–Fri, spring and autumn daily). Admission is charged per vehicle.

In the refuge is **Allee House**, a well-preserved brick plantation house, built in the Queen Anne style in 1753, at *Dutch Neck Rd; tel: (302) 736-4266*. Open weekends. Admission: free.

DOVER

Delaware's capital city since 1777, Dover has a fine green at South State St surrounded by some of the city's grand historic and government buildings. It was in the Golden Fleece Tavern at The Green that delegates to the Delaware Constitutional Convention in 1787 voted to ratify the American Constitution – the first state to do so, and ever since Delaware has been known as the First State.

Today, Dover's visitor attractions range from stock-car racing, a US Air Force museum, an Amish market, and the 1920s Victrola Museum, to an agricultural museum which reveals that corn cobs pre-dated the toilet roll in farm privies.

Don't leave town without exploring the historic and architectural delights of The Green, Federal St, Duke of York St, William Penn St, Legislative Ave and The Plaza. Amish people who farm in the area drive their well-turned-out horse-drawn buggies through the tree-shaded streets.

TOURIST INFORMATION

Delaware Tourism Office, *99 King's Hwy, Dover, DE 19903; tel: (302) 739-4271* or *(800) 441-8846.* **Delaware Visitor Center**, *Federal St; tel: (302) 739-4266.* A slide show on Delaware State Museums can be seen. The Sewell C. Biggs Museum of American Decorative Arts, on site, has changing exhibitions.

Statewide tourist information is available. The gift shop specialises in Delaware products and souvenirs.

ARRIVING AND DEPARTING

All major roads in Delaware lead to Dover. Hwy 13 and Rte 1 cross the city north–south and Rte 8 crosses east–west.

GETTING AROUND

Many of Dover's sights are within the city centre, which is fairly compact, and others are within a short drive. A public bus system operated by **Delaware Administration for Regional Transit** (DART) serves Dover and the surrounding area.

STAYING IN DOVER

The du Pont Highway (Hwy 13) is where the budget–moderate chain motels and the usual crop of quick-serve eateries are, and where you will find the **Dover Mall**, with a range of shops and restaurants.

SIGHTSEEING

Guided walking tours of Dover are operated by **Dover Heritage Trail**, *PO Box 1528, Dover, DE 19903; tel: (302) 678-2040.* The company's Old Dover Historic District Tour includes the Legislative Hall, the Hall of Records and Christ Church. The Victorian Dover Historic District Tour includes the Governor's House and Richardson and Robbins Cannery.

Blue Hen Tours, *159 S. Fairfield Dr., Dover, DE 19901; tel: (302) 697-7519,* provides hospitality packages in Kent and Sussex Counties and customised tours.

Delaware Supreme Court, *The Green; tel: (302) 739-4155,* the state's

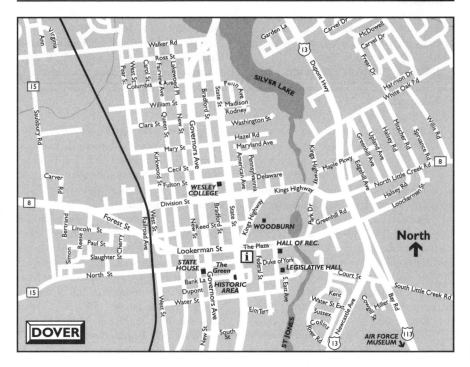

highest court, is a brick building dated 1909–12. Open Mon–Fri, admission free.

Kent County Court House, *38 The Green; tel: (302) 739-4266*, built in 1874, was the county's third court. It stands on the site of a 1691 Court House, which replaced an earlier one. Also on the site for about 140 years (until 1863) was a tavern with an inn sign depicting King George III. Open Mon–Fri. Admission: free.

The Old State House, *The Green; tel: (302) 739-4266*; visitors to the 1792 building, which contains a court room and legislative chamber, learn how people were affected by legislative and judicial decisions. The Governor's ceremonial office is on view, along with period furniture and other items, which include a geometrical staircase. The State House was restored to its original appearance in 1976 as part of Delaware's celebration of the 200th

anniversary of the signing of the Declaration of Independence. Open Tues–Sat 1000–1630. Admission: donations.

Legislative Hall, *Legislative Ave* (one block east of The Green); *tel: (302) 739-5807*, was built in 1932. The General assembly meets on the first floor, the Governor's offices are on the floor above. Paintings of former governors and of World War II heroes from Delaware are displayed. Open Mon–Fri. Admission: free. In front of the Legislative Hall, on *Capital Sq.*, stands Delaware's replica of the **Liberty Bell**.

Woodburn, the Governor's House, *151 King's Hwy; tel: (302) 739-5656*, is a striking Georgian mansion built in 1791 and the official residence of the Governor since the mid-1960s. It was used in the 19th century as a station on the Underground Railroad – the movement which helped runaway slaves. The grounds are open to the public daily. House open Sat 1430–1630. Admission: free.

Johnson Victrola Museum, *Bank Lane and New St* (behind Meeting House Galleries); *tel: (302) 739-4266*. An original oil painting of Nipper, the dog listening to a 'talking machine' who became the internationally recognised trade mark of His Master's Voice, is exhibited. The museum – a Delaware State Museum – is a tribute to Eldridge Reeves Johnson, a Delaware inventor, businessman and philanthropist who founded the Victor Talking Machine Company in 1901. It is designed as a 1920s Victrola dealer store and contains a collection of talking machines. Through displays of Victrolas, early records and other memorabilia, it reveals Johnson's life story. The museum shop has much fascinating material. Researchers can use the museum's archives and library by appointment only – *tel: (302) 739-5316*. Open Tues–Sat 1000–1530. Admission: donation.

Meeting House Galleries I and II, *316 S. Governor's Ave; tel: (302) 739-4266*, are Delaware State Museums, owned and administered by the state. Gallery I unfolds 12,000 years of Delaware's archaeology in a former Presbyterian church built in 1790. Exhibits include artefacts from the Island Field Site, a Native American burial ground near Bowers Beach south-east of Dover. Gallery II, in the adjacent 1880 Sunday-school building, has a *Main Street, Delaware* feature, depicting small town life illustrated with occupations followed by citizens and portraying the economics and culture of Delaware communities in the early 1900s. Open Tues–Sat 1000–1530. Admission: donation.

Christ Episcopal Church, *S. State St and Water St; tel: (302) 734-5731*. In the graveyard of the 1734 church is a monument to Caesar Rodney, a signatory to the Declaration of Independence. Open Mon–Fri. Admission: free. **Constitution Park**, adjacent to *Constitution Pl., S. State St*, is a small park with an impressive bronze sculpture of a 12-ft quill resting on a 4-ft cube on which the Constitution is inscribed.

Spencer's Bazaar, *South and New Sts; tel: (302) 734-3441*. Homemade sausages, cakes, bread, preserves and farm produce of the Amish community attract locals and visitors to the auction and flea market. Open Tues and Fri.

Dover Downs International Speedway, *Hwy 13 (1 mile north of Dover); tel: (302) 674-4600*, has NASCAR (stock car) meetings in June and Sept. Harness racing is held at Dover Downs Nov–Mar. Slot machines – more than 500 of them – are a popular draw all year. Open Mon–Sat 0800–0200, Sun 1300–0200.

Dover Air Force Base, *Hwy 113 (2 miles south of Dover); tel: (302) 677-3355 or 3376*. Vintage aircraft significant in aviation history can be seen at the **Air Force Base Museum**, accessed by the base's main gate – security police will direct you. Dover AFB opened in 1941 and has grown to become the eastern US hub of strategic airlift. The world's largest cargo aircraft, the C-5A Galaxy, is often seen flying above Dover, and tours can be made of the plane. The **Aircraft Center** displays artefacts which reflect the history and evolution of the Dover base. Planes which saw service in World War II and Vietnam are exhibited. Among these is the C-47 Gooney Bird, which took part in the D-Day and Arnhem troop drops, the Commando drop in Norway, the Berlin Airlift and the first glider assault across the Rhine. Another aircraft, a C-54M, was built in World War II and used in the Pacific Theatre, then modified to haul coal in the Berlin Airlift. It is the last of its type

History on The Green

William Penn, the English Quaker who founded Pennsylvania, designated The Green at Dover in 1683. It was not until 1722 that the square was laid out according to his orders, and, surrounded by important old buildings, it exudes history.

At the outbreak of the American Revolution in 1776 men mustered here for service and marched to Washington to join the Continental Army. When the Declaration of Independence was read to crowds gathering at The Green in 1776, the people celebrated by publicly setting fire to a portrait of King George III. It was in the Golden Fleece Tavern on The Green that delegates to Delaware's Constitutional Convention met and voted to ratify the US Constitution. The tavern no longer exists.

in existence. The O-2A served in Vietnam and took part in the Bat 21 rescue. A B-17G – one of the few remaining – has been restored to typical World War II configuration. Photography is permitted in the museum, and serious researchers can examine aircraft, documents and artefacts by appointment. Reservations are required for tours. The gift shop sells books, posters and souvenirs. Open Mon–Sat 0900–1600. Admission: free.

Delaware Agricultural Museum, *866 N. du Pont Hwy* (Hwy 13 at *N. State St*); *tel: (302) 734-1618*. Thousands of exhibits in the museum's main hall take the visitor through 200 years of farming history on the Delmarva Peninsula (Delaware, Maryland and Virginia). An typical 1890s village is re-created, with each building presenting 'echoes of the past' – a whistle from a steam train, gossip in the barbershop, children's laughter at the school, hammering at the blacksmith's shop, prayers at the church. The museum, a private, non-profit organisation, has grown tremendously since it opened in 1980. Exhibits include a 1700s log house, early farm machinery, horse-drawn farm wagons and countless artefacts from the domestic and industrial aspects of farm life – many from the 1790s when 90 per cent of all Americans lived by farming, com-

pared with fewer than two per cent today. Among the special events that take place during the year are special studies of developments which have an impact on farming, workshops on 19th-century arts and crafts, living history events with costumed interpreters, lectures, children's programmes and summer camps. Unusual items in the gift shop range from pewterware ornaments to sun bonnets and 19th-century reproduction clothing. Open Mon–Fri 1000–1600 (Jan–Mar), Tues–Sat 1000–1600 (Apr–Dec), Sun 1300–1600. General admission $3, seniors 60-plus and children 10–17 $2, 6–9 $1. Special events admission $5, seniors $3, children 6–17 $2.

John Dickinson Plantation, *Kitts Hummock Rd* (Rte 68 south-east of Dover Air Force Base off Hwy 113); *tel: (302) 739-3277*. This mansion, completed in 1806, and plantation, interprets through costumed guides the daily life of the Dickinson family, their tenants and slaves. John Dickinson, who helped frame the US Constitution and was a signatory to it, grew up in the mansion beside the St Jones River. The original 1740 brick-built house caught fire in 1804 and Dickinson re-built it. A museum shop and visitor centre are on site. Open Tues–Sat 1000–1530, Sun 1330–1630. Closed Sun in Jan and Feb. Admission: donations.

DOVER–OCEAN CITY

This route travels from the capital of Delaware to Maryland's seaside playground, providing an opportunity to see the historic port of Lewes and catch up on some tax-free shopping at Rehoboth Beach. South of Rehoboth, on the narrow strip of land that separates Rehoboth Bay from the Atlantic Ocean, lie the tiny coastal communities of Dewey Beach, Bethany Beach and Fenwick Island, as well as the Delaware Seashore State Park.

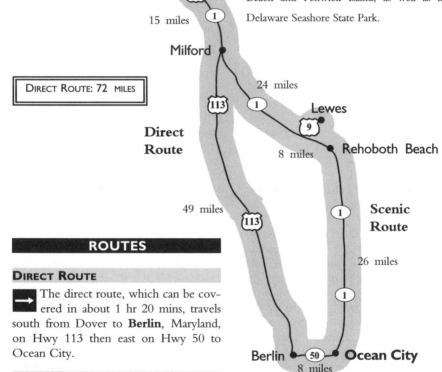

DIRECT ROUTE: 72 MILES

Dover

113

15 miles   1

Milford

24 miles

113   1

Lewes

9

Direct
Route

8 miles   **Rehoboth Beach**

49 miles   113

Scenic
Route   1

26 miles

1

Berlin 50 **Ocean City**

8 miles

296

ROUTES

DIRECT ROUTE

→ The direct route, which can be covered in about 1 hr 20 mins, travels south from Dover to **Berlin**, Maryland, on Hwy 113 then east on Hwy 50 to Ocean City.

SCENIC ROUTE

→ The more interesting route, which adds a mere three miles to the trip, follows Hwy 113 south to **Milford**, then follows Rte 1 for 19 miles to Belltown, where Hwy 9 leads east for 3 miles into **Lewes**. From Belltown, Hwy 1 continues south for 5 miles to **Rehoboth Beach**, where a local loop road also takes in **Dewey Beach** then returns to Hwy 1, which continues south to reach **Ocean City** (see p. 235) in 26 miles.

A brief diversion west from Hwy 113 just south of Dover takes you to **Frederica**, a small town dating from

1770. It is known as the Cradle of Methodism in America, as the New World Chapter of Methodism was established here in the 1780s. **Barratt's Chapel Museum**, a mile north of the town on Hwy 13; *tel: (302) 335-5544,* is open on weekend afternoons.

TOURIST INFORMATION

Tourist Information: Kent County Convention and Visitor Bureau, *9 E. Lockerman St, Dover; tel: (302) 734-1736,* covers the first part of this route, north of Milford.

MILFORD

Tourist Information: Milford Chamber of Commerce, *PO Box 805, Milford, DE 19963; tel: (302) 422-3344.*

Milford is bisected by the Mispillion River, which forms the boundary between Kent and Sussex counties. The town, dating from 1700, grew out of river transportation and shipbuilding businesses.

LEWES

Tourist Information: Lewes Chamber of Commerce and Visitors Bureau, in the *Fisher-Martin House, 120 Kings Hwy, Lewes, DE 19958; tel (302) 645-8073.*

ACCOMMODATION AND FOOD

Lewes has at least half a dozen motels and a number of bed and breakfast inns and homes in the district.

Cape Henlopen Motel, *Savannah and Anglers Rds, Lewes; tel: (302) 645-2828,* is centrally located and convenient for Delaware Bay and the historic district. Moderate. **Captain's Quarters Motel**, *406 Savannah Rd; tel: (302) 645-7924,* open Apr–Nov, has ten units, each with two double beds. Moderate.

Inn at Canal Square, *122 Market St at Front St, Canal Sq., Lewes; tel: (302)* *645-8499.* Expensive late June–early Sept, lower rates rest of year. The property also offers the *Legend of Lewes*, a houseboat with two cabins, two baths and a modern galley. **Anglers Motel**, *110 Anglers Rd and Market St, Lewes; tel: (302) 645-2831,* overlooks Lewes-Rehoboth Canal. Summer rates moderate, lower rest of year.

Bay Moon Bed and Breakfast, *128 Kings Hwy, Lewes; tel: (302) 644-1802;* gourmet breakfast, complimentary wine. Open Apr–Dec, packages and discounts. Moderate. **Wild Swan Inn**, *525 Kings Hwy, Lewes; tel: (302) 645-8550.* Bed and breakfast in a Queen Anne-style house. Moderate. **Blue Water House**, *407 E. Market St; tel: (9302) 645-7832.* Closest Bed and Breakfast to the beach. Children permitted. Open year round. Moderate.

There are 159 campsites with water hook-ups in **Cape Henlopen State Park**; *tel: (302) 645-2103.* Open Apr–Oct; $15 a night.

A quick bite at McDonald's, a relaxed family meal or fine dining amid Victorian antiques – Lewes can provide them all.

Rose and Crown Restaurant and Pub, *108 Second St, Lewes; tel: (302) 645-2373,* an Old English-style establishment serving seafood, steaks and a range of important beers. Moderate. **Gilligan's Harborside Restaurant and Bar**, *Front and Market Sts, Lewes; tel: (302) 645-7866,* offers waterfront dining and canalside bar. Open daily in summer, closed Dec–Feb. Moderate. **The Lighthouse Restaurant**, *Anglers Rd, Lewes; tel: (302) 645-6271.* Overlooks the harbour. Open all year for breakfast, lunch and dinner. The Drawbridge Bar is popular and an outside barbecue is used in season. Moderate to pricey.

SIGHTSEEING

Named after the town in Sussex, England,

297

Lewes is the most northerly of a string of Delaware coastal towns. It is Delaware's oldest settlement – the Dutch arrived in 1631. Many old buildings have survived.

For information of guided and self-guided **tours**, mid June–early Sept, Tues–Sat, contact **Lewes Historical Society**, *110 Shipcarpenter Square and 3rd St; tel: (302) 645-7670*.

Cape Henlopen State Park, *42 Cape Henlopen Drive, Lewes; tel: (302) 645-8983*, One mile east of Lewes is Delaware's largest state park – almost 4000 acres. Delaware Bay and the Atlantic Ocean meet along its shoreline. It has 4 miles of sandy beaches and high dunes, the Pinelands Trail, the Seaside Nature Trail, a picnic pavilion and a quarter-mile fishing pier. Five aquariums provide a close-up look at aquatic life found in the bay and ocean at the Seaside Nature Center. An observation tower put up as part of the coastal defence system in World War II, is open Apr–Oct. Daily vehicle entrance fee payable from late May–early Sept and at weekends in May, Sept and Oct. Nature Center open year round.

De Vries Monument and Fort Site, *Pilottown Rd*. This commemorates the 28 Dutch settlers under de Vries who arrived in 1631, set up the whaling colony of Zwaandendael, and erected a fort. Reputedly they had been there only a few months when a Native American tribe burned down the stockade and massacred all the settlers.

Zwaanendael Museum, *Savannah Rd and Kings Hwy, Lewes; tel: (302) 645-1148*. The richly-ornamented building with carved stonework was constructed in 1931 and based on the City Hall in Hoorn, the Netherlands. It commemorates the 300th anniversary of the first European settlement in Delaware. It has artefacts relating to the original settlement, the 1812 British

bombardment of Lewes, the Cape Henlopen lighthouse and the seafaring heritage and shipwrecks of the area. The name *Zwaanendael* means Valley of the Swans. Open Tues–Sat 1000–1630, Sun 1330–1630. Donations accepted.

Cape May–Lewes Ferry, *Lewes Terminal, Cape Henlopen Drive; tel: (302) 644-6030*. The boarding point for the 16-mile 70-min cruise to the southern tip of New Jersey is near the entrance to Cape Henlopen State Park, a mile east of Lewes. The ferry service began in 1964 when four Virginia ferries were made redundant by the opening of the Chesapeake Bay Bridge-Tunnel. The Delaware River and Bay Authority bought them, added to their number and has since replaced them with new vessels. By Apr 1992 the 20 millionth passenger had been transported across the bay. A daily service operates year round. Single fare for foot passengers over the age of 12 years is $4.50 ($8 return). For cars and pick-ups the one-way charge is $18; off-season (Dec–Mar) $15. Reservations for vehicles recommended at least 24 hrs in advance (processing fee).

The tall ship **Jolly Rover;** *tel: (302) 644-1501*, sets sail for public trips thrice daily in summer from Lewes Memorial Park. **Sunset Cruises**; *tel: (302) 645-8262* depart daily from July–early Sept and at weekends in spring and fall from Fisherman's Wharf, by the Drawbridge. Dinner cruises and dolphin- and whale-watching cruises are also available.

Queen Anne's Railroad, *703 Kings Hwy, Lewes; tel: (302) 644-1720*. Regular trips in a train hauled by a steam locomotive operate from the railway station just west of Stango Park, Lewes, mid June–early Sept. Excursions with a boxed lunch are offered. From May–Fall on weekend evenings, the Royal Zephyr Dinner Train sets out for a 2½ hr ride with

Ferry Rescue

Before the days of fast highways, the quickest route between Wilmington and Philadelphia was by water. The Delaware River and Delaware Bay channels were susceptible to sand shoals, and even in these days of echo sounders and high technology, ships have been known to go aground.

On Memorial Day 1990 (the last Monday in May), the liner *Regent Star* with 900 passengers went aground some 25 miles up river. *MV Delaware*, one of the vessels in the Lewes-Cape May ferry service, made a two-hour off-course voyage to assist the stricken vessel. By skilful positioning in difficult conditions, her crew was able to lead all the liner's passengers to safety.

The Delaware Bay channel and the east–west and north–south sea channels converge just off Cape Henlopen. The Cape Henlopen Light was the second lighthouse in the New World, built between 1763 and 1767. It lasted for nearly 160 years before falling (literally) victim to shifting sands in 1926.

The stone fireplace from the lighthouse was incorporated in the Council Room at Lewes City Hall.

elegant dining and entertainment. Diners are expected to dress appropriately.

Lewes Historical Complex is a group of restored buildings that have been moved to *Shipcarpenter Square* and are maintained by **Lewes Historical Society**, *110 Shipcarpenter Square; tel: (302) 645-7670*. Open mid June–early Sept, Tues–Fri 1000–1500, Sat 1000–1230. Guided tours by appointment. The properties are:

Burton–Ingram House, *Shipcarpenter and Third St*. Built about 1789, this house, the main section of which is constructed of hand-hewn timbers and cypress shingles, was moved to the site from *Second St* in 1962. An original wing destroyed by fire in 1922 has been replaced with a section of a house of the same period. Early portraits, Chippendale furniture and an interesting staircase can be seen. **Doctor's Office**, *Shipcarpenter Sq*. Originally a doctor's office in *Savannah Rd*, this 1850 structure in the Greek Revival style is now on its third site in Lewes. It became a tailor's shop and later a newsagent's, surviving a major fire in 1971. It is now once more fitted out as a turn-of-the-century doctor's office, forming a medical and dental museum.

Next door is the **Plank House**, moved from *Pilottown Rd* in 1963. Although its date is unknown, the log cabin construction is believed to be early Swedish. It has been restored and is presented as an early settler's cabin. Its neighbours are **Ellegood House**, now a gift shop selling hand-crafted items, a **blacksmith's shop** now serving as an extension to the gift shop, and **Thompson's Country Store** in *Third St*, where tickets for the Historical Complex are on sale. Thompson's was built in Thompsonville, Delaware, around 1800, and was run as a country store there by the Thompson family from 1888 to 1962, when it was moved to Lewes and re-opened by the Society. The store has many of its original fittings and looks much as it did when it operated on a full-time basis.

The Hiram Burton House, *Second St and Shipcarpenter Square*. The oldest part of the house is the 18th-century kitchen with furnishings donated from a private collection. In the house is a reading room with works on Delaware history.

Rabbit's Ferry House, *Third St*. Moved to the site from a rural part of

299

Lewes called Rabbit's Ferry in 1967, this house is in two sections, the smaller of which is a one-room farmhouse dating from the early 1700s. It has a sleeping loft, original cypress shingles, woodwork and fireplace panelling. Most of the larger section, added in the 1750s, is original.

The admission charge for the Historical Complex includes the **Lightship Overfalls** on the Lewes-Rehoboth Canal at *Front St*, by the US Lifesaving Station. It was donated to the Historical Society in 1973 by the US Coast Guard. The 1938 sea-going lightship, which formerly saw service off Boston, Massachusetts, was re-named *Overfalls* when it was moved to Lewes, after a lightship which patrolled the entrance to Delaware Bay from 1892–1961. **Cannonball House Marine Museum**, *118 Front St, Lewes; tel: (302) 645-1873*, also included in the tour, was in existence by 1797, and was struck by a cannonball during the British bombardment of Lewes in the War of 1812. The building contains the **Marine Museum**, which has some fascinating nautical exhibits.

1812 Memorial Park, *Front St* (opposite Post Office). This is the site of a War of 1812 defence battery, marked by a granite monument and four large guns. A smaller gun is believed to have come from a pirate vessel. On the lower terrace is a World War I gun, presented by the American Legion in 1930.

REHOBOTH BEACH

Tourist Information: Rehoboth Beach/Dewey Beach Chamber of Commerce (housed in the former railway station), *PO Box 216, 501 Rehoboth Ave, Rehoboth Beach, DE 19971; tel: (302) 227-2233* or *(800) 441-1329*.

A **Park & Ride Transit System**; *tel: (302) 226-2001*, operates from late May to early Sept along Hwy 1 between Lewes and Dewey Beach and into Rehoboth Beach, with stops in the town centre and mile-long boardwalk. The parking lot is guarded and the service runs 24 hrs a day.

Jolly Trolley of Rehoboth, *tel: (302) 227-1197*, runs approximately every 30 mins between Rehoboth and Dewey. **First State Webfooters** hold year-round walking events, starting from the Atlantic Sands Hotel on the boardwalk; *tel: (302) 945-2020*.

Wheelchairs designed for beach use are available for disabled travellers through the **City Hall**; *tel: (302) 227-5534*.

Factory-direct shopping can save large sums on quality goods at **Rehoboth Outlet Center**, *Hwy 1 at Midway, Rehoboth Beach; tel: (302) 644-2600*. There is a wide range of merchandise on sale from many big name stores. A food court offers refreshment and relaxation.

As well as art galleries, antique and craft shops, the in-town shopping mall offers more unusual items like sea shells, embroidered monograms, flags, wickerwork furniture and coins – some from ships wrecked in the area long ago.

ACCOMMODATION AND FOOD

Visitors are recommended to make reservations well in advance, especially in July and Aug, when most motels require a three-day minimum weekend stay. If you have no reservation, you may find greater availability if you arrive on a Thur or Sun. Cottages and apartments should be reserved several months in advance.

Accommodation includes guest houses, inns, hotels, motels, condominiums, apartments, bed and breakfast homes and a retreat centre. The Chamber of Commerce has listings. Hotel chains in Rehoboth Beach are *BW* and *EL*.

There is no shortage of eateries, though

some close in winter. Cheap and budget-priced sub shops, low-cost breakfast shacks with plates piled high, good family fare and restaurants for special occasions – the choice is there.

Blue Moon Restaurant, *35 Baltimore Ave; tel: (302) 227-6515*, is one of the classiest. Its wines have a good reputation. Open daily (Feb–Dec). Another is **Garden Gourmet**, *Hwy 1 and Church St; tel: (302) 227-4747*, set in a Victorian farmhouse. **Sea Horse Restaurant**, *State Rd and Rehoboth Ave; tel: (302) 227-7451*, is open daily, year-round. Fri night seafood buffet. Baystar Dinner Theatre entertainment Mar–Dec. Moderate.

Dogfish Head Brewings and Eats,

320 Rehoboth Ave; tel: (302) 226-BREW, serves home-made beer with your hickory-grilled seafood, steaks and pizzas. Moderate.

Dewey Beach, just south of Rehoboth Beach, also has a good selection of accommodation and restaurants, and is continually growing. Its southern neighbour is the long and narrow **Delaware Seashore State Park**, surrounded by the Atlantic Ocean and Rehoboth Bay. There are more than 400 campsites in the park. The **campground**; *tel: (302) 539-7202*, is open year-round, with full service from mid Mar–mid Nov.

SIGHTSEEING

Of the beach communities along the 24-miles of Delaware's Atlantic coast, Rehoboth Beach is the one with the video games, rides, nightlife and bandstand. The name sounds Biblical – and it is. Rehoboth appropriately enough means 'room enough'. Permanent residents number fewer than 1300, but people swarm in from Washington, DC at the first sign of spring and throughout the hot weather, giving the resort its 'Nation's Summer Capital' tag. This is very much a beach resort, with the accent on things to do. Band concerts on **Rehoboth Ave Bandstand**; *tel: (302) 227-6181*, take place in summer, starting at 2000 on weekend and some weekday evenings.

Bay Fishing and Crabbing Aboard the Sand Dollar; *tel: (302) 945-3345,* runs half-day trips 0800 and 1300. The 49-passenger vessel also runs evening cruises to Lewes along the Lewes-Rehoboth Canal.

Other activities include sailing, parasailing, surfing, biking and nature tours. The **Chamber of Commerce**; *tel: (302) 227-2233,* has details and information on hire of equipment.

301

Maull House Legend

Maull House is not normally open to the public, but it is included in the annual Christmas House Tour organised by Lewes Historical Society on the first Sat in Dec.

The early type of Dutch house in *Pilottown Rd; tel: (302) 645-7670*, is believed to have been built around 1739, and restoration work began in the 1960s. The early woodwork is greatly admired.

Three of the four Maull sons became prominent river pilots in the 18th century – an important job for Lewes men, guiding cargo ships to and from the ports of Wilmington and Philadelphia.

It is said that in 1803 Napoleon Bonaparte's brother, Jerome, with his bride, Betsy, were aboard a ship which had put into Lewes Harbor for repairs one stormy night, and took refuge at Maull House. According to legend, a dinner of roast goose was served, but Betsy would not relax until her own silver candlestick had been fetched from the ship.

WILMINGTON–PHILADELPHIA

On the face of it, there isn't much between Wilmington and Philadelphia except what appears on the map to be 30 community-crowded miles. But the map deceives. The short distance between the two cities is rich in history and interest and the countryside hilly, green and forested. The port of Chester on the Delaware River, about halfway along the direct route, is Pennsylvania's oldest settlement. At Chadds Ford, on the scenic route, Washington's Colonial Army suffered an early setback when it was defeated by the British on the Brandywine Battlefield in 1777.

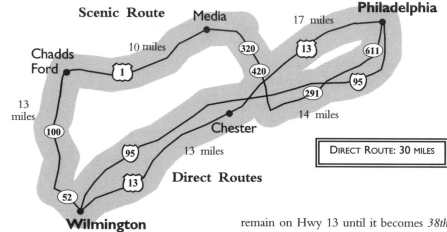

DIRECT ROUTE: 30 MILES

ROUTES

DIRECT ROUTES

➡ The quickest route – about 30 mins – is I-95 north, but Hwy 13, running parallel with the interstate for much of the way, will take you through historic **Chester** and provide a glimpse of riverside life along the way.

From downtown Wilmington follow *10th St* east for ten blocks then head north (turn left) on Hwy 13. Beyond Chester remain on Hwy 13 until it becomes *38th St* on the outskirts of Philadelphia, then turn right on to *Market St*, which leads to City Hall, the Liberty Bell and Old City.

SCENIC ROUTE

▪▪▶ Heading away from the river at Wilmington and following Hwy 1 for much of the way to Philadelphia adds about 10 miles to the journey, which can be covered in around an hour, depending on traffic as one nears Philadelphia. From downtown Wilmington follow Rte 52 west for 3 miles then head north on Rte 100, which intersects with Hwy 1 after 10 miles at **Chadds Ford**. Head east on

Hwy 1 to reach **Media** in a further 10 miles. Just beyond Media, after passing under I-476, turn right on to Rte 320, after 200 yards turn left on to Rte 420, which continues south for 6 miles, passing through **Morton** and **Prospect Park** to reach Rte 291 at **Essington**. Rte 291 east (turn left) passes Philadelphia International Airport and after 7 miles intersects with *Broad St* (Rte 611 north) which leads to City Hall in the heart of **Philadelphia**.

CHESTER

Tourist Information: Delaware County Convention and Visitors Bureau, *200 E. State St, Suite 100, Media, PA 19063; tel: (610) 565-3679 or (800) 343-3983.* Information on events in the region is obtainable on the bureau's 24–hr **Funline**, *tel: (610) 565-3666.* The bureau is the source of information on accommodation, dining and attractions for all places on this route.

ACCOMMODATION

Howard Johnson Hotel, *1300 Providence Rd* (Exit 6 from I-95); *tel: (610) 876-7211.* This hotel has an indoor pool and exercise equipment. Restaurant open Mon–Fri 0600–2300 (from 0700 Sat–Sun). Bar open from 1100. Moderate.

SIGHTSEEING

Established by the Swedish Trading Company, the city was first known as Upland. William Penn arrived here in 1682 to begin colonisation of lands granted to him by King Charles II and re-named it after the city in Cheshire, England. Today, Chester is a busy port and shipbuilding centre.

Penn Memorial Landing Stone, *Front and Penn Sts, Chester.* The stone marks the spot where William Penn landed on 28 Oct 1682.

Morton Homestead, *100 Lincoln Ave, Prospect Park* (Rte 420 south, off Hwy 13, 4 miles east of Chester); *tel: (610) 583-7221.* The log house was built around 1655 by forebears of John Morton, a signatory to the Declaration of Independence. Outdoor exhibits feature the life of Pennsylvania's Swedish pioneers. Open daily. Admission charge.

Caleb Pusey Home, *Landingford Plantation, 15 Race St, Upland* (northern outskirts of Chester); *tel: (610) 874-5665.* The only remaining house in Pennsylvania actually visited by William Penn. It was built in 1683 for the manager of Penn's mill. It stands on 27 acres of original plantation, which it shares with a 1790 log house and a mid-18th-century stone schoolhouse now used as a museum. Open Sat–Sun 1300–1700 (May–Sept). Admission charge.

CHADDS FORD

Tourist Information: as Chester.

ACCOMMODATION AND FOOD

Best Western Concordville Hotel, *Hwys 1 and 322*, 2 miles east of Chadds Ford; *tel: (610) 358-9600 or (800) 522-0070*, offers complimentary continental breakfast. Indoor pool, sauna, health spa. Moderate. **Brandywine River Hotel**, *Hwy 1 and Rte 100, Chadds Ford; tel: (610) 388-1200.* This Victorian-style hotel has 30 rooms and 10 suites with fireplaces. Complimentary breakfast. Moderate.

Chadds Ford Ramada Inn, *Hwys 1 and 202, Glenn Mills*, 2 miles north-east of Chadds Ford; *tel: (610) 358-1700.* Geared mainly for business travellers, the hotel offers complimentary continental breakfast Mon–Fri. Restaurant and tavern. **Chadds Ford Inn**, *Hwy 1 and Rte 100; tel: (610) 388-7361.* Fresh seafood, beef and innovative pasta dishes are the specialities in this

18th-century inn. Wyeth art is on show. Lunch Mon–Sat, dinner daily, brunch Sun; moderate–pricey.

Hank's Place, *Hwy 1 and Rte 100, Chadds Ford; tel: (610) 388-7061.* Old-fashioned, home-style breakfasts, lunches and dinners. Budget. **Pace One Restaurant and Country Inn**, *Thornton and Glenn Mills Rds, Thornton; tel: (610) 459-3702.* Located in a renovated 1740s fieldstone barn, the restaurant serves country cuisine and has an extensive wine list. Open for lunch and dinner. Moderate.

SIGHTSEEING

Barns Brinton House, *Hwy 1, Chadds Ford; tel: (610) 388-7376.* Guides in colonial costume give tours of the brick structure, built around 1714 and now restored as an 18th-century tavern. Open Sat–Sun 1200–1800 (May–Sept). Admission: $2.

Brandywine Battlefield State Park, *Hwy 1, Chadds Ford; tel: (610) 459-3342.* This is where George Washington's Continental Army suffered defeat at the hands of British Gen. William Howe and his troops on 11 Sept 1777. The Visitors Center tells the tale in exhibits and audiovisual presentations. Nearby are farmhouses used as quarters by Washington and Lafayette. Open Tues–Sat 0900–2000, Sun 1200–2000 (late May–early Sept); Tues–Sat 0900–1700, Sun 1200–1700 (rest of year). Admission: $3.50.

Brandywine River Museum, *Hwy 1, Chadds Ford; tel: (610) 388-7601.* The works of three generations of the Wyeth family (see also Wilmington chapter, pp.279–286) can be seen in this Civil War-era grist mill, which opened as an art museum in 1967. The mill, which has a restaurant and a fine museum shop, is set in wildflower gardens and is a venue for craft fairs, concerts, lectures and events. Open daily 0930–1630. Admission: $5.

John Chads House, *Rte 100,* quarter-mile north of Hwy 1; *tel: (610) 388-7376.* The house was built around 1725 for farmer and ferryman John Chads, after whom the village was named. Guides describe 18th-century life and there are demonstrations of baking in a beehive oven. Open Sat–Sun 1100–1800 (May–Sept). Admission: $2.

MEDIA

Tourist Information: details as for Chester, p. 303.

Roughly half-way on our scenic route, Media makes a good stopover, with a choice of accommodation, plenty of eating places and shops, and some interesting attractions.

ACCOMMODATION AND FOOD

McIntosh Motor Inn, *Hwy 1 and Rte 352; tel: (610) 565-5800.* The inn has 84 rooms. Restaurant nearby. Budget. **Media Inn**, *435 E. Baltimore Park* (Hwy 1 and Rte 252); *tel: (610) 566-6500;* restaurant, complimentary continental breakfast. Budget–moderate.

Motel Providence, *Providence Rd* (Rte 252) *and Franklin St; tel: (610) 566-6480.* The motel has 41 rooms, an apartment and 18 self-catering units. Budget–moderate.

D'Ignazio's Towne House, *117 Veterans Sq.; tel: (610) 566-6141.* Filled with memorabilia and antiques, this has been a popular restaurant since 1951, specialising in pasta, steaks and seafood. Nightly piano bar. Moderate.

Peking Restaurant, *6 W. State St; tel: (610) 892-0115.* Chinese cuisine in a cosy café setting in downtown Media. The same management has another Peking Restaurant, specialising in the cuisine of northern China, in the **Granite Run Mall**, *1037 W. Baltimore Pike; tel: (610) 566-4110.* Budget.

Pinocchio's Restaurant, *131 E. Baltimore Pike; tel: (610) 566-4895.* Family restaurant offering pizzas, strombolis (an Italian fast-food concoction), entrées and daily specials. Budget. **Plumstead Inn**, *26 W. State St; tel: (610) 566-2212.* A favourite restaurant and bar since 1960. Open for lunch, dinner and late snacks. Budget. **The Sweet Potato Cafe**, *4 W. State St; tel: (610) 891-1460.* Healthy fare includes baked goods and low-fat and no-fat dishes. Open Mon–Sat. Cheap.

SIGHTSEEING

Delaware County Institute of Science, *11 Veterans Sq; tel: (610) 833-3599* or *833-2985.* Natural history museum featuring minerals, shells, fossils, birds, animals and plantlife of the county and other regions. Open Mon, Thur and Sat 0900–1300. Admission: free.

Franklin Mint Museum, *Franklin Center, Hwy 1; tel: (610) 459-6168.* One of the world's largest private mints displays collections of works in bronze, pewter, precious metals, crystal and porcelain, as well as books, dolls, jewellery and furniture. There are original works by Andrew Wyeth and Norman Rockwell. Open Mon–Sat 0930–1630, Sun 1300–1630. Admission: free.

Ridley Creek State Park, *Sycamore Mills Rd* (off Rte 252 north); *tel: (610) 892-3900.* Hiking, cycling, fishing, sledding and skiing in 2600 acres of woodland and meadows. Picnic sites. Admission: free. Within the park is the **Colonial Pennsylvania Plantation**, a living history museum where farm life of the late 18th century is re-created. Open Sat–Sun 1000–1600 (mid Apr–Nov). Admission charge.

HARRISBURG

Harrisburg is not the most exciting state capital in the US, even if its capitol building, with a dome modelled on that of St Peter's in Rome, is considered by some to be the finest in the land. True, the city has an attractive park, a promenade flanking the Susquehanna River for four miles, some grand public buildings and what is claimed to be the world's longest and widest stone arch bridge, but it remains a workaday city with a population of around 52,000, dependent upon industry, commerce and state politics. The explorer Etienne Brulé passed the site of the city during a trip down the Susquehanna in 1615, but it was more than a century later when the first settler, John Harris, arrived. The town was established by his son in 1785 and it became the state capital in 1812. Harrisburg became the focus of international attention in 1979 when an accident at the Three Mile Island nuclear power station caused concern over the safety of nuclear reactors. Today, most of the area's tourists are attracted by neighbouring Hershey, headquarters of the famous chocolate company with its associated theme park, entertainment centres and resorts.

TOURIST INFORMATION

Harrisburg–Hershey–Carlisle Tourism and Convention Bureau, *114 Walnut St, PO Box 969, PA 17108-0969; tel:* *(717) 232-1377.* **Hershey Information Center**, *300 Park Blvd, Hershey, PA 17033; tel: (800) HERSHEY*, has lots of information on the Hershey chocolate company, theme park, attractions and resorts. (See Sightseeing, p. 310).

ARRIVING AND DEPARTING

Harrisburg lies at the conjunction of a number of major highways, including three interstates. I-81 approaches from West Virginia and Maryland in the south-west and from New York state in the north-east. Hwy 15 approaches from the south-west from Frederick, MD, via Gettysburg, PA (see Washington–Harrisburg, pp. 97–106) – and from New York State in the north. I-76 comes from Pittsburgh in the west and Philadelphia in the east. I-78, coming from New Jersey via Allentown in the east, intersects with I-81 19 miles east of Harrisburg. I-83 provides a fast route from Baltimore in the south.

STAYING IN HARRISBURG

Accommodation

The area embracing Harrisburg and Hershey is rich in accommodation options, with an abundance of motels and inns. Some bed and breakfast homes are to be found in surrounding communities. Hotel chains in the area include: *BW, CI, DI, EL, HJ, Hd, Hn, QI, Ra, Rd, RI, RR, Sh, S8.*

Harrisburg Hotel on Market Square, *23 S. Second St; tel: (717) 234-5021 or (800) 588-0101.* Centrally located, the ten-storey hotel offers free garage parking. It has an indoor pool, exercise equipment, a gift shop and rooftop patio. The restaurant is open daily 0630–1400 and 1700–2200. Bar opens 1130–0100. Moderate.

Harrisburg Hilton and Towers, *1 N. Second St; tel: (717) 233-6000*, is a 15-storey hotel with 341 rooms and suites. Amenities include indoor pool, exercise equipment and valet parking. Restaurant opens daily 0630–2300 and the bar 1100–0100. A shopping arcade links the hotel to the Strawberry Hill Mall. Moderate–expensive.

Hampton Inn, *4230 Union Deposit Rd, Harrisburg* (near Exit 29 from I-83); *tel: (717) 545-9595*, has a heated pool and a coin laundry. Complimentary continental breakfast. Adjoining restaurant open 24 hours. Moderate.

Hershey Lodge, *W. Chocolate Ave and University Dr., Hershey, PA 17033; tel: (717) 533-2211*. This is the chocolate city's family resort, set among 33 rolling acres, with 457 guest rooms, three restaurants, lounge, nightclub, indoor and outdoor pools, exercise facilities, games room, tennis, golf and a cinema. Shuttle service to Hershey attractions and early admission to Hersheypark (see p.310). Open all year round. Moderate–expensive; packages available.

Hotel Hershey, *PO Box 400, Hotel Rd, Hershey, PA 17033; tel: (717) 533-2171*. Just 2 mins by car from Hersheypark, this is the accommodation showpiece of the Hershey enterprises. Completed in 1933, the hotel is styled after the 19th-century grand hotels of the Mediterranean. It has 241 guest rooms, 17 suites and a guest house. Its Circular Dining Room has original stained-glass windows overlooking formal gardens. The Fountain Cafe, opened in 1994 to provide guests with a second dining option for the first time in 60 years, provides a panoramic view of the

town of Hershey. Casual eating is provided by the Club House Cafe, overlooking the first tee of the hotel's nine-hole golf course, and the Iberian Lounge. Recreational facilities include indoor and outdoor pools, jogging and walking trails, cycle rentals, tennis, horse-drawn carriage rides and an exercise room. In winter there are toboggan and sled rentals and cross-country skiing. Pricey; themed weekend packages available.

Radisson Penn Harris, *1150 Camp Hill Bypass, Camp Hill; tel: (717) 763-1117*. The hotel is 1½ miles from downtown Harrisburg on Hwy 11/15 west of the Susquehanna River. Its 250 guest rooms are contained on two sprawling levels and the grounds hold parking spaces for 1000 vehicles. Pool and fitness facility. Two full service restaurants open daily 0630–2200 and there is room service. Bar opens 1500–0200. The **Comedy Club** provides entertainment by stand-up comedians. Moderate–expensive.

Pheasant Field Bed and Breakfast, *150 Hickorytown Rd, Carlisle, PA 17013; tel: (717) 258-0717*. Four guest rooms available in a cosy old farmhouse. Full breakfast; tennis court. Moderate.

Pinehurst Inn, *50 Northeast Dr, Hershey, PA 17033; tel: (717) 533-2603 or (800) 743-9140*. Built by Milton Hershey to provide a home for orphaned boys, the inn has 15 rooms and is non-smoking. Complimentary continental breakfast; lunch available. Budget.

White Rose Motel, *1060 E. Chocolate Ave, Hershey, PA 17033; tel: (717) 533-9876*. This totally non-smoking motel has 24 rooms with refrigerators and private patios or balconies. Heated pool; gift shop. Complimentary coffee, restaurant nearby. Budget.

Hershey KOA, *PO Box 449, Hershey, PA 17033; tel: (717) 367-1179*. Six miles

307

south of Hershey, on Rte 743, the campsite has 160 sites for RVs and tents as well as seven cabins. Pool open daily June–early Sept. Amenities include snack bar, store, TV theatre, recreation room, fishing pond. Open Apr–Oct.

Jonestown KOA, *500 Old Rte 22 E., Jonestown, PA 17038; tel: (717) 865-2526.* Well sign-posted, the campsite is 5 miles south of Exit 1 from I-78. It offers shaded sites for RVs and tents and also has cabins available. Pool open daily May–early Sept. Snack bar, mini-golf, free movies. Free shuttle service to Hersheypark with discounted admission. Open mid Mar–Oct.

Hershey Highmeadow Campground, *Rte 39,* two miles west of Hersheypark; *tel: (717) 566-0902.* The chocolate empire's official campsite covers 55 acres of scenic countryside with 297 sites for RVs and tents. Amenities include an outdoor pool, children's wading pool and a country store. Open year-round.

Eating and Drinking

Travellers are never far from an eating place in this corner of Pennsylvania. Thanks to its tourist attractions, Hershey probably offers the widest and easiest range of choices for visitors.

Alfred's Victorian Restaurant, *38 N. Union St, Middletown; tel: (717) 944-5373.* Italian and continental cuisine, specialising in homemade pastas, steaks and seafood, served in an appropriately furnished Victorian mansion with antique chandeliers. Open Mon–Fri 1130–1400 and 1700–2200, Sat 1700–2200, Sun 1500–2100. Lunch budget–moderate, dinner moderate–pricey.

Berkley's-The Place, *3745 N. 6th St, Harrisburg; tel: (717) 232-4131.* Fresh seafood, veal and steak are specialities here. Open Mon–Sat 1100–1500 and 1630–

2200, Sun 1630–2100. Lunch is cheap to budget, dinner budget–moderate.

Dimitri's, *1311 E. Chocolate Ave, Hershey; tel: (717) 533-3403.* Greek and continental cuisine, with the emphasis on seafood and steak. Open daily 1100–2300. Lunch cheap–budget, dinner budget–pricey.

Union Canal House, *107 S. Hanover St, Union Deposit Village* (near Hershey); *tel: (717) 566-0054.* Angus steaks, crab cakes and roast duckling head the continental menu in this family-owned restaurant, which has three dining rooms. Open Mon–Sat 1600–2200. Budget–pricey.

SIGHTSEEING

Pride of the Susquehanna, *Harrisburg Area Riverboat Society, 116 Pine St, Harrisburg; tel: (717) 234-6500.* Cruises along the Susquehanna River from City Island Park last around 45 mins. Open Sat–Sun 1300–1600 (May and Sept), Tues–Sun 1200–2000 (June–Aug). Fare: $4.75. Two-hour dinner cruises (phone for details): $32.50.

Harrisburg's skyline is dominated by the massive, 272 ft high dome of **The Capitol**, *N. Third and Walnut Sts; tel: (717) 787-6810.* The Italian Renaissance building covers two acres and contains 651 rooms. Daily tours start at the main entrance at *Third* and *State Sts.* Admission: free.

Other public buildings on the 45-acre Capitol Hill site may be visited. Most contain interesting works of art or decorative features. The **South Office Building** contains the striking murals, *Penn's Treaty With the Indians* and *The Industries of Pittsburgh*, by Edward Trumbull.

The State Museum of Pennsylvania, *Third and North Sts,* north of the Capitol Building; *tel: (717) 787-4978.* Part of the Capitol Hill complex, the museum

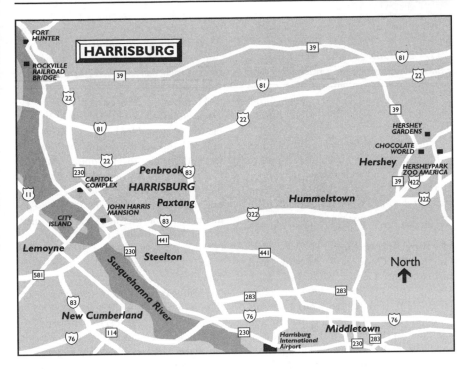

is housed in an imposing six-storey circular building. Four floors of galleries contain exhibits of technology, industry and Indian life, a pioneer country store and natural history and geology displays. There are collections of antique cars and period carriages. There is also a planetarium in which public shows take place Sat–Sun (admission charge). Among the most striking exhibits in the museum is Rothermel's *The Battle of Gettysburg*, one of the largest framed paintings in the world. Open daily. Admission: free.

Fort Hunter Park, *N. Front St*, (6 miles north of downtown Harrisburg); *tel: (717) 599-5751*. The 37-acre park is the site of a fort built by the British in 1754 as unrest mounted at the start of the French and Indian War. The grounds contain buttonwood trees, which were standing at the time of William Penn, and several

19th-century rustic buildings, including a blacksmith's shop and a tavern dating from 1800. The Pennsylvania Canal runs through the park. Also in the park is the **Fort Hunter Mansion**, a Federal-style stone mansion built in sections between 1786 and 1870. The mansion contains exhibits of period clothing, furnishings and toys. Open daily. Admission charge.

Indian Echo Caverns, *Hwy 322, Hummeltown* (10 miles east of Harrisburg); *tel: (717) 566-8131*. Impressive formations of stalagmites and stalactites. Picnic site and playground. Open daily 0900–1745. Admission: $7.

John Harris Mansion, *219 S. Front St, Harrisburg; tel: (717) 233-3462*. Home of the city's founder, the stone mansion houses a collection of historical artefacts and 19th-century furnishings. Open Mon–Sat. Admission charge.

Museum of Scientific Discovery, *Strawberry Sq., Third and Walnut Sts; tel: (717) 233-7969*. About 100 hands-on exhibits demonstrate the principles of and developments in mathematics, science and technology. Open Tues–Fri 0900–1700, Sat 1000–1700, Sun 1200–1700. Admission charge.

Rockville Bridge, *Hwy 22*, 4 miles north of downtown Harrisburg, is said to be the longest and widest stone arch bridge in the world at 3810 ft. It carries four tracks of the Penn Central Railroad's main line across the Susquehanna River.

Hershey Attractions

Hershey's Chocolate World and Information Center, *300 Park Blvd, Hershey; tel: (717) 534-4900* or *(800) HERSHEY*. This is the official visitors centre of Hershey Foods Corporation, and staff here can help you make the most of your stay in the area by providing information on accommodation and dining options, as well as attractions. Visitors to the centre can take a 12-min simulated factory tour ride – with a free sample at the end – and learn about the history and production of chocolate. Chocolate World also encompasses a shopping village, café and full-service restaurant. Open Mon–Sat 0900–1700 (Oct–Apr); daily 0900–2000 (May–Sept). Admission: free.

Founders Hall, *Milton Hershey School, off Hwy 322; tel: (717) 534-3500*. The hall was built as a tribute to the chocolate tycoon Milton Snavely Hershey, whose vision led to the building of a school for needy children. Exhibits tell the story of his philanthropy. Open daily 0900–1700. Admission: free.

Hershey Gardens, *Hotel Rd* (near the Hotel Hershey); *tel: (717) 534-3439*. What began as a 3½-acre plot planned by Milton Hershey's wife Catherine has blos-

somed into ten themed gardens covering 23 acres. They are noted for spectacular displays of blooms, especially tulips and roses. Open daily 0900–1700 (Apr–Oct). Admission: $4.25.

Hershey Museum, *170 W. Hersheypark Dr.; tel: (717) 534-3439*. The life of Milton Hershey, the man who founded the company and the town, is featured in the main exhibit, *Built On Chocolate*. This also displays the development of chocolate bar wrappers, cocoa tins, and the town itself. The museum includes Milton Hershey's original collection of Native American and Pennsylvania German artefacts. Open daily 1000–1700 (Sept–May); daily 1000–1800 (June–Aug). Admission: $4.25.

Hersheypark, *100 W. Hersheypark Dr.* (Rte 743 and Hwy 422); *tel: (717) 534-3090* or *(800) HERSHEY*. Opened in 1907 as an entertainment centre for workers at the Hershey chocolate factory, the 100-acre park encompasses more than 50 rides and attractions, games, shops, cafés and restaurants. Five theatres present Broadway-style revues, and top name entertainers perform everything from country to rock and roll. Entertainment is also provided by a marching band and 15 life-sized Hershey's product characters. Open daily 1000–1800, 2000 or 2200 (mid May–Aug); closes 2300 weekends (July–Aug). Open Sat–Sun 1000–2000 or 2200 (Sept). Admission: $26.45 (concessions for consecutive days and late admission).

ZooAmerica, within Hersheypark; *tel: (717) 534-3860*. This 11-acre wildlife park contains more than 200 animals in five areas depicting five climatic regions of North America. Open daily 1000–2000 (June–Aug); daily 1000–1700 (Sept–May). Admission: $4.75 (included with Hersheypark admission).

HARRISBURG–PHILADELPHIA

This is a fascinating journey, heading from the banks of the Susquehanna River, through the Pennsylvania Dutch Country, where horse-drawn Amish buggies share the road, across the wide rural vistas of Lancaster and Chester counties to Valley Forge and sad memories of a bitter winter for George Washington's army. Then it continues down through a succession of suburbs to the city of Philadelphia.

> DIRECT ROUTE: 109 MILES

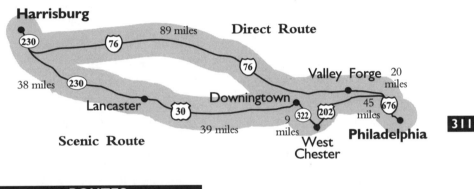

ROUTES

DIRECT ROUTE

➡️ Apart from a few miles at the start, this is an all-interstate route which can be accomplished in 2 hours. From downtown Harrisburg follow Rte 230 (*Front St*) south for 7 miles, then head east on I-76. Continue on I-76 for 100 miles then pick up I-676 for a 2-mile run east into downtown Philadelphia. Take the *15th St* exit and follow *15th St* south to Philadelphia Visitors Center and City Hall.

SCENIC ROUTE

➡️ This route – a distance of 131 miles – can be covered in less than 3 hours, but sightseeing, especially in the Pennsylvania Dutch Country around Lancaster, will distract all but the most worldweary of travellers.

From downtown Harrisburg follow Rte 230 south and continue for 38 miles to **Lancaster**, where you should pick up Hwy 30 east. Follow the highway east for 39 miles to **Downingtown**, where a right turn on to Hwy 322 south leads to **West Chester** in 9 miles. Leave West Chester on Hwy 202 north for 25 miles to **King of Prussia** and **Valley Forge**. To reach **Philadelphia** from King of Prussia pick up I-76 east and continue for 20 miles to I-676 and downtown as above.

VALLEY FORGE

Tourist Information: Valley Forge Convention and Visitors Bureau, *600 W. Germantown Park, Suite 130, Plymouth Meeting, PA 19462; tel: (610) 834-1550 or (800) 441-3549.* **Valley Forge Country Funline**; *tel: (610) 834-8844*, is a 24-hr source of information on what's happening in the area. Valley Forge is best known as the place where hundreds of George Washington's troops died of malnutrition and exposure during the bitterly cold 1777-1778 winter.

ACCOMMODATION AND FOOD

The area's accommodation and dining opportunities are fortified by options available in nearby King of Prussia. Hotel chains in the area include *CI, CM, Hd, HJ. Sh.* **The Court and Plaza**, a huge shopping complex of two malls, *at Rte 202 and N. Gulph Rd, King of Prussia*, has more than a dozen restaurants catering for all tastes and budgets. Open Mon–Sat 1000–2130, Sun 1100–1700. **Comfort Inn at Valley Forge**, *550 W. DeKalb Pike* (Hwy 202), *King of Prussia; tel: (610) 962-0700 or (800) 222-0222*, is a new motel with complimentary continental breakfast, coin laundry, exercise equipment. Moderate.

Sheraton Plaza Hotel, *N. Gulph Rd and First Ave, King of Prussia; tel: (610) 265-1500.* Resort-style hotel with rooms and suites, pool, tennis courts, exercise facilities. Restaurant open daily 0630–2230, bar 1100–0130. Expensive.

Carlucci's, *795 W. DeKalb Pike, King of Prussia; tel: (610) 265-0660.* An Italian-American menu features seafood, steak and home-made pasta. Open Mon–Sat 1100–2200, Sun 1000–2100. Moderate.

Kennedy Supplee Restaurant, *1100, W. Valley Forge Rd* (opposite Valley Forge Historical Park main entrance); *tel: (610) 337-3777.* French and Northern

Italian dishes served in seven elegant dining rooms in a mid-19th century Italianate mansion. Men required to wear jackets. Open Mon–Fri 1130–1400, 1730–2230, Sat 1730–2230. Lunch budget–moderate, dinner moderate–pricey.

Town and Country Grill, *888 Chesterbrook Blvd, Wayne* (close to Valley Forge Historical Park); *tel: (610) 647-6700.* Singing bartenders and a pianist provide entertainment as weekend diners tuck into pasta and fish dishes. On other occasions the atmosphere is agreeably casual. Open Mon–Thur 0630–2200, Fri 0630–2300, Sat 0700–1100, 1200–1430, 1700–2300, Sun 0700–1400, 1700–2100. Budget–moderate.

SIGHTSEEING

The area's biggest attraction is, of course, the **Valley Forge National Historical Park**, *intersection of Valley Forge Rd and Rte 23; tel: (610) 783-1077.* An 18-min film and exhibits in the visitor centre tell the story of the Continental Army's winter encampment ordeal in 1777–78. A map is available for a 10-mile self-guided driving tour of the park. Audio-cassette guides are also on sale and bus tours leave from the visitor centre. Sights include reconstructed military huts, the Artillery Park where the army stored its cannons and the house Washington used as his headquarters. The park contains jogging, cycling and hiking trails and picnic areas. Open daily 0900–1700. Admission: $2 charge to see Washington's headquarters.

Valley Forge Historical Society Museum, *Rte 23; tel: (610) 783-0535.* A collection of items owned by George and Martha Washington as well as Colonial artefacts and military equipment. Open Mon–Sat 0930–1630, Sun 1300–1630. Admission: $1.50.

Mill Grove, *Audubon and Pawlings Rds,*

Audubon (north of Valley Forge National Historic Park); *tel: (610) 666-5593.* Built in 1762, this was the home of the naturalist, John James Audubon. It contains reproductions, original prints, paintings of birds and wildlife and the double-elephant folio of his masterpiece, *Birds of America.* Open Tues–Sat 1000–1600, Sun 1300–1600. The adjoining 170-acre **Audubon Wildlife Sanctuary**, has a marked hiking trail, and is open Tues–Sun 0700–dusk. Admission: free.

LANCASTER

Tourist Information: Pennsylvania Dutch Convention and Visitors Bureau, *501 Greenfield Rd, off Hwy 30, Lancaster, PA 17601; tel: (717) 299-8901.* This is the main source for all information about Lancaster County, with lots of brochures, maps and direct telephone links to local hotels. Its magazine-style *Visitors Guide* is one of the best of its kind. There is a $2 charge to see *There Is A Season*, a 15-min audio-visual introduction to Pennsylvania Dutch Country. Open daily 0900–1700. The **Downtown Visitors Information Center**, is located at *S. Queen and Vine Sts, Lancaster.* The **Tourist Information Center** on *Rte 272* (Exit 21 of the Pennsylvania Turnpike), *Denver; tel: (717) 768-7482,* dispenses information about northern Lancaster County.

The **Mennonite Information Center**, *2209 Millstream Rd, Lancaster, PA 17602; tel: (717) 299-0954,* is mainly an information centre about the Mennonite Church – but also has information on accommodation in inns and Mennonite guest houses. Visitors may watch a 20-min video about the Amish and Mennonite people and their commitment to a way of life based on traditional German rural lifestyles of the age before spontaneous combustion and electricity. Mennonite

guides are on hand to join visitors in their cars and take them on a tour of country roads, craft shops and produce stands. Open Mon–Sat 0800–1700.

ACCOMMODATION

Accommodation is plentiful in Pennsylvania Dutch Country – including town houses, farmhouses, tourist homes, guesthouses and campsites. Hotel chains include *BW, CI, DI, EL, HJ, Hn, QI, Ra, S8.*

Downtown Lancaster's most central accommodation is the **Hotel Brunswick**, *Chestnut and Queen Sts; tel: (717) 397-4801* or *(800) 233-0182.* It has rooms and suites, lounge, health club, bar and coin laundry. The restaurant is open daily 0700–1330 and 1700–2100. Free covered parking. Moderate.

Willow Valley Family Resort, *2416 Willow St Pike* (3 miles south of Lancaster on Rte 222); *tel: (717) 464-2711* or *(800) 444-1714,* has air-conditioned rooms, some non-smoking, restaurants open daily 0600–2100, heated pools, shopping arcade and free laundry facilities. It also has tennis courts, a golf course, fitness centre and spa. Guests receive a free Lancaster County tour kit with maps and brochures and there are free tours of the Pennsylvania Dutch Country. Moderate.

Historic Strasburg Inn, *Rte 896, Strasburg* (8 miles south-east of Lancaster, off Hwy 30); *tel: (717) 687-7691* or *(800) 872-0201.* This colonial-style inn consists of five buildings overlooking scenic Amish country, in the quaint village of Strasburg. The inn has two restaurants, bar, gift shop and heated outdoor pool. Moderate.

Garden Spot Motel, *2291 Hwy 30 E.* (3 miles east of downtown); *tel: (717) 394-4736.* This motel has a coffee shop and ground level rooms with outdoor seating. Restaurants and attractions are within walking distance. Budget–moderate.

313

Candlelight Inn Bed and Breakfast, *2574 Lincoln Hwy E.* (Hwy 30), *Ronks; tel: (717) 299-6005*. Five miles out of Lancaster, this large country home is furnished with Victorian antiques and oriental rugs and surrounded by Amish farmland. Candle-lit breakfast. Moderate.

Equestrian Estates Horse Farm B&B, *221 Schultz Rd* (off Hwy 222, 4 miles south of downtown); *tel: (717) 464-2164*. Suites with Jacuzzis are a feature of this restored 1800s farm and carriage house. Horses and streams surround the farm and Sunday church services are held in a barn. Full breakfast. Moderate.

Witmer's Tavern, *2014 Old Philadelphia Pike (Rte 340); tel: (717) 299-5305*. Lancaster's oldest inn, dating from 1725, has antique-furnished rooms with fireplaces, and beds with traditional quilts. Continental breakfast. Moderate.

Beacon Camping, *Rte 772, off Rte 340*, half-mile north-west of the village of Intercourse; *tel: (717) 768-8775*. Quiet, shady sites for tents and RVs, with full hook-up facilities. Restrooms, showers, playground and game room. Cabins and trailers available. Tours.

Country Acres Family Campground, *20 Leven Rd, Gordonville* (just off Hwy 30 E, between the villages of Paradise and Soudersburg); *tel: (717) 687-8014*, offers shaded sites with full hook-ups and a separate area for tents. Pool, playground, laundry room. Tours.

Flory's Cottages and Campground, *N. Ronks Rd*, (half-mile north of Hwy 30 E, 1 mile south of Rte 340); *tel: (717) 687-6670*. More than 70 sites with full hook-ups. Rooms (some non-smoking), furnished cottages and mobile homes available, farmland tours.

Old Mill Stream Camping Manor, *2249 Hwy 30 E.* (near Dutch Wonderland); *tel: (717) 299-2314*. About 2½ miles east of Lancaster, this large campsite has shaded sites with modern facilities, pavilion with sun deck, playground and games room.

EATING AND DRINKING

Lancaster and the surrounding areas enjoy a wide range of eating places, offering everything from wholesome Amish fare to high continental cuisine. Amish restaurants do not serve alcohol.

Amish Barn Restaurant, *Rte 340* between Bird-in-Hand and Intercourse; *tel: (717) 768-8886*. Traditional Pennsylvania Dutch cuisine – including bread and apple dumplings and home-baked pies – served family-style or á la carte at breakfast, lunch and dinner. Open daily (Apr–Dec), Fri–Sun (Jan–Mar). Moderate.

Bird-in-Hand Family Restaurant, *2760 Old Philadelphia Pike (Rte 340), Bird-in-Hand; tel: (717) 768-8266*. Pennsylvania Dutch cooking served at breakfast, lunch and dinner buffets. Open Mon–Sat 0600–2000. Budget.

Bube's Brewery and The Catacombs Restaurant, *102 N. Market St, Mount Joy (*11 miles west of Lancaster on Rte 230); *tel: (717) 653-2056*. Since this is the only brewery in the US to have survived the Prohibition years intact you might expect the theme to be G-men and gangsters. In fact, it's medieval, with serfs, wenches and minstrels – the ambience influenced, no doubt, by the fact that the restaurant is in vaulted catacombs 40 ft below ground. Entertainment accompanies dinners of steak and seafood. Two other restaurants in the brewery, which may be toured, offer more conventional service. Open daily. Budget–pricey.

Family Style Restaurant, *Rte 30 E*, (3 miles east of Pennsylvania Dutch CVB); *tel: (717) 393-2323*, serves buffet breakfast and lunch and an all-you-can-eat dinner.

Beer and wine available. Open daily 0800–2000. Budget–moderate.

Groff's Farm Restaurant, *650 Pinkerton Rd, Mount Joy; tel: (717) 653-2048*. The reputation of this family-run restaurant, located in a 1756 farmhouse, is widespread. The cuisine is Mennonite, with home-cured ham, fresh seafood and home-baked pastries. Wines and spirits available. Open Tues–Fri 1130–1330 and 1700–1930; Sat 1130–1330, dinner sittings 1700 and 2000. Reservations essential for dinner, advisable for lunch. Lunch budget, dinner moderate–pricey. **Washington House**, at the Historic Strasburg Inn, Strasburg (see p.313)*; tel: (717) 687-7691* or *(800) 872-0201*. Fine, fireside dining in Colonial-style surroundings. Specialities include steaks, crab cakes and wild game. Open Mon–Sat 0700–1400, 1700–2100; Sun 0700–2100. Bar open daily 1130–2100. Moderate–pricey.

ENTERTAINMENT

Amish Experience Theatre and Homestead, *Rte 340* at Plain and Fancy Farm between Bird-in-Hand and Intercourse; *tel: (717) 768-8400*, is a dinner theatre with a difference. Before or after a traditional family-style meal, diners watch a spectacular multi-media production of *Jacob's Choice*, an emotional examination of Amish life. Open daily.

Dutch Apple Dinner Theatre, *510 Centerville Rd, at Rte 30 W, Lancaster; tel: (717) 898-1900*. Full-length Broadway shows with professional performers and a candle-lit buffet, feature in this intimate theatre. Performances Tues–Sun, matinées Wed, Thur, Sat.

Rainbow Dinner Theatre, *3065 Lincoln Hwy E. (Hwy 30), Paradise; tel: (800) 292-4301*. Buffet-style food is served at the table during professional performances of comedies and musicals.

Matinées Mon–Fri, evening shows Sat–Sun.

Fulton Opera House, *12 N. Prince St, Lancaster; tel: (717) 397-7425*. This 19th-century theatre, a National Landmark, is said to be the oldest in continuous use in the country. Recently restored, it now houses the Actors' Company of Pennsylvania, The Fulton Theatre Company, the Lancaster Opera and the Lancaster Symphony Orchestra.

Sight and Sound Entertainment Centre, *Rte 896, Strasburg; tel: (717) 687-7800*. The nation's largest Christian entertainment theatre seats nearly 1400 people, boasts a 100-ft stage and surround-sound and features concerts and lavish shows with spectacular effects and live animals based on Bible stories.

SHOPPING

Few visitors will be able to resist the temptation to window-shop, at least among the plethora of arts, crafts and antique shops in Lancaster County. Amish quilts, dolls and furniture are popular buys, especially as most establishments can arrange shipment home. The area also has a number of farm and antique markets and retail outlets.

Amish Barn Gift Shop, *Rte 30 between Bird-in-Hand and Intercourse; tel: (717) 768-3220*, has a wide selection of gifts, handicrafts, quilts, wall hangings and collectables. Open daily 0800–2000.

Amish Country Traditions, *442 Strasburg Pike, Lancaster; tel: (717) 687-9270*. Amish quilts of all styles and sizes are displayed in an old farmhouse, also crafts and furniture. Open Mon–Sat 1000–1700.

Amishland Prints, *3471 Old Philadelphia Pike, Intercourse; tel: (717) 768-7273* or *(800) 999-9660*. Original drawings and prints depicting Amish life and landscapes by the artist and folklorist, Xtian Newswanger.

315

Bird-in-Hand Farmers' Market, *Rte 340, Bird-in-Hand; tel: (717) 393-9674*, sells meat, baked goods, homemade articles, clothing and shoes. Snack counter. Open Fri–Sat year round, plus Wed (Apr–Nov) and Thur (July–Oct).

Central Market, *Penn Sq., downtown Lancaster; tel: (717) 291-4739*. The oldest publicly owned farmers' market in the US, selling local produce, crafts and flowers. One hour free parking at *N. Prince St* parking garage. Open Tues, Fri 0600–1630, Sat 0600–1400.

Country Market at Intercourse, *3504 Old Philadelphia Pike, Intercourse; tel: (717) 768-8058*, is the place where local Amish families sell handmade items and furniture. Xtian Newswanger's Amishland prints also available.

Dutchland Quilt Patch, *The Village of Dutch Delights, Hwy 30 E., Soudersburg; tel: (717) 687-0534*. More than 250 quilts and wall hangings displayed, together with pillows, dolls and other crafts. Quilting demonstrations. **Old Country Store**, *3510 Old Philadelphia Pike, Intercourse; tel: (717) 768-7107*, has one of the largest quilt selections in the area and local crafts.

Olde Mill House Shoppe, *105 Strasburg Pike, Lancaster; tel: (717) 299-0678*, sells folk art, 18th-century furnishings, lighting, pottery and country accessories.

Rockvale Square Outlets, *Hwy 30 east and Rte 896; tel: (717) 293-9595*. Brand name goods, including designer fashions and home accessories, at 30–70% below normal retail prices. Open Mon–Sat 0930–2100, Sun 1200–1700.

Tanger Outlet Center at Millstream, *Hwy 30 east*, 2½ miles east of Pennsylvania Dutch CVB Information Center; *tel: (717) 392-7202*. More stores offering discounts of 30–70%. Open Mon–Sat 0930–0900, Sun 1100–1800.

SIGHTSEEING

Tours

Aerial Tours; *tel: (717) 394-6570*, makes a 30-mile tour by light aircraft over some of the most beautiful farmland in Lancaster County, with views of Amish farms. Tours daily 0900–1700.

Amish Country Tours, *Plain and Fancy Farm, Hwy 340 E.; tel: (717) 392-8622*. Air-conditioned, guided bus tours of the county's back roads with an opportunity to meet Amish people. Tickets also available at local hotels. Tours daily. **Red Rose Excursions**, *Hwy 30 E. between Oregon Pike and Hwy 222; tel: (717) 397-3175*. Plain People guides meet visitors in their cars for a personal tour of the back roads, where they can meet members of Amish, Mennonite and Brethren communities. Tours Mon–Sat 0900–2100.

Aaron and Jessica's Buggy Rides, *Plain and Fancy, Rte 340 E. between Bird-in-Hand and Intercourse; no tel*. Country rides in Amish and Mennonite carriages driven by members of local communities; Mon–Sat. **Abe's Buggy Rides**, *Rte 340, ½ mile east of Rte 896; no tel*. Tours of Amish country in an Amish family carriage, Mon–Sat 0800–dusk. Admission: $10. **Ed's Buggy Rides**, *Rte 896, Strasburg; tel: (717) 687-0360*. A 3-mile buggy ride through Amish farmlands and scenic back roads. Admission: $6.50.

Historic Lancaster Walking Tour, *Downtown Visitor Center, S. Queen and Vine streets, Lancaster; tel: (717) 392-1776*. Costumed guides lead 90-min tours through the city's historic district. Tours Mon–Sat 1000 and 1330, Sun 1330 (Apr–Oct); by appointment during rest of year. Admission: $5.

Attractions

The Amish Village, *Rte 896, 2 miles*

north of Strasburg; tel: (717) 687-8511. Guided tours of an Amish house, blacksmith's shop, one-room schoolhouse, operating smokehouse and waterwheel. There are farm animals, a picnic area and gift shops. Open daily 0900–1700 (spring and autumn), 0900–1800 (summer). Admission: $5.50.

Choo–Choo Barn, *Rte 741 E., Strasburg; tel: (717) 687-7911*. A miniature layout of Lancaster County, with an extensive model rail system and animated scenes, including a house fire and a parade. Railroad Supermarket and speciality shops nearby. Open daily 1000–1700 (Apr–Dec). Admission: $3.

Demuth Foundation Museum, *114 E. King St, Lancaster; tel: (717) 299-9940*. The restored 18th-century home and studio of the modernist artist Charles Demuth encompasses a gift shop and the nation's oldest operating tobacconist's store, opened in 1770. Admission: free.

Dutch Wonderland, *2249 Hwy 30 east, Lancaster; tel: (717) 291-1888*. Popular amusement park with 22 rides, botanical gardens, shows and performances by the Great American High Diving Team. Open daily end May–early Sept; weekends spring and autumn. Admission charge. **Gast Classic Motorcars Exhibit**, *421 Hartman Bridge Rd, Rte 896, Strasburg; tel: (717) 687-9500*. Nostalgic self-indulgence for car buffs, this is a changing exhibition of more than 50 antique, classic, high-performance and sports cars, with lots of chrome and fins. Open daily 0900–2100 (end May–early Sept), Sun–Thur 0900–1700, Fri–Sat 0900–2100 (Sept–May). Admission: $6.

Hans Herr House, *1849 Hans Herr Dr., Willow St* (off Hwy 222, 5 miles south of Lancaster); *tel: (717) 464-4438*. Considered the finest example in North America of medieval-style German architecture, the house dates from 1719 and appears in several paintings by the artist Andrew Wyeth (see also p.304), who was descended from the Herr family. Today, it contains the Lancaster Mennonite Historical Society's visitor centre. There are 45-min tours of house and grounds. Open Mon–Sat 0900–1600 (Apr–Nov). Admission: $3.50.

Heritage Center Museum, *Penn Sq, Lancaster; tel: (717) 299-6440*. The Old City Hall now houses examples of the work of local craftsmen through the ages – from the Pennsylvania long rifle, to clocks and furniture. Open Tues–Sat 1000–1600. Admission: donation.

Landis Valley Museum, *2451 Kissel Hill Rd, Lancaster* (off Oregon Pike); *tel: (717) 569-0401*. Some 15 historical buildings, including a country store and a farmstead, show what 19th-century rural life was like in Pennsylvania Dutch country. Articles produced during demonstrations of spinning, weaving, tinsmithing and other crafts are sold in the museum gift shop. Open Tues–Sat 0900–1700, Sun 1200–1700 (May–Oct). Admission: $7.

Lancaster Newspapers Newseum, *28 S. Queen St, Lancaster; tel: (717) 291-8600*. An exhibition of news presentation past and present, with displays of printing equipment and old and new production methods. Freely accessible for self-guided tours.

National Toy Train Museum, *Paradise Lane* (off Rte 741), *Strasburg; tel: (717) 687-8976*. Models of antique and modern trains are put through their paces on five operating layouts, and hundreds of locomotives and rolling stock are exhibited. Open daily 1000–1700 (May–Oct and Christmas week), Sat–Sun 1000–1700 (Apr and Nov–mid Dec). Admission: $3.

People' Place, *3513 Old Philadelphia Pike, Intercourse; tel: (717) 768-7171*. The

317

beliefs and lifestyle of the Mennonite, Amish and Hutterite people are interpreted in this cultural centre. It features a 30-min audio-visual presentation, hands-on museum, bookshop and an arts and crafts gallery. Open Mon–Sat 0930–2130 (end May–early Sept); Mon–Sat 0930–1700 (rest of year). Admission: $3.50.

Railroad Museum of Pennsylvania, *Rte 741, Strasburg* (opposite Strasburg Rail Road station); *tel: (717)687-8628*. The museum is home to about 80 locomotives, coaches and freight cars displayed. There are colourful displays of uniforms and artefacts. Open Mon–Sat 0900–1700, Sun 1200–1700. Closed Mon Nov–Apr.

Strasburg Rail Road, *Rte 741, Strasburg; tel: (717) 687-7522*. Said to be the oldest short line in the US, the 9-mile run from Strasburg to Paradise is covered by a steam locomotive pulling antique wooden coaches. Passengers can lunch in the dining car or buy box lunches at the station before boarding. Departures daily every 30 mins (Apr–Oct), Sat–Sun only (Nov–Mar). Closed first two weeks in Jan. Round trip fare: $7.

Wheatland, *1120 Marietta Ave* (Rte 23, 1½ miles west of downtown Lancaster)*; tel: (717) 392-8721*. This restored 1828 Federal mansion was the home of James Buchanan, 15th President of the US. The house is furnished exactly as it was during his lifetime. Open daily 1000–1600 (Apr–mid Dec). Admission: $3.50.

WEST CHESTER

Tourist Information: Chester County Tourist Bureau, *601 Westtown Rd, Suite 170. West Chester, PA 19382; tel: (610) 344-6365*. A quiet university and residential city, West Chester is close to three important Revolutionary War sites: Brandywine, Paoli and Valley Forge.

Abbey Green Motor Lodge, *1036 Wilmington Pike; tel: (610) 692-3310*, has cottages with kitchenettes. Restaurant nearby. Budget.

Duling-Kurtz House and Country Inn, *146 S. Whitford Rd, Exton; tel: (610) 524-1830*. Continental breakfast is included at this 15-room inn. The formal restaurant noted for its continental cuisine. Moderate–expensive.

Holiday Inn West Chester, *943 S. High St; tel: (610) 692-1900*. This hotel has rooms and suites, a pool and children's activities. Room service, restaurant open daily 0630–2200; bar 1600–0200. Moderate.

Dillworthtown Inn, *1390 Old Wilmington Pike; tel: (610) 399-1390*, is a restored colonial house now serving as a restaurant specialising in seafood and game dishes. The wine cellar is said to be stocked with 14,000 bottles. Open Mon–Sat 1730–2200, Sun 1500–2100. Moderate–pricey.

Lenape Inn, *junction of Rtes 52 and 100; tel: (610) 793-2005*, offers relaxed dining in a restaurant with chandeliers, vaulted ceilings and views of the Brandywine Creek. Serves continental cuisine. Open Mon–Sat 1130–2200, Sun 1400–2100. Lunch budget–moderate, dinner moderate–pricey.

Magnolia Grill, *West Goshen Shopping Center, 971 Paoli Pike; tel: (610) 696-1661*, is the place for a family meal, with seafood, sandwiches and omelettes in a jolly, New Orleans setting. Open Mon–Thur 0900–2100, Fri–Sat 0900–2130, Sun 0900–1700. Cheap breakfast, lunch cheap–budget, dinner cheap–moderate.

Book-lovers will not want to miss **Baldwin's Bookbarn**, *865 Lenape Rd; tel: (610) 696-0816*. Some 300,000 used and rare books are housed in a stone barn dating from 1822.

318

Anyone returning to Philadelphia after a gap of a few years will be gratified to find some impressive improvements. The Birthplace of the Nation is presented in the film Independence, shown at the visitor centre of the Independence National Historical Park. Visitors are taken through every stage of the development and emergence of an independent nation with the signing of the Declaration and of the Constitution.

The park – known as America's Most Historic Square Mile – covers a four-block area which includes Independence Hall, where the Declaration was signed, Carpenters' Hall, site of the first Continental Congress in 1774, and the Liberty Bell, that symbol of US freedom, and many other historic attractions.

Penn's Landing, a Delaware River waterfront park, with ice skating, historic ships, restaurants and nightclubs, is where William Penn landed. He went on to found the state, having received the title to the land from King Charles II in 1681. The following year he named the nation's first planned city and port Philadelphia – 'City of Brotherly Love'.

The city was the nation's capital from 1791–1800, but as Washington and New York City became major political and commercial centres, Philadelphia was elbowed out and went into decline.

W.C. Fields commented wryly that he had 'spent a month in Philadelphia one day'. That sort of reputation took a lot of living down. Now the city has pulled itself up by the bootlaces, prospered, invested in its future and put itself on the tourism map for its entertainments and award-winning restaurants as well as its history.

TOURIST INFORMATION

Philadelphia Visitors Center, *16th St and John F. Kennedy Blvd; tel: (215) 636-1666.* Open daily, except Christmas Day, 0900–1700 (to 1800 in summer). For information on hotel packages and a calendar of events write to **Philadelphia Visitors Center**, *1515 Market St, Suite 2020, Philadelphia, PA 19102; tel: (800) 537-7676.*

Independent National Historical Park Visitors Center, *3rd and Chestnut St; tel: (215) 597-8974.* Open daily 0900–1700. For its foreign language hotline and emergency translation service, available 24 hours a day, *tel: (215) 879-5248.*

ARRIVING AND DEPARTING

Airport
Philadelphia International Airport, *tel: (215) 937-6800,* 8 miles from Center City, is served by major airlines, with 1200 flights daily to more than 100 cities in the US and abroad. The airport has four **Thomas Cook Currency Services** locations; *tel: (800) CURRENCY.*

Airport Rail Line operates to and

319

from Center City daily every half-hour 0530–2325. Fare: $5. The journey takes about 25 mins from Center City (*Market East, Suburban* and *30th St Stations*). Taxi fare between the airport and Center City is $20.

By Car

Philadelphia is accessible by the Pennsylvania Turnpike (I-76), the New Jersey Turnpike and the Delaware Expressway (I-95).

By Boat

Riverbus; *tel: (800) 634-4027.* Passenger ferry services run between Philadelphia and Camden, New Jersey. Ferries leave every 30 mins from Penn's Landing and the Camden waterfront next to New Jersey State Aquarium. Fare $2 one way.

By Train

SEPTA (Southeastern Pennsylvania Transportation Authority); *tel: (215) 580-7800,* is a convenient means of getting around the city and suburbs. The authority also runs subway services, commuter lines and buses. Exact fare is required – the basic fare on most routes is $1.60, transfers $0.40. You can buy tokens – $5.75 for five, $11.50 for ten, or a $5 Daypass which gives unlimited travel for a day on all city vehicles, plus one way on the airport line. Senior citizens ride buses and streetcars free and pay $1 on trains.

Philadelphia is a hub of **Amtrak's** North-east Corridor; *tel: (800) USA-RAIL,* with services to and from Boston, New York, Baltimore and Washington and connections to points west and east.

Parking in downtown Philadelphia is both difficult and expensive. The **PHLASH Downtown Loop** is a SEPTA (see 'By Train', above) initiative providing visitors with a safe and easy way to get to shops, restaurants, hotels, and attractions of the downtown area in a distinctive purple tourist bus. Cost: $1.50 for a one-way ride. One-day passes are available for $3 from selected hotels and attractions or on boarding the bus. PHLASH buses have low floors and ramps, and each can take two wheelchairs. The service runs daily in summer, 1000–1800, and six days a week the rest of the year.

Getting a taxi in the daytime rarely presents a problem, but the night-time service is less reliable. Taxi companies include **Yellow Cab**; *tel: (215) 922-8400,* **Quaker City Cab**, *tel: (215) 238-9500.* Cost is a basic $2 and between $1.80 and $2.30 per mile.

Accommodation

Hotel chains in Philadelphia's **Center City** (the area bordered by the Delaware and Schuylkill Rivers, and *Vine* and *South Sts*), and its suburbs, include *BW, CI, DI, ES, Hd, HJ, Hn, Ma, RC, Rd, Rm, Sh, TL.*

It is not easy to find budget-priced accommodation in Philadelphia, although it is worth inquiring about hotels' discount packages.

The **Bank Street Hostel**, *32 S. Bank St; tel: (215) 922-0222,* charges $15 a night plus a small charge for the compulsory sleeping bag liner.

Antique Row Bed and Breakfast, *341 S. 12th St; tel: (215) 592-7802,* offers good value and full breakfast in a 180-year-old townhouse. Budget–Moderate.

Bag and Baggage Bed and Breakfast, *338 S. 19th St*, one block south of *Rittenhouse Sq.* Moderate.

Omni Hotel at Independence

PHILADELPHIA

DELAWARE

95

2nd St

3rd St

Spring Garden St

4th St

Callowhill St

5th St

Ben Franklin Bridge

676

Christopher Columbus Blvd

PENN'S LANDING

COLUMBUS MEMORIAL

VIETNAM WAR MEMORIAL

MUSEUM & INDEPENDENCE SEAPORT

95

Race St

Vine St

ARCEN THEATRE

Arch St

Market St

BISHOP WHITE HOUSE

POWEL HOUSE

PHYSICK KEITH HOUSE

KOSCIUSZKO NATIONAL MEMORIAL

Front St

6th St

7th St

FRANKLIN'S GRAVE

U.S. MINT

Franklin Square

NAT MUS. OF AMERICAN JEWISH HISTORY

INDEPENDENCE CONGRESS, OLD CITY & PHILOSOPHICAL HALLS

ARMY-NAVY MUSEUM

NEW HALL

Dock St

3rd St

4th St

Pine St

EDGAR ALLEN POE NATIONAL HIST. SITE

North

WHYY/FORUM THEATRE

U.S. FEDERAL BUILDING

LIBERTY BELL

NORMAN ROCKWELL MUSEUM

Independence National Historical Park

TODD HOUSE

Washington Square

TOMB OF THE UNKNOWN SOLDIER

SOCIETY HILL PLAYHOUSE

5th St

8th St

9th St

10th St

11th St

Walnut St

Spruce St

Locust St

AFRO-AMERICAN HIST. & CULT. MUSEUM

CHINESE CULTURAL CENTRE

GRAFF HOUSE

Chestnut St

Sansom St

Locust St

HENRY GEORGE HOUSE

Lombard St

South St

321

GREYHOUND BUSTERMINAL

READING TERMINAL MARKET

FORREST THEATRE

PHILADELPHIA ARTS BANK

PENNSYLVANIA CONVENTION CENTRE

Filbert St

12th St

13th St

10th St

Noble St

Hamilton St

11th St

12th St

13th St

14th St

QUAKER INFORMATION CENTRE

CITY HALL

TEMPLE CENTRE CITY

ACADEMY OF MUSIC

MERRIAM THEATRE

UNIVERSITY OF THE ARTS

CATHEDRAL OF SAINTS PETER & PAUL

Race St

Cherry St

Arch St

15th St

16th St

17th St

FREE LIBRARY OF PHILADELPHIA

ACADEMY OF NATURAL SCIENCES MUSEUM

MUSEUM OF AMERICAN ART OF THE PENNSYLVANIA ACADEMY OF THE FINE ARTS

Logan Circle

Vine St

Mt Vernon St

Green St

Spring Garden St

Hamilton St

Callowhill St

GOLDIE PALEY GALLERY AT MOORE COLLEGE OF ART

FRANKLIN INSTITUTE SCIENCE MUSEUM

STOCK EXCHANGE

Winter St

18th St

19th St

20th St

Rittenhouse Square

CURTIS INST. OF MUSIC

PLAYS & PLAYERS

CIVIL WAR LIBRARY & MUSEUM

TEMPLE THEATRE

ACADEMY OF VOCAL ARTS

ROSENBACH MUSEUM & LIBRARY

RODIN MUSEUM

The Benjamin Franklin Parkway

Pennsylvania Av

Fairmount Park

Eakins Oval

676

Market St

JFK Blvd

Ludlow St

Sansom St

Chestnut St

Walnut St

Locust St

Spruce St

Delancey St

Lombard St

South St

Bainbridge St

Fitzwater St

21st St

22nd St

23rd St

Arch St

24th St

25th St

26th St

Pine St

30th ST STATION

SCHUYLKILL

PHILADELPHIA MUSEUM OF ART

Eakins Oval

500 m

500 yds

0

0

Park, *401 Chestnut St; tel: (215) 925-0000,* is a Four-Diamond hotel in Independence National Historic Park. Each room has a view of the park. Expensive–pricey.

Penn's View Inn, *Front and Market Sts; tel: (215) 922-7600.* European-style hotel overlooking Delaware River; 27 rooms, some with Jacuzzi and fireplace. The award-winning restaurant has a large wine bar. Weekend packages available. Moderate–pricey.

Thomas Bond House, *129 S. 2nd St; tel: (215) 923-8523.* Restored guesthouse, circa 1769, in Independence National Historical Park owned by the National Parks Service. Price includes continental breakfast weekdays, full breakfast weekends. Moderate–expensive.

The Latham, *135 S. 17th St; tel: (215) 563-7474,* is a Center City hotel with well-appointed rooms with newspaper in the morning. Expensive–pricey, but offers weekend packages and off-season rates.

Holiday Inn Express Midtown, *1305 Walnut St; tel: (215) 735-9300.* Half the guest rooms are for non-smokers at this Three-Diamond hotel. Free deluxe breakfast bar. Moderate.

Radisson Hotel Philadelphia Airport, *500 Stevens Dr.; tel: (610) 521-5900.* One of the newer airport hotels with rooms and mini-suites, and a quick and reliable free shuttle service between the hotel and airport, where a frequent rail service will get you into the city in 20 min. Free parking. Expensive.

Eating and Drinking

Visitors to Philadelphia are utterly spoilt for choice, with a whole atlas of cuisines offered by dozens of restaurants, especially in the **Waterfront** and **Historic District**, the business district and *South St.*

A Philadelphia institution for more than 130 years and the city's oldest seafood house is the **Old Original Bookbinder's Restaurant**, *125 Walnut St; tel: (215) 925-7027.* It serves live lobsters, fresh fish and meat. The valet parking is free at lunchtime. Moderate–pricey.

Spaghetti Warehouse, *1026 Spring Garden St; tel: (215) 787–0784.* A 15-layer baked lasagna, more than 12 different pastas, and veal Parmagiana are among the affordable choices. Eat in or meals to go. Budget.

Hikaru, *607 S. 2nd St; tel: (215) 627-7110,* one of a number of good Japanese restaurants in town. Specialities include sushi, tempura, sukiyaki and teriyaki. Moderate.

Elephant and Castle Pub and Restaurant (at Holiday Inn Select), *18th and Market Sts; tel: (215) 751-9977.* A variety of British fare and 18 beers on draught. Open from breakfast to dinner, with a late-night menu available, too. Moderate.

Bassett's Original Turkey, *Gallery Food Court, 9th and Market Sts; tel: (215) 574-1690.* The bird, not the country. They oven-roast them and carve succulent slices for meals or well-stuffed sandwiches. Freshly baked breads sliced to order. Eat in or take out. Budget.

Tang's, *429 South St; tel: (215) 928-0188.* Award-winning Chinese restaurant with fresh flowers, candlelight and a good wine list with your orange chicken, fresh lobster or satay duck. Budget–moderate.

Moriarty's Restaurant and Bar, *1116 Walnut St; tel: (215) 627-7676.* The ads say this is the Best Kept Irish Secret in Town, but the food is mostly good American wings and burgers. However, they're big on beer which is served at the 60 ft bar. Budget.

New Delhi Indian Restaurant and Sweets, *4004 Chestnut St; tel: (215) 386-*

1941. Traditional North Indian cuisine with tandoori specialities. Daily lunch and dinner buffets. Budget–moderate.

Happy Roaster, *118 S. 16th St at Sansom St; tel: (215) 563-1481.* offers American, continental and Russian fare, and a claim to the best-stocked bar in town. Moderate–pricey.

Brigid's, *726 N. 24th St; tel: (215) 232-3232.* The menu includes Duck Chambord, Bouillabaise Ostendaise and a splendid collection of Belgian beers. Moderate–expensive.

Slim Cooper's Lounge and Restaurant, *6402 Stenton Ave; tel: (215) 224-0509.* The food is American and Southern/Soul. Live jazz Fri 1700–2100. Budget.

Jim's Steaks, *400 South St; tel: (215) 928-1191.* They've turned steak rolls into an art form in this art deco-style cafeteria. Cheap.

Money

Thomas Cook Currency Services, *1800 John F. Kennedy Blvd; tel: (215) 563-5544.* See also under 'Airport', p.319.

ENTERTAINMENT

High quality professional theatre is found at a number of Philadelphia venues, and the city is especially renowned for its music.

The **Philadelphia Orchestra** under Wolfgang Sawallisch, Peter Nero and the **Philly Pops** and the **Opera Company of Philadelphia** – with which Pavarotti and other top stars frequently appear – all perform at the **Academy of Music**, *Broad and Locust Sts; tel: (215) 893-1999 or 735-7506.* The **Pennsylvania Ballet**; *tel: (215) 551-7000,* also performs at this magnificent opera house.

The **Forrest Theatre**, *1114 Walnut St; tel: (215) 923-1515,* and the **Merriam**

Theatre, *250 S. Broad St; tel: (215) 732-5446,* at the University of the Arts, feature shows on their way to Broadway or on national tour.

Other venues where highly professional performances are staged include: **The Walnut Street Theatre**, *9th and Walnut Sts; tel: (215) 574-3550*; the **Philadelphia Theatre Company**, *1714 Delancey St; tel: (215) 592-8333*; the **Philadelphia Festival for New Plays**, *3680 Walnut St; tel: (215) 898-3900,* and the **Wilma Theatre**, *2030 Sansom St; tel: (215) 963-0345.*

The **Freedom Theatre**, *1346 W. Broad St; tel: (215) 765-2793,* founded in 1966, makes a statement on African American issues and accomplishments.

Philadance – the Philadelphia Dance Company, *9 N. Preston St; tel: (215) 387-8200,* has earned high esteem as a modern contemporary dance company.

The **Delaware River Waterfront** is the newest part of the city for **nightclubs**, where they have mushroomed recently. Most of them are near the Benjamin Franklin Bridge, where a water taxi service ferries people to the hot spots. *South St*

323

The Millenium

Philadelphia is poised to greet the new millenium with its new $300 million Avenue of the Arts, with opera, ballet and music venues, a new sports and entertainment centre, a fun centre, several more art galleries, theatres and hotels, and a $1 billion improvement programme for Philadelphia International Airport. Many of these projects were completed in 1995 and 1996 and are up and running. The opening of the Constitution Center on Independence Mall is scheduled for 1998.

continues to be one of the city's liveliest areas after dark.

The monthly *Philadelphia Where* magazine gives details of current entertainment in the performing arts and sports. There should be a copy in your hotel room. The city newspapers, *Philadelphia Daily News* and the *Philadelphia Inquirer*, also have information about what's on.

SHOPPING

Philadelphia is a city of neighbourhoods – more than 100 in all. Some, like **Germantown** and **Society Hill**, are mainly residential and of historic significance, but most have shops that add to their individual character.

Rittenhouse Square is one of 5 original squares laid out by William Penn. The square, with its statuary and fountains, at *18th and 19th Sts* on *Walnut St*, is surrounded by exclusive boutiques and smart restaurants. On *9th St*, between *Christian* and *Washington Sts*, in the heart of South Philadelphia, is the site of the **Italian Market** – the place to buy meat, produce and baked goods and such delicacies as Sicilian pepper cheese and pasta salads.

Sorrelle Cianfero; *tel: (215) 772-0739*, runs behind-the-scenes tours of the market, Tues–Sat and Sun mornings. New Age bookshops, antique shops and the off-beat shops that appeal to anyone looking for the unusual are found along trendy *South St*.

Market St in Center City is a great shopping centre, and the splendid architecture of **Hecht's** department store, gives it some added status.

Nearby is **The Gallery**, *at 9th and Market Sts*, claimed to be the nation's biggest enclosed city shopping centre with anchor stores J.C. Penney, Clover and Strawbridge and Clothier.

Reading Terminal Market, *12th and Arch Sts; (tel: (215) 922-2317*, has become a lunchtime rendezvous, having 23 ethnic eateries and 80 merchants. Established more than a century ago, it is noted for its groceries and fresh fish, meat and farm produce.

Fifteen mins drive north-east of Center City is **Franklin Mills Mall**, *tel: (215) 632-1500* (see map, left), where over 200 outlet stores offer generously discounted goods include Benetton and Spiegel.

SIGHTSEEING

Tours

A number of companies offer guided tours, including the following:

African American Historical Tours, *4601 Market St; tel: (215) 748-3222*. Five tours focus on the history of the African-American in Philadelphia and

Jewellery Row

For a close-up look at diamonds, sapphires, rubies, emeralds and countless other gems – and the chance to choose stones and settings for an individual ring or brooch – go to Jewellery Row, established in 1851 and said to be the oldest diamond district in the US.

Formerly open only to the trade, Jewellery Row now welcomes the public to visit more than 300 jewellers' shops, where diamond cutters, setters, polishers, designers and goldsmiths work. Jewellery may be bought at discounted prices.

Jewellery Row is one block from Independence Hall on *Sansom St* between *7th* and *8th Sts*, and on *8th* St between *Chestnut* and *Walnut Sts*. Individual shop hours may vary, but generally they are open Mon–Sat 0930–1700 (Wed to 2030) and Sun 1100–1700.

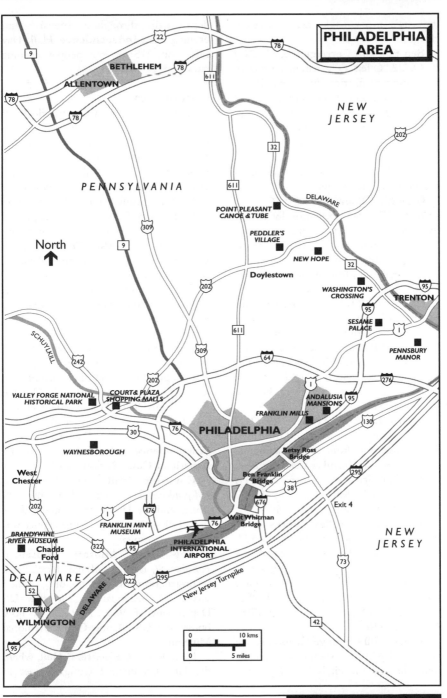

PHILADELPHIA
AREA

9

22

78

611

BETHLEHEM

ALLENTOWN

78

78

78

NEW
JERSEY

202

PENNSYLVANIA

32

611

DELAWARE

309

POINT PLEASANT
CANOE & TUBE

North

PEDDLER'S
VILLAGE

NEW HOPE

32

202

Doylestown

WASHINGTON'S
CROSSING

95

TRENTON

SCHUYLKILL

611

309

95

SESAME
PALACE

1

325

242

64

PENNSBURY
MANOR

202

309

1

276

VALLEY FORGE NATIONAL
HISTORICAL PARK

COURT & PLAZA
SHOPPING MALLS

ANDALUSIA
MANSIONS

95

FRANKLIN MILLS

PHILADELPHIA

130

30

76

WAYNESBOROUGH

Betsy Ross
Bridge

295

West
Chester

Ben Franklin
Bridge

38

202

676

Exit 4

1

476

FRANKLIN MINT
MUSEUM

76

Walt Whitman
Bridge

NEW
JERSEY

BRANDYWINE
RIVER MUSEUM

95

PHILADELPHIA
INTERNATIONAL
AIRPORT

322

73

Chadds
Ford

322

295

DELAWARE

New Jersey Turnpike

52

DELAWARE

WINTERTHUR

42

WILMINGTON

95

0   10 kms

0   5 miles

the city's major landmarks. Admission charge.

Ben Franklin Carriage Co; *tel: (215) 923-8522*. Offers fully narrated tours of the historic district in horse-drawn Victorian carriages. Tours start at *5th and Chestnut Sts, Independence National Historic Park*, daily 0900–1800. Evening tours start 1900 daily from *2nd and Lombard Sts*. A courtesy van collects visitors from anywhere in the city. Admission charge, from $25 for up to four people.

Gray Line Tours; *tel: (215) 569-3666* or *(800) 577-7745*. Professionally guided tours of historic, contemporary and cultural Philadelphia and nearby areas depart three times daily from *30th St Station* and there are pick-ups from most Center City hotels.

Old Town Trolley Tours, *60 Laurel St; tel: (215) 928-TOUR*. Trolleys move in a loop covering 15 stops, including Liberty Bell Pavilion, Independence Park Visitors Center and Philadelphia Museum of Art, and passengers may board and alight at will. Tours daily every 30 min. Admission: $15.

Penn's Landing Trolley; *tel: (215) 627-0807*, run a 20-min round trip along the historic waterfront aboard authentic antique streetcars. Board at *Columbus Blvd, Dock St* or *Spruce St*. Open Thur–Fri 1100–dusk (July–Aug); Sat–Sun 1100–dusk (Apr–Nov). Admission: $1.50.

Philadelphia Trolley Works, *1119 N. Bodine St; tel: (215) 923-8517*. Victorian-style trolleys loops through the historic area, Center City and the waterfront, making 19 stops, including most hotels. Passengers may step on and off as they choose. Operates daily 0900–1700. Admission: $10.

Society Hill Carriage Company; *tel: (215) 627-6128*. Horse-drawn carriage tours through the city's historic district

depart daily throughout the day and evening from **Independence Hall**. Day rides from $15 for four people, evening rates from $20.

Historic Park
Independence National Historic Park covers the area between Benjamin Franklin Bridge and *South St*, and the *Waterfront* and *8th St* and encompasses some of the most hallowed historical shrines in the US. Buildings within the park are open daily 0900–1700 year round and admission is free. Tour maps and information on events and attractions are available at the **Visitor Center**, *3rd and Chestnut Sts*, and park rangers and guides are provide historical information.

Highlights of the park include:

Liberty Bell Pavilion, *Market St, between 5th and 6th Sts*. The pavilion houses the famous bell which was rung to mark the first reading of the Declaration of Independence on 8 July 1776.

Independence Hall, *Chestnut St, between 5th and 6th Sts*. Built in 1732 as the Pennsylvania State House, the hall was used by the Second Continental Congress 1775-83. Here, the **Declaration of Independence** was adopted and the **American Constitution** written.

Congress Hall, *6th St, next to Independence Hall*, was where the US Senate and the House of Representatives met, 1790–1800, when Philadelphia was the nation's capital.

New Hall Military Museum, *Chestnut St, between 3rd and 4th Sts*, is a reconstruction of the building which served as headquarters for the US Department of War, 1791–92. It now houses the US Marine Corps Memorial Museum.

Next door is **Carpenters' Hall**, where the First Continental Congress met in

1774. It contains original chairs and exhibits of early tools.

Franklin Court, *bounded by Chestnut and Market Sts, and 3rd and 4th Sts*, is a tribute to Benjamin Franklin on the site of the great man's house. It features a print shop and bindery, a museum and the B. Free Franklin Post Office.

Christ Church, *2nd and Market Sts*, has been the centre of an active Episcopalian parish since 1695. George Washington and Benjamin Franklin were among the Revolutionary worshippers who occupied pews here.

Christ Church Burial ground, *5th and Arch Sts*, is said to contain the remains of more colonial and Revolutionary War leaders than any other non-military cemetery in the US. Tradition says throwing a penny on the grave of Ben Franklin will bring good luck.

Declaration House, *7th and Market Sts*, is a reconstruction of the house in which Thomas Jefferson stayed and drafted the Declaration of Independence. Visitors may view a short film on the life and times of Jefferson.

Thaddeus Kosciuszko National Memorial, *3rd and Pine Sts*. Kosciuszko was a champion of American and Polish freedom and one of the first foreign volunteers to join the Revolutionary Army. The townhouse in which he rented a room during the winter of 1797-98 has been restored as a memorial to him.

Other Attractions

Independence Seaport Museum, *Columbus Blvd and Walnut St; tel: (215) 925-5439*. Historic ships can be toured, the building of boats traditionally used in local waters can be watched, and visitors can even weld and rivet a ship's hull and 'scull' along a simulated Schuykill River. There are also many nautical exhibitions

on display. Open daily 1000–1700. Admission to the museum and historic ship zone is $7, the museum only costs $5.

A **Riverpass** ticket giving access to the museum, historic ship zone, Riverbus Ferry and the New Jersey State Aquarium at Camden is $15 (concessions for seniors and children).

Fairmount Park, *starting at Benjamin Franklin Parkway; tel: (215) 685-0000*. This is acclaimed as the world's largest landscaped city park – 8900 acres of meadows, woodland, creeks and trails to explore containing a number of Early American mansions, numerous sports facilities and other places of interest open to the public. The mansions are open all year. Admission: $2.50.

On some evenings in June and July the Philadelphia Orchestra (see p.323) performs in an open-air amphitheatre at the **Mann Music Center**, near Ohio House at George Hill. Major attractions within Fairmount Park include Philadelphia Museum of Art, Philadelphia Zoo and the Horticultural Center.

Philadelphia Museum of Art, *26th St and Benjamin Franklin Parkway; tel: (215) 763-8100*, or for a recorded list of daily events *684-7500*. Masterpieces of paintings, sculpture, drawings, glassware, silver, furniture and other works are exhibited in a neo-classical building. The museum, founded in 1876, has arts from Asia, Europe and the US spanning more than 2000 years. The renowned modern collection of Impressionism and Post-Impressionism includes sculptures by Rodin and Degas. Open Tues–Sat 1000–1700 (Wed to 2045), Sun 1000–1300. Admission $7; Sun free.

Philadelphia Zoo, *3400 W. Girard Ave; tel: (215) 243-1100*. More than 1400 animals, birds, reptiles and amphibians from around the world are featured in

327

Carnivore Kingdom, Bear Country, World of Primates and other sectors. Open daily 0930–1700. Admission: $8.

Academy of Natural Sciences, *1900 Benjamin Franklin Pkwy; tel: (215) 299-1000.* Dinosaur bones have a permanent home here. A picture of the prehistoric giants' lives is seen through videos, interactive exhibits and fossils. Dioramas of wild animals in authentic habitats, a look at rocks, gems and minerals and a hands-on nature centre are among the attractions. Open Mon–Fri 1000–1630, Sat, Sun and public holidays 1000–1700. Admission: $6.50.

Edgar Allan Poe National Historic Site, *532 N. 7th St at Spring Garden St; tel: (215) 597-8780.* Poe lived in Philadelphia for six years before moving to New York in 1844 and some of his most famous works – including *The Fall of the House of Usher* and *The Murders in the Rue Morgue* – were published during this time. The small, brick-built house, the only one of his Philadelphia homes still standing, has exhibits and an audio-visual programme on the author. Open daily 0900–1700. Admission: free.

Norman Rockwell Museum, *601 Walnut St at 6th and Sansom Sts; tel: 9215) 922-4345.* More than 600 works by Norman Rockwell, including all the *Saturday Evening Post* covers he painted, are featured in the original Curtis Publishing Building. Rockwell sold his first cover to the company in 1916, when he was 22. His career spanned nearly 60 years. Prints are on sale in the museum gift shop. Open Mon–Sat 1000–1600, Sun 1100–1600. Admission: $2.

Afro-American Historical and Cultural Museum, *701 Arch St; tel: (215) 574-0380.* Opened in 1976 to present a collection interpreting African-American culture in an Afro-American neighbour-hood, the museum attracts 350,000 visitors a year. Open Tues–Sat 1000–1800. Admission: $4, senior and children $2.

Please Touch Museum, *210 N. 21st St; tel: (215) 963-0667.* This is the first museum in the US for children under eight – so from the age of 12 months all visitors pay the adult admission fee of $6.95. Only those under one go free. Strollers and buggies are not allowed. Fun and education go hand in hand. Adults and children can explore together. Tots can take the wheel of a real SEPTA bus, operate a crane, visit a Russian kindergarten, listen to lullabies from around the world, shop for groceries and cook them in a child-size kitchen. Open daily 0900–1630.

Institute of Contemporary Art, *36th and Sansom Sts; tel: (215) 898-7108.* Changing exhibitions are staged at this leading art museum, where video art comes into its own with sculpture, painting, photography and other media. Open Wed 1000–1900, Thur–Sun 1000–1700. Admission: $3, students over 12 and seniors $1.

Historical Society of Pennsylvania, *1300 Locust St; tel: (215) 732-6201,* documents Philadelphia's history from the 1660s to the 20th century through some 500 displayed items. The Trolley Car Theatre presents videos of turn-of-the-century Philadelphia. Open Tues and Thur–Sat 1000–1300, Wed 1300–2100. Admission fee is $2.50, students and seniors $1.50.

National Archives Branch, *9th and Market Sts, Room 1350; tel: (215) 597-3000.* Open for research, visits and tours, this is where federal records from Delaware, Maryland, Pennsylvania, Virginia and West Virginia are stored. Open Mon–Fri 0800–1700 and on the first and third Sat of each month 0800–1200. Admission: free.

PHILADELPHIA–NEW YORK

Those visiting the Capital Region may pick New York City as the starting or finishing point for their touring holiday. Equally, having journeyed to the eastern US, many travellers will not want to miss one of the great cities of the world. Fortunately the New Jersey Turnpike (a toll road) makes the 107 miles between New York and Philadelphia an easy 2 hr drive. Add a few more hours to that time for a detour to the gambling resort of Atlantic City.

DIRECT ROUTE: 107 MILES

329

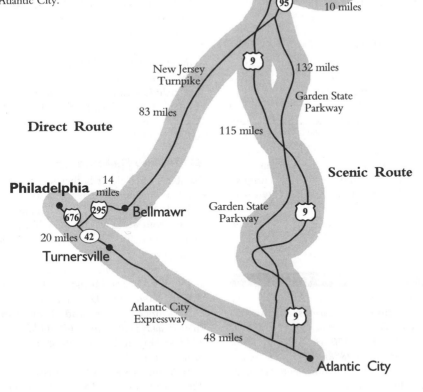

New York City

Newark

78

95   10 miles

9   132 miles

New Jersey
Turnpike

Garden State
Parkway

83 miles

115 miles

Direct Route

Scenic Route

14
miles

Philadelphia

676   295   **Bellmawr**

Garden State
Parkway

9

20 miles   42

Turnersville

Atlantic City
Expressway

9

48 miles

Atlantic City

ROUTES

DIRECT ROUTE

➡ From Philadelphia follow I-676 to exit 27. Turn left onto I-295 for a mile and at the next exit turn right, passing through **Bellmawr** before reaching the New Jersey Turnpike.

Follow the Turnpike north-east to Newark. **Newark International Airport** is located alongside the New Jersey Turnpike, with Hwy 81 connecting the two. From Newark take I-78 to cross to Manhattan.

If you are heading home via **John F. Kennedy Airport**, leave Manhattan by the Queens Midtown Tunnel at *38th St* and *Second Ave*, and take the Long Island Expressway. At Exit 13 take the Van Wyck Expressway to JFK Airport.

SCENIC ROUTE

330

⇢ An alternative route along the New Jersey coast takes in the gambling resort of **Atlantic City**.

From Philadelphia leave by I-676 and Rte 42 to join the Atlantic City Expressway at Turnersville. The Atlantic City Expressway (Toll) links Philadelphia to Atlantic City and the Garden State Parkway (Toll) and New Jersey Turnpike (Toll)/I-95 run from Atlantic City on to New York.

An alternative route is via US Hwy 9. Philadelphia to Atlantic City is 68 miles, Atlantic City to New York 142 miles.

ATLANTIC CITY

Tourist Information: Atlantic City Convention & Visitors Authority, *2314 Pacific Ave, Atlantic City, NJ 08401; tel: (609) 449-7130 or toll-free (800) BOARDWK or (888) AC-VISIT*. It has information on city tours, entertainment and cultural activities.

The minimum age for participating in gambling is 21.

ACCOMMODATION

The action is at 12 huge, elegant **casino hotels**, each offering at least 500 rooms and six restaurants. Of these, **Trump's Castle** and **Harrah's** are in the marina area; the others are along the Boardwalk, including **Bally's Park Place**, **Caesars**, **Claridge**, **The Grand**, **Merv Griffin's Resorts**, **Sands**, **Showboat**, **Trop-World**, **Trump Plaza** and **Trump Taj Mahal**. Rooms are expensive to pricey, with rates highest in summer, lowest in winter.

Chain motels in Atlantic City or nearby towns include *BW, CI, DI, EL, HJ, Hd, QI, RI, Rm, Sh, S8* and *TL*. These offer moderate to expensive rooms. Campsites are available nearby in Pleasantville and Mays Landing.

Many hotels offer lower one- or two-night package rates (especially midweek) that include casino coins and free or discounted show tickets, meals and parking. Ask the Visitors Authority what is currently available.

EATING AND DRINKING

Gamblers often don't bother to leave the hotel at mealtime, relying instead on casino-hotel restaurants, which range in cuisine from steaks to seafood, Chinese to French and Italian, and in price from budget to pricey.

If you're venturing out, try the seafood at **Dock's Oyster House**, *2405 Atlantic Ave; tel: (609) 345-0092; moderate*.

The pricey **Knife and Fork Inn**, *Atlantic and Pacific Aves; tel: (609) 344-1133*, serving steaks and seafood, has been open since 1927.

In Venice Park, **Old Waterway Inn**, *1700 West Riverside Dr; tel: (609) 347-*

1793, serves up moderate–pricey seafood, steaks and pasta.

Follow the locals to the **White House Sub Shop**, *2301 Arctic Ave; tel: (609) 345-1564*, whose photo-covered walls advertise 75 years' worth of famous patrons, budget. Along the Boardwalk you'll find hot dogs, pizza, candy floss and other seaside fast foods.

EVENTS

The **Miss America Pageant**, started in 1921 to extend the summer season, is held mid-Sept in the Convention Center and broadcast nationwide and is one of the city's chief claims to fame.

There's a **Marathon Swim** in early Aug; music and food festivals dot the summer calendar.

SIGHTSEEING AND ENTERTAINMENT

The northern tip of Absecon Island has been a seaside resort since the 1850s, when a newly built railroad helped the masses escape the steamy summers of Philadelphia and New York City. In 1870 the famous Boardwalk appeared – to keep sand from trailing into the station and fancy hotels of the nouveau riches – and an American icon was born.

The city's street names (such as *Baltic Ave* and *Park Place*) have been immortalised on the 'Monopoly' game board in 25 languages, and its Miss America Pageant (see above) has become a part of the American psyche. But it was casino gambling, introduced in 1976, that rescued the rundown, has-been resort town and turned it back into a top tourist destination.

Atlantic City today is an East Coast version of Las Vegas, with 24-hour casino action and glittery shows featuring bigname entertainers such as singers Liza Minelli, Aretha Franklin, Linda Ronstadt, Julio Eglesias, Wayne Newton and comics Bill Cosby and Joan Rivers. Buy show tickets at casino box offices or (for a fee) from **Ticketmaster**, *tel. (800) 736-1420*. Lesser-known entertainment runs almost continuously in hotel lounges.

Gamblers can earn points toward discounts on food, room rates and shows by using a **casino card**, such as 'Harrah's Gold Card'. (Indeed, savvy players may ask to place their card in your slotmachine, so the points won't go to waste.) Ask at each casino courtesy desk how to obtain one.

The 4½-mile **Boardwalk** is the place for strolling, bicycling and peoplewatching – or let an attendant push you in a three-wheeled, wicker 'rolling chair' ($5–$25 for two, depending on distance). The sandy beaches offer bathing, boating and other aquatic sports in Gulf Streamwarmed waters of the Atlantic Ocean.

For kids, there's the roller coaster and Ferris wheel on **Steel Pier** and **Storybook Land** theme park in Pleasantville, among other amusements. There's golfing at 22 public courses nearby and saltwater fishing, either from a chartered boat or the shore.

For the culturally inclined, **Garden Pier**, along the Boardwalk, houses the **Atlantic City Art Center**, with exhibitions in three galleries, and the **Historical Museum**; *tel: (609) 347-5839*.

Noyes Museum; *tel: (609) 652-8848*, *Lily Lake Rd, Oceanville*, 15 min north, offers a collection of fine art by southern New Jersey artists and vintage duck decoys.

An excursion to **Cape May**, a 40–45-mile drive to the southernmost tip of New Jersey, offers a glimpse at the architecture and ambience of America's Victorian era.

331

NEW YORK CITY

If New York is your air gateway to the Capital Region, it's well worth rounding off your vacation with one or two days in the city. The Big Apple is a tonic, a stimulant, an energiser. With skyscrapers and slums, it's both fascinating and frustrating, but never boring.

TOURIST INFORMATION

The New York Convention & Visitors Bureau (NYCVB) operates a **Visitor Information Center,** *2 Columbus Circle* (southwest Central Park), *New York, NY 10019; tel: (212) 397-8222* or toll-free *(800) NYC-VISIT (692-8474),* open Mon–Fri 0900–1800, Sat–Sun and holidays 1000–1500.

When calling, choose the **New York by Phone** option for automated information about hotels, restaurants, sightseeing attractions, events, theatre, shopping and services. Multilingual counsellors are available Mon–Fri 0900–1800, Sat, Sun and holidays 1000–1500.

Bronx Tourism Council, *880 River Ave, Suite 3, Bronx, NY 10452; tel: (718) 590-3518.* **Meet Me in Brooklyn,** *30 Flatbush Ave, Suite 427, Brooklyn, NY 11217; tel: (718) 855-7882.* **Queens Tourism Council,** *P.O. Box 555, Queens Borough Hall, Queens, NY 11424; tel: (718) 647-3387* or *(800) 454-1329.* **Staten Island Chamber of Commerce,** *130 Bay St, Staten Island, NY 10301; tel: (718) 727-1900.*

WEATHER

New York is just about at sea level and its coastal weather can be fairly unpredictable. Summers can be hot and relatively humid, though the once predictable 'August heat wave' is now apt to come at any time during the summer months. The average July temperature is 68–85°F. The average Jan temperature is 26–38°F.

ARRIVING AND DEPARTING

Airports

John F. Kennedy International Airport (JFK), the main airport for international flights as well as many domestic connections, is about 15 miles southeast of New York City. Several US airlines handle all flights from their own terminals; most non-US airlines use the international terminal, which has four Thomas Cook locations. Ground transportation, *tel: (800) 247-7433;* parking information, *tel: (718) 656-5699.* By yellow (metered) cab, it's 5–10 mins from airport hotels and 25 mins to an hour or more from midtown Manhattan, depending on traffic, weather, time of day and day of week. Average fare $35, includes $3 tunnel/bridge toll and tip. Car/limo service, $25, plus toll and tip.

Bus connections: **Carey Airport Express** buses, $13, depart every half hour from airport terminals; travel time 1 hr minimum. Stops in Manhattan are **Grand Central Terminal,** *Park Ave* and *42nd St* (on Manhattan's East Side) and **Port Authority Bus Terminal,** *42nd St* and *Eighth Ave* (West Side); *tel: (718) 632-0500.* Some of the large chain hotels (*HL, Sh, MA*) run shuttle buses (ask at Ground Transportation Centre).

Connections from JFK to other area airports: To LaGuardia, there's a Carey bus every 30 mins, $10. To Newark International, take the **Princeton Airporter;** *tel: (609) 587-6600,* $19 per person.

LaGuardia Airport, serving domestic destinations only – including hourly shuttle flights to Washington, D.C. – is about 8 miles northeast of NYC. Ground transportation, *tel: (800) 247-7433;* parking information, *tel: (718) 533-3400.*

By yellow cab, it's 10–30 mins from midtown Manhattan with an average fare of $20. Car/limo service is $15. Bus connections: **Carey Airport Express buses,** $9, depart every half hour from airport terminals; travel time half an hour minimum. Stops in Manhattan are on the East Side at *Park Ave* and *42nd St* near Grand Central Terminal and on the West Side at **Port Authority Bus Terminal**, *42nd St* and *Eighth Ave; tel: (718) 632-0500.* A variety of hotels run shuttle buses and Gray Line runs shuttle buses from the airports to your hotel.

Bus connections to other area airports: To JFK – Carey bus every 30 mins, $9.50. To Newark International – Princeton Airporter, $19 per person; *tel: (609) 587-6600.*

Newark International Airport, which has one international and two domestic terminals, is in New Jersey, about 16 miles southwest of New York City. Ground transportation, *tel: (800) 247-7433;* parking information, *tel: (201) 961-4751.*

By taxi, it's 30–45 mins from midtown Manhattan. Average fare $30–$40. Car/limo service is $25. Bus connections: **Olympia Trails Express Bus,** *tel: (212) 964-6233,* departs every 20–30 mins for Manhattan, $8, with stops downtown at World Trade Center, midtown at Grand Central and at Penn. Station (frequency varies with time of day and day of week). **NJ Transit,** *tel: (201) 762-5100,* runs an express bus, $7, about every 15 mins to Port Authority Bus Terminal, *Eighth Ave* and *42nd St.*

Bus connections to other area airports: To JFK, take the Princeton Airporter, $19 per person, *tel: (609) 587-6600.*

By car
To leave Manhattan and head south east to New Jersey and Philadelphia, drive via the **Lincoln Tunnel** midtown (entrance *Ninth Ave* at *41st St*) to **I-495,** and after 3 miles join the I-95/New Jersey Turnpike which travels south to Philadelphia. Alternatively, take the **Holland Tunnel** downtown (entrance at *Canal St*) and continue on 12th St to I-78, cross Newark Bay and join 1-95. From Manhattan's lower tip, take the **Brooklyn Battery Tunnel** to Brooklyn and along **I-278** south, across the **Verrazano Narrows**.

Getting to the airports: For **JFK,** leave Manhattan via the Queens Midtown Tunnel (entrance at *38th St* and *Second Ave*), then take the Long Island Expressway. If there is no traffic, take Exit 22 (Grand Central Parkway), then Exit 13 to Van Wyck Expressway to JFK. In heavy traffic, take Exit 19 (Woodhaven Blvd) to Belt Parkway and follow signs to JFK. For **LaGuardia**, take the Queens Midtown Tunnel to the Long Island Expressway to Brooklyn-Queens Expressway to Grand Central Parkway to the airport. For **Newark**, take the Lincoln Tunnel (entrance *Ninth Ave* at *41st St*), follow signs to New Jersey Turnpike and then to Newark airport (Exit 13A).

By helicopter
New York Helicopter, *tel: (800) 645-3494.* Manhattan heliports: Downtown; *tel: (212) 248-7240.* E. 34th St; *tel: (212) 889-0986.* W. 30th St; *tel: (212) 563-4442.*

333

By train

Train connections from cities in this book arrive at **Pennsylvania (Penn.) Station,** between *Seventh* and *Eighth Ave* and *31st–33rd St (West Side),* which also serves commuters to New Jersey and Long Island and train travellers from other US cities. A speedy Metroliner, *tel: (800) 523-8720,* services Washington, DC. A club car seat costs extra, but you get meal and beverage service and more comfort. To find up-to-date details of rail services if you live outside North America, consult the latest edition of the bi-monthly *Thomas Cook Overseas Timetable,* available from Thomas Cook Publishing.

By bus

Port Authority Bus Terminal, *Eighth Ave* and *42nd St* (near the theatre district); *tel: (212) 564-8484,* is where buses to other parts of the country, on major lines, arrive and depart. The two major long-haul bus lines are **Greyhound**; *tel: (212) 971-6300* or *(800) 231-2222,* and **Adirondack Trailways**; *tel: (212) 967-2900* or *(800) 225-6815.*

GETTING AROUND

With a population of 7 million and growing, metro New York is congested with traffic and pedestrians. Driving to attractions is not advised. With the aid of public tranport for longer distances, the best way to see the city and feel its energy is on foot.

A long and narrow island (12.5 miles long and 2.5 miles wide), Manhattan's streets and avenues are relatively simple to navigate – providing you know some basic facts and the lingo that goes with them: *Fifth Ave* runs north-south and divides Manhattan into **East Side** and **West Side.** Avenues run north and south, with mostly one-way traffic; even-numbered streets tend to run east and odd-numbered

ones west. **Uptown** is an area – from the 60s on up – as well as a direction, as in going with the ascending street numbers. **Downtown** is the lower (southern-most) part of Manhattan and also refers to travelling in the direction of descending street numbers. Both are invaluable when using the subway. **Midtown** is the middle part of Manhattan – from the 30s to the 60s, between the East River and the Hudson River. **Crosstown** is a direction, as in travelling across the island (east or west). If you're walking, remember that crosstown blocks are twice as long as up or downtown ones.

Manhattan neighbourhoods

The Battery, at the lowest tip of the island, is where the city was founded. **Battery Park City** is residential, and the area is also where the terminals are located for ferries that serve Staten Island, Governors Island, the Statue of Liberty and Ellis island. The **Lower Broadway** area, just north of the Battery, encompasses the World Trade Center and the World Financial Center complexes. **Wall St** is a specific street as well as a generic name for the financial district, which at its northern boundary includes *Fulton St* and the South St Seaport.

Next come City Hall and the court buildings and **Chinatown,** where the narrow, winding streets yield butchers, bakers and Chinese greengrocers. There are news-stands and souvenir shops as well as unmistakably Chinese-style public telephone booths. **Canal St** divides Chinatown and **Little Italy,** which shows off its cultural heritage, mainly with restaurants, cafés, bakeries and grocers.

Proceeding uptown, there is the **Lower East Side,** an area known as a ghetto for late 19th-century and early 20th-century immigrants of all kinds, but

MANHATTAN

LINCOLN CENTRE FOR
THE PERFORMING ARTS

CENTRAL
PARK

FRICK COLLECTION

E 72nd St

W 60th St
W 58th St
W 56th St
W 54th St
W 52nd St
W 50th St
W 48th St
W 46th St
W 44th St
W 42nd St
W 40th St
W 36th St
W 34th St

Columbus
Circle

CENTRAL
PARK ZOO

Fifth Av

Madison Av

Third Av

Lexington Av

Second Av

First Av

E 66th St

E 62nd St

E 60th St

E 58th St

E 56th St

E 54th St

E 52nd St

E 50th St

E 48th St

E 46th St

E 44th St

E 42nd St

E 40th St

CARNEGIE
HALL

AMERICAN CRAFT
MUSEUM

MUSEUM OF
MODERN ART

MUSEUM OF
TV & RADIO

ROCKEFELLER
CENTER

ST PATRICK'S
CATHEDRAL

INTREPID
SEA-AIR-SPACE
MUSEUM

Lincoln Tunnel (toll)

Twelfth Av

Eleventh Av

Tenth Av

Ninth Av

Eighth Av

Seventh Av

Av of the Americas

Dyer Av

HUDSON

JACOB JAVITS
CONVENTION
CENTER

Franklin Roosevelt Dr

W 30th St
W 28th St
W 26th St
W 22nd St
W 20th St

West St

Tenth Av

Ninth Av

Eighth Av

MACY'S

MADISON
SQUARE
GARDEN

PENN
CENTRAL
STATION

NEW YORK
PUBLIC LIBRARY

PIERPONT
MORGAN LIBRARY

EMPIRE STATE
BUILDING

GRAND CENTRAL
TERMINAL

UNITED
NATIONS
HQ

Queen's Midtown
Tunnel (toll)

495

E 36th St
E 34th St
E 32nd St
E 30th St
E 28th St
E 26th St
E 24th St
E 22nd St
E 20th St

Broadway

Madison
Square Park

North

W 14th St

Gansevoort St

Bank St

Christopher St

Barrow St

Greenwich Av

Seventh Av

Av of the Americas

Fifth Av

University Pl

Park Av

EAST

T. ROOSEVELT
BIRTHPLACE

POLICE ACADEMY
MUSEUM

CON EDISON
ENERGY MUSEUM

W 10th St

W 8th St

Washington
Square

Fourth Av

Third Av

E 14th St

E 10th St

E 8th St

E 6th St

E 4th St

Av A

Av B

Av C

Av D

Tompkins
Square

Holland Tunnel
(toll)

W Houston St

FIRE
MUSEUM

NEW MUSEUM OF
CONTEMPORARY ART

GUGGENHEIM
MUSEUM SOHO

E Houston St

Stanton St

Rivington St

Delancey St

Broome St

Grand St

Second Av

First Av

Columbia St

Franklin Roosevelt Drive

Watts St

Vestry St

Laight St

Greenwich St

Hudson St

Varick St

W Broadway

Church St

Broadway

Spring St

Broome St

Grand St

Kenmare St

Bowery

Elizabeth St

Mott St

Forsyth St

Allen St

Essex St

Hester St

Canal St

Canal St

East Broadway

Williamsburg Bridge

Duane St

Reade St

Chambers St

Centre St

Elk St

Park Row

St James Pl

Pike St

Rutgers St

Jackson St

WORLD TRADE
CENTER

CITY HALL

Barclay St

West St

Trinity Pl

Broadway

Nassau St

Fulton St

Madison

East River Drive

Manhattan Bridge

Brooklyn Bridge

STOCK
EXCHANGE

FEDERAL
RESERVE BANK

FEDERAL HALL
NATIONAL MUSEUM

SMITHSONIAN NATIONAL
MUSEUM OF THE
AMERICAN INDIAN

East River Drive

95

95

0   1 km

0   1/2 mile

mostly Jews from Eastern Europe. **Orchard St** is famous for bargain shopping, with many restaurants and businesses still retaining their ethnic flavour. The **SoHo Cast-Iron District** was designated a historic district by the New York City Landmarks Preservation commission in 1973 and is an architectural treasure trove; SoHo is short for 'South of Houston St' (pronounced HOW-ston).

Gramercy Park is a beautiful European-style square and its surroundings have a fascinating history of famous former residents and establishments such as **Pete's Tavern**, *66 Irving Pl* (which claims to have been a favoured haunt of author O. Henry), and the private **Players Club**, *16 Gramercy Park South*. **Greenwich Village**, with its distinctive Washington Arch, was originally the bohemian home of writers and artists, with residents such as O. Henry, Edgar Allan Poe and Mark Twain. At the southeast corner of **Washington Square** is the main building of New York University and nearby the small clubs and cafés of *Macdougal* and *Bleecker Sts*.

Central Park separates the **Upper East Side** from the **Upper West Side** (Central Park West, the gentrified *Columbus* and *Amsterdam Aves* and, at *110th St*, the Columbia University campus). **Morningside Heights** and **Harlem** have some of the city's poorer residential neighbourhoods, though Harlem also has historic points of interest (See Sightseeing). From Washington Square upwards, the streets are laid out on a strict grid. In lower Manhattan, keep a street map handy, because the older streets are a jumble of names and directions.

Public Transport

Buses and subways are, by far, the most expedient method for getting around Manhattan and to the other boroughs.

The major lines on the **subway** network are the **IRT**, **IND** and **BMT**, plus the **Shuttle** between Grand Central (East Side) and Times Square (West Side). The **No. 7 (Flushing) Line,** also serves as a shuttle between Grand Central, Fifth Ave and Times Square, and then it continues into the borough of Queens. **Express trains** stop only at major stations, sometimes as far as 30 blocks apart); **Local trains** are not practical for longer distances, as they stop at major stations as well as everywhere in between, on an average of every eight blocks.

Drawbacks: the subway system is very extensive (more than 400 stations) and can be confusing, though markings are now colour-coded and vastly improved). Avoid using subways during rush-hours (0730–0900 or 1700–1830) when they can be unpleasantly hectic and crowded or – very important! – late at night, after 2300. Another caveat: Be prepared to climb lots of steep steps.

Tokens can be purchased in booths in the station. A single token costs $1.25, but may also be purchased in a ten-pack, which comes in handy, depending on the length of your visit. The same tokens are used on city buses.

Free maps are available and 24-hour subway and bus information is provided by the **New York City Transit Authority,** *tel: (718) 330-1234.*

Buses are a more scenic way of getting from point to point. The fare – a token or $1.25 in exact change – is deposited as you board. If your journey requires you to go uptown/downtown as well as crosstown, ask the driver for a (free) **transfer**, but mind that you re-board at a transfer point (marked on the back of the transfer). Most buses have wheelchair lifts. The Express version of a city bus is marked 'Limited Stops'. Otherwise buses stop every other

336

block. Maps are available and frequency is noted on signs at bus stops. Again, avoid rush hours.

Taxis are more expensive (fares increase with distance covered, plus a $0.50 evening surcharge) but are a more comfortable and convenient alternative, and can be cheaper than the subway if three or more are travelling together.

Driving in New York City

DON'T. Free parking is practically non-existent, and garages are expensive or inconveniently located. Local drivers can be erratic, impatient and discourteous and, with frequent gridlock, it can take up to half an hour just to get across town.

If bringing a car into Manhattan is unavoidable, here are two of the largest parking garages: **GMC (Garage Management Corp.)** has 53 locations; *tel: (212) 888-7400,* **Kinney System** has over 130 facilities; *tel: (800) 836-6666.* For information about current street parking regulations, *tel: (212) 442-7080.*

STAYING IN NEW YORK CITY

Accommodation

Manhattan's 100,000–plus rooms include the most luxurious and elegant, the moderate and the safe-and-affordable. The New York Visitors Information Center has a handy, comprehensive hotel guide (with map indicating locations), prices and services available at up to 100 hotels in every price range.

At the high end are the pricey **Four Seasons**, *57 E. 57th St, New York, NY 10022; tel (212) 758-5700;* the **Peninsula**, *700 Fifth Ave, New York, NY 10019; tel: (212) 247-2200;* **The Mark**, *25 E. 77th St, New York, NY 10021; tel: (212) 744-4300,* and the **Ritz Carlton**, *112 Central Park South, New York, NY*

10019, tel: (212) 757-1900. There are expensive *BW* and *HJ* and a variety of budget choices.

If location is the key, theatre district hotels include the pricey **Macklowe,** *141 W. 44th St, New York, NY 10036; tel. (212) 768-4400,* two *Sh* and *RM.* Near Lincoln Center are the pricey *RA* and expensive **Mayflower**, *15 Central Park West, New York, NY 10023; tel: (212) 265-066.* On the Museum Mile, is the pricey **Stanhope**, *995 Fifth Ave, New York, NY 10028; tel: (212) 288-5800,* as well as the moderate–expensive **Wales**, *1295 Madison Ave, New York, NY 10028; tel: (212) 876-6000.* In the financial district are the expensive **Vista**, *3 World Trade Center, New York, NY 10048; tel: (212) 938-9100,* **Millenium**, *55 Church St, New York, NY 10007; tel: (212) 693-2001,* and *Hd.*

Two moderate finds on the East Side, midtown, are the **Pickwick Arms**, *230 E. 51st St, New York, NY 10022; tel: (212) 355-0300,* and **Quality Hotel Fifth Ave**, *3 E. 40th St, New York, NY 10016; tel: (800) 228-5151.*

The **YMCA** offers group rates and package programs, including room, breakfast and a variety of meals; sightseeing and exursions are available, with an Airport Hospitality Service – The Y's Way Student Information Desk – on the ground floor of the International Arrivals Building at Kennedy Airport. Two locations in Manhattan are **YMCA-Vanderbilt**, *224 E. 47th St, New York, NY 10017; tel: (212) 756-9600,* and **YMCA-West Side,** *5 W. 63rd St, New York, NY 10023; tel: (212) 787-4400.* Students may request a multilingual catalogue from **The Y's Way International**, *224 E 47th St, New York, NY 10017, tel: (212) 308-2899.*

Another budget alternative is **HI**, *891*

337

Amsterdam Ave at W. 103rd St, New York, NY 10025; tel: (212) 932-2300. Rates for members of Hostelling International start at $20 and include use of garden, library, laundry room, coffee bar and cafeteria. For non-members, rates are slightly higher.

Eating and Drinking

New York restaurants comprise the most sophisticated international blend with authentic ethnic ingredients from all over the world. As higher prices don't always dictate quality, be wary of expensive 'name' restaurants in busy tourist areas that provide heavy ambience while skimping on quality. Like most things in New York, a meal can be costly.

For an extensive, up-to-date listing of restaurants (by location and price) consult local newspapers, *New York* magazine, *WHERE* (available free in hotel lobbies) and *Times Square Restaurant Guide* (listing more than 200 establishments).

The **Deli** is short for delicatessen, but no one calls it that. It's a good source for takeout – generous sandwiches, with side orders of coleslaw or macaroni salad and a hot or cold beverage. Eat your meal in a charming, off-the-street pocket park, maybe at a table near a mini-waterfall. Some of the most authentic delis can be found on the Lower East Side, which also has the famous Jewish kosher eatery, moderate **Ratner's Dairy Restaurant**, *138 Delancey St; tel: (212) 677-5588,* (closed Fri evening and Sat for Sabbath). Other outstanding delis: budget **Katz's** (since 1888), *205 E. Houston St; tel: (212) 254-2246,* and the moderate **Carnegie**, *854 Seventh Ave; tel: (212) 757-2245,* and **Stage Deli**, *834 Seventh Ave near 53rd St; tel: (212) 245-7850.*

Near the financial district, the **South St Seaport** has good quality sit-down restaurants as well as take-away opportuni-

ties and a great view of the Brooklyn and Manhattan bridges. In the main seaport complex, the moderate **North Star Pub** serves English meat pies, pasties and bangers, made by Peter Myers in his shop.

Some restaurants are more memorable than others and, though sometimes more expensive, are worth it. One, the **Tavern on the Green**, at the edge of Central Park at *67th St; tel: (212) 873-3200,* is as affordable as you want it to be for an à la carte Sunday Brunch (book ahead for the Crystal Room). A reasonable outdoor meal, with a lovely view of the Lincoln Center complex and fountain, can be had at one of the sidewalk restaurants along **Broadway**, between *64th* and *66th Sts*.

A fun place for dinner is moderate-pricey **Asti's**, *13 E. 12th St off Fifth Ave; tel: (212) 242-9868.* The waiters and bartenders at the family-owned restaurant entertain customers with opera arias. Open early Sept–late June (closed summers). In the theatre district, near the Palace Theater, are two family-style restaurants: **The Olive Garden**, across the street at *47th St and Broadway; tel: (212) 246-4517* (café) or *(212) 333-3254* (restaurant), and **Langan's,** around the corner at *150 W. 47th St; tel: (212) 869-5482.*

Some fabulous aerial views can be enjoyed over cocktails. **The View**, on the 48th floor (accessed by glass-walled elevators) of the **Marriott Marquis Hotel**, *1535 Broadway at 45th St, New York, NY 10036; tel: (212) 398-1900,* in the heart of the theatre district, is a revolving cocktail bar from which to see glowing sunsets over the Hudson River and the neon lights of Times Square. A pleasant indoor and outdoor view of the Manhattan skyline, United Nations gardens, UN Plaza and the East River can be had from the **Top of the Tower** 26th-floor cocktail lounge in the **Beekman Tower Hotel**,

338

49th St and *First Ave; tel: (212) 355-7300.* Also in Midtown, lower to the ground, are the glass walled **Sun Garden** and **Crystal Fountain** bar/restaurant at the **Grand Hyatt Hotel,** *E. 42nd St; tel: (212) 883-1234,* overhanging the sidewalk next to Grand Central Station.

In Chinatown, **20 Mott,** *20 Mott St; tel: (212) 964-0380,* for dim sum or dinner, and **Golden Unicorn**, *18 E. Broadway; tel: (212) 941-0911,* are a good starting point among the many possibilities. In Little Italy, there's **Joey Paesano**, *136 Mulberry St; tel: (212) 966-3337,* budget, for good value, and **SPQR**, *133 Mulberry St; tel: (212) 925-3120,* moderate. Also explore the offerings of **Little India**, a district on Lexington Ave between *27th* and *29th Sts*, where **Madras Mahal**, *104 Lexington Ave; tel: (212) 684-4010,* is outstanding.

SoHo has upmarket art galleries, luxury lofts and in-crowd restaurants for those who want to see and be seen. Moderate American meals are at **American Renaissance**, *260 W. Broadway; tel: (212) 343-0049.*

Gourmet foods can be purchased at: **Balducci's**, *6th Ave and 9th St; tel: (212) 673-2600,* **Dean and Deluca**, *560 Broadway at Prince St; tel: (212) 254-8776,* **Macy's Cellar**, *Herald Sq. and 34th St; tel: (212) 494-2647,* **Manganaro's**, *488 Ninth Ave at 37th St; tel: (212) 563-5331,* originators of the six-ft 'hero' sandwich.

Communications

Manhattan's main office is at *Eighth Ave and 33rd St,* near Penn. Station. More central, sizeable ones are also at *44th St and Lexington Ave* near Grand Central Station, and *55th St and Third Ave.*

Money

Thomas Cook Currency Services are located at *1590 Broadway and 48th St; tel: (212) 265-6049; 317 Madison Ave and 42nd St; tel: (212) 883-0400; Harold Sq. at 1271 Broadway and 32nd St; tel: (212) 679-4365; 29 Broadway; tel: (212) 363-6206; and 511 Madison Ave; tel (212) 753-0662.* All offer the MoneyGram Service.

ENTERTAINMENT

New York is THE place when it comes to entertainment. For complete listings and current best bets, consult the entertainment sections of local newspapers or pick up a copy of *New York* magazine or *WHERE* comprehensive and free in hotel lobbies). Free theatre brochures are available at the ticket offices of the Broadway theatres. Some hotel lobbies have ticket agencies.

Seats at a Broadway show go for an average of $25 (balcony seat) to $75 (stalls). Half-price, same-day tickets (cash only) are available at two locations of **TKTS**, *W 47th St and Broadway* (in the theatre district), open Mon–Sat 1500–2000, Wed and Sat matinees 1200–1400, Sun 1200–1900, and downtown, where queues are shorter, at *2 World Trade Center,* open Mon–Fri 1100–1730, Sat 1100–1530. This can either be time-consuming (but worth it) if you get 'on line' (New York-ese for queueing) early in the afternoon. Or arrive at 1945, when lines have usually gone, and see what's left. Excellent entertainment is also found at less centrally located **Off-Broadway**, where theatres are smaller and seats generally less expensive.

Three major performance halls are part of the **Lincoln Center** for the Performing Arts complex, *62nd to 65th Sts,* between *Broadway* and *Amsterdam Ave.* There's opera and ballet at **The Metropolitan Opera House,** *tel: (212) 362-6000,* and **New York State Theater**, *tel: (212)*

339

870-5570. **Avery Fisher Hall**, *tel: (212) 875-5030,* is home to the New York Philharmonic Orchestra. Two legendary entertainment halls are **Carnegie Hall**, *Seventh Ave and 57th St; tel: (212) 247-7800,* and **Radio City Music Hall**, *50th St and Sixth Ave; tel: (212) 247-4777.*

Nightlife

There are many other ways to stay entertained in Manhattan. **Live shows** with dinner: **Michael's Pub**, *211 E. 55th St; tel: (212) 758-2272;* Harlem's **Cotton Club**, *West Side Highway at W. 125th St; tel: (212) 663-7980;* **Tatou**, *151 E. 50th St; tel: (212) 753-1144.* **Jazz: Bradley's**, *70 University Place at 10th St; tel: (212) 228-6440;* **Blue Note**, *131 W. Third St near Sixth Ave; tel: (212) 475-8592;* **Village Vanguard**, *178 Seventh Ave South at 11th St; tel: (212) 255-4037.* **Comedy: Caroline's**, *1626 Broadway near 50th St; tel: (212) 757-4100.* **The Improvisation**, *433 W 34th St; tel: (212) 279-3446;* **Dangerfield's**, *1118 First Ave at 61st St; tel: (212) 593-1650).*

Events

The Metropolitan Opera holds outdoor concerts in city parks in all five boroughs during June, the New York Philharmonic holds its free summer parks concerts in Aug and **Shakespeare in the Park** events are held July–Aug at Delacorte Theater in Central Park. The **US Open Tennis Championships** are held late Aug–early Sept at Flushing Meadow Park, Queens.

The **New York Film Festival** takes place at Lincoln Center in late Sept–early Oct. The **New York Marathon** fills the streets (and hotels) with runners in early Nov. Radio City Music Hall holds its **Christmas Spectacular** early Nov–Jan, with the lighting of a giant Christmas tree

at Rockefeller Center early Dec. On **New Year's Eve,** Times Square is jammed with revellers.

Sports

Madison Square Garden, *Seventh Ave and 33rd St; tel: (212) 465-6000,* is the home of the New York Knickerbockers (Knicks) basketball team and New York Rangers hockey team. Tickets are sold out well in advance of games; for schedules and information: **Knicks**, *tel: (212) 465-JUMP.* **Rangers**, *tel: (212) 308-NYRS.*

New York has two professional baseball teams, which play Apr–Oct. The Mets play at **Shea Stadium**, *126th St and Roosevelt Ave, Flushing, Queens; tel: (718) 507-8499* (subway: *Willets Point/No. 7 Flushing line*). The Yankees play at **Yankee Stadium**, *161 St and River Ave, Bronx; tel: (718) 293-6000* (subway: *IND D or C local trains or the Lexington Ave IRT No. 4 train*).

Both the New York Giants and the New York Jets professional football teams play Sept–Dec at **Giants Stadium Meadowlands Sports Complex** in Rutherford, N.J.; *tel: (201) 935-3900* (Buses leave from Port Authority Bus Terminal).

SHOPPING

New York tempts shoppers at every turn with all kinds of merchandise. The main shopping artery is *Fifth Ave*, with fashionable stores such as F.A.O. Schwarz, Bergdorf Goodman, Tiffany's, Bally, Steuben, Saks Fifth Avenue, Barnes & Noble and Lord & Taylor. Other notables are **Bloomingdale's**, *Lexington Ave and 59th St,* **Macy's** – the world's largest department store – at *Herald Square, 34th St and Broadway* and the popular **Barney's**, one at *Seventh Ave and 17th St* and the other at *61st St and Madison Ave.*

Shopping centres include the glitz and marble **Trump Tower**, *Fifth Ave off 57th St*, **A&S Plaza**, *33rd St and Sixth Ave* near *Herald Square*, and the **SoHo Emporium**, *375 W. Broadway* in lower Manhattan. Some of Manhattan's most stylish shops (Georg Jensen, Polo) are found along *Madison Ave*.

Discounted merchandise can be found in the **Orchard St Bargain District** on the Lower East Side; *tel: (212) 995-VALU*; **Daffy's** (two), *Madison and 44th St* and *Fifth Ave and 18th St*. Also, downtown, near the World Trade Center, and **Century 21**, *22 Cortland St*. A popular and convenient discount outlet is the 150-shop **Woodbury Common**, *Route 32, Central Valley, NY; tel: (914) 928-7467, (NY State Thruway Exit 16)* with public transportation available from Port Authority bus terminal, *tel: (800) 631-8405*

SIGHTSEEING

Tours
Methods of touring vary. For a legitimate bird's-eye view, there's Air Pegasus Heliport, **Liberty Helicopter**, *W. 30th St and 12th Ave; tel: (212) 967-6464*, $49–$139. Since Manhattan is an island, water tours are among the most popular. The **Circle Line** boats, with frequent sailings from *Pier 83 at West 43rd St; tel: (212) 563-3200*, $9–$18, have been taking visitors on guided tours around Manhattan for 50 years. On board is a snack bar with cocktails, souvenirs, guidebooks and film. Extra special are Harbor Lights cruises and music cruises. Along the streets of New York, **Gray Line** tours have double-decker buses or trolleys, *900 Eighth Ave at 53rd St, tel: (212) 397-2600*; impromptu horse and buggy rides through Central Park from *59th St* and *Fifth Ave* in a

Hansom carriage, and – just because it's New York - **Olympia 'Rent-a-limo – Drive it yourself"** with hourly rates from $30 to $60 – for a 10-passenger super-stretch limo, *tel: (212) 995-1200*.

Lower Manhattan
There is great concentration of attractions here: Take a Circle Line ferry from Battery Park to Liberty Island in New York Harbor. You can climb the 300 steps into the **Statue of Liberty's** crown, and learn how she was constructed, but be aware that it takes several hours to reach the top. Take an earlier boat if you're planning to make the climb.

Stop at **Ellis Island Immigration Museum**; *tel: (212) 363-3200*. Stroll through the stone canyons of narrow *Wall St*, see the **New York Stock Exchange** and **Trinity Church**. Walk around the informative observation deck at the **World Trade Center**, 110 floors up. The **South St Seaport**, with its fleet of historic ships, is also in the area, as are City Hall and the courts, **Chinatown** and **Little Italy**.

341

Midtown
Here are such wonders as the **Empire State Building**, *Fifth Ave and 34th St; tel: (212) 736-3100*, where not only do you have views from the 86th- and 102nd-floor observatories, $2–$4, you can take the Skyride, a flight-simulator where visitors (wearing seatbelts) feel as if they are in a plane that takes off from the top of the building. Take a multilingual tour of the **United Nations**, *E. 46nd St and United Nations Plaza (First Ave); tel: (212) 963-7713*, open daily 0915–1645, $3.50–$6.50 (subway: *Grand Central*). Tour **NBC Studios**; *tel: (212) 664-4000*, open daily 0930–1630, $8.25, and nearby **Radio City Music Hall**, *tel: (212) 632-4041*,

open daily 1000–1700, tours every 30–45 min, $6–$12, before resting up at at **St. Patrick's Cathedral**, *Fifth Ave* and *50th St*, regardless of your religious beliefs.

Uptown

On the upper West Side, visit **The Cloisters** at Fort Tryon Park on the Hudson River. At *West 122nd St*, is **Riverside Church** with its 400-ft high tower. Take a **Harlem Gospel** or **Soul Food and Jazz** tour, *tel: (212) 757-0425*.

MUSEUMS

New York is a cultural centre and for passionate museum goers, there is much to see. These are only the highlights:

Upper West Side

The **American Museum of Natural History and Hayden Planetarium**, *Central Park West at 79th St, New York, NY 10024; tel: (212) 769-5100*, open Sun–Thur 1000–1745, Fri–Sat 1000–2045, $4–$6, the most child-friendly museum in the city, has two new dinosaur halls and a NatureMax Theatre presenting large-screen (70mm) IMAX films. The **Children's Museum of Manhattan**, *212 W. 83rd St, New York, NY 10024; tel: (212) 721-1234*, open Mon, Wed, Thur 1530–1730, Fri, Sat, Sun 1000–1700, $5, has 'please touch' exhibits and special events of interest to children. **Studio Museum in Harlem**, *144 W. 125th St, New York, NY 10027; tel: (212) 864-4500*, open Wed–Fri 1000–1700, Sat–Sun 1300–1600, $1–$5, has changing exhibits of art and artifacts of black America and the African Diaspora.

Upper East Side

The **Metropolitan Museum of Art**, *Fifth Ave and 82nd St, New York, NY 10028; tel: (212) 979-5500*, open

Tues–Thur, Sun 0930–1715, Fri, Sat 0930–2045, $3.50–$7, is the the *grande dame* of museums, with the Temple of Dendur as its centrepiece. The **Solomon R. Guggenheim Museum**, *Fifth Ave at 88th St, New York, NY 10128; tel: (212) 423-3500*, open Sun–Wed 1000–1800, Fri, Sat 1000–2000, $4–$7, is a designated landmark building, design ed by US architect Frank Lloyd Wright in 1950 and known for its grand spiral ramp, where the art is displayed. This is modern art at its most contemporary. The Guggenheim has a **branch** at *575 Broadway, downtown; tel: (212) 423-3500*, open Wed–Fri, Sun 1100–1800, Sat 1100–2000, $3–$5, with changing avant-garde exhibits.

The Jewish Museum, *1109 Fifth Ave at 92nd St, New York, NY 10128; tel: (212) 423-3200*, open Sun–Thur 1100–1745, Tue 1100–2000, $6, covers 4000 years of Jewish history. **The Museum of the City of New York**, *Fifth Ave at 103rd St, New York, NY 10029; tel: (212) 534-1672*, open Wed–Sat 1000–1700, Sun 1300–1700, founded in 1933, spans New York history from its settlement to the present.

Midtown West Side

Aboard a World War II aircraft carrier, **The Intrepid Sea–Air–Space Museum**, *Pier 86, 12th Ave and W. 46th St, New York, NY 10036; tel: (212) 245-2533*, open Wed–Sun 1000–1700, $5–$10, showcases early aviation and World War II history. The **Museum of Modern Art**, *11 W. 53rd St, New York, NY 10019; tel: (212) 708-9400*, open Sat–Tues 1100–1800, Thur–Fri 1200–2030, $5–$8, has a comprehensive collection of 20th-century art, including works by Picasso and Matisse. You can hear and watch more than 70 years of radio and TV at the **Museum of Television and Radio**, *25*

W. 52nd St, New York, NY 10019; tel: (212) 621-6800, open Tue–Sun 1200–1800, Thur 1200–2000, $5.

Midtown East Side
The Pierpont Morgan Library, *29 E. 36th St, New York, NY 10016; tel: (212) 685-0610,* Tue–Sat 1030–1700, Sun 1300–1700, $5, is a gem on the inside and out. The pink marble, Renaissance-style building contains books, manuscripts, paintings and art objects. **The Museum of American Illustration**, *128 E. 63rd St, New York, NY 10021; tel: (212) 838-2560,* open Sat 1200–1600, Tue 1000–2000, Wed–Fri 1000–1700, free, has a collection of contemporary and historic magazine, book and advertising illustrations.

Downtown
Lower East Side Tenement Museum, *90 Orchard St, New York, NY 10002; tel: (212) 431-0233,* open Tue–Fri 1100–1700, 1100–1800, $5–$7, shows New York's colourful immigrant history, with renovated tenement apartments and photos. **New York City Fire Museum**, *278 Spring St, New York, NY 10013; tel: (212) 691-1303,* open Tue–Sat 1000– 1600, $0.50–$3, is a renovated 1904 fire station with all the trimmings. The **New York Police Museum**, same address; *tel: (212) 477-9753,* open by appointment only, free, has police-related paintings, photos, uniforms and firearms dating back to Colonial times.

National Museum of the American Indian, *Alexander Hamilton US Customs House near Battery Park, New York, NY 10004; tel: (212) 668-6624,* open daily 1000–1700, free, has the world's largest collection of Native American artifacts.

The **Museum for African Art**, *593 Broadway, New York, NY 10012; tel: (212)*

966-1313, open Tues–Fri 1030–1730, Sat 1200–2000, Sun 1200–1800, $4, has a permanent collection like no other, especially on sub-Saharan art.

Manhattan is one of five boroughs that comprise New York. The other four:

The Bronx
North of Manhattan, the many parks of **The Bronx** make it New York's greenest borough. Although its notoriety once came from the rubble-strewn South Bronx, the borough has undergone a remarkable renaissance. **The Bronx Museum of the Arts**, *1040 Grand Concourse; tel: (718) 681-6000,* open Wed 1500–2100, Thu–Fri 1000–1700, Sat–Sun 1000–1800, $3, reflects the cultural diversity. Another major attraction is **The Bronx Zoo**, *Bronx River Pkwy (Exit 6) at Fordham Rd, Bronx, NY 10460; tel: (718) 367-1010,* (take Liberty Bus; *tel: (718) 652-8400,* or Metro North trains; *tel: (212) 532-4900,* from Grand Central Station), open Mon–Fri 1000–1700, Sat, Sun, holidays 1000–1730; $3–$6.75. Adjacent to the zoo is the vast **New York Botanical Garden**, *Southern Blvd at Mosholu Pkwy, Bronx, NY 10458; tel: (718) 220-8700.* The best public transport access to The Bronx is via subway (IRT), bus or Metro North commuter train.

Brooklyn
At the other end of the **Brooklyn Bridge** (built in 1883), is the most populated (2.5 million) of the boroughs. It's rich in ethnic communities and accents – it's the land of 'dese and dose' (these and those) and 'toidy toid and toid' (33rd and Third). Woody Allen and Barbra Streisand were born here. Brooklyn has museums and parks and, on the Atlantic Ocean, the **Coney**

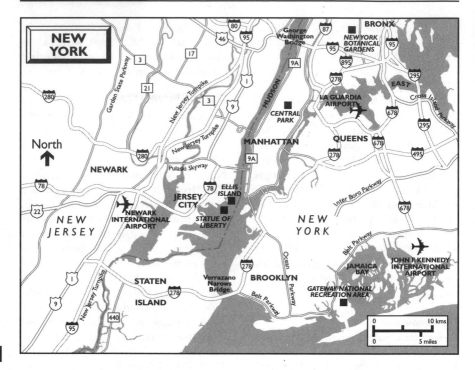

NEW
YORK

North ↑

NEWARK

NEW
JERSEY

NEWARK
INTERNATIONAL
AIRPORT

JERSEY
CITY

STATEN

ISLAND

Garden State Parkway

New Jersey Turnpike

New Jersey Turnpike

Pulaski Skyway

ELLIS
ISLAND

STATUE OF
LIBERTY

Verrazano
Narows
Bridge

George
Washington
Bridge

HUDSON

CENTRAL
PARK

MANHATTAN

9A

BRONX

NEW YORK
BOTANICAL
GARDENS

LA GUARDIA
AIRPORT

QUEENS

EAST

Inter Boro Parkway

NEW
YORK

BROOKLYN

Belt Parkway

Ocean Parkway

Belt Parkway

JAMAICA
BAY

GATEWAY NATIONAL
RECREATION AREA

JOHN F. KENNEDY
INTERNATIONAL
AIRPORT

Cross Island Parkway

0   10 kms
0   5 miles

344

Island amusement park, with the Cyclone, boardwalk and famous Nathan's hot dogs. One of the most beautiful sights of all can be seen only from this borough, from the promenade in Brooklyn Heights: the spectacular **Manhattan skyline**. Best public transport access to Brooklyn is by bus, subway or the Long Island Railroad.

Queens

The largest of the boroughs in area, Queens is well known as the site of the **1939 and 1964 World's Fairs**, in Flushing Meadow's Corona Park, where some of the exposition structures still remain, and its tennis centres – the formerly used **Forest Hills** and the modern **National Tennis Center,** *Flushing Meadow Park* (subway: *Willets Point*/No. 7 *Flushing Line); (718) 760-6200,* where the US Open Tennis Championships are held

every Sept. The complex is a 30-min sub-way ride from Grand Central Station in Manhattan and shares the same stop with **Shea Stadium,** home of the city's other famous baseball team, The 1986 World Champion New York Mets (see Sports). Queens is linked to Manhattan by four bridges and the Queens Midtown Tunnel, with public transportation provided by bus, subway and Long Island Railroad.

Staten Island

The only other island borough, Staten Island is a pleasant 20-min ride by ferry from downtown Manhattan. Don't forget your camera as you'll have one of the best views of the downtown skyscrapers as you depart from the aft deck of the **Staten Island Ferry**, *Whitehall St, next to Battery Park in Manhattan; tel: (212) 806-6940,* which runs daily every 20–30 mins, $0.50.

DRIVING DISTANCES AND TIMES

Approximate distances between regional centres and air gateway cities are given following the most direct routes. Driving times are meant as an average indication only. They do not include allowance for stops or breaks en route.

Baltimore to . . .	Miles	Km	Hours
Dover	86	138	1¾
Harrisburg	76	122	1½
New York	200	320	4
Norfolk	227	363	4½
Philadelphia	99	158	2
Richmond	150	240	3
Washington, DC	39	62	¾

Dover to . . .			
Baltimore	86	138	1¾
Harrisburg	131	210	2½
New York	177	283	3½
Norfolk	190	304	3¾
Philadelphia	76	122	1½
Richmond	202	323	4
Washington, DC	96	154	2

Harrisburg to . . .			
Baltimore	76	122	1½
Dover	131	210	2½
New York	198	317	4
Philadelphia	105	168	2
Richmond	244	390	5
Washington, DC	133	213	2¾

New York to . . .			
Baltimore	200	320	4
Dover	177	283	3½
Harrisburg	198	317	4
Philadelphia	101	162	2
Richmond	353	565	7
Washington, DC	239	382	4¾

Norfolk to . . .	Miles	Km	Hours
Baltimore	227	363	4½
Dover	190	304	3¾
Philadelphia	266	426	5¼
Richmond	94	150	2
Roanoke	250	400	5
Washington, DC	190	304	3¾

Philadelphia to . . .			
Baltimore	99	158	2
Dover	76	122	1½
Harrisburg	105	168	2
New York	101	162	2
Norfolk	266	426	5¼
Richmond	254	406	5
Washington, DC	138	221	2¾

Richmond to . . .			
Baltimore	150	240	3
Dover	202	323	4
Harrisburg	244	390	5
New York	353	565	7
Norfolk	94	150	2
Philadelphia	254	406	5
Roanoke	168	269	3½
Washington, DC	111	178	2¼

Roanoke to . . .			
Norfolk	250	400	5
Richmond	168	269	3½
Washington, DC	246	394	5

Washington, DC to . . .			
Baltimore	39	62	¾
Dover	96	154	2
Harrisburg	133	213	2¾
New York	239	382	4¾
Norfolk	190	304	3¾
Philadelphia	138	221	2¾
Richmond	111	178	2¼
Roanoke	246	394	5

345

HOTEL CODES

AND CENTRAL BOOKING NUMBERS

The following abbreviations have been used throughout the book to show which chains are represented in a particular town. Cities and large towns have most except HI. Central booking service phone numbers are shown – use these numbers while in the USA to make reservations at any hotel in the chain. Where available, numbers that can be called in your own country are also noted.

(Aus = Australia, Can = Canada, D = Germany, F = France, Ire = Republic of Ireland, NZ = New Zealand, SA = South Africa, UK = United Kingdom, WW = worldwide number.)

BW	**Best Western**		Can *(800) 465 4329*		Ire *(800) 557 474*
	(800) 528 1234		Ire *(800) 553 155*		NZ *(800) 443 333*
	Aus *(800) 222 422*		NZ *(800) 442 222*		UK *(800) 191991*
	Can *(800) 528 1234*		SA *(011) 482 3500*	**Rm**	**Ramada**
	Ire *(800) 709 101*		UK *(800) 897121*		**(800) 228 2828**
	NZ *(09) 520 5418*	**HI**	**Hostelling**		Aus *(800) 222 431*
	SA *(011) 339 4865*		**International**		Can *(800) 854 7854*
	UK *(800) 393130*		(information only)		Ire *(800) 252 627*
CI	**Comfort Inn**		Can/US *(800) 444 6111*		NZ *(800) 441 111*
	(800) 228 5150		UK *(0171) 248 6547*		UK *(800) 181737*
	Aus *(008) 090 600*	**HJ**	**Howard Johnson**	**RI**	**Residence Inn**
	Can *(800) 221 2222*		**(800) 654 2000**		**(800) 331 3131**
	Ire *(800) 500 600*		Aus *02 262 4918*		Aus *(800) 251 259*
	NZ *(800) 808 228*		UK *(0181) 688 1418*		Ire *(800) 409 929*
	UK *(800) 444444*	**Hn**	**Hilton**		NZ *(800) 441035*
Cr	**Clarion**		**(800) 445 8667**		UK *(800) 221222*
	(800)-CLARION		Aus *(800) 222 255*	**RR**	**Red Roof Inns**
	or as Comfort Inn		Can *(800) 445 8667*		**800 843 7663**
CM	**Courtyard by**		NZ *(800) 448 002*	**Sh**	**Sheraton**
	Marriott		SA *(011) 880 3108*		**(800) 325 3535**
	(800) 321 2211		UK *(0345) 581595*		Aus *(800) 073 535*
DI	**Days Inn**	**Hy**	**Hyatt**		Ire *(800) 535 353*
	(800) 325 2525		**(800) 233 1234**		NZ *(800) 443 535*
	D *069 41 2525*		Aus *(800) 131 234*	**SR**	**Stouffer**
	F *1 44 77 88 03*	**Ma**	**Marriott**		**Renaissance**
	UK *(01483) 440470*		**(800) 228 9290**		as Ramada
EL	**Econo Lodge**		Aus *(800) 251 259*	**St**	**Stouffer**
	(800) 221 2222		Can *(800) 228 9290*		**(800)-HOTELS-1**
ES	**Embassy Suites**		NZ *(800) 441 035*	**S8**	**Super 8**
	(800) 362 2779		UK *(800) 221222*		WW *(800) 800 8000*
	Aus *02 959 3922*	**Om**	**Omni**	**TL**	**Travelodge**
	Can *416 626 3974*		**(800)-THE-OMNI**		**(800) 578 7878**
	NZ *09 623 4294*	**QI**	**Quality Inn**		Aus *(800) 622 240*
	SA *11 789 6706*		**(800) 228 5151**		Ire *(800) 409 040*
	UK *01992 441517*	**QS**	**Quality Suites**		NZ *(800) 801111*
Hd	**Holiday Inn**		as Quality Inn		SA *(011) 442 9201*
	(800) 465 4329	**Rd**	**Radisson**		UK *(0345) 404040*
	Aus *(800) 221 066*		**(800) 333 3333**		

CONVERSION TABLES

DISTANCE

km	miles	km	miles
1	0.62	30	21.75
2	1.24	40	24.85
3	1.86	45	27.96
4	2.49	50	31.07
5	3.11	55	34.18
6	3.73	60	37.28
7	4.35	65	40.39
8	4.97	70	43.50
9	5.59	75	46.60
10	6.21	80	49.71
15	9.32	90	55.92
20	12.43	100	62.14
25	15.53	125	77.67

1km = 0.6214 miles
1mile = 1.609 km

METRES AND FEET

Unit	Metres	Feet
1	0.30	3.281
2	0.61	6.563
3	0.91	9.843
4	1.22	13.124
5	1.52	16.403
6	1.83	19.686
7	2.13	22.967
8	2.4	26.248
9	2.74	29.529
10	3.05	32.810
14	4.27	45.934
18	5.49	59.058
20	6.10	65.520
50	15.24	164.046
75	22.8	246.069
100	30.48	328.092

WEIGHT

Unit	kg	Pounds
1	0.45	2.205
2	0.90	4.405
3	1.35	6.614
4	1.80	8.818
5	2.25	11.023
10	4.50	22.045
15	6.75	33.068
20	9.00	44.889
25	11.25	55.113
50	22.50	110.225
75	33.75	165.338
100	45.00	220.450

1kg	=	1000g
100g	=	3.5oz
1oz	=	28.35g
1lb	=	453.60g

FLUID MEASURES

Litres	Imp.gal.	US gal.
5	1.1	1.3
10	2.2	2.6
15	3.3	3.9
20	4.4	5.2
25	5.5	6.5
30	6.6	7.8
35	7.7	9.1
40	8.8	10.4
45	9.9	11.7
50	11.0	13.0

1 litre(l)=0.88 imp.quarts
1 litre(l)=1.06 US quarts
1 imp. quart = 1.14 l
1 imp. gallon= 4.55 l
1 US quart = 0.95 l
1 US gallon = 3.81 l

MENS' SHIRTS

UK	Europe	US
14	36	14
15	38	15
15.5	39	15.5
16	41	16
16.5	42	16.5
17	43	17

MENS' SHOES

UK	Europe	US
6	40	7
7	41	8
8	42	9
9	43	10
10	44	11
11	45	12

Unit	mm	cm	metres
1 inch	25.4	2.54	0.025
1 foot	304.8	30.48	0.304
1 yard	914.4	91.44	0.914

To convert cms to inches, multiply by 0.3937
To convert inches to cms, multiply by 2.54

MENS' CLOTHES

UK	Europe	US
36	46	36
38	48	38
40	50	40
42	52	42
44	54	44
46	56	46

LADIES' SHOES

UK	Europe	US
3	36	4.5
4	37	5.5
5	38	6.5
6	39	7.5
7	40	8.5
8	41	9.5

LADIES' CLOTHES

UK	France	Italy	Rest of Europe	US
10	36	38	34	8
12	38	40	36	10
14	40	42	38	12
16	42	44	40	14
18	44	46	42	16
20	46	48	44	18

TEMPERATURE

Conversion Formula: $°C \times 9 \div 5 + 32 = °F$

°C	°F	°C	°F	°C	°F	°C	°F
-20	-4	-5	23	10	50	25	77
-15	5	0	32	15	59	30	86
-10	14	5	41	20	68	35	95

INDEX

References are to page numbers. **Bold** numbers refer to the planning maps at the end of the book; e.g. **3:B4** means square B4, map page 3.

349

READER SURVEY

If you enjoyed using this book, or even if you didn't, please help us improve future editions by taking part in our reader survey. Every returned form will be acknowledged, and to show our appreciation we will give you £1 off your next purchase of a Thomas Cook guidebook. Just take a few minutes to complete and return this form to us.

When did you buy this book? _____

_____

Where did you buy it? (Please give town/city and if possible name of retailer)

_____

When did you/do you intend to travel in the Capital Region?

_____

    For how long (approx.)? _____

    How many people in your party? _____

Which cities, towns, national parks and other locations did you/do you intend mainly to visit?

_____

_____

351

_____

_____

Did you/will you:
    ☐ Make all your travel arrangements independently?
    ☐ Travel on a fly-drive package?
Please give brief details: _____

_____

Did you/do you intend to use this book:
    ☐ For planning your trip?
    ☐ During the trip itself?
    ☐ Both?

Did you/do you intend also to purchase any of the following travel publications for your trip?
    A road map/atlas (please specify) _____
    Other guidebooks (please specify) _____

_____

Have you used any other Thomas Cook guidebooks in the past? If so, which?

_____

Please rate the following features of On the Road around the Capital Region for their value to you (Circle VU for 'very useful', U for 'useful', NU for 'little or no use'):

The 'Travel Essentials' section on pages 15–37	VU	U	NU
The 'Driving in the Capital Region' section on pages 38–44	VU	U	NU
The 'Touring Itineraries' on pages 54–64	VU	U	NU
The recommended driving routes throughout the book	VU	U	NU
Information on towns and cities, National Parks, etc	VU	U	NU
The maps of towns and cities, parks, etc	VU	U	NU
The colour planning map	VU	U	NU

Please use this space to tell us about any features that in your opinion could be changed, improved, or added in future editions of the book, or any other comments you would like to make concerning the book:

352

Your age category: ☐ 21–30 ☐ 31–40 ☐ 41–50 ☐ over 50

Your name: Mr/Mrs/Miss/Ms
(First name or initials)
(Last name)

Your full address: (Please include postal or zip code)

Your daytime telephone number: _____

Please detach this page and send it to: The Project Editor, On the Road around the Capital Region, Thomas Cook Publishing, PO Box 227, Peterborough PE3 6PU, United Kingdom.

We will be pleased to send you details of how to claim your discount upon receipt of this questionnaire.

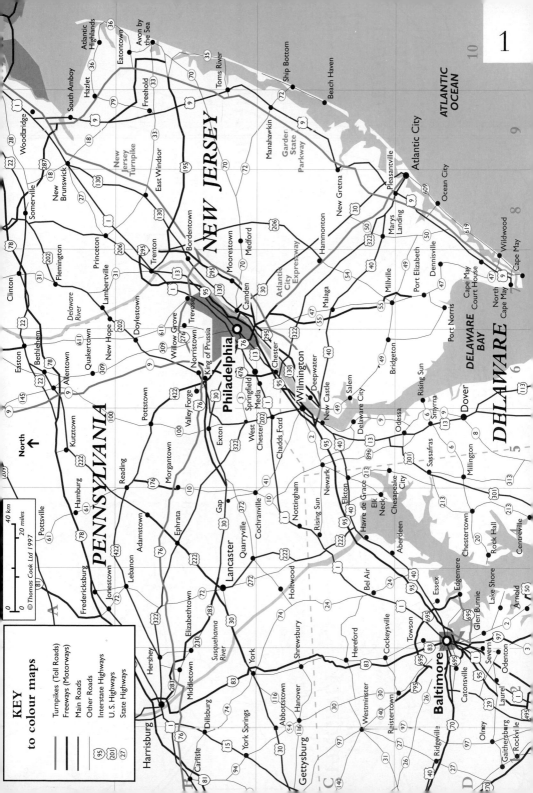

1

ATLANTIC OCEAN

NEW JERSEY

PENNSYLVANIA

DELAWARE

DELAWARE BAY

KEY to colour maps

	Turnpikes (Toll Roads)
	Freeways (Motorways)
	Main Roads
	Other Roads
95	Interstate Highways
201	U.S. Highways
27	State Highways

40 km
20 miles
© Thomas Cook Ltd 1997

North

Atlantic Highlands
Avon by the Sea
Eatontown
South Amboy
Hazlet
Woodbridge
Freehold
Toms River
Ship Bottom
Beach Haven
New Brunswick
Somerville
Clinton
Flemington
East Windsor
Manahawkin
Garden State Parkway
Atlantic City
Ocean City
Princeton
Lambertville
Trenton
Bordentown
Moorestown
Medford
New Gretna
Hammonton
Pleasantville
Marys Landing
Dennisville
Wildwood
Cape May
Easton
Bethlehem
Allentown
New Hope
Doylestown
Norristown
King of Prussia
Camden
Malaga
Millville
Port Elizabeth
North Cape May
Kurztown
Quakertown
Willow Grove
Trevose
Philadelphia
Chester
Wilmington
Deepwater
Bridgeton
Rising Sun
Port Norris
Pottstown
Valley Forge
Springfield
Media
New Castle
Salem
Delaware City
Odessa
Smyrna
Dover
Reading
Exton
West Chester
Chadds Ford
Newark
Elkton
Sassafras
Millington
Morgantown
Gap
Cochranville
Nottingham
Rising Sun
Havre de Grace
Elk Neck
Chesapeake City
Chestertown
Rock Hall
Centreville
Lebanon
Ephrata
Quarryville
Holtwood
Aberdeen
Edgemere
Lancaster
Adamstown
Hamburg
Pottsville
Fredericksburg
Jonestown
Elizabethtown
York
Shrewsbury
Bel Air
Cockeysville
Towson
Essex
Lake Shore
Arnold
Hershey
Middletown
Hanover
Hereford
Baltimore
Glen Burnie
Catonsville
Severn
Odenton
Harrisburg
Carlisle
Dillsburg
York Springs
Gettysburg
Abbottstown
Westminster
Raistertown
Severna
Laurel
Gaithersburg
Rockville
Olney
Ridgeville
Reistertown

Susquehanna River

Delaware River

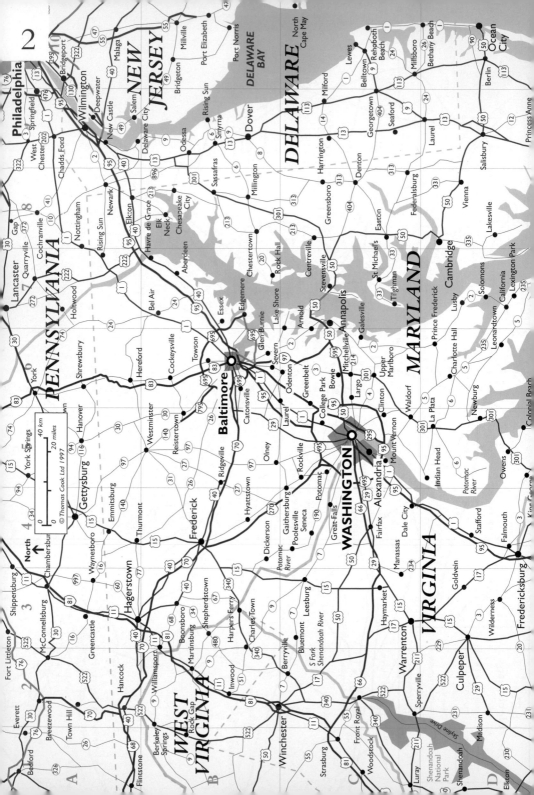

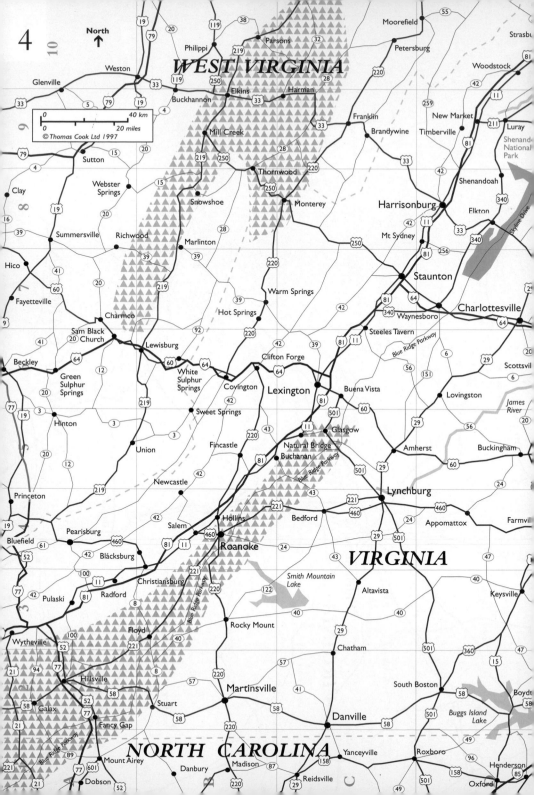